AMERICAN SILVER FLATWARE 1837-1910

AMERICAN SILVER FLATWARE 1837-1910

NOEL D. TURNER

San Diego
A. S. Barnes & Company, Inc.
In London:
The Tantivy Press

Manufactured in the United States of America

For information write to:

A. S. Barnes & Company, Inc.
P.O. Box 3051
La Jolla, California 92038

ISBN: 498 06580 4
Library of Congress Catalogue Card Number: 68-27217

4 5 6 7 8 9 84 83 82

To my friend Bertha,
Mrs. Walter Bruce,
without whose patience and understanding
this book could not have been completed.

Contents

Preface

Long before his *Life with Father* returned late 19th century family life to the American scene, Clarence Day commented, in *This Simian World*. "Curiosity is a valuable trait . . . but the curiosity of the simian is as excessive as the toil of an ant."

Such curiosity is responsible for these pages.

A few unidentified pieces of Victorian silver flatware, inherited without an explanatory note, started the progression of questions, one following the other, ant-like.

First came the question of defining the pieces of silver. Once the purpose of each piece had been determined, it was impossible to avoid the chicken-and-egg query: had Victorian manners dictated the manufacture of the pieces, or had the pieces influenced Victorian manners? And with the identification of the patterns, there came the question of nomenclature: had silver patterns been named like their contemporary Pullman Palace cars, or had there been some logic in the choices?

Scout-ant explorations revealed that I was not alone in my curiosity, and there was comfort in the company of others who were equally confused by the microcosm of Victorian living that the many-faceted silverware reflected. Among dealers and collectors there was much interest, but little information, frequent fantasies, and few facts. Little had been written about the compact, movable, and practically indestructible miniature world of knives and forks and spoons during the time of Victoria Regina. But as the fragments of information were assembled from newspaper clippings, forgotten catalogs, long overlooked etiquette books, and contemporary accounts of social and business events, it became increasingly clear that silverware mirrored accurately all the decorative motifs the 19th century had held dear, that the pieces echoed a period of ostentation and good living, of overly bounteous meals made possible by a more leisurely pace on the one hand, and excessive toil on the other. Equally, the myriad implements traced the development of an industry, and of a country, during those years—development that created, and in turn was created by a rising middle class. The many grades in which the ware was made reflected the upward mobility of Americans; their widespread use, the democratic leveling process. These Victorian trends continued well into the Edwardian years, and for this reason, the history presented here has been carried to 1910.

Every effort has been made to make this pioneer work as complete and comprehensive as possible. But many of the companies that manufactured sterling and electroplated wares are no longer in business; there have been mergers and consolidations, each of which has diminished existing records. Even those companies with a continuous existence through a century and a quarter or more find that there are periods for which historical reports are incomplete. Catalogs have been destroyed as the flatware they featured has become obsolete; trade journals that reported developments within the industry have stopped publication, and their files have disappeared. The encyclopedic sections of this book involved tens of thousands of separate entries. It is hoped that each of these is accurate; any errors are unintentional and regretted—but perhaps only human. Insofar as it is possible, omissions will be corrected in future editions, if additional information becomes available. In some cases, facts about related products have been omitted from this volume after much deliberation. Pearl-handle tableware, for example, enjoyed periods of popularity during the 19th century, but research discloses that much of this ware was imported, and American manufacturers used a completely different system of nomenclature, incompatible with that employed for sterling and electroplated flatware, to designate designs and qualities. This material may be presented in another volume, should collector interest warrant, even though its nature has prevented inclusion in this book.

The final compilation of this record of the facts and foibles of the Victorian silver chest could not have been completed without the help of many individuals, companies and institutions. Among those who assisted are the staffs of The Center for Research Libraries, The John Crerar Library, The Newberry Library in Chicago, The Art Institute of Chicago, and the Chicago Historical Society; The Cincinnati Historical Society, called the Ohio Historical and Philosophical Society when the work began; The Detroit Institute of Arts; The Illinois State Historical Library in Springfield; The William Henry Smith Memorial Library of the Indiana State Historical Society; The Indiana State Library; The Michigan Historical Commission; The Historic Mobile Preservation Society of Mobile, Alabama; The New York Historical Society; Cooper Union Museum; The State Historical Society of Wisconsin; The Free Library and The Franklin Institute in Philadelphia; The Library of Congress in Washington, and the Victoria & Albert Museum in London; Public Libraries in Chicago, Cincinnati, New York City, San Francisco, St. Louis, Providence, R.I., North Attleboro, Mass., Bridgeport and Waterbury, Conn., Keene, N.H., Dickinson County, Mich., Madison, Ind., and Aurora, Freeport and Rockford, Ill.

Much of the credit for this reconstruction of past trends in the design, production and merchandising of flatware is owed to *Jewelers' Circular-Keystone*. For 100 years, this magazine and its predecessor publications, including *The Watchmaker & Jeweler, Jewelers' Circular, Jewelers' Weekly, The Keystone* and *The Connoisseur,* have carefully reported the history of the jewelry and related trades; these records were made available through the interest and kind cooperation of Mr. Lansford F. King, the publisher, and Mr. Donald S. McNeil, the editor.

Dr. Elliot Evans, Curator of The Society of California Pioneers, contributed helpful information about western American silverware and manufacturers; Betty C. Monkman, Registrar in the Office of the Curator, The White House Collection, helped in tracing the Dolly Madison and Cleveland era flatware, and supplied photographs of these pieces.

An invaluable collection of catalogs and early designer scrapbooks was loaned by Mr. Frank Perry of Oneida, Ltd. Through the courtesy of Mr. John R. Blackinton of R. Blackinton & Company, Mr. Clarence V. Lau, Mr. W. Dan Lemeshka, Mr. Roy J. Wood and Mrs. Florence Rafuse of The Gorham Company, Mr. E. P. Hogan of The International Silver Company, Mr. S. Kirk Millspaugh of Samuel Kirk & Son, Mr. D. C. Lunt of Lunt Silversmiths, Mr. Stafford P.

Osborn of Reed & Barton, Mr. Howard J. Hickingbotham of Shreve & Company, Mr. Austin F. Grant of Frank Smith Silver Co., Mr. Charles Stieff II of the Stieff Company, Miss Joanna Brown of Tiffany & Company, Mr. Arthur Roy of the Towle Manufacturing Company, and Miss Arlene Hershey of Wallace Silversmiths, the historical collections of these pioneer silver manufacturers were opened for examination and research.

Mr. Edward B. McAlpine of the Manchester Silver Company, Mr. Jerome Weissner of National Silver Company, Mr. John A. Ekstrom of Albert Pick Co., Mr. R. J. Nolan of Saart Bros. Co., Mr. Nelson Kaiser of Simons Bros. Co., Mr. Paul V. Happold of E. J. Towle Company, and Mr. William Bass of The Web Silver Company were generous with time and information.

Mr. Richard W. Dirksen of Freeport, Illinois, Senator Everett W. Dirksen of Pekin, Illinois and Washington, D.C., Mr. R. W. Sheets of Rockford, Illinois, Mr. Alexander W. Macy of New York City, and Mr. Willard Soderlund of Norway, Michigan offered valued assistance, as did Mrs. Bert Carlson of Marshall Field & Company in Chicago. Lebolt & Co., C. D. Peacock, and Spaulding & Company, all of Chicago, Herschede Jewelers of Cincinnati, and Mermod-Jaccard-King of St. Louis were among the jewelers who contributed historical material. Antique dealers in many parts of the country permitted examination of catalogs and silver flatware in their stocks; among them, Andrew Farmelo of Worcester, Mass., Nora Flemington of Iron Mountain, Mich., Emma Grutzmacher and Blanche Holly of Chicago, Kathleen Harvey of Evanston, Ill. and Frank Palmer of Mt. Vernon, Ohio were most helpful.

A collection of Victorian wholesale jewelry catalogs owned by John Plain & Company, and made available through the kindness of Mr. Thomas Karon, provided many of the illustrations; others came from the Sears, Roebuck and Company library of the firm's early catalogs. Permission to photograph unusual examples of flatware in their private collections was granted by Mrs. Charles (Jane Lightfoot) Beaumont of Penn Yan, N.Y., Mrs. Carl (Donna) Felger of College Park, Md., Spencer Franc and Joan Goodwillie of Chicago, and Mrs. W. G. (Clara) Price of Breezewood, Pa. Several of the collateral illustrations were made available by the New York Central System (now Penn-Central) and the Santa Fe Railway; The Palmer House and The Brown Palace hotels; and by Miss Constance Rita Weber. Jane Lightfoot Beaumont, co-author of *Early American Plated Silver,* also loaned original reference materials which were most helpful.

Among the many competent and cooperative photographers who assisted, Gwen Daly, Tom Newman, Paul Ihde and Kelly Powell were most frequently called upon; particular gratitude is due Anthony Pozniak, whose photocopy skill and patience made it possible to reproduce hundreds of frequently faded or otherwise damaged old illustrations and other documents.

The careful work of those who earlier searched out American silversmiths, whose individual contributions are credited in the section of this book devoted to these craftsmen, is gratefully acknowledged, as is the research assistance of Willard Thompson.

The encouragement and help offered by Dorothy T. Rainwater and Henry Valent, attorney in Watkins Glen, N.Y., during a particularly trying period is greatly appreciated.

The anecdote at the beginning of Chapter 5 is reprinted with the permission of Mr. Ben Botkin and *The New York Times;* derivations of the term "Kettle Drum" are from Russell Lynes' *The Domesticated Americans,* for which permission was granted by Harper & Row, Publishers, Inc.; the quotation that closes Chapter 9 is used with the permission of Harcourt, Brace & World, publishers of Mary McCarthy's *The Group.* Quotations from early etiquette books, not otherwise identified in Chapter 8, are from Arthur M. Schlesinger's *Learning How to Behave;* The Macmillan Company, publishers of this book, kindly granted permission to use these excerpts.

1

Preludes and Precedents

In 1731, more than a century before the appearance of the complex silver place settings of the Victorian years, Jonathan Swift, in *Polite Conversations,* wrote: "Fingers were made before forks, and hands before knives." His indictment of the trivialities of the table, just beginning to assume importance in society, was sound, but somewhat simplified.

The most primitive man had used a pointed stick for spearing food, forked sticks for removing food from fire, sharp-edged stones and shells for cutting food that resisted tearing between the hands; he had utilized chips and shells and gourds for transmitting liquids. These were the earliest ancestors of the fork, the knife, and the spoon, early supplements to the fingers, the clenched hand for tearing and the cupped hand for sipping.

The familiar bowl-and-handle spoon was probably the first eating tool to be developed. Etruscan spoons, dating from 700 B.C., are not unlike the ones we use today, and early knives designed to serve as weapons as well as food spears, with a handle to protect the user's palm from the sharpened blade, are as old as metal-working. The early Greeks were known to have had forks, and a two-tined fork of gold was brought to Italy by a Greek princess in 1071. But while forks of gold or silver appear in inventories from the 11th century on, these seem to have been used only for special foods, such as ginger, berries, or fruit. In the inventory of Charles V of France, it is explained that the gold and silver forks were used only for eating mulberries and foods likely to stain the fingers; it was not until the 16th century that forks began to replace fingers for carrying food to the mouth. The practice began in Italy, probably in Venice, and the new fashion gradually spread to the rest of the continent. Major C. T. P. Bailey in *Knives & Forks,* a 1927 publication of the Victoria & Albert Museum, quotes from an earlier book, published in London in 1611, in which an early English traveler, Thomas Coryat of Adcomb, reported:

> I observed a custom in all those Italian Cities and Townes through which I passed, that is not used in any other country that I saw in my travels, neither do I thinke that any other nation of Christendom doth use it, but only Italy. The Italian, and also most strangers that are commorant in Italy, doe alwaies, at their meales use a little fork when they cut the meate; for while with their knife, which they hold in one hand, they cut the meate out of the dish, they fasten their forke, which they hold in their other hand, upon the same dish, so that whatsoever he be that sitteth in the company of others at meate, should unadvisedly touch the dish of meate with his fingers, from which all at the table doe cut, he will give occasion of offense unto the company as having transgressed the lawes of good manners, insomuch for his error

he shall at least be browbeaten, if not reprehended in words. This forme of feeding I understand is generally used in all places in Italy, their forks being for the most part made of yron or steele, and some of silver, but those used only by gentlemen.

Coryat pointed out later in his book that he had embraced the Italian custom of forking his food after he returned home, and that it had aroused much curiosity among his friends. Since they were undoubtedly gentlemen, it was undoubtedly to the silversmith of their choice that they carried their requests for duplicates of this unique implement.

Meanwhile, the early pronged or pointed stick had developed in two other directions; it became the spit, useful in cooking, and, in the east, developed into chopsticks, the parallel of the western fork. Among the earliest tableware services, dating from the 14th century, are those consisting of a single fork and a matched set of knives; the fork used for serving, the knives and fingers for eating.

Sets of knives and forks, with handles fitting together for convenience in travelling. The center pair have handles that serve as sheaths for the blade and tines. *Courtesy Victoria & Albert Museum.*

Set of knives and one fork; the fork was used for serving, the knives for eating; late 17th century. Handles are of silver, the case of ivory, inlaid with silver wire and colored ivory and composition material. *Courtesy Victoria & Albert Museum.*

By the time the fork came into popular use in the 17th century, sets of a knife, fork, and spoon were treated as highly personal tools, and were carried about by their owners and used not only at home but in other houses where they might be guests or at inns when traveling. Such sets were made with cases, and later, were designed so that they might be folded, with the handle of the knife and fork acting as a protective shield for the sharp blade and tines.

The pistol-grip handle, still greatly admired for the way it fits the hand, and the wide, flared top commonly used even today for fork and spoon handles, were originally designed to sheath the sharp and pointed working members of traveling tableware.

These portable implements continued to be popular into the early days of American colonization, and were made by some of the early silversmiths in the Colonies. One such set, made by John Coney, who worked in Boston until 1722, is in the Boston Museum of Fine Arts. It closely resembles earlier English sets of "pocket tools."

During the 18th century, the personalized, portable tableware sets continued to be popular with travelers, but well-equipped houses began to include, among other appointments, knives, forks, and spoons for guests as well as family. Since these pieces traveled only from knife box to table to scullery and back again to the sideboard, the folding feature was dispensed with; but even the fixed handles retained the wide shapes of the earlier sheath handles, a narrow throat terminating in a flaring, broad top. The pistol-grip handle continued in popularity from the early 18th century into the reign of George III; during these years it gradually became more ornate, with scrolls and leaf decoration. Accompanying forks and spoons were often made in what has come to be called the Old English pattern; a curved top, with a ridge through the center, running from the tip of the handle to the top of the bowl or tines. Some silversmiths gradually eliminated the ridge, forming a flat, round-topped handle; others experimented with a pointed tip, while some offered a straight, clipped top, tapered slightly at the sides to form a coffin shape. Decoration was generally simple and austere; an engraved crest, initials, or occasionally a motif borrowed from architectural or furniture decoration. The feather edge was used on some pieces, and lightly etched or engraved designs, sometimes called "Bright Cut" were used effectively on others.

The straight handle for knives began to replace the pistol-grip late in the 18th century, and in a few years, spoons and forks began to carry the same designs as those on knives. The day of the silver service had begun, and the silversmiths of the 18th century carried their craft to all great houses and many lesser establishments on the continent, in England and America.

Most 18th century forks had three prongs, but four-pronged forks had been made in earlier years, during the reign of Charles II. Some of these continued to be made and used throughout the 18th century, while the two-pronged fork, probably the type that was first made, appeared as a serving piece, and even in table forks made of the simpler metals, well into the 19th century. Early

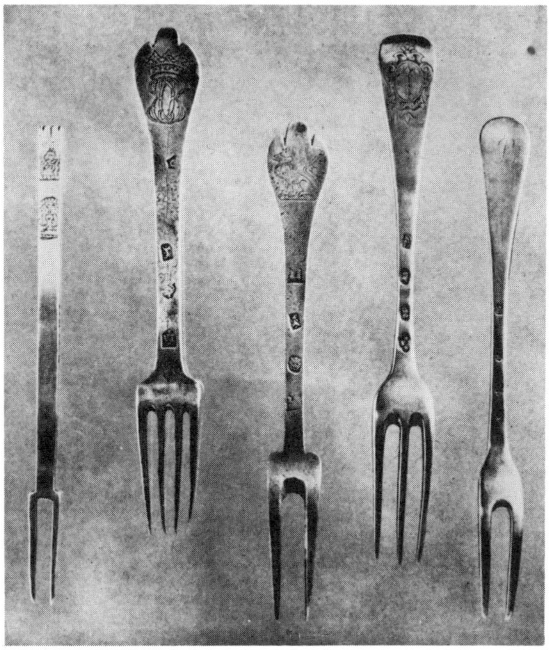

Silver forks made between 1632 and 1719, all bearing hallmarks of London or Edinburgh. The styles indicate that the number of tines offers no guide to relative antiquity of forks. *Courtesy Victoria & Albert Museum.*

18th century forks were generally small; after a time they grew larger, and, by the end of the century, were made in two sizes, table forks and dessert forks. By this time, solid silver tableware had become an accepted embellishment for the homes of the English gentry, and leading families in the colonies followed the custom established by their peers. The services were generally specially commissioned, and an order might range from a single teaspoon to an elaborate service for 12 or 24. The most complete of these usually consisted of what were called table knives, table forks, tablespoons, and teaspoons. These were supplemented, more and more frequently by dessert knives and forks, and, occasionally, by a set of marrow spoons with long, narrow bowls and channeled stems. Serving pieces were simple, and beautifully designed; usually a soup ladle, one or more serving forks, several serving spoons, and sometimes a platter spoon. Punch and toddy ladles were called for in some cases, and a gentleman's well-equipped table might also have a device, similar in appearance and function to an apple corer, called a cheese or butter taster or tester. Silver skewers, too, sometimes appeared at the table; these had been substituted, in the kitchen, for the iron skewer used in the actual cooking. The sucket fork and spoon was disappearing, although this ingenious tool, with a spoon at one end for eating the syrup, and prongs at the other for spearing the fruit or sweetmeat that swam in the sweet liquid, had been one of the earliest aids to eating a food that could be delicious —but difficult. In more modest homes, pewter was the accepted metal for spoons, and forks and knives were generally made of steel or iron, often with handles of wood or bone.

2

People: Personalities and Partners

From the time of Demetrius, the Biblical silversmith who opposed the Apostle Paul on the grounds that Christianity would encroach on the commerce of those who worked in the precious metal for the glorification of Diana of the Ephesians, those who plied the craft seem to have been part artist, part tradesman, part banker, part craftsman. The silversmiths of the early 19th century were no exception, particularly in the smaller communities. They could turn a hand to work in almost any metal, combining their craft with clockmaking and locksmithing. Some even served as oculists and dentists. But it was in the role of banker to the community that their services were most often remarked in the literature of the day; Samuel Johnson is credited by Boswell with the remark: "If he does really think that there is no distinction between virtue and vice, why, sir, when he leaves our houses let us count our spoons," while Lord Macaulay referred to the type of "diners-out from whom we guard our spoons."

The silver spoon represented the tangible evidence of wealth, for it was to the silversmith that the village housewife carried her carefully hoarded stock of silver coins to be made into a teaspoon or two. It was to the silversmith that the wealthy merchant or large landowner turned, to provide safekeeping for his excess silver money. Whether made into teapots, pitchers, bowls, and porringers called "hollow ware," or spoons and forks called "flatware," the silver retained its intrinsic value and still could be used and displayed. Yet in case of theft, its distinctive design combined with crests, monograms, and initials made it more easily identifiable than the commonly circulated coinage.

Banking and silversmithing had been combined in England for centuries. Samuel Kirk, who founded the Baltimore firm bearing his name, was descended from a long line of silversmiths and bankers. During the early 1800s, when he was setting up his business, silversmiths outnumbered bankers, and the 2500 or more who carried on the craft in various parts of the still-new country were frequently called upon to turn coins into silver spoons.

Along with a reputation for integrity, and an unusual degree of manual dexterity, the silver craft called for a knowledge of metallurgy and a more than passing acquaintance with a wide variety of tools. They were an inventive lot, and many were mechanically inclined. As machine methods replaced handwork in other industries, the U. S. Patent office was bombarded with devices for the mechanization of silversmithing, many of which helped establish one of the earliest "assembly-line" type of production industries in the country. As early as 1801, a method of manufacturing spoons was patented by a

Typical coin silver spoon patterns, late 18th century to mid-19th century. Top, from left: Joseph Moulton (1814–1903), William Moulton (1772–1861), William Moulton (1720–1793), Abel Moulton (1784–1840), F. Koldewey (c. 1840–1850), Kirk & Smith (c. 1815), T. J. Brown (c. 1835–1845). Below, Clement Oskamp (c. 1840). *Moulton spoons, courtesy Towle Mfg. Co.; Kirk & Smith spoon, courtesy Samuel Kirk & Son, Inc.; Koldewey spoon, courtesy W. V. Thompson; Oskamp spoon, courtesy Cincinnati Historical Society.*

T. Bruff. Other patents were granted to I. Bisbee of Bath, Massachusetts in 1809 and to J. Ridgeway of Groton, Massachusetts in 1814 for machines to make spoons. Also in 1814, J. Owings of Baltimore patented an impressed roller for making knives, spoons, etc., and within a few years R. Butcher of Philadelphia registered a method of making tableware from tin plates, pewter in sheets, sheet silver, etc. Another new method for making spoons came from A. Little in Bridgeton, N.J., in 1830, and, in 1833, T. Mix of Cheshire, Connecticut patented a new mold for casting spoons in quantity. Three years later, William Mix, this time from Prospect, Connecticut, offered an improved method of casting these utensils, and other patents, for machines for manufacturing silver spoons continued to be granted to various members of the Mix family, in Prospect and Wallingford, Connecticut until 1866. It was William Mix, in the early 1800s, who had rigged a buff wheel made with layers of rags, powered by a water wheel, to give his hand-made spoons a high polish, and his little village the nickname of "Ragville." And it was a member of the Mix family who had moved to Tariffville, Connecticut to join the youthful Cowles Manufacturing Company in one of the first electroplating efforts ever made in America, at a time when the youthful Asa Rogers, one of the three Rogers Brothers, was a partner in the same firm. That was in 1845, and Asa Rogers had earlier worked for the firms of Church & Rogers, and Rogers & Cole, producing coin silver pieces in the shops where his brother William was already a partner. By 1847, William and Simeon Rogers had been joined by their brother Asa, and the firm of William Rogers & Co. was already established in Hartford. It was the beginning of what was to become one of the best known names in the Victorian silver world, and the start of one of the most complex and confusing series of corporate identities the country has ever seen. William Rogers had established his own business in 1836, and it had become William Rogers & Co. in 1841, when Simeon Rogers joined the firm. By 1847, Asa Rogers had also become a partner, and in 1853 the Rogers Brothers Manufacturing Co. was organized; in 1854, the senior William Rogers transferred some of his stock to his son, William H. Rogers. A year later, in 1855, Simeon departed, to organize his own business, and the original William Rogers & Co. partnership was dissolved. In 1856, the younger William Rogers became a

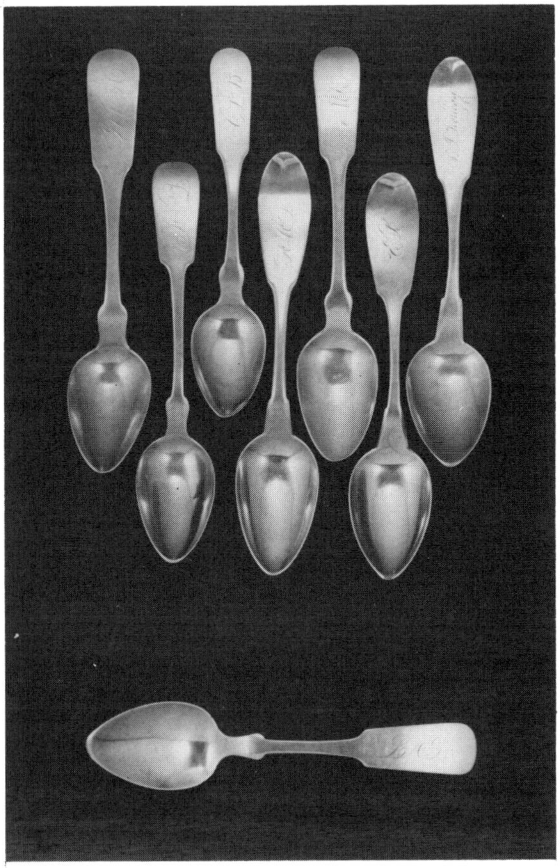

Coin silver spoons produced by William, Asa and Simeon Rogers before 1846. The Rogers Brothers were pioneers in the development of electroplated wares after 1847. *Courtesy International Silver Company.*

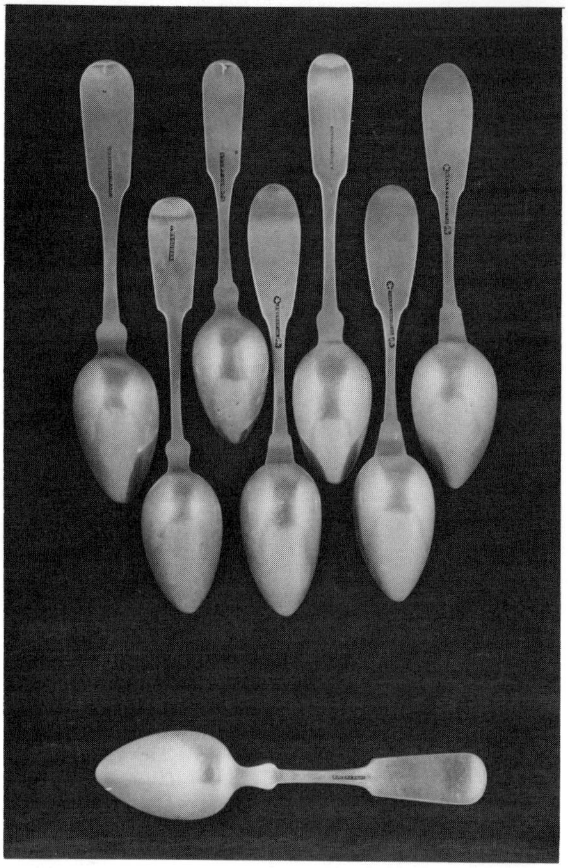

Marks used on early coin silver ware made by the three Rogers brothers before 1846. Their later trademark on plated ware became one of the most famous of all Victorian silver marks. *Courtesy International Silver Company.*

partner in William Rogers & Son, and father William Rogers became a partner in the new firm of Rogers, Smith & Co. The son, William Henry Rogers, became a director of Rogers, Smith & Co. in 1858, and, during the same year, brothers Simeon and Asa Rogers organized the firm of Rogers & Bro. at Waterbury, Connecticut. In 1861, Rogers Brothers Manufacturing Company was merged with Rogers, Smith & Company, and in 1862, both firms became a part of the Meriden Britannia Company. Meanwhile, although the Meriden Britannia Company had acquired the rights to the 1847 Rogers Bros. trademark, the William Rogers Manufacturing Company and Rogers & Bro. continued in business, and a son joined Simpson, Hall, Miller & Co., letting that firm use his name on its plated flatware line, and adding a William Rogers brand to the already complicated scene. In 1866, C. Rogers & Bro. began business in Meriden and as late as 1897, advertised management by the "only living Rogers Brother." In the ensuing years, as new generations of the family established themselves, other companies incorporating the Rogers name were organized. These included the Rogers Cutlery Company in 1871; the Rogers & Hamilton Co. in 1886, the F. B. Rogers Silver & Cutlery Company in 1884, and finally, about the turn of the century, the firms of William A. Rogers, Ltd., William G. Rogers, William H. Rogers, The F. B. Rogers Silver Co., Frank W. Rogers (whose trademark was William Rogers Son), The Rogers Silver Plate Company, the Simeon L. & George H. Rogers Co. and J. Rogers & Company. Most of these companies were eventually absorbed into the International Silver Company; Oneida, Ltd., took over William A. Rogers, Ltd., J. Rogers & Company, and the Simeon L. & George H. Rogers Company.

But long before this corporate complex developed, the early Victorian patent holders included names that were to become familiar throughout the country as the silver business grew: R. Wallace, J. L. & J. D. Frary, and Zephaniah A. Leonard and William Crossman, early partners in the firm that later became Reed & Barton.

Among the other silversmiths who were active in small shops during the early years of the 19th century, many were to lend their talents and their names to manufacturing firms supplying prodigious quantities of silverware before the end of the century. Samuel Kirk, who started the famous firm in Baltimore, worked in that city in 1815.

Jabez Gorham, whose son founded the Gorham Manufacturing Company, was already established in Providence in 1825. William B. Durgin, whose company later was merged with that of Gorham, was a silversmith in Concord, N. H. At this time in Newburyport, Massachusetts, Joseph Moulton IV, representing the fourth generation of the Moulton family to pursue the trade in America, had a bright young apprentice, Anthony Towle.

This same apprentice of the Moultons started his own business in 1855, became a partner in the firm of Towle & Jones in 1857, and by 1879 was operating a jewelry store under the name of Anthony F. Towle & Son. Spoons were made in the back shop of the establishment, and in 1880 this part of the business became the A. F. Towle & Son Manufacturing Co. Three years later the organization was split into two companies; The Towle Manufacturing Company, which has remained in Newburyport ever since that time, and The A. F. Towle & Son Company. The latter firm moved to Greenfield, Massachusetts in 1890, and in 1902 was succeeded by the Rogers, Lunt & Bowlen Company, a corporation formed by George Rogers, a Greenfield manufacturer, and George C. Lunt, who had been associated with the Anthony F. Towle enterprises since 1882. This company is known today as Lunt Silversmiths.

These 19th-century companies were not alone in tracing ancestry to earlier silversmiths. In some cases, it appears that there were breaks in the tradition, but descendants returned to the craft practiced by their families long before. William H. Manchester of Providence, R. I., for example, founder of another silver company still bearing his surname, is said to have counted among his ancestors one Malcolm Manchester, who served the first Queen Elizabeth as a hammer man. In her service, it is reported, he "lost an arm and lost a leg, but lost none of his skill as a silversmith."

Other silversmiths of the early 19th century became pioneers in the still-new jewelry retailing and wholesaling operations. The Marquand Brothers—Frederick, Isaac, and Joseph—were famous for the delicacy and balance of their spoons and forks about 1820. They later formed the firm of Marquand & Company, which eventually through the years, as other partners were admitted, became Black, Starr & Frost. Clement Oskamp, a silversmith in the new western metropolis of Cincinnati, later became a partner in the firm of Oskamp, Nolting & Company.

It was during the first year of Queen Victoria's reign that young Elijah Peacock journeyed from London, where his father was a clockmaker, to the little town of Chicago, on the shores of Lake Michigan. The shop he opened there was largely devoted to clock repairs, and specialized in the adjustment of chronometers for Great Lakes sailing vessels. But before Chicago was linked to the east by telegraph in 1848 or by railroad in 1852, the Peacock store was handling silverware and fine jewelry. This firm, bearing the name of C. D. Peacock, a son of the founder, was incorporated in 1860, and was one of the first retail establishments to market silver flatware stamped with the name of the store.

Throughout the later Victorian years, this practice of double-trademarking silverware was followed by many retail establishments, for the names and reputations of leading jewelers in a city were often better known than the names of distant manufacturers. Most flatware marked in this manner also carried the trademark of the silversmith as well. Store-marking continued well into the 20th century, but posed many problems for the jewelers. The multiplicity of pieces and patterns, combined with the many grades and weights of flatware, entailed the stocking of enormous inventories. In addition, special

Coin silver pieces made by silversmiths in Mobile, Alabama. Most of the popular early Victorian patterns are represented in this collection. *Courtesy Historic Mobile Preservation Society.*

orders, frequently for wedding or anniversary gifts, might be returned or exchanged by the recipients, and those pieces which were marked with the store name could not be returned to the manufacturer or sold through another outlet.

In some cases, a retail store name became synonymous with that of a manufacturer; Charles L. Tiffany, for example, was already a partner in the firm of Tiffany & Young in 1837, and the growing store sold almost all of the output of John Moore, who had begun the manufacture of silverware in 1827. The relationship continued when the store became Tiffany & Company in 1853, and in 1868, when Tiffany was incorporated, the Moore firm became a part of the organization, and Edward C. Moore, a son of the founder, became a director and officer of Tiffany & Company.

Whether it stems from the durability of the metal itself, from the integrity forged into the products, or from an innate ability to adapt to changing industrial, social, and economic patterns, the longevity of so many of the early silversmithing firms is a phenomenon unusual in American business history, and a tribute to the respect the industry has won through many years.

3

Pewter, Britannia and Brass

In many of Sir William Gilbert's collaborations with Sir Arthur Sullivan, the libretto achieved its humor, if not its lilt, through quick reversals of familiar facts. Such was the case in *The Gondoliers,* with the lines:

> When every blessed thing you hold
> is made of silver, or of gold,
> You long for simple pewter.

The days of "simple pewter" were not long gone in 1889 when *The Gondoliers* was first performed. The theatre audiences of the day could readily recall a farm or village household where the mistress, scouring her never-quite-bright pewter spoons, had often expressed a longing to exchange them for silver. And the housewives in the audience, content with their spoons of the new silver plate or sterling, could join in the laughter that greeted such a seemingly preposterous statement.

The alloy known as pewter, a mixture of tin with lead, brass, or copper, had been known and used by the ancient Egyptians, Chaldeans, Greeks, and Chinese; the Romans had brought pewter vessels to England about 100 B.C. After the dissolution of the Roman Empire, the art of pewter making seems to have disappeared, until about 1000 A.D. Pewter is mentioned in English records as early as 1076, and after 1473 the establishment of pewterers' guilds standardized quality and increased production. Three grades were generally recognized; *Fine pewter* consisted of 80 percent tin and 20 percent brass or copper; *hollow ware pewter,* consisted of 80 percent tin and 20 percent lead, and *trifle pewter* was an alloy of 60 percent tin and 40 percent lead. Later, the alloy for trifle pewter was changed to 83 parts tin to 17 parts antimony, and this became the raw material for spoons and similar small articles. Antimony, during the 17th century, virtually replaced copper in making flatware, and the best hard metal pewter contained over 90 percent tin, with less than 8 percent antimony and 2 percent copper.

While guild and government regulations doubtlessly played a part in maintaining the quality of English pewter, it was the mines in Wales and Cornwall, supplying the world's purest tin, that made the high quality possible. And that tin was zealously guarded!

The earliest pewterers in the American colonies could visualize a constantly growing market for pewter products, but raw materials were virtually impossible to obtain. There were no tin mines; the few copper and lead mines had low yields and high recovery costs; tin imported from England was subject to a five percent *ad valorem* duty, while pewter manufactured in England entered colonial ports duty-free. But the thrift of the colonial settlers, combined with the daily use which wore out most pewter after five or six years, favored the American pewterers. No matter how badly bent, how deeply dented, or how worn pewter might be, it could always be melted down, re-alloyed, and reworked. Through necessity, the pewter craftsmen operated as traders, taking in old pewter as part payment for each sale, thereby conserving a stock of raw material. They became expert junkmen, too, for the alloy used in each piece accepted in trade had to be determined—often by guess.

Like silversmithing, the craft required skill learned through apprenticeship. It required an unusually large investment in molds made of brass or iron, soldering irons, and other tools—including wheels, lathes, ladles, and anvils. In the American Colonies, it required a knack for Yankee trading, for the sale of the products might, in addition to bringing in old pewter, bring in furs or a firkin of butter, farm produce, or fruit.

Early pewterers worked in many metals, with little specialization in the wares. Plates, teapots, and spoons, looking glass frames, lather boxes, and buttons all might come from the same small crafts shop. The business, too, was often combined with retail trade in other items. Ashbil Griswold, one of the early 19th-century pewterers who had been an apprentice of Thomas Danforth, dealt in shoes and cigars, cashmere and goose feathers, during the years when he was putting his touch mark on hundreds of pieces of fine pewter in his Connecticut establishment. A jewelry and watch repair shop was combined with the pewter workshop of Isaac Babbitt in Taunton, Massachusetts, in the early 1820s. Despite the problems with which the craft was beset, it was one that attracted apprentices who realized that it represented what was known as "a steady trade." The population was growing, and each new mouth to be fed meant a new demand for pewter tableware, along with the constant replacement business. So, for periods of up to seven years, such young men as Isaac Lewis, Lemuel Curtis, James Frary and some of the sons of Hiram Yale of Yalesville worked and learned their trade in small shops throughout New England. It was during the lifetime of these young men that the pewter business was to be largely eclipsed by new alloys. These same men brought about the founding of what were to become some of America's leading silver firms during the Victorian era.

For some years, English manufacturers had been exporting to the United States numerous articles fabricated of a new "white metal." It was closely related to pewter, apparently, but afforded a harder surface with a more silvery sheen; it took a brighter polish, and possessed better working qualities. The new alloy was made in Sheffield, and James Vickers, an English manufacturer, seems to have first used it for spoons and vegetable forks in 1769. By the beginning of the 19th century, The Sheffield Directory listed more than a dozen firms making "white metal" products. In 1804, the firm of James Dixon was organized, and for a time set the standards for quality and styling of these products in the United States. Spurred on by examples set in other industries, the hard, silvery, and shining metal products began to be made in factories. While the alloy was still hand-crafted in most respects, the various stages were becoming separated, and the individual workman found himself repeating a specialized operation rather than carrying a single piece to completion. The formulation of the new metal was a closely guarded secret in most of these early English factories, but gradually the various mixtures came to be called by a common name—Britannia Metal.

Large quantities of the fabricated goods were being exported to the United States, and more and more of the American pewterers' old customers were demanding the shiny new metal. Many a young man who had com-

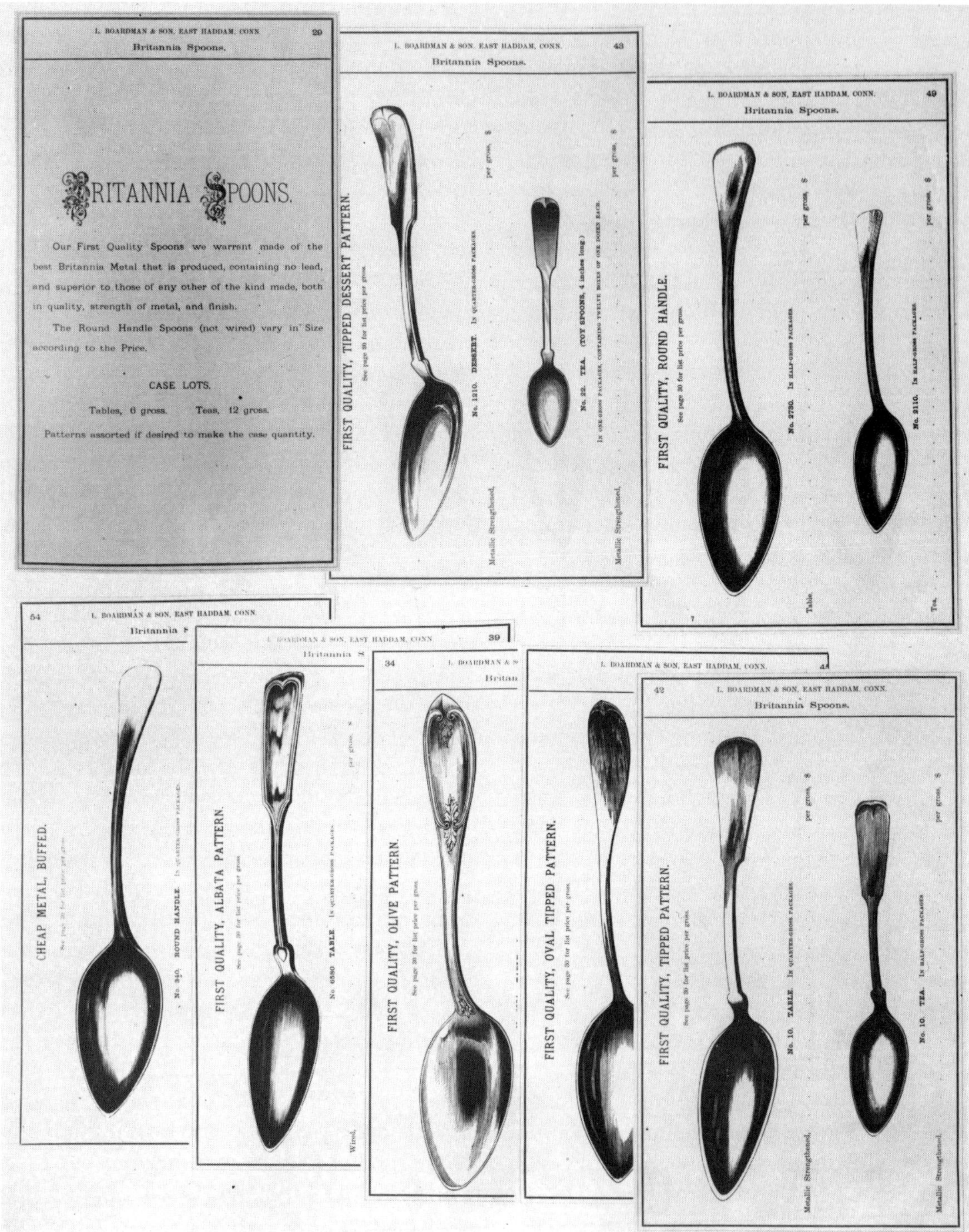

Britannia spoons in various patterns made by Luther Boardman & Son as late as 1880. Such spoons are often mistakenly called "pewter," and frequently believed to have been made much earlier.

pleted his pewterer's apprenticeship was intrigued by the secret of Britannia; experiments were constantly carried on in an effort to discover the magic proportions of the various metals used in the alloy. Some of these ingredients were still difficult to obtain. Restrictions on the export of the ores from the Welsh and Cornish tin mines had not been relaxed; lead production was still limited, and the available sources of other minerals were not always dependable. Some tin was entering the United States from Spain and the West Indies, and expanding world trade from New England seaports was slowly making other raw materials accessible to the metal working shops in the states bordering the Atlantic.

As early as 1814, a few one-and-two man shops in Salem, Massachusetts had begun limited production of Britannia ware. Later in that decade, Isaac Babbitt, working in a little shed back of his father's jewelry store in Taunton, pulled his first successful sheet of Britannia-like metal between a set of jeweler's hand rolls. In 1824, with William Crossman, a friend and neighbor, he formed the firm of Babbitt & Crossman for the production of Britannia metal products.

Through the years, the partners and principals changed along with the products, as the company became successively Babbitt, Crossman & Company; Crossman, West & Leonard; Taunton Britannia Manufacturing Company; Leonard, Reed & Barton; and, after 1840, Reed & Barton. While Babbitt's name early disappeared from the corporate signature, he was memorialized in every Victorian silver factory and other shop powered by waterwheel or steam. "Babbitt Metal" in the bearing boxes bore the brunt of the wear imposed by the complex system of pulleys, shafts, and belts which transferred power from the central source to the individual machines.

Elsewhere in New England, men like Rufus Dunham in Maine, Roswell Gleason in Massachusetts, and Ashbil Griswold in Connecticut were making the transition from the crafting of pewter articles to the manufacture of Britannia Metal products, too. A number of Griswold's earlier apprentices had settled in the area around Meriden, and the growing Britannia industry in the community included the firms of James A. Frary & Company, I. C. Lewis & Company, Curtis & Lyman, and in nearby Wallingford, John Munson's factory.

None of the firms was large, and none of them maintained any salesmen. The Connecticut peddler, dealing in notions and small wares of all kinds, still worked his way from farmhouse to farmhouse, from village to village, with a loaded wagon of ivory combs, pewter buttons, tinware, and Britannia pieces. The supplies came from the workshops and small factories, and were replenished as the peddlers made their more or less regular rounds.

But the country was growing, and the area that one man, a horse and wagon could cover was limited, so a pair of Meriden brothers had formed the firm of H. C. Wilcox & Co. to market the output of the various Britannia producers in the little city. They were a far-sighted and commercially minded pair, alert to the role that salesmen would play when more of America's small factories and shops would turn to mass production methods, as had already happened in England. To justify the capital investment that factory methods would entail, the Wilcox brothers knew that faster sales and broader markets would have to be developed; an industrialized economy could not be built on casual patrons whose orders were filled individually. So it was largely at the instigation of the Wilcox firm that, in 1852, most of the small Britannia firms in the Meriden area were brought together to form the Meriden Britannia Company. And it was largely through the efforts of Horace Wilcox, who had sold some of the

Rogers Brothers new silver-plated spoons as early as 1848, that the Meriden Britannia Company entered the silver business in 1862, and through an additional series of consolidations, became the International Silver Company in 1898.

Among the apprentices trained by Captain William Mix was young Robert Wallace. By 1833, he was making Britannia spoons in a rented grist mill in Cheshire, Connecticut, and within a year he had obtained a bar of a new alloy called German silver from Dr. Fouchtwanger, a chemist who had come to New York from Germany. After having the bar rolled in Waterbury, young Wallace produced some four dozen spoons, the first to be made of this new material in America. Encouraged by Deacon Almer Hall of Wallingford, who was later to be head of Hall, Elton & Co., R. Wallace moved his operation to Hall's home town, where production of R. Wallace & Son and Wallace Silversmiths flatware has continued to the present time. Until 1877, when the firm began its own plating operations, customers for the unplated German silver products included Hall, Elton & Co., the Fred H. Curtis Co. Meriden Britannia Co. and others.

Since the manufacture of many of the early pieces of electroplated flatware paralleled the Wallace experience, it is often difficult to credit a single firm or maker with the entire production of these pieces. In 1852, for example, a year or two after a branch of the Oneida Community had been established beside the Quinnipiac river in Connecticut, the stream was dammed to form the present Community Lake in Wallingford, and the water power used to produce tinned iron spoons in the "Olive" and "Lily" patterns. Within a year, by 1853, unplated steel spoon blanks were being sold to the new Meriden Britannia Co., eight miles away. This relationship continued until 1877, when the Oneida Community colony in Wallingford established its own plating plant—a factory which was later moved to Niagara Falls, and finally to its present location in Oneida, N.Y.

Meanwhile, from the early 1800s on, the practitioners of individual crafts had tended to concentrate in certain areas, and as the crafts shops grew into small factories, specific industries became associated, in the public mind, with specific towns. Thus Danbury was known as a "hat city," New Haven as a "buggy city," and Waterbury, Connecticut, had early become known as a "brass city." Like pewter and Britannia, this alloy, too, was a forerunner of silver plate.

It was from Waterbury, in the 1820s, that the Scovill family, who were engaged in the manufacture of brass buttons, sent a young clerk to England to learn all he could about brass casting and brass rolling. This young man, Israel Holmes, later became production manager for the Scovill company, and, through the years, was successfully associated with firms of Holmes & Hotchkiss, Brown & Elton, Walcott Brass Company, and The Waterbury Brass Company. In 1851, he organized the firm of Holmes & Tuttle, and in 1853 the firm of Holmes, Booth & Haydens, which boasted the largest brass rolling mill in the United States. The Civil War boomed the production of brass, and at the end of the war, seeking new outlets, this company turned to the production of nickel silver, which was superseding Britannia Metal, both as a base for silver-plated knives, forks, and spoons and as cheaper unplated flatware. Within a few years, Holmes, Booth & Haydens was producing completed silverware, and the earlier Holmes & Tuttle firm eventually became the American Silver Company.

Israel Holmes' son, Colonel C. E. L. Holmes, had established a rolling mill in New York City after the Civil War with his brother-in-law, George Edwards. Along with sheet copper and brass, their firm of Holmes & Griggs rolled nickel silver. This production, in turn, led to the purchase of a silver company in Stratford, Connecticut, which would provide an outlet for the New York rolling mill's production. Within a few years, the new firm absorbed still another Bridgeport silver company, and the Holmes & Edwards Silver Company was established in Bridgeport.

The transitions were normal ones for well-managed companies. The silver business was constantly increasing as frontiers were pushed farther west, the population expanded, and the economy shifted from one based on mercantile enterprises to an increasingly complex industrial system. A new middle class was rising, and, like Americans before and after this time, was constantly demanding something better than the products the previous generation had employed. Pewter had given way to Britannia, and Britannia to silver plate on more and more tables across the nation.

But for a long time after the end of the Civil War, the unplated spoons and knives and forks of the various white metals were not completely supplanted in many homes; steel was used for some tableware, frequently combined with wooden handles, and the new aluminum ware enjoyed a brief flurry of popularity. But while pewter had been all but forgotten, except in isolated homesteads where a spoon mold might be used to recast and reuse worn tableware, Britannia Metal continued to be produced well into the 1890s. The newer nickel silver, sold under a variety of names that included German Silver, Alpacca Silver, Alaska Silver, and Mexican Silver continued to be featured in mail order catalogs well into the 20th century. It was serviceable and popular for smaller hotels and restaurants, for "everyday" use in farmhouses, and for city kitchens. It was described, in one of the mail order catalogs of the 1890s, as:

> The cheapest and best flatware made. The Alaska Silverware is not plated, but is the same solid metal through and through, and will hold the same color as long as there is any portion of the goods left. The metal is very dense and tough, is almost as white as genuine silver, takes a beautiful polish, and requires no care as does silver plated ware. You can scrape kettles or pots, or subject it to any kind of service without fear of damage. We have this year added a beautiful engraved pattern, which is equal in appearance and artistic finish to any of the best silver plated or solid silver goods on the market.

The selling was sound, but of necessity it was based on a comparison with what had become the standard for tableware—silver plate or solid silver. America's housewives had not been sated with the precious metals, to a point where they would as yet "yearn for simple pewter," or for any of its substitutes!

4

Properties, Production, and Processing

When, in 1860, Ralph Waldo Emerson paraphrased an earlier comment of Dr. Johnson with the words "The louder he talked of his honor, the faster we counted our spoons," he emphasized again the intrinsic value that Victorians recognized in their silver tableware. Silver was synonymous with valued coins; it was comparatively rare, and therefore desirable.

But its value in the market place was only one of the qualities that had from the earliest times made silver so desirable for the fabrication of eating implements; its physical properties provided additional appeal. Of all the usual metals, silver has the highest heat conductivity; instant adjustment to temperature change makes it friendly to the hand and to the mouth, and kind to the food it transfers. It gives off no substances which stain or affect the flavor of foods. Psychologically, it is a warm and intimate metal; it possesses a luminosity that is deep and friendly. The same balance of refraction and diffusion that affords this luminous quality gives it a special affinity for the talents of the designer, and its molecular structure permits a wide range of finishes, ornamentation, and refinement. Silver is a workable metal; it can be beaten, drawn, stamped, cast, incised, and oxidized, permitting almost limitless design possibilities. It requires only minute adulteration to assure durability, yet it gives an impression of being almost sensuously soft. All these properties have combined, through the years, to make tableware of silver a symbol of elegance and personal achievement.

Even so stalwart a champion of modesty and thrift as Benjamin Franklin admitted the appeal of silverware. After extolling the frugality and industry of his wife in his *Autobiography,* Franklin continued:

> We kept no idle servants, our table was plain and simple, our furniture of the cheapest. For instance, my breakfast was for a long time bread and milk (no tea), and I ate it out of a twopenny earthen porringer, with a pewter spoon. But mark how luxury will enter into families, and make progress, in spite of principle: being call'd one morning to breakfast, I found it in a China bowl, with a spoon of silver! They had been bought for me without my knowledge by my wife, and had cost her the enormous sum of three-and-twenty shillings, for which she had no other excuse or apology to make, but that she thought her husband deserv'd a silver spoon and China bowl as well as any of his neighbors.

That luxury continued to make progress is attested by his next sentence:

> This was the first appearance of plate

and China in our house, which afterward, in a course of years, as our wealth increased, augmented gradually to several hundred pounds in value.

Pure silver is too soft to use in articles subject to handling, but the desirability of the metal for many purposes early led to the establishment of standards governing the permissible alloy. As early as the beginning of the 16th century, Henry VIII and Edward VI had brought silversmiths from Germany to England to help establish a standard formula for use in minted coins. The Germans, who were known as Easterlings, arrived at a figure of 92.5 percent pure silver, which was called the Easterling Standard. English silversmiths shortened the term to Sterling Standard, and in 1562 Queen Elizabeth made this percentage official for all English coins. In the United States, the U.S. Mint Act of 1792 established a standard of 892-4/10 fine for Coin Silver, which is generally defined as 900/1000 pure silver, 100/1000 added copper. It was not until 1906 that the Stamping Act made the Sterling Standard official for the United States, but the term "Sterling" had appeared on some silverware produced in this country before that time.

During the late 18th century, a group of Irish silversmiths who worked in Baltimore had used it, but most 18th-and early 19th-century silversmiths used the terms *Coin, Pure Coin, Coin Silver, Dollar,* or *Standard* on their wares. Other quality marks used in this country included the terms *11 Oz.* and *10.15,* meaning 11 ounces and 10 ounces, 15 pennyweight of silver in the pound troy.

Some of the silverware produced by the firm of John C. Moore for Tiffany & Company in 1854 and 1855 was marked "English Sterling 925-1000," along with the name of Tiffany & Co., but the first habitual use of the sterling stamp on silverware produced in the United States appears to have been on the wares of William Gale & Sons from 1856. The Gale company used a stamp reading "925 Sterling." The Gorham Manufacturing Co. adopted the Sterling mark in 1868. It appeared intermittently on the wares of various manufacturers during the 1870's and 1880s, but by the 1890s most manufacturers had switched from the various coin designations and ounce markings to a "925/1000" or a "Sterling 925/1000" mark. 1895 advertisements for Gorham products explain the difference between "Coin" and "Sterling" standards; the mark of Samuel Kirk & Son was changed from 11 Oz. to 925/1000 in 1896; Tiffany & Co. used a "Sterling 925/1000" mark consistently after 1875.

A system of hallmarks such as has been used in England since the 14th century was never established in the United States, except for a brief period from 1814 to 1830, when the silversmiths of Baltimore—then, as now, a silver producing center—set up a system which identified the city, the smith, and the year in which a particular piece was produced. The Baltimore mark, and the dominical or date letters employed during those years, are illustrated under the Kirk & Smith and Samuel Kirk listings in the *Manufacturers, Trade Marks and Trade Names* section of this book.

Although no hallmark system was officially adopted in the United States, English hallmarks influenced the design of many trademarks. Some frankly imitated the firmly established marking system of the British Isles; others adapted the form, frequently substituting company initials for the British symbols. Few employed the scholarship evident in the mark of The Gorham Company, where the anchor is emblematic of the State of Rhode Island, the lion adapted from the English sterling mark, and the Old English "G" representative of both the company name and, (in the English date sequence) the year of its founding, 1831. This mark was used on some pieces as early as 1848; it has been used consistently since 1868.

The early Victorian silversmiths worked almost entirely by hand. Coins were brought in, melted down to provide the raw material, and rolled into sheets. Blanks of flat metal were then cut, and shaped by placing the blanks on a matrix of proper form, covered by a round punch, which could be dealt a sharp blow with a hammer to form a spoon bowl. Further hammering and filing with more delicate tools completed the shaping of the piece. Finishing was a hand operation, as it is today in many fine silver factories. The signs of the earlier working—hammer or file marks, irregularities in the surface—were removed by hand operations; these included stoning with pumice and bluestone, sand bobbing, brushing and buffing to prepare the piece for its final polishing.

The craft was taught through an apprentice system, and it is to apprentices of the early Victorian years that many of the country's great silver companies owe their existence. It is to this apprentice system, too, that the exquisitely wrought small pieces in coin silver, generally spoons, must be credited. These miniatures, often referred to as "toy" silverware or identified as "doll pieces," were actually the work of apprentices, and represented a kind of final examination for those who were about to be allowed to carry on the trade without the close supervision of the master silversmith for whom they worked. Unlike the miniature chests and chairs of the Victorian period, which were usually salesmen's samples, these small silver pieces were not used in selling or treated as samples. They were executed simply to show that the apprentice worker had acquired sufficient skill to take on commissions, and, after approval by their masters, the apprentice was permitted to sell them, usually at about 25 cents apiece. The miniature evidences of skill were made in the same patterns as the larger teaspoons, and, while they are comparatively rare, single examples still appear occasionally. The Essex Institute in Salem, Massachusetts and the Cooper Union Museum in New York City are among the museums boasting collections of this "silver-in-the-little."

Various methods of molding spoons had been devised during the 18th and early 19th centuries, and early Victorian inventors had patented a number of machines utilizing multiple molds. None of these were entirely satisfactory, but a system credited to William Gale, which permitted the forming of spoons from flat sheets of silver through the use of a drop hammer, came into limited use after 1821. Improvements to the original equipment, and supplementary aids to this early factory method were gradually developed, so that by mid-century most silverware factories were equipped with some form of this machine method. But the very nature of the product precluded the elimination of hand work, and most of the early factories continued to be composed of collective groups of hand-craft men.

It was not until the decade before the Civil War that most silverware manufacturers adopted machine techniques. The drop hammer, combined with upper and lower dies, both of which contained the ornament, made possible a far wider variety of designs, but the nature of the process and the equipment employed limited patterns to comparatively flat surfaces with shallow depressed motifs or low embossing.

During the 1890s, the shaped die came into almost universal use. This die permitted a far wider range of designs, and added greater depth to the design elements. It also permitted the flatware to be shaped at the same time that the pattern was rendered. This feature, in turn, made it economically feasible to develop the multiplicity of pieces that comprised the complete silver flatware service of the late Victorian days.

But each new stride toward mechanization

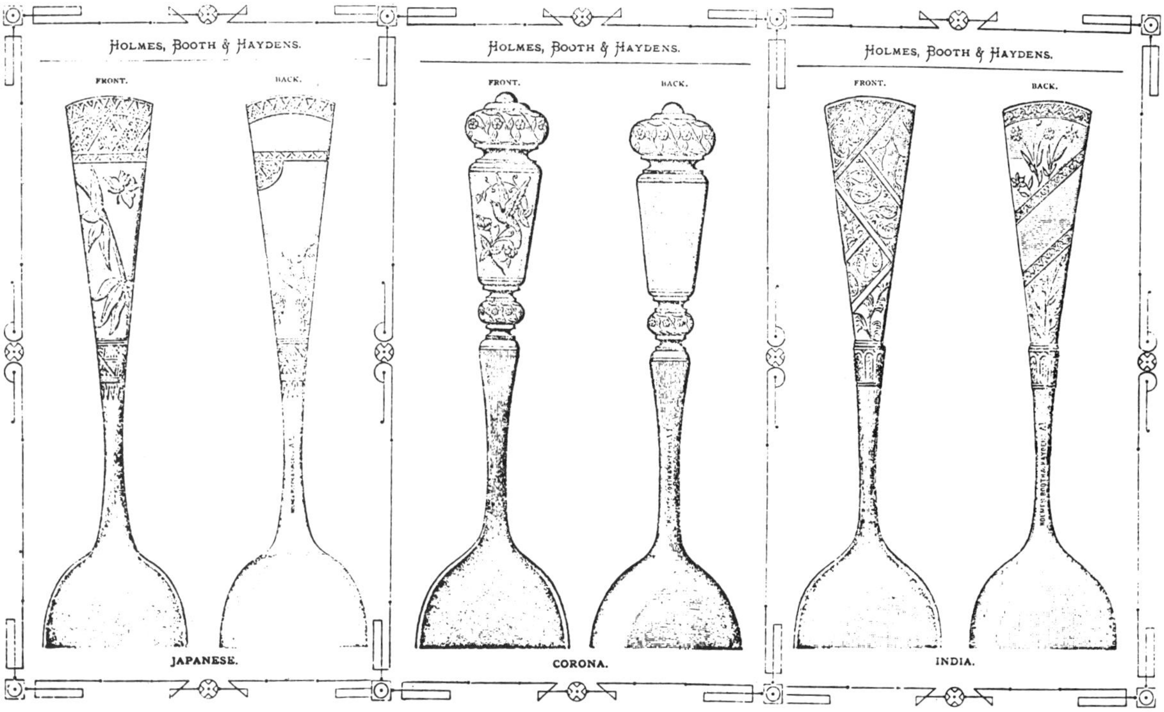

The use of two-part dies permitted inexpensive decoration of both the front and back of flatware handles. The new development doubled the number of illustrations in manufacturers' catalogs, for both sides of each new pattern had to be shown.

of the industry required further inventive skill to solve new problems. In the case of the shaped die, a method had to be devised to retain the temper of the fork and spoon shaft while the handle was heated to a point where it could be subjected to the impression of the die. In 1895, Elijah Talman invented a device for heating the end to be struck with the pattern while keeping the remainder of the article water-cooled to maintain the temper of the metal, and his improved system of "hot stamping" came into general use.

So-called hollow handles for flatware had been developed during the 18th century, and by 1820 had become virtually standard on many pieces in solid silver services. Most knives were equipped with handles of this type, made to approximate the pattern of the spoons and forks. In some cases, early in the 19th century, these hafts, as they were called, were the products of specialized factories, sold to the silver manufacturer for use with the forks and spoons he made; in other cases, they were manufactured in the same factory as the rest of the pieces. The vast majority were stamped from thin sheets of sterling silver. The two halves were struck from dies, and soldered together; where the work is fine, this solder line is invisible even with a magnifying glass. The central cavity was generally filled with a mixture of shellac strengthened with powdered pumice and poured in while the mixture remained semi-liquid. The tang of the knife blade or fork shaft was inserted—

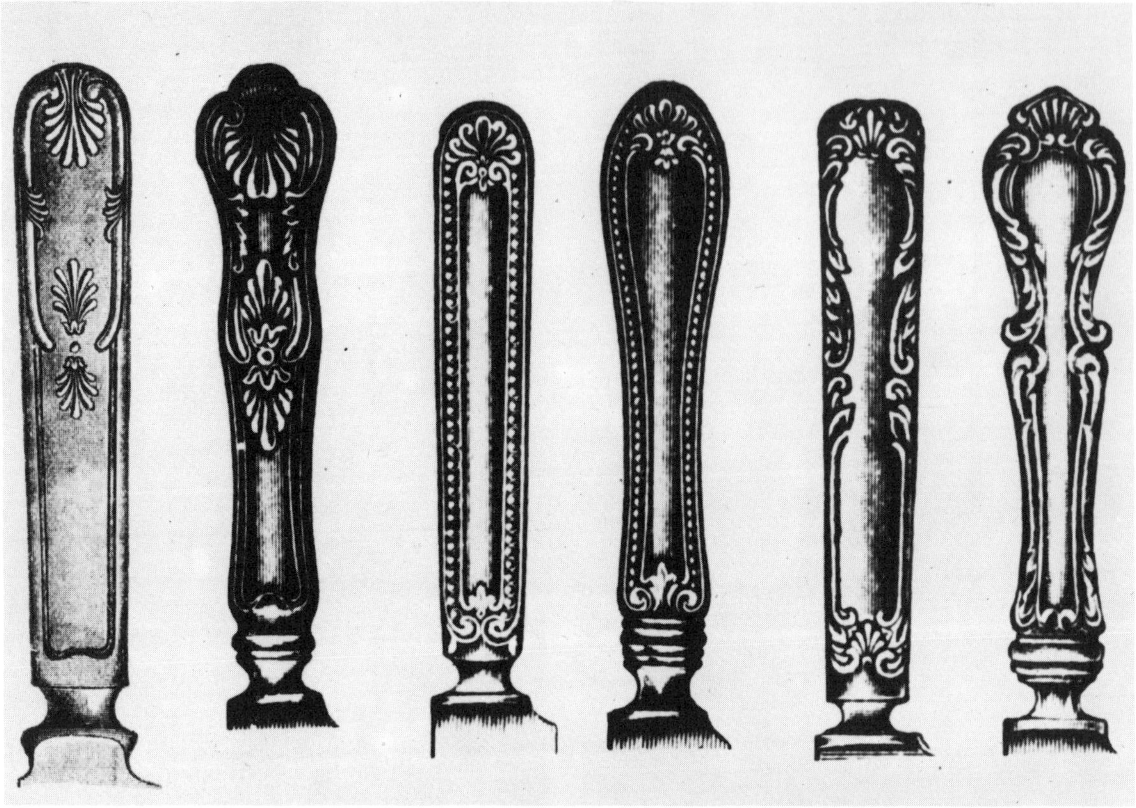

Buyers might select either solid or hollow handles in many patterns in electroplate. Solid handles were simple in outline, but decorated to match other pieces. From left, "King," "Stuart," and "Joan," all 1835 R. Wallace.

sometimes with an additional bolster covering the joint between handle and blade or shaft—so that when the cement hardened, the handle was securely fixed. The "filler" of the hollow handle varied with the maker; in addition to the shellac-pumice cement, some firms used compositions of resin or other substances that would remain in a semi-liquid state while the work was in process, but would harden after a period of setting.

Throughout the mid- and late-Victorian years, improvements in the manufacture of hollow handles occupied both designers and production men. Many new methods for stamping the half units, soldering them together, and attaching the blades and shafts were patented, but it was not until many years later in the 1930s, that hollow handles were successfully made in one piece.

One of the Yales of Yalesville, Connecticut, during the first half of the 19th Century, had arrived at an improvement in the earlier English method of soldering the two halves together by silver-brazing. This procedure was followed with minor variations throughout the Victorian years. The system was not foolproof; the annealing process might soften the two pieces, and weaken the handle. Small pieces of the silver solder, or other brazing material when it was used, might break off inside the handle with a resultant rattle each time the piece was moved. But despite the deficiencies, hollow handles were popular, for they permitted heavy, ornate decoration, and without making a piece unwieldy or unduly heavy, gave an impression of massive solidity compatible with the heavy walnut and mahogany tables that silver services were designed to grace. During the last years of the 19th century, all manner of knives and forks, and even some spoons, (to say nothing of a wide variety of fancy pieces) boasted hollow handles—mute reminders to a dinner guest that the host had happily paid the premium price these intricately fashioned accoutrements commanded.

Machine stamping, or raising of the pattern, gave the designer a free hand in filling the demand for increasingly ornate patterns. Unlike most manufacturing where the rule is that the simpler the product the easier it is to produce in volume, the shaped die encouraged increased ornamentation. Mechanically, the process was not unlike the hammering procedure employed by hand craftsmen; but the machine, with the aid of handwork at the finishing point, could turn out thousands like the one model, once the dies had been completed. It was just as easy to produce heavily decorated patterns as it was to manufacture the plain and simple ones.

Nor was the role of the machine denied by the producers; it was an age when the wonders of machine production could still arouse admiration. As production of silverware and silver-plated ware followed new frontiers, manufacturers boasted of the size of their factories, rolling mills, and drop hammers. In the late 60s, for example, the Aurora Silver Company, from its site on the Fox River in Illinois, issued a broadside pointing out that its "Rolling Mill is the only one of its kind west of Cincinnati," and featuring the 20,000 square feet of floors in the factory. Manned, as were so many of the western factories, by pioneers from Connecticut, the Aurora firm was repeating the standard advertising formula of the earlier eastern silver manufacturers, whose catalogs and broadsides often devoted as much space to the factory as they did to the product.

The decade following the end of the Civil War brought other changes to the silver business, too. Up to this time, solid silver tableware had found its way to very few middle class families; most could boast only a coin silver spoon or two. The metal itself was expensive; this in itself was enough to discourage most middle income buyers. The price of the metal effectively discouraged the application of factory methods to the fabrication of silver services, since factory methods precluded a mass market for the product. Among the wealthy, where custom-made solid silver services had not been replaced by the factory-produced, less costly electroplated services, there was a limited demand easily filled by the silversmiths who had continued the handcraft methods. But for about 30 years, electroplated table silver had enjoyed a virtual monopoly; it had rapidly replaced Britannia ware, just as Britannia ware had replaced pewter.

The silver plate was attractive, it wore well, it served its purpose admirably; but the characteristic American striving for something better for each new generation again made itself felt. This ambition was helped along by several other factors in the late 1870s; all combined to increase the availability and popularity of solid silverware.

By the mid-70s, silver mining had assumed tremendous proportions. The opening of the Comstock Lode in 1859, and metallurgical process improvements that lowered production and recovery costs and made it possible to use ores of lower grade, brought lower prices. There was a decreased demand for monetary silver from Europe. The steady level of silver prices, which had been maintained at between $1.32 and $1.36 an ounce from 1850 to 1872, began to decline, and with each new drop in price, the difference in cost between solid silver and top grade electroplate decreased.

Lower prices for the precious metal itself meant little until factory methods could convert the silver into silver services, so more and more silversmiths established factories. There had been pioneers; even before the Civil War, such firms as Kirk, Tiffany, and Gorham had featured solid silver products, and had done much to broaden the market. As late as 1872, jobbing firms like that of B. F. Norris & Co. in Chicago had solicited the custom-crafting of coin silver. In its catalog for that year, the Norris firm listed charges ranging from $3.00 for making up a dozen teaspoons in "plain work" to $5.00 for a shell-bowl soup ladle in "figured work"; to these prices was added the desired number of ounces of silver at $1.60 an ounce "made up." But despite the pioneer factories, it was undoubtedly the drop in silver prices after 1875 that hastened the advent of the power press and the decline of the hand hammer in the fabrication of solid silver flatware.

While mechanization broadened the market, it was the press of competition that led to the wide variety of weights in which sterling silver was offered.

Most of the older firms producing solid silverware had continued the pricing practice of the earlier English and American silversmiths; the prices of completed pieces were determined by their weight. The cost of spoons or other flatware was quoted "by the ounce," sometimes as a single piece, sometimes in terms of "weight per dozen." It was not until October of 1897 that *The Keystone* was able to announce that:

> Several leading manufacturers of sterling silverware have announced to the trade that their spoons and forks, which were formerly sold by weight, will hereafter be sold after the manner of other goods, by the piece or dozen.

The article continued, after quoting opinions of some of the concerned manufacturers:

> There is by no means general agreement, however, among the sterling silverware manufacturers as to the advisability of selling to the trade by the dozen instead of by weight as formerly . . . and the retailer will do well to note the method adopted by the particular manufacturers in whose product he is interested.

ANNUAL PRICE LIST. 15

COIN SILVER.

FOR MAKING KNIVES, FORKS, SPOONS, &c., TO ORDER.

FIGURED WORK.

Table Forks and Spoons	per doz.	$9 00
Dessert Forks and Spoons	"	7 50
Tea and Coffee Spoons	"	4 50
Salt and Mustard Spoons	"	4 50
Sugar Shells	"	10 00
Preserve Spoons	"	24 00
Sugar Sifters	"	24 00
Butter, Tea and Dessert Knives	"	10 00
Children's Forks	"	7 50
Pickle Forks	"	6 50
Pickle Forks, with blade	"	9 00
Soup Ladles, plain bowl	each	4 50
Soup Ladles, shell bowl	"	5 00
Oyster Ladles, shell bowl	"	4 00
Oyster Ladles, plain bowl	"	3 50
Gravy Ladles	"	1 50
Cream Ladles	"	1 00
Sugar Tongs, claw	"	2 25

PLAIN WORK.

Table Spoons	per doz.	6 00
Dessert Spoons	"	4 50
Tea Spoons	"	3 00
Table Forks	"	9 00
Dessert Forks	"	7 50
Sugar Spoons	"	7 50
Cream Ladles	each	75
Gravy Ladles	"	1 00
Soup Ladles	"	3 50
Oyster Ladles	"	2 50

At the present rate of Gold, for Silver made up, $1.60 per ounce.

To ascertain the price of Spoons, Forks, etc., add to the above price for manufacture the number of ounces of silver you wish at $1.60 per ounce.

WE BUY OLD GOLD AND SILVER.

Old Silver, per ounce	1 15
California Gold, per pwt	1 00
Pike's Peak Gold, per pwt	1 00
18 kt. Gold, per pwt	90

Weight determined cost of coin silver flatware. The customer selected the pieces, chose plain or figured work, then added the cost of the number of ounces of silver to be used in making up the order. This price list is from an 1871 catalog.

For a number of years, pricing remained a matter of compromise; most manufacturers finally arrived at a system where price was determined by the number of ounces of silver used in each dozen teaspoons. As new firms entered the field, light weights and low prices became weapons for the newcomers, and even many reputable old manufacturers were forced to offer as many as five different grades, or weights, of sterling, which might range from 5 to 12 ounces in a single pattern and a single line.

But the foes of the practice of selling silverware by weight continued to marshal their arguments; in the same article in which he had discussed factory methods for silver production, Mr. Johnston wrote, in the *English Magazine of Art:*

> So long as the buyer asks the weight of a piece, and how many shillings the ounce, the maker will try to put in as much solid silver and as little workmanship as possible. Can anything more truly sad and inartistic be imagined? If weight of silver is required, in the name of heaven buy your metal by the ingot; but to go to an artist to buy his produce by the scales is insulting as well as foolish.

Still, in Mr. Johnston's opinion, this was but one of the reasons for "the decline in the art of English silversmithery" during the latter part of the 19th century; his article, reprinted in *The Jewelers' Weekly* continued to another cause:

> . . . the custom, which we trust is on the wane, of melting up old silver by each generation, and having it made into new plate. This is probably the natural consequence of buying by the ounce, but so long as the practice is continued we can hardly expect a workman to bestow upon a piece the loving care and constant thought that are necessary to make a work of art of it. No art can flourish under such discouragement, and so long as every heir, upon succeeding to his heritage, has his father's silver recast and his mother's jewels reset for his bride, just so long shall we have silver and jewelry worthy of such treatment. No man will put his whole heart into work which he knows is ephemeral.

Despite Mr. Johnston's protests, England was not alone in the practice of melting down old silver "to have it recast." In the United States, even The President's House in Washington was not immune to such action, according to a story appearing in *The New York Journal* under a Washington dateline of March 27, 1897, reprinted shortly after in *The Jewelers' Weekly:*

> President and Mrs. McKinley were surprised shortly after their installation in the

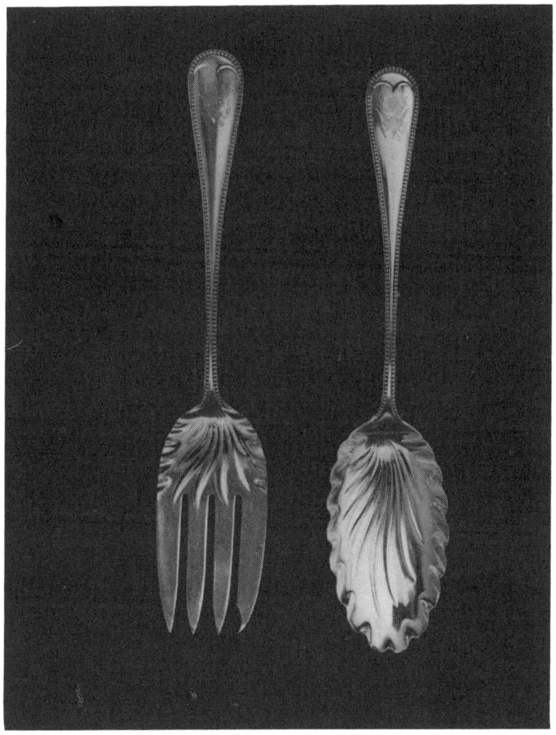

Matching serving forks and spoons, apparently added at a later date, supplement the two sizes of forks and spoons reportedly made from the Dolly Madison silver during the Cleveland administration. *Courtesy The White House Collections.*

White House to learn that the old Dolly Madison spoons and forks that had been part and parcel of the Executive Mansion belongings ever since that famous woman held sway there, had some time since been melted down.

This historic silver, together with various odd bits that from time to time had in past administrations been added to the White House possessions, had been converted into a set of forks and spoons used at the cabinet dinner last Thursday evening.

It had been urged from time to time by the successive mistresses of the White House that the stock of White House silver was not only incongruous as to size and shape, but in most instances a positive burden to use at table.

It was claimed that the forks and spoons were not only clumsily constructed, but, having been made originally more with regard to weight than intrinsic beauty, the use of them throughout a meal was a weariness to the flesh.

This state of affairs had been tolerated long enough, Mrs. Cleveland thought, therefore she decided to inaugurate a reform. The Dolly Madison spoons formed a part of this motley but valuable collection of White House Plate. After it had been duly weighed, a messenger was dispatched to one of the large local silversmiths on Pennsylvania Avenue asking for an estimate of the number of forks and spoons, respectively, in tea and dessert sizes, could be made from the collection.

When this reply was returned to the White House it was accompanied by a request on the part of the firm that it be allowed to retain the Dolly Madison spoons, these to be considered as an equivalent to payment for remodeling the balance of the plate. This offer was refused.

Then the enterprising firm named a price, a fancy figure, which it was willing to pay for the Dolly Madison spoons. This offer was also refused. It is understood that the shrewd silversmiths wanted to preserve the Dolly Madison spoons as relics of great historical value, esteeming them as really worth their weight in gold to any antiquarian collector if retained in their original shape.

But Mrs. Cleveland would consent to no interference with her plans. She sent the silver to the mint, and had it melted into ingots. The silversmiths were then requested to furnish affidavits that they would use the silver ingots and no other silver in making the new lot of spoons and forks. This was an unusual demand, but White House custom is worth keeping, and it was complied with.

The new silver is simple but handsome in design. About the edges of the forks and spoons runs a beading which is the only ornamentation of the kind in their make up. On the handles, in repousse work, is the coat of arms of the United States, and beneath this is engraved "President's House." Both the design and ornamentation are of Mrs. Cleveland's suggestion.

Although present White House records neither confirm nor deny the stories published in 1897, dated pieces corresponding to those

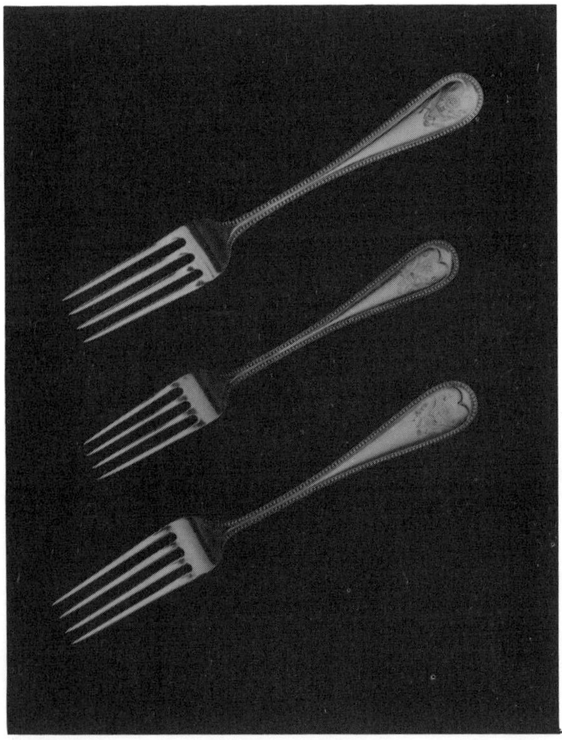

White House silver matching the description of the pieces ordered by Mrs. Grover Cleveland, and made by melting down the Dolly Madison spoons and forks with which the President's House had originally been equipped. *Courtesy The White House Collections.*

described are still a part of the White House service; forks in two sizes, and some of the serving forks and spoons are still in use. The pieces apparently ordered by Mrs. Cleveland in 1895, made by Harris & Shafer, were supplemented in 1896, 1898, and 1899 by pieces of similar design made by Galt & Brother. At some later date, all of the pieces, except for the serving spoons and forks, were gilded, and today are part of the "gold service" at the White House.

Jewelers in many cities encouraged the "trading in" of old silver as part of the purchase price of new, matched flatware services. Some of the pieces acquired in this manner were undoubtedly sold to other customers, but much of the old silver found its way to secondary smelters and "salvage" operations, while making it easier for the mistresses of establishments less pretentious than the White House to own gleaming new sterling services.

Unlike the earlier transitions from pewter to Britannia to silver plate, the arrival of

Reverse of the Cleveland White House silver has marks of Washington silversmiths; each piece is engraved "President's House" and dated. *Courtesy The White House Collections.*

mass-produced sterling did not completely displace the plated service. One result was a greater emphasis on design; another was a trend toward specialization on the part of manufacturers. It took only a few years for firms engaged in the production of both sterling and plated wares to realize that the buyer tended to confuse in his own mind, the lower priced products with the more expensive, or, conversely, to associate the name of the manufacturer with one or another of his products —but seldom with both. This situation, in turn, led to intensified promotional work directed not alone to the retailers as so much previous advertising had been, but to the customer himself.

The increased number of factories was aided, no doubt, by the new and increased sources of power. The early factories had been located on rivers, preferably where a sufficient "head" would permit the use of waterwheels to power the equipment that was most frequently assembled by the proprietor and his helpers at the site. But waterpower was not the only source. In the early 1840s, when John Gorham had first been admitted to a partnership in his father's firm, power was provided by a horse on a treadmill in the cellar of the factory. When a particular operation required additional power, a factory hand would call down through a speaking tube, "Get up, Dick"! The development of the steam engine permitted more freedom in the location of factories; and the silver industry, through early experience with the "plating dynamo," was among the first to explore and utilize electricity for operating increasingly complex machines.

Regardless of wider markets, increased production, and improved distribution; despite the size of the rolling mills and factories, the silver industry is one from which the role of the craftsman has never been eliminated. Even today, in plants throughout New England, in the rolling hills fringing the Mohawk Valley, where Oneida, Ltd. is located, in the dark brick castle in Forest Hill, N.J. where Tiffany sterling is made, in factories from Massachusetts to Maryland, the traditional skills of the early silversmiths continue in many of the operations.

In the creation of any pattern, design is of course the result of skill and originality, of talent possessed by the artist-designer. Once a pattern is selected, a handmade spoon is carved and hand-chased by a master craftsman, who must also be a talented artist. Thus a design on paper takes on definite form. A large master model is then carved for use on the die-cutting machine, and this again must be done by skilled hands. When the model is completed and approved, steel dies must be made for each item of flatware; these are roughed out in blocks of steel on a die-cutting machine, and again patient, skilled hands are required to turn the rough die into a carefully finished tool. Once completed, the dies must be hardened to stand the continual pounding of the drop presses. This is accomplished by a series of heat treatments alternating with brine baths. Even for today's somewhat simplified flatware services, as many as 120 special dies must be made; the infinitely more complex services of the late Victorian years often required three or four times as many.

Whether the dies are used to form sterling silver pieces, or to form the nickel silver which will be plated with silver, this preparation is but a preliminary to the actual manufacturing process. The metal must be mixed and melted, rolled and cleaned, annealed and properly gauged, time and again, until the sheets are ready for cutting and shaping, grade rolling and stamping. And at each stage in production, a trained eye and a skilled hand must supplement the work of the machine. As the process continues through the many steps in striking the design, stamping the bowls and tines, facing spoon bowls to assure a smooth finish, buffing with sand and cloth, the craftsman is a participant. In many factories, even today, stoning by hand with pumice and bluestone is a regular step in the production of fine silver, as is hand filing to remove the flask after shaping, and setting the shape of fork and spoon handles with blows of a wooden mallet. Numerous inspections by individuals trained to perceive imperfections so minute that they would escape the eye of the average person are standard factory procedures.

In decorating, hand engraving is still practiced in some plants, and the fine art of hand chasing to form decoration in relief, remains another province of the craftsman. In hand chasing, raising the pattern from beneath starts with sketching the outlines of the design on the outside, then raising the gross design from the reverse side by using a foot-powered "snarling iron." Hot tar and pitch fills the piece, and when cooled, provides the necessary resiliency for hammer blows on the opposite side. A series of small tools, tapped by a hammer handled with skill, deftly provide rich ornament in sharp relief.

In steps such as these, the ancient art of the silversmith has been preserved. This pride in craftsmanship is perhaps one of the reasons why pride of ownership continues to be a dominating characteristic in the possession of fine silver.

5

Plating and Platers

Writing in the *New York Times Book Review*, B. A. Botkin relates one of the earliest "shaggy" anecdotes—about a horse, not a dog—from the *California Pioneer* of 1854:

> (A friend) was describing to us the other day the wonderful qualities of a horse that he had trained, as he expressed it, "to do everything." Said he, "I taught him to sit at a bench by a table, and eat boiled rice with a silver fork." "Impossible!" said we. "How *could* a horse eat with a silver fork!" "Well," replied Pinto, "hem! I don't mean exactly a *silver* fork. It was one of those plated ones, you know—cost about eight dollars a dozen."

That jokes involving plated tableware were circulating in the far west only a few years after the first successful silver-plated spoons were produced in the Atlantic states is testimony to the rapid acceptance these new implements achieved. For years a demand for a product that would fill the gap between pewter and solid silver had been developing, particularly among those of moderate means.

In England, an accident had led to the partial fulfillment of this demand. In 1742, a mechanic named Thomas Boulshover, while mending a knife blade in a garret in London, had inadvertently fused silver and copper. His invention, soon taken over by manufacturers in Sheffield, rapidly became popular and widely known as "Sheffield Plate." It was produced by fusing, with intense heat, a thin sheet of silver to one or both sides of a thicker sheet of copper. The metals were not amalgamated; they were distinct, but not separate. The composite metal could be rolled down to the desired thickness for fabrication, then treated like a silver sheet to form all manner of hollow ware. The edges, where the copper was exposed, were covered with a sterling silver band or border, and the finished tea sets, trays, and candle sticks achieved all the brilliance and beauty of solid silverware. As the bulk of the metal was copper, pieces of Sheffield Plate could be priced within the reach of many families who could never afford solid silver, and a wide market for the products opened in England and in America. The exposed copper edge posed a problem in adapting the sheets to flatware, however, and the use of Sheffield Plate was largely limited to shaped hollow handles for knives and serving pieces.

About 100 years later, in 1840, a patent was granted to the firm of G. R. and H. Elkington in England for a method of "coating copper and certain other metals, by means of a solution of silver in connection with a galvanic current." The process, which dissolved the oxide of silver in a solution of cyanide of potassium, so that it could reform itself on copper, nickel, or Britannia metal, had first been discovered by a young medical student named John Wright. Later, as a practising physician

Early example of English electroplating; a large dinner fork made and plated by the Elkingtons, owners of the patented process in Great Britain. The Elkington mark appears on the reverse side of the fork. *Courtesy Spencer W. Franc.*

in Birmingham, Wright had sold his invention to Henry Elkington.

The new process of electroplating got off to a slow start in England, but the "Elkington patent of 1840" aroused great interest across the Atlantic among American silver workers. The process had been sketchily described in a series of articles in the *Bulletins* of the Franklin Institute in Philadelphia; and the improvement in coating various metals had been discussed at length in letters, conversations, and magazine articles.

John O. Mead, who manufactured Britannia ware articles in Philadelphia, was abroad in 1837. He brought home with him a Smee battery (one of several devices in use at the time for generating an electrical current) and began his own electroplating experiments. Within five years, he had developed a workable plating technique, and in 1845 he formed a partnership with Asa and William Rogers. The firm of Rogers & Mead, set up in Hartford, Connecticut, was short-lived, and within a few years John Mead was manufacturing silver plated-ware in Philadelphia under his own name. The firm of John O. Mead shortly after became J. O. Mead & Sons and finally Filley, Mead & Caldwell.

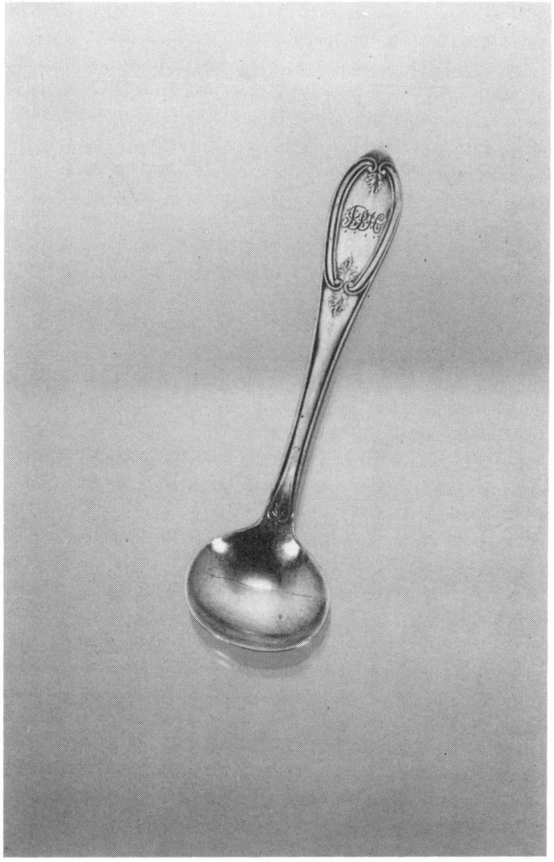

Salt spoon made by J. O. Mead, probably the first successful electroplater in the United States, and an early partner of William Rogers. *Collection of Jane Lightfoot Beaumont; Kelly Powell photo.*

Meanwhile, as early as 1842, Whitfield Cowles and his son William had begun the manufacture of silver-plated ware in Granby, Connecticut, and in 1845 William Cowles, with Asa Rogers, James Isaacson and John Johnson, had formed the Cowles Manufacturing Company for the manufacture of silver-plated goods.

In 1847, the three Rogers brothers—Asa, William and Simeon—began producing electroplated spoons in Hartford, Connecticut. Their earlier experience as silversmiths, manufacturers of Britannia ware, and partners in the Mead and Cowles firms, had fitted them for the venture, and Asa had hit upon the use of German silver—a mixture of copper, nickel, and zinc—as an especially good base for silver plating. The quality of their products far excelled that of the earlier platers, and in a short time established a standard for housewives who had previously preferred coin silver, tinplate, or Britannia spoons.

The success of the new products quickly attracted others. In 1848, Reed & Barton brought an electroplater, who had been trained in Connecticut, to the company's plant in Taunton, Massachusetts; as early as 1840, the factory had been equipped to produce 100 dozen spoons of nickel silver each week. Much of this production was diverted to silver plating as soon as a "plating room" could be completed, for, like others in the Britannia business, Reed & Barton realized that the popularity of the new silverware foretold the end of the Britannia business as such.

Others, too, were fascinated by the new process and products. John Gorham, who had served an apprenticeship with his father in the shop founded in 1825, became a partner in 1841, and by 1850 was convinced that there was a place for machinery in the production of silverware. Two years later, on a trip to Europe, he visited the plants of Dixon & Sons and the Elkingtons, and observed at first hand the plating processes. On the same journey he worked beside skilled metallurgists in London, and hired an expert molder, along with other metal working artisans for the growing plant in Providence. By 1865, the company was producing electro-plated ware as well as solid silver products.

The flexibility and adaptability of the new process intrigued not only the customers but the producers themselves. The plating, properly handled, was compact and solid; the operator could form any thickness desired by the simple means of prolonging the operation. Within a few years, this facility led to the production of electroplated ware in several grades. While a coating of only .001 inch will produce a satisfactory finish if it is applied uniformly, competitive selling and a desire to provide long, satisfactory use even in hotels and other commercial establishments soon led to the establishment of various grades of silver plate. These were determined by the quantity of pure silver required to coat each gross of teaspoons, and applied, relatively, to other pieces as services became more complex.

Standard Plate, Extra Plate, Double Plate, and Triple Plate were common designations for four grades of silver plate, with an increased quantity of silver electro-deposit on each. "A-1" was a common designation for Standard Plate; numerical references, following the makers stamps were sometimes substituted for the words "Double Plate" or "Triple Plate." The Rockford Silver Plate Company used the numeral "5," following the company imprint, to indicate double plate—the usual practice at the time, calling for 2-1/2 ounces of silver for each gross of teaspoons in standard plate. Rogers, Smith & Co. and 1847 Rogers Brothers wares carried different numerals on different pieces; "4," "6," and "8" stamped, respectively, on teaspoons, dessert spoons, and forks, and tablespoons and medium forks, indicated double plate; "6," "9," and "12" on the same pieces marked them as triple plate.

L. Boardman & Son, in an 1880 catalog, explained that: "Our ELECTROPLATED WARE is *heavily plated on all parts alike with pure Silver, on the finest quality of Nickel Silver,* and hand burnished. The goods are carefully weighed before and after depositing the silver thereon, insuring us no hesitation in warranting the full amount of silver on the goods as represented." On Standard Plate, the company used "4-*," on tablespoons, table and medium forks; "3-*," on dessert spoons and forks, and "2-*," on teaspoons; on Double Plate, the same pieces were marked "8-*," "6-*," and "4-*;" the better grade, which Boardman called "Treble Plate," was stamped "12-*," "9-*," and "6-*." A further note indicated that "Quadruple Plate" would furnished to order.

The William A. Rogers Company, on the other hand, used an "X," "XX," and "XXX" on the Horseshoe Brand of flatware produced by the company to indicate standard, double, and triple plate. Grades were further designated by special brand names; the highest grade was stamped W. A. Rogers (Horseshoe); popular grade flatware was stamped 1881 (Wreath) Rogers (Wreath); medium grade was stamped (Cross) W. R. (Key-

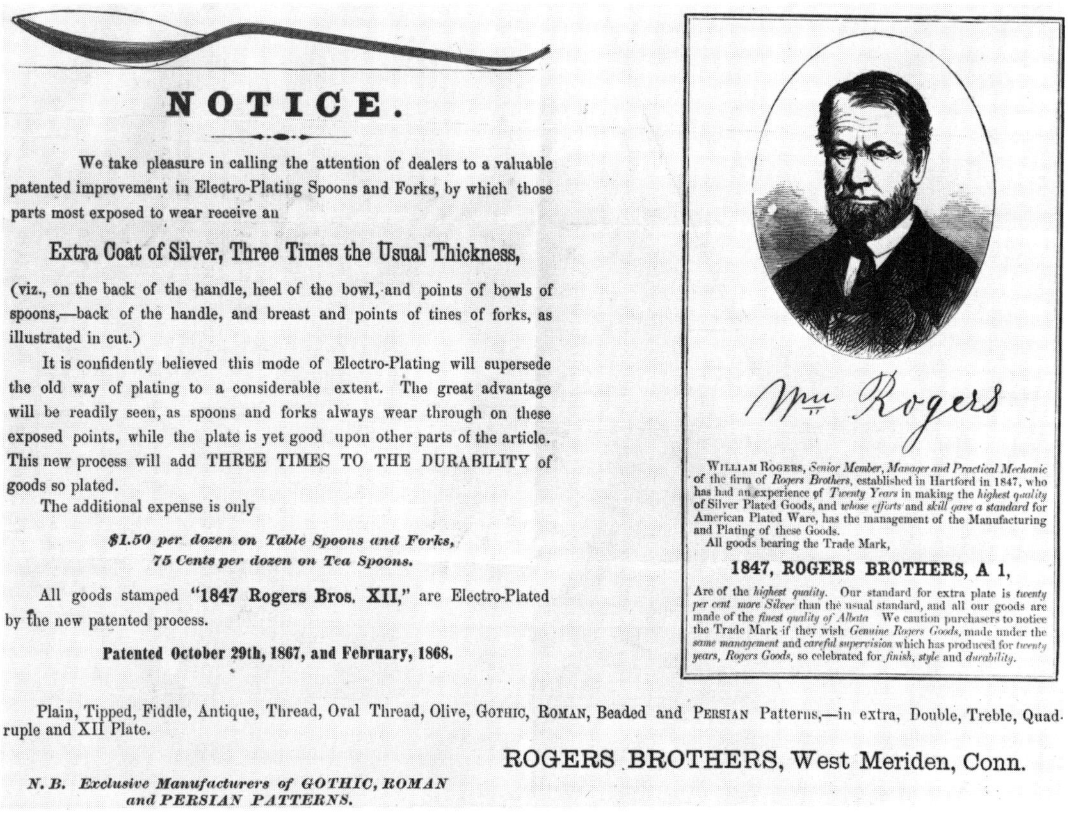

NOTICE.

We take pleasure in calling the attention of dealers to a valuable patented improvement in Electro-Plating Spoons and Forks, by which those parts most exposed to wear receive an

Extra Coat of Silver, Three Times the Usual Thickness,

(viz., on the back of the handle, heel of the bowl, and points of bowls of spoons,—back of the handle, and breast and points of tines of forks, as illustrated in cut.)

It is confidently believed this mode of Electro-Plating will supersede the old way of plating to a considerable extent. The great advantage will be readily seen, as spoons and forks always wear through on these exposed points, while the plate is yet good upon other parts of the article. This new process will add THREE TIMES TO THE DURABILITY of goods so plated.

The additional expense is only

$1.50 per dozen on Table Spoons and Forks,
75 Cents per dozen on Tea Spoons.

All goods stamped **"1847 Rogers Bros. XII,"** are Electro-Plated by the new patented process.

Patented October 29th, 1867, and February, 1868.

Wm Rogers

WILLIAM ROGERS, *Senior Member, Manager and Practical Mechanic* of the firm of *Rogers Brothers*, established in Hartford in 1847, who has had an experience of *Twenty Years* in making the *highest quality* of Silver Plated Goods, and *whose efforts* and *skill gave a standard* for American Plated Ware, has the management of the Manufacturing and Plating of these Goods.

All goods bearing the Trade Mark,

1847, ROGERS BROTHERS, A 1,

Are of the *highest quality*. Our standard for extra plate is *twenty per cent more Silver* than the usual standard, and all our goods are made of the *finest quality of Albata* We caution purchasers to notice the Trade Mark if they wish *Genuine Rogers Goods*, made under the *same management* and *careful supervision* which has produced for *twenty years, Rogers Goods*, so celebrated for *finish, style* and *durability*.

Plain, Tipped, Fiddle, Antique, Thread, Oval Thread, Olive, GOTHIC, ROMAN, Beaded and PERSIAN Patterns,—in extra, Double, Treble, Quadruple and XII Plate.

ROGERS BROTHERS, West Meriden, Conn.

N. B. Exclusive Manufacturers of GOTHIC, ROMAN and PERSIAN PATTERNS.

Broadside distributed by Rogers Brothers about 1868. While the handbill featured the new "XII" plating process, four other grades of electroplate were offered. *Courtesy of The New York Historical Society, New York City.*

stone), and the cheaper grade flatware bore an Oxford Silver Plate Co. or an Extra Coin Silver Plate stamp.

William Rogers & Son used another letter series; goods in standard plate were stamped "A" or "A-1," in double plate "AA," and in triple plate "AAA."

Separate brand names for varying grades of silver plate were a popular device: the Williams Brothers Manufacturing Co. used Our Very Best, Lion Brand, Stag Brand, and Williams Triple Plate; the American Silver Company, World Brand for its better grade, H & T Co. for its popular grade; similar designations were used by many other manufacturers. The practice permitted penetration of the market at all price levels, and made it possible for a single company to sell to jewelry stores, department stores, and mail order houses simultaneously, in a period when each type of retail outlet was bitterly denounced by each of the others.

The battle for competitive advantages continued to bring improvements to silver-plated flatware. One of the earliest was the development of sectional plating, which added extra silver plate at the points most exposed to wear—bottoms and tips of spoon bowls, tine tips and bottom of forks, and the back of the handle on both spoons and forks. Rogers, Smith & Company and 1847 Rogers Brothers marked this ware with a XII following the brand name; William A. Rogers added an SXR to indicate that pieces in the company's Horseshoe Brand were "Sectional Reinforced" and Triple Plated. Announcements of the designation indicated that teaspoons produced in this grade were guaranteed to strip not less than 3 ounces of pure silver to the gross.

As competition increased, a Quadruple Plate was developed and marketed by a number of firms, including Meriden Britannia Company's 1847 Rogers Brothers operation; William A. Rogers countered with an SXXXR grade, "guaranteed to be plated with FULL SIX OUNCES of pure silver per gross. Parts most exposed to wear are *reinforced* with an *additional heavy plate,* making them equal in service to quadruple plate." "Quintuple Plate" was one of the competitive answers.

While this battle raged within the Rogers clan, George Edwards, the president of the Holmes & Edwards Silver Company in Bridgeport, Connecticut, was reading an article in the *Scientific American* about a patent that

INJUNCTION.

Important Decision of the Supreme Court of Errors,

STATE OF CONNECTICUT.

Manufacturers prohibited from using the same combination of numbers, or such imitation as have similarity to the Trade-marks of L. BOARDMAN & SON, used on BRITANNIA SPOONS.

L. BOARDMAN & SON VS. MERIDEN BRITANNIA CO.

Petition for Injunction to restrain the respondents from selling, or offering for sale, any Britannia Spoons having thereon any label prepared in imitation of any of the labels of the petitioners, like those used (at the date of the petition) by the respondents—that is, labels similar in shape, color, size, and style, with certain specified numbers printed thereon, which the petitioners claimed as their TRADE-MARKS.

At the February Term of the Superior Court for Middlesex County, Conn., 1868, the Hon. Miles T. Granger, one of the Judges of the Superior Court in said State, was appointed a Committee to hear the parties and their evidence, and report to said Court the facts alleged respectively by the parties, which he should find to be proved and true. That at the September Term of said Court, 1868, said Committee made his report, which was accepted, and the question as to what decree should be rendered thereon, was reserved for the advice of the Supreme Court of Errors, which Court advised that judgment be rendered in favor of the petitioners.

The Supreme Court of Errors say:

. . . . "We entertain no doubt that the labels thus arranged, adopted, and used constitute legal trade marks and are entitled to protection.

. . . . "The presumption of a designed imitaton, arising from the similarity of the spoons, the resemblance of the labels, and the identity of the numbers, would be very strong if all these circumstances were found to exist in reference to only one kind; but when the case finds, as it does, that they exist in respect to several different kinds, the presumption is vastly strengthened. . . . . It is true the respondents put their own name on the labels used by them, in place of that of the petitioners; but that is not sufficient to destroy the effect of the imitation in other respects, especially in respect to the numbers.

"The importance attached to these numbers is further shown by the fact that since the temporary injunction the respondents have used the same numbers with a cypher prefixed.

"On the whole, we are satisfied that, although the name of the imitator was substituted for that of the original proprietors, and that the imitation in other respects may not be exact, a resemblance exists, which was designed to mislead, and which, under the circumstances, was well calculated and likely to produce that result.

"Have the petitioners suffered damage? On this point there is no room to doubt. . . . . The circumstance that the respondents now prefix a cypher to the numbers would hardly vary the result. Their motive is apparent. They may succeed in reaping some advantage from the numbers as thus used, but it is manifest that it will be at the expense of the petitioners.

"We advise judgment for the petitioners."

In conformity to this advice, the Superior Court, at its February Term, 1869, passed the following decree:

"And now this Court doth find the facts set forth in said report to be true, as found by said Committee; and by the advice of the Supreme Court of Errors, doth thereupon order and decree that the said Meriden Britannia Company, the respondents, their workmen, attorneys, servants, and agents, and each and every one of them, are hereby strictly enjoined and commanded, under a penalty of TEN THOUSAND DOLLARS, that from henceforth they and each of them do wholly and entirely cease and desist from selling or offering for sale any Britannia spoons manufactured by any other parties than said petitioners, in packages having thereon any labels prepared in imitation of any of the said labels of the petitioners, like those used by the respondents, as described in said petition; and for selling or offering for sale any such Britannia spoons in packages with labels and numbers thereon, so nearly like those used by the petitioners as aforesaid, as are calculated to induce the purchasers thereof to believe they are the genuine manufacture of the petitioners."

Litigation between rival manufacturers was frequent and often furious. This decision was publicized in newspapers and catalogs, mailed to dealers, and presented in person by salesmen representing the Boardmans.

had been granted to the Warner Brothers of Syracuse, New York. The August 20, 1887, issue carried a small-type item reading:

> The invention herewith illustrated provides a method of manufacturing plated ware in which parts most exposed to wear are filled with precious metal or alloy, as for instance, the bottom of the bowl of a spoon or the back of the handle of a fork, these being the usual points of rest from which the plating on such articles generally wears off the quickest. In such goods, and all plated flatware of a similar kind, a recess is made at the points of rest, or places of greatest wear, and this recess is filled, in the process of manufacture, with fine or coin silver, or other metal used in plating, so that, after the whole is plated, abrasions of these parts will not, as in the ordinary plated ware, expose the base metal or alloy of which the article is mainly composed. The illustration shows the method of inserting this silver filling in a standard type of silverplated tea spoon.

The following morning, Mr. Edwards dispatched a trusted employee to Syracuse, and, after receiving a favorable report on the operation in the small Warner shop, arranged for the purchase of the patent rights, securing, at the same time, the services of the inventor, William Warner. There were many technical difficulties to be overcome before the process was completely feasible for commercial production, but by the time of the Columbian Exposition in Chicago in 1892-93, the company was awarded a gold medal for the greatest improvement in plated flatware in 100 years, and the Holmes & Edwards Sterling Inlay trademark had won new acclaim in the silver trade.

In 1898, Reed & Barton's George Brabrook patented another system for silver inlays in plated ware; other companies countered with "silver filled" methods, many of which were variations on the sectional method of plating. Through it all, most manufacturers continued to produce at least four separate grades of plated ware, compounding the inventory problems as the number of pieces in each pattern ranged between 100 and 150.

At the same time, as silver prices dropped and the sterling silver producers increased in number, becoming more competitive with each other, more and more firms found that production costs on their top grades of plated ware forced them to price these grades almost as high as sterling silver.

This dilemma was resolved by Oneida Community about the turn of the century. While the Oneida Community was not new to the production of silverware, the plant at Niagara Falls, New York, had in the past produced only the lower-priced wares. When the decision to compete with the older, firmly established companies was made, it was decided that a new line would be made in only one grade, and that it would compete only with what was popularly known as Triple Plate. The decision was a sound one; the biggest volume in the silverware business at the time was in the grade called "Extra Plate," using 2-1/2 ounces of silver per gross of teaspoons, but Oneida executives knew that the real cost of making plated ware came from the shaping and polishing. Except for the fact that triple plate had to be left in the plating bath for a longer period, each of the steps in production was the same for standard, extra plate, or triple; the principal difference in the cost of manufacturing was in the price of the silver itself. The new line was made in a grade called "Triple Plus," using something over 6 ounces of silver per gross of teaspoons. The heavier plating, combined with distinctive patterns, set the keynote for an unprecedented selling plan; firm resale prices for both jobber and wholesaler, and an advertising campaign that was revolutionary for its time, helped establish Oneida Community, or Community Plate, as a quality line.

There were new developments in base metals, too. The Rogers Brothers original im-

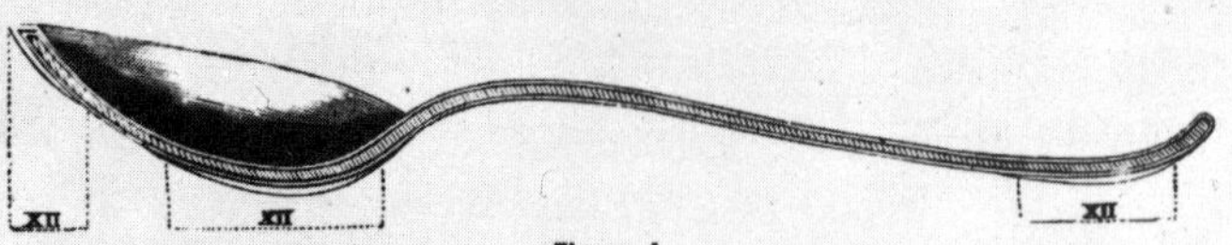

Figure 1.

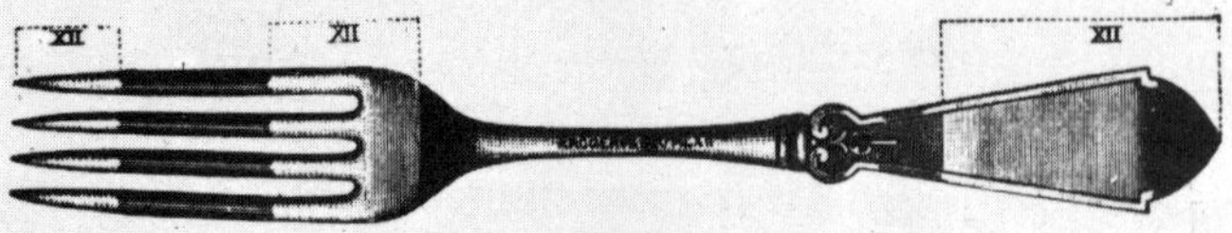

Figure 2.

Figures 1 and 2 show a Nickel Silver Spoon and Fork with the XII plate on, as they appear before the final plating; the appearance is the same as regular goods, in plate or solid silver.

XII OR SECTIONAL PLATE.

(PATENTED.)

The forks and spoons made by this valuable process are by far the most economical to users—the article being plated the heaviest on the parts most exposed to wear, as seen in the above cuts. They are more serviceable, and dealers will find it greatly to their advantage to keep them in stock and explain their merits to purchasers.

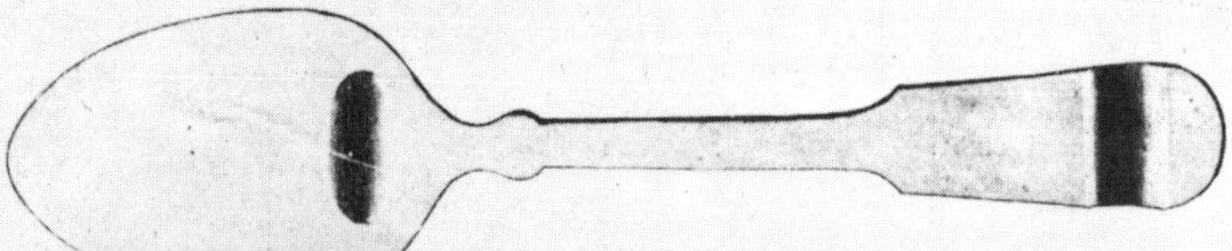

METAL BLANK CUT READY TO INLAY OR FILL WITH SILVER.

SPOON SILVER INLAID READY FOR PLATING.

SECTIONAL VIEW OF STERLING SILVER INLAID TEASPOON.

The trade will find this a very satisfactory brand to handle. The patterns are desirable, and with our strong guarantee (a copy of which is enclosed in each package) are easily sold and bound to prove satisfactory to the purchaser. If you are not familiar with our goods, send for Catalogue and prices.

When ordering Silverware be sure to mention pattern wanted
SOLID SILVER
SOLID SILVER
BLANK METAL
SILVER FILLED SILVERWARE
is better than any other silverware because the inner blank, or composition metal, is the highest grade and the nearest approach to solid silver yet discovered. You will have no misshapen, bent and ugly looking silverware on account of a little rough usage. The tough metal protects it. The stamping process under hydraulic pressure brings out the patterns and fancy work better.
MOST IMPORTANT OF ALL, you are securing for your money more intrinsic value than is offered by any other line or make. WE GUARANTEE TRIPLE QUALITY TO GIVE YOU FIFTEEN YEARS OF ACTUAL SERVICE.

Improvements in plating techniques were demonstrated with cut-away illustrations and semi-technical drawings in price lists, catalogs, and early advertisements.

provement on the Elkington methods had been in the use of an improved nickel silver formula as a base for silver plating. Its advantages had been obvious from the start of the business, for it worked well, provided a good base, was dense and hard, and, even when the plating wore off with use, continued to show white metal with a silvery sheen. Nothing ever quite replaced nickel silver, but formulae were changed and improved over the years, and, at various times, other metals were tried by many companies. Brass had its day; steel was tried; the white metal alloys, containing various amounts of tin, copper, lead, antimony and bismuth, underwent constant experimentation. But for quality flatware, the combination of copper, nickel, and zinc—generally about two-thirds copper, with a varying proportion of the other two elements—maintained its leadership.

After the initial experiments and early production with the Smee Battery, or other constant voltaic batteries of the type J. F. Daniell had invented in 1836, the electrical current used in the electro-deposit of metals became a subject for scrutiny, too. The most important early change in this direction was the plating dynamo, which was invented and patented in 1842 by J. S. Woolrich of Birmingham, England. This patent, like many others affecting the electroplating process, was acquired by the Elkington firm, which for years maintained a firm grip on the electroplating business in England through control of the original patent as well as subsequent patents covering improvements in the process. While many other manufacturers produced plated ware in England, they all operated under licenses granted by the Elkingtons, and for many years English electroplate was manufactured without the benefits and hazards of the competitive situation which had developed in the United States. The plating dynamo made possible the increased electrical charge which, properly controlled, vastly improved the tenacity of the plate. The early battery, like that used by the Rogers Brothers in 1848, produced only about five amperes per square foot of surface; dynamos and later generators were to produce up to three thousand amperes, distributed at a rate of 15 to 30 amperes per square foot of surface. And tanks, from the original ones holding only five or six gallons of solution, increased in size as increased production was demanded, until a single tank, perhaps part of a complex of such tanks, might hold 3,000 gallons or more.

Unlike Sheffield Plate, where the plating process was the first step in production with fabrication of the articles following, in electroplating the plating process is the last step, except for final finishing and polishing. Consequently, the production procedures followed in making solid silver flatware are conducted with the base metal instead of silver. For many years, during the early and mid-Victorian periods, the working characteristics of the base metals in use at the time affected the design of the pieces, the patterns with which they were embellished, and even the pieces themselves. The solid-handle knife, for example, was much more economical to produce than was its hollow-handle counterpart. Even as late as the 1890s, silverplated "sets" in the lower price ranges were often sold with patterned fork and spoon handles, but plain-handled knives, or the solid-handle knives carried the pattern in shallow embossing. Many manufacturers offered a choice of solid- or hollow-handle knives, with the hollow-handle knives commanding a premium price.

In design, the "deep patterns" associated with sterling silver were usually difficult to reproduce in nickel silver, although many firms began doing creditable jobs by the early 1890s. A number of such patterns were made available by the late 90s, and the early Edwardian years saw the development of a number of patterns duplicating the intricacies of sterling ware, as heat treating, die-casting

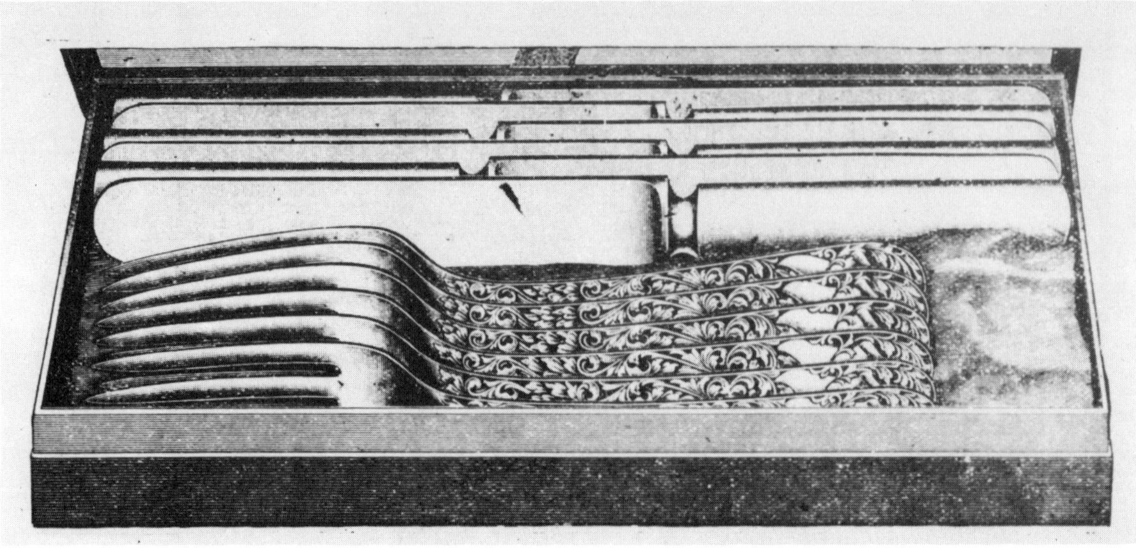

Patterned forks and spoons often were combined with plain, solid-handle knives to make up inexpensive sets of electroplated table silver.

and stamping techniques were improved.

Unlike the earlier progressions, where Britannia ware supplanted pewter, German silver supplanted Britannia in flatware, and silver plate took over almost completely from the earlier base alloys (as well as from Sheffield Plate), silver plate has never been completely routed from the tableware scene. Handsome, durable, and economical, silver-plated flatware has remained in favor for well over a century. The reasons for its continued popularity were perhaps best summarized in the English *Art Journal* of 1875:

Far from checking artistic development, electroplating has encouraged it, by permitting the manufacture of works of Art, at a relatively low price, that monarchs might hesitate to purchase if made in solid metal. The extraordinary progress which this branch of industry has made in the past quarter of a century is most remarkable. The electro-plated goods of white alloys are practically little inferior to those made of solid silver. When properly executed they are nearly as durable, and at the same time far cheaper, than the goods of which they are imitations.

6

Promotion

"The trumpet's silver sound" to which Sir Walter Scott referred in *Marmion* might well have been lifted from its poetic context to describe many of the selling efforts of the Victorian silver firms; for trumpet they did, sending a silver sound throughout the land.

The earliest Victorians heard little of the trumpeting, however. Most advertising for coin silver wares and the first silver plate was by word of mouth, as the skill of this or that silversmith was discussed and passed on, or a traveler described the new silver-plated spoons seen at the farmhouse where the previous night had been spent. Discreet advertisements appeared in local newspapers, generally describing only the location of the silversmith or listing the type of wares he made. One departure from this practice might have been noted in 1847, when the following advertisement appeared in newspapers, not only in Hartford, but in New Haven and other Connecticut towns as well:

> FORKS, SPOONS, KNIVES, LADLES—all silverplated on the finest quality of German Silver in the most thorough manner. WM. ROGERS & CO. No. 4 State Street, Hartford, Connecticut.

Other editors chose to treat the new development as news; the *New York Commercial Advertiser*, in 1846, carried the following story:

> SILVER AND NOT SILVER: We have seen this morning some specimens of table and dessert knives, and forks, spoons, etc., with which we would like to try an experiment. With profound respect for the tact and experience of our lady readers, we have no doubt that we could deceive them with the articles referred to, only that conscience is a "respected friend" with us—one whom we care not to offend.
>
> The specimens of art shown to us are manufactured by the Cowles Manufacturing Company, at Tariffsville, Conn. The body of them is of fine German silver, of almost steel-like hardness, and over this, by a peculiar process, is deposited a plating of pure silver. The deposition of silver can be made of any thickness, according to the price which the purchaser may be willing to pay. With the ordinary thickness, which we are assured will outwear usage for a number of years, the price is only about one-fourth that of solid silver.
>
> And yet it would take a practiced eye, to discover that they are not of solid silver, for the plating is of considerable thickness, the German silver beneath is of equal whiteness with the pure metal, the patterns, style, finish, etc. are facsimiles of the most highly wrought silver, and the body of the articles is indeed harder. For steamboats, hotels, boarding houses, and indeed for private families also, they appear to be elegant and economical.
>
> We learn that the company has an established agent here, Mr. F. R. Anderson, 31 Liberty Street, who will doubtless be glad to show these beautiful articles to anyone who may call upon him.

The *Hartford Courant* had repeated the story, thoughtfully appending an additional paragraph which read:

> We fully endorse the above from the Commercial Advertiser. The articles manufactured by the Cowles Manufacturing Company are equal in appearance to those of pure silver, and are becoming celebrated throughout the country. Their agents in this city, are Messrs. Wm. Rogers & Co. No. 4 State Street.

Whether the reporter for the *Commercial Advertiser* influenced the silver manufacturers with his suggestion, or had been influenced himself in his interview with their agent, there is little doubt that hotels and boarding houses were among the first sales targets for the new silverware. Silver-plated spoons, and forks, and knives were available to private families; stores in the larger cities stocked them, and they were carried to smaller communities and farms by the peddlers who continued to ply their trade. But the efforts of most manufacturing firms were directed toward the establishments that would buy in larger quantities.

The boarding house was already accepted as an appurtenance to elegant city living in the 1830s. Mrs. Trollope, on her visit to the United States, deplored them as detrimental to wholesome family life at the same time that they established extravagant standards of living for the young couples who chose these early forerunners to the apartment hotel for their first homes. Many of the boarding houses were set up in mansions that the original owners had been unable to keep; most were run by widows who found "the boarders" a way to maintain a house and a standard of living that might be economically impossible any other way. Formal drawing rooms and large dining rooms characterized the better of these residences, and it was to the dining rooms, with

The "United States" was typical of the hotels Mrs. Trollope found in the 1830s. In less than a generation, elaborate new establishments catered to mobile Americans.

their daily multitude of substantial Victorian meals, that the silver manufacturers sent their wares. Not all of the boarding houses of the day were elegant, and certainly many were not well run. But the appeal of the comparatively effortless living offered by a good boarding house continued throughout the Victorian years, and the houses hosted young couples not yet settled in a permanent home, widows and widowers no longer maintaining homes, and a varied group of temporary and transient guests. It was a big market, and the electroplaters pursued it vigorously.

A generation after his mother had decried the boarding house, Anthony Trollope, in a kindlier vein, commented on the new palaces that were then starting to serve the still migratory Americans. In his *North America,* Trollope devoted an entire chapter to hotels. He explained his reason in the opening lines:

> . . . in the States the hotels are so large an institution, having so much closer and wider bearing on social life than they do in any other country, that I feel myself bound to treat them in a separate chapter as a great

national feature in themselves. They are quite as much thought of in the nation as the legislature, or judicature, or literature of the country; and any falling off in them, or any improvement in the accomodations given, would strike the community as forcibly as a change in the constitution, or an alteration in the franchise.

After comparing continental and English hostelries—and pointing out that those in France are the most expensive in the world, and possess every luxury save that of comfort, and that in England "the port is still bad and the beef too often tough"—Trollope describes the frequency with which large establishments were encountered in 1861:

Hotels in America are very much larger and more numerous than in other countries. They are to be found in all towns, and I may almost say in all villages. In England and on the continent we find them on the recognized routes of travel and in towns of social and commercial importance. On unfrequented roads and in villages there is usually some small house of public entertainment in which the unexpected traveler may obtain food and shelter, and in which the expected boon companions of the neighborhood smoke their nightly pipes, and take their nightly tipple. But in the United States of America the first sign of an incipient settlement is an hotel five stories high, with an office, bar, a cloak-room, three gentlemen's parlours, two ladies' parlours, a ladies' entrance, and two hundred bedrooms.

Leaping into his own answer to his own question, "Whence are to come all the sleepers in these two hundred bedrooms," Mr. Trollope found that Americans had not changed greatly in a generation:

When the new hotel rises up in the wilderness, it is presumed that people will come there with the express object of inhabiting it. The hotel itself will create a population,—as the railroads do. With us the railroads run to the towns; but in the States the towns run to the railways. It is the same thing with the hotels.

Housekeeping is not popular with young married people in America, and there are various reasons why this should be so. Men there are not fixed in their employment as they are with us. If a young Benedict cannot get along as a lawyer at Salem, perhaps he may thrive as a shoemaker at Thermopylae. Jefferson B. Johnson fails in the lumber line at Eleutheria, but hearing of an opening for a Baptist preacher at Big Mud Creek moves himself off with his wife and three children at a week's notice. Aminadab Wiggs takes an engagement as a clerk at a steamboat office on the Pongawonga River, but he goes to his employment with an inward conviction that six months will see him earning his bread elsewhere. Under such circumstances, even a large wardrobe is a nuisance, and a collection of furniture would be as appropriate as a drove of elephants. . . . I think I may allege that the mode of life found in these hotels is liked by the people who frequent them. It is to their taste. They are happy, or at any rate contented at these hotels, and do not wish for household cares.

Obviously, one of the household cares avoided by hotel residents was the preparation of meals. After commenting favorably on dinners he had enjoyed in private homes in America, and granting that Americans "are by no means indifferent to their comestibles," the English visitor described hotel dining:

The mode of eating is as follows. Certain feeding hours are named, which generally include nearly all day. Breakfast from six to ten. Dinner from one till five. Tea from six till nine. Supper from nine till twelve. When the guest presents himself at any of these hours, he is marshalled to a seat, and a bill is put into his hand containing the names of all the eatables then offered for his choice. The list is incredibly and most unnecessarily long. Then it is that you will see care written on the face of the American hotel liver, as he studies the program of the coming performance. With men this passes off unnoticed, but with young girls the appearance of the

May 23, 1900. THE JEWELERS' CIRCULAR-WEEKLY. 17.

EIGHT NEW AMERICAN LINERS

OF THE

International Navigation Company's

FLEET ARE TO BE FURNISHED WITH

"HOLMES & EDWARDS' STERLING SILVER INLAID"

SPOONS, FORKS, ETC.

The "St. Paul" and "St. Louis," on their completion several years ago, were furnished with "Sterling Inlaid" goods. Although the test has been an unusually severe one, and makers of other grades of goods have used every endeavor to secure the order, the International Navigation Co. are so well pleased with this quality that they decided to equip all of the eight new steamers with "Sterling Silver Inlaid" goods. Two of the liners go into commission at once, the remainder as quickly as possible.

Spoons and Forks that will withstand the hard usage of steamer, hotel or restaurant to the satisfaction of the owner, are certain to prove a most economical and durable quality for private use. They are "Warranted 25 years."

If you do not sell "Inlaid" goods you are omitting a desirable and salable line. Send for catalogue, which explains how "Sterling Silver Inlaid" spoons and forks are made and shows patterns and prices.

DINING SALOON, STEAMER "PARIS."

INTERNATIONAL SILVER CO.,

SUCCESSOR TO

HOLMES & EDWARDS SILVER COMPANY,

BRIDGEPORT, CONN.

New York, 9, 11, 13 Maiden Lane.

CHICAGO. ST. LOUIS. SAN FRANCISCO.

Keen competition marked the selection of silverware for an ocean liner, railroad, or hotel. Such sales were not only substantial; they also offered great promotional opportunities for the successful bidder.

thing is not attractive. The anxious study, the elaborate reading of the daily book, and then the choice proclaimed with clear articulation. "Boiled mutton and caper sauce, roast duck, hashed venison, mashed potatoes, poached eggs and spinach, stewed tomatoes. Yes; and waiter,—some squash"! There is no false delicacy in the voice by which this order is given, no desire for a gentle whisper. The dinner is ordered with the firm determination of an American heroine, and in some five minutes' time all the little dishes appear at once, and the lady is surrounded by her banquet.

These hundreds of hotels, each with hundreds of guests, serving almost continuous meals, certainly represented the mass market Horace Wilcox and other early silver salesmen dreamed about, and it was to these caravansaries that sales efforts were directed. During the years immediately preceding the Civil War, and for a decade afterward, most flatware manufacturers looked on the hotel trade as a primary source of sales. It was not until the late 60s and early 70s that it became apparent to many of these firms that silverware on the hotel table might influence the choice of silver for the home. In *The Whitesmiths of Taunton,* George Sweet Gibb relates the following:

A large new hostelry nearing completion was an irresistable magnet which with silent force attracted silverware men from near and far. A salesman's letters tell of one such experience. In the spring of 1875, as the finishing touches were being put on the Palace Hotel in San Francisco, salesmen mysteriously began to arrive in town. Long before bidding was opened by the owners, salesmen from Tiffany's, The Meriden Britannia Company, Gorham, and Reed & Barton had established themselves and their samples. Tension mounted as the time for submitting bids approached, and devious pressures were exerted to obtain "inside" information and assistance. Each salesman watched with guarded suspicion the movements of his competitors. J. H. Rines, representing Reed & Barton, wrote: "The dealers here all enquire every day if its settled yet, and I would prefer that you not lose the order as your sales would probably be affected by it."

In the days when hotels like the Palmer House in Chicago, the Astor House in New York, and Willard's in Washington were but a few of the great hotels being built, the hotel owners demanded heavy silver plate that would match in elegance the often exceedingly luxurious appointments with which the establishments were being outfitted. Since the constant use required durable ware, and maintenance demanded simplicity, the hotel flatware of the Victorian years avoided much of the over-ornamentation that marked some pieces intended for other markets. The hotel trade also encouraged the development of certain pieces and patterns for the household market; in some lines, the same patterns might carry two names—one for the hotel trade, in a commercial grade plate, and the other in standard plate for the household market.

Many of the newly affluent received their first introduction to some of the newly de-

The second Palmer House, opened in Chicago during the 1870s, provided a gold table service for banquets and special dinners, in addition to elaborate silver services in the dining rooms and restaurants. *Courtesy The Palmer House.*

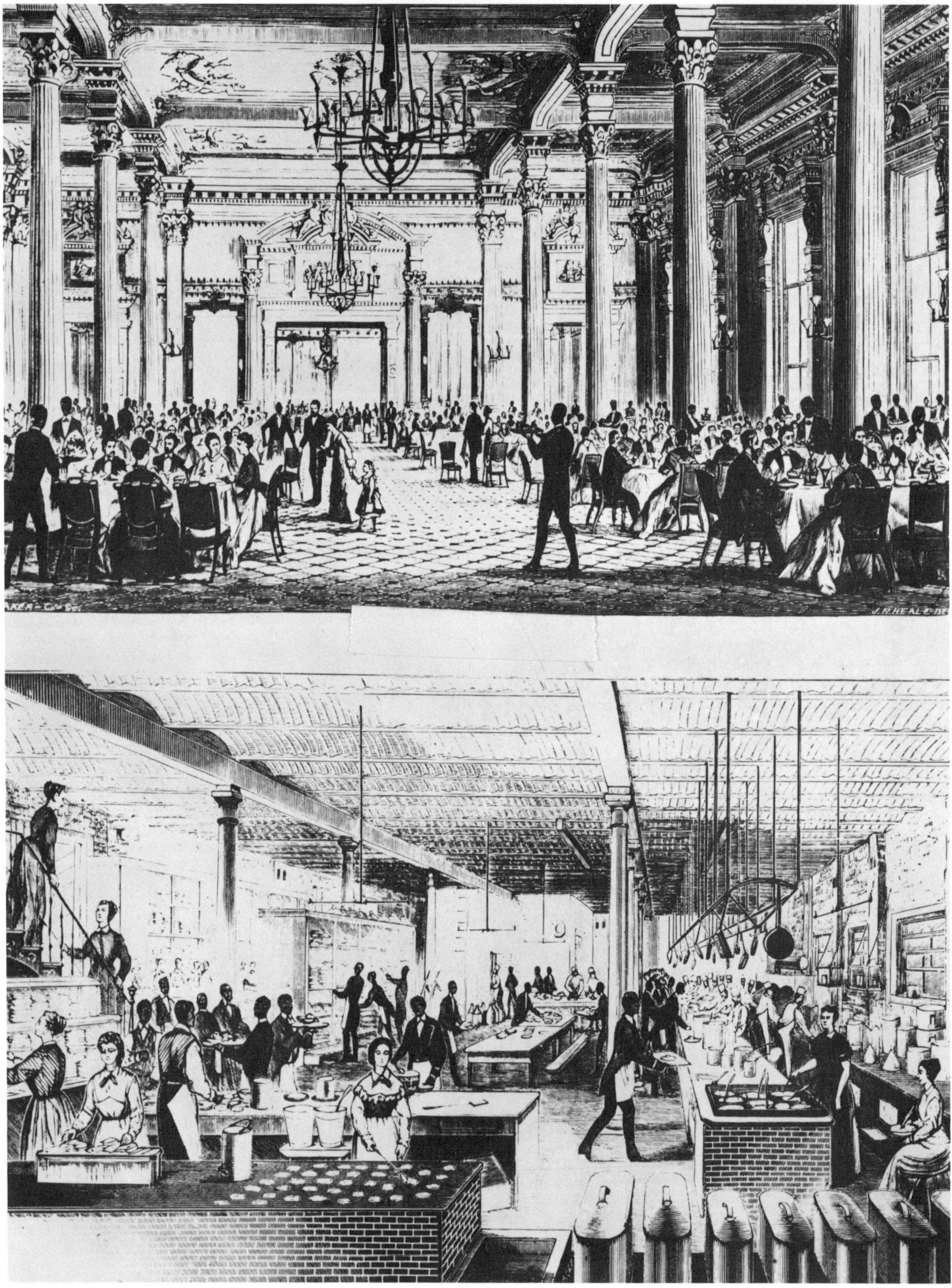

The main dining room and one of the kitchens of The Palmer House in Chicago during the early 1870s. Such hotel dining rooms influenced the design of silver flatware and popularized many new pieces. *Courtesy The Palmer House.*

signed specialized pieces of silverware, too, in elegant hotels, on steamships, or on the dining cars that appeared on more and more American railways after 1868, when the Chicago & Alton made its first dining car available to an entire trainload. The oyster fork, for example, was a requirement of the commercial establishments before 1860, and within a few years the small coffee spoon had become an almost standard appurtenance of the hotel dining room, although it would be some years before the lines "You can have your upper classes, with their devilish demi-tasses" would be popularized in A. Baldwin Sloane's parody, *Heaven Will Protect the Working Girl.*

The prestige attendant upon outfitting fine hotels continued throughout the Edwardian years; as late as 1907, Dominick & Haff, in an advertisement in *The Jewelers' Circular*, boasted that "the order placed with us for the new 'Plaza Hotel' New York City will be the finest and most extensive service of this kind ever produced."

New hotels, proud of fine appointments, publicized the flatware, too. Souvenir booklets prepared for formal openings and distribution to guests frequently mentioned the source of the hotel's silver service. A booklet bound in white leather, published just after the opening of the Brown Palace in Denver, for example, stated:

> The collection of hard metal service, numbering many hundred pieces, is from Reed & Barton, of Taunton, Mass., and New York City. Modeled to carry out the general effect of the main design, each is unique in detail, with the general outline of the antique.

Surrounded by Limoges and Haviland china, and the Val St. Lambert cut glass which the hotel boasted, such table appointments were bound to impress those who dined at these establishments.

Once exposed to this new sophistication,

The menu card of the "Lusitania" was typical of the dining service aboard Edwardian luxury liners. Silver services used on the steamships influenced many passengers in the purchase of similar pieces for home use. *Courtesy C. R. Weber.*

it was only natural that returned travelers turned to the home-town jeweler to supply the same new pieces before the next dinner party. Thus the profitable business of catering to the silver needs of the traveling public became a subtle sort of advertising, too.

That the saturation of public eating places with silverware was affecting manners is attested, too, by the contrasting reports of the Trollopes, a generation apart. Mrs. Frances Trollope, describing the dinner hour on a Mississippi River steamboat in 1828, wrote:

> The total want of the usual courtesies of the

Dining equipment at The Brown Palace Hotel in Denver included Limoges china, Val St. Lambert cut glass, and a silver service specially designed and made by Reed & Barton. *Courtesy The Brown Palace.*

> table, the voracious rapidity with which the viands were seized and devoured, the strange uncouth phrases and pronunciation; the loathsome spitting, from the contamination of which it was absolutely impossible to protect our dresses; the frightful manner of feeding with their knives, till the whole blade seemed to enter the mouth; and the still more frightful manner of cleaning the teeth afterwards with a pocket knife, soon forced us to feel that we were not surrounded by the generals, colonels and majors of the old world; and that the dinner hour was to be anything rather than an hour of enjoyment.

A generation later, in 1861, the good lady's son, Anthony, reported his experiences in Lexington, Kentucky—not with the "generals, colonels and majors" his mother had found wanting in manners:

> . . . I found in the hotel to which I went seventy-five teamsters belonging to the army. The landlord apologized for their presence, alleging that other accommodations could not be found for them in the town . . . while I was at supper, the seventy-five teamsters were summoned into the common eating room by a loud gong, and sat down at their meal at the public table. They were very dirty; I doubt whether I ever saw dirtier men; but they were orderly and well-behaved, and but for their extreme dirt might have passed for the ordinary occupants of a well-filled hotel in the West. Such men, in the States, are less clumsy with their knives and forks . . . than are Englishmen of the same rank.

The upward social mobility of Americans, on which Trollope commented in the same chapter, had again been demonstrated for the author—this time with tableware! Nickel silver and silver-plated knives and forks and spoons had become accessible to family tables in the smallest hamlet, for the peddler had begun to be replaced with print. The catalogs of the silver companies could reach more customers than the individual drummer. The simple price list with a few woodcuts or lithographs introduced during the 1850s had made it possible for the storekeeper in even the most remote crossroads to order tableware for his customers. These were in general use within a few years, but it was the development of the "patent patterns" in the late 60s that led to the production of the elaborately engraved tomes which marked silver selling through the later Victorian years. The new patterns, patented and produced by only one manufacturer, made style as well as quality a factor in silver purchases. Among the more elaborate of these was the 1871 edition of the Meriden Britannia Company's catalog. This was followed by Reed & Barton's first catalog in the grand manner in 1877; this effort was promptly matched by the Meriden Britannia Company with a new edition in 1878, and surpassed by an even larger book in 1883. The elaboration was infectious; even the smaller companies produced ornately illustrated catalogs, like that of Luther Boardman's 1880 catalog, which boasted hard-cover cloth binding and gilt edges for each page.

The development of the great, cloth-bound and fully illustrated volumes reached a climax

Pages from an 1857 catalog of the Rogers Bros. Manufacturing Company. The catalog, probably the first produced by the famous brothers, is a beautiful example of lithography, and illustrates early electroplate patterns and pieces in actual size. (Approximately one-quarter size shown here.) *Courtesy The International Silver Company.*

in 1885, when Reed & Barton spent something over $100,000 for 7000 copies of its most ambitious and comprehensive catalog.

Within a few years, services had become so elaborate, and most patterns were made in so many different pieces, that no one catalog could do justice to an entire line, so manufacturers brought out individual catalogs for each pattern. Those for the early 90s were beautiful examples of the engraver's art, and most of the catalogs illustrated up to 150 pieces, in full size, of a selected pattern. Some of them, notably a series produced by the Towle Manufacturing Company, combined historical notes in narrative form, relating pertinent background for the pattern illustrated with the illustrations of the service. By the mid-90s, photo-engraving appeared, and even more realistic reproductions enhanced the pages as the earlier line drawings disappeared.

Easier travel by steamship and railroad

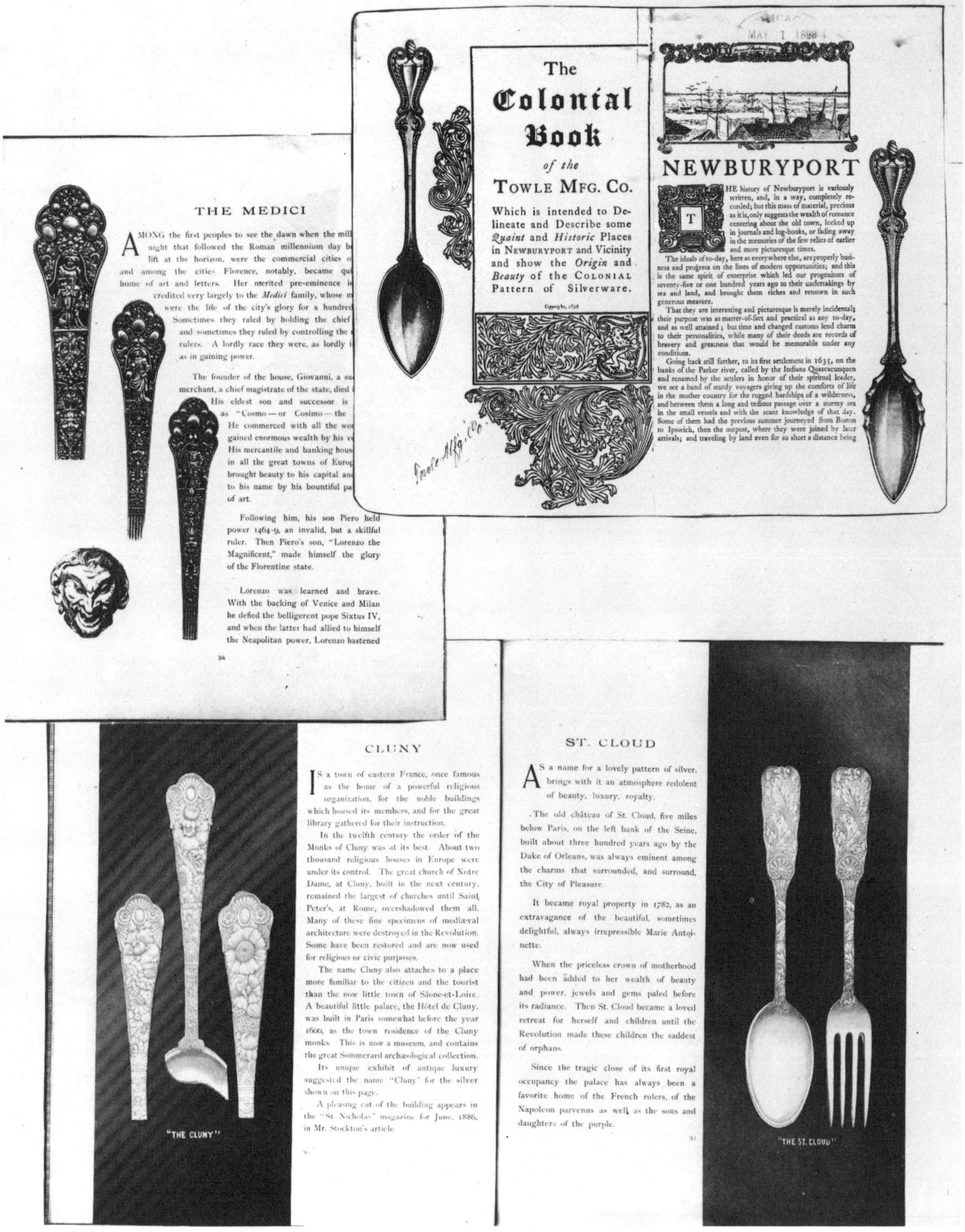

THE MEDICI

AMONG the first peoples to see the dawn when the mill
night that followed the Roman millennium day b
lift at the horizon, were the commercial cities o
and among the cities Florence, notably, became qui
home of art and letters. Her merited pre-eminence is
credited very largely to the *Medici* family, whose m
were the life of the city's glory for a hundred
Sometimes they ruled by holding the chief
and sometimes they ruled by controlling the
rulers. A lordly race they were, as lordly i
as in gaining power.

The founder of the house, Giovanni, a su
merchant, a chief magistrate of the state, died
His eldest son and successor is
as "Cosmo — or Cosimo — the
He commerced with all the wo
gained enormous wealth by his v
His mercantile and banking hous
in all the great towns of Europ
brought beauty to his capital an
to his name by his bountiful pa
of art.

Following him, his son Piero held power 1464-9, an invalid, but a skillful ruler. Then Piero's son, "Lorenzo the Magnificent," made himself the glory of the Florentine state.

Lorenzo was learned and brave. With the backing of Venice and Milan he defied the belligerent pope Sixtus IV, and when the latter had allied to himself the Neapolitan power, Lorenzo hastened

34

The Colonial Book of the Towle Mfg. Co.

Which is intended to Delineate and Describe some *Quaint* and *Historic* Places in Newburyport and Vicinity and show the *Origin* and *Beauty* of the Colonial Pattern of Silverware.

Copyright, 1898

NEWBURYPORT

THE history of Newburyport is variously written, and, in a way, completely recorded; but this mass of material, precious as it is, only suggests the wealth of romance centering about the old town, locked up in journals and log-books, or fading away in the memories of the few relics of earlier and more picturesque times.

The ideals of to-day, here as everywhere else, are properly business and progress on the lines of modern opportunities; and this is the same spirit of enterprise which led our progenitors of seventy-five or one hundred years ago to their undertakings by sea and land, and brought them riches and renown in such generous measure.

That they are interesting and picturesque is merely incidental; their purpose was as matter-of-fact and practical as any to-day, and as well attained; but time and changed customs lend charm to their personalities, while many of their deeds are records of bravery and greatness that would be memorable under any conditions.

Going back still further, to its first settlement in 1635, on the banks of the Parker river, called by the Indians Quascacunquen and renamed by the settlers in honor of their spiritual leader, we see a band of sturdy voyagers giving up the comforts of life in the mother country for the rugged hardships of a wilderness, and between them a long and tedious passage over a stormy sea in the small vessels and with the scant knowledge of that day. Some of them had the previous summer journeyed from Boston to Ipswich, then the outpost, where they were joined by later arrivals; and traveling by land even for so short a distance being

"THE CLUNY"

CLUNY

IS a town of eastern France, once famous as the home of a powerful religious organization, for the noble buildings which housed its members, and for the great library gathered for their instruction.

In the twelfth century the order of the Monks of Cluny was at its best. About two thousand religious houses in Europe were under its control. The great church of Notre Dame, at Cluny, built in the next century, remained the largest of churches until Saint Peter's, at Rome, overshadowed them all. Many of these fine specimens of mediæval architecture were destroyed in the Revolution. Some have been restored and are now used for religious or civic purposes.

The name Cluny also attaches to a place more familiar to the citizen and the tourist than the now little town of Sâone-et-Loire. A beautiful little palace, the Hôtel de Cluny, was built in Paris somewhat before the year 1600, as the town residence of the Cluny monks. This is now a museum, and contains the great Sommerard archæological collection.

Its unique exhibit of antique luxury suggested the name "Cluny" for the silver shown on this page.

A pleasing cut of the building appears in the "St Nicholas" magazine for June, 1886, in Mr. Stockton's article.

ST. CLOUD

AS a name for a lovely pattern of silver, brings with it an atmosphere redolent of beauty, luxury, royalty.

The old château of St. Cloud, five miles below Paris, on the left bank of the Seine, built about three hundred years ago by the Duke of Orleans, was always eminent among the charms that surrounded, and surround, the City of Pleasure.

It became royal property in 1782, as an extravagance of the beautiful, sometimes delightful, always irrepressible Marie Antoinette.

When the priceless crown of motherhood had been added to her wealth of beauty and power, jewels and gems paled before its radiance. Then St. Cloud became a loved retreat for herself and children until the Revolution made these children the saddest of orphans.

Since the tragic close of its first royal occupancy the palace has always been a favorite home of the French rulers, of the Napoleon parvenus as well as the sons and daughters of the purple.

32

"THE ST. CLOUD"

Catalogs of silver manufacturers at about the turn of the century were frequently devoted to a single pattern. Such volumes explained the source of the design, and were generally elaborately illustrated.

THE NEW YORK CENTRAL
DINING CAR SERVICE.

LUNCHEON

MUTTON BROTH WITH RICE

CUCUMBERS PIN-MONEY PICKLES RADISHES
CHOW CHOW QUEEN OLIVES

BAKED BLUEFISH STUFFED, TOMATO SAUCE

BAKED CHICKEN PIE, FAMILY STYLE
CORN FRITTERS WITH MAPLE SYRUP
BOILED OX TONGUE WITH SPINACH

ROAST RIBS OF BEEF ROAST HAM, CHAMPAGNE SAUCE

BOILED POTATOES STEWED TOMATOES BOILED ONIONS
NEW GOLDEN WAX BEANS BOSTON BAKED BEANS

COLD MEATS, ETC.
ROAST BEEF CHICKEN LAMB SMOKED BEEF TONGUE
BEECH-NUT HAM BONELESS SARDINES
PICKLED LAMBS' TONGUES

LETTUCE SALAD POTATO SALAD

BREAD AND BUTTER CUSTARD PUDDING, WINE SAUCE
BANANAS BERRIES CALIFORNIA ORANGES ASSORTED CAKES
NEAPOLITAN ICE CREAM ORANGE MARMALADE
BENT'S WATER CRACKERS H. & P. DINNER BISCUITS
ROQUEFORT AND EDAM CHEESE
TEA HORLICK'S MALTED MILK COFFEE

MEALS ONE DOLLAR.

"LITHIA POLARIS"—PURE SPRING WATER FREE.

The drinking water served on the New York Central Dining Cars is from the celebrated "Polaris Springs" of the Boonville Mineral Spring Co., on the Rome, Watertown & Ogdensburg Division, in the foot-hills of the Adirondack Mountains. It has been analyzed by eminent chemists, and is absolutely pure.

A SOUVENIR MENU.

A copy of this Menu card in an envelope ready for mailing will be furnished free, on application, by the conductor in charge of this car.

A turn-of-the-century menu card used by the New York Central. Railroad dining car silverware was generally designed and manufactured for a specific line, and contracts to supply these transportation systems with flatware were eagerly sought. *Courtesy New York Central System.*

made the Expositions of the Victorian years natural centers for the display of craftsmanship, and, like other manufacturers, the silver industry sponsored exhibits at all of them. As early as 1851, the English electroplating firms had shown the "application of silver to sculpture," in the Great International Exhibition of that year, and American silver companies followed this precedent. While the exhibition of standard production items at such events as the annual Massachusetts Charitable Mechanics Association exhibits in Boston, the Franklin Institute exhibits in Philadelphia, the American Institute in New York, and the New York Crystal Palace Fair of 1853, had elicited favorable acknowledgements of the skill of the silver companies, and the awards made at these affairs had been publicized by the winners, it was not until the Philadelphia Centennial Exposition of 1876 that the special "exhibition pieces" were presented. At that fair, Reed & Barton showed a massive "Progress Vase," four feet long and three feet high, along with a second piece of sculpture depicting a trotting horse and sulky: The Meriden Britannia Company offered the "Buffalo Hunt," an equally ornate and even larger

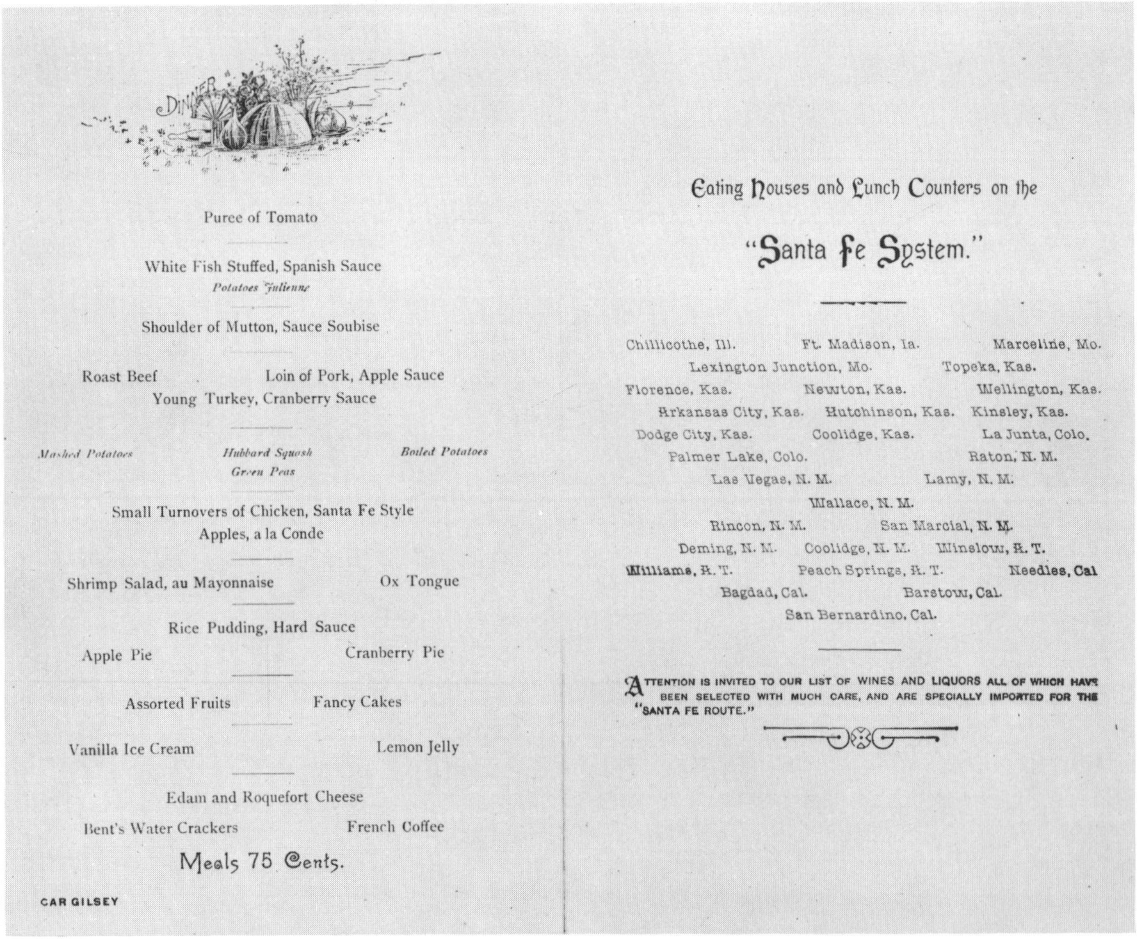

Dinner

Puree of Tomato

White Fish Stuffed, Spanish Sauce
Potatoes Julienne

Shoulder of Mutton, Sauce Soubise

Roast Beef   Loin of Pork, Apple Sauce
Young Turkey, Cranberry Sauce

Mashed Potatoes   *Hubbard Squash*   *Boiled Potatoes*
Green Peas

Small Turnovers of Chicken, Santa Fe Style
Apples, a la Conde

Shrimp Salad, au Mayonnaise   Ox Tongue

Rice Pudding, Hard Sauce
Apple Pie   Cranberry Pie

Assorted Fruits   Fancy Cakes

Vanilla Ice Cream   Lemon Jelly

Edam and Roquefort Cheese

Bent's Water Crackers   French Coffee

Meals 75 Cents.

CAR GILSEY

Eating Houses and Lunch Counters on the

"Santa Fe System."

Chillicothe, Ill.   Ft. Madison, Ia.   Marceline, Mo.
Lexington Junction, Mo.   Topeka, Kas.
Florence, Kas.   Newton, Kas.   Wellington, Kas.
Arkansas City, Kas.   Hutchinson, Kas.   Kinsley, Kas.
Dodge City, Kas.   Coolidge, Kas.   La Junta, Colo.
Palmer Lake, Colo.   Raton, N. M.
Las Vegas, N. M.   Lamy, N. M.
Wallace, N. M.
Rincon, N. M.   San Marcial, N. M.
Deming, N. M.   Coolidge, N. M.   Winslow, A. T.
Williams, A. T.   Peach Springs, A. T.   Needles, Cal
Bagdad, Cal.   Barstow, Cal.
San Bernardino, Cal.

ATTENTION IS INVITED TO OUR LIST OF WINES AND LIQUORS ALL OF WHICH HAVE BEEN SELECTED WITH MUCH CARE, AND ARE SPECIALLY IMPORTED FOR THE "SANTA FE ROUTE."

Menu cards used by The Santa Fe Railway in 1888 and 1889. Dining Cars and railway "Eating Houses" featured elaborate meals, and introduced many customers to specialized flatware pieces. *Courtesy The Santa Fe Railway.*

piece; The Gorham Manufacturing Company presented a monumental "Century Vase," five feet long and four feet high. As the centers of displays of flat and hollow ware, these pieces attracted enormous crowds, and served to familiarize the visitors with the wonders in silver they might enjoy in their own homes. Similar exhibits graced the Louisiana Purchase Exposition in New Orleans in 1885, the International Cotton Exposition of 1881 in Atlanta, the International Exposition in Omaha in 1898, and the Columbian Exposition in Chicago in 1893. As the world's fairs increased in size, so did the exhibits of the silver makers; at the Chicago Exposition, the Meriden Britannia Company occupied an "Octagonal structure of mahogany thirty-two feet in diameter and forty feet high," crowded, according to contemporary reports in the jewelry trade press, with novelty pieces, and with the trademark of the company, "1847 Rogers Bros. A1" represented in spoons and forks.

Visitors from distant states thronged the Midway at these affairs, and, when they carried home their souvenir spoons, they also carried an impression of the new elegance silverware was bringing to everyday life. Once home again more and better silverware represented another ambition to be fulfilled.

Among the astute merchandisers of the late 19th century, the housewives' ambition to own silverware was not overlooked by purveyors of soups and cereal, tea and tonics. "Premium" selling—the inclusion of an unrelated gift item with the sale of a staple—was already established, and silver-plated tableware soon became one of the most popular of the premium items. Included in a large package of cereal, exchanged for a coupon, a part of a package, or a specified number of soap wrappers, a silver fork or spoon provided the incentive for the housewife to change to another brand of food product, or convince her grocer that he should stock another kind of tea. The premium silver-plated ware was often a standard pattern, perhaps one that had been available for some years and was no longer "news" in regular silver sales channels. In some cases a special pattern was designed as a premium, and was available only to the purchasers of a specific brand of food product. Such a pattern was Oneida Community's "Cereta," a full-blown iris motif that was distributed for years by the American Cereal Company with packages of Quaker Oats. Illustrated on packages, shown

Quaker Oats used the first silver flatware specifically designed as a premium. The "Cereta" pattern was designed and made by Oneida Community; Quaker Oats advertised the ware widely in newspapers and magazines. *Courtesy Oneida, Ltd.*

OFFICE OF THE

STANDARD SILVER WARE CO.,

MANUFACTURERS AND JOBBERS OF

FINE ELECTRO

SILVER PLATED WARE,

→SPOONS, FORKS,←

→KNIVES, ETC.←

Factories at Wallingford, Naubuc, Hartford, Conn.; and Brooklyn, N. Y.

BOSTON OFFICE, - - 86 WASHINGTON STREET.

KIND READER :

As your name has been handed to us, together with first-class recommendations, we take pleasure in enclosing you this circular, giving full particulars of our goods and sincerely hope you will be benefited thereby. As we desire to have our goods introduced into your locality at once, directly from us or through our agent, we have thought best to enclose you one of our Certificate Circulars, which we give you ***gratis***, which entitles you to a Sample Casket or Agent's full outfit, only requiring ***$1.25***, being a little more than the actual cost of postage, packing, &c., with the hope you will either accept an Agency or procure us a good, reliable Agent to introduce our goods. Therefore, we hope none of our friends will seek to take advantage of us by procuring our goods upon this Certificate offer without returning us a favor by assisting us to make sales. If you send for a Sample Casket, we Guarantee that an Agency at our hands will *pay* you *better* and be more *satisfactory* than any business in which you can engage, as our goods are staple, and sell at every house.

Remember we make this Certificate offer in order to have our goods introduced, and for profit we depend entirely upon future sales. This *method* is a first-class way for an agent to commence business. If you cannot act as agent, or secure us an agent, you can help us to make sales in your locality by having one of our Caskets and showing it to your neighbors and friends and telling them the *prices*. Now do not imagine or class our Reliable House with the hundreds of swindlers that swarm the country to-day. If, after you send and get a Sample Casket of Cutlery, you do not find everything as we represent, do not hesitate, but return the goods, and we will refund you your money. Therefore you see, we recompense you splendidly for any and all favors you show us. If we cannot induce you to take advantage of this golden opportunity, will you be kind enough to hand this Circular and Certificate to some one whom you think would make us a good agent. Hoping to receive an early reply, and that you will see best to take advantage of this *Extraordinary Offer*, we beg leave to remain,

Very truly yours,

Standard Silver Ware Co

Handbill distributed by wholesale house soliciting door-to-door salesmen for electroplated flatware. Such houses frequently implied that they manufactured their own wares, listing locations of factories from which they bought private label merchandise. *Courtesy of The New York Historical Society, New York City.*

in newspaper and magazine advertisements, and featuring the maker's name and reputation, these early premium offers effectively supplemented the silver companies' own advertising efforts.

More and more, as new patterns and new pieces joined the early products of the silver manufacturers, the firms turned to the trade journals of the jewelry industry to carry the news of the latest designs, the newest fashion whim represented in silver flatware, and improved production methods. The silver business had become big business, and competition for the favor of the leading jeweler in every locality was keen. As a link between the manufacturer and the user, as the man who could build the mass sales needed to maintain mass production, the jeweler had displaced the wagon salesman; between visits of its own representatives, the silver business turned to the trade journals to remind him of their wares.

By this time, and on into the 20th century, the role of advertising was becoming accepted by the manufacturers. Ingenious plans to increase dealer's advertising in individual markets were developed by William Snow, who had joined the Meriden Britannia Company in 1892, and served as advertising manager when the firm became the International Silver Company. It was Mr. Snow, too, who first used full color in magazine pages to advertise silverware, and, in 1909 dramatized the leadership of the Rogers Brothers name in the silver plate world with "The 1847 Girl" who presided over exhibitions of the products of the company at expositions and in jewelry stores. But it was Oneida, Ltd. who first grasped the importance of the "pretty girl" in printed selling, when the New York company addressed its advertising to younger women just after the turn of the century. Oneida, too, first used endorsements of leading socialites like Mrs. Belmont, and celebrities like Irene Castle, then at the height of her fame as a dancer, to add distinction to silver plate.

7

Patterns

It is conceivable that Alexander Pope might have foreseen the day when his "Yielding metal flow'd to human form" might grace the tables of a multitude of the rich and powerful he so greatly admired; from his early 18th-century writing table, he could hardly have imagined that in little more than a century even many moderately comfortable households would share these sometimes fantastically wrought designs in table silver. Nor was the buyer limited to designs depicting the human form; biologically impossible animals, insects and sea serpents vied with florals from no earthly garden, verdure from no terrestrial glade.

So familiar have these ornate mid-Victorian designs become that it is easy to overlook much of the beautifully proportioned, handsomely-worked ware that was produced by individual silversmiths and commercial establishments between 1837 and 1910.

Throughout the early Victorian period, solid silver tableware patterns bore a close resemblance to their 18th-century counterparts. Variations in style were minor, but generally marked enough to distinguish the Victorian pieces from their predecessors. Spoon bowls became more pointed, less egg-shaped. This trend, which had started about 1810, had become marked by 1825, and continued to be a recognizable characteristic until the late 1850s. The handles, viewed in profile, developed a curve. Most 18th-century spoons had handles which were comparatively flat from bowl to tip, so that the length of the handle lies parallel to the table top. There were occasional departures; tips frequently flared upward during the middle years of the 18th century, and some were turned down after 1775, but in practically every design, the shank of the handle remained straight.

Another distinguishing characteristic in the design of coin silver pieces appeared between 1810 and 1820, and had become general by the 1830s. This is the shoulder at the junction of the bowl and shaft; very few early Victorian spoons or forks were made without it, and it was continued in many patterns until after 1900. Some earlier silversmiths had used it for a brief period around 1775–1780, but it had generally disappeared again on almost all later 18th-century pieces.

Handles continued to be wide, a carry-over from the very early folding tableware, and tips were round, oval, and coffin shaped. The fiddle shape became popular, and the patterns—generally limited to the top of the handle—began to offer more variations. Designs included plain, rat-tail, and tipped; threaded borders and threaded tips were seen more often. What is commonly called the tipped design—the slightly scrolled, shallow embossing resembling a musical brace—was treated to many variations; some silversmiths made fork and spoon handles with plain tops, but used the tipped design on the back of the handles, calling these "Reverse Tip" or "French Tip."

Plain tips were frequently ordered, and an increasing number of silversmiths engraved rather delicate patterns—conventionalized floral or shell designs most frequently—on many pieces. This engraving was of the "Bright Cut" type, and compared favorably with almost any of the 18th-century work. Initials and monograms were commonly employed. These usually appeared on the top of the handle, but were not infrequently found on the back. The practice is readily understandable when we recall that the coin silver pieces frequently represented the family bank account as well as its tableware; initials, monograms, and distinctive patterns made the ware more readily recognizable in case of theft.

In Baltimore, Samuel Kirk had introduced his Repousse work in 1824. This intricately fashioned pattern, anticipating a trend by 50 years or more, had rapidly become known as "Baltimore silver." Other silversmiths in the United States adapted prevailing English styles; John Polhemus, for example, is generally credited with making the first American "Kings" pattern, a classic design of French origin popularized in England, and still made by many firms.

Pinpointing the date of early Victorian coin silver patterns is difficult. Practically all of these pieces were custom made, until the late 50s and early 60s, and earlier spoons or forks might be matched, as family finances permitted, 10, 20, or even 30 years later. Nor were all pieces in a family service necessarily made by the same silversmith. The practitioners of the craft were also mortal, and one or more of their apprentices might carry on in the same location, working for the same customers, making the same patterns, changing only the name or initial marked on the back of the shaft after the master's death. Even geography was no particular barrier; family mobility is not, after all, an invention of the 20th century. Families moved, most often westward, and the coin silver pieces they possessed were small enough and light enough to be readily moved too. If they prospered in the new location, the pieces might be supplemented by others made by a silversmith in the new neighborhood; if they failed, the silver might afford the grub-stake needed to move on to try again.

The spoon-mold afforded a certain degree of standardization, but since the mold itself was most often a hand made affair, and the finishing was done by hand, even the pieces made by the same man may show wide variations.

Among plated pieces, all of which are dated after the mid-1840s, the earliest patterns were almost exact duplicates of the coin silver pieces being produced at that time.

The earliest of these were "Plain," "Threaded," and "Tipped," all originally produced by the Rogers Brothers, in 1847, all of which continued to be produced by various manufacturers throughout the Victorian and Edwardian periods.

During the next three years, the Rogers Brothers introduced the "Olive," "Antique," "Fiddle," "Windsor," and "Silver" patterns. This group of patterns became standard in the trade, along with the ten other patterns the firm produced during the next two decades, for the unplated pieces of base metal were sold to other electroplaters, who plated and finished the pieces, and gave them their own backstamps. This practice continued well into the late 1860s, so that on most plated ware produced before 1870, identical patterns may bear the stamp of any one of the early plating firms.

These patterns, numbering about 20, offered many housewives their first opportunity to own silverware for the family table, and they were extremely popular.

Until about 1850, the patterns reflected the popular taste in architecture and household furniture of the early Republic. Where ornament was used, the designs were as symmetrical as the London-produced plates showing the plans of Palladio for facades and porticoes; details borrowed from the Brothers Adam, or from MacIntire, who borrowed from *them,* tended to be light and delicate. It is questionable that the resemblances were premeditated; new buildings and new chairs or chests may have exerted an almost subconscious influence, the handbooks of Asher Benjamin may have offered some guidance to silversmiths as well as carpenters, but on the whole the silver industry at no point was called upon to set trends. Silverware was an accessory, albeit a necessary one, and the tastes of a given day in housing and furniture, in draperies and decoration, determined the popularity of a particular pattern in silver. Since it was one of the earliest of the "mass production" industries, the manufacturers could not afford to gamble on designs calculated to change tastes; they could only follow trends set by others, and adapt to the metal the prevailing modes in domestic design and decoration.

There were exceptions, of course. Some of the patterns introduced by manufacturers who *anticipated* trends at first shocked their competitors. But as these patterns caught the public fancy, the same competitors developed similar styles of their own. In other cases, patterns of exceptional design, beautifully adapted to the metal, continued as favorites—and best sellers—through many different fashion trends in home design and decoration. Many of these were developed during the last years of the 19th century, after the industry had enjoyed 50 years of growth.

About 1850, as the country entered the mid-Victorian years, the influences that were bringing about changes in architecture and interior design, in furniture and furnishings, made themselves felt in silverware, too.

The "Tuscan" and "French Oval" patterns, both introduced in 1852, each reflected, in its own way, the two courses domestic design was to follow for many years.

On the side of "Tuscan" stood the Classicists, the group of architects and builders and cabinetmakers who looked to the glories of ancient Greece and Rome for their inspirations. The foundations for this movement had been established during the late years of the 18th century, but it was not until after 1820 that the movement gathered its full momentum in residential design. Until about 1860, the Classic Revival, or Greek Revival as it is often called, made its mark, particularly in those areas which were newly established at this time.

In furniture, the designs of John Hall, as set forth in *The Cabinet Makers Assistant,* brought a conglomerate of curves and vaguely Greco-Roman details to massive mahogany-veneered pieces. From 1840, when his book was published in Baltimore, for more than a decade, his influence was visible in the products of the newly-built, steam-powered, bandsaw-equipped furniture factories, which suddenly put new furniture with a certain formality within reach of a new middle class. Even the customers of the dwindling group of old-line cabinet makers ordered furniture in the same style, and much of it found its way through the wooden porticoes of the miniature temples that more and more Americans called home.

While the Greek Revival might be termed a part of the Romantic movement in America, more new homeowners found their romance in the adaptations of Andrew Jackson Downing and Alexander Jackson Davis—represented, in silverware, by the "French Oval" pattern. Downing's books on landscape gardening, as well as cottage and country residences, espoused the cause of the Gothic, the Tudor, the Swiss, and the Italian Villa, with bows to the Egyptian and Moorish. He preached a doctrine of adapting architecture to the site and to the owner; he broke with formality in landscaping, and the rigid symmetrical plan of previous American houses; and, for a generation after his death in 1852, he remained a dictator of taste from the Atlantic to the westernmost frontier. Davis, favorite architect of the imperious Downing, favored the Gothic and Italian styles, and imposed them with charm on the families of wealth and influence through the 1840s and 50s. Concurrently, after 1844, cabinetmakers like John Henry Belter and critics like Arthur Gilman opened new avenues to the purchasers of home furnishings; Belter, through his elaborately carved, intricately worked designs, and Gilman, whose plea was heeded by furniture manufacturers throughout the land, by his argument for eclecticism. He felt that designs that were new and distinctly American would be arrived at only by a blending of many older forms.

With such a variety of possible stage settings, it is understandable that the classic "Tuscan" pattern in silverware, and the more romantic "French Oval" pattern, with its suggestion of a trefoil arch, should make their concurrent entrances to public acclaim that would last for many years. Even more to the point is the neat straddling of the two disparate decorating camps—a facility that the silver industry was to demonstrate more and more often through the years of Victoria's reign.

Between 1852 and 1860, "Beaded," "Oval," "Shell," and "Roman" patterns followed the Classic trend; "Gothic" and "St. Charles," the Romantic school. The scroll design of the latter forecast scores of Victorian patterns.

During the years when these patterns were being introduced, there was less competition from overseas for the fledgling industry. English suppliers had originally dominated the Britannia business, at first because of the quality of the ware, and later because of the styling. By the middle 1830s, American producers had developed a satisfactory alloy, but continued to copy English styles, openly advertising that exact copies were offered for sale. As electroplate replaced Britannia, the English manufacturers failed to recover the market, for the transition to silver plate was rapid. Sporadic attempts to sell the new English electroplated wares were made, and catalogs of firms like Henry Wilkinson & Co. were distributed on both sides of the Atlantic. That the patterns these catalogs displayed influenced American design cannot be doubted, when pages from the English editions of the mid-1850s are compared with patterns presented by American makers a few years later.

Another source of British influence on design is found in the pages of publications like Ackerman's *Designs for Gold & Silversmiths,* published in 1836, or the *Pattern Book for Jewellers, Gold-and Silversmiths,* published in London in the 1880s. The product of an enterprising printer, A. Fischer, the pattern book was "complete in 25 fortnightly parts," constituting a veritable correspondence course in baroque design for craftsmen working in precious metals. Examination of the flatware sections of these and similar guides published at about the same time indicates that the sin of over-ornamentation was not committed solely in America, nor was it caused entirely by the demands of an artistically unsophisticated public. While no such guides, so far as is known, were published in the United States, Ameri-

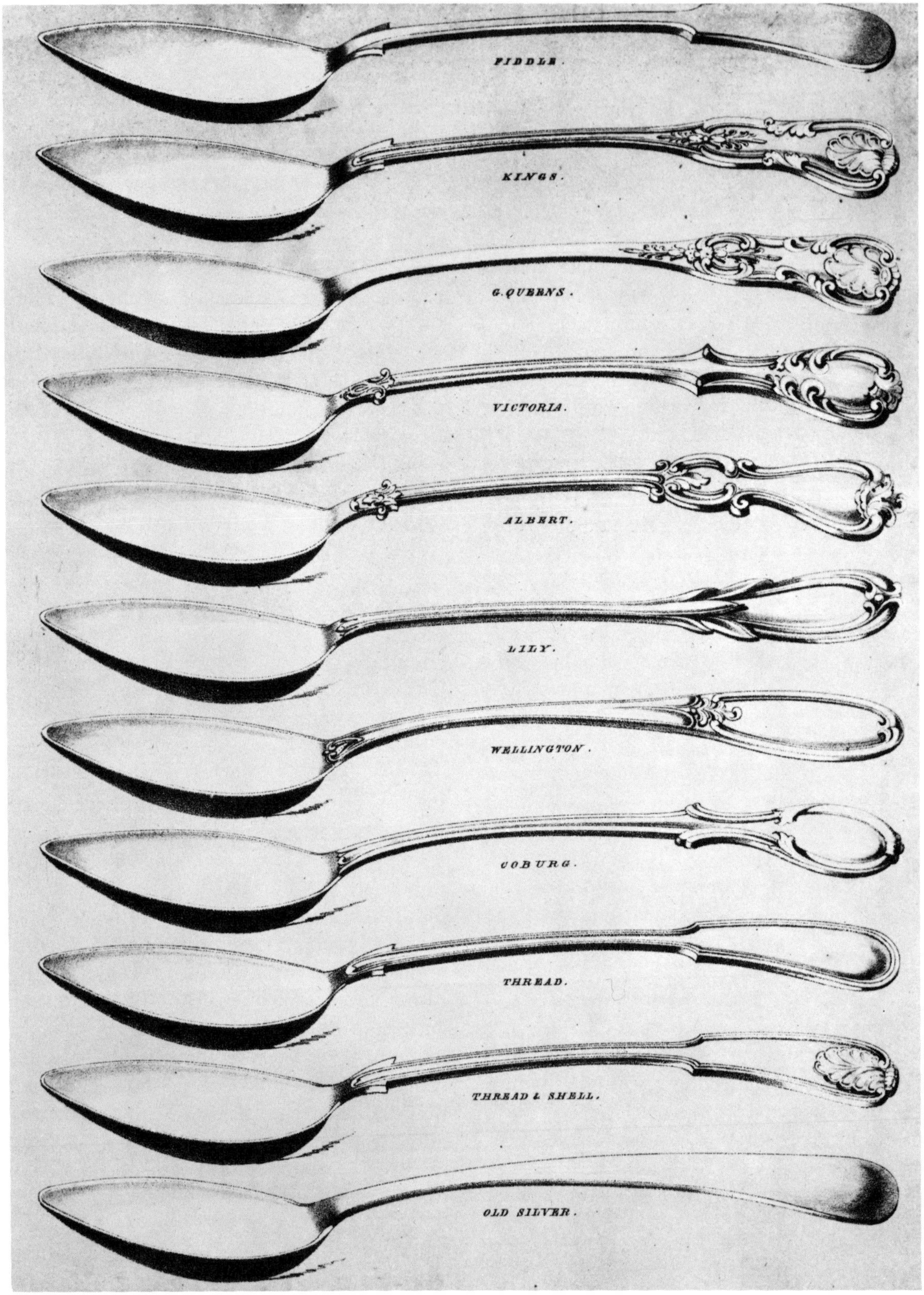

An 1855 catalogue of Henry Wilkinson & Co. showed patterns favored by English buyers of that period. Similar designs were offered by most manufacturers in the United States during the same years.

Silver cutlery.

Design for silver knife, fork and spoon.

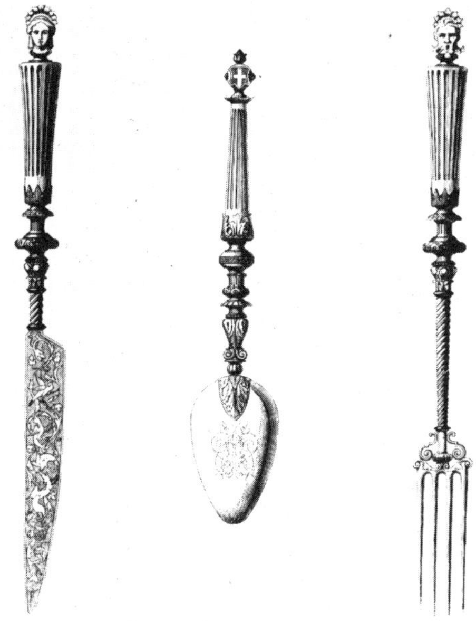

Silver cutlery in Renaissance style.

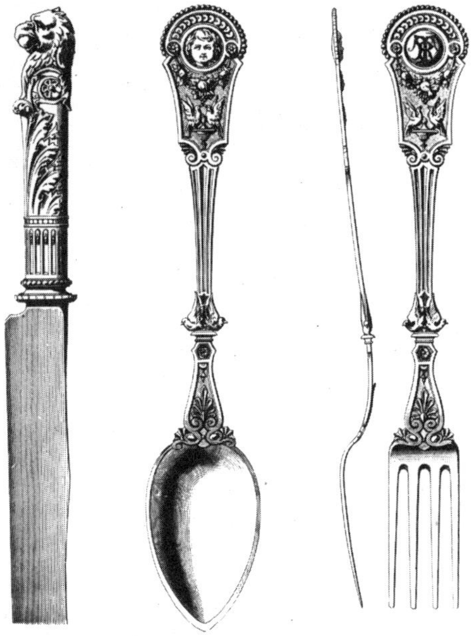

Silver knife, fork and spoon.

Four pages from the *Pattern Book for Jewelers, Gold and Silversmiths* show the ornate decoration with which much mid-Victorian silver was embellished. Illustrations are approximately one-third the size of the original pages offered by A. Fischer of London in 1883.

can silversmiths were among the subscribers to the overseas service. While the suggested designs undoubtedly provided complex exercises in fabrication, they confirm the comment of an early 20th century critic of Victorian silver who believed that design was irreparably impaired when it was transferred from the craftsman's bench to the drawing board, and the designing function removed from the men who best understood the medium.

Rapid improvement in world wide communications by mid-century, and the increased knowledge of archaeological discoveries helped introduce fresh influences from classical antiquity. The diggings at Bernay in 1830, the recoveries at Hildesheim in 1868, and the discoveries at Chaourse and Bascoreale later in the century, all contributed metalwork from classical antiquity for adaptation.

By 1860, new influences were affecting design, forecasting the agglomerate that was to mark all the later years of Victoria's rule. Both England and the United States had entered a period of world trade; publications in both countries, conversations at dinner and tea tables, and the very food at these tables, were spiced with references to far-off, romantic places. Steamships and railroads had brought previously undreamed-of comfort to travel, and all who could afford it, traveled and brought home their souvenirs; those who could not go in person collected pictures and scrapbooks to attest to their interest in the wide, wide world. For their tables both travelers and stay-at-homes paid homage to far-off places by buying silver patterns named for Egypt and Armenia, Assyria, and Persia. That the designs did not always reflect the artistic achievements of older cultures was not too important; they were names in the news, and they brought to the isolated farm wife, as well as her city sister, glamour that would gleam in lamplight and gaslight, at supper or high tea.

When, in 1866, Japan began trade with the western nations, a near-craze for Oriental items struck the domestic scene. The fad encompassed many decorating forms; they ranged from cheap paper fans printed in garish colors and inexpensive china with comparatively well done transfer designs, to the handsome wallpapers of such understanding designers as Bruce Talbert. The producers of silver flatware were not exempt from the movement, and patterns were soon designated as "Japanese," "Oriental," "Orient," and "Mikado." Some manufacturers seized on the stylized art forms of the East as still another way to make silverware compatible with the newest trend in home decor. Delicately poised cranes joined stiff sprays of cherry blossoms to prove that the East and West could meet.

During the same decade, improvements in manufacturing processes made possible the development of more intricately fashioned designs; the new processes enabled many more silver manufacturers to fabricate their own patterns completely from blanks to finished ware. While the earlier patterns continued to be marketed by almost all firms, the new patented designs, exclusive to a single company were added. Patented flatware patterns were not new; some silversmiths had been granted patents for "spoon designs" as early as 1801, and many early 19th-century silversmith designers—William Gale, Michael Gibney and John Cox among others—had registered patent patterns between 1830 and 1850. But as machines increased silverware production, competition based on design as well as on workmanship entered the silver trade, and patterns like the "Ribbon" of Theodore Evans & Co. and the "Roman Medallion" of Reed & Barton reflected this new trend.

There was no question but that the buying public was the final judge of the merit of any

Heavy ornamentation, gilding, and enamel work were all recommended for silver flatware in the pattern books sold to mid-Victorian silversmiths in England and the United States. Commercially produced wares reflected these same trends in design.

flatware pattern. Writing in *Harper's New Monthly Magazine* for September, 1868, James Parton explained the process of design selection:

> The informing soul of all this dwells in the Designing Room. To perfect utility until it becomes elegance; to produce forms novel and pleasing, *because* they are perfectly convenient; to devise ornaments which shall truly harmonize with the object they are intended to adorn; always to keep a little in advance of the public taste, so as to educate while delighting it—these are the constant aims of the designer of an establishment like this. The triumphs aimed here are such as the whole silver-using public can appropriate. The most signal success of this kind ever achieved, perhaps, was the Gorham Company's well-known "Cottage Pattern" of forks and spoons, designed in a happy moment by a member of the company some years ago. When the head of a celebrated house first saw this design, his experienced eye perceived at a glance all its merit, and after looking at it for some time in silence, he exclaimed with professional enthusiasm, "This is an inspiration!" It is amusing for a person ignorant of their business to witness the delight with which a fortunate conception of this kind is hailed by those who are competent to judge of it. Such a spoon and fork for example, as the Gorham Company's "Medallion Pattern," which has had a great run among persons fond of the original and peculiar, causes a stir and excitement in Maiden Lane when it is first exhibited. Its merits are canvassed like a new book when the copies first come from the bindery, or of a new picture when it is first hung in the Academy. Its fate is soon determined. When the representatives of leading houses have examined it they generally express their opinion of its merits by the number they order. When the pretty "Rosette" pattern was first shown, a few weeks ago, at the warerooms of this company, a large dealer gave eloquent utterance to his approval in words like these: 'Send me forty dozen.'"

The 1870s introduced another result of the effect of technical developments on design. The installation of flat dies, with both the upper and lower dies contributing to the ornament, ushered in a whole new school of silver flatware patterns, reflecting styles and trends which would continue well into the 90s.

Shallow embossing, elaborately patterned, characterized the new development, which shared honors with engraved patterns. The engraving itself—sometimes, on the more expensive lines, done by hand, but more often a simulated engraving made possible by the new dies—achieved a complexity silverware had never before displayed.

Some of these patterns, in both the embossed and engraved styles, reflected the Eastlake influence—not always as it had been propounded by the English architect, but as it

Designs infringing on popular patented patterns were not unknown. Injunctions were widely publicized after a design had been successfully defended in the courts.

was interpreted by the furniture manufacturers. When his *Hints on Household Taste* appeared in bookstores in 1872, the terms Eastlake employed to describe the design and decoration of houses rapidly became the descriptive clichès of the then younger generation. Their demands for things in "the Eastlake style" brought forth a few of the straightforward furnishings he advocated, but far more pieces embellished with the shallow gouge-work and non-functioning straps he found as deplorable as the glued-on decoration he openly opposed. The cursory machine carving of oak dressers and chairs, the depthless carving with which brownstone sills and lintels were tortured, found many of their counterparts in the flat, low embossing of the popular silverware patterns of the day.

The work of his contemporary, William Morris, fared better in its interpretation in solid and electroplated flatware. The over-all, naturalistic floral and foliage patterns he favored in fabrics and wallpaper were well adapted to both the new technology and the medium. These new silverware patterns found a ready market, and were among the patterns that retained their popularity through many subsequent changes in fashions in home furnishings.

These complex designs, intertwining floral and foliage motifs, provided a basis for still another pattern innovation in the late 70s and early 80s, one which was to be revived and repeated in new interpretations for many years. This was the pattern with a design motif that permitted individual variations for each type of knife and fork and spoon in the table service.

Among the earliest of these patterns was the "Medallion" of Hall, Elton & Co., introduced before 1867. Like many of the popular "Medallion" patterns, this design featured Roman heads; unlike most of the other flatware bearing the name, these heads ranged from the familiar Centurion to a delicately feminine young woman, might face either right or left, and varied from piece to piece. The supplementary decoration of scrolls and beading also varied with each size of spoon and fork.

Probably the first such pattern in sterling, was "Japanese," introduced by Tiffany & Company in 1871, and later called "Audubon." Each piece in the complete service featured a different bird, developed in the classic Oriental style, and the back of each piece was given individual treatment.

Among the early variations, produced in both electroplate and sterling, was the Rogers, Smith & Co. "Embossed" pattern, a floral design in which a different flower was featured on each type of place and serving piece, and the 1847 Rogers Brothers "Lucerne," a plated, engraved pattern with a fruit motif varied from piece to piece. A later elaboration in plated ware is represented by the 1835 R. Wallace "Floral" pattern; in sterling, Reed & Barton's "Les Cinq Fleurs" and "Les Six Fleurs." Simpson Hall, Miller & Company's "Mille Fleurs" and George W. Shiebler's "Fiorito" presented different floral arrangements for the individual pieces included in a service. "Fiorito," for example, depicted a peony on the teaspoon, a poppy on the dessert spoon, an anemone on the coffee spoon, a violet on the afternoon teaspoon, a wild rose on the oyster fork, with similar variations for each piece in the complete service. In the "Mille Fleurs" pattern by Simpson, Hall, Miller & Co., the tea rose appeared on the teaspoon and the sugar spoon, clematis on the coffee spoon, hibiscus on the dessert spoon, and a daisy on the tablespoon. The butter knife featured a poppy, the medium fork a sweet pea, and the dessert fork a California mariposa lily; geographically as well as horticulturally, the pattern offered something for everyone!

The Gorham Company employed a French sculptor named Heller to design and prepare dies for three of the patterns in which variations of a single theme are carried from piece to piece; "Mythologique," in which 24 separate panels represent Ancient Greek myths; "Versailles," inspired by murals in the Palace of Versailles; and "Paris," based on a variety of motifs popular during the Louis XVI period.

Such highly individualized patterns, produced on a commercial scale, offered the well-to-do some of the distinction achieved by the truly rich in their custom-made services, always individually designed for the family, and frequently designed specifically for one of the great houses built during the last two decades of the 19th century. So elaborate were these great services, that the costs of the dies alone were staggering; dies for the W. K. Vanderbilt service cost over $10,000; other magnificient made-to-order services produced between 1870 and 1890 included the J. W. McKay service, for which the dies cost $9,000, and that for the Bradley Martins, with an $11,000 price tag on the mechanical production molds.

Such expenditures were not particularly breathtaking in an era when charges for decorating a house might suddenly exceed the estimate by over $100,000 "for changes in the treatment of the smaller rooms," as did Stanford White's in the case of the Payne Whitney's Fifth Avenue residence; nor could the owners of these mansions, furnished with the plunder of palaces in a dozen European cities, expect their tables to reflect the currently correct culture without such silver services. The chairs might be genuine *Louis Quatorze,* the tapestries commissioned by Marie Antoinette, but only a special service, designed in the prevailing style of the house, would see the dinners for innumerable guests through the innumerable courses demanded by the times.

Such services included settings for from 50 to 300 places; each place setting ranged from a minimal 12 to a socially secure 25 pieces, and the flatware was usually supplemented by compotes and candelabra, trays and tureens, and, often, by service and salad and other plates for individual service.

Nor was solid silver sufficient; many of the great houses in New York and Newport, Chicago and Cincinnati, St. Paul and San Francisco boasted gold services for entertaining. Such tableware was not, of course, made of solid gold; like pure silver, the metal is too soft to use for pieces subjected to frequent handling. In making these impressive appointments, sterling silver was plated with gold. These dining displays of precious metal were probably inspired by an 18th-century silver-gilt process called *Vermeil,* which had enjoyed great popularity among wealthy families on the continent and in England. The original process involved the use of mercury, which often blinded the workers; for this reason, production was banned in the early years of the 19th century, and could be revived only when new methods of plating were developed in the later Victorian years.

While many of the gold services were made to order by such firms as Tiffany & Co., in New York and George Shreve in San Francisco, standard sterling silver flatware patterns were also gold plated by many companies, and, by 1890, featured in catalogs of wholesalers like Oskamp, Nolting & Co. of Cincinnati. Gold tableware was available to all who could afford it—and, each year, more families had the means.

For every Vanderbilt who might commission a Hunt to design a French Gothic chateau, each Villard who could turn to the firm of McKim, Mead and White for an Italian Renaissance pallazzo, there were a thousand moderately successful men who might turn to the lesser architectural lights for their own small castles on narrow fronts just off Fifth Avenue in New York, around the corner from Prairie Avenue in Chicago, on the far-out stretches of Summit Avenue in St. Paul. And there were tens of thousands who could afford to translate the lace of Gothic stone into fretwork wood, the marble of the Renaissance into iron cast in a foundry. For the first time in the history of the nation, the post-Civil War period had brought to a mass market an era of free choice.

Rigid rules regarding the "correct" styles in which to live were relaxing, and the new home owner could select from—and be confused by—an increasingly wide choice of architectural styles and furniture fashions. The trend was encouraged by those who catered to the newly rich and the newly well-to-do. The group included architects and art dealers, purveyors of carriages and carpets, wallpaper and window shades—each marketing his own particular brand of taste to those who would be cultured as well as wealthy.

Like other emporiums, jewelry stores glittered with new offerings. Windows and cases gleamed with dozens of new silverware patterns, and old customers were bewildered by new names attached not only to the array of patterns, but to the new pieces etiquette demanded, and even to the package labels themselves. New manufacturers had entered the field, and with them more new designers bringing more new patterns.

Most of the new companies concentrated on the production of solid silver ware, but there were some new entries in the electroplating business, too. The mail-order houses were distributing their early catalogs, and most of them gave high priority to table silver, further broadening the market. Some of the silver companies were engaged almost entirely in supplying the needs of the growing Sears, Roebuck and Montgomery Ward mail-order customers, but even the pages of these catalogs continued to feature the names of silver firms already familiar in the hinterland along with the "private label" brands.

When, in the mid-1870s, solid silver lines were added to the products of the electroplating firms, some companies offered the same patterns in both the solid and the plated product. This phase was short-lived; as Walter Edmonds comments in *The First Hundred Years*, a history of the Oneida Community and Oneida, Ltd., "a girl clerk in a jewelry store pointed out . . . that no woman wanted to pay good money for silver that her hired girl might buy at a fraction of the price." Soon, separate patterns distinguished the products, and the curious neighbor or knowing guest found it unnecessary to eye the back of a fork surreptitiously to determine the quality of the "taste" of the hostess or the liberality of the host. Robert Chapman, in *The Portrait of a Scholar* admitted to this universal weakness of the time when he wrote:

> When I dine out and find my soup embellished by a notable spoon, as may often happen to those who dine in Colleges or Inns of Court, my manners are seldom proof against temptation. I contrive a furtive scrutiny of the underside.

Even after most manufacturers no longer duplicated patterns in their own plated and sterling lines, there was still room for confusion. Pirating of patterns was not unknown, and litigation between rival firms over patented patterns was reported regularly in the trade press. In other cases, startlingly close resemblances appeared, as was the case with sterling "Lancaster" and an electroplated pattern called, appropriately for such commercial warfare, "York Rose." Names, too, were frequently repeated, although applied to completely different designs. "Antique" was used to describe many patterns by different manufacturers of both sterling and electroplated wares. The name "Victoria," of course, was almost in the public domain during these years, and it, too, was used by six manufacturers of solid silver and by at least four electroplaters. No less than three firms added a "Prince Albert" to the firmly entrenched "Victoria," and even the Queen's faithful "Hagie" was immortalized in sterling. The horticulturally derived designations were well represented; "Violet," "Oak," and "Rose"—even "American Beauty," the long-stemmed symbol of elegance in the floral world—appeared several times, while the more romantically inclined could choose "Forget—me—not" in sterling or electroplate.

Designs hand engraved on the "Antique" or "Windsor" pattern in sterling or electroplate were popular with Victorian housewives.

The vogue for French furniture, expressed both in the importation of antiques for the homes of the wealthiest, and in reproductions and adaptations with varying degrees of authenticity, was reflected in another group of patterns for silverware. The succession of the Houses of Valois and Bourbon might almost be traced in silver flatware names introduced during the 1880s and 90s, and, if the First Republic was ignored, the Consulate and First Empire were recalled by several firms, in patterns called both "Empire" and "Napoleon."

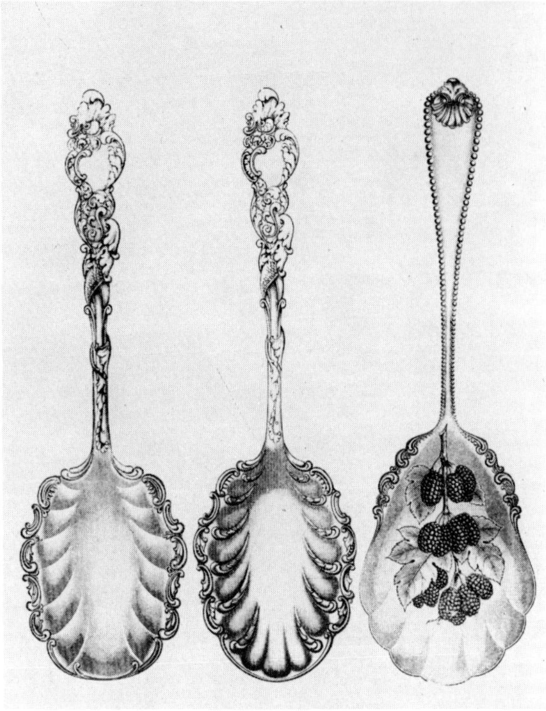

Optional ornamentation was offered by many manufacturers. The "Columbia" berry spoon could be ordered with or without the engraved bowl; either style might have either a silver or a gilt bowl. Gold inlay was featured in other patterns, in addition to plain, gilt, or engraved bowls.

One of these, a "Napoleon," produced in sterling silver, was given a gold finish reminiscent of the *vermeil* popular in France during the mid-1700s, and further embellished by a wreath inlaid with enamel, as were several other patterns produced during the late 1880s and early 1890s. These elegant services crowned the gilding and gold-plating touches which frequently appeared on a part of other plated and sterling patterns, where the tines of serving forks, or the bowls of ladles and berry spoons were adorned with the more precious metal.

Even the glitter of gold and the colorful display of enamel found competition in still another pattern innovation, that of filigree work. Deceptively delicate in appearance, this tableware was actually strengthened by the intricate system of trusses and counterstrains inherent in the design itself. Much of this work was done by silversmiths trained during long European apprenticeships, but at least one manufacturer offered a variety of filigree patterns produced on a commercial basis. Even this firm, The Dirksen Silver Company, was headed by a man who had been painstakingly trained by his father, who, in turn, had mastered this particular skill as a young man in Germany.

The Dirksen products were displayed and won many awards at such expositions as the Columbian in Chicago and the Mid-winter Fair in San Francisco; some of the displays were retained by museums in those cities after the expositions closed; another collection of Dirksen silver filigree became the property of The Smithsonian Institution. The graceful openwork patterns were understandably popular with the mistresses of houses where not one, but *two* sets of Brussels lace curtains were *de rigueur* at parlor windows, and eyelet embroidery or delicate lace was used lavishly through all the rooms.

Literary tastes of the times inspired other patterns. Parlors and libraries were suitably enriched by sets of Sir Walter Scott ensconced in Gothic bookcases, and his influence carried over into the dining room with sets of "Abbotsford," "Ivanhoe," "Waverly," or "Kenilworth" flatware. Longfellow, that conventional and kindly contemporary, was honored with "Evangeline" and "Standish." With a new emphasis on culture came an increased interest in universities and colleges; "Oxford" and "Cambridge" joined "Harvard" and "Yale" in jewelry stores and wholesalers' catalogs.

Nor were current events ignored. The playgrounds of the rich and socially elect were remembered in silverware names like "Elberon," "Newport" and "Saratoga." The Flaglers' developments in Florida, aided by the architectural firm of Carrère & Hastings, brought the Spanish Renaissance into the news of the 1880s and '90s; patterns named "Alhambra" and "Seville" quickly followed.

Some 50 years before, Mrs. Trollope had commented on the "evident fondness which Americans shew for titles"; the wave of trans-Atlantic weddings and their ensuing coronets for American brides, seem to have strengthened this fondness, and to have impressed silver designers during these years. "Countess" was available in electroplate, as were "Marquis" and "Marquise"; the more rank-conscious could look to sterling, and choose from at least three patterns named "Duchess" or "Duchesse," six called "Princess," and almost any number of "Queens." Even brides less well endowed with worldly goods than a Consuelo Vanderbilt could adorn their tables with a "Marlborough"—in sterling.

Opera, the concert stage, and theatre were not overlooked; "Verdi," "Jenny Lind," and "Garrick" were among the newsworthy patterns available to the patrons of these arts.

The very terms used to describe the most elaborate new homes and the most elegant new furnishings were repeated in flatware pattern names; "Rococo" and "Arabesque" competed with "Florentine" and "Renaissance." The classic orders were completed when "Doric" and "Ionic" joined the earlier "Tuscan" about 1870, and "Corinthian" came along a few years later.

As the 19th century drew to a close, silver design was influenced by two diverse movements; Arts Nouveau and the Colonial revival.

The Art Nouveau movement had its beginnings in France during the 90s, and reached its peak in the United States during the early 1900s. Sponsors of the style advocated a complete break with the influence of conventional, historical art; interpretations tended to be highly individualized, generally based on naturalistic forms. In sterling flatware, Art Nouveau patterns ranged from the simple, graceful "Wave" of George W. Shiebler, to the ornate "Lily" of The Whiting Mfg. Co. A few silver companies acknowledged the source of the pattern influence in the name; Durgin's "New Art" was one such pattern. In electroplated ware, Reed & Barton's "Modern Art" paid similar homage to the movement, while designs like the 1835 R. Wallace "Floral" and Williams Bros. "Peerless" reflected the overseas action. Meanwhile, a reversal of taste that had been quietly developing for many years suddenly gathered momentum, and Americans re-discovered their own beginnings.

Exhibits that had been gathered for the Philadelphia Centennial Exposition in 1876 undoubtedly contributed to the new interest in the houses and household effects of the Colonies and early Republic, but as early as 1856, a Philadelphia writer had described the vogue for reviving and displaying old furniture and the ordering of new pieces "exactly in imitation." He ascribed the fashion's beginnings to Boston, and there is, of course, evidence that well-established New Englanders and residents of other Atlantic areas had proudly maintained their antique furniture throughout the Victorian years, perhaps as a conservative protest against the extravagances of the time, perhaps as a symbol of the traditions and long standing family background that were about all that new post-war money could not buy.

Others maintain that the colonial revival resulted from the establishment of American schools and institutes for design; certainly the first graduates of these schools were coming of age at the time, and, at least in the design rooms of many of the silver manufacturers, were beginning to replace their European-trained predecessors and superiors. It was natural that they should reexamine the arts of their own country, the crafts of their own ancestors, with eyes newly trained to perceptive evaluation.

Some of the early favorites among the flatware patterns had never been completely submerged by the more ornate of the Victorian patterns, of course. The firms of Gorham and Kirk and Towle had continued to produce simple designs almost directly derived from the early silversmiths who founded these companies. The 90s, when the architects turned again to 18th-century houses for inspiration, and fine furniture makers began turning out reproductions of Chippendale and Sheraton and Hepplewhite pieces, saw many other silver manufacturers adapting the earlier designs. The silver patterns were not limited to reproductions; almost every manufacturer found a motif in the delicate carving of Bulfinch or the Adams. The great southern houses were examined for themes; the woodwork in Melrose, the handsome plantation house outside Natchez, provided the scrollwork theme for the silver pattern that bears its name.

Simplified patterns were adopted by the electroplaters, too, and comparatively plain patterns were included in almost every catalog by 1900. The simplicity of some of these patterns was deceptive, for their "plain" surfaces frequently represented a new skill in adapting designs and planes to emphasize the refractive qualities of silver.

Along with the renewed interest in the products and designs of the 18th century had come a renewed appreciation for the earlier English Sheffield hollow ware, and collections of these pieces were enthusiastically assembled. Trays and teapots, salvers and sugar bowls, all with the characteristic borders that had served the functional purpose of covering the copper exposed at the edges of the sheets of Sheffield, were exhibited and used in many American homes. Many of the pieces had utilized a naturalistic grapevine border, and the flatware designers seized on this theme. By 1905, most manufacturers had made a "grape pattern" available to their customers, designated by names like "Vintage," "La Vigne," "Moselle," or—surprisingly—"Grape."

By 1910, too, another reaction to the overornamentation of the previous 50 years had set in. Sparked by the California firm of Greene & Greene, whose large houses in the western states used natural wood, an open plan, and emphasized functional, structural details for decoration, the "California Bungalow" swept across the country, furnished, most frequently, with the new furniture called "Mission." Though most of it was factory-produced, it emphasized the construction of each piece, with exposed mortise-and-tenon features, square lines, and flat, natural, wood surfaces. Hardware was frequently exposed, and, more often than not, given a hand-hammered appearance. Accessories were muted, and the handcrafted look was sought in everything from curtains to ceramics to table silver.

For large houses, designed and decorated by professionals, furniture and accessories were often hand-made and custom designed; these customers often turned to the individual silversmithing studios like that of The Boston Society of Arts and Crafts, the Handicraft Shop in Wellesley Hills, or the shop of Miss Jane Carson and Miss Mildred Watkins in Cleveland, Ohio. These establishments and a number of others were described in 1906 in *Good Housekeeping Magazine,* in a long article which concluded:

> Better than the freshness of the pattern which makes these examples of craftsman silver attractive, is the knowledge that the same intelligence which planned the design in nearly every case, followed the piece of work to its completion, according to the quality of the metal, respecting its limitations and modifying the pattern in accordance therewith. The hammer marks which often are vaguely present but help to reveal the texture of the metal. The

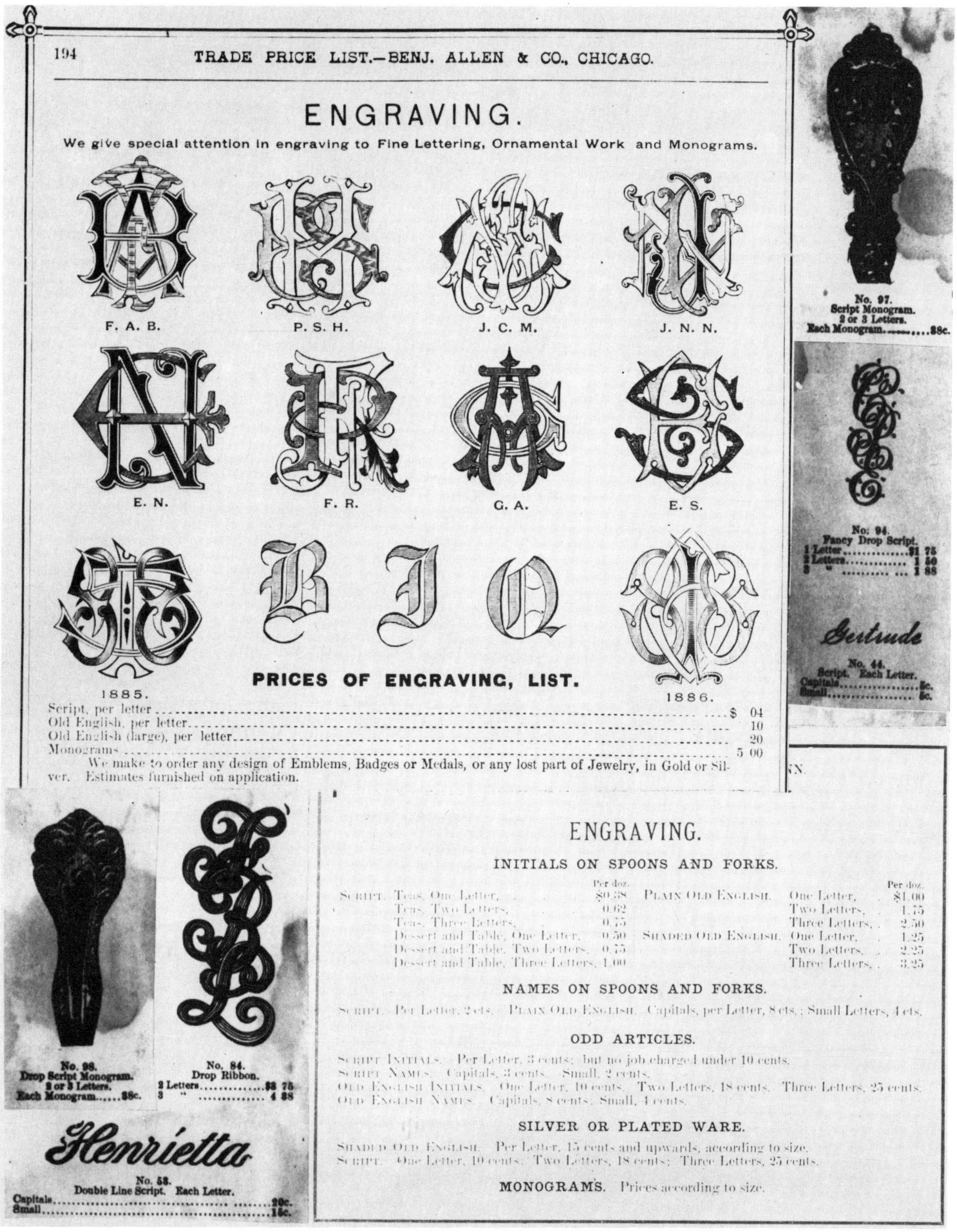

194 TRADE PRICE LIST.—BENJ. ALLEN & CO., CHICAGO.

ENGRAVING.

We give special attention in engraving to Fine Lettering, Ornamental Work and Monograms.

PRICES OF ENGRAVING, LIST.

Script, per letter	$ 04
Old English, per letter	10
Old English (large), per letter	20
Monograms	5 00

We make to order any design of Emblems, Badges or Medals, or any lost part of Jewelry, in Gold or Silver. Estimates furnished on application.

No. 97.
Script Monogram.
2 or 3 Letters.
Each Monogram.........88c.

No. 94.
Fancy Drop Script.
1 Letter..........$1 75
2 Letters.......... 1 50
3 " 1 88

Gertrude

No. 44.
Script. Each Letter.
Capitals..........5c.
Small..........5c.

No. 98.
Drop Script Monogram.
2 or 3 Letters.
Each Monogram......88c.

No. 84.
Drop Ribbon.
2 Letters..........$3 75
3 " 4 88

Henrietta

No. 58.
Double Line Script. Each Letter.
Capitals..........20c.
Small..........15c.

ENGRAVING.

INITIALS ON SPOONS AND FORKS.

		Per doz.			Per doz.
Script.	Teas, One Letter,	$0.38	Plain Old English.	One Letter,	$1.00
	Teas, Two Letters,	0.62		Two Letters,	1.75
	Teas, Three Letters,	0.75		Three Letters,	2.50
	Dessert and Table, One Letter,	0.50	Shaded Old English.	One Letter,	1.25
	Dessert and Table, Two Letters,	0.75		Two Letters,	2.25
	Dessert and Table, Three Letters,	1.00		Three Letters,	3.25

NAMES ON SPOONS AND FORKS.

Script. Per Letter, 2 cts. Plain Old English. Capitals, per Letter, 8 cts.; Small Letters, 4 cts.

ODD ARTICLES.

Script Initials. Per Letter, 3 cents; but no job charged under 10 cents.
Script Names. Capitals, 3 cents. Small, 2 cents.
Old English Initials. One Letter, 10 cents. Two Letters, 18 cents. Three Letters, 25 cents.
Old English Names. Capitals, 8 cents; Small, 4 cents.

SILVER OR PLATED WARE.

Shaded Old English. Per Letter, 15 cents and upwards, according to size.
Script. One Letter, 10 cents; Two Letters, 18 cents; Three Letters, 25 cents.

MONOGRAMS. Prices according to size.

Elaborate monograms were high fashion during the late Victorian years. Gifts and presentation pieces often were engraved with the full name of the recipient.

practical requirements of durability and utility are adequately met by hand wrought silver. Its finish lacks the high polish on which the first finger print is a blemish. Instead it is slightly dulled so that it does not lose luster from daily use, but rather gains in beauty of surface from its handling, so that each succeeding generation to which it comes, finds the well-made example of the true silversmith increasingly beautiful.

The article sensibly pointed out that opportunities for learning the silversmith's craft at that time were rare; that the expense of equipping a shop was heavy, the material expensive, the necessary tools available only when specially made; and that "to do worthy work, to compete with the factory product, years of manual labor are indispensable, to say nothing of the knowledge of design, which is necessary to lift the silversmith from the plane of artisan to that of artist—and unless the silversmith is that he is no true craftsman."

Fortunately for the young housewife described in the article as "alert for the adornment of her table," it was not necessary for her to buy the "hand wrought spoon, of a commercial value of some ten or twenty dollars" described as an example of conspicuous consumption by Thorstein Veblen in *"The Theory of the Leisure Class"*; by 1910, many of the silver factories were turning out patterns with "hammer marks vaguely present" and "slightly dulled," to conform to the new demands of the newest brides.

The cycle had been completed; in something less than 75 years, the colonial forms and the hand-crafted look reigned almost supreme in flatware design again.

CATALOG OF FLATWARE PATTERNS

In the following pages, illustrations of Victorian and Edwardian flatware patterns are arranged under "Sterling" and "Electroplate" sections.

At the beginning of the catalog, a group of "Standard Patterns" is shown; these patterns were made by many different firms, over a period of many years, in both solid silver and electroplate. Where a manufacturer made one or more of these patterns, a note directing attention to this page will be found on the pages illustrating other patterns of the firm.

Where an identical pattern was made by more than one company prior to 1910—either through the sale or merger of the original firm, or the sale of patterns, patents and dies—the pattern is shown with the products of the original manufacturer. Here again, a note directing attention to the firm that introduced the pattern will be found on those pages devoted to the products of successor companies. These sequences are carried to 1910; later purchases, mergers, etc., are detailed in the *Manufacturers, Trade Marks and Trade Names* section of this book, where the sequence of company and trade mark ownership is carried up to date.

Some patterns were made in both sterling and electroplate, by the same company. In such cases, cross references between the sterling and electroplate pages showing the products of the firm are carried in the captions.

This section is planned solely as a guide to the identification of patterns; consequently, illustrations may not do full justice to the artistic achievement inherent in many of the old flatware designs. Many compromises were necessary in order to achieve some uniformity of reproduction quality. The original illustrations came from hundreds of sources, and ranged from early lithographs, wood cuts and steel engravings to modern photographs of old pieces. In many cases, any reproduction was dependent on the sometimes limited facilities of a given library or museum; in other cases, deterioration of the original illustration affected the quality of the copy. Finally, where it was necessary to choose between delineation of identifying characteristics and an artistic presentation, identification won out.

Standard Patterns

Standard Patterns

Standard patterns were made by many companies and produced in both sterling and electroplate. *Top (l. to r.)*: Threaded Oval (Oval Thread, Oval Threaded), Oval, Olive, Kings, Lily, French Thread, Threaded (Plain Threaded, Plain Thread, Thread), Fiddle Tip (Fiddle Tipped, Fiddle Tip't). *Bottom (l. to r.)*: Old English, Antique (French Antique), Windsor, Shell, Plain, Reverse Tip (French Tip), Plain Tipped (Tipped, Tip't), Fiddle.

Sterling

Alvin Mfg. Co.

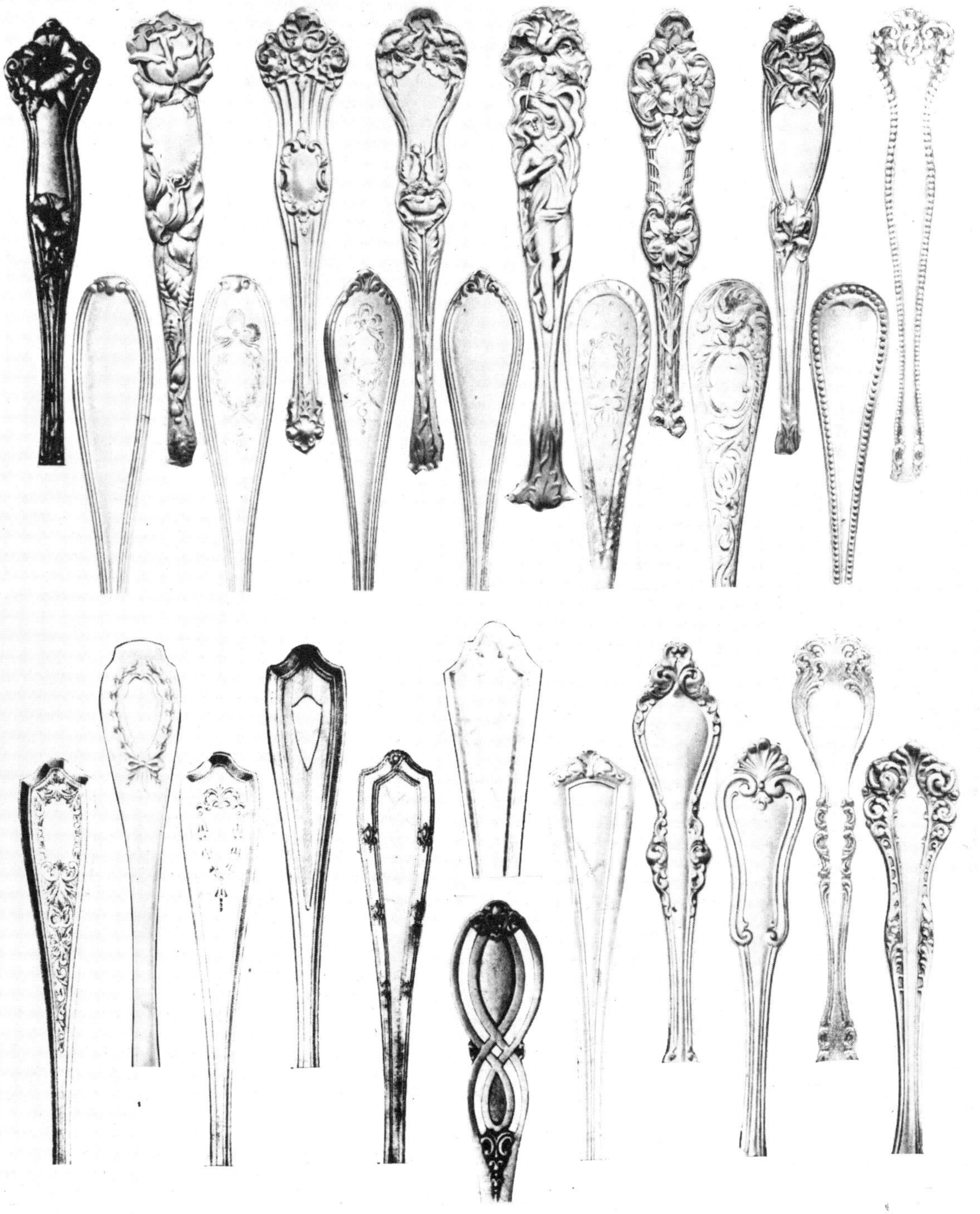

ALVIN MFG. CO.: *Top row (l. to r.)*: Morning Glory, Bridal Rose, Viking, Majestic, Raphael, Orange Blossom, Fleur de Lis, Raleigh. *Second row (l. to r.)*: Wm. Penn, Wm. Penn No. 7, Evangeline No. 7, Evangeline, Antique No. 3, Antique No. 6, Virginia. *Third row (l. to r.)*: Apollo, Delaware, Hamilton, Lorraine, Marseilles. *Fourth row (l. to r.)*: Lady Beatrice, Roanoke, Francis I, Chippendale (Old), Josephine, Suffolk, Florentine. See also Peter L. Krider Co., Simons Bros. Co., and Variations sections.

Alvin Mfg. Co. R. Blackinton & Co.

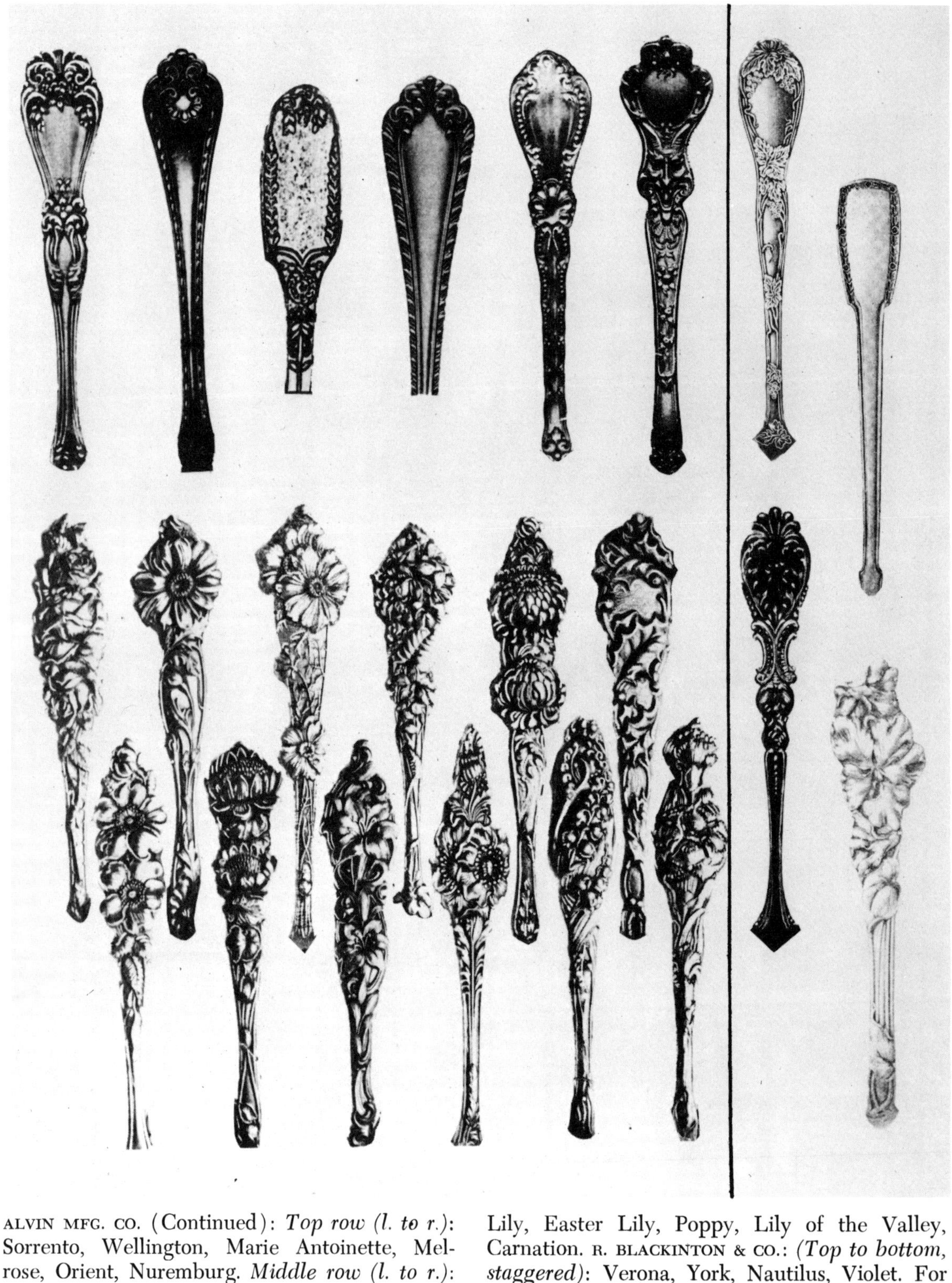

ALVIN MFG. CO. (Continued): *Top row (l. to r.)*: Sorrento, Wellington, Marie Antoinette, Melrose, Orient, Nuremburg. *Middle row (l. to r.)*: Rose, Daisy, Cosmos, Violet, Chrysanthemum, Holly. *Bottom row (l. to r)*: Wild Rose, Water Lily, Easter Lily, Poppy, Lily of the Valley, Carnation. R. BLACKINTON & CO.: *(Top to bottom, staggered)*: Verona, York, Nautilus, Violet. For Alvin Mfg. Co. see also Peter L. Krider Co., Simons Bros. Co. and Variations sections.

Campbell-Metcalf Silver Co. | Albert Coles & Co. | Coles & Reynolds | Dirksen Silver Co.

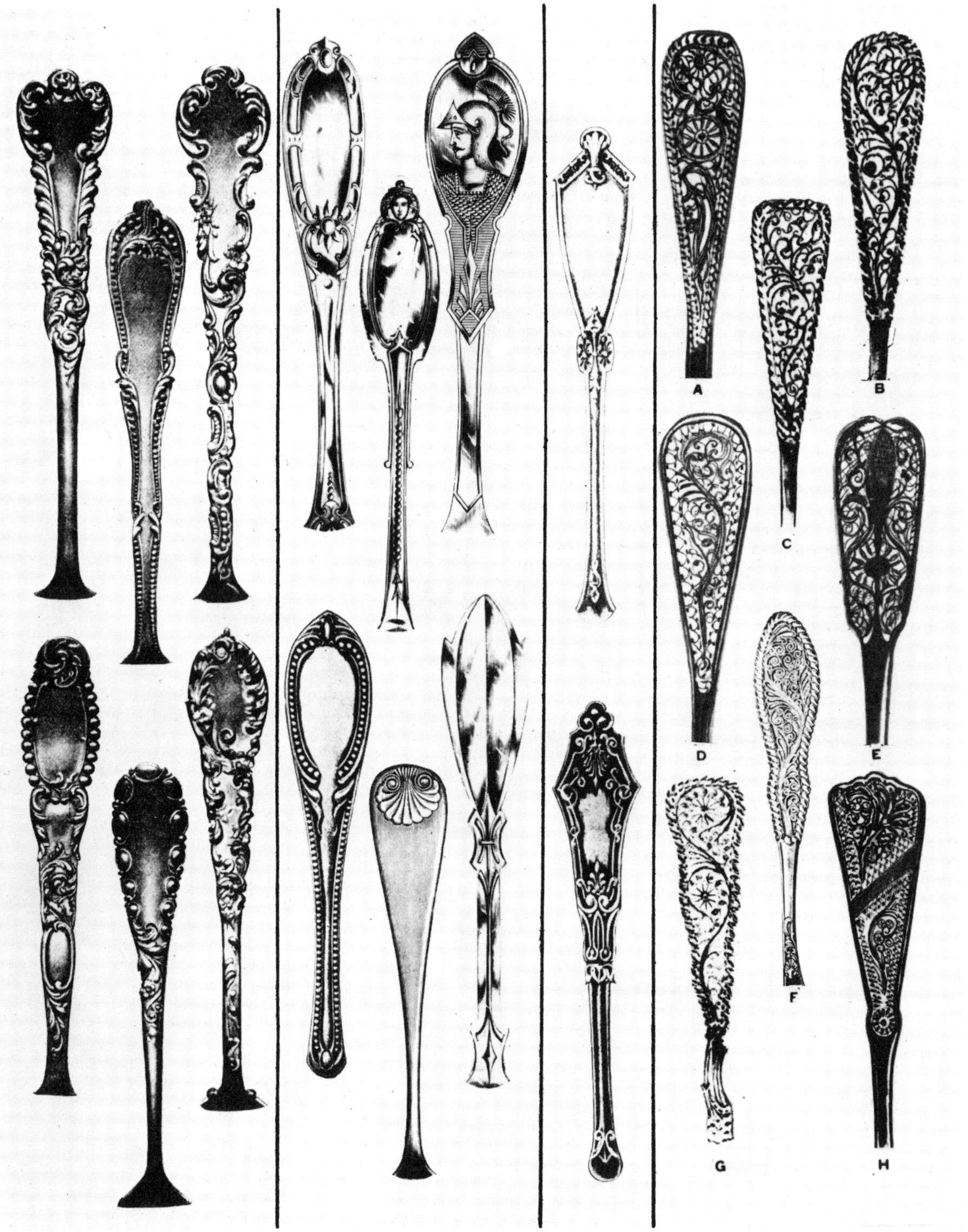

CAMPBELL-METCALF SILVER CO.: *Top row (l. to r.)*: Eton, Geneva. *Second row*: Colonial. *Third row (l. to r.)*: Priscilla, Rococo. *Bottom*: Stuart. ALBERT COLES & CO.: *Top row (l. to r.)*: Jenny Lind, Ivanhoe. *Second row*: Kenilworth. *Third row (l. to r.)*: Mayflower, Palace. *Bottom*: Nautilus. COLES & REYNOLDS: *Top*: Doric. *Bottom*: Empress. DIRKSEN SILVER CO.: Patterns were not named by manufacturer; letters indicate pattern designations. For Albert Coles & Co. see also Coles & Reynolds, Standard Patterns sections. For Coles & Reynolds see also A. & W. Wood and Standard Patterns sections.

Dominick & Haff

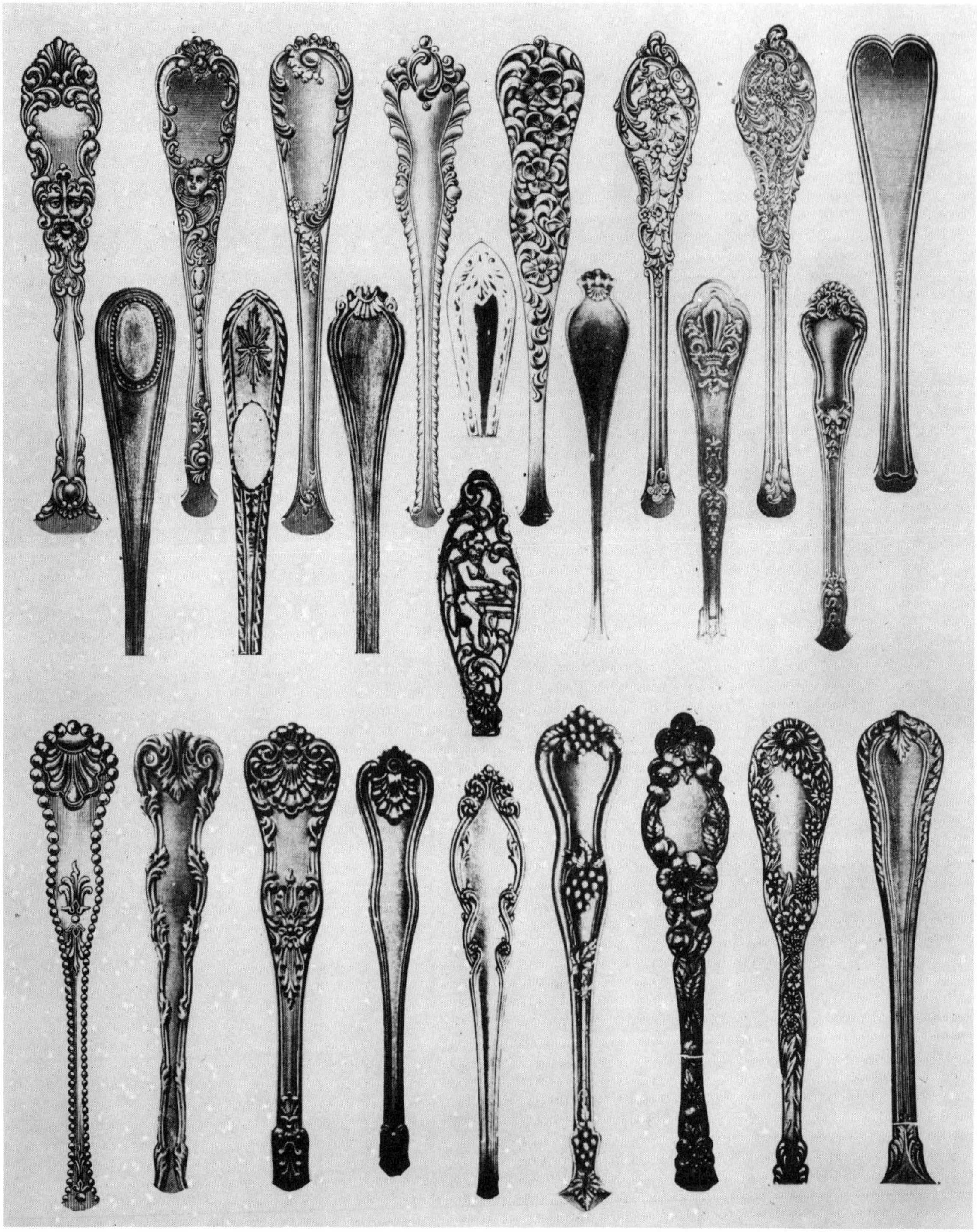

DOMINICK & HAFF: *Top row (l. to r.)*: Renaissance, Cupid, Louis XIV, Mazarin *(Top center*: Marie Antoinette), Rococo, Trianon (Pierced) (Reed & Barton Florentine Lace), Trianon (Solid), Tudor. *Middle row (l. to r.)*: Medallion, 1776, Century. *Lower Center*: 1900 (Reed & Barton Labors of Cupid), Corona, Versailles, Imperial. *Bottom row (l. to r.)*: Charles II, Victoria, New Kings, Alexandra, Gothic, Grape Vine (Grape), Blossom, No. 10, Acanthus. See also Wm. Gale & Sons, John R. Wendt, and Standard Patterns sections.

Wm. B. Durgin Co.

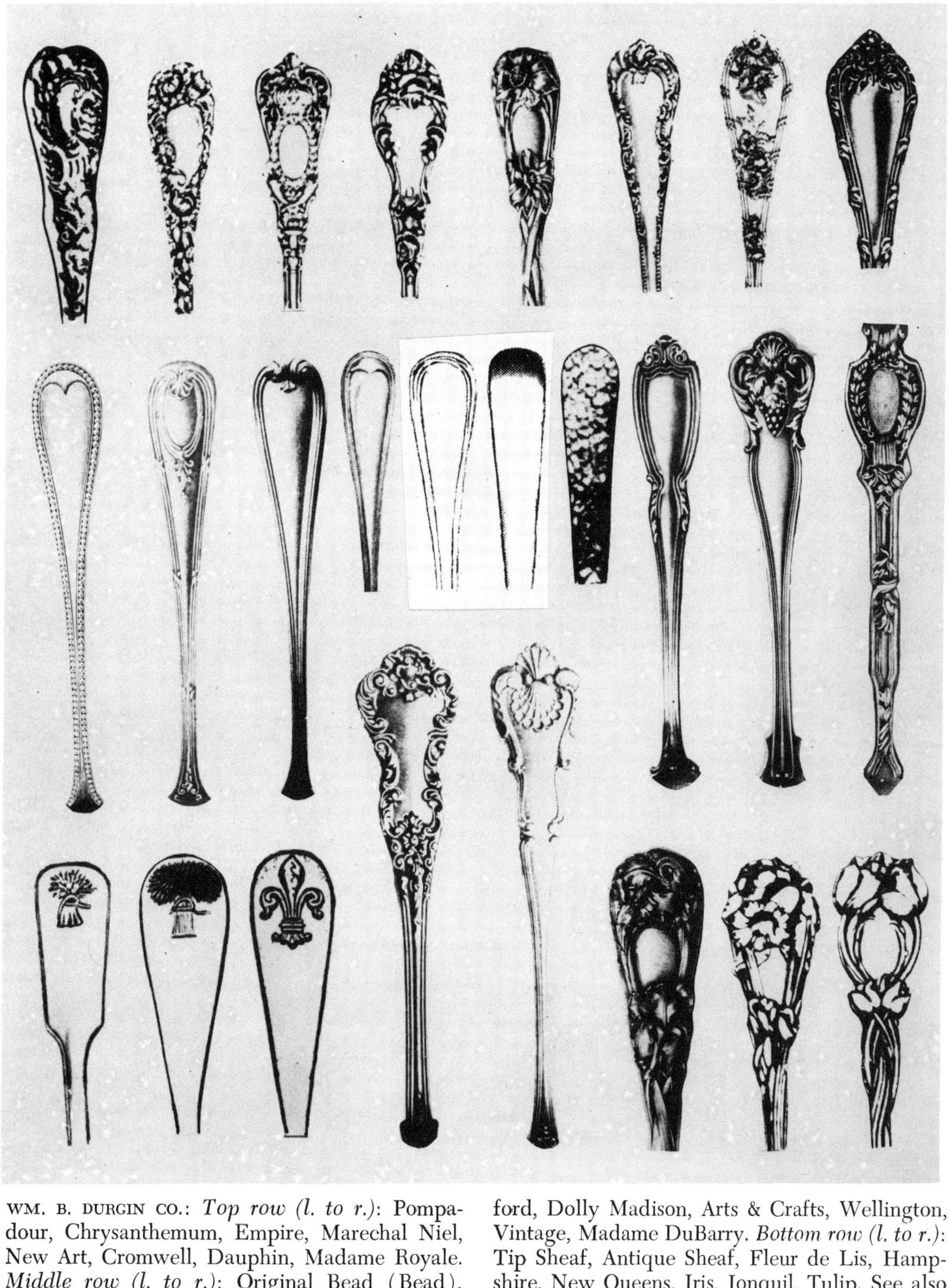

WM. B. DURGIN CO.: *Top row (l. to r.)*: Pompadour, Chrysanthemum, Empire, Marechal Niel, New Art, Cromwell, Dauphin, Madame Royale. *Middle row (l. to r.)*: Original Bead (Bead), Navarre, Standish (New), Standish (Old), Bradford, Dolly Madison, Arts & Crafts, Wellington, Vintage, Madame DuBarry. *Bottom row (l. to r.)*: Tip Sheaf, Antique Sheaf, Fleur de Lis, Hampshire, New Queens, Iris, Jonquil, Tulip. See also Standard Patterns section.

WM. B. DURGIN CO. (Continued): *Top row (l. to r.)*: Colfax, Victorian. *Second row (l. to r.)*: Fairfax, Chatham. *Third row (l. to r.)*: Fairfax Engraved, Essex. *Bottom row (l. to r.)*: Fairfax Engraved No. 2, Lenox. THEO. EVANS & CO.: Ribbon. FESSENDEN & CO.: *Top row (l. to r.)*: Greenwich, Alice. *Second row (l. to r.)*: No. 88 (Newport), LaProvence, Avon. *Third row (l. to r.)*: Narcissus, Daisy, McKinley. *Bottom row (l. to r.)*: Old Rose, Tulip, Tremont, Marie Louise. WM. GALE & SONS: *Top to bottom, staggered*: Italian, Mayflower, Olive, Tuscan. For Wm. B. Durgin Co., Theo. Evans & Co., Wm. Gale & Sons see also Standard Patterns section.

Gorham Mfg. Co.

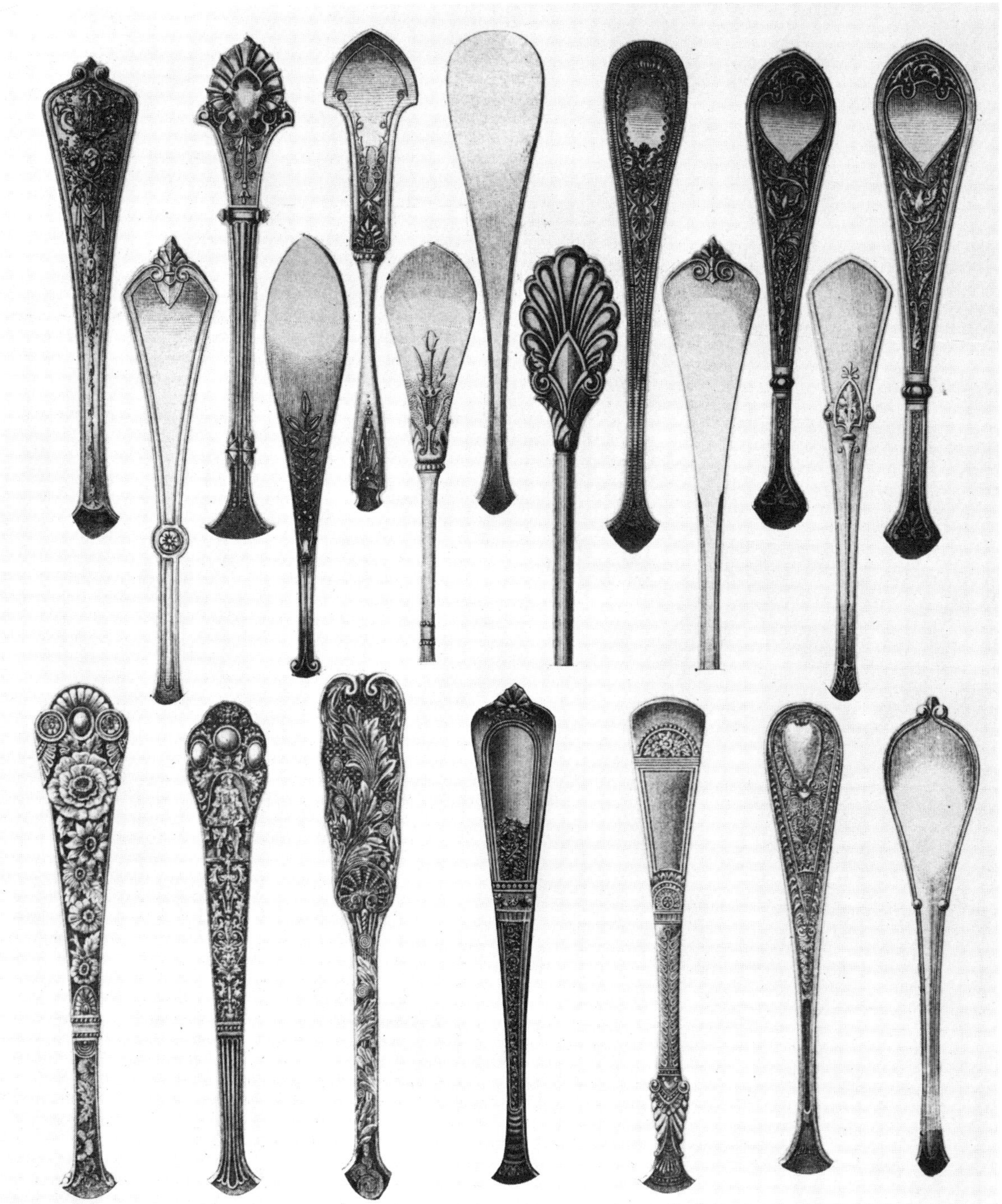

GORHAM MFG. CO.: *Top row (l. to r.)*: Lady Washington, Louis XIV, Corinthian, Gorham, Knickerbocker Engraved, Raphael Small, Raphael. *Middle row (l. to r.)*: Rosette, Palm, New Tipt, Grecian, Queens, Swiss. *Bottom row (l. to r.)*: Cluny, Medici, St. Cloud, Domestic, Empress, Hindostanee (Hindustani), Cottage. See also Wm. B. Durgin Co., Graff, Washbourne & Dunn, Whiting Mfg. Co., Standard Patterns and Variations sections.

Gorham Mfg. Co.

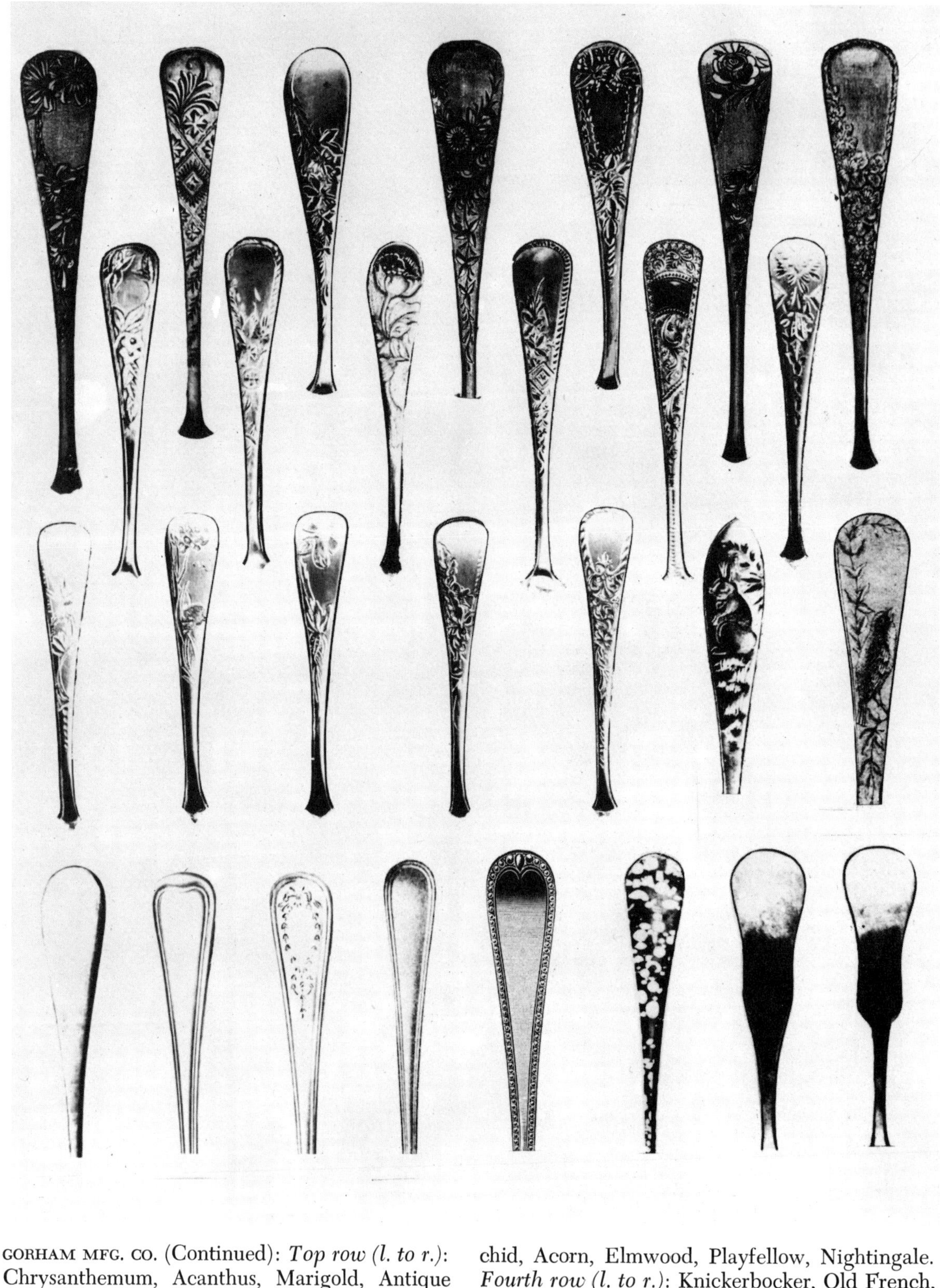

GORHAM MFG. CO. (Continued): *Top row (l. to r.)*: Chrysanthemum, Acanthus, Marigold, Antique No. 15, London, Jac Rose, Cherry Blossom. *Second row (l. to r.)*: Clematis, Marguerite, Knickerbocker Etched, Antique No. 8, Tudor, Diana. *Third row (l. to r.)*: Poppy, Carnation, Orchid, Acorn, Elmwood, Playfellow, Nightingale. *Fourth row (l. to r.)*: Knickerbocker, Old French, Jefferson, Hamilton, Newcastle, Cairo, French Tipped, Old Fiddle. See also Wm. B. Durgin Co., Graff, Washbourne & Dunn, Whiting Mfg. Co., Standard Patterns and Variations sections.

Gorham Mfg. Co.

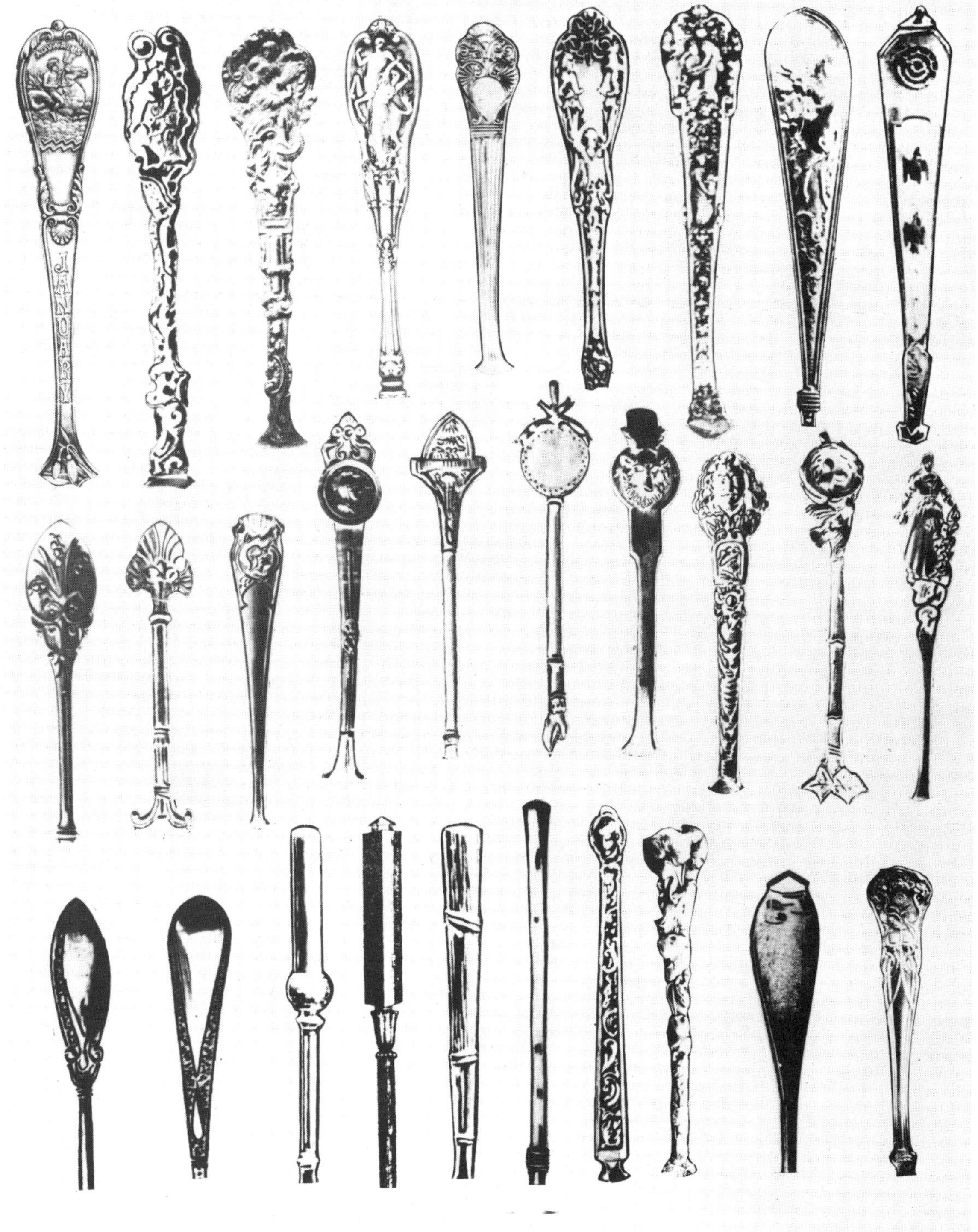

GORHAM MFG. CO. (Continued): *Top row (l. to r.)*: Zodiac, Hizen, Versailles, Mythologique, Milan, Paris, Coligni, Aurora, Japanese. *Middle row (l. to r.)*: Lily of the Valley, Lotus, H111, Medallion, Ivy, Lady's, Saxon Stag, Old Master, Bird's Nest, Nuremburg. *Bottom row (l. to r.)*: Persian, Eva, Dowager, Isis, Bamboo, Angelo, Florence, Violet, Italian, Astor. See also Wm. B. Durgin Co., Graff, Washbourne & Dunn, Whiting Mfg. Co., Standard Patterns and Variations sections.

Gorham Mfg. Co.

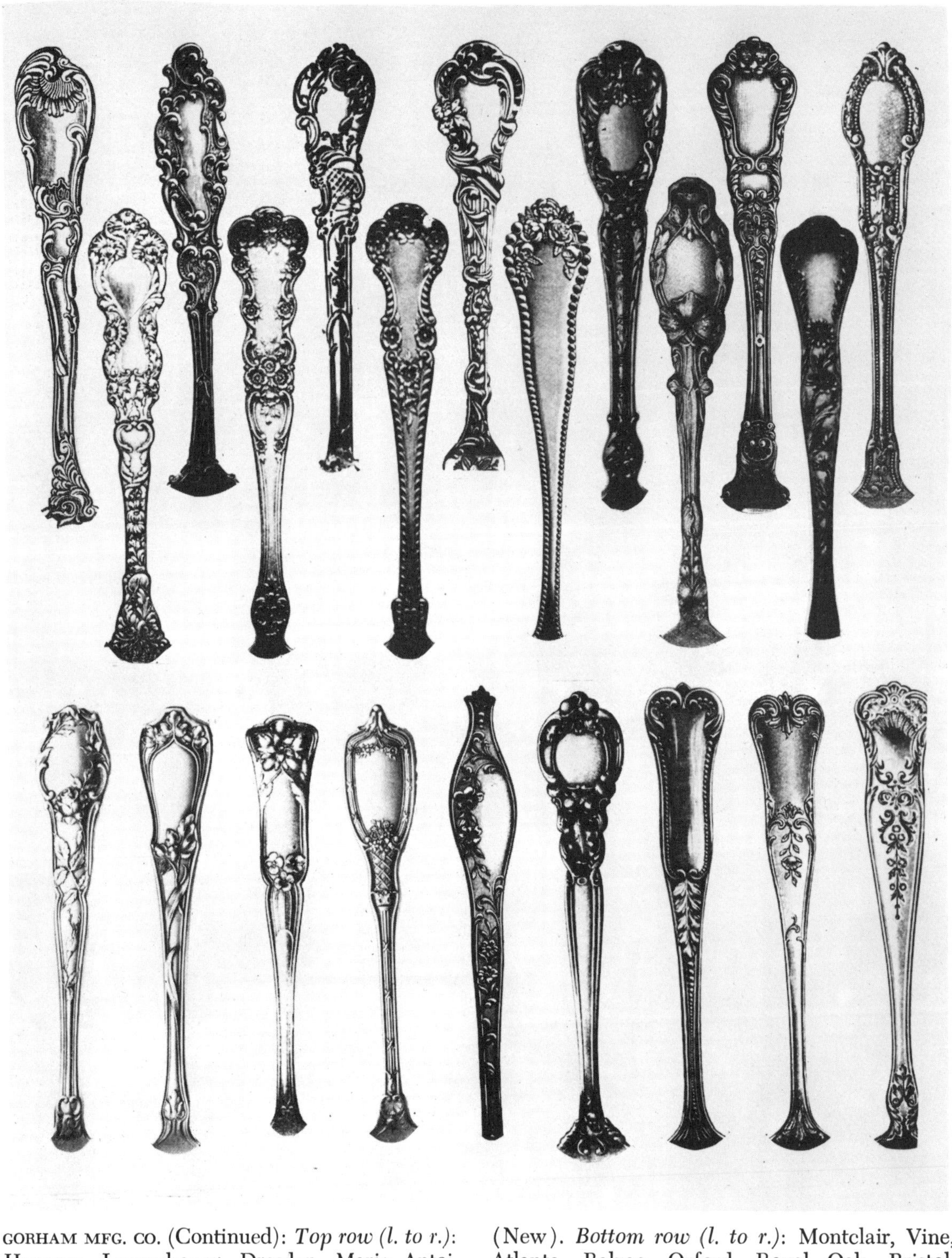

GORHAM MFG. CO. (Continued): *Top row (l. to r.)*: Hanover, Luxembourg, Dresden, Marie Antoinette, Florentine, Baronial, Tuileries. *Middle row (l. to r.)*: Imperial Chrysanthemum, Buttercup, Cambridge, Lancaster, Virginiana, Marguerite (New). *Bottom row (l. to r.)*: Montclair, Vine, Atlanta, Balzac, Oxford, Royal Oak, Bristol, Plymouth, Maryland. See also Wm. B. Durgin Co., Graff, Washbourne & Dunn, Whiting Mfg. Co., Standard Patterns and Variations sections.

Gorham Mfg. Co.

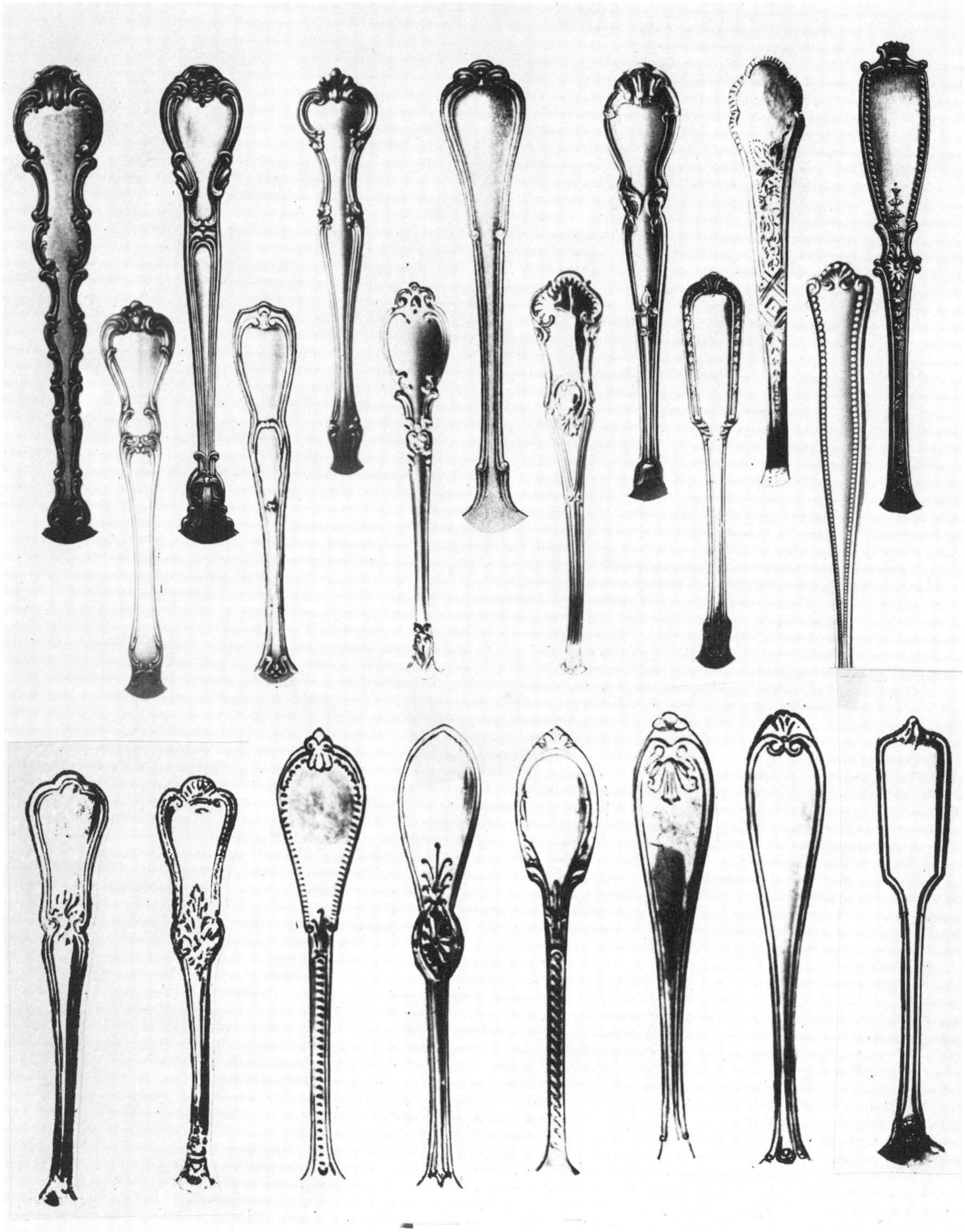

GORHAM MFG. CO. (Continued): *Top row (l. to r.)*: Strasbourg, Chantilly, Cromwell, Norfolk, Portland, Grape, Bedford. *Middle row (l. to r.)*: Buckingham, LaModele, Lenox, Regent, Chesterfield, Pembroke. *Bottom row (l. to r.)*: Imperial, Kensington, Beaded, Ionic, Roman, Josephine, Princess, Melrose. See also Wm. B. Durgin Co., Graff, Washbourne & Dunn, Whiting Mfg. Co., Standard Patterns and Variations sections.

Gorham Mfg. Co.

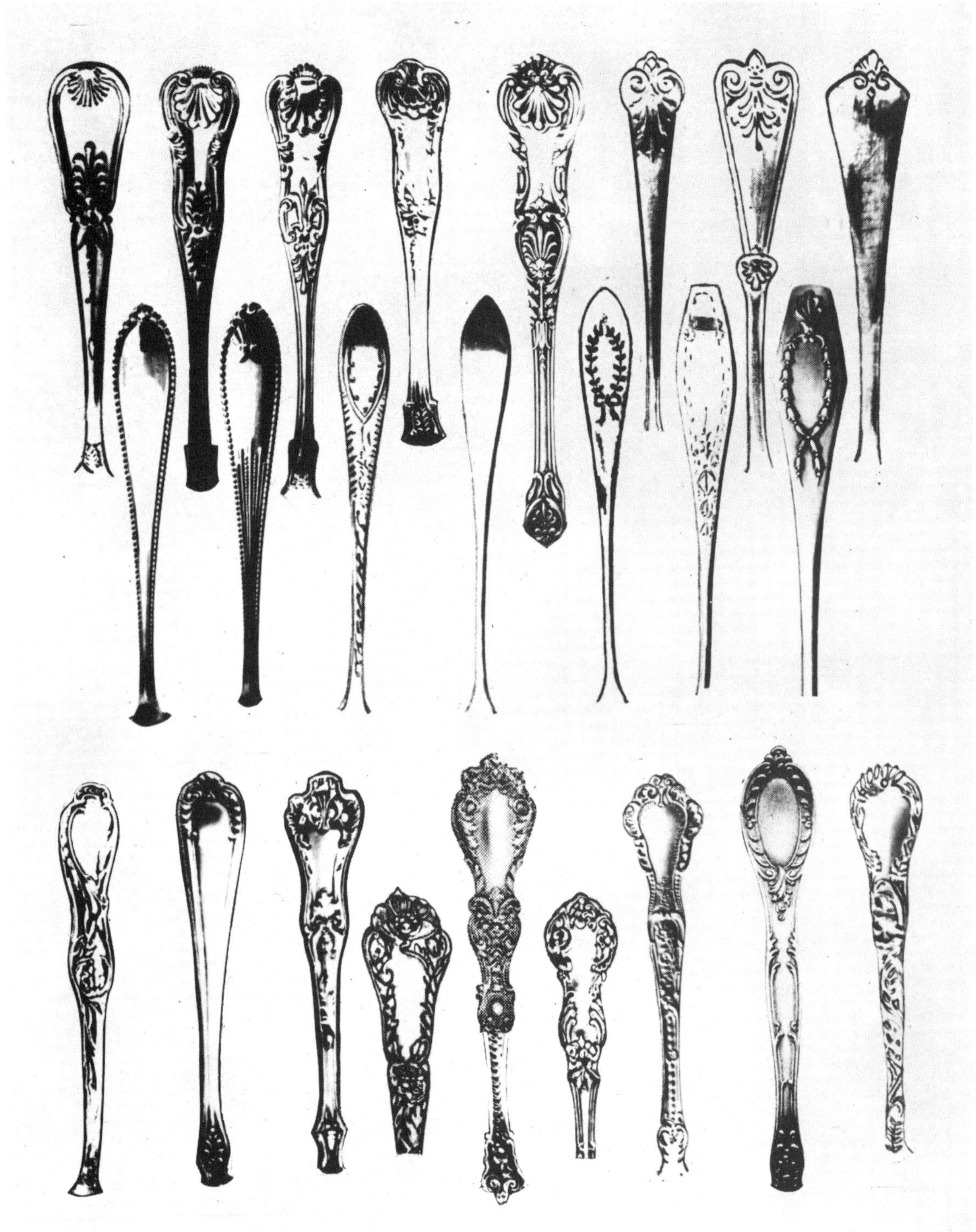

GORHAM MFG. CO. (Continued): *Top row (l. to r.)*: Kings I, Kings II, Kings III, New Queens, King George, 83, Pompeii, Fleur de Lis. *Middle row (l. to r.)*: Virginia, Chippendale, Old Newport, Mothers, Mothers Engraved, Priscilla, Wreath. *Bottom row (l. to r.)*: Rouen, Chester, Patrician, Poppy (New), Henry II, Fleury, Louis XVI, Old Colony, Meadow. See also Wm. B. Durgin Co., Graff, Washbourne & Dunn, Whiting Mfg. Co., Standard Patterns and Variations sections.

Gorham Mfg. Co.

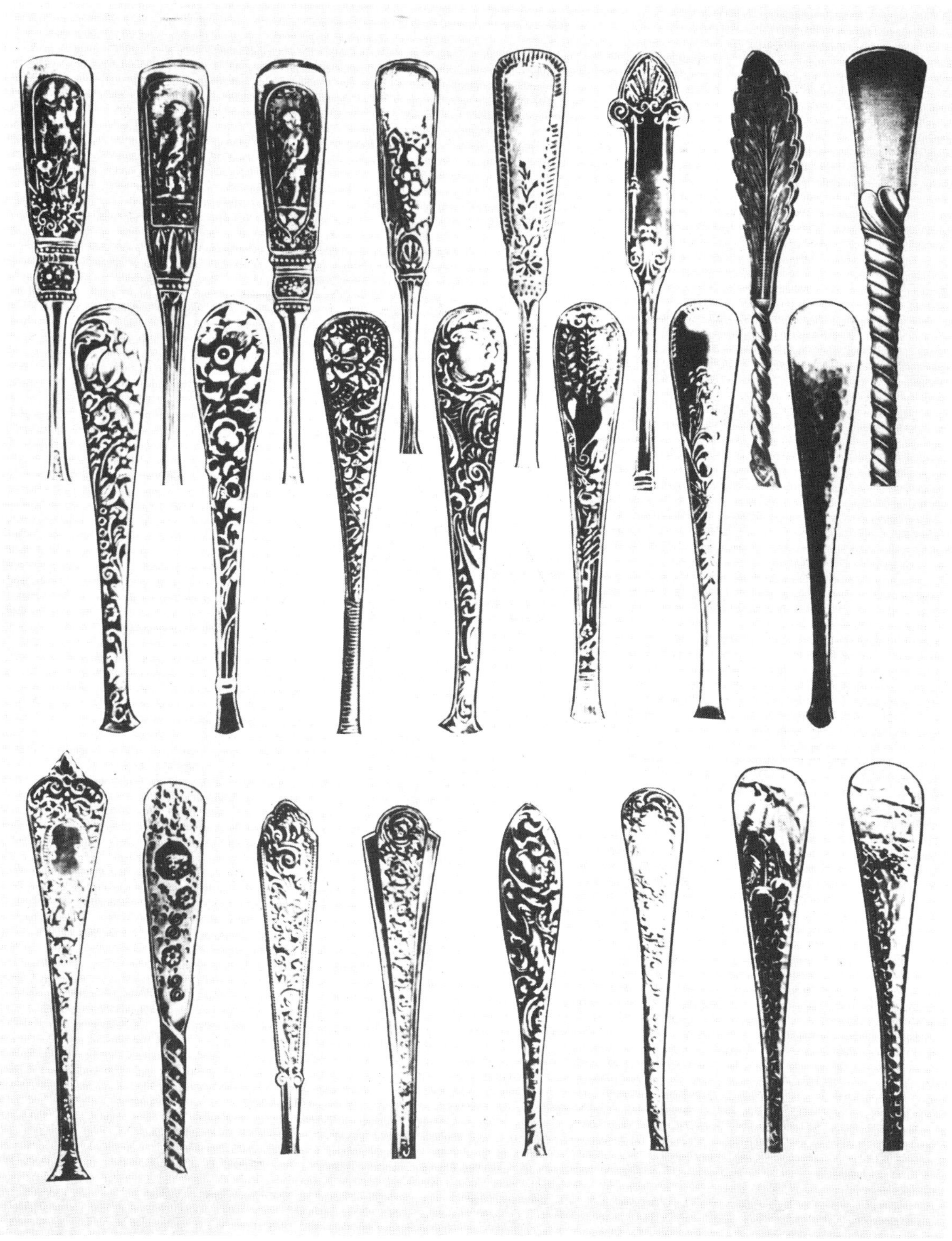

GORHAM MFG. CO. (Continued): *Top row (l. to r.)*: Fontainebleau, Piper, Gilpin, H 83, Daisy, Byzantine, Leaf, Colonial. *Middle row (l. to r.)*: Tulip, Eglantine, Delhi, Berlin, Laurel, Hawthorne, Antique Hammered. *Bottom row (l. to r.)*: Queen Anne, Hamburg, Scandinavian, Floral, French, Douglass, Antique Hammered Applied, Antique Hammered Applied No. 2. See also Wm. B. Durgin Co., Graff, Washbourne & Dunn, Whiting Mfg. Co., Standard Patterns and Variations sections.

Graff, Washbourne & Dunn | Heer-Schofield Co. | Howard Sterling Co. | Samuel Kirk & Son

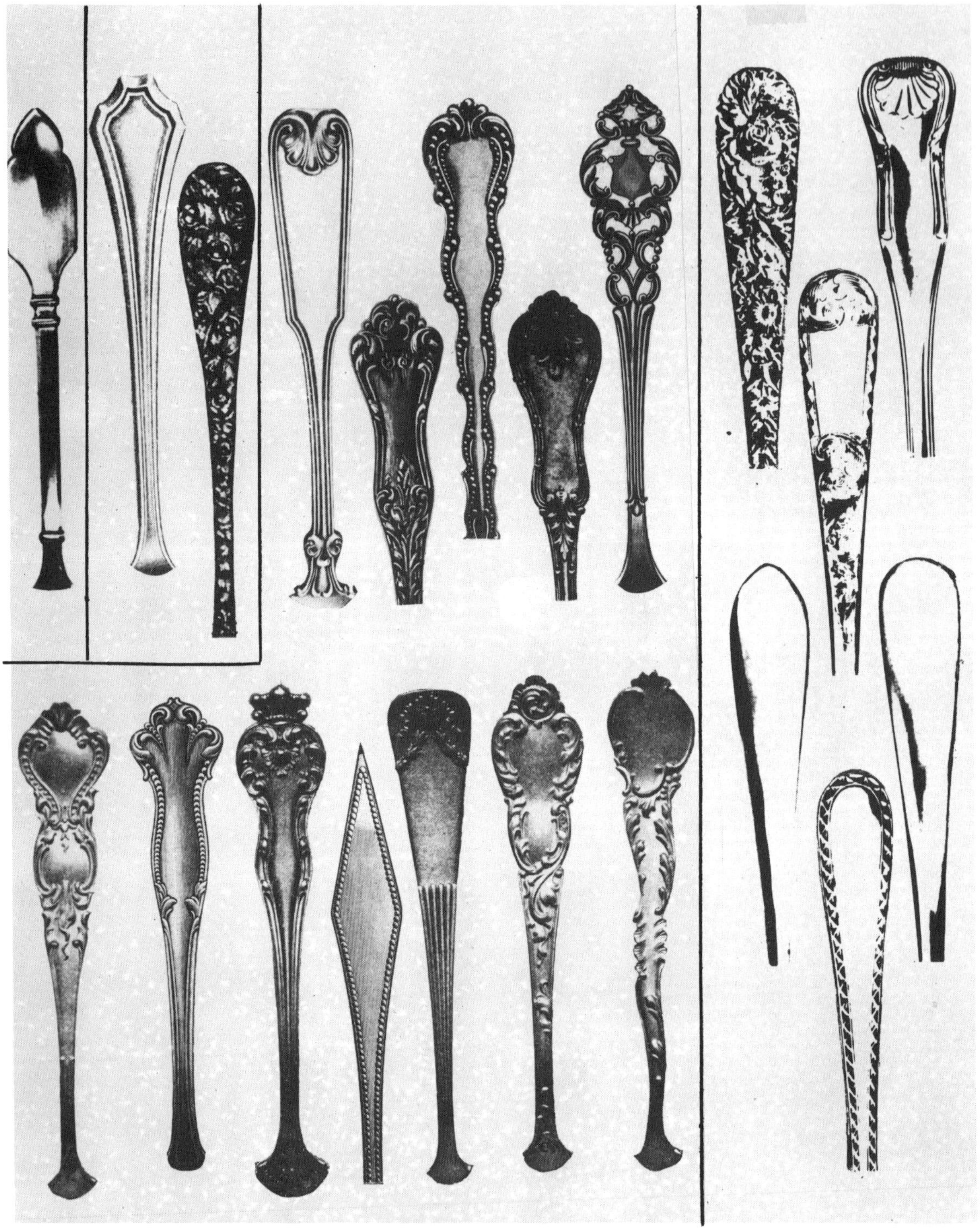

GRAFF, WASHBOURNE & DUNN: Robert Bruce. HEER-SCHOFIELD CO.: *(l. to r.)*: Virginia Dare, Baltimore Rose. HOWARD STERLING CO.: *Top row (l. to r.)*: 1776, LaFayette, York. *Middle row (l. to r.)*: Monarque, Josephine. *Bottom row (l. to r.)*: Dauphin, Hope, Queen, Washington, First Empire, Lorraine, Watteau. SAMUEL KIRK & SON: *Top row (l. to r.)*: Repousse, Kirk King (King). *Second row*: Mayflower. *Third row (l. to r.)*: Wadefield, Old Maryland Plain. *Bottom*: Winslow. For Howard Sterling Co., Samuel Kirk & Son see also Standard Patterns section.

J. B. & S. M. Knowles Co.

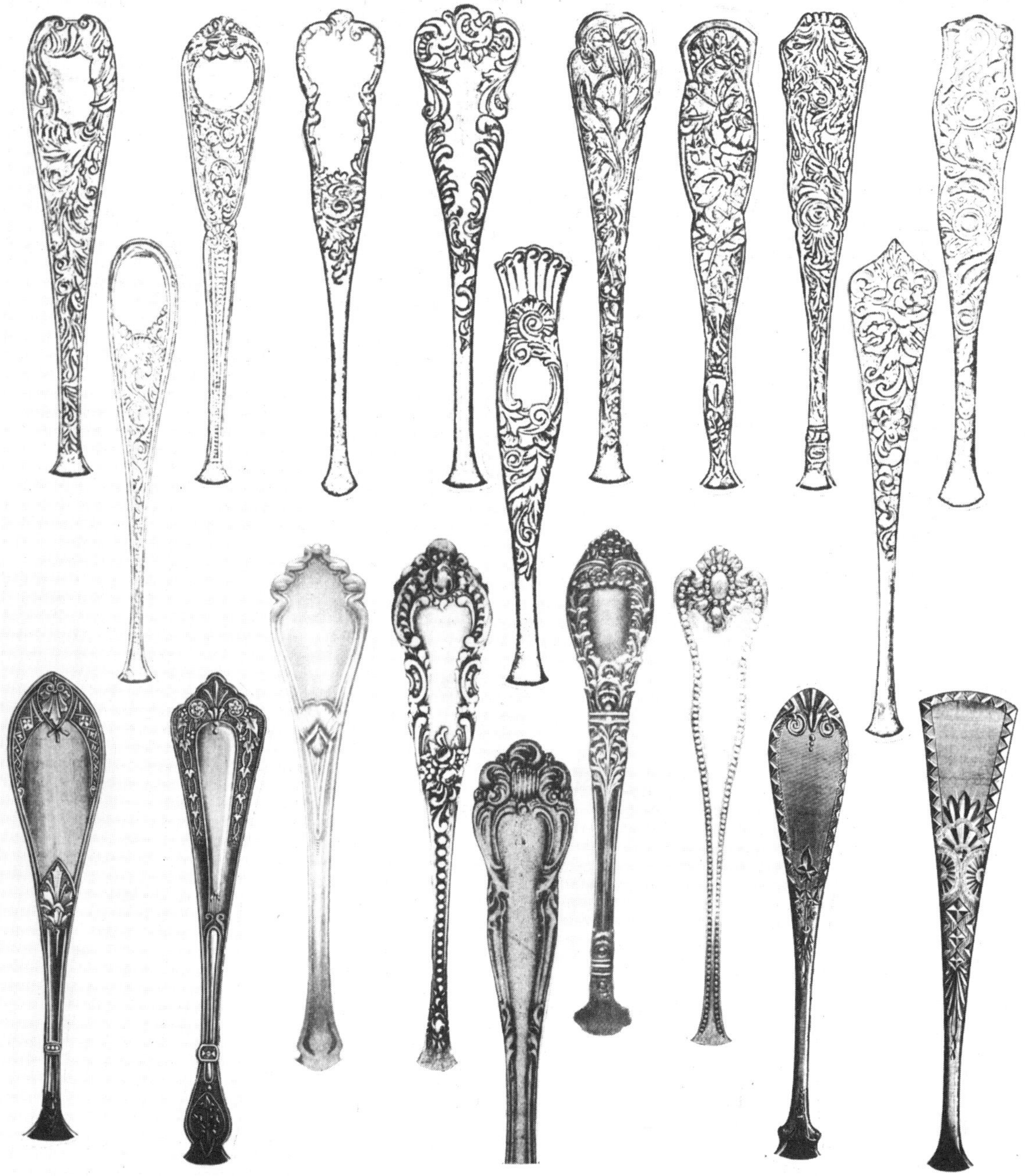

J. B. & S. M. KNOWLES CO.: *Top row (l. to r.)*: Aeolian, Webster, Lenox, Argo, No. 90, Rose, Tudor, Trianon. *Second row (l. to r.)*: Coronet, King, Essex. *Third row (l. to r.)*: Sweet Pea, Apollo, Roman, Lexington. *Bottom row (l. to r.)*: Crescent, Clinton, Angelo, Mayflower, Agate. See also Webster & Knowles, Knowles & Ladd, Standard Patterns sections.

Knowles & Ladd | Peter L. Krider Co. | Landers, Frary & Clark | Lebolt & Co. | Manchester Mfg. Co. | W. H. Manchester & Co.

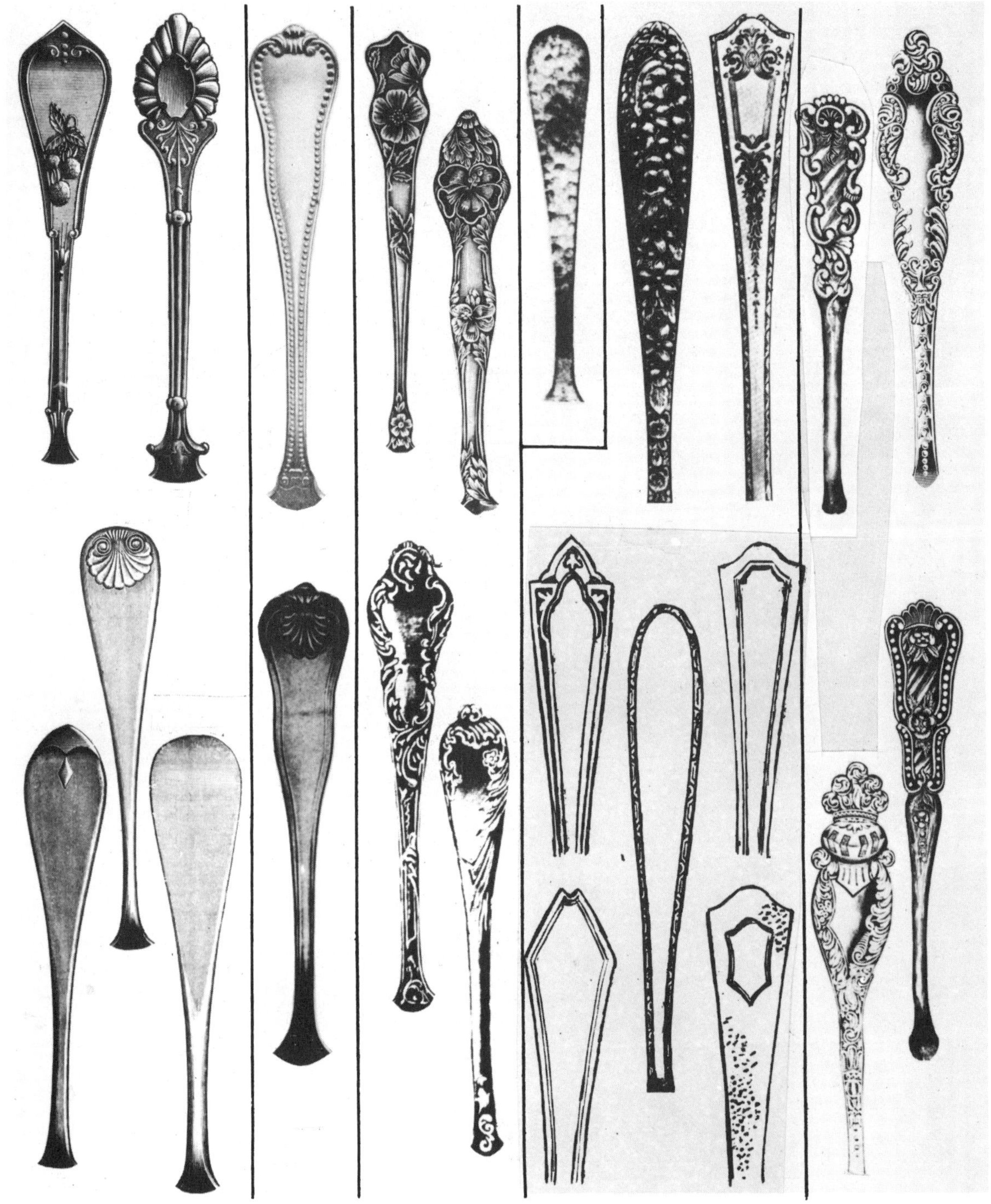

KNOWLES & LADD: *Top row (l. to r.)*: Queen, Emperor. *Middle*: Shell. *Bottom row (l. to r.)*: Antique, Warren. PETER L. KRIDER CO.: *Top*: Bead. *Bottom*: Thread Shell. LANDERS, FRARY & CLARK: *(Top to bottom, staggered)*: Landers No. 1, Landers No. 2., No. 2160, No. 2159. LEBOLT & CO.: LeBolt. MANCHESTER MFG. CO.: *Top row (l. to r.)*: Southern Rose, Princess. *Middle row (l. to r.)*: Doric, Manchester, Mary Warren. *Bottom row (l. to r.)*: Dixie, Priscilla (Priscilla Hammered). W. H. MANCHESTER & CO.: *(Top to bottom, staggered)*: LaFayette, Washington, Webster, Spartan. For Knowles & Ladd, see also Webster & Knowles and Standard Patterns sections. For Peter L. Krider Co. see also Standard Pattern sections. For Manchester Mfg. Co. see also W. H. Manchester & Co. and Standard Patterns sections.

Mauser Mfg. Co. | Jos. Mayer & Bro. | Newburyport Silver Co. | John Polhemus

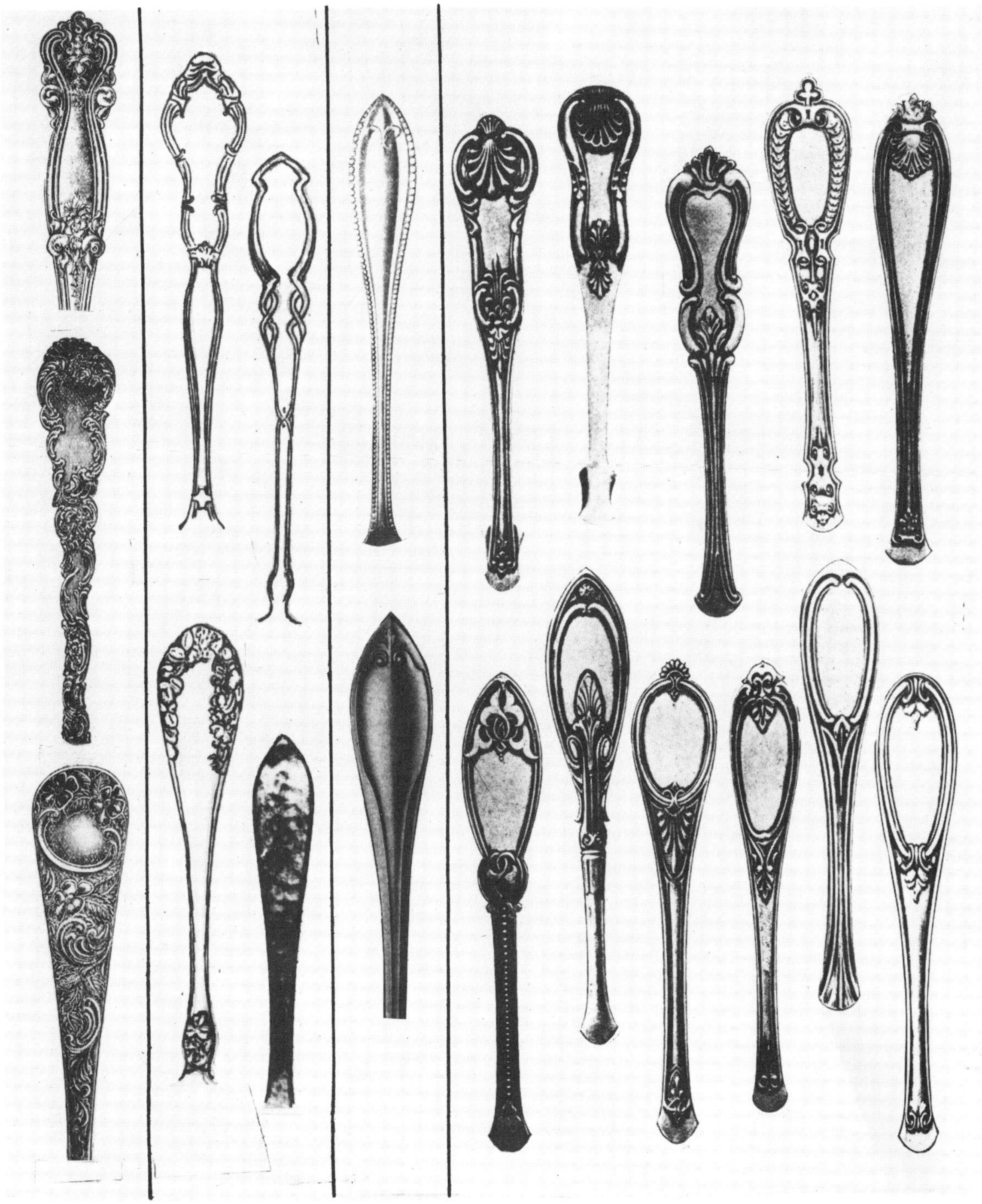

MAUSER MFG. CO.: *(Top to bottom)*: Emperor, Junior Rococo, Oneida. JOS. MAYER & BRO.: *(Top to bottom, staggered)*: Olympian, 1909, Clover Blossom, Mission. NEWBURYPORT SILVER CO.: *(Top to bottom)*: Betsy Ross, Fleur de Lis. JOHN POLHEMUS: *Top row (l. to r.)*: King's, Queen's, Prince Albert, Armor, Shell. *Bottom row (l. to r.)*: Oriental, Ruby, Honeysuckle, Neptune, Cottage, Empire. For Mauser Mfg. Co., Newburyport Silver Co., and John Polhemus, see also Standard Patterns section.

John Polhemus Reed & Barton

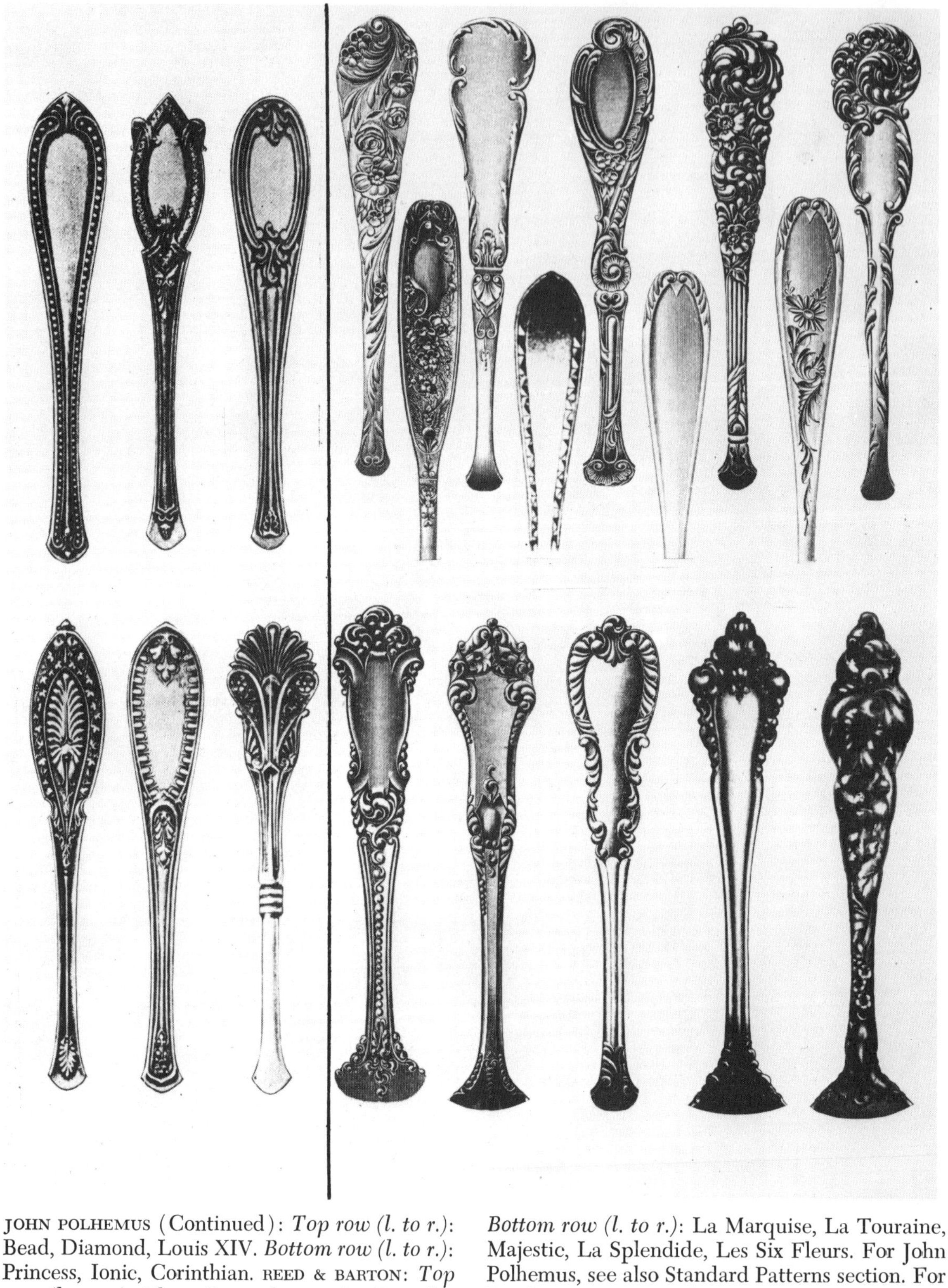

JOHN POLHEMUS (Continued): *Top row (l. to r.)*: Bead, Diamond, Louis XIV. *Bottom row (l. to r.)*: Princess, Ionic, Corinthian. REED & BARTON: *Top row (l. to r.)*: Flora, Luxembourg, La Rocaille, Trajan, La Reine. *Middle row (l. to r.)*: Empire, Four Georges, Athenian, Athenian Engraved. *Bottom row (l. to r.)*: La Marquise, La Touraine, Majestic, La Splendide, Les Six Fleurs. For John Polhemus, see also Standard Patterns section. For Reed & Barton, see also Dominick & Haff, Standard Patterns and Variations sections.

Reed & Barton

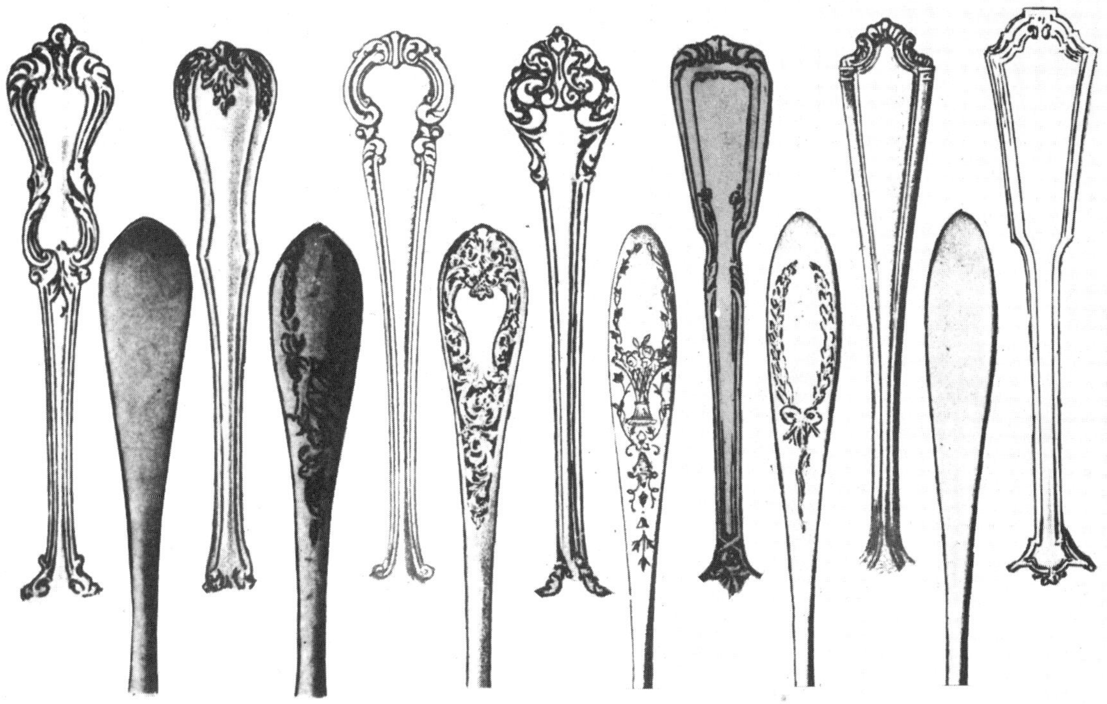

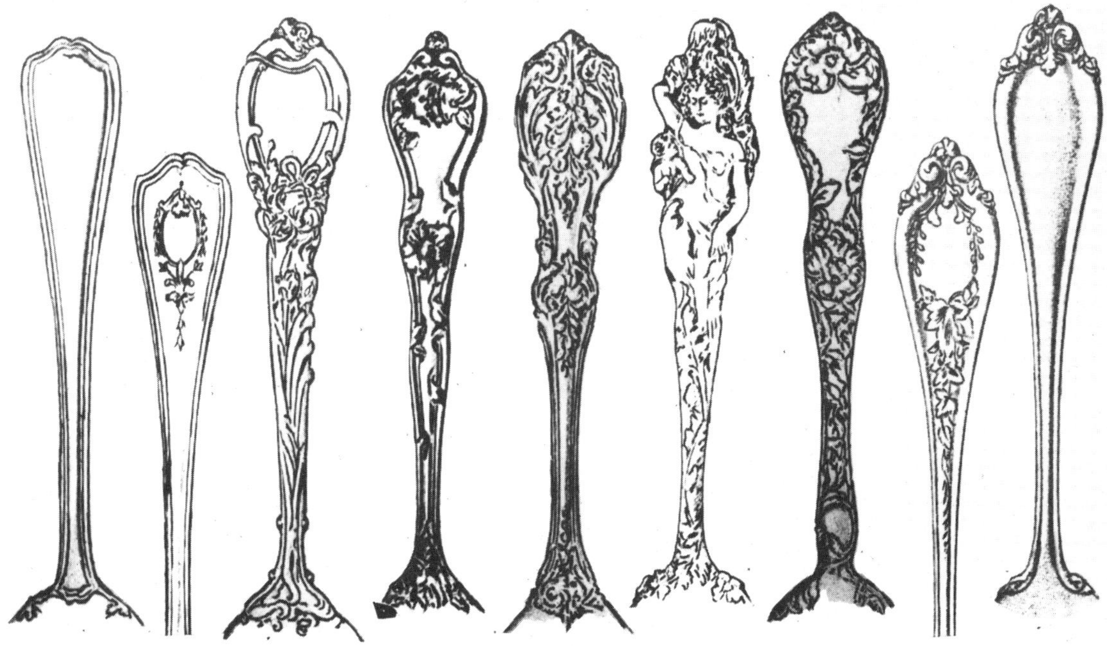

REED & BARTON (Continued): *Top row (l. to r.)*: Marlborough, Devon, La Comtesse, L'Elegante, Chambord, St. George (Chased), Jacobean. *Middle row (l. to r.)*: English Antique, English Antique Engraved, English Antique Etched, French Antique Watteau Engraved, French Antique Engraved, French Antique. *Bottom row (l. to r.)*: Hepplewhite, Hepplewhite Engraved, La Parisienne, Intaglio, Francis I, Love Disarmed, Les Cinq Fleurs, La Perle Engraved, La Perle. See also Dominick & Haff, Standard Patterns and Variations sections.

1847 Rogers Bros. (Meriden Britannia Co.) Rogers, Lunt & Bowlen Henry Sears & Son

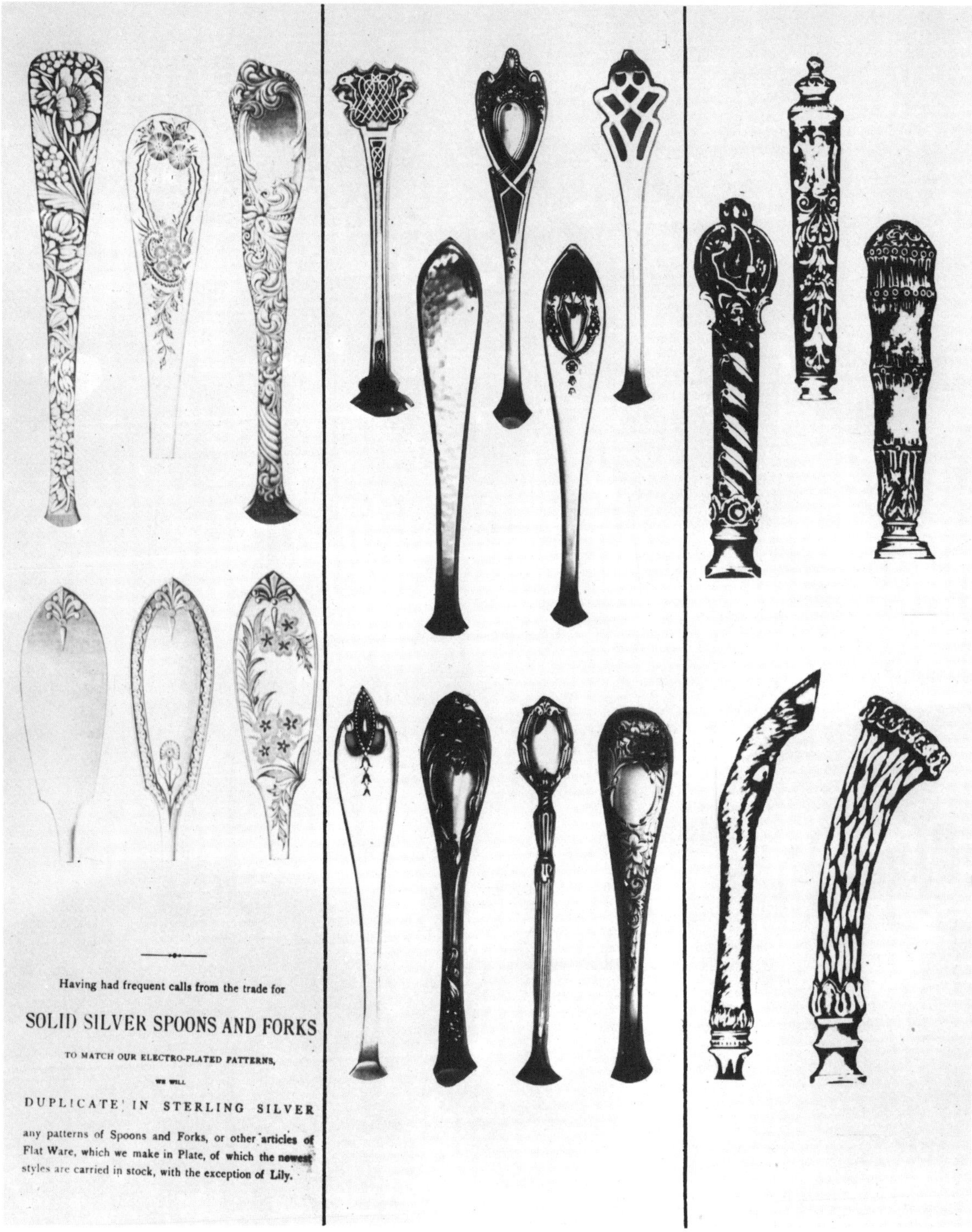

Having had frequent calls from the trade for
SOLID SILVER SPOONS AND FORKS
TO MATCH OUR ELECTRO-PLATED PATTERNS,
WE WILL
DUPLICATE IN STERLING SILVER
any patterns of Spoons and Forks, or other articles of Flat Ware, which we make in Plate, of which the newest styles are carried in stock, with the exception of Lily.

1847 ROGERS BROS. (MERIDEN BRITANNIA CO.): *Top row (l. to r.)*: Embossed, Marlboro (Satin Engraved), Ivanhoe. *Bottom row (l. to r.)*: Shell Tipped, Figured French, Gladstone (Satin Engraved). ROGERS, LUNT & BOWLEN: *Top row (l. to r.)*: Celtic, Monticello, Pynchon (Ye Pynchon). *Middle row (l. to r.)*: Jefferson Hammered, Mount Vernon. *Bottom row (l. to r.)*: Virginia, Narcissus, Sheraton, Dorothy Q. HENRY SEARS & SON: *Top*: Egyptian. *Middle row (l. to r.)*: Scroll, Bamboo. *Bottom row (l. to r.)*: Deer Foot, Deer Crown. For 1847 Rogers Bros. (Meriden Britannia Co.) see also Electroplate Sections for Rogers Bros., Rogers Bros. Mfg. Co., Rogers, Smith & Co., 1847 Rogers Bros. (Meriden Britannia Co.). Any of the electroplate patterns introduced by these companies prior to 1879 were available in sterling, per 1879 catalog note reproduced above. The goods could be stamped "1847 Rogers Bros." or "Rogers, Smith & Co." See also Standard Patterns and Variations sections. For Rogers, Lunt & Bowlen (Lunt Silversmiths) see also Standard Patterns and A. F. Towle & Son Co. sections.

Joseph Seymour Sons & Co.

JOSEPH SEYMOUR SONS & CO.: *Top row (l. to r.)*: Fiddle Tipt, Kentucky Tipt, French Tipt, Honeysuckle, Wreath, Cottage, Prairie Flower. *Middle row (l. to r.)*: Square Handle Engraved, Union, Duchess, Diadem. *Bottom row (l. to r.)*: Twist Engraved, Wheat Engraved, Rose Engraved, Lily Engraved, Woodbine Engraved, Patrician, Windsor Engraved. See also Standard Patterns.

George W. Shiebler & Co.

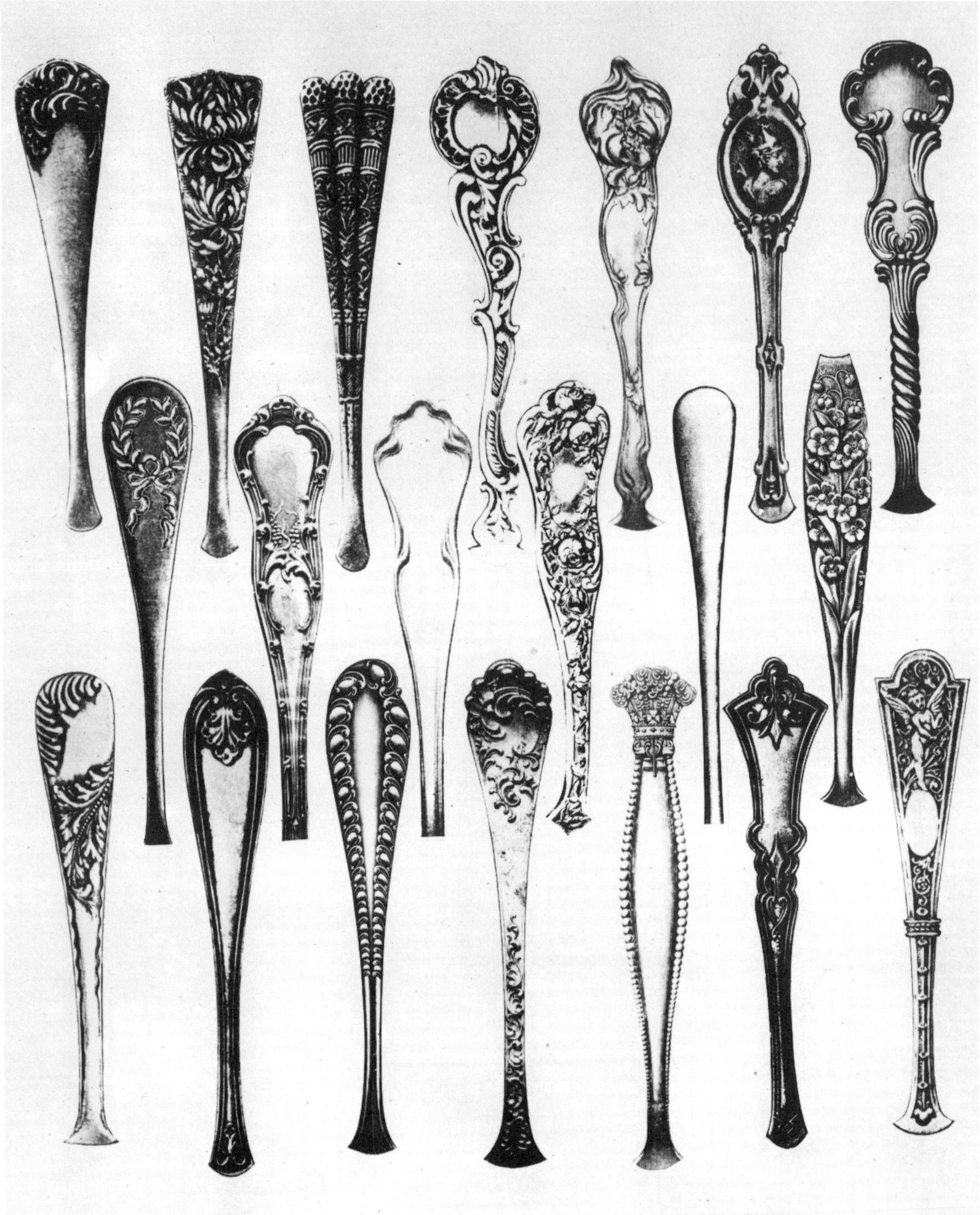

GEORGE W. SHIEBLER & CO.: *Top row (l. to r.)*: Marie Antoinette, Chrysanthemum, Luxembourg, Rococo, Fiorito, Medallion, Louvre. *Middle row (l. to r.)*: Napoleon, Gothic (Salisbury), Wave, American Beauty, Penn, Flora. *Bottom row (l. to r.)*: Acanthus, Leaf, Victoria, Maintenon, Sandringham, Clematis, Cupid. See also Albert Coles & Co., Coles & Reynolds, A. & W. Wood, John Polhemus, Standard Patterns and Variations sections.

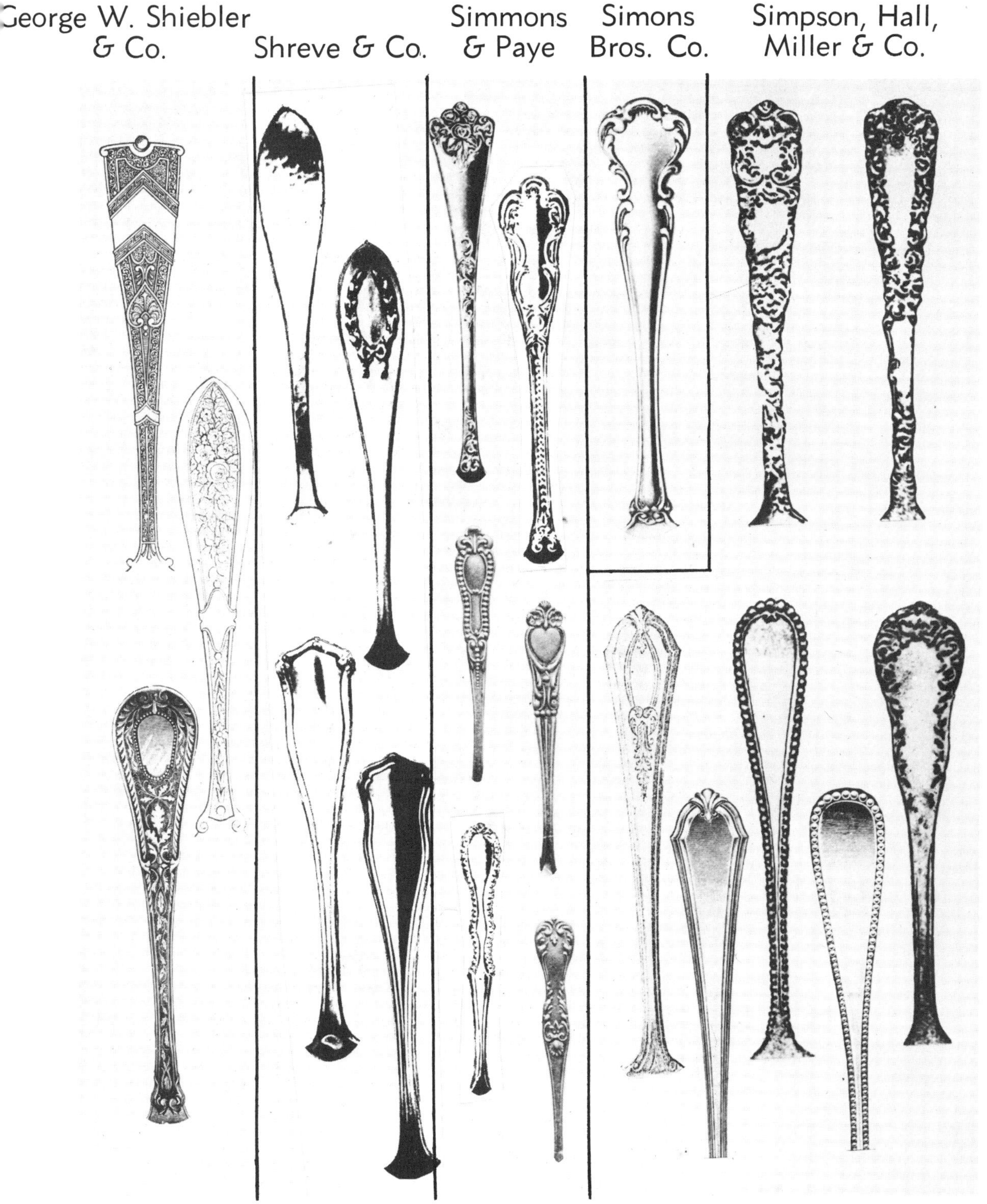

GEORGE W. SHIEBLER & CO. (Continued): *(Top to Bottom, staggered)*: Amaryllis, Montezuma, Gipsy. SHREVE & COMPANY: *(Top to Bottom, staggered)*: Antique, Napoleonic, Dolores, Winchester. SIMMONS & PAYE: *Top (l. to r.)*: No. 6, No. 8. *Middle (l. to r.)*: No. 598, No. 599. *Bottom (l. to r.)*: No. 6198, No. 601. SIMONS BROS. CO.: Flanders. SIMPSON, HALL, MILLER & CO.: *Top row (l. to r.)*: Dresden, Venus. *Middle row (l. to r.)*: Copley, Cambridge, Diana. *Bottom row (l. to r.)*: Shirley, Luzon. For George W. Shiebler & Co. see also Albert Coles & Co., Coles & Reynolds, A. & W. Wood, John Polhemus, Standard Patterns and Variations sections. For Simons Bros. Co. see also Peter L. Krider Co. For Simpson, Hall, Miller & Co. see also Standard Patterns and Variations sections.

Simpson, Hall, Miller & Co.

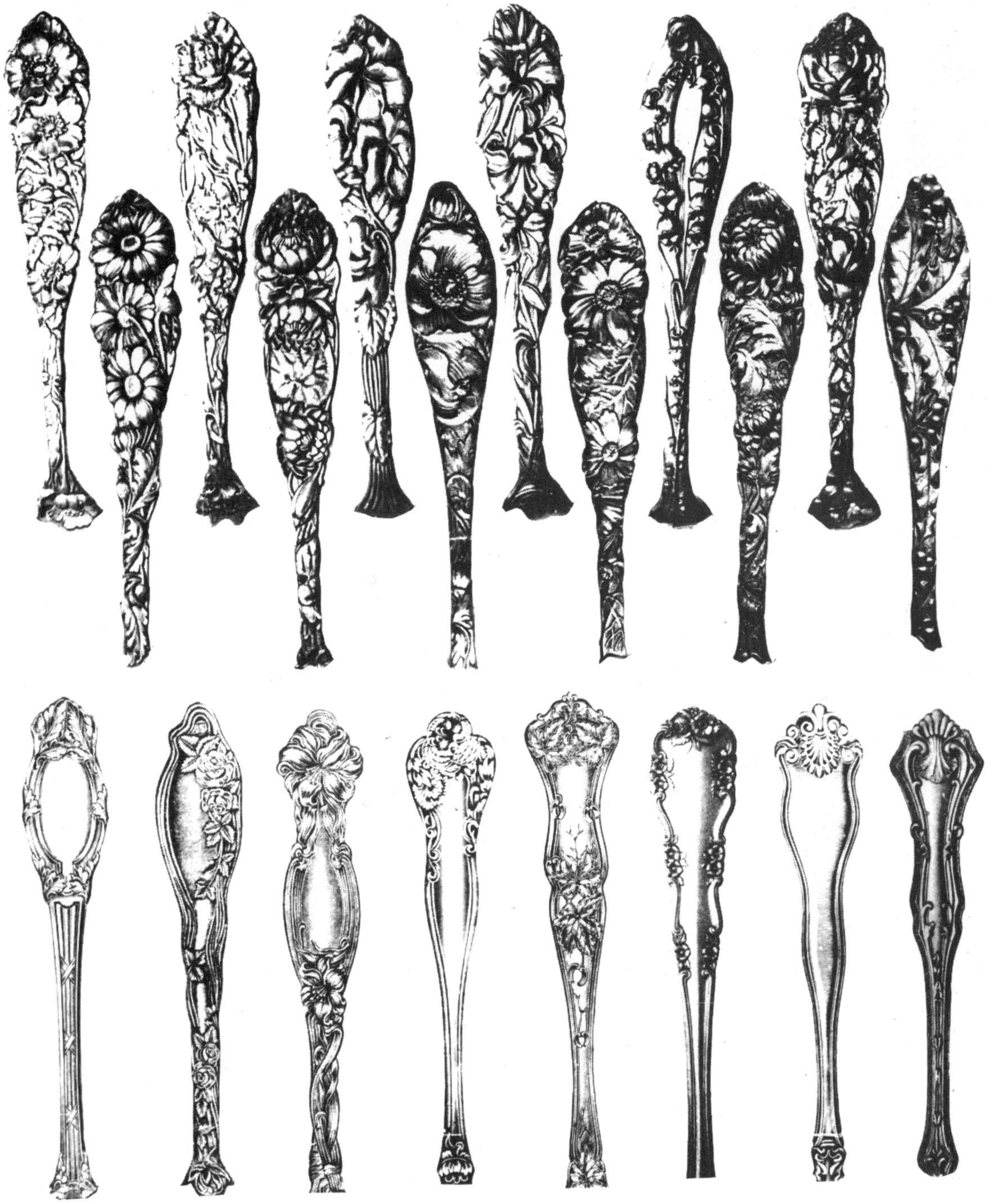

SIMPSON, HALL, MILLER & CO. (Continued): *Top row (l. to r.)*: Wild Rose, Carnation, Violet, Easter Lily, Lily of the Valley, Rose. *Middle row (l. to r.)*: Daisy, Water Lily, Poppy, Cosmos, Chrysanthemum, Holly. *Bottom row (l. to r.)*: Abottsford, Mille Fleurs, Frontenac, Stratford, Edgewood, Rosalind, Winchester, Duchesse. See also Standard Patterns and Variations sections.

Simpson, Hall, Miller & Co.

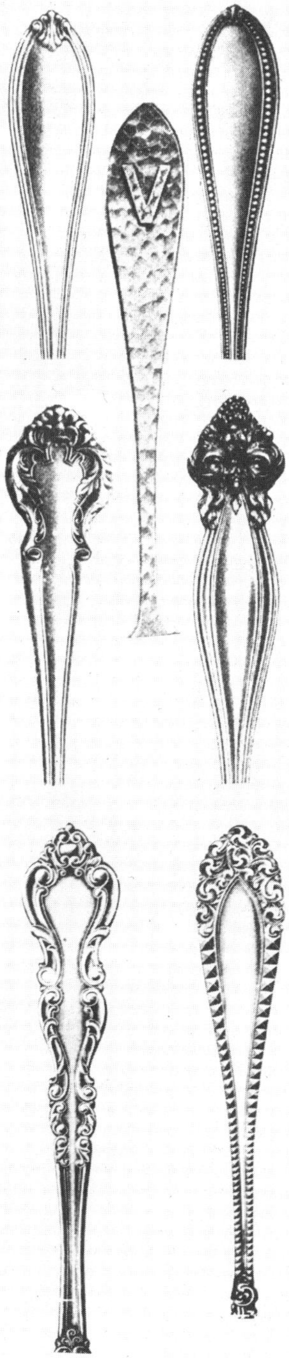

Frank W. Smith Co.

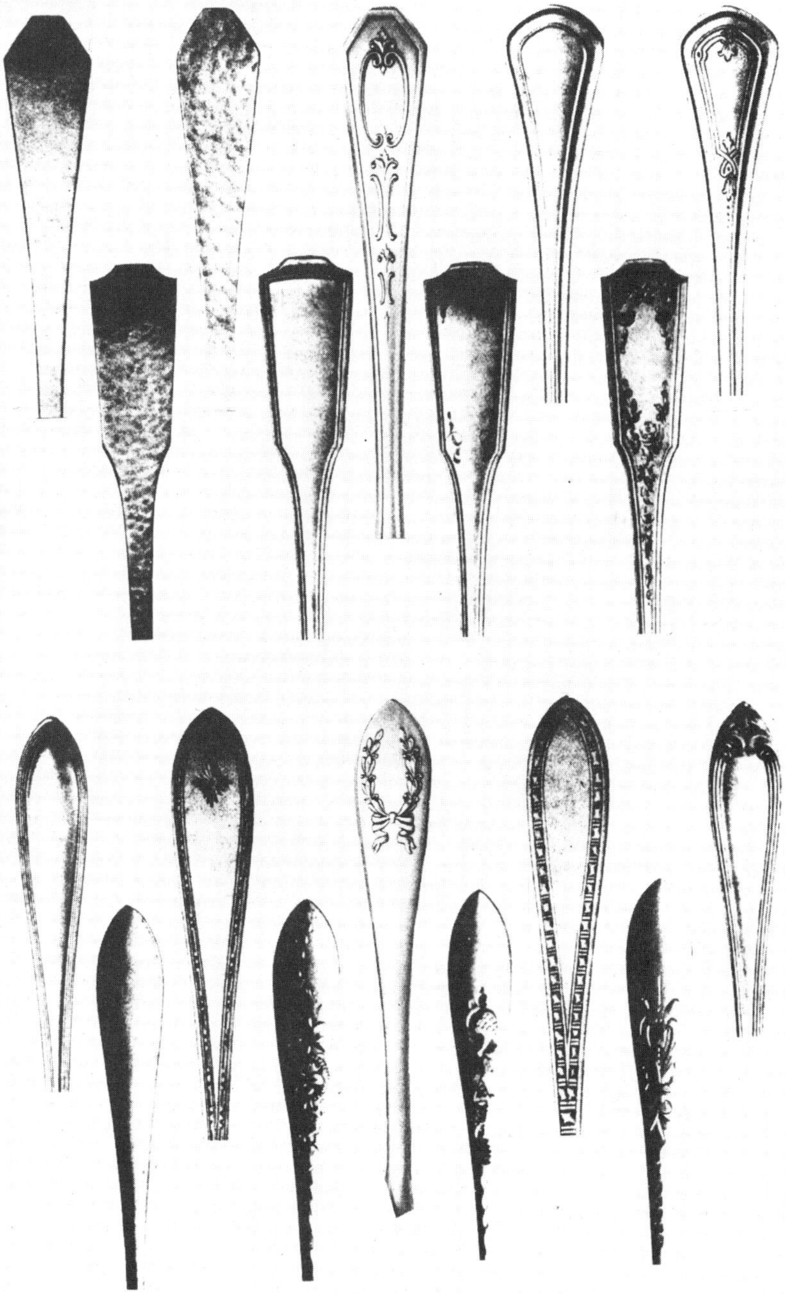

SIMPSON, HALL, MILLER & CO. (Continued): *Top row (l. to r.)*: Margaret, Vandyke (Vandyke, Applied Initial), Trumbull. *Middle row (l. to r.)*: Cedric, Jeanne d' Arc. *Bottom row (l. to r.)*: Warwick, Kenilworth. FRANK W. SMITH CO.: *Top row (l. to r.)*: Bostonia, Vergennes Kraft, Vergennes, Mayflower, Mayflower (Hand Chased). *Second row (l. to r.)*: Lincoln Kraft, Lincoln, Lincoln Engraved, Lincoln Kraft Engraved. *Third row (l. to r.)*: Pilgrim, Salem, Laurel, Beverly, No. 14. *Bottom row (l. to r.)*: Martha Washington, Martha Washington Lily, Martha Washington Star, Paul Revere Engraved. For Simpson, Hall, Miller & Co. and Frank W. Smith Co. see also Standard Patterns.

Frank W. Smith Co.

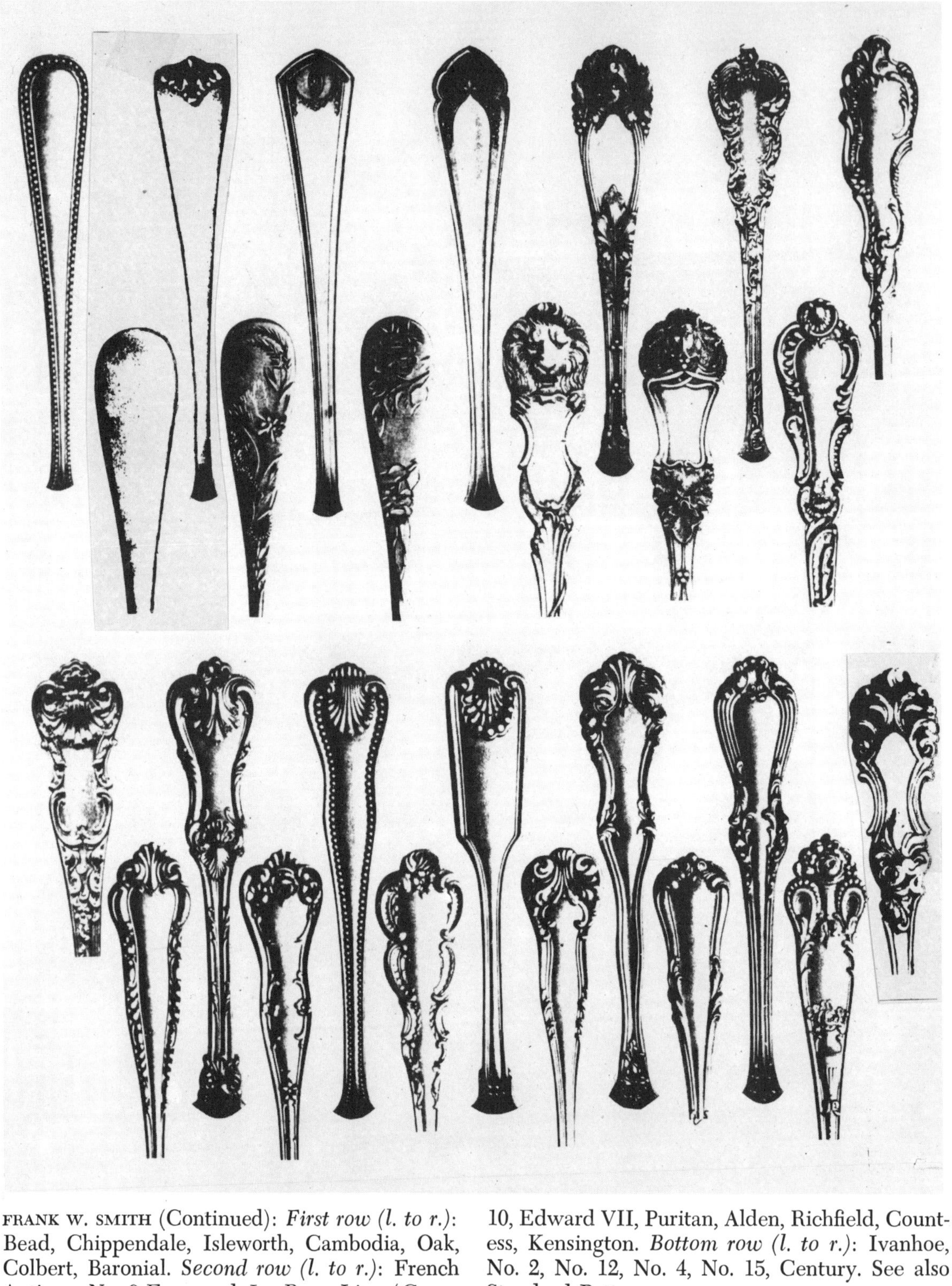

FRANK W. SMITH (Continued): *First row (l. to r.)*: Bead, Chippendale, Isleworth, Cambodia, Oak, Colbert, Baronial. *Second row (l. to r.)*: French Antique, No. 9 Engraved, Jac Rose, Lion (Coeur de Lion), Ivy, Crystal. *Third row (l. to r.)*: No. 10, Edward VII, Puritan, Alden, Richfield, Countess, Kensington. *Bottom row (l. to r.)*: Ivanhoe, No. 2, No. 12, No. 4, No. 15, Century. See also Standard Patterns.

Frank W. Smith Co. | The Stieff Company | Tiffany & Co.

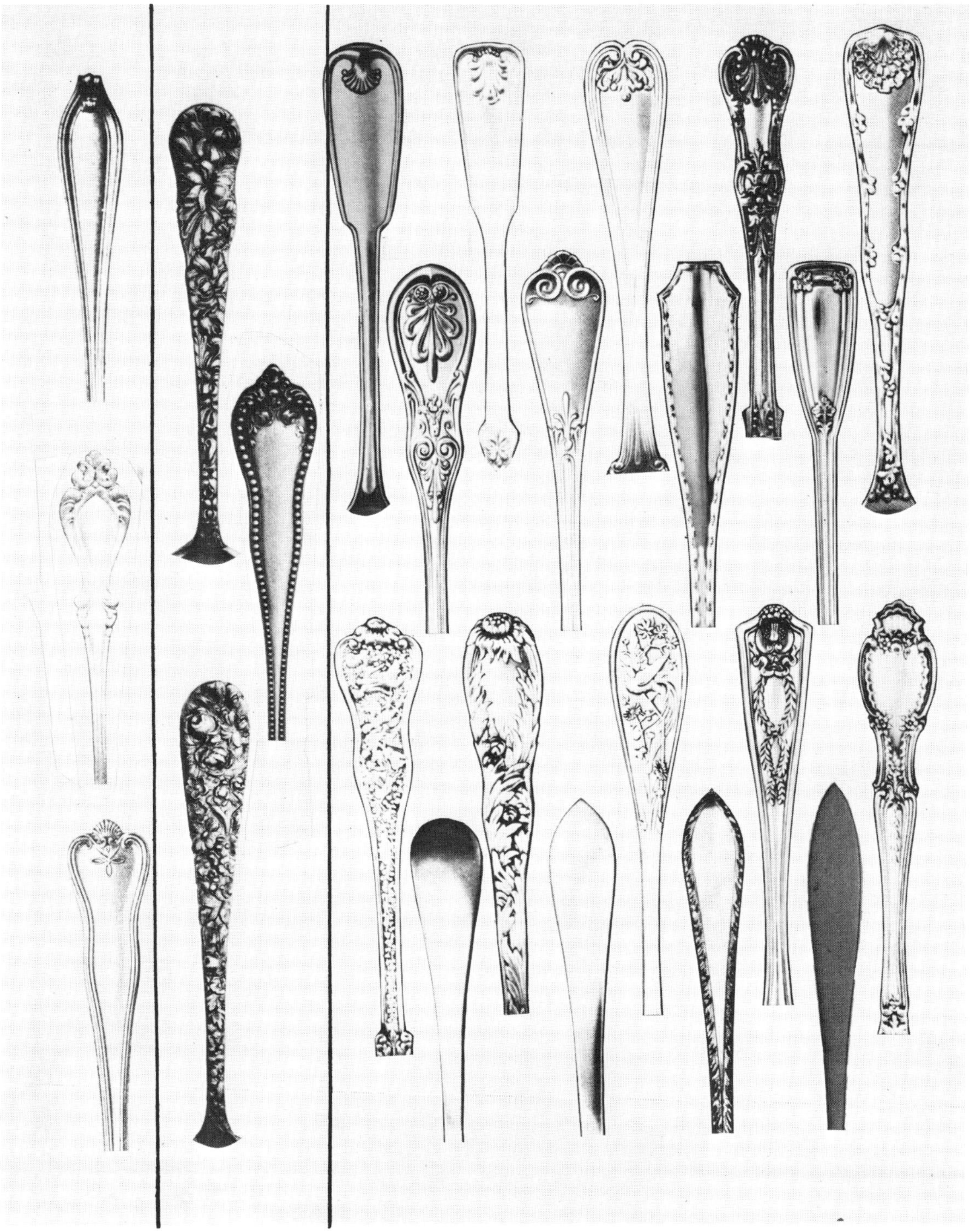

FRANK W. SMITH CO.: (Continued): *(Top to bottom)*: Martha Randolph, Nordica, Priscilla. THE STIEFF COMPANY: *(Top to bottom, staggered)*: Chrysanthemum, Victoria, Maryland (Rose). TIFFANY & CO.: *Top row (l. to r.)*: Palm, Shell & Thread, Colonial, English King, Wave Edge. *Second row (l. to r.)*: Cook (Saratoga), Tiffany (Beekman), Marquise, St. Dunstan. *Third row (l. to r.)*: Olympian, Chrysanthemum (Indian Chrysanthemum), Japanese (Audubon), Winthrop, Richelieu. *Bottom row (l. to r.)*: King William, Faneuil, Faneuil No. 95 (Feather Edge), Queen Anne. For Frank W. Smith Co. and The Stieff Company see also Standard Patterns section.

A. F. Towle & Son Co. The Towle Mfg. Co.

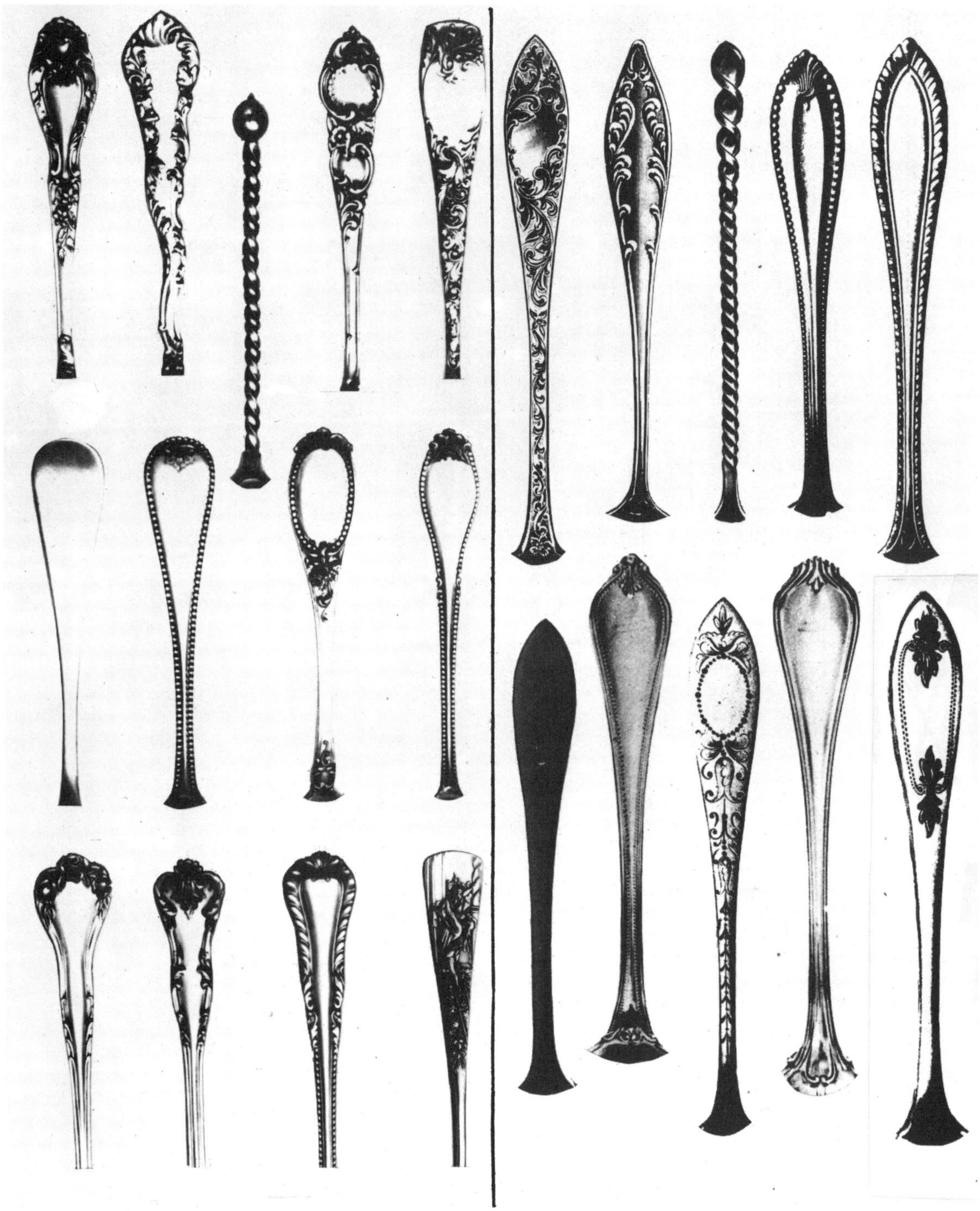

A. F. TOWLE & SON CO.: *Top row (l. to r.)*: Verona, Elaine, Ball Twist Sterling, Navarre, Greenfield. *Middle row (l. to r.)*: Warren, Priscilla, Wentworth, Provence. *Bottom row (l. to r.)*: Tudor, Chatelaine (Enid), Old Dominion, Juliet. THE TOWLE MFG. CO.: *Top row (l. to r.)*: Auvergne, Essex, No. 128, Cordova, Godroon. *Bottom row (l. to r.)*: LaFayette, Newbury (Old Newbury), LaFayette Engraved, Paul Revere, Madame LaFayette. For A. F. Towle & Son Co. see also Standard Patterns. For The Towle Mfg. Co. see also Standard Patterns and Variations sections.

The Towle Mfg. Co.

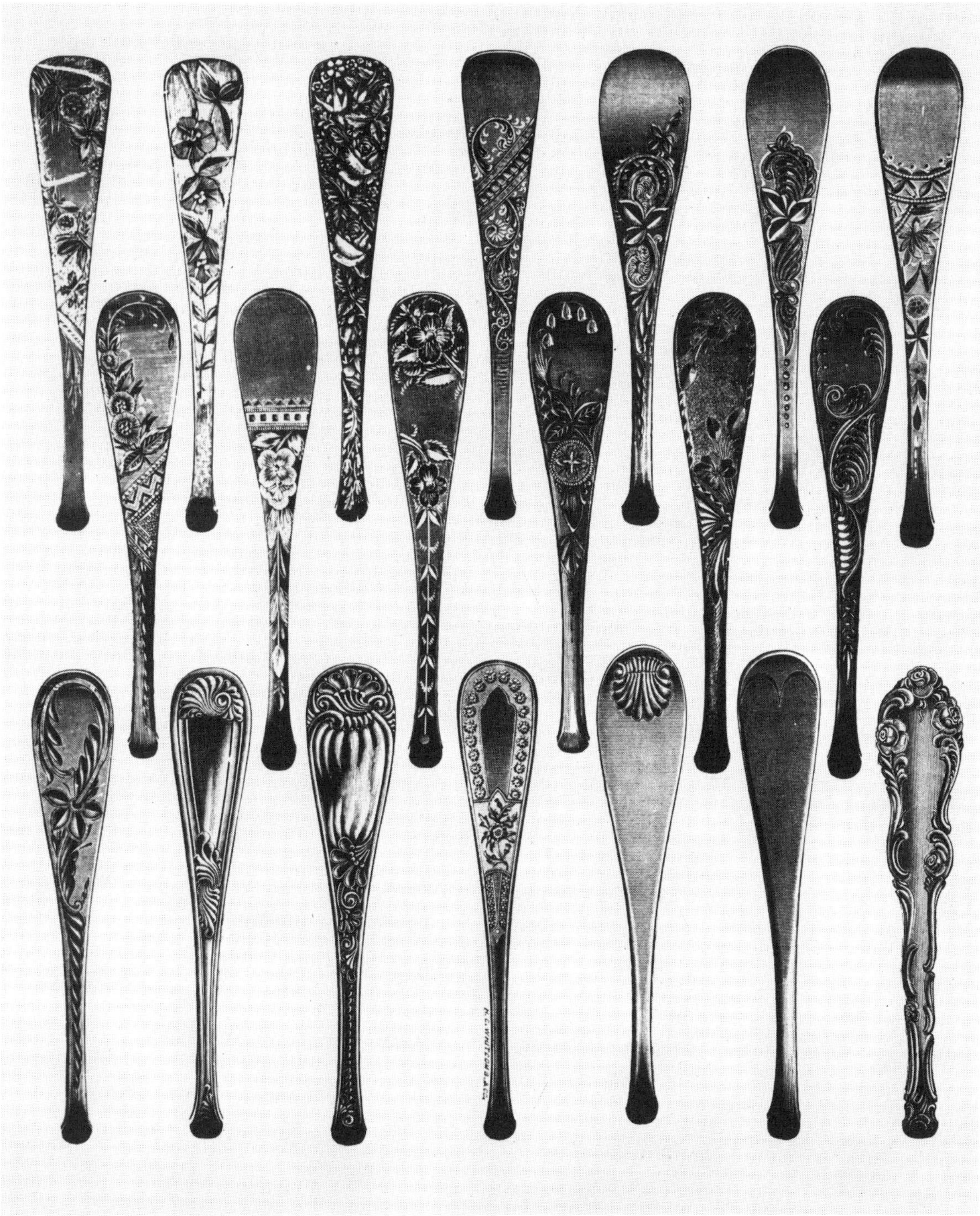

THE TOWLE MFG. CO. (Continued): *Top row (l. to r.)*: No. 62, No. 63, Arlington, Scroll, Clifton, Gladys, No. 50. *Middle row (l. to r.)*: No. 38, No. 39, No. 43, Lily, Clover, Argyll. *Bottom row (l. to r.)*: Florence, Lenox, Glenmore, Victor (Daisy), Shell, Antique, Old English. See also Standard Patterns and Variations sections.

The Towle Mfg. Co.

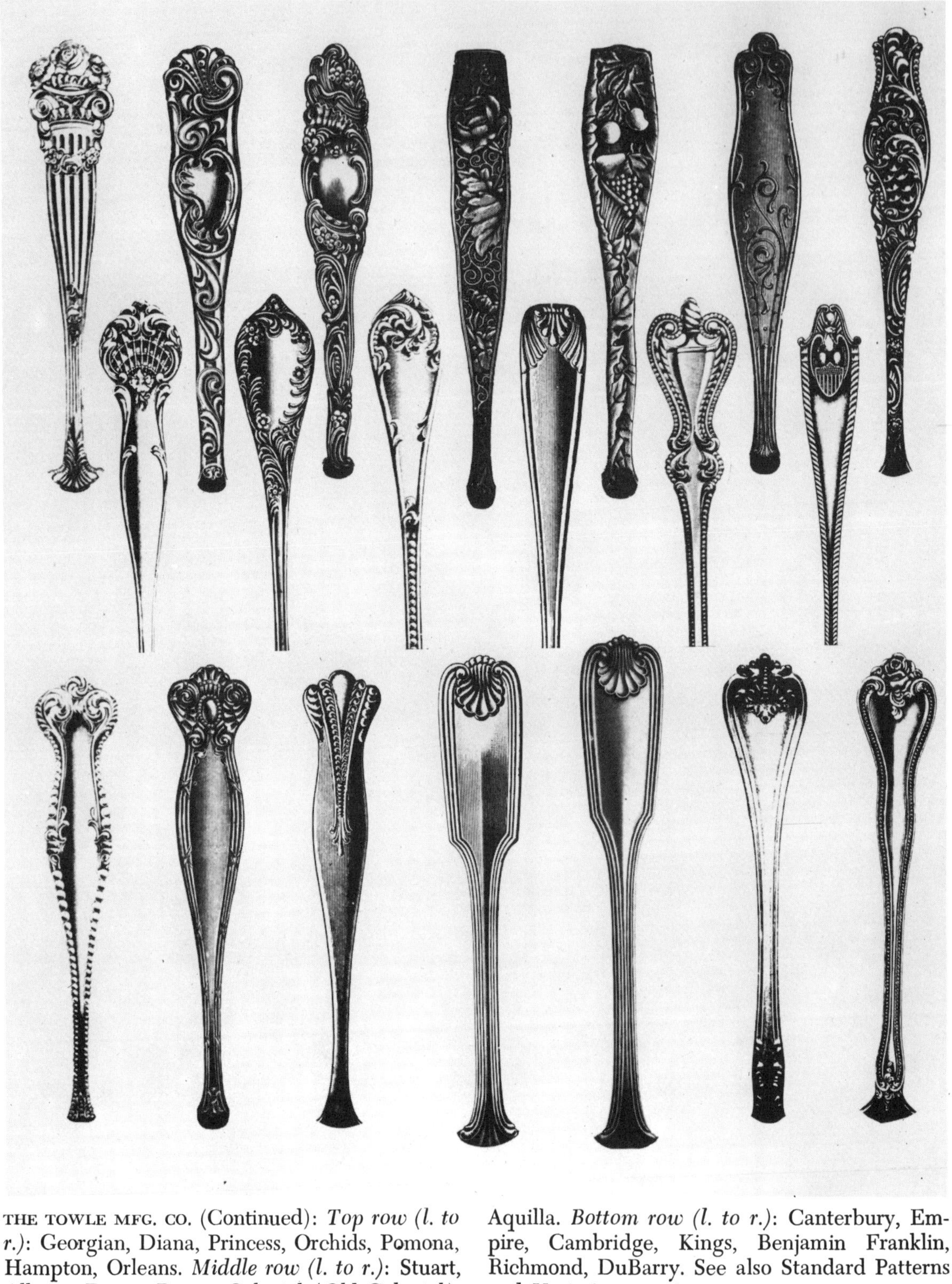

THE TOWLE MFG. CO. (Continued): *Top row (l. to r.)*: Georgian, Diana, Princess, Orchids, Pomona, Hampton, Orleans. *Middle row (l. to r.)*: Stuart, Albany, Dover, Rustic, Colonial (Old Colonial), Aquilla. *Bottom row (l. to r.)*: Canterbury, Empire, Cambridge, Kings, Benjamin Franklin, Richmond, DuBarry. See also Standard Patterns and Variations sections.

Tuttle Silver Co. | W. K. Vanderslice Co. | R. Wallace & Sons

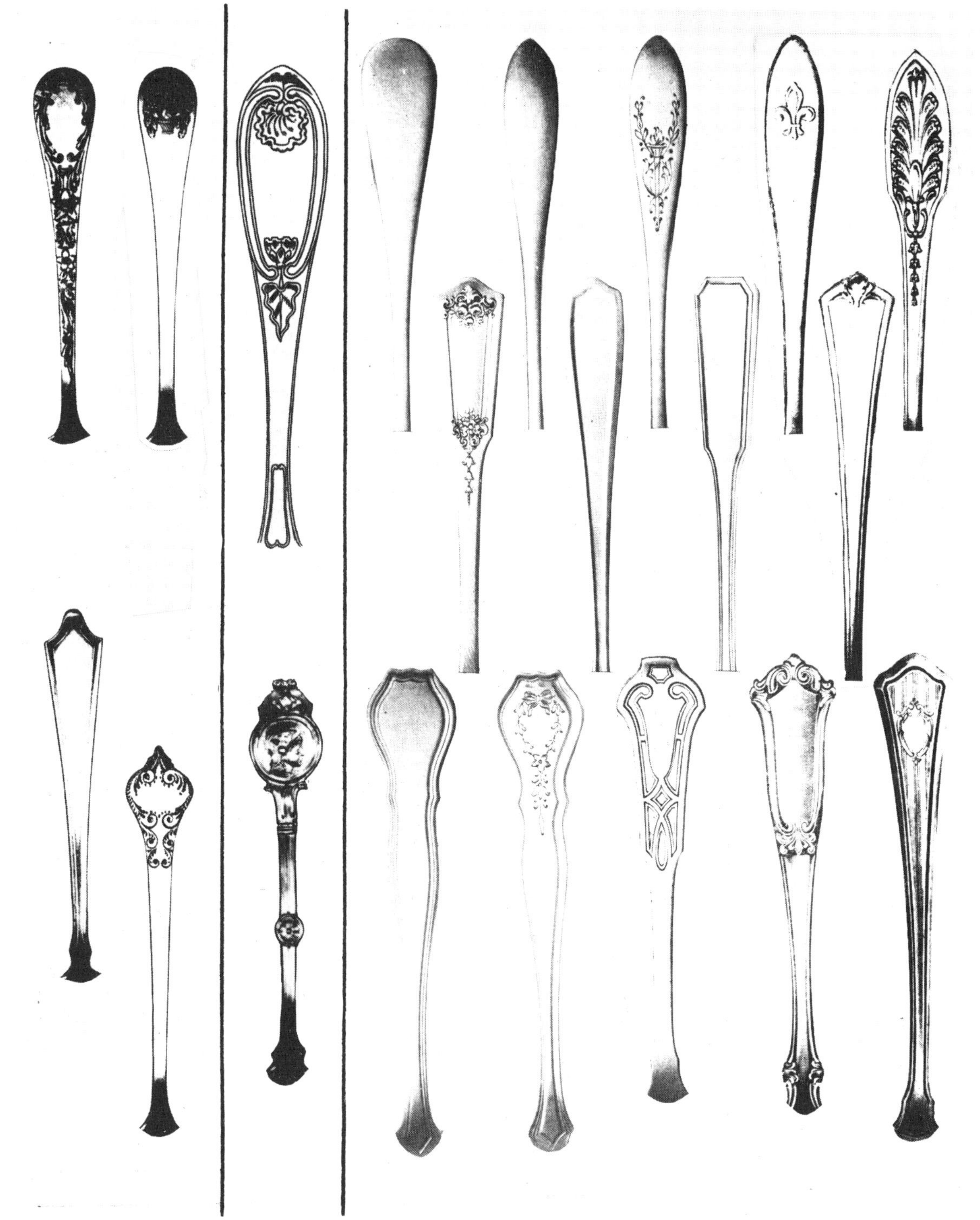

TUTTLE SILVER CO.: *(Top to bottom, staggered)*: Georgian, Basket of Flowers, Aberdeen, Charles II. W. K. VANDERSLICE CO.: *(Top to bottom)*: Vanderslice No. 1, Medallion. R. WALLACE & SONS: *Top row (l. to r.)*: Sherwood, Puritan, Priscilla, No. 40, No. 42. *Middle row (l. to r.)*: No. 43, No. 44, No. 45, No. 41. *Bottom row (l. to r.)*: Nile, Cairo, No. 300, Saxon, Hamilton. For W. K. Vanderslice Co. and R. Wallace & Sons see also Standard Patterns section. *(Vanderslice "Medallion" courtesy Blasdel Collection, Society of California Pioneers. Photo by Roy D. Graves.)*

R. Wallace & Sons

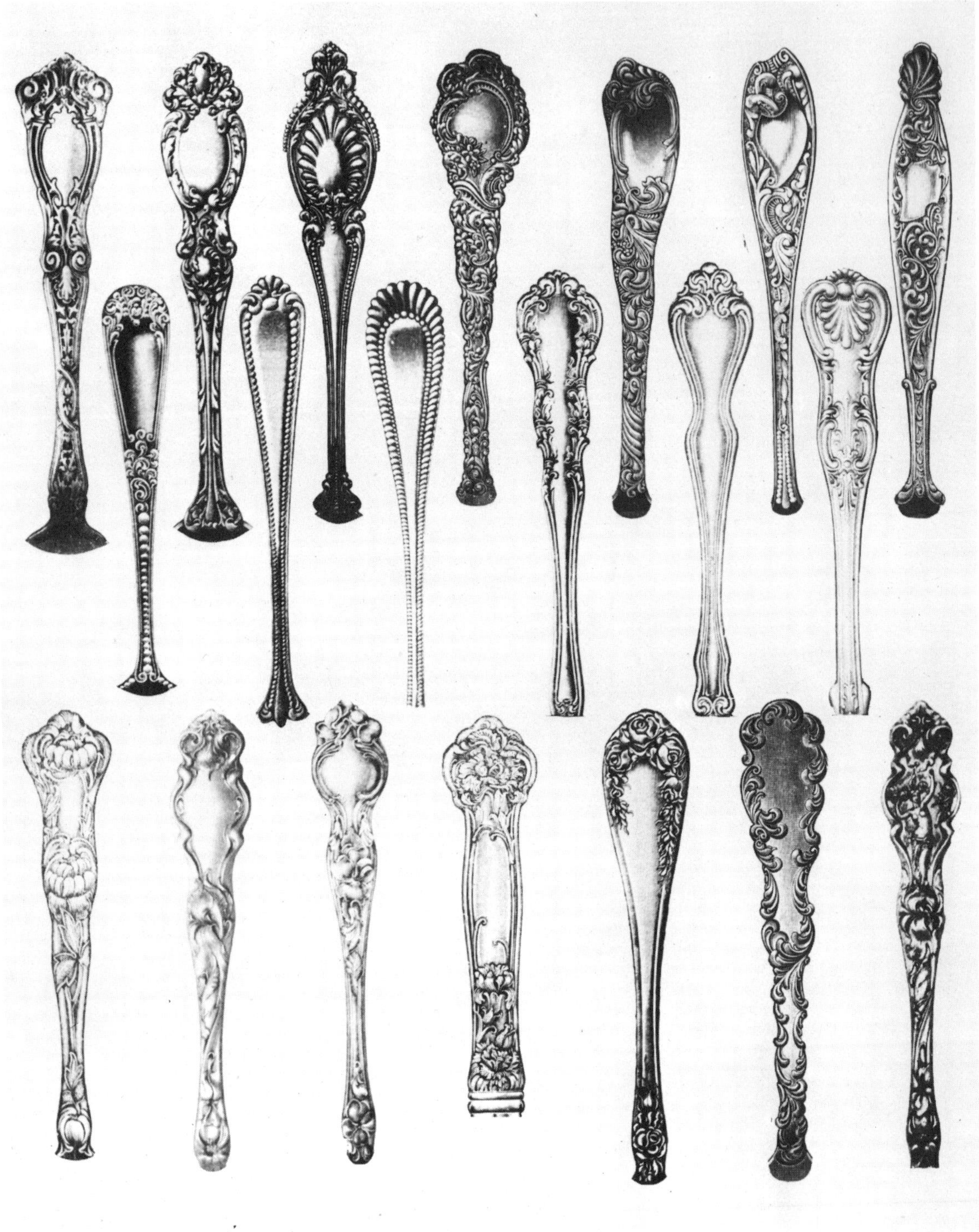

R. WALLACE & SONS (Continued): *Top row (l. to r.)*: Berain, Lucerne, Sappho, Louvre, Ivanhoe, Bessie, Rodney. *Middle row (l. to r.)*: Somerset, No. 4, Atalanta, Irving, Hampton, Kings. *Bottom row (l. to r.)*: Peony, Eton, Violet, Carnation, Rose, Waverly, Irian. See also Standard Patterns.

R. Wallace & Sons | Watrous Mfg. Co. | Watson, Newell & Co.

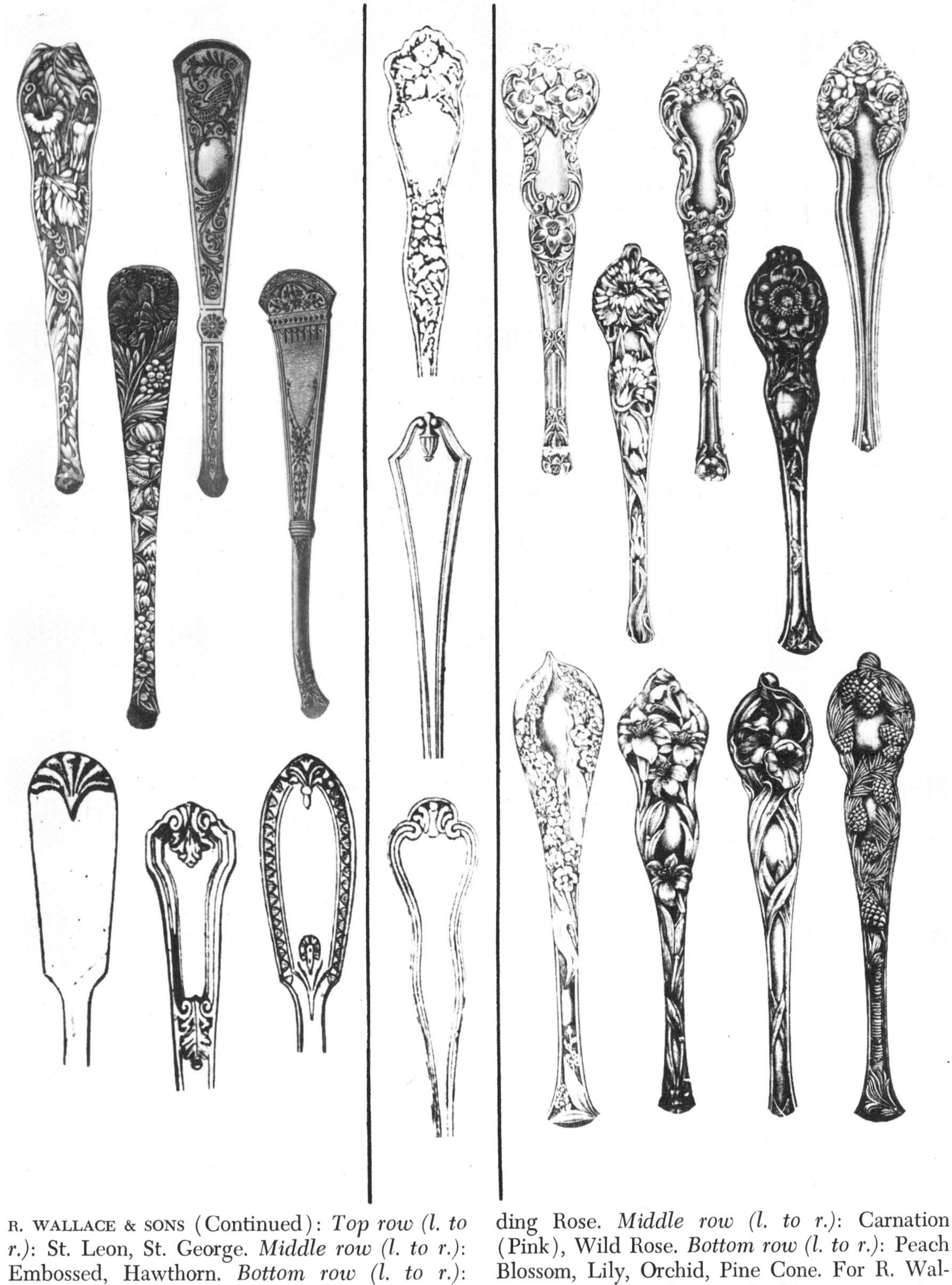

R. WALLACE & SONS (Continued): *Top row (l. to r.)*: St. Leon, St. George. *Middle row (l. to r.)*: Embossed, Hawthorn. *Bottom row (l. to r.)*: Figured Tipped, Corinthian, Figured Shell. WATROUS MFG. CO.: *(Top to bottom)*: Althea, Dorchester, Richmond. WATSON, NEWELL & CO.: *Top row (l. to r.)*: Bridal Flower, Meadow Rose, Wedding Rose. *Middle row (l. to r.)*: Carnation (Pink), Wild Rose. *Bottom row (l. to r.)*: Peach Blossom, Lily, Orchid, Pine Cone. For R. Wallace & Sons see also Standard Patterns section. For Watson, Newell & Co. see also Standard Patterns and Variations sections.

Watson, Newell & Co.

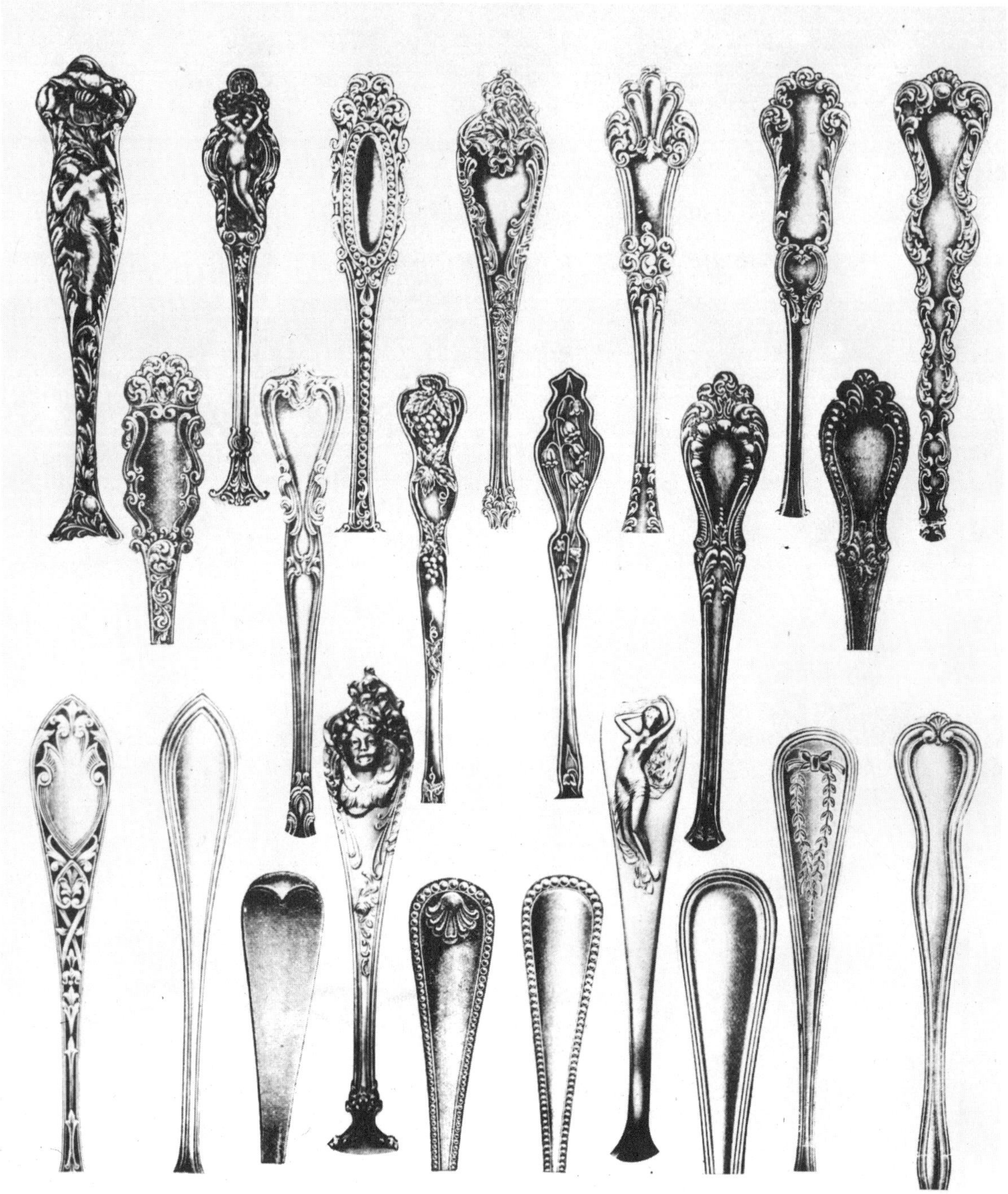

WATSON, NEWELL & CO. (Continued): *Top row (l. to r.)*: Psyche, Phoebe, Eugenie, Altair, Olympia, Oakland, St. Louis. *Middle row (l. to r.)*: Victoria (Old), Victoria (New), Grape, Lily of the Valley, Princess, Jefferson. *Bottom row (l. to r.)*: Orleans, King Phillip, Tipped, Cherub, Dorchester, Plymouth, Watson No. 1, Commonwealth, Commonwealth Engraved, Mt. Vernon. See also Standard Patterns and Variations sections.

Watson, Newell & Co.

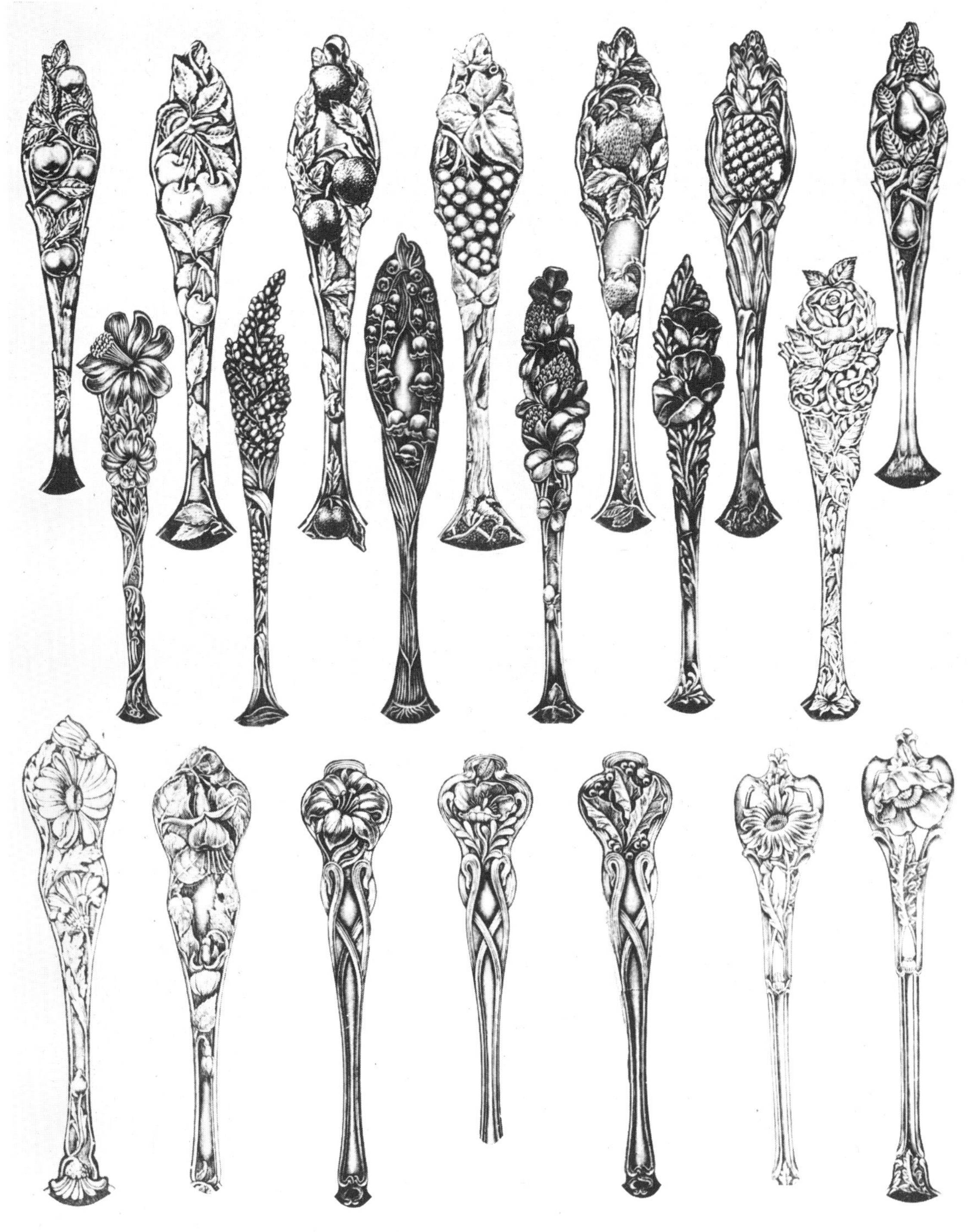

WATSON, NEWELL & CO. (Continued): *Top row (l. to r.)*: Fruit series: Apple, Cherry, Orange, Grape, Strawberry, Pineapple, Pear. *Middle row (l. to r.)*: Floral Series No. 1: Columbine, Golden Rod, Lily of the Valley, Sweet Clover, Poppy, Rose. *Bottom row (l. to r.)*: Floral series No. 2: Daisy, Fuchsia; Floral series No. 3: Easter Lily, Poppy, Holly; Floral series No. 4: Daisy, Poppy. Examples of fruit and floral series patterns. See also Standard Patterns and Variations sections.

Webster & Knowles | Wendell Mfg. Co. | John R. Wendt | F. M. Whiting Co.

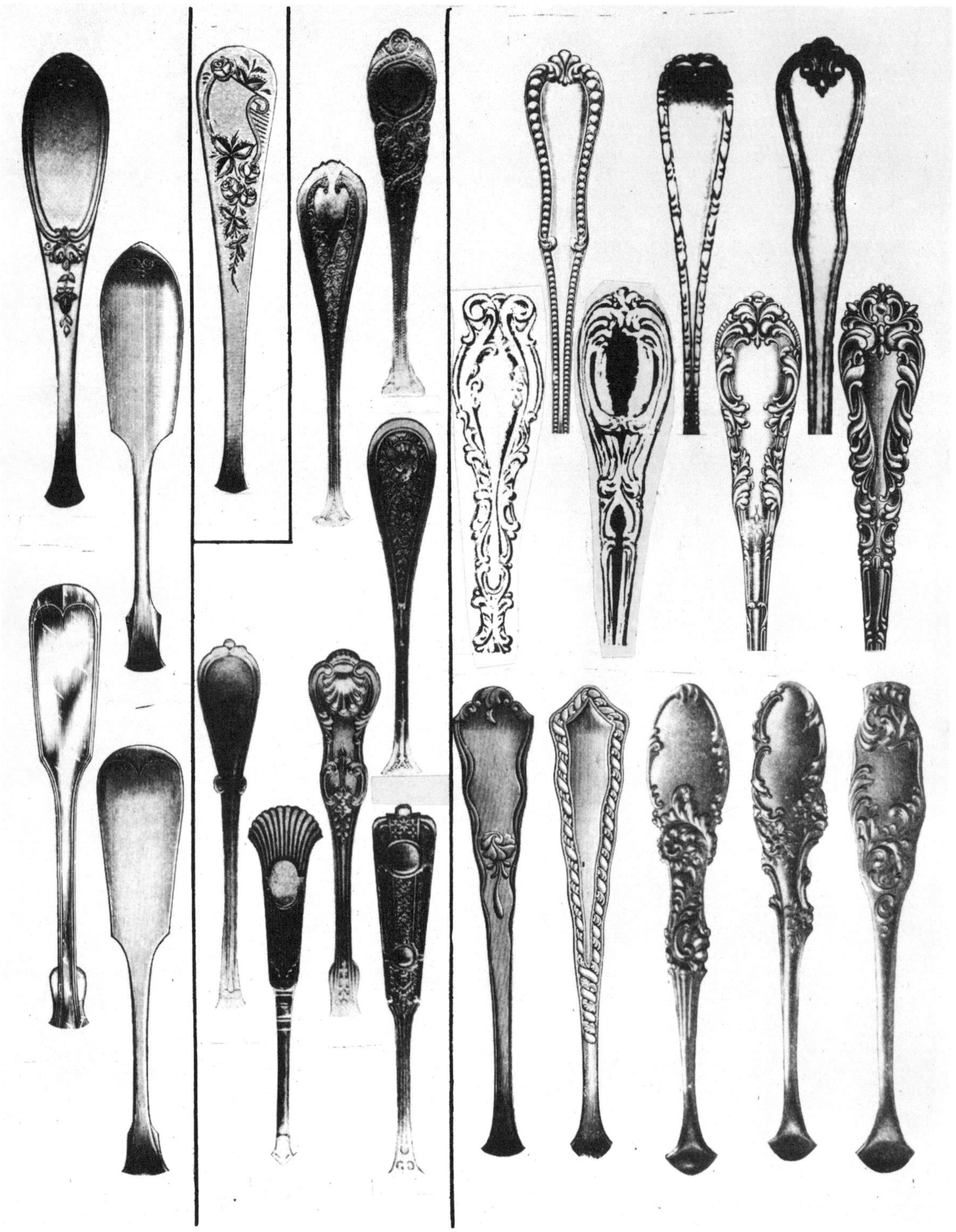

WEBSTER & KNOWLES: *(Top to bottom, staggered)*: Pineapple, Connecticut, French Thread, Straight Tipped. WENDELL MFG. CO.: Rose. JOHN R. WENDT: *Top*: Moresque. *Second row*: Florentine. *Third row*: Bird. *Fourth row (l. to r.)*: Cottage, King's. *Bottom row*: Osiris, Ribbon. F. M. WHITING CO.: *Top row (l. to r.)*: Marlborough, 99, Puritan. *Middle row (l. to r.)*: Josephine, Florence, Flemish, Athene. *Bottom row (l. to r.)*: Gothic, Helena, Tyrolean, Orleans, Esther. For Webster & Knowles, see also Knowles & Ladd and Standard Patterns sections. For F. M. Whiting Co. see also Standard Patterns section. For Wendell Mfg. Co. see also Mauser Mfg. Co., Simmons & Paye, Standard Patterns.

F. M. Whiting Co.

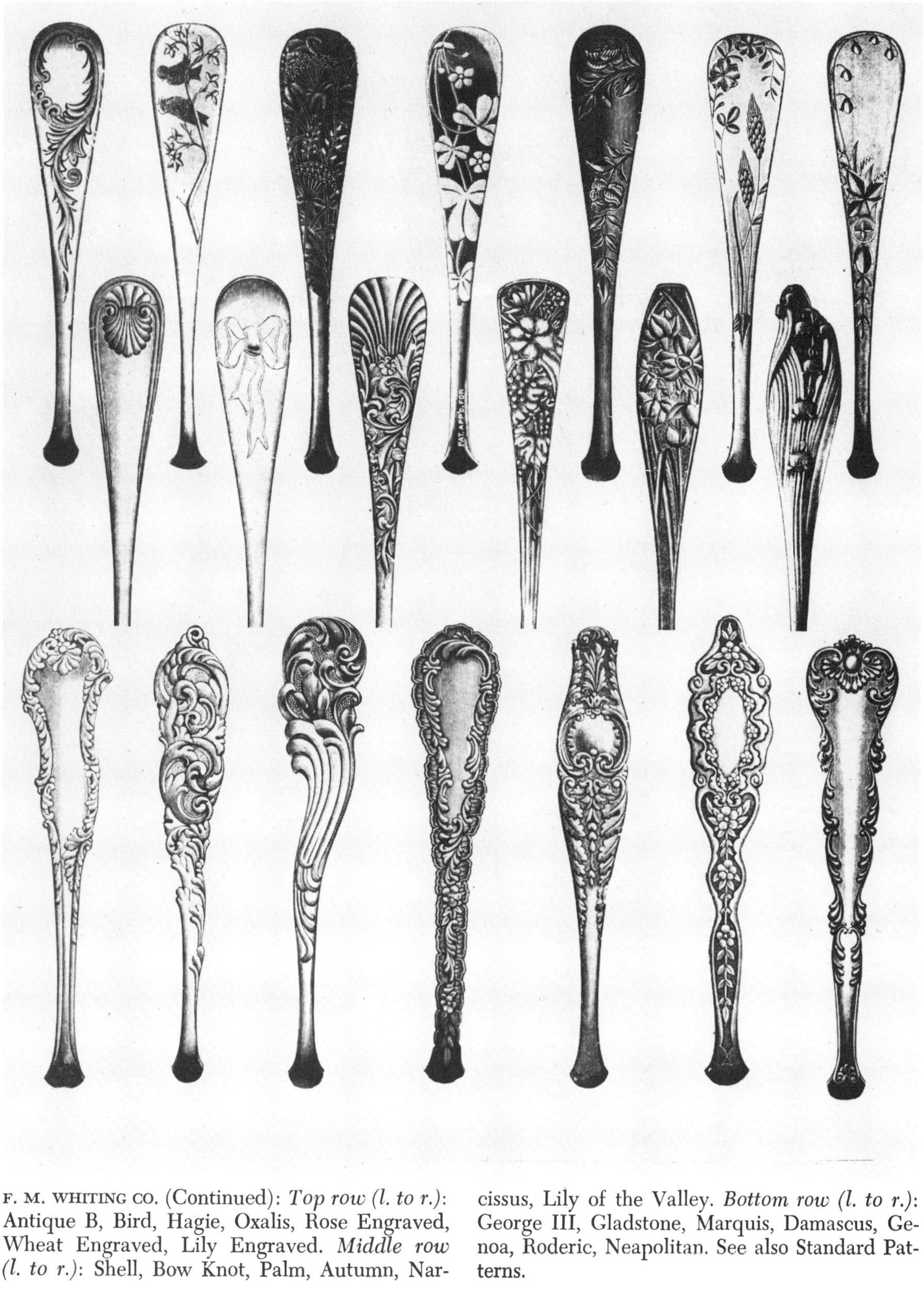

F. M. WHITING CO. (Continued): *Top row (l. to r.)*: Antique B, Bird, Hagie, Oxalis, Rose Engraved, Wheat Engraved, Lily Engraved. *Middle row (l. to r.)*: Shell, Bow Knot, Palm, Autumn, Narcissus, Lily of the Valley. *Bottom row (l. to r.)*: George III, Gladstone, Marquis, Damascus, Genoa, Roderic, Neapolitan. See also Standard Patterns.

The Whiting Mfg. Co.

THE WHITING MFG. CO.: *Top row (l. to r.)*: Home, Grape, Cox, Le Cordon, Antique Engraved, Antique Twist. *Middle row (l. to r.)*: Olive, Mask, Indian, Bead, Fancy Tip, Italian. *Bottom row (l. to r.)*: Tuscan, Empire, Gibney, New Honeysuckle, Honeysuckle, New Jap. See also John R. Wendt, Standard Patterns and Variations sections.

The Whiting Mfg. Co.

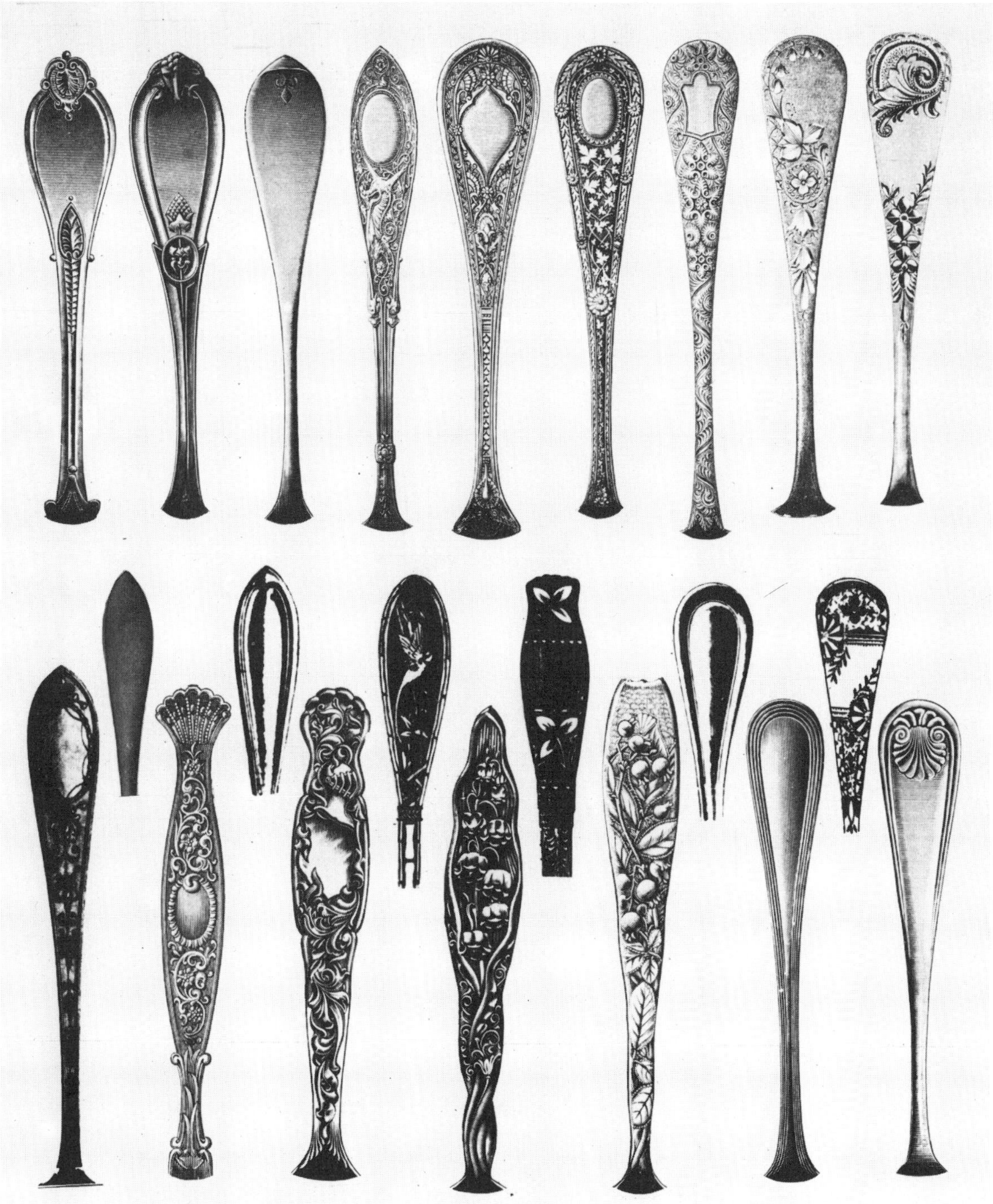

THE WHITING MFG. CO. (Continued): *Top row (l. to r.)*: Armor, Grecian, Antique Tip, Arabesque, Persian, Laureate, Antique (Chased), Antique (Lily Engraved), Antique (M2 Engraved). *Middle row (l. to r.)*: Colonial, Fairfield, Japanese (Jap), Gem Leaf, Eastlake, Antique Rosette. *Bottom row (l. to r)*: Adam, Hyperion, Heraldic, Lily of the Valley, Berry, Villa, Athenian. See also John R. Wendt, Standard Patterns and Variations sections.

The Whiting Mfg. Co.

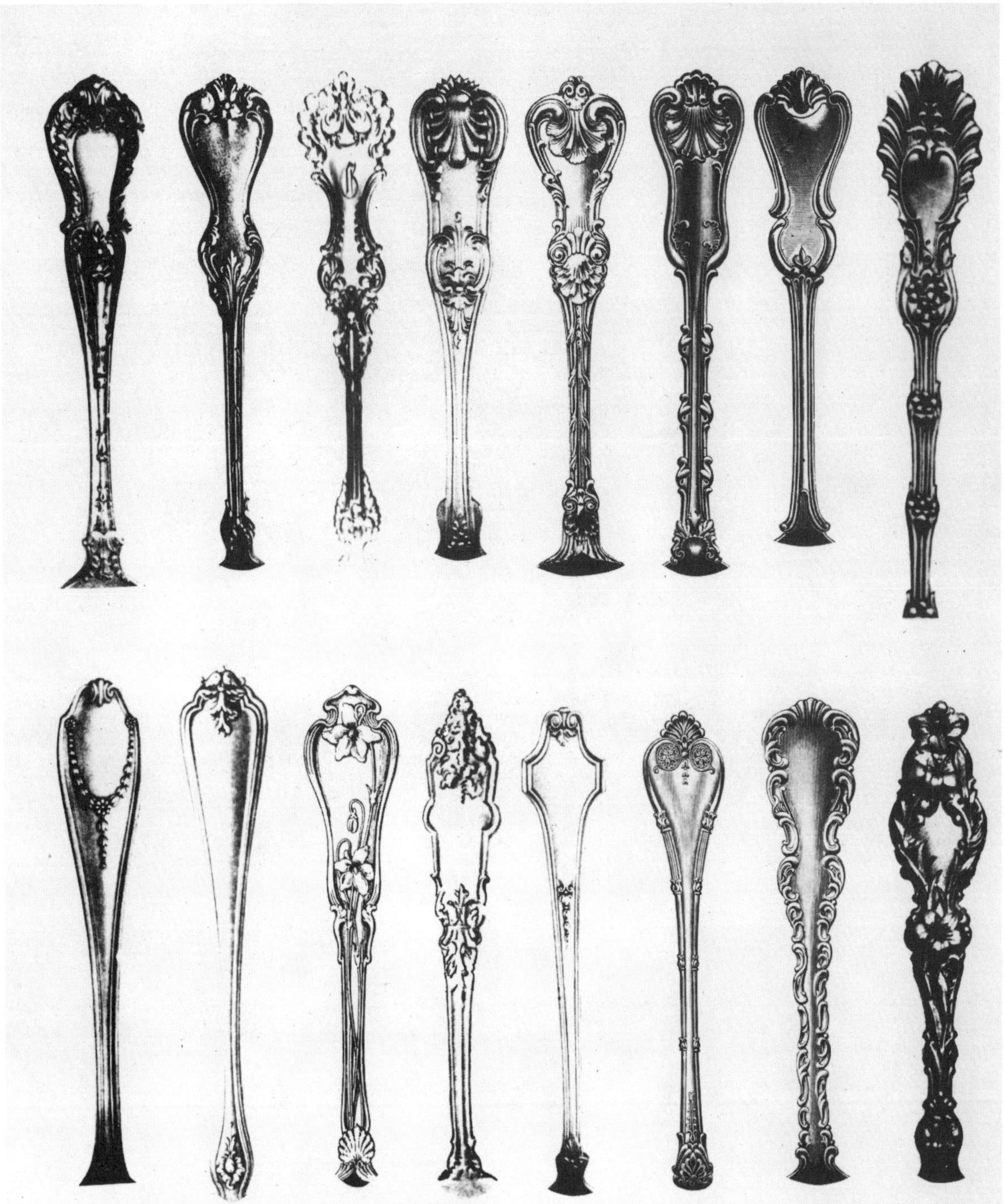

THE WHITING MFG. CO. (Continued): *Top row (l. to r.)*: Dorothy Vernon, Duke of York, Pompadour, Old King, King Edward, Imperial (Imperial Queen), Prince Albert, Radiant. *Bottom row (l. to r.)*: Wedgwood, Duchess, Violet, St. Germaine, Burlington, New Empire, Louis XV, Lily. See also John R. Wendt, Standard Patterns and Variations sections.

The Whiting Mfg. Co.

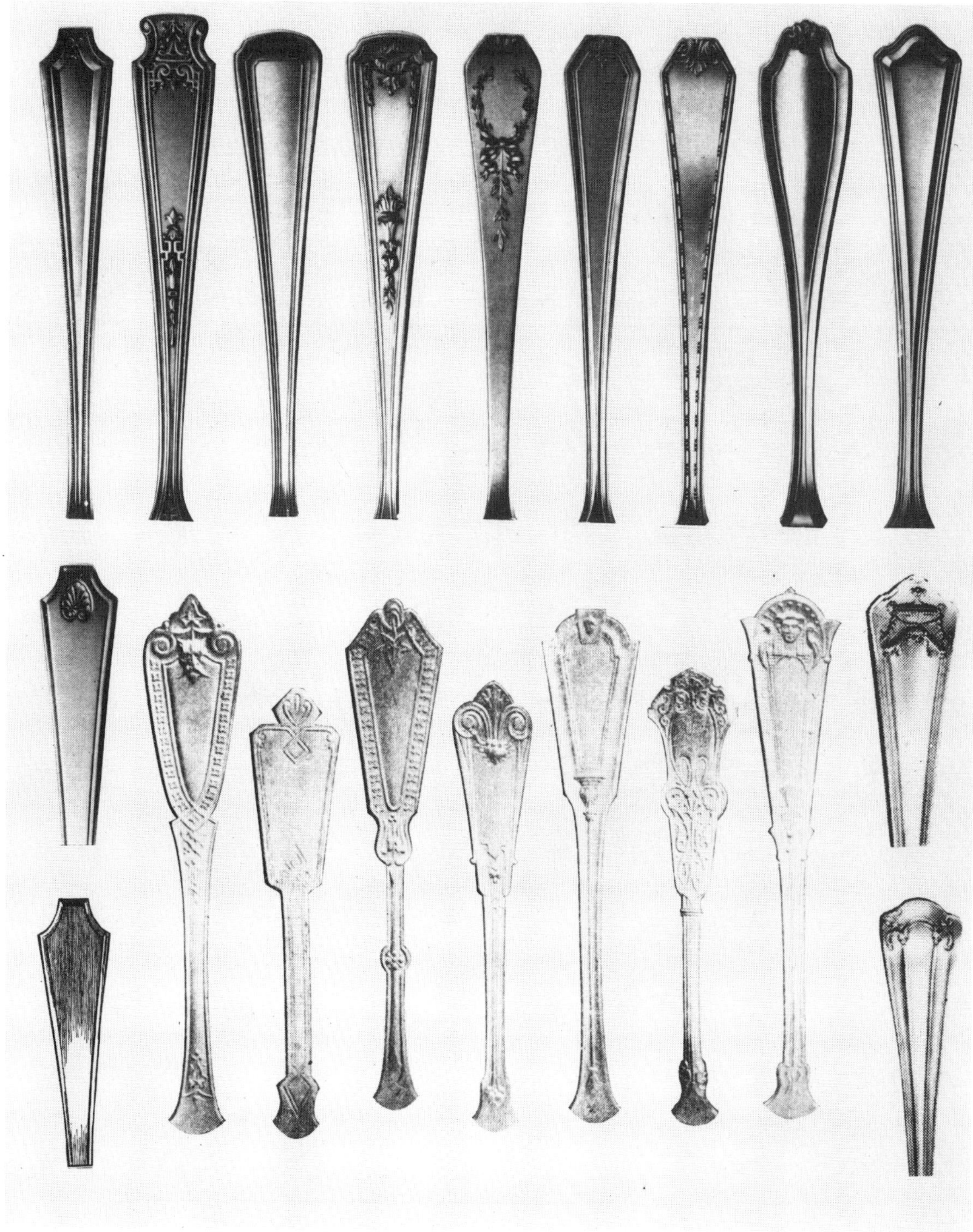

THE WHITING MFG. CO. (Continued): *Top row (l. to r.)*: King Albert, Mandarin, Livingston, Oriana, Madame Jumel, Lady Baltimore, Madame Morris, Stratford, Portland. *Middle, left*: Newport. *Middle, right*: Pompeiian. *Bottom row (l. to r.)*: Jenny Lind, Ivy, Diamond, Rosette, Fruit, Keystone, Alhambra, Egyptian, Stuart. See also John R. Wendt, Standard Patterns and Variations sections.

Wilcox & Evertsen | Roger Williams Silver Co. | A. & W. Wood | Wood & Hughes

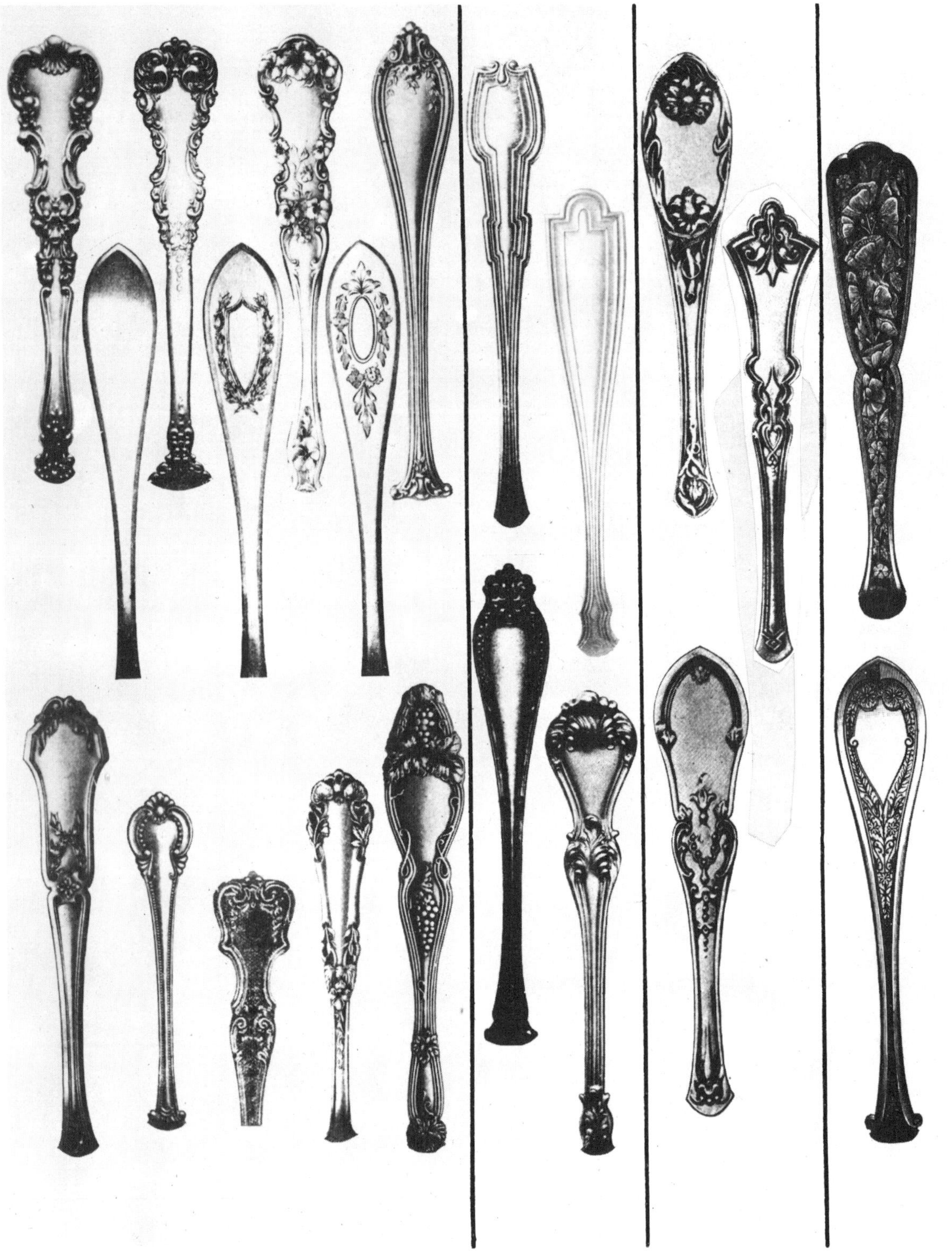

WILCOX & EVERTSEN: *Top row (l. to r.)*: Avalon, Revere, Pansy, Florence. *Middle row (l. to r.)*: John Winthrop, Napoleon, Beverly. *Bottom row (l. to r.)*: La Rochelle, Irene, Litchfield, Marcell, Cloeta. ROGER WILLIAMS SILVER CO.: *(Top to bottom, staggered)*: Venice, Imperial, Florence, Corinthian. A. & W. WOOD: *(Top to bottom, staggered)*: Lily, Clematis, Dew Drop. WOOD & HUGHES: *(Top to bottom)*: Byzantine, Marguerite. For Roger Williams Silver Co. see also Howard Sterling Co. and Standard Patterns sections. For Wood & Hughes see also Wm. Gale & Sons and Standard Patterns sections.

Wood & Hughes

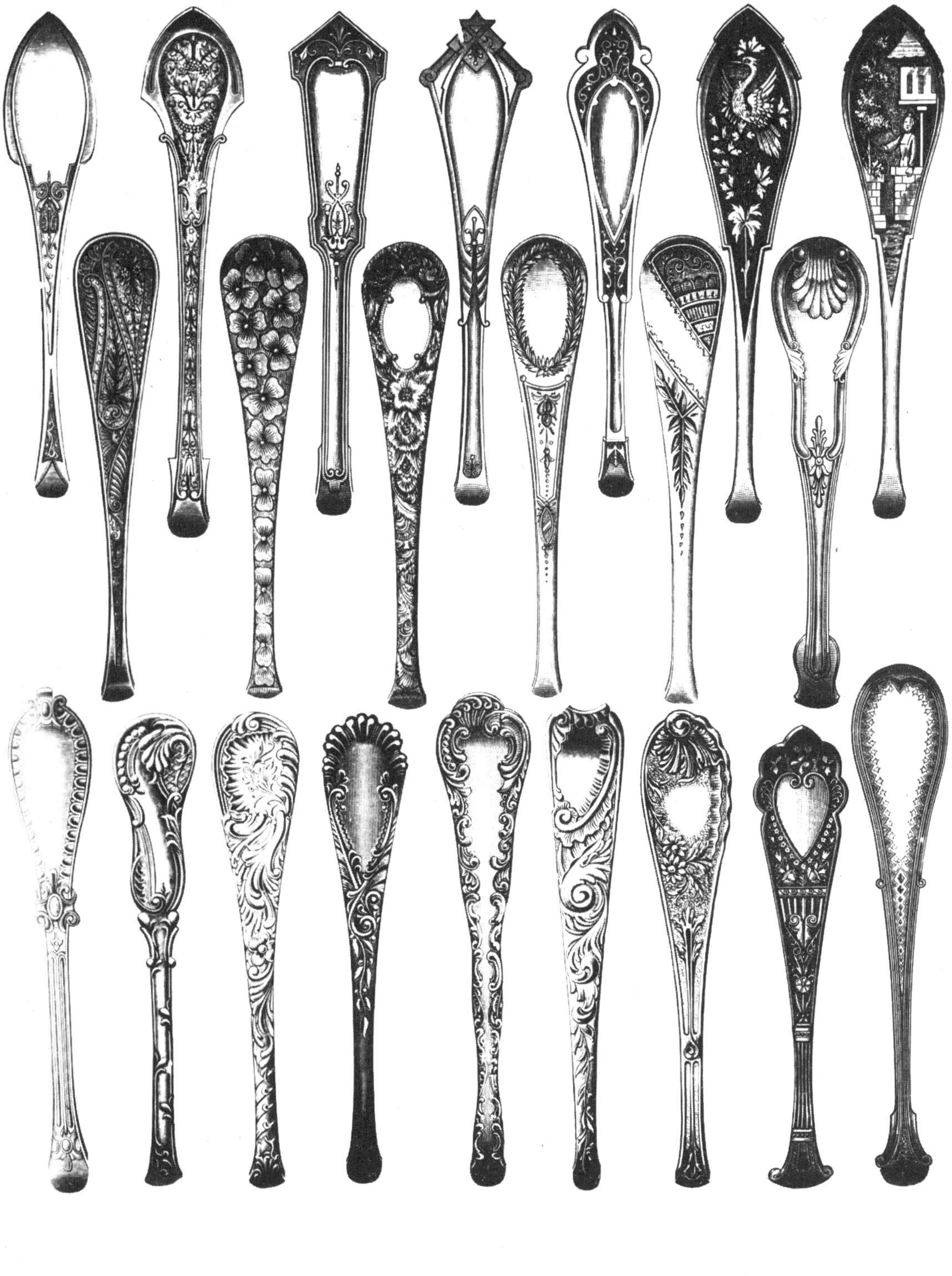

WOOD & HUGHES (Continued): *Top row (l. to r.)*: Zephyr, Angelo, Humboldt, Viola, Venetian, Japanese, Celestial. *Middle row (l. to r.)*: Cashmere, No. 45, No. 8, No. 30, No. 3, New King. *Bottom row (l. to r.)*: Gadroon, Princeton, Louvre, Victoria No. 85, Louis XV, Luxembourg, Undine, Murillo, Cellini. See also Wm. Gale & Sons, Standard Patterns sections.

Electroplate

Alvin Mfg. Co. | American Silver Co.

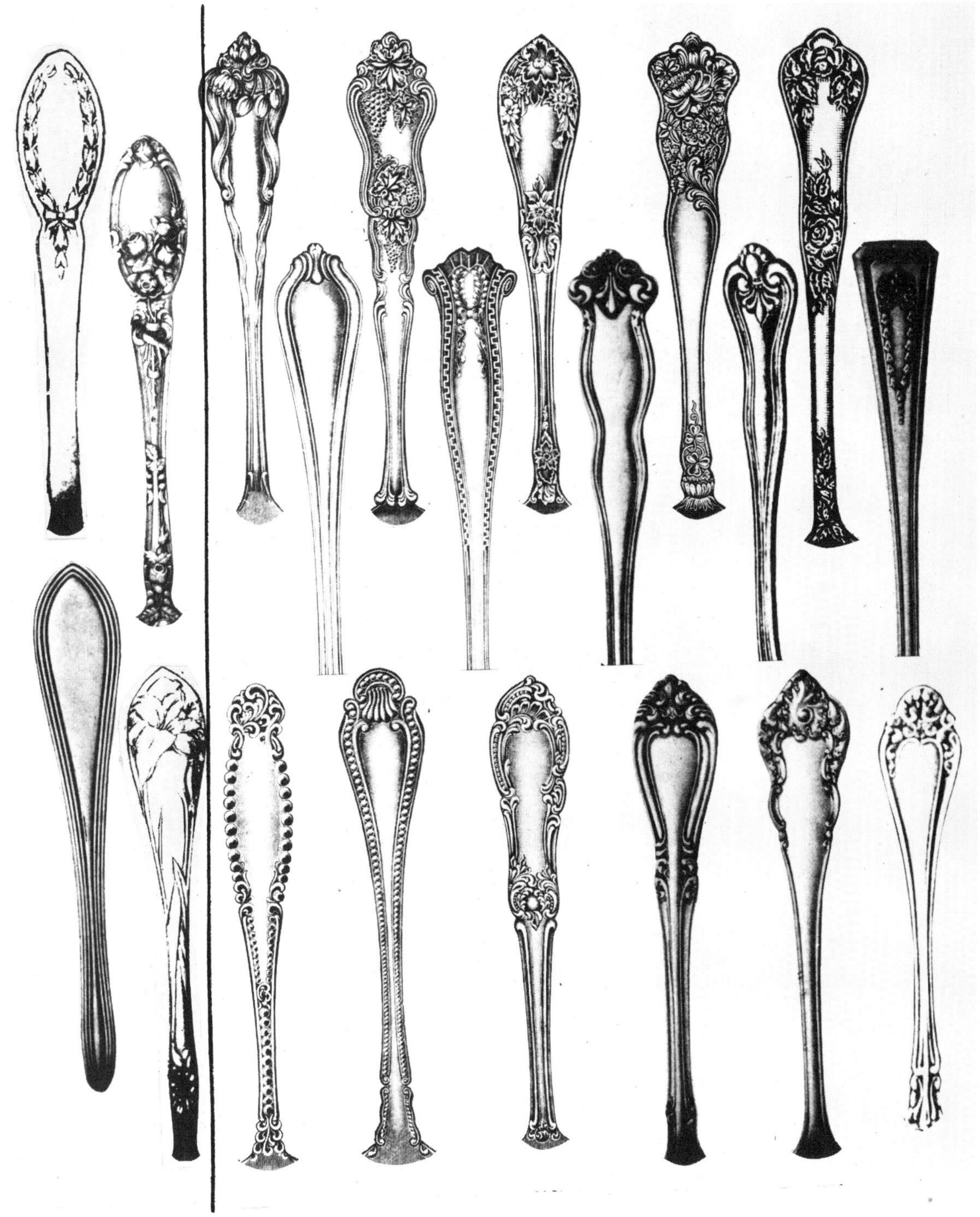

ALVIN MFG. CO.: *(Top to bottom, staggered)*: Diana, Brides Bouquet, Lexington, Easter Lily (Lily). AMERICAN SILVER CO.: *Top row (l. to r.)*: Nenuphar, Moselle, Corona, Wildflower, Rosalie. *Middle row (l. to r.)*: Monticello, Marathon, Ponce de Leon, Vincent, Roanoke. *Bottom row (l. to r.)*: St. Paul, Tours, Loraine, Berlin, Laurence, Oregon. For American Silver Co., see also Standard Patterns section.

Associated Silver Co. | Aurora Silver Plate Co. | Benedict Mfg. Companies | E. A. Bliss Co.

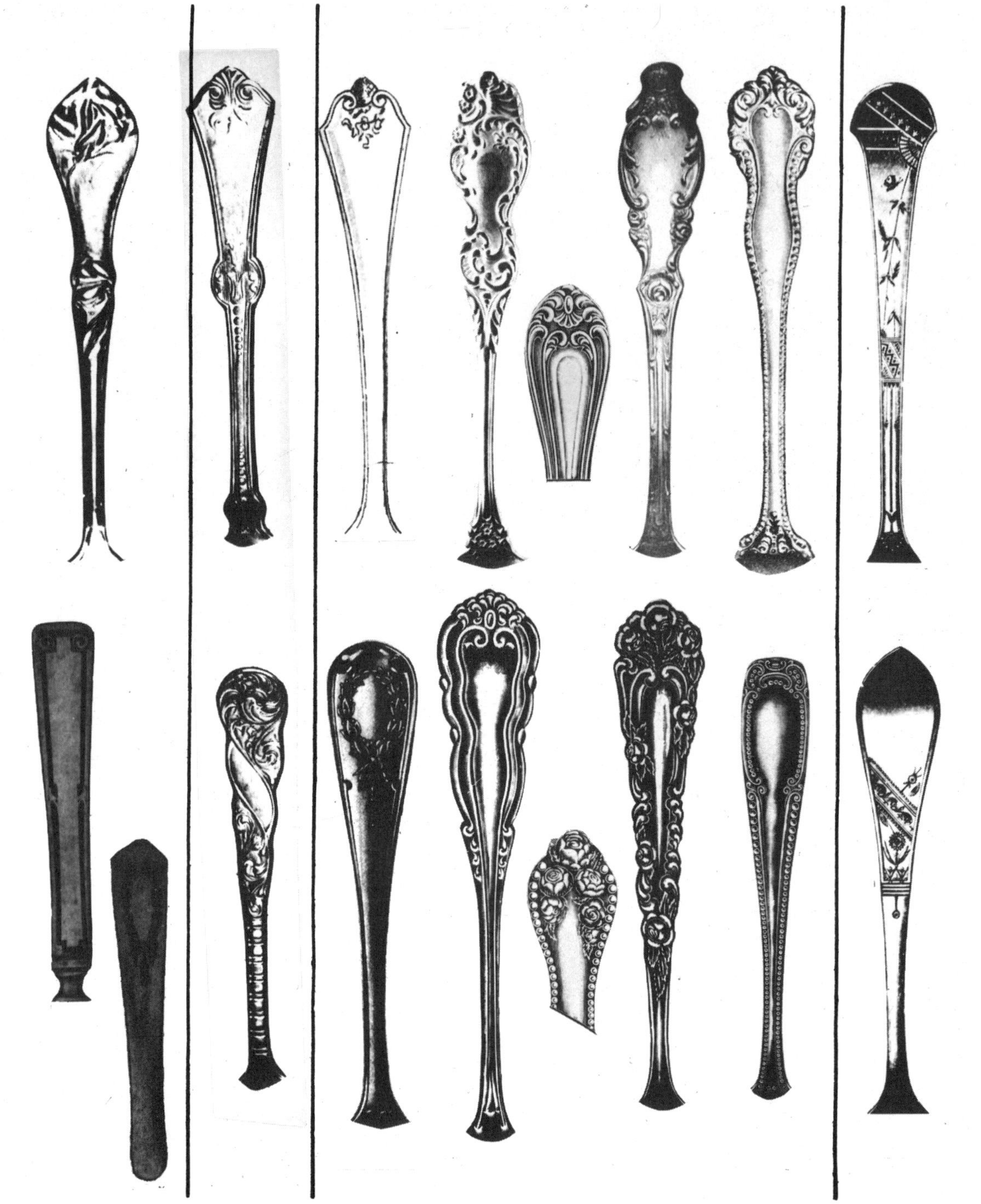

ASSOCIATED SILVER CO.: *(Top to bottom, staggered)*: Sweet Pea, Victory, Marjo-Nell. AURORA SILVER PLATE CO.: *(Top to bottom)*: Aurora No. 1, Royal. BENEDICT MFG. COMPANIES.: *Top row (l. to r.)*: Salem, Benedict No. 1, Solvay, DeWitt, Benedict No. 2. *Bottom row (l. to r.)*: Fairfax, LaFayette, LaFrance Rose, American Beauty, Benedict No. 3. E. A. BLISS CO.: *(Top to bottom)*: Boston, Japanese. For Aurora Silver Plate Co., Benedict Mfg. Companies, and E. A. Bliss Co. see also Standard Patterns section.

L. Boardman & Son — Cambridge Silver Plate Co. — Derby Silver Co.

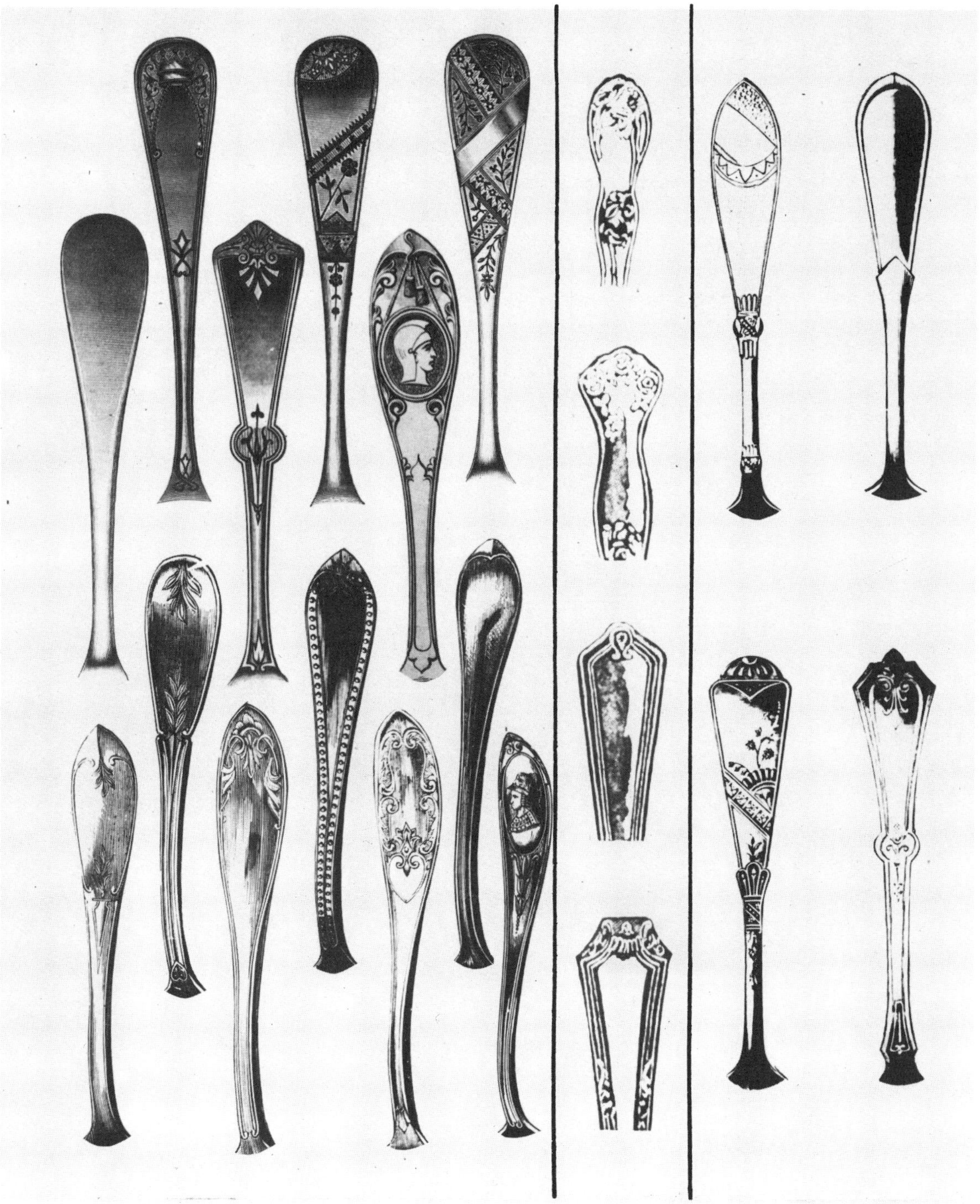

L. BOARDMAN & SON: *Top row (l. to r.)*: Imperial, Warwick, Breton. *Second row (l. to r.)*: French, Persian, Medallion. *Third row (l. to r.)*: Brunswick, Beaded, French Tipped. *Bottom row (l. to r.)*: New Pattern, Silver, American, Medallion No. 2. CAMBRIDGE SILVER PLATE CO.: *(Top to bottom)*: Holyoke, Elmwood, Dunster, Newtown. DERBY SILVER CO.: *Top row (l. to r.)*: Pompeiian, Derby. *Bottom row (l. to r.)*: Harvard, Empress. For L. Boardman & Son and Cambridge Silver Plate Co. see also Standard Patterns section. For Derby Silver Co. see also 1847 Rogers Bros. (Meriden Britannia Co.), Rogers Bros., Rogers Bros. Mfg. Co. and Standard Patterns sections.

Forbes Silver Co. | Glastonbury Silver Co. | Gorham Mfg. Co. | Griffon Cutlery Co. | Hall, Elton & Co.

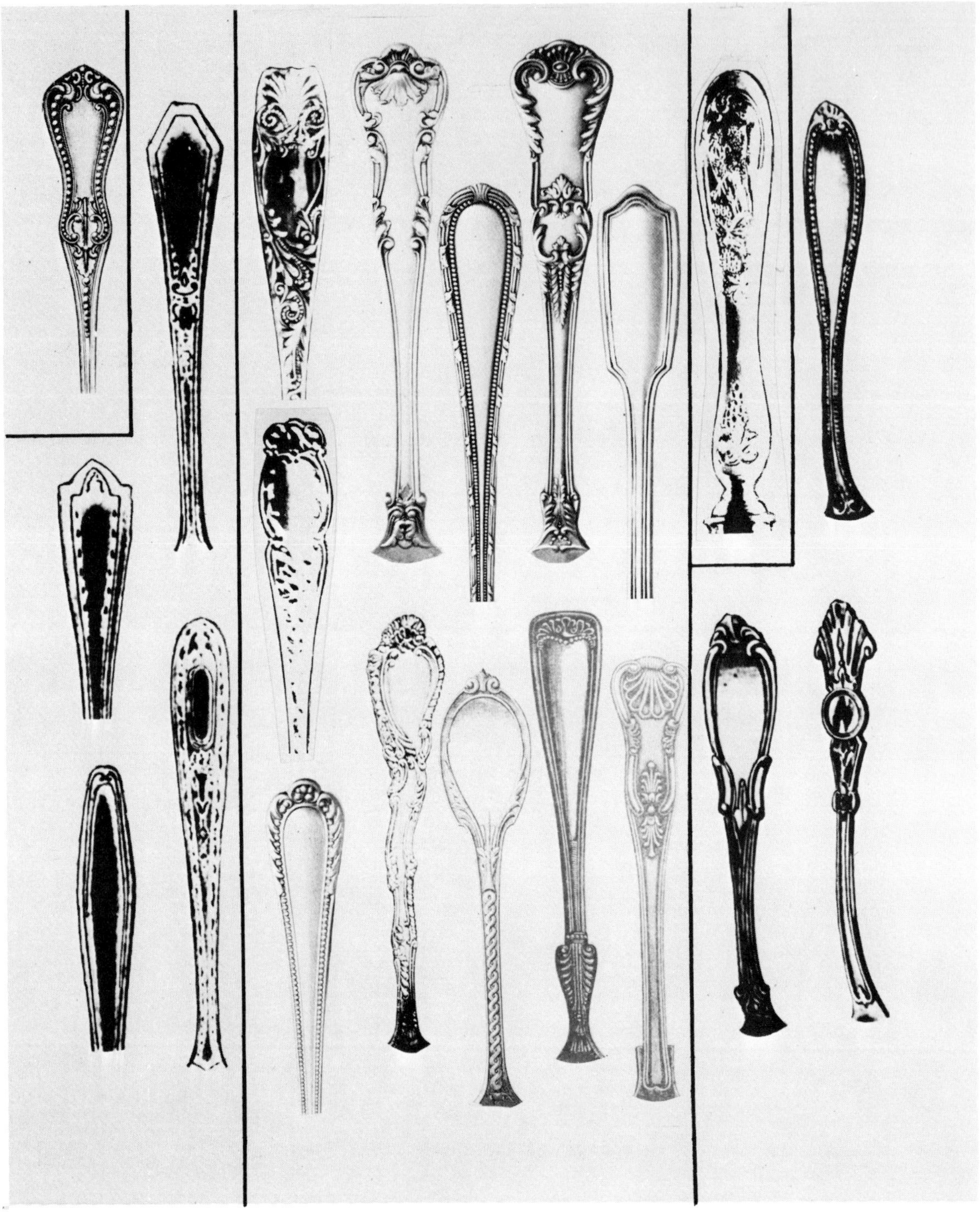

FORBES SILVER CO.: Clovis. GLASTONBURY SILVER CO.: *Top, right*: Pearl. *Middle, left*: Leona. *Bottom (l. to r.)*: Lucille, Queen Bertha. GORHAM MFG. CO.: *Top row (l. to r.)*: Royal, Regent, Richmond. *Middle row (l. to r.)*: Carolina, Empire, Stanhope. *Bottom row (l. to r.)*: Winthrop, Saxony, Roman, Princess Louise, Kings. GRIFFON CUTLERY CO: Griffon No. 1. HALL, ELTON & CO.: *Top*: Beaded. *Bottom (l. to r.)*: Florence, Egyptian. For Forbes Silver Co., Glastonbury Silver Co., and Hall, Elton & Co. see also Standard Patterns section. For Gorham Mfg. Co. see also Gorham Mfg. Co. Sterling and Standard Patterns sections.

Hall, Elton & Co. | Holmes, Booth & Haydens | The Holmes & Edwards Silver Co.

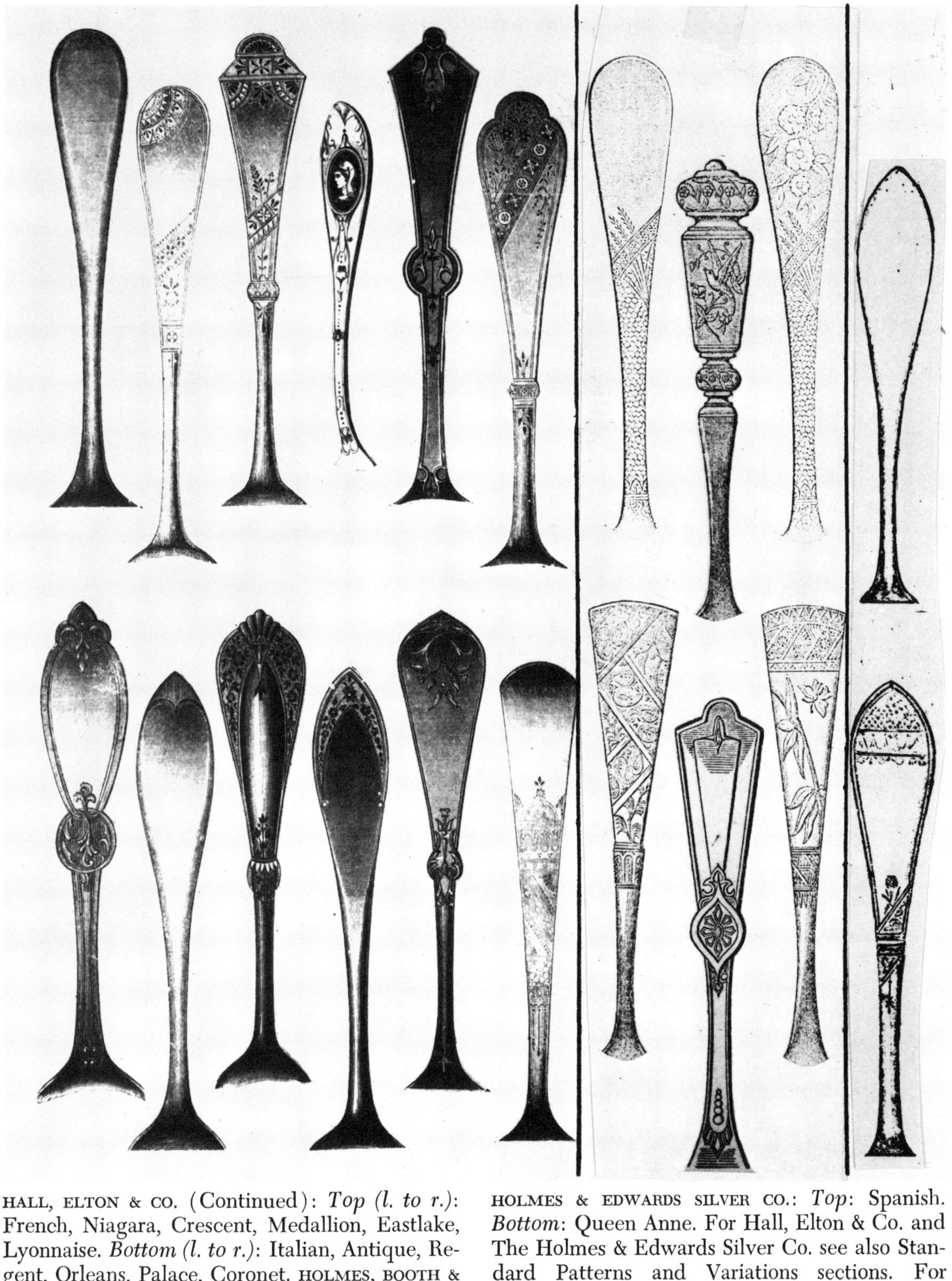

HALL, ELTON & CO. (Continued): *Top (l. to r.)*: French, Niagara, Crescent, Medallion, Eastlake, Lyonnaise. *Bottom (l. to r.)*: Italian, Antique, Regent, Orleans, Palace, Coronet. HOLMES, BOOTH & HAYDENS: *Top (l. to r.)*: Palace, Corona, Corinth. *Bottom (l. to r.)*: India, Roman, Japanese. THE HOLMES & EDWARDS SILVER CO.: *Top*: Spanish. *Bottom*: Queen Anne. For Hall, Elton & Co. and The Holmes & Edwards Silver Co. see also Standard Patterns and Variations sections. For Holmes, Booth & Haydens see also Standard Patterns section.

The Holmes & Edwards Silver Co.

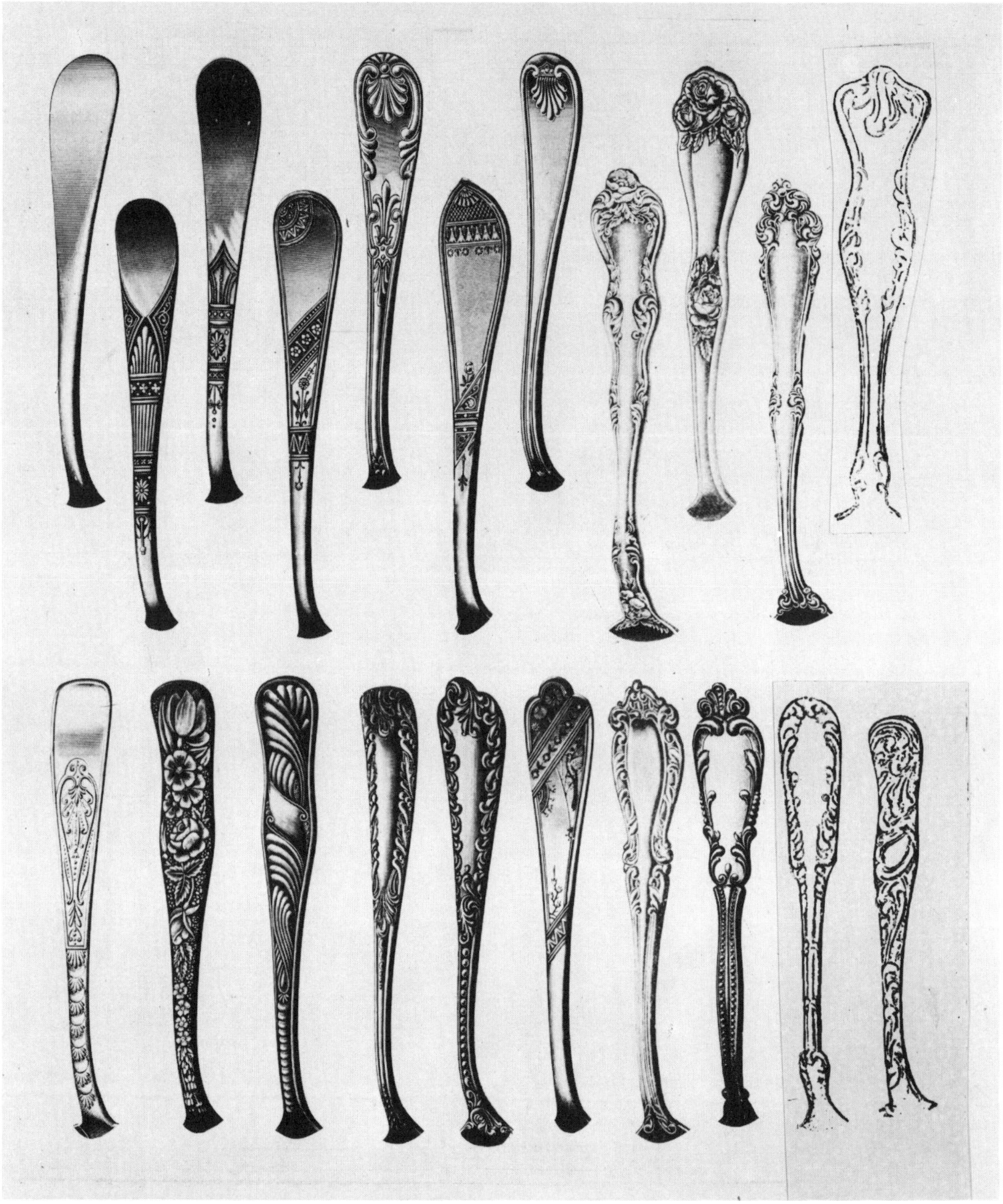

THE HOLMES & EDWARDS SILVER CO. (Continued): *Top row (l. to r.)*: Perfect, Mayflower, King, Shell Thread, American Beauty Rose, Westfield. *Middle row (l. to r.)*: Leader, Angelo, Queen, Orient, Imperial. *Bottom row (l. to r.)*: Greek, Flower, Warner, Irving, Liberty, Eastlake, Nassau, Marina, Montauk, Triumph. See also Standard Patterns and Variations sections.

The Holmes & Edwards Silver Co. | Lakeside | Landers, Frary & Clark | Mc Glashan, Clarke & Co.

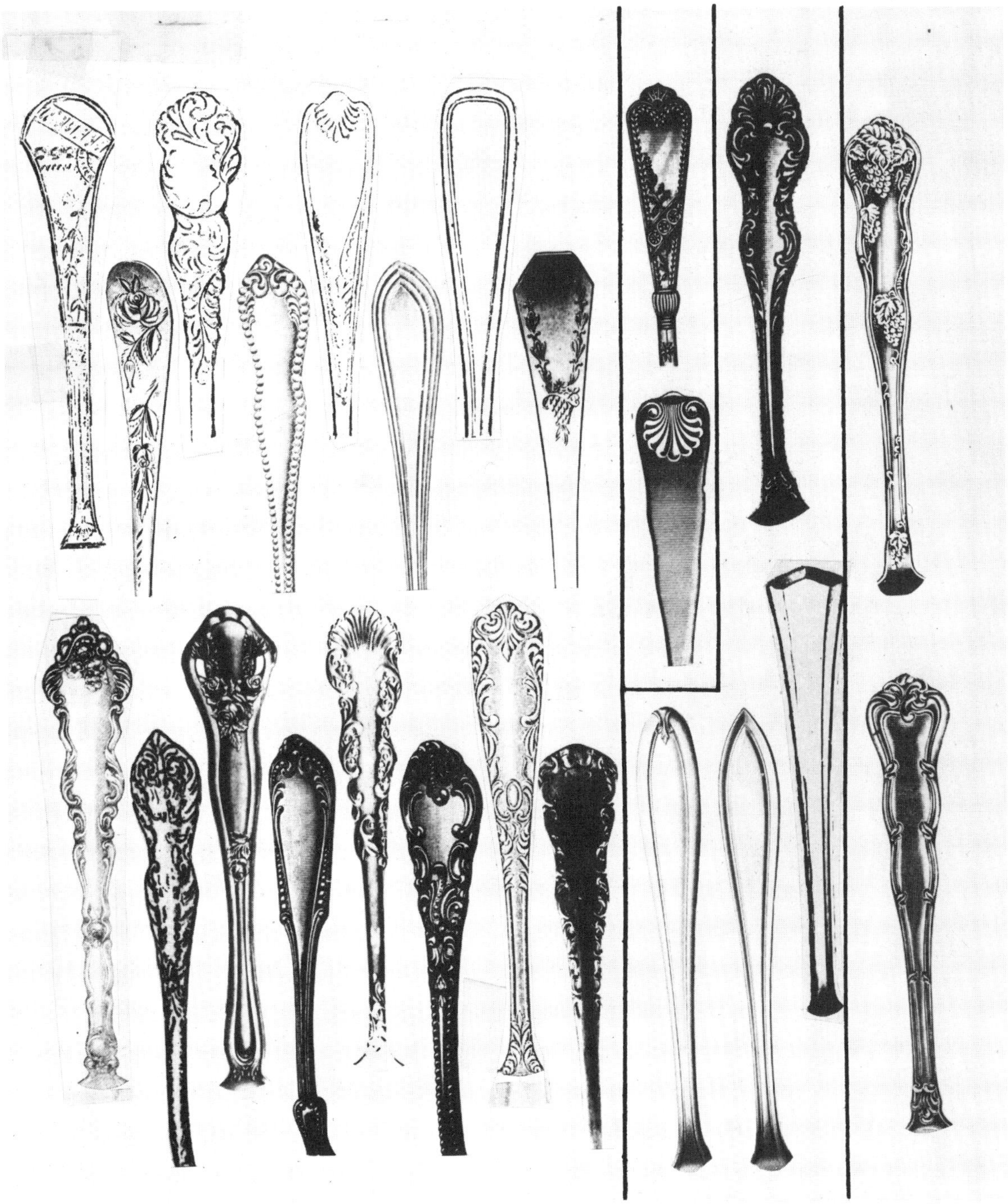

THE HOLMES & EDWARDS SILVER CO. (Continued): *Top row (l. to r.)*: Japanese, Rialto, Minnehaha, Thread Hotel. *Second row (l. to r.)*: Jac Rose, Pearl, Washington, Carolina. *Third row (l. to r.)*: LaFayette, Dolly Madison, Waldorf, Eugene. *Bottom row (l. to r.)*: Delsarte, Unique, Lincoln, Lashar No. 1. LAKESIDE: *Top*: Chicago. *Bottom*: Shell. LANDERS, FRARY & CLARK: *Top*: No. 1731. *Middle right*: Farmington. *Bottom row (l. to r.)*: Newington, Saybrook. MCGLASHAN, CLARKE & CO.: *Top*: Grape. *Bottom*: Elsmere. For The Holmes & Edwards Silver Co. see also Standard Patterns and Variations sections. For Lakeside, Landers, Frary & Clark, and McGlashan, Clarke & Co. see also Standard Patterns section.

Niagara Silver Co. | Niagara Falls Silver Co. | Oneida Community

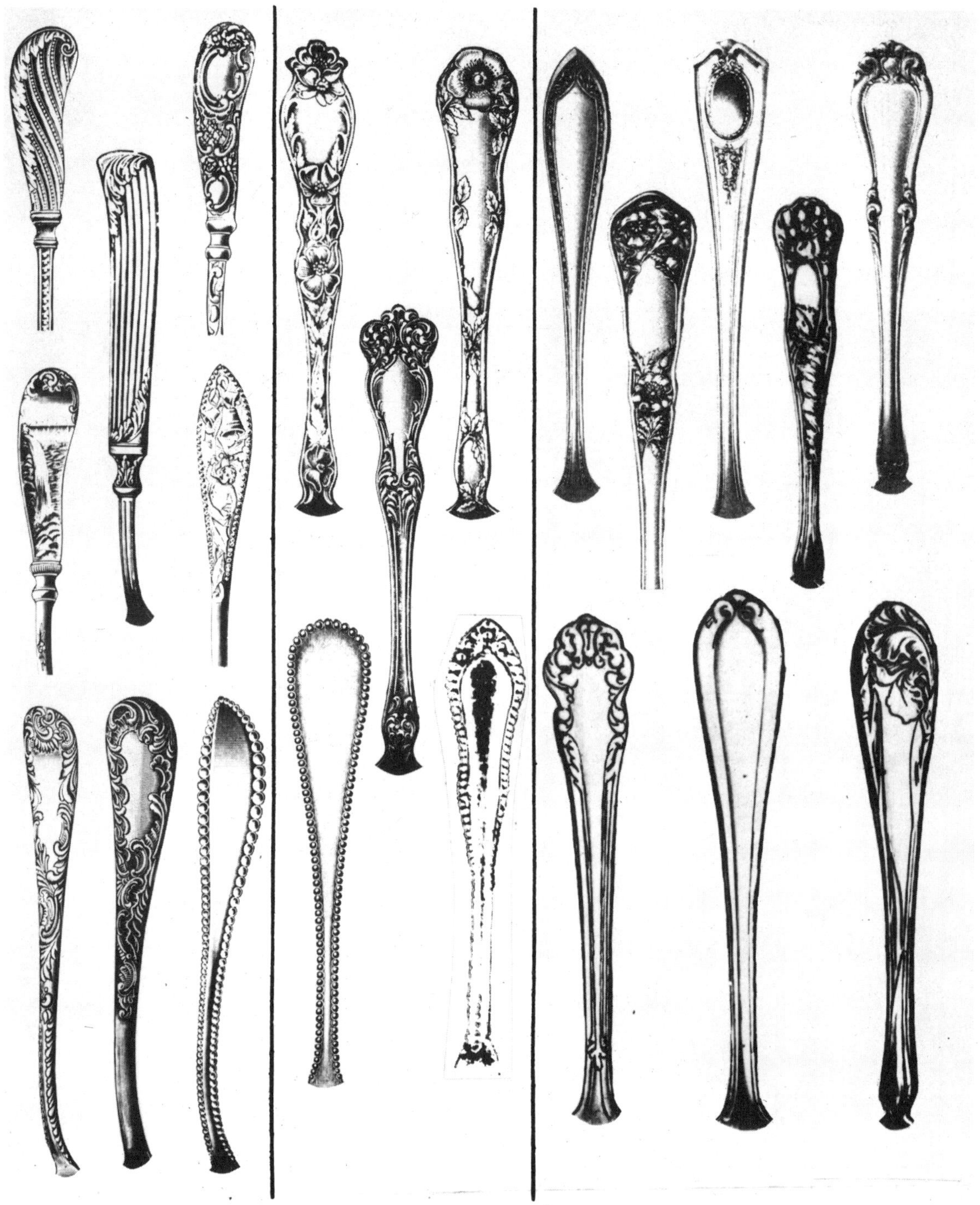

NIAGARA SILVER CO.: *Top row (l. to r.)*: Cinderella, Gladys. *Middle row (l. to r.)*: Cascade, Iroquois, Beaded Cherub. *Bottom row (l. to r.)*: Vernon, Tacoma, Alberta. NIAGARA FALLS SILVER CO.: *Top row (l. to r.)*: Adams, Wild Rose. *Middle*: Essex. *Bottom row (l. to r.)*: Colonial, Niagara Falls No. 1. ONEIDA COMMUNITY: *Top row (l. to r.)*: Sheraton, Louis XVI, Kenwood. *Middle row (l. to r.)*: Wildwood, Cereta. *Bottom row (l. to r.)*: Avalon, Classic, Fleur de Luce (Flower de Luce). For all companies on this page see also Standard Patterns section.

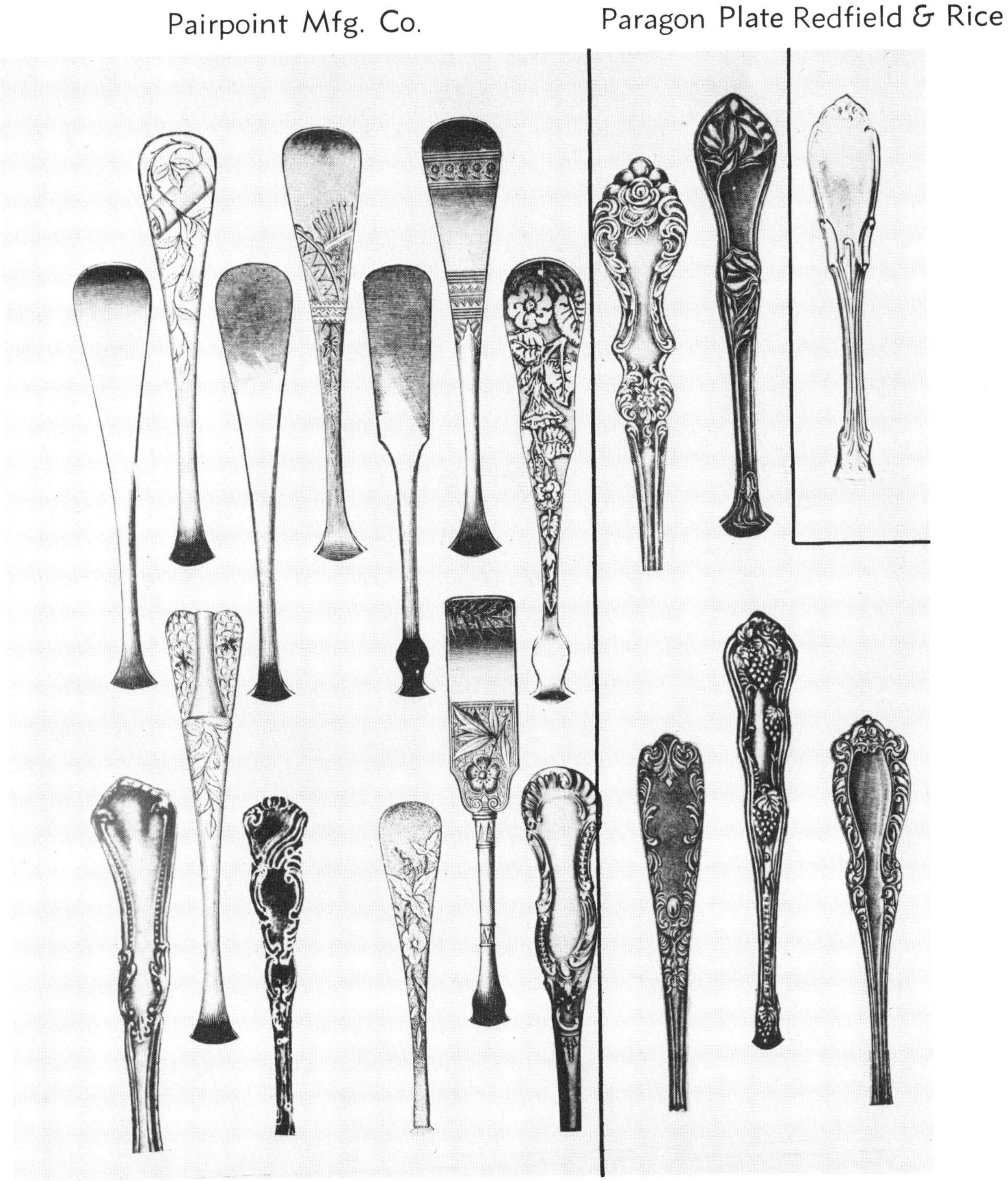

PAIRPOINT MFG. CO.: *Top row (l. to r.)*: Essex, India, Ascot. *Second row (l. to r.)*: Brighton, Dover, Plain, Morning Glory. *Third row (l. to r.)*: Laurion, Croyden. *Bottom row (l. to r.)*: Clifton, Erminie, Mistletoe, Arlington. PARAGON PLATE: *Top (l. to r.)*: Rose, Sweet Pea. *Bottom (l. to r.)*: Colonial, Muscatel, Fleur de Lis. REDFIELD & RICE: Florence. For all companies on this page see also Standard Patterns section.

Reed & Barton

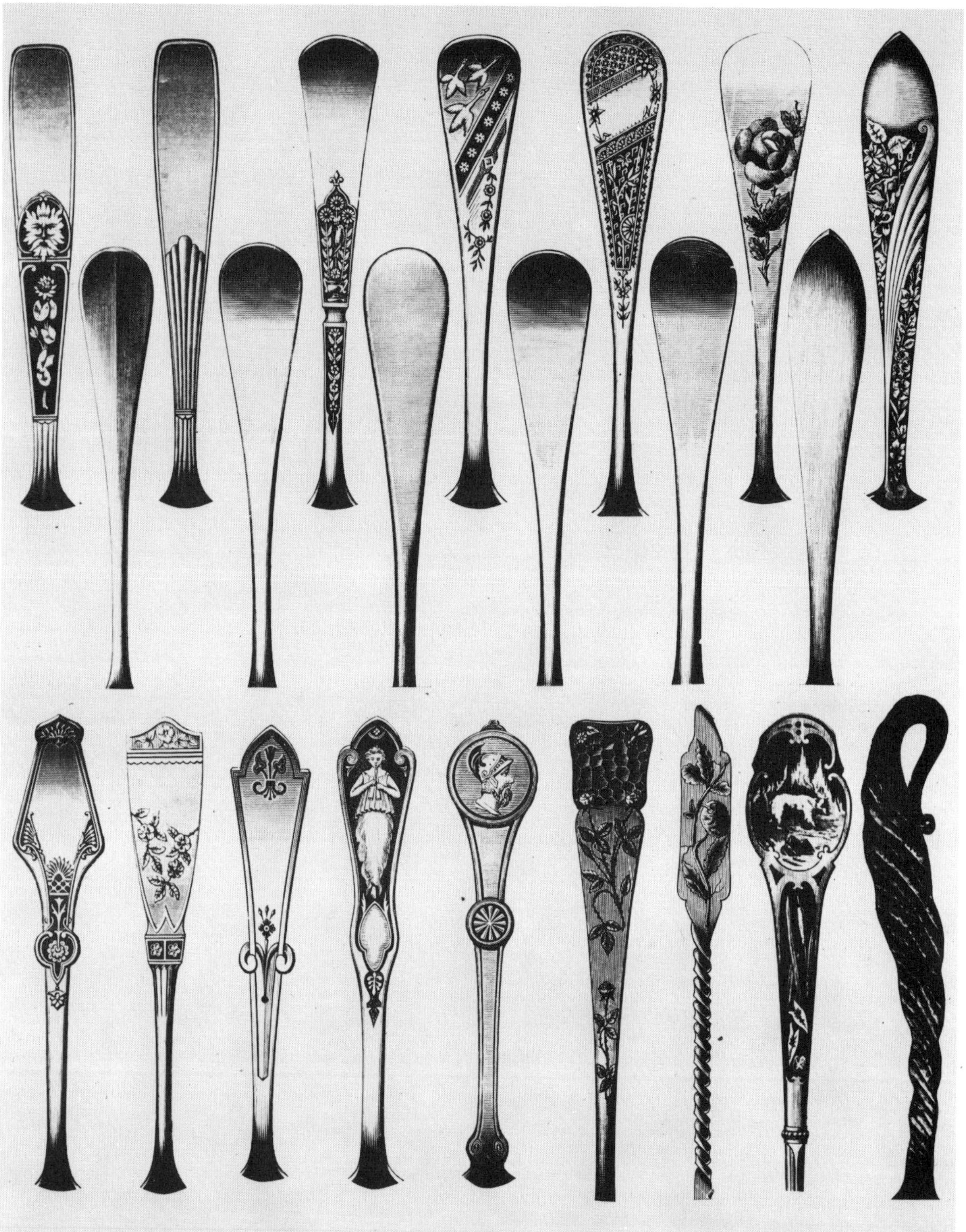

REED & BARTON: *Top row (l. to r.)*: Italian, Vendome, Unique, Japanese, Brilliant, Bijou, Cashmere. *Middle row (l. to r.)*: Spanish, Florence, Oxford, Palace, French, Brunswick. *Bottom row (l. to r.)*: Orient, Parisian, Gem, Pearl, Roman Medallion, Russian, Swiss, Arctic, Venetian. See also Standard Patterns.

Reed & Barton   Rockford Silver Plate Co.

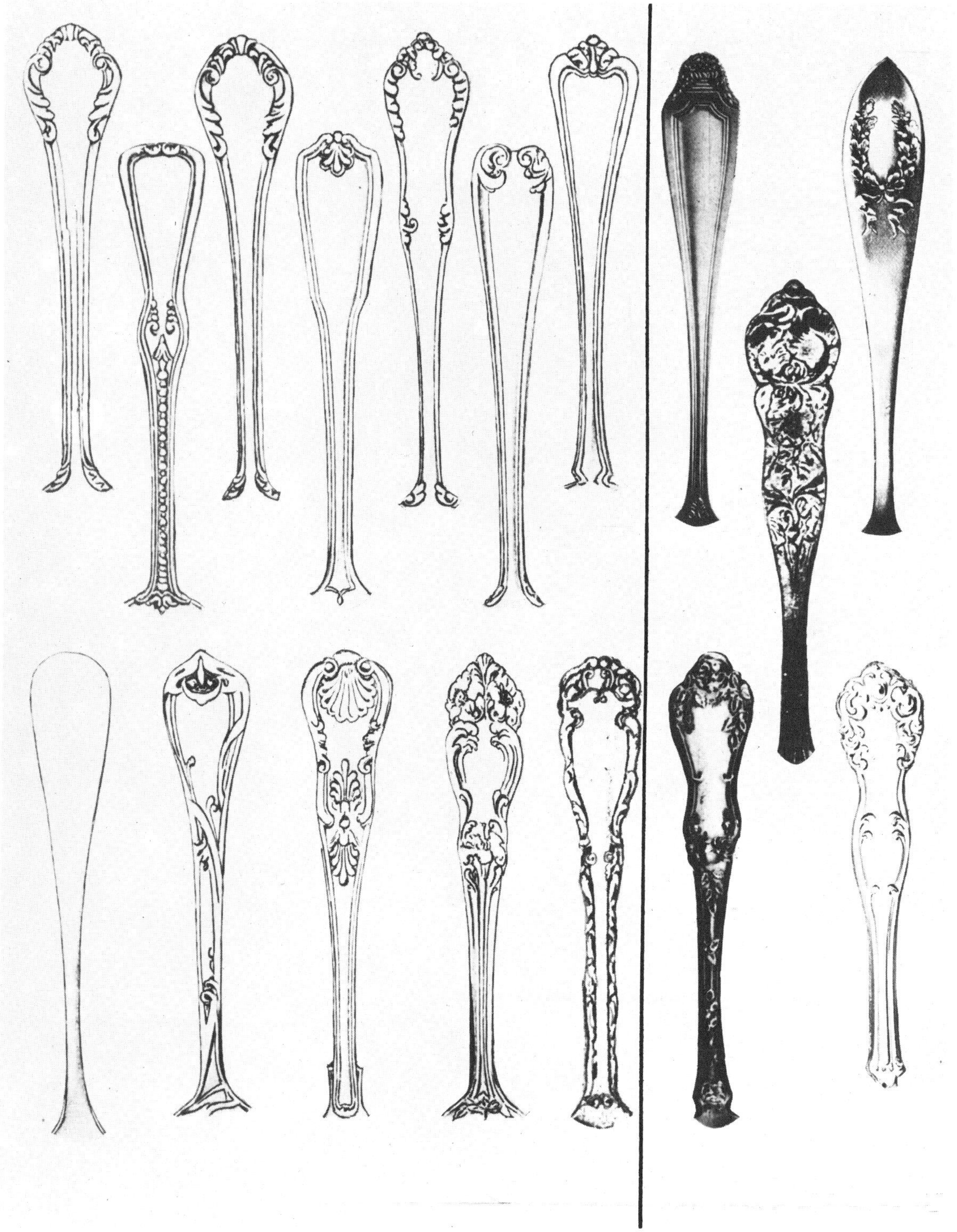

REED & BARTON (Continued): *Top row (l. to r.)*: Cecil, Royal, Carlton, Alden. *Middle row (l. to r.)*: LaMode, Commonwealth, Belmont. *Bottom row (l. to r.)*: LeGrand, Modern Art, Kings, Tiger Lily, Rex. ROCKFORD SILVER PLATE CO.: *Top row (l. to r.)*: Hawthorne, Fairoaks. *Middle*: Louvre. *Bottom row (l. to r.)*: Rosemary, Rockford No. 1. For Reed & Barton see also Standard Patterns section. For Rockford Silver Plate Co. see also Pairpoint Mfg. Co., Williams Bros. Mfg. Co., and Standard Patterns sections.

Rogers & Bro.

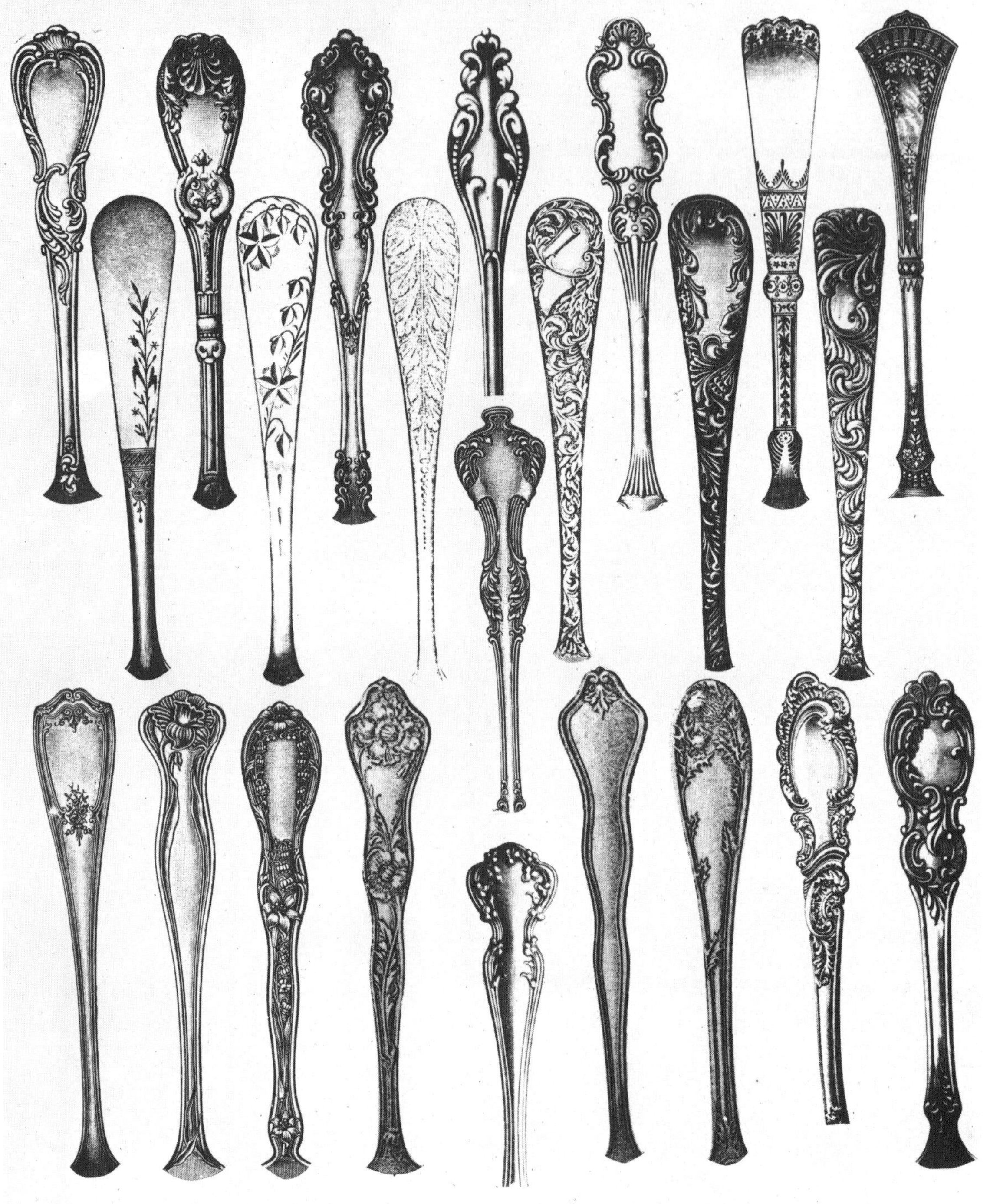

ROGERS & BRO.: *Top row (l. to r.)*: Navarre, Tuxedo, New Century, Cornell, Flemish, Attica, Crown. *Middle row (l. to r.)*: Spray, Belle, Acanthus, Crest, Victoria, Crystal, Nevada. *Bottom row (l. to r.)*: Verona, Mystic, Florette, Poppy, Belmont, Elton, Thistle, Aldine, Princeton. See also 1847 Rogers Bros. (Meriden Britannia Co.), Rogers Bros., Rogers Bros. Mfg. Co., Rogers, Smith & Co., Rogers & Hamilton, Wm. Rogers Mfg. Co., Standard Patterns and Variations sections.

Rogers & Bro. Rogers Bros. Rogers Bros. Mfg. Co. 1847 Rogers Bros. (Meriden Britannia Co.)

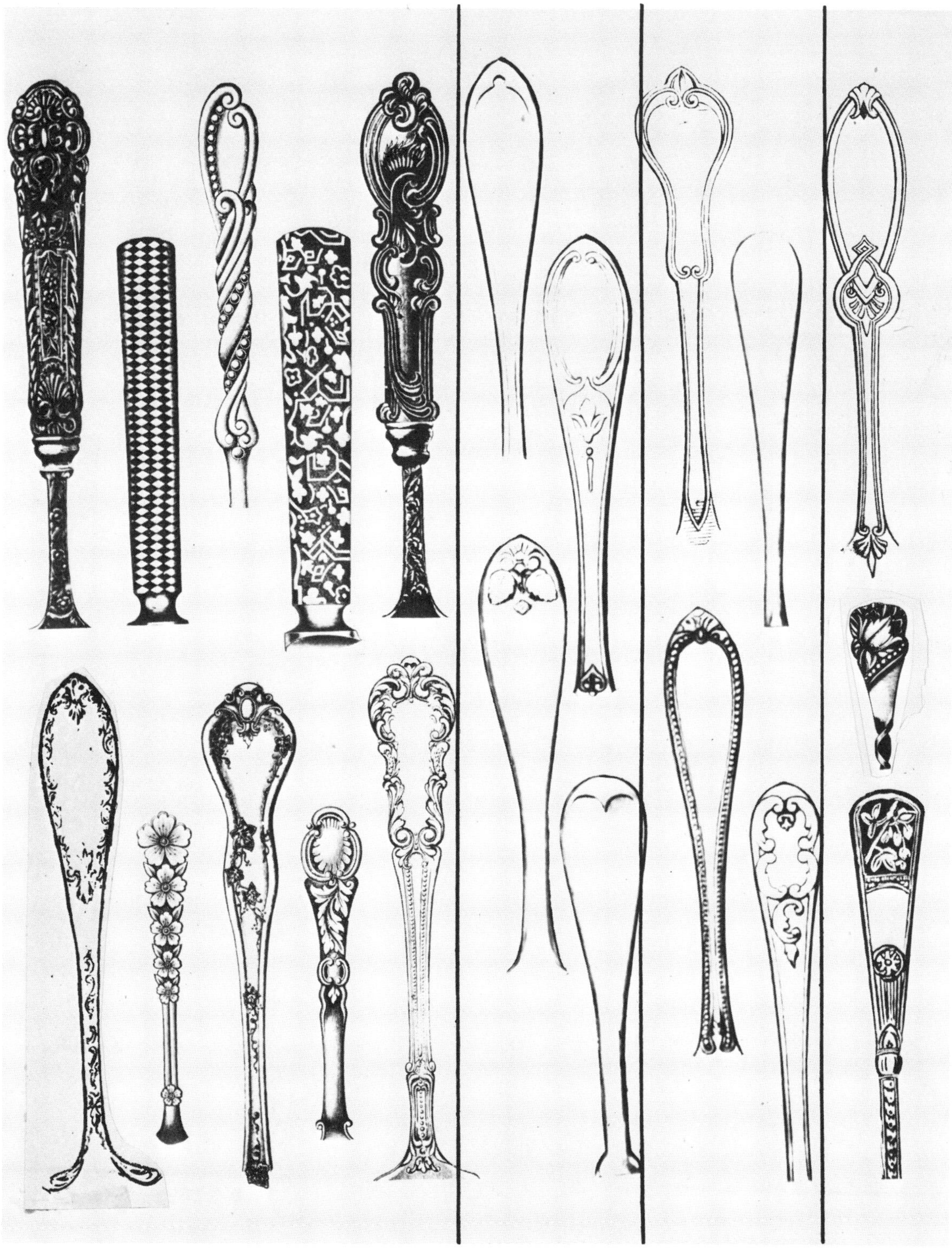

ROGERS & BRO. (Continued): *Top row (l. to r.)*: Ionic, Diamond, Colonade, Eastlake, Rajah. *Bottom row (l. to r.)*: Harold, Primrose, Ivy, Plaza, Halcyon. ROGERS BROS.: *(Top to bottom, staggered)*: French Oval, Tuscan, Silver, Antique. ROGERS BROS. MFG. CO.: *(Top to bottom, staggered)*: Gothic, Spanish, Beaded, St. Charles. 1847 ROGERS BROS. (MERIDEN BRITANNIA CO.): *(Top to bottom)*: Roman, Floral, Nevada. For Rogers & Bro. see also 1847 Rogers Bros. (Meriden Britannia Co.), Rogers Bros., Rogers Bros. Mfg. Co., Rogers, Smith & Co., Rogers & Hamilton, Wm. Rogers Mfg. Co., Standard Patterns and Variations sections. For 1847 Rogers Bros. (Meriden Britannia Co.) see also Rogers Bros., Rogers Bros. Mfg. Co., Rogers & Bro., Rogers, Smith & Co., Rogers & Hamilton, Simpson, Hall, Miller & Co. (Wm. Rogers Eagle Brand), Wm. Rogers Mfg. Co., Standard Patterns and Variations sections.

1847 Rogers Bros. (Meriden Britannia Co.)

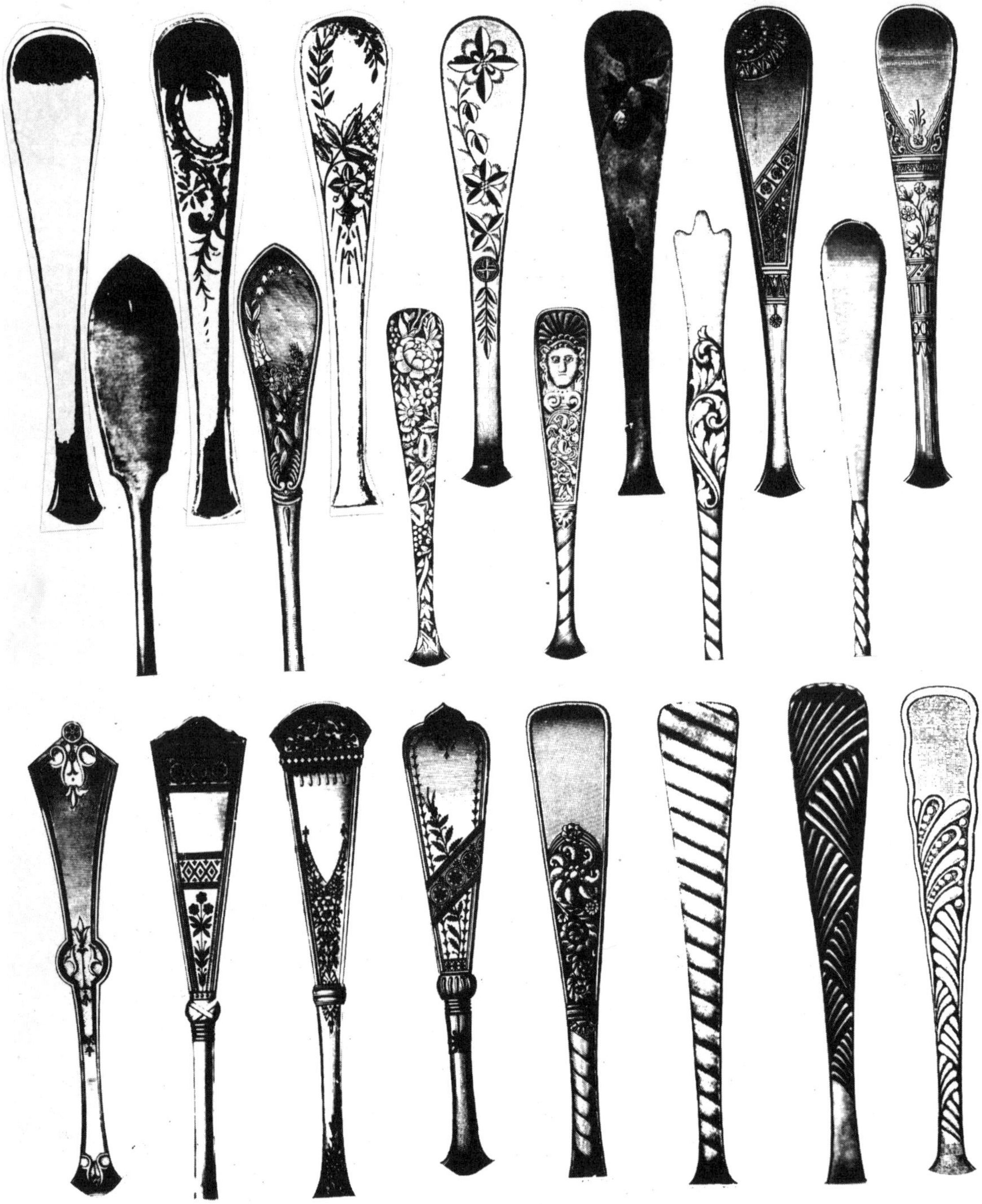

1847 ROGERS BROS. (MERIDEN BRITANNIA CO.) (Continued): *Top row (l. to r.)*: Hoffman, Diana, Armenian, Linden, Lucerne, Saratoga, Lorne. *Middle row (l. to r.)*: Shell Tipped, Lily, Embossed, Assyrian Head, Lenox, Windsor Twist. *Bottom row (l. to r.)*: Persian, Laurel, Imperial, Newport, Assyrian, Dundee, Brunswick, Louis XV. See also Rogers Bros., Rogers Bros. Mfg. Co., Rogers & Bro., Rogers, Smith & Co., Rogers & Hamilton, Simpson, Hall, Miller & Co. (Wm. Rogers Eagle Brand), Wm. Rogers Mfg. Co., Standard Patterns and Variations sections.

1847 Rogers Bros. (Meriden Britannia Co.)

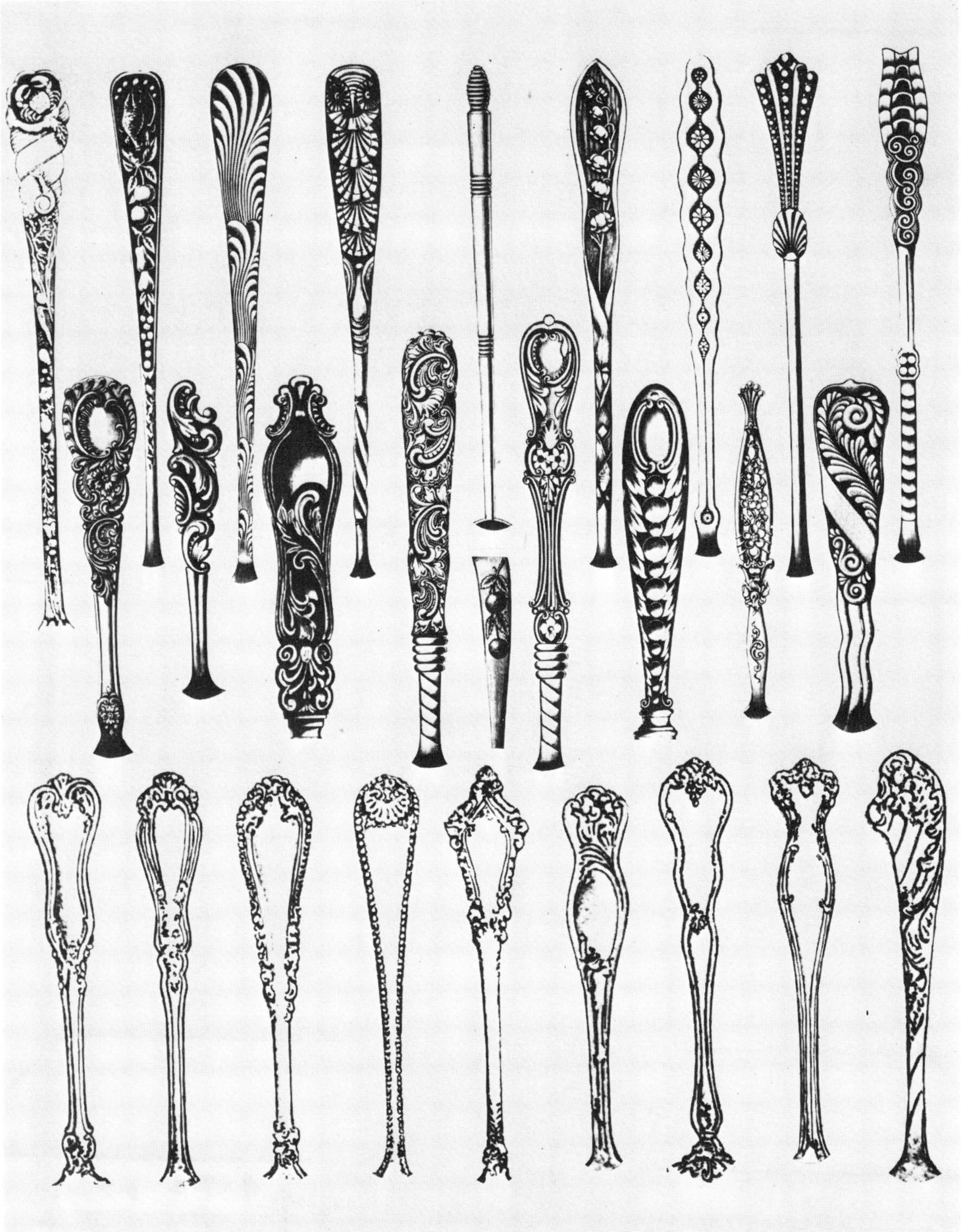

1847 ROGERS BROS. (MERIDEN BRITANNIA CO.) (Continued): *Top row (l. to r.)*: Shrewsbury, Game, 1890, Owl, Delmonico, Lily of the Valley, Pearl, Ruby, Lorraine. *Middle row (l. to r.)*: Harvard, Vassar, Grecian, Parisian, Fruit, Columbian, Moselle, Tolland, Florentine. *Bottom row (l. to r.)*: Ashford, Olympia, Norfolk, Milan, Flanders, Daffodil, Concord, Forget-me-not, Scythian. See also Rogers Bros., Rogers Bros. Mfg. Co., Rogers & Bro., Rogers, Smith & Co., Rogers & Hamilton, Simpson, Hall, Miller & Co. (Wm. Rogers Eagle Brand), Wm. Rogers Mfg. Co., Standard Patterns and Variations sections.

1847 Rogers Bros. (Meriden Britannia Co.)

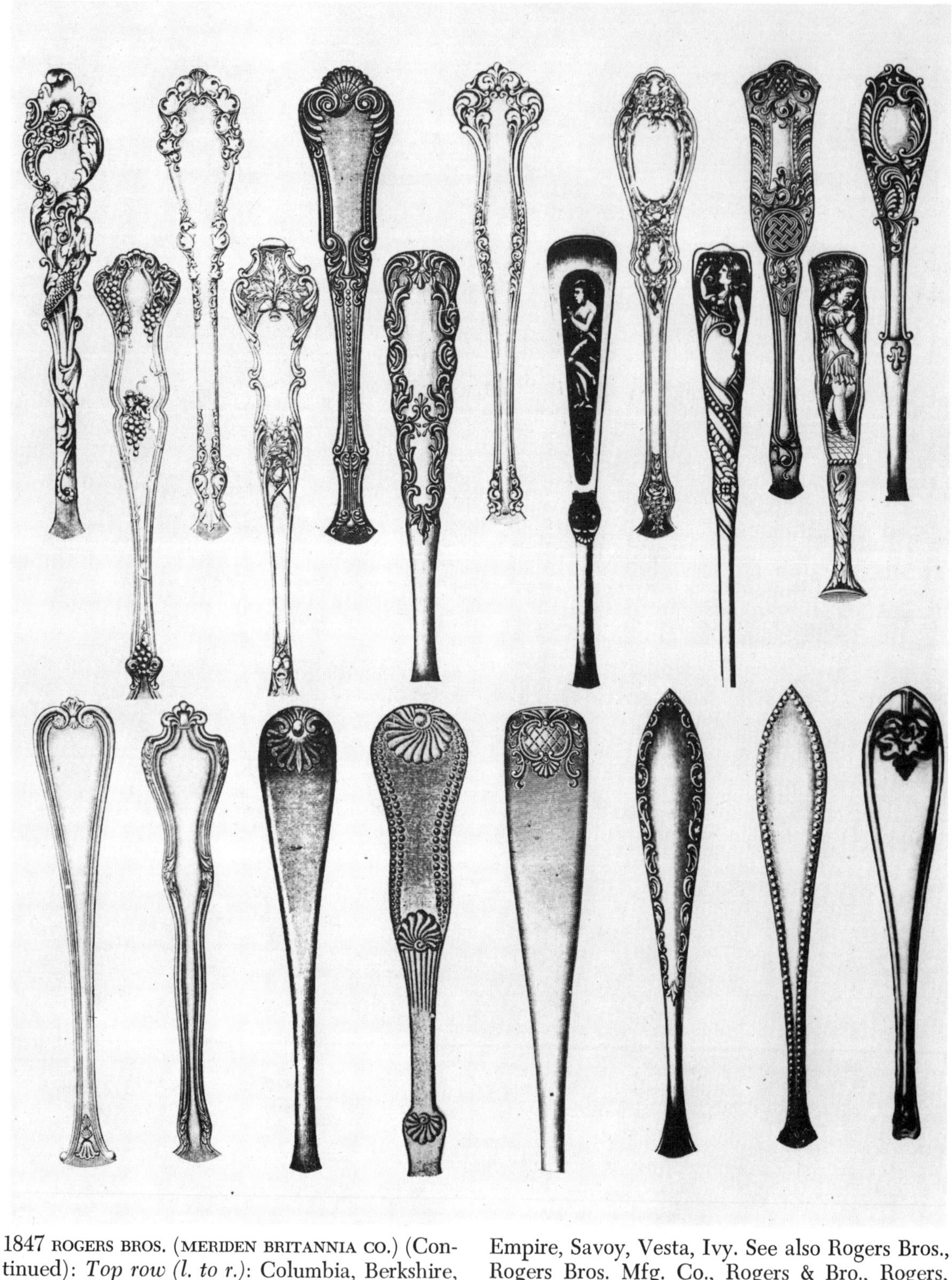

1847 ROGERS BROS. (MERIDEN BRITANNIA CO.) (Continued): *Top row (l. to r.)*: Columbia, Berkshire, Lotus, Avon, Sharon, Romanesque, Moline. *Middle row (l. to r.)*: Vintage, Charter Oak, Portland, Arcadian, Siren, Fairie. *Bottom row (l. to r.)*: Priscilla, Faneuil, Shell No. 2, Etruscan, Empire, Savoy, Vesta, Ivy. See also Rogers Bros., Rogers Bros. Mfg. Co., Rogers & Bro., Rogers, Smith & Co., Rogers & Hamilton, Simpson, Hall, Miller & Co. (Wm. Rogers Eagle Brand), Wm. Rogers Mfg. Co., Standard Patterns and Variations sections.

C. Rogers & Bro. Rogers Cutlery Co.

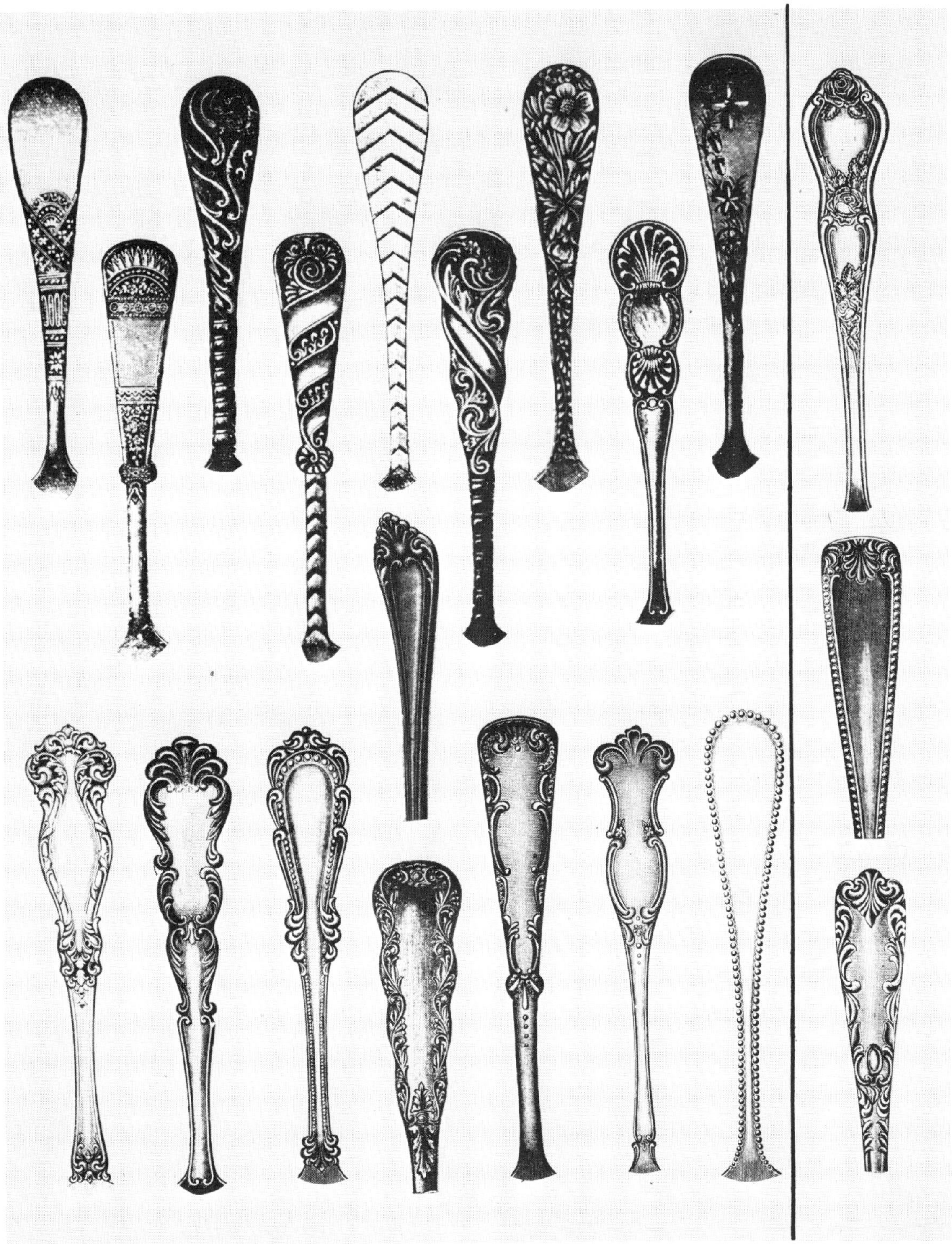

C. ROGERS & BRO.: *Top row (l. to r.)*: Winthrop, Savarin, Lenox, Mayflower, B. Engraved. *Middle row (l. to r.)*: Westminster, Belmont, Eucla, Royal, Naples. *Bottom row (l. to r.)*: Newton, Regent, Milton, Imperial, Utica, Victor, Pluto. ROGERS CUTLERY CO.: *(Top to bottom)*: Rose, Orleans, Marquise. For C. Rogers & Bro. see also 1847 Rogers Bros. (Meriden Britannia Co.), Rogers Bros., Rogers Bros. Mfg. Co., and Standard Patterns sections. For Rogers Cutlery Company see also Standard Patterns section.

Rogers & Hamilton   Simeon L. & George H. Rogers Co.

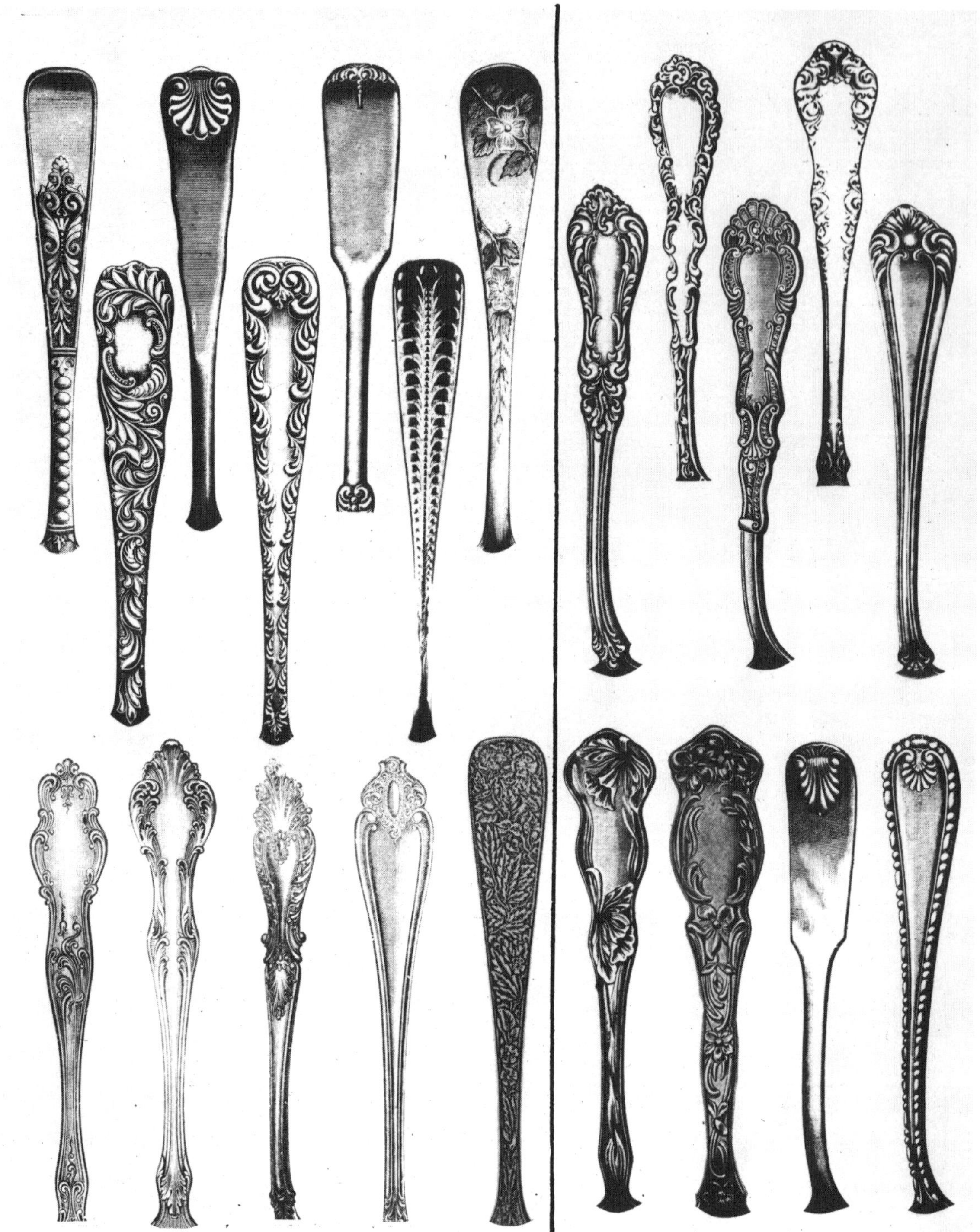

ROGERS & HAMILTON: *Top row (l. to r.)*: Cardinal, Shell, Ideal, Harlequin. *Middle row (l. to r.)*: Monarch, Majestic, Acanthus. *Bottom row (l. to r.)*: Tudor, Doric, Raphael, Marquise, Normandie. SIMEON L. & GEORGE H. ROGERS CO.: *Top row (l. to r.)*: Warren, Simeon No. 1. *Middle row (l. to r.)*: Lakewood, Franklin, Puritan. *Bottom row (l. to r.)*: Orchid, Violet, Shell, Princess. For Rogers & Hamilton see also 1847 Rogers Bros. (Meriden Britannia Co.), C. Rogers & Bro., Rogers & Bro., Wm. Rogers Mfg. Co., Standard Patterns and Variations sections. For Simeon L. & George H. Rogers Co. see also Standard Patterns section.

Simeon L. & George H. Rogers Co. | Rogers, Smith & Co. | William A. Rogers, Ltd.

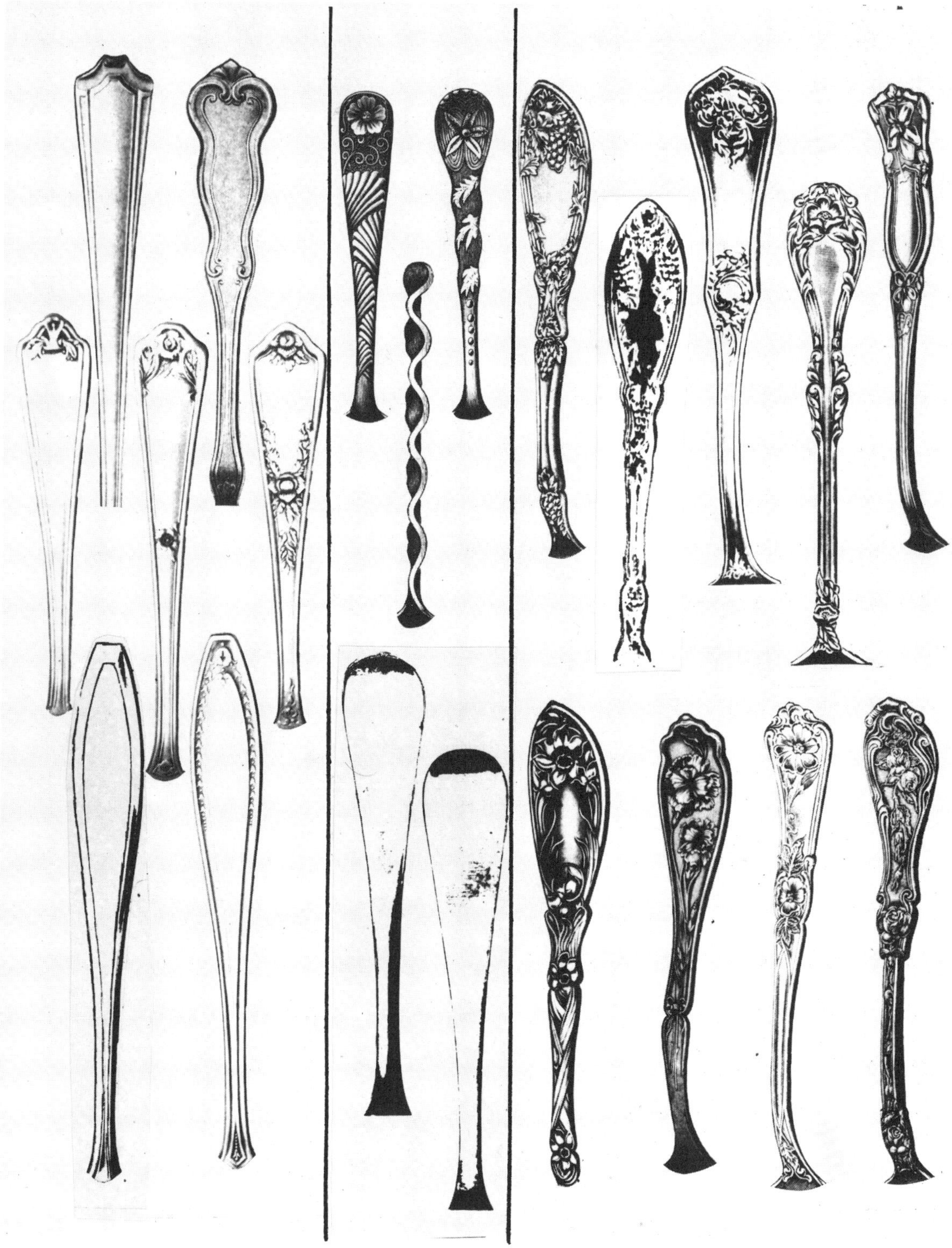

SIMEON L. & GEORGE H. ROGERS CO. (Continued): *Top row (l. to r.)*: Lexington, Colonial. *Middle row (l. to r.)*: Laureate, Lois, Minerva. *Bottom row (l. to r.)*: Adonis, Webster. ROGERS, SMITH & CO.: *Top row (l. to r.)*: Daisy, Coral. *Middle*: Venetian. *Bottom (l. to r.)*: Sherwood, Puritan. WILLIAM A. ROGERS, LTD.: *Top row (l. to r.)*: La-Vigne, Garland, Violet. *Middle row (l. to r.)*: La Concorde, Hanover. *Bottom row (l. to r.)*: Narcissus, Carnation, Grenoble, Glenrose. For Simeon L. & George H. Rogers Co. see also Standard Patterns section. For Rogers, Smith & Co. see also 1847 Rogers Bros. (Meriden Britannia Co.) electroplate and sterling, Standard Patterns and Variations sections. For Wm. A. Rogers, Ltd. see also Pairpoint Mfg. Co., W. H. Rogers Corp., Niagara Silver Co. and Standard Patterns sections.

William A. Rogers, Ltd.

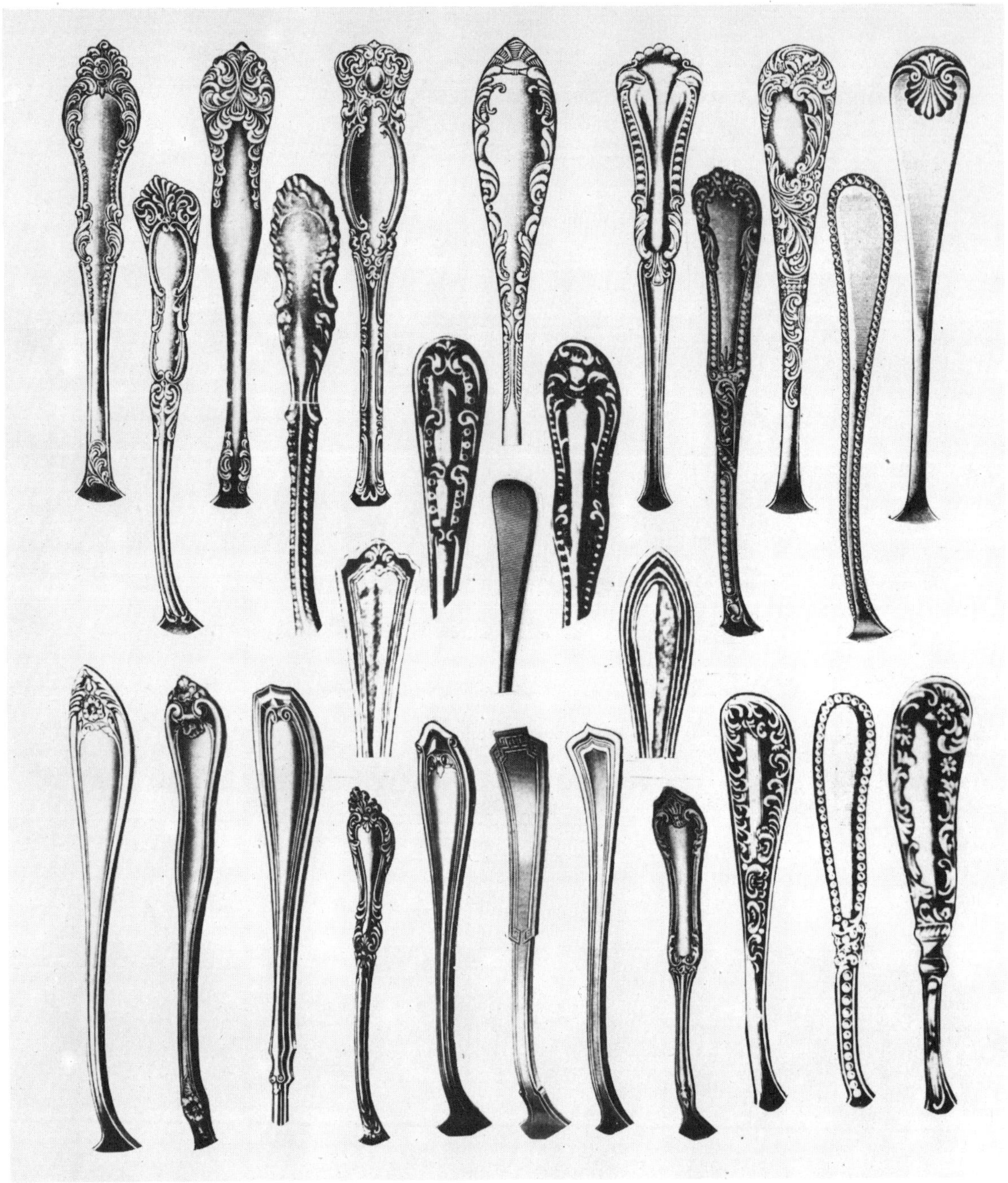

WILLIAM A. ROGERS, LTD. (Continued): *First row (l. to r.)*: Carlton, Lenora, Warwick, Rhinebeck (St. Elmo), Marcella, Elmore, Shell. *Second row (l. to r.)*: Ardsley, Elberon, Helena, Bernice, Orient, Eudora (Linden). *Third row (l. to r.)*: Raleigh, Brighton, Standish. *Bottom row (l. to r.)*: Greylock, Leyland, Biltmore, Arundel, Abington, Grecian, Revere, Suffolk, Raymond, Mabel, Elsie. See also Niagara Silver Co., Pairpoint Mfg. Co., W. H. Rogers Corp., and Standard Patterns sections.

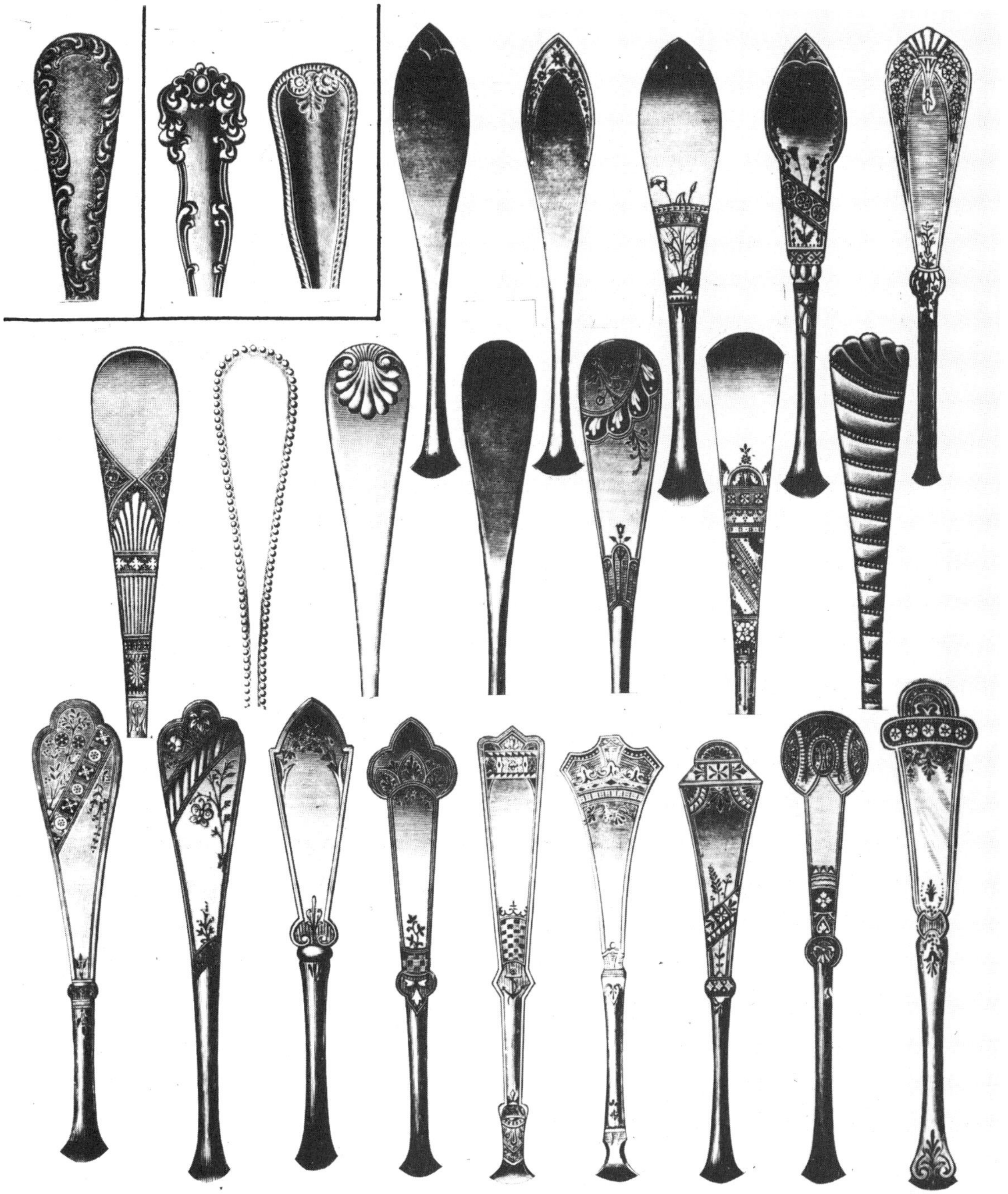

W. F. ROGERS (ROGERS CUTLERY CO.): Alton. W. H. ROGERS CORP.: *(l. to r.)*: Helena, Columbia. WM. ROGERS MFG. CO.: *Top row (l. to r.)*: Antique, Imperial, Lilian, Hartford, Regent. *Middle row (l. to r.)*: Peerless, Essex, Sultana, French, Rival, Coronet, San Diego. *Bottom row (l. to r.)*: Lyonnaise, Berlin, Princess, Countess, Anchor, Regal, Eastlake, Danish, Venetian. For W. F. Rogers (Rogers Cutlery Co.) and W. H. Rogers Corp. see also Standard Patterns section. For Wm. Rogers Mfg. Co. see also Rogers Bros., Rogers Bros. Mfg. Co., 1847 Rogers Bros. (Meriden Britannia Co.), Rogers & Hamilton, Rogers, Smith & Co., Rogers & Bro., Simpson, Hall, Miller & Co. (Wm. Rogers Eagle Brand), Standard Patterns and Variations sections.

Wm. Rogers Mfg. Co.

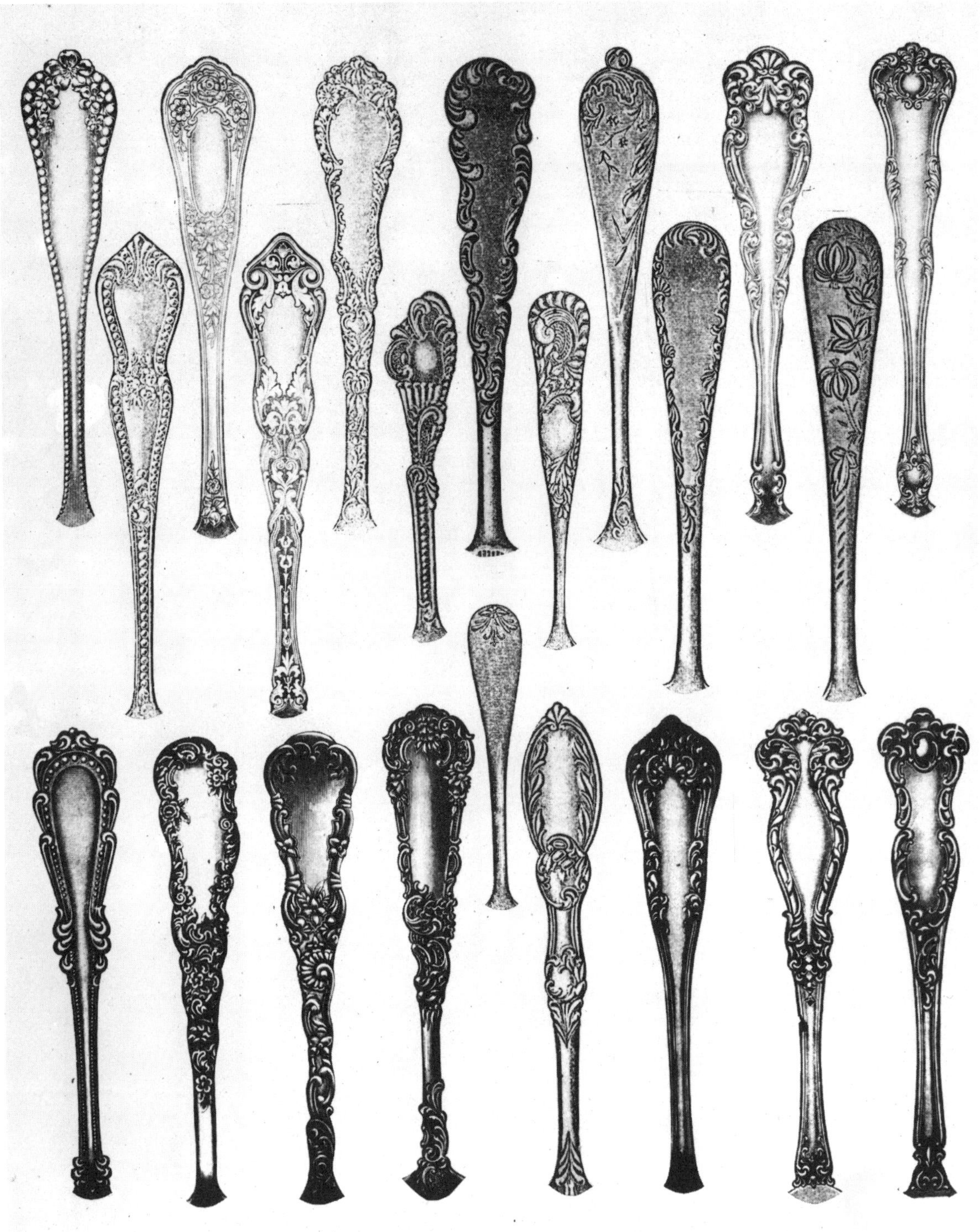

WM. ROGERS MFG. CO. (Continued): *Top row (l. to r.)*: Mayflower, Beauty, Chevalier, Cromwell, Columbus, Lexington, Argyle. *Middle row (l. to r.)*: Beaded, Alhambra, Pequot, Ceres *(Center, below)*, Gem, Victoria, Tiger Lily. *Bottom row (l. to r.)*: Chelsea, Florida, Harvard, Yale, Ormonde, America, Raleigh, Oxford. See also Rogers Bros., Rogers Bros. Mfg. Co., 1847 Rogers Bros. (Meriden Britannia Co.), Rogers & Hamilton, Rogers & Bro., Rogers, Smith & Co., Simpson, Hall, Miller & Co. (Wm. Rogers Eagle Brand), Standard Patterns and Variations sections.

Wm. Rogers Mfg. Co. | Salem Silver Plate Co. | Sears (Sears, Roebuck & Co.) | Simpson, Hall, Miller & Co. (Wm. Rogers Eagle Brand)

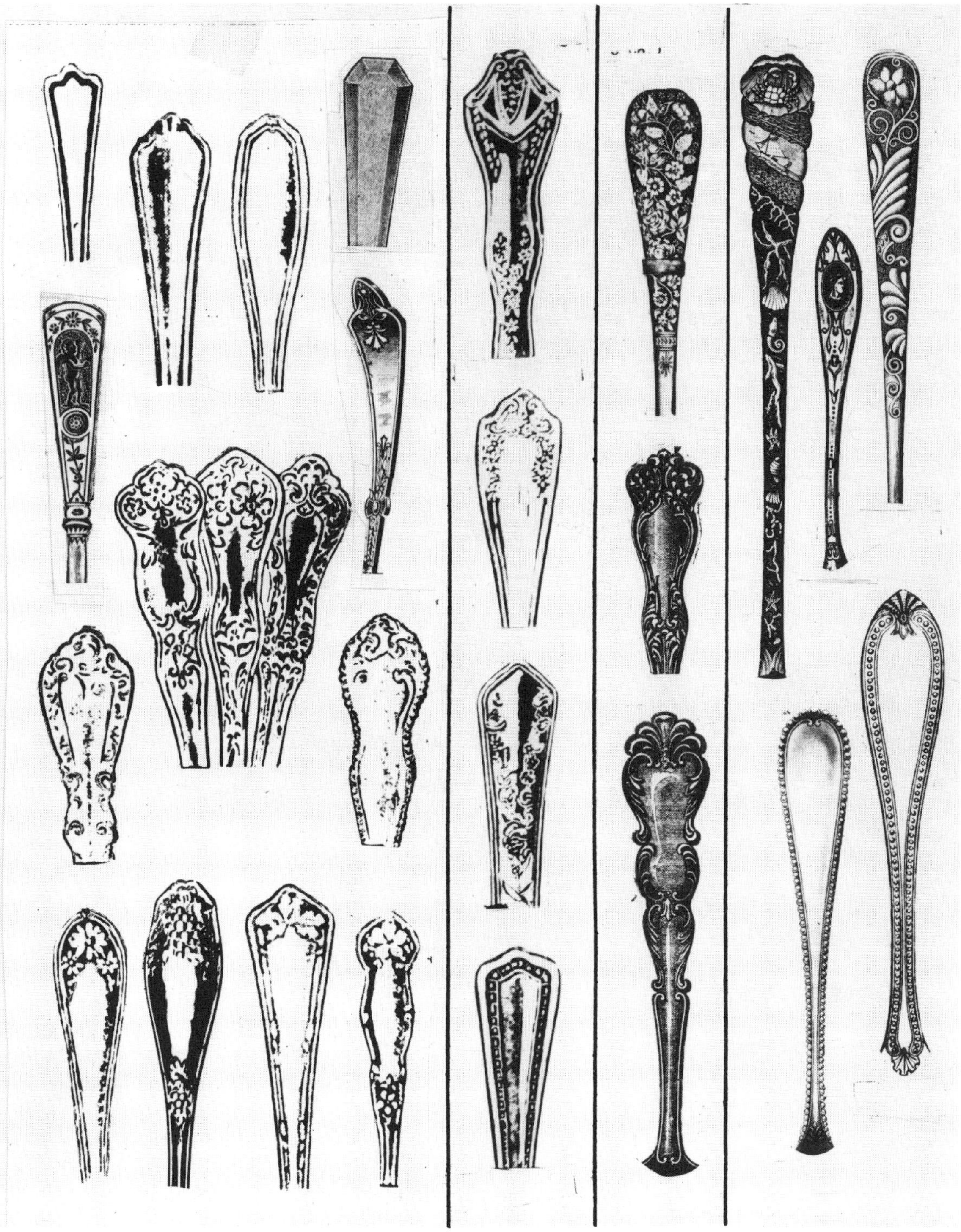

WM. ROGERS MFG. CO. (Continued): *Top row (l. to r.)*: Manchester, Puritan, Clinton, Lincoln. *Second row, left*: Cupid, *right*: Silver, *center group of three*: Daisy, Flower, Florentine. *Third row, left*: Plymouth, *right*: Arbutus. *Bottom row (l. to r.)*: New Daisy, Isabella, Oak, Arbutus. SALEM SILVER PLATE CO.: *(Top to bottom)*: Endicott, Conant, Dunbar, Broadfield. SEARS (SEARS, ROEBUCK & CO.): *(Top to bottom)*: Standard, Adell, Glasgow. SIMPSON, HALL, MILLER & CO.: *Top (l. to r.)*: Saddle Rock, Medallion, Blue Point. *Bottom (l. to r.)*: Seville, Beaded. For Wm. Rogers Mfg. Co. see also Rogers Bros., Rogers Bros. Mfg. Co., 1847 Rogers Bros. (Meriden Britannia Co.), Rogers & Bro., Rogers & Hamilton, Rogers, Smith & Co., Simpson, Hall, Miller & Co. (Wm. Rogers Eagle Brand), Standard Patterns and Variations sections. For Sears see also Standard Patterns section. For Simpson, Hall, Miller & Co. (Wm. Rogers Eagle Brand) see also Standard Patterns and Variations sections.

Simpson, Hall, Miller & Co. (Wm. Rogers Eagle Brand)

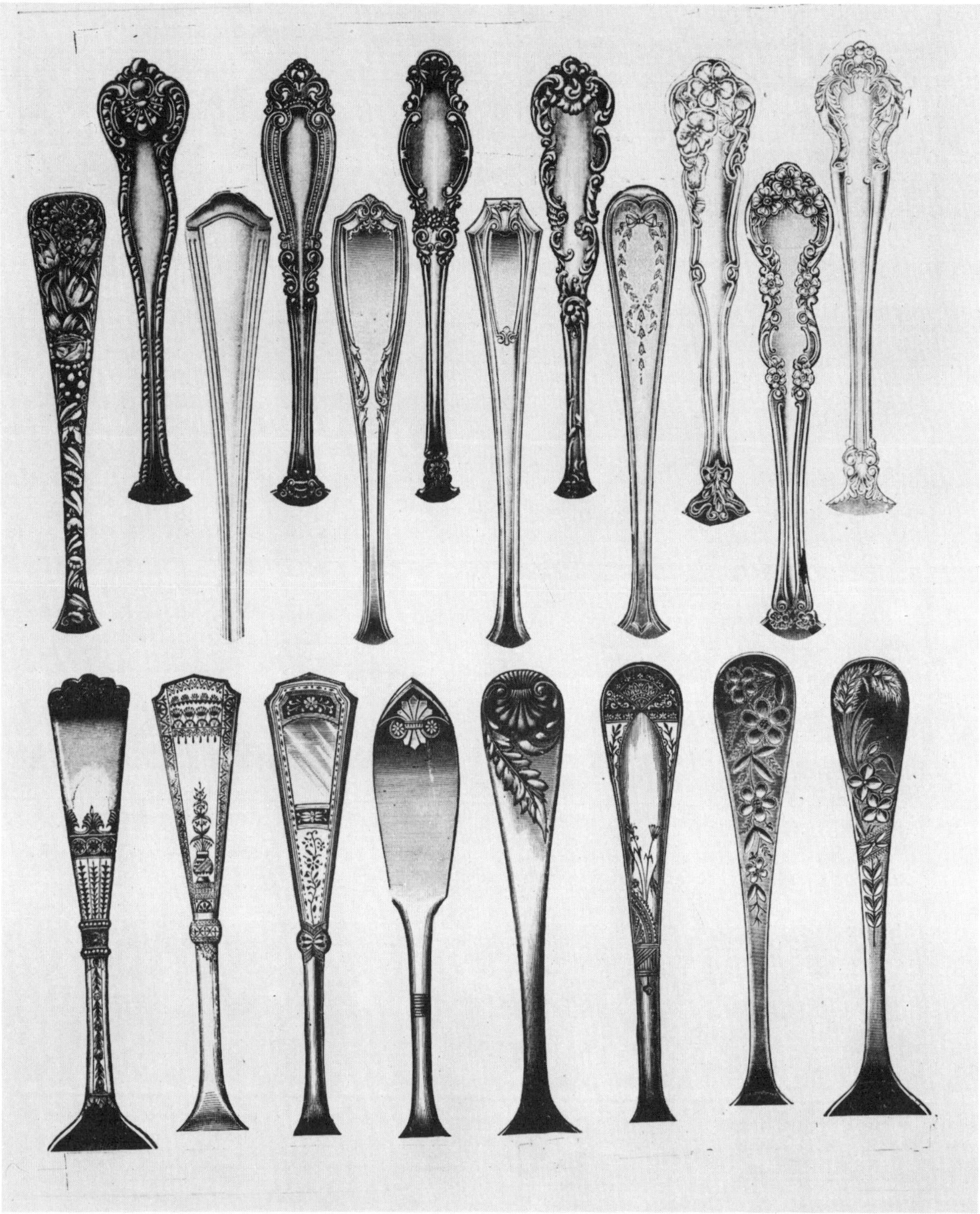

SIMPSON, HALL, MILLER & CO. (WM. ROGERS EAGLE BRAND) (Continued): *Top row (l. to r.)*: York, Blenheim, Melrose, Cordova, Berwick, Cedric. *Middle row (l. to r.)*: Magnolia, Randolph, Concord, Carrollton, Garrick, Hardwick. *Bottom row (l. to r.)*: Athens, Geneva, Countess, French, Queen, St. James, Mikado, St. Augustine. See also Rogers Bros., Rogers Bros. Mfg. Co., Wm. Rogers Mfg. Co., Standard Patterns and Variations sections.

E. H. H. Smith Silver Co.

Stratford Silver Co.

A. F. Towle & Son Co.

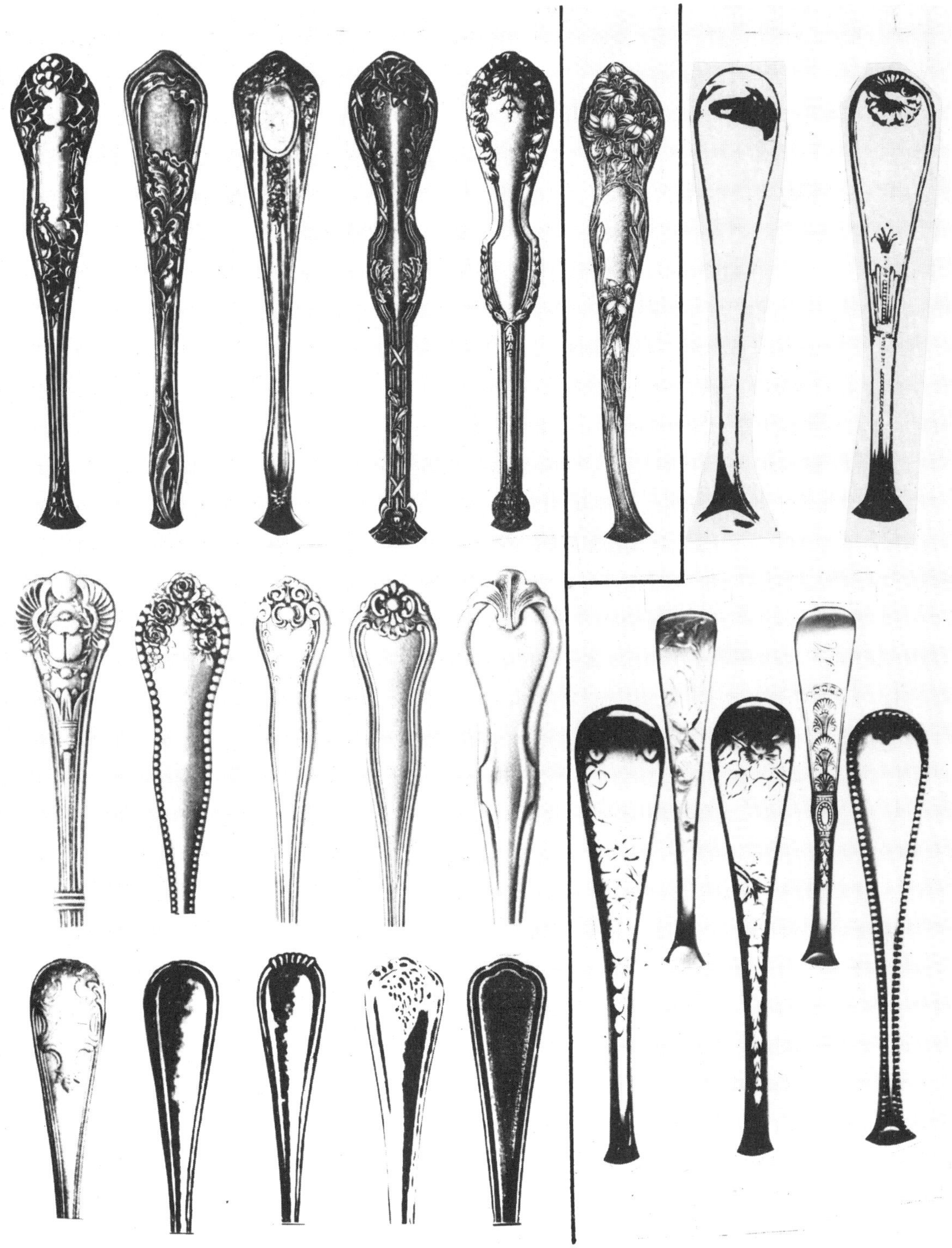

E. H. H. SMITH SILVER CO.: *Top row (l. to r.)*: Holly, Iris, Dorothy Vernon, Oak, Louis XVI. *Middle row (l. to r.)*: Antique Egyptian, York Rose (Rose), Marseilles, Verdi, Flemish. *Bottom row (l. to r.)*: Martha Washington, New Model (Portia), Lincoln, Wistaria, Mission. STRATFORD SILVER CO.: Lilyta. A. F. TOWLE & SON CO.: *Top row (l. to r.)*: Warren, Shell No. 2. *Middle row (l. to r.)*: No. 80, Samoset. *Bottom row (l. to r.)*: Windsor Engraved No. 5, Windsor Engraved No. 43, Priscilla. For all companies on this page, see also Standard Patterns section.

A. F. Towle & Son Co. Towle Mfg. Co. James W. Tu

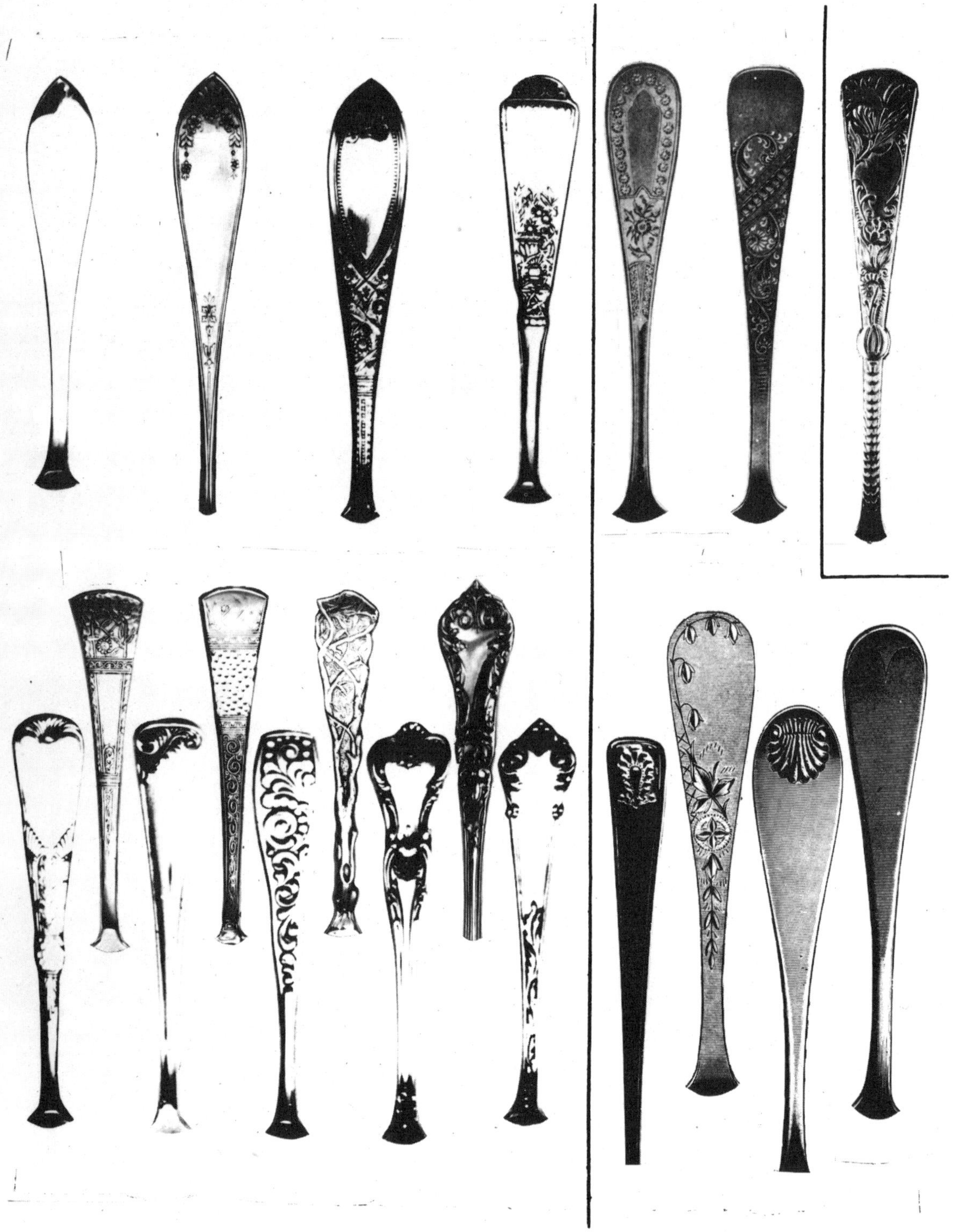

A. F. TOWLE & SON CO. (Continued): *Top row (l. to r.)*: Warwick, No. 300, No. 83, Kremlin. *Middle row (l. to r.)*: Arbutus, Grenada, Rustic, Eltham. *Bottom row (l. to r.)*: Clyde, Climber, Ionic, Arundel, Raleigh. TOWLE MFG. CO.: *Top row (l. to r.)*: Victor, Chester. *Middle row (l. to r.)*: Engraved '05, Antique. *Bottom row (l. to r.)*: Norwood, Shell. JAMES W. TUFTS: Tufts No. 1. For all companies on this page see also Standard Patterns section.

1835 R. Wallace | The Wallingford Co. | E. G. Webster & Bro.

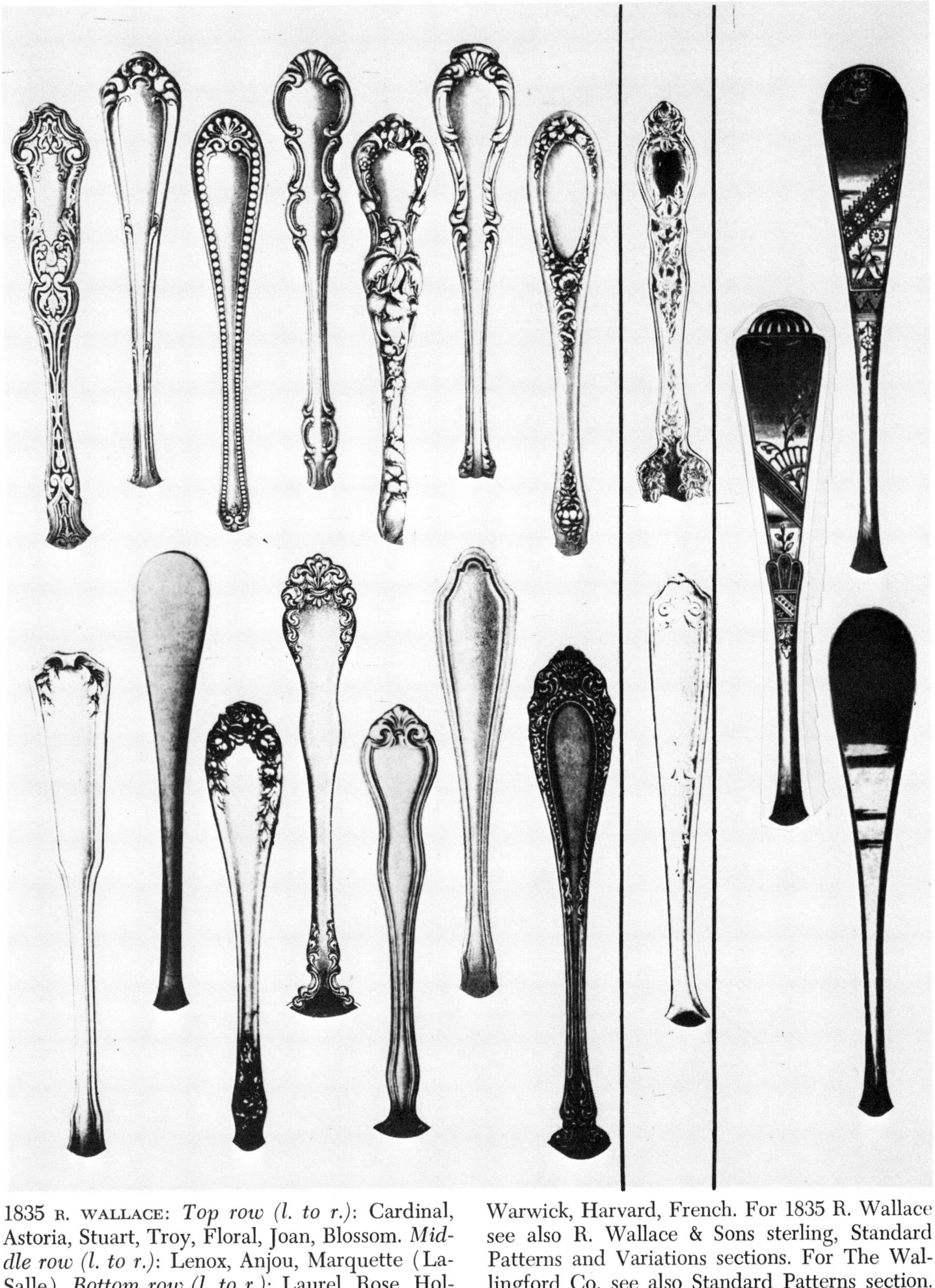

1835 R. WALLACE: *Top row (l. to r.)*: Cardinal, Astoria, Stuart, Troy, Floral, Joan, Blossom. *Middle row (l. to r.)*: Lenox, Anjou, Marquette (LaSalle). *Bottom row (l. to r.)*: Laurel, Rose, Holland, Virginia. THE WALLINGFORD CO.: *(Top to bottom)*: Wallingford No. 1, Wallingford No. 2. E. G. WEBSTER & BRO.: *(Top to bottom, staggered)*: Warwick, Harvard, French. For 1835 R. Wallace see also R. Wallace & Sons sterling, Standard Patterns and Variations sections. For The Wallingford Co. see also Standard Patterns section. For E. G. Webster & Bro. see also Derby Silver Co. and Standard Patterns sections.

Williams Bros. Mfg. Co.

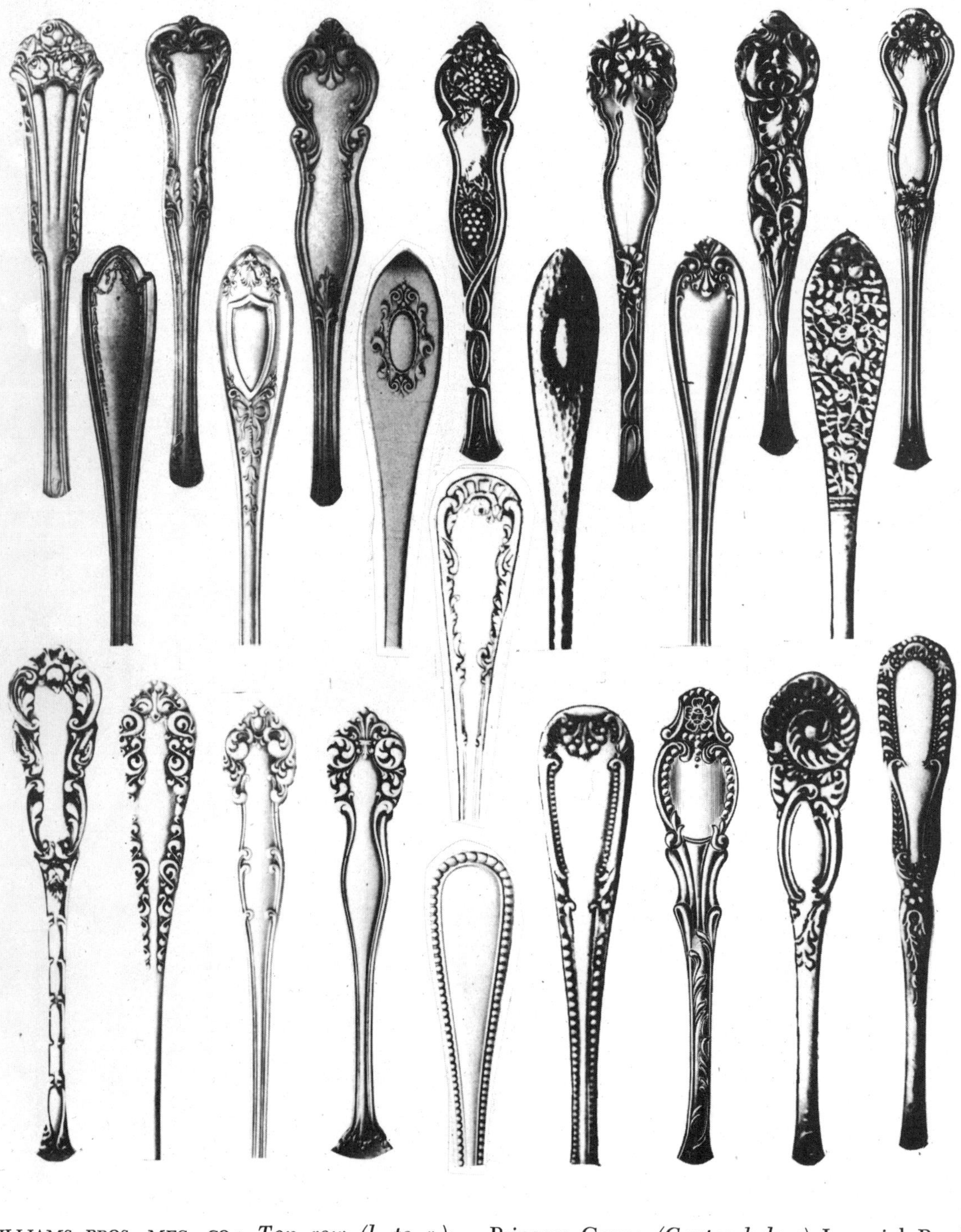

WILLIAMS BROS. MFG. CO.: *Top row (l. to r.)*: Queen Victoria, Queen Elizabeth, Queen Anne, Vineyard, Peerless, Louvre, Paragon. *Middle row (l. to r.)*: Shirley, Queen Helena (Alma), Princess, Genoa. *(Center, below)*, Imperial, Pearl, Valada. *Bottom row (l. to r.)*: Rosalind, Priscilla, Como, Norma, Beaded, Geisha, Kensico, Plastron, Luxfer. See also Standard Patterns section.

Variations

Alvin Mfg. Co. Gorham Mfg. Co.

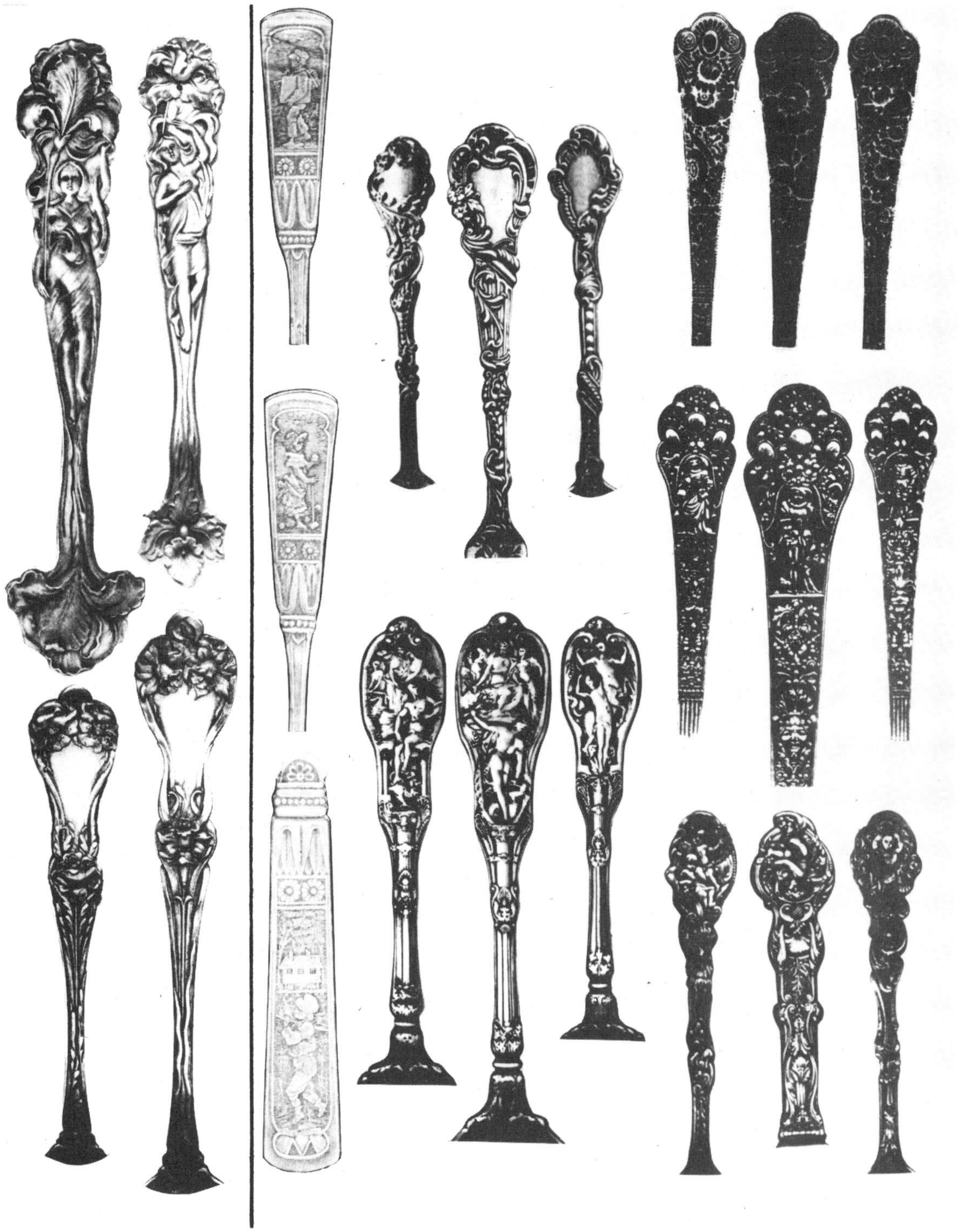

Examples of variations of design within a single pattern. ALVIN MFG. CO.: *Top*: Raphael. *Bottom*: Majestic. GORHAM MFG. CO.: *Left*: The Piper. *Center, top*: Marie Antoinette. *Center, bottom*: Mythologique. *Right, top*: Cluny. *Right, middle*: Medici. *Right, bottom*: Versailles.

Gorham Mfg. Co.

GORHAM MFG. CO.: *Top (l. to r.)*: Patterns A, B, C, D, E, F, G, H, I, J, K and L; after dinner coffee spoons sold as a set. *Bottom (l. to r.)*: Versailles, No. 26, Floral series: Forget-me-not, Lilly, Rose, Pansy, Daisy, Passion Flower; No. 14, Three Kings. The Floral Series made up a set; the other patterns in this row were available in "assorted dozens" in coffee spoon and afternoon tea spoon sizes.

Gorham Mfg. Co.

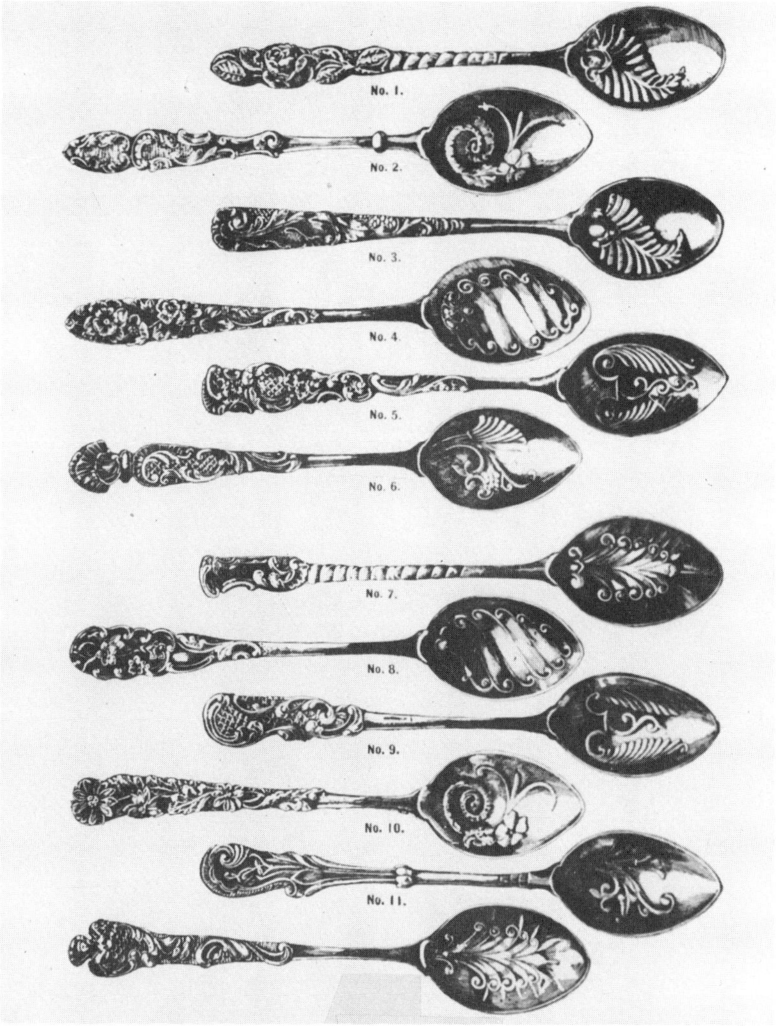

GORHAM MFG. CO. Sterling silver English 5 o'clock Tea Spoons.

Gorham Mfg. Co. — Hall, Elton & Co. — The Holmes & Edwards Silver Co.

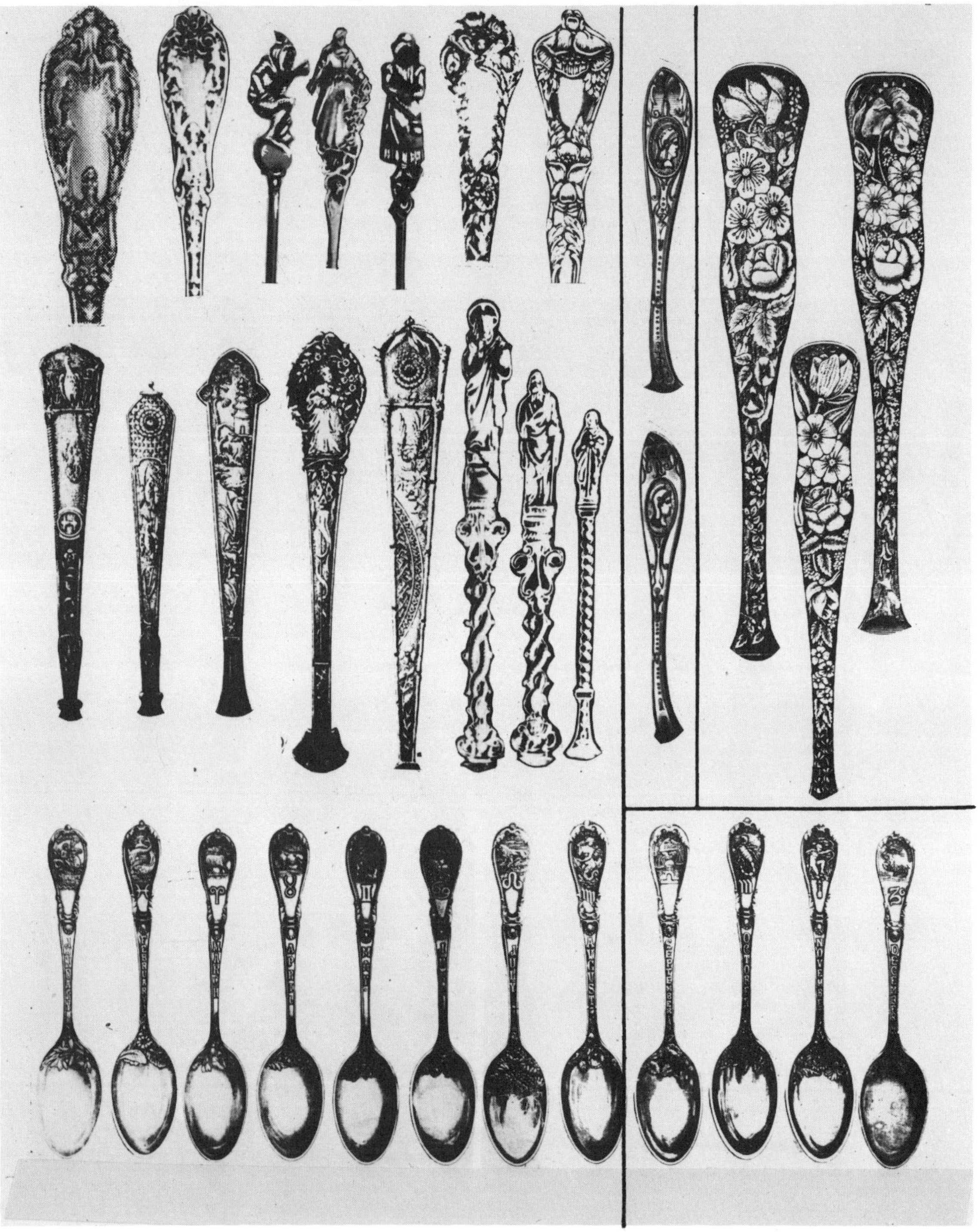

Examples of variations of design within a single pattern. GORHAM MFG. CO.: *Top row (l. to r.)*: Paris (2), Nuremburg (3), New Poppy (2). *Second row (l. to r.)*: Japanese (5), Master, Apostle Large, Apostle Small. *Bottom row, across page*: Zodiac, with birth month flowers listed below each variation. (Two-thirds scale). HALL, ELTON & CO.: Variations of Medallion pattern. THE HOLMES & EDWARDS SILVER CO.: Variations of Flower pattern.

Reed & Barton

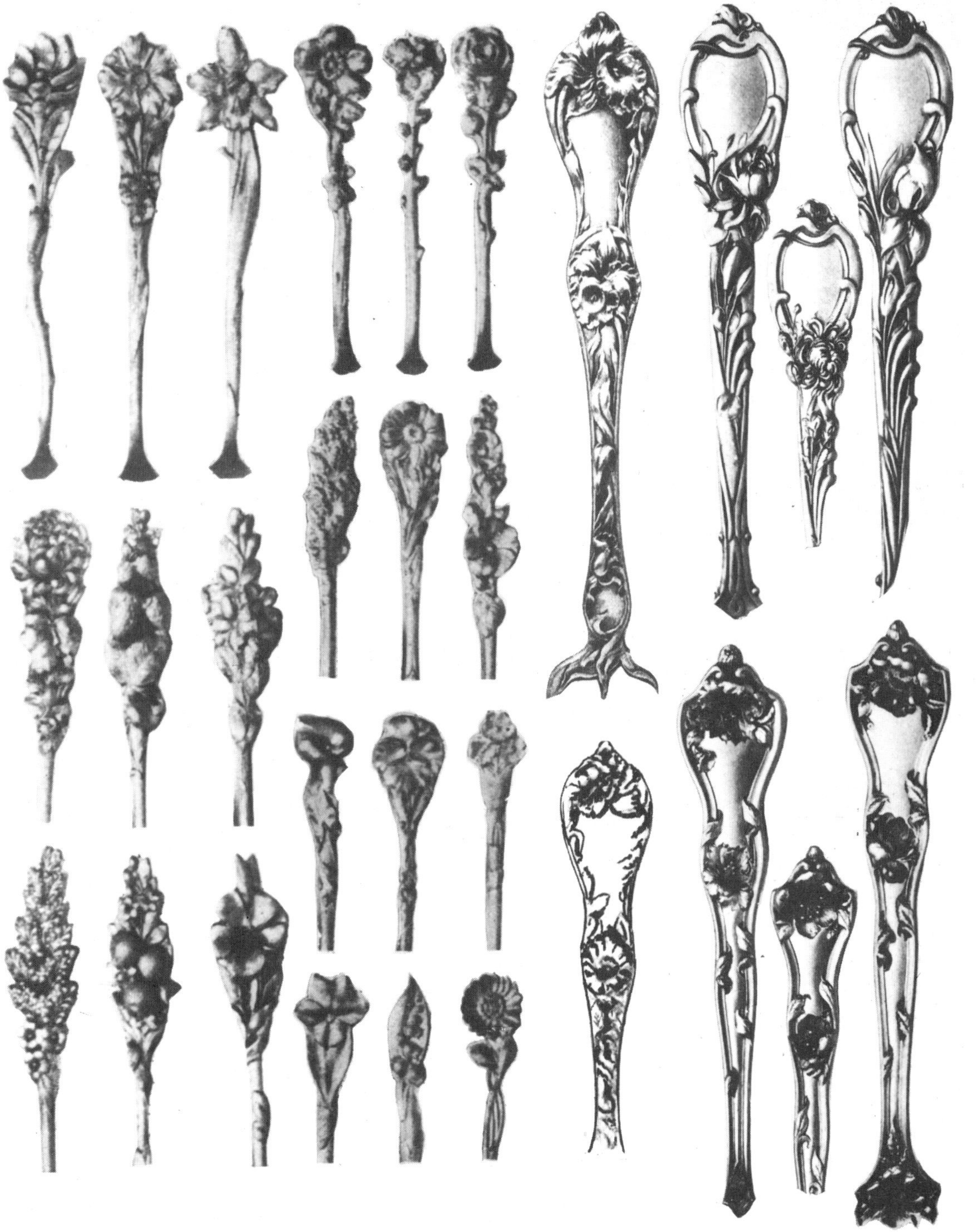

Examples of variations in specialty spoon sets and in standard production patterns. REED & BARTON: *Left*: 9 variations in Harlequin pattern P.M. Teaspoons: *Top (l. to r.)*: Magnolia, Bachelor Button, Orchid. *Middle (l. to r.)*: Chrysanthemum, Strawberry, Mayflower. *Bottom (l. to r.)*: Goldenrod, Orange Blossom, Myrtle. *Left Center*: 12 variations in Harlequin pattern Coffee Spoons: *Top (l. to r.)*: Wild Rose, Apple Blossom, Tree Rose. *Second row (l. to r.)*: Goldenrod, Daisy, Hollyhock. *Third row (l. to r.)*: Calla Lily, Pansy, Forget-me-not. *Bottom row (l. to r.)*: Violet, Lily of the Valley, Water Lily. *Right Center*: *(Top and bottom)*: Les Cinq Fleurs. *Right*: *Top*: La Parisienne. *Right*: *Bottom*: Intaglio.

1847 Rogers Bros.—Rogers, Smith & Co.

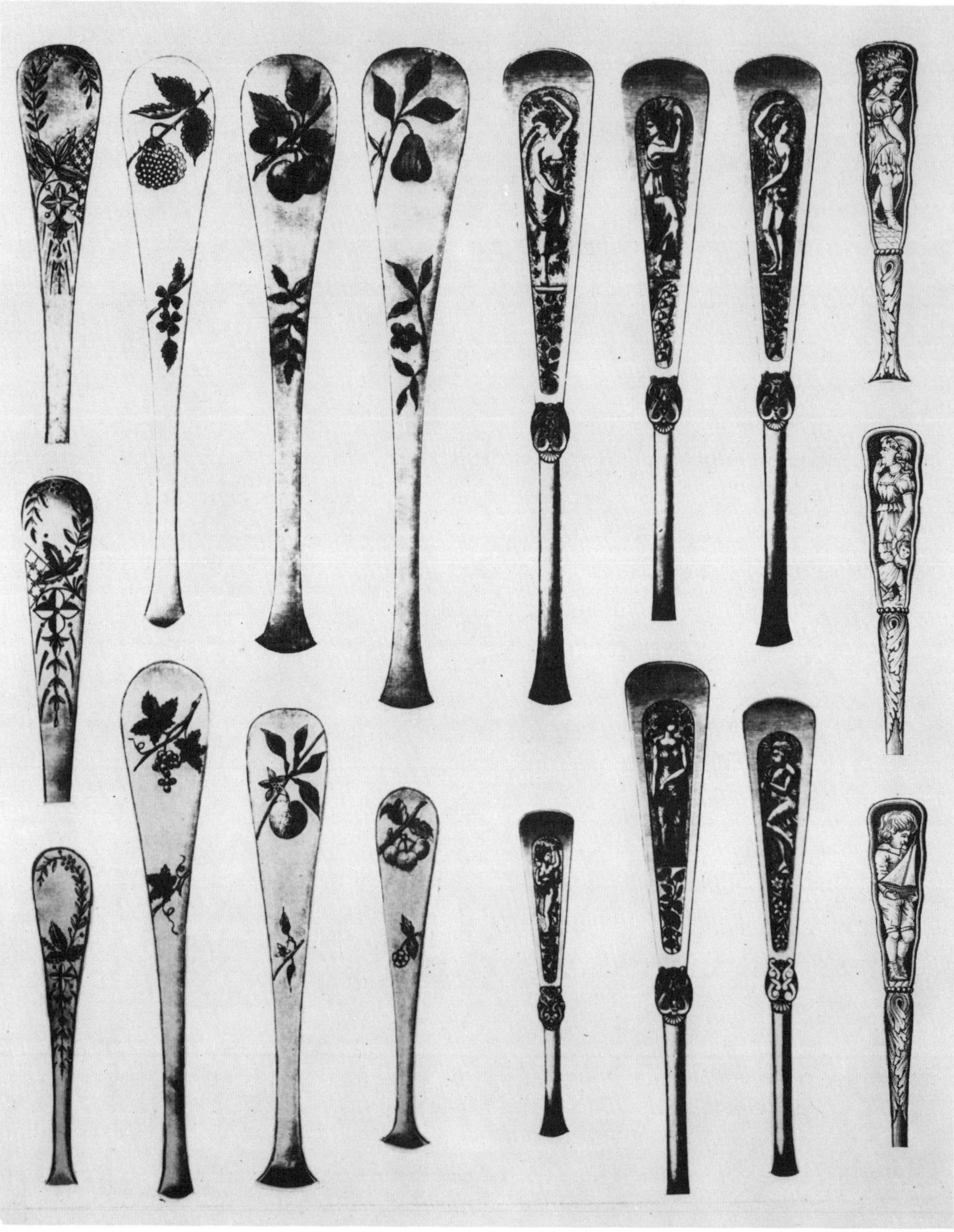

Examples of variations within standard production patterns and specialty patterns. 1847 ROGERS BROS.—ROGERS, SMITH & CO.: *Left (top to bottom)*: Armenian. *Left center*: Lucerne. *Right Center*: Arcadian. *Right (top to bottom)*: Fairie.

1847 Rogers Bros.—
Rogers, Smith & Co.

Wm. Rogers Eagle Brand
(Simpson, Hall,
Miller & Co.)

Wm. Rogers Mfg. Co.

Examples of variations within standard production flatware patterns. 1847 ROGERS BROS.—ROGERS, SMITH & CO.: *Left*: Embossed. WM. ROGERS EAGLE BRAND (SIMPSON, HALL, MILLER & CO.): *Right Center*: Magnolia. WM. ROGERS MFG. CO.: *Right*: Lyonnaise.

George W. Shiebler Co.

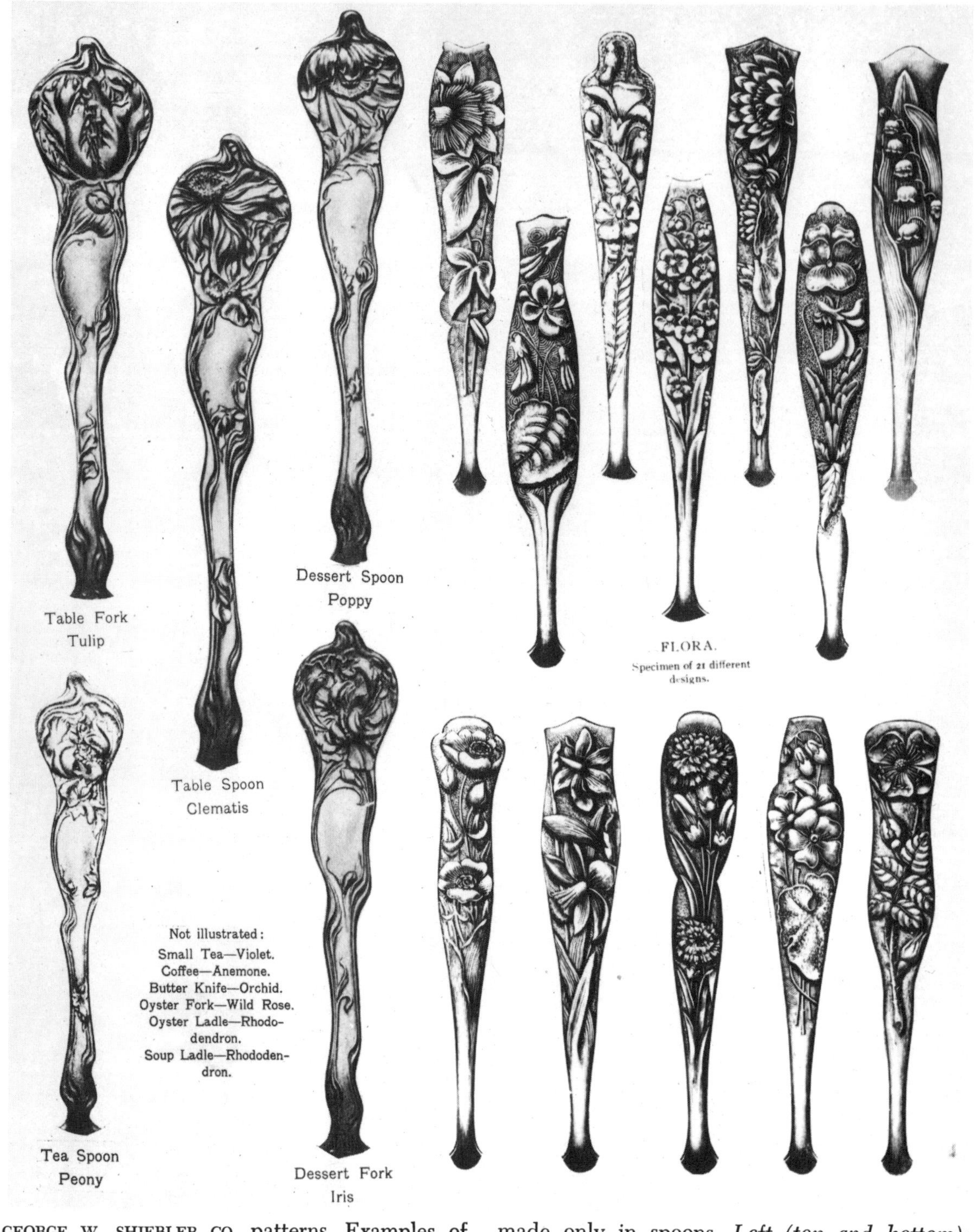

GEORGE W. SHIEBLER CO. patterns. Examples of variations on a design theme within a single pattern and in a specialty pattern. Flora was made only in spoons. *Left (top and bottom)*: Fiorito. *Right (top and bottom)*: Flora.

Simpson, Hall, Miller & Co.

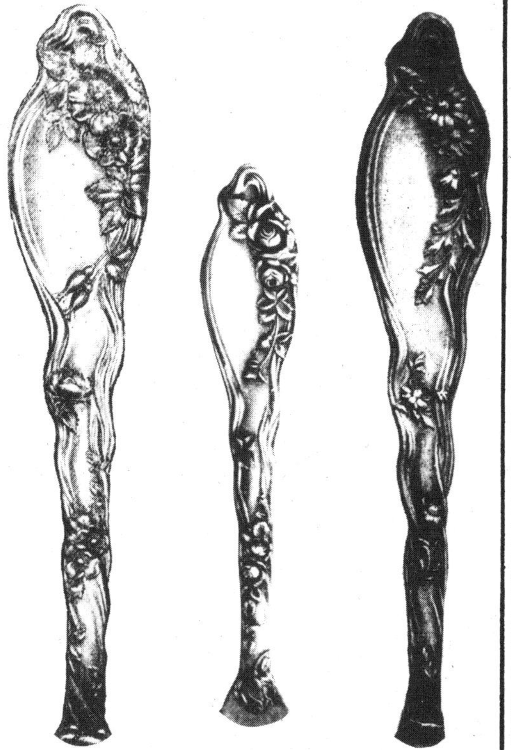

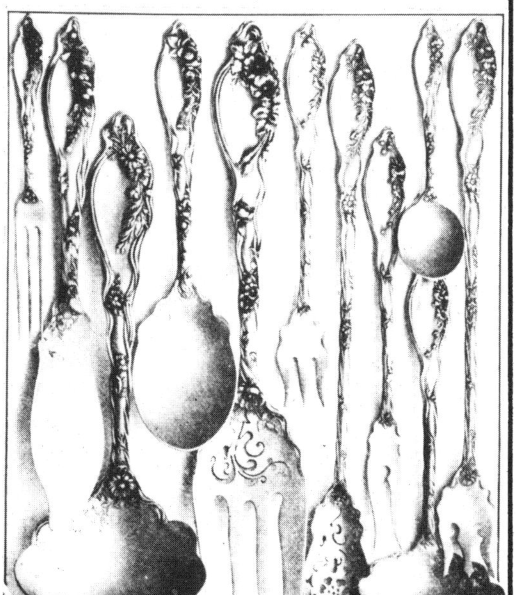

Tiffany & Co.

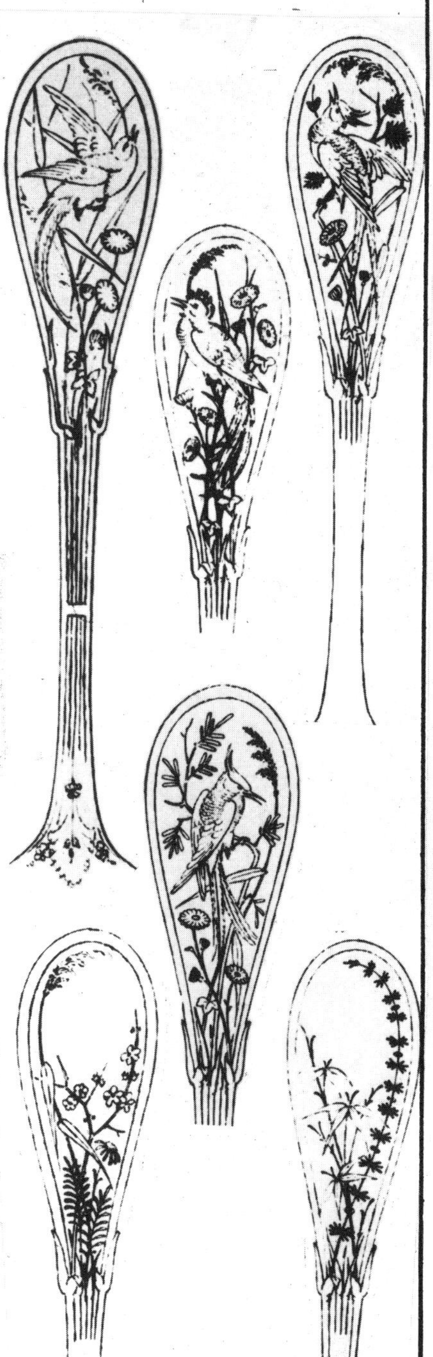

Towle Mfg. Co.

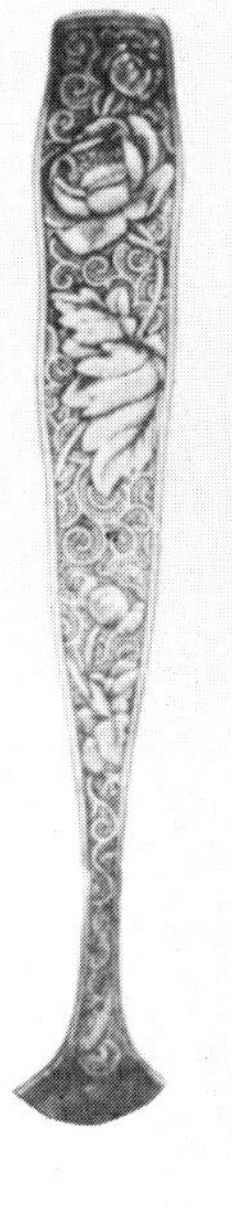

Examples of variations within a design theme. SIMPSON, HALL, MILLER & CO.: *Left*: Mille Fleurs. Handles at top are ¾ actual size; examples of the various pieces (bottom) are approximately ⅜ actual size. TIFFANY & CO.: *Right Center:* Japanese (Audubon). Original designer sketches for various pieces, front and reverse. TOWLE MFG. CO.: *Right*: Orchids pattern variations.

1835 R. Wallace

Watson, Newell & Co.

Whiting Mfg. Co.

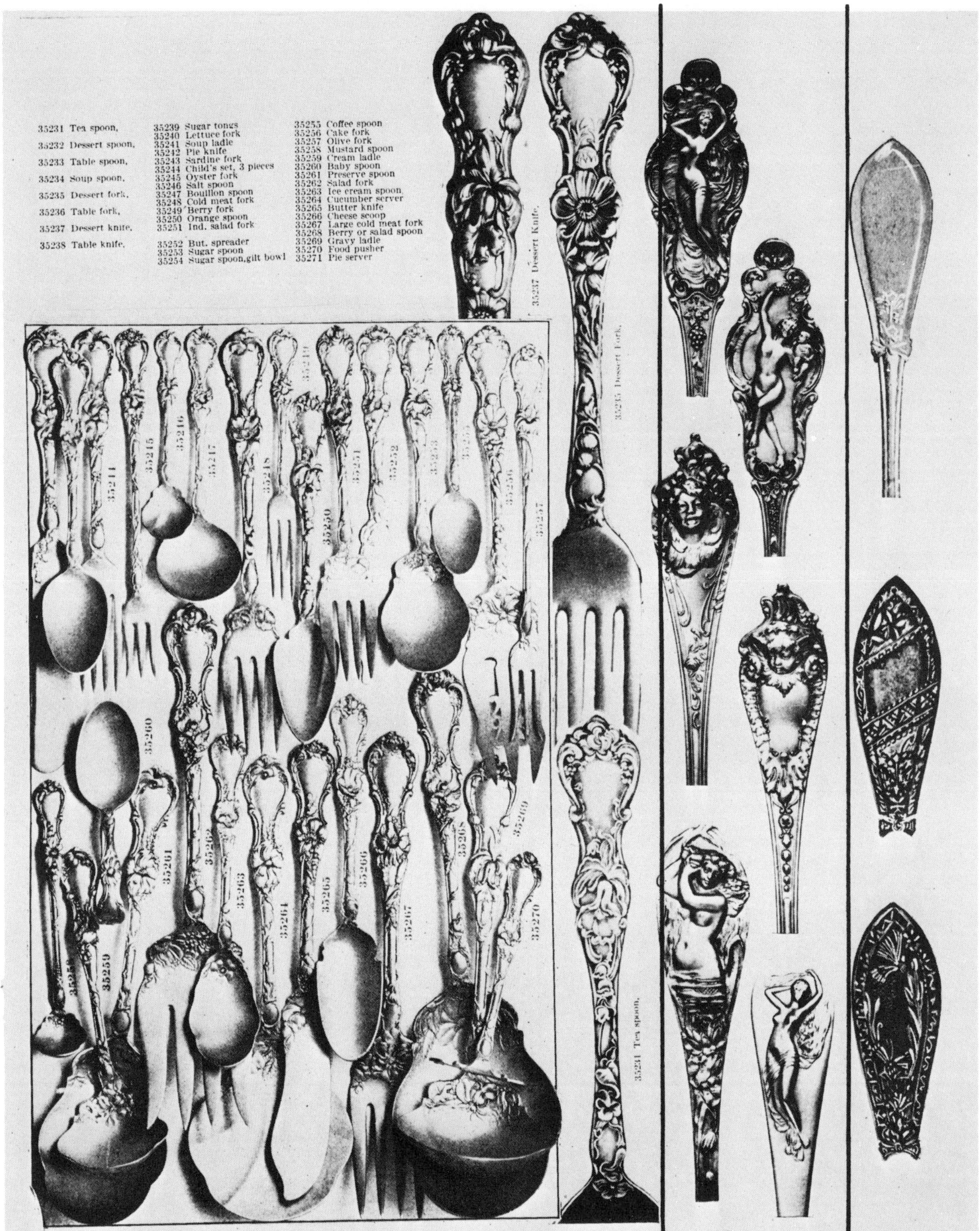

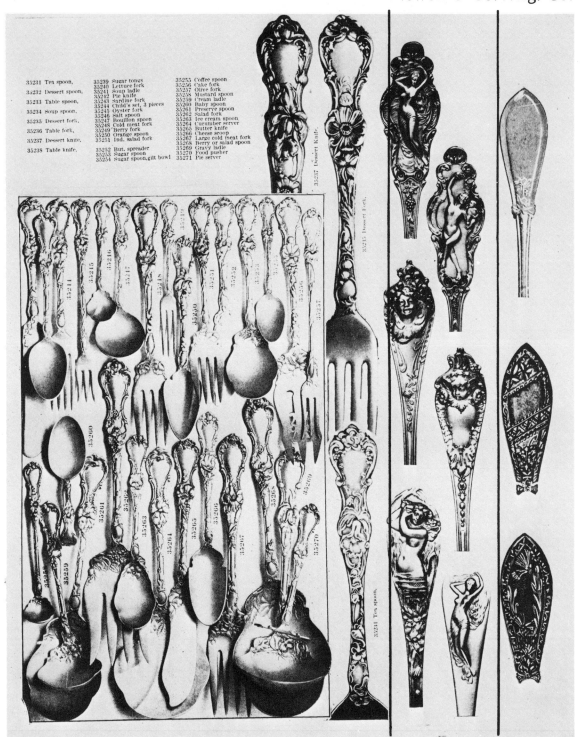

Examples of variations within a design theme. 1835 R. WALLACE: *Left*: Floral. Knife, fork and spoon handles are ¾ actual size; examples of other pieces, approximately ⅜ actual size, indicate the many variations possible in a complete service.

WATSON, NEWELL & CO.: *Right Center (top to bottom, staggered)*: Phoebe, Cherub, Watson No. 1. WHITING MFG. CO.: *Far right (Top to bottom)*: Italian, Italian J, Italian K.

8

Pieces

When Charles Lutwidge Dodson, under his pseudonym of Lewis Carroll, wrote the line, "They pursued it with forks and hope," he attributed it to the mild-mannered baker who was hunting the Snark to serve with greens. He might well have used the same line to describe the plight of many guests at contemporary Victorian dinners, where stern, social orthodoxy decreed that "a knife or spoon is never used when a fork will suffice." Judged by the controversy that raged through the press of the time, many of the guests relied more on hope than on the implement as they pursued ice cream, berries, and other elusive foods with the correct but ill-adapted fork.

But the arbiters of fashion were not alone responsible for the changing patterns of etiquette that brought a bewildering array of forks and spoons and knives to the late Victorian table; changing patterns of eating and entertaining, rapidly altering economic and social conditions, even an increasing abundance and availability of many foods, contributed to the new concept of the art of dining.

At the beginning of the Victorian period, silver services were comparatively simple, as was serving at the table. In the section devoted to "Furniture of the Table" in *The American Chesterfield,* published in 1828 in Philadelphia by John Grigg, thc following extract describes table setting in a fashionable house:

> Every person at table should be provided with knife and fork, plate, bread, &c.; and, before every meat dish, a carving knife, fork and spoon; and a spoon before every dish of vegetables. At the corners of the table, spoons, a salt cellar, and small spoon for the salt; and, if pickles are there placed, a small knife and fork. If the table is large, the furniture of the corners should likewise be placed at short and convenient intervals. It has lately become common, in our Atlantic towns, and particularly at tables where light wines are used with water as a long drink, to place, at convenient distances around the table, bottles of Sauterne, Claret or other light wine (the corks slightly drawn and inserted slightly in the bottle) and goblets of water. This is found, by experience, to be an admirable arrangement for convenience, and gives the waiters more time to attend, among other duties, to the frequent changes of plates which modern refinement has introduced.
>
> On the sideboard should be arranged, in order, all those articles of furniture which are necessary for the table. These are, the great supplies of knives and forks, plates of different sizes, spoons, bread, &c., &c.; but, in a particular manner, the castors. These should always consist of five bottles, at least; viz; cayenne pepper, black pepper, mustard, vinegar and sweet oil. Let the castors be *filled* —not half filled—with condiments of good quality, that is, the *sweet* oil not rancid, nor the vinegar *sweet,* nor the pepper in grains

> like hailstones, nor the mustard stale; and one word more, madame, before we dismiss the castors—*a little spoon for the mustard, though it be of wood—and—and—remember the salt spoons.*

After a word of caution regarding industry among servants, and a discussion of the rules of waiting, *The American Chesterfield* continues:

> If there is soup for dinner, according to the number of the company, lay each person a flat plate, and a soup plate over it; a napkin, fork, knife and spoon; and to place the chairs. If there is no soup, the soup plate may be omitted.

There can be no doubt that *The American Chesterfield* was directed toward the sons of American families of established wealth and position; that is made clear by the references to forks in the table settings. Writing in *Harper's New Monthly Magazine* in 1868, James Parton explained:

> From spoons, Jabez Gorham advanced to fruit knives, butter knives, thimbles, napkin rings and combs—the only articles commonly made by American silversmiths thirty years ago. Silver forks were then scarcely known in the United States. They had been an article of luxury among the nobility of France for a century or more, and had been introduced from that country into England; but in the United States, as recently as 1835, their use was confined to persons who possessed considerable wealth. They were not common at that time in any but the best hotels, and not one person in ten had ever seen them used.

But for that one person in ten, and for those who dined with him, specialization of table flatware was beginning. To the table knife and fork and spoon of the early 18th century had already been added the dessert knife and fork; the teaspoon, and with it, the caddy spoon; ladles for sauce and soup, the sugar tongs, and serving spoons. Early 19th-century America saw a growing demand for pickle forks, and sometimes pickle knives, for salt spoons and mustard spoons, and for the long handled dressing spoon or platter spoon, to reach deep into the cavity of the spit-cooked bird. These were sometimes called basting spoons, but it was a careless housewife who permitted her silver that near the flames!

In some households, the new English fashion for separate fish knives was being followed; these had been introduced in London in 1820. Although it would be 50 years before the separate fish fork was introduced, more and more people were ordering second sets of table forks to be used with these new knives; this accounts for the occasional appearance today of a service for 12 with 24 table forks. The fish trowel had been developed earlier, during the reign of George III, when Whitebait had become fashionable; this serving piece had gradually evolved into the asymmetrical fish knife, which was joined by a serving fork by 1830. Such specialization was but a beginning, for within a generation even the pattern for serving meals was to change radically, and with this change came many new demands on silversmiths and electroplaters.

Anthelme Brillat-Savarin, in his *Physiology of Taste,* published in 1825, had introduced a new "ordinance of the table," which he is said to have devised during his exile in the United States during the last years of the 18th century. Prior to the introduction of his new theory, meals had been served in what was called the Italianate style, which had been brought to the French court by Catherine de'Medici. In this style, apparently revived from the Roman Empire, all food was prepared, then placed helter-skelter on the table. There might be separate "services" or "plates," but since each service might include fish, fowl, game, fruits, and sweets, there was little point in keeping them apart.

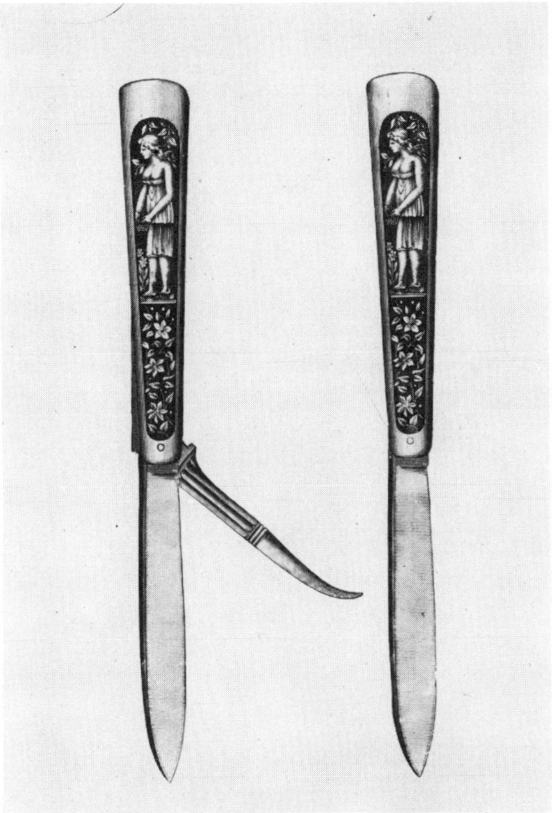

Pocket fruit knives were sometimes made with handles closely resembling popular flatware patterns. Such knives sometimes included a nut pick as well as a fruit knife blade.

Under Savarin's system, which has now become so common that few people realize how original it was at the time of its introduction, the old "services" became "courses," each consisting of only one fundamental food, and these were arranged in a logical order. The logic was Savarin's; if anyone questioned why fish should come before meat, or a stew before a roast it was because Savarin said that was the way it should be —and Savarin was confident of his own taste. He stressed the necessity of having the wines complement the food, and taught that every meal should be a festive occasion with gay, cheerful conversation and a well-chosen group. The new scheme was adopted to a limited extent throughout Europe during the ensuing years; it made its appearance in the United States about mid-century, but was not generally accepted until after the War between the States.

At least one silverware manufacturer paid his debt to Savarin by naming a tableware pattern after him; there seems to be no record of the dedication of one of the numerous books on decorum and etiquette to the French master, but that was surely merely an oversight on the part of the authors and publishers for whom a whole new field had opened.

"A Woman of Fashion," writing one of these countless guides to social acceptance which poured forth at this time, stated that:

> The comfortable, pot-luck, "come-early-and-stay-to-dinner" sort of society is not included in this manual, naturally. Certain communities —perhaps the happiest and most hearty—make their own dinner table laws, and live up or down to them. They ladle out your brimming soup, or possibly eliminate that preliminary, and begin by hacking off a generous slice of beef for you. You pass up your plate, or reach over somebody's, shove things about, do anything you like at such boards, and are happy. But these need no rules. The newspaper's answers to correspondents, as to how to dispose of your knife and fork when you pass your plate for a second helping, are all such as they require.

But even "such as they" were making their requirements known to silver manufacturers —and their demands were being met by carving sets, which, even though used to "hack off a generous slice of beef," were matched to the knife and fork at each place; the ladles for the brimming serving of soup, too, were designed to complement each place setting.

The confusion attendant on new manners of dining brought forth a rash of etiquette books; 28 separate manuals appeared in the 1830s, 35 in the 1840s, and 38 more in

Despite the ridicule of such magazines as *Life* during the 1880s and 1890s, the formal dinner remained a popular form of entertaining at home—for those whose homes were adequately equipped and staffed.

the 1850s—apart from revisions and 'later editions'. And as the population and new fashions spread, so did the books! In the 1870s 46 came forth from publishers, 51 more in the 80s, 43 in the 90s, and 65 between 1900 and World War I.

> "Nowhere has the growth of luxury in this country been more apparent," exulted a contemporary, "than in the pomp and circumstance which now accompanies modern dinners." In contrast to simpler times, the guest found at his place—"a bewildering array of glass goblets, wine and champagne glasses, numerous forks, knives and spoons."

The ordeal of dining involved many traps for the unwary, to which the etiquette editors devoted loving attention. The question of the knife *versus* the fork gained fresh urgency with the introduction of the French or silver fork in place of the steel variety. According to the social arbiters, both refinement and safety recommended the primacy of the fork, although there were dissenters.

By the 1870s, dinners consisted of from 5 to 18 courses, and the meal might be expected to be prolonged for up to two hours. *Decorum: A Practical Treatise on Etiquette*, published in 1878, had these helpful hints for guest and host:

> Soup is the first course. All should accept it even if they let it remain untouched, because it is better to make a pretense of eating until the next course is served than to sit waiting or compel the servants to serve one

SCENE: RECEPTION IN PHILADELPHIA.

Young Gentleman: WAITER, BRING ME A SPOON FOR THE ICE CREAM INSTEAD OF THIS FORK.
Waiter (from New York): OXCUSE ME, I CLEAN FORGOT I VAS THIS NIGHT IN PHILADELPHIA.

TO THE MANNER BORN.

Mr. Primus: WHO IS THAT GIRL EATING SO ENTHUSIASTICALLY OVER YONDER AT THE OTHER TABLE?
Miss Secunda: WHY, THAT IS MISS BLACKHILL, GRANDDAUGHTER OF THE DAKOTA MILLIONAIRE. SHE LOOKS AS IF SHE HAD ALWAYS HAD WHAT SHE WANTED, DOESN'T SHE?
Mr. Primus: WELL, YES. SHE LOOKS LIKE A GIRL WHO WAS BORN WITH A SILVER KNIFE IN HER MOUTH.

Public interest in newly fashionable silver flatware pieces vied with changing table manners, as reflected in these cartoons in *Life* during the 1880s.

before the rest. Fish follows the soup, and must be eaten with a fork unless fish knives are provided. After soup and fish come the side dishes, which must be eaten with a fork only, although the knife may be used for cutting anything too hard for a fork. Pastry should be eaten with a fork. Everything that can be cut without a knife should be cut with a fork alone. Pudding may be eaten with a fork or spoon. Ice requires a spoon. Cheese *must* be eaten with a fork. Never bite fruit. An apple, pear or peach should be peeled with a silver knife, and all fruit should be broken or cut. Never pare an apple or a pear for a lady unless she desires you, and then be careful to use your fork to hold it; you may sometime offer to *divide a very large pear* with or for a person.

The dilemma presented by the necessity for cutting everything possible with a fork alone was again solved by the manufacturers; in 1869, Reed & Barton patented the "cutting fork", a fork with one broad, sharpened tine which acted like a knife blade. It was offered originally in dinner and dessert fork sizes, and later became the standard form, in smaller size, for the pie or pastry fork; in a larger version, it became the cold-meat fork.

Despite the new inventions, warnings against the use of the knife continued. Most of the authorities on decorum agreed with the author, who, writing in 1878, stated that "a knife should never, on any account, be put into the mouth. Many even well-bred people in other particulars think this is an unnecessary regulation; but when we consider it a rule of etiquette, and that its violation causes surprise and disgust to many people, it is wise to observe it." To illustrate his point, the author quoted a letter from William Makepeace Thackeray to a gentleman in Philadelphia:

The European continent swarms with your people. They are not all as polished as Chesterfield. I wish some of them spoke French a little better. I saw five of them at supper in Baslc thc other night with their knives down their throats. It was awful! My daughter saw it, and I was obliged to say, "My dear, your great, great grandmother, one of the finest ladies of the old school I ever saw, applied cold steel to her wittles. It's no crime to eat with a knife," which is all very well; but I wish five of 'em at a time wouldn't."

This was from Thackeray, who was *not* included among the members of English literary "Silver Fork School"—the group of English novelists who were felt to give undue importance to etiquette and the externals of social intercourse. Among the more distinguished members were Lady Blessington, Lord Lytton, Lord Beaconsfield, and, of course, Mrs. Trollope!

Among the dissenters, a Mrs. Farrar, wife of a professor at Harvard, and the author of *The Young Lady's Friend,* fought a losing battle when she insisted, patriotically, that "Americans have as good a right to their own fashions as the inhabitants of any other country." She went on in defense of the practice of eating with a knife "providing you do it neatly and do not put in large mouthfuls or close your lips tight over the blade." As late as 1889, *Life* magazine, in a satirical sketch, pointed out that James Russell Lowell had departed from "the American idea . . . he ate his pie with a fork when he dined at Windsor."

By the middle 1880s, most proponents of the knife had conceded defeat, but, heady with victory, the arbiters of fashion threw the fork into a new conflict, this time with the spoon.

The true devotee of fashion," asserted one of these high priests in 1887, "does not dare to use a spoon except to stir his tea or eat his soup, and meekly eats his ice cream with a fork and pretends to like it.

In the decade following the Civil War,

silver services had been somewhat expanded; catalogs generally listed butter knives and butter picks, so that the diner's own knife was no longer used to cut butter served in a slab, or his own fork to spear the butter ball. To the tea and tablespoon had been added the small coffee spoon, for use with the demi-tasse. Silver fruit knives appeared in great variety, some designed as pocket pieces, handy for a Sunday afternoon stroll through the orchard. Some of these ingeniously added a nut pick, another piece which was frequently made to match the table service and nut crack. Grape shears had come into general use at the table, and the oyster fork as well as the individual fish fork had begun to appear more and more frequently.

Manufacturers soon tried to outdo one another in the variety of pieces produced. As early as 1880, for example, Reed & Barton manufactured 20 different varieties of spoons, 12 different forks, and 10 different knives. The complete flatware line consisted of 57 distinct items. Inventory problems were enormous, for most of the pieces were made in four grades and more than a dozen patterns. When pieces, grades and patterns were all taken into consideration, the number of items in this one flatware line totaled 3,560! And with most manufacturers, the variety increased throughout the 1890s, as *Etiquette for Americans* pointed out in 1898:

As to the manner of "setting" the table,

Diagram of a Table Laid for a Formal Dinner

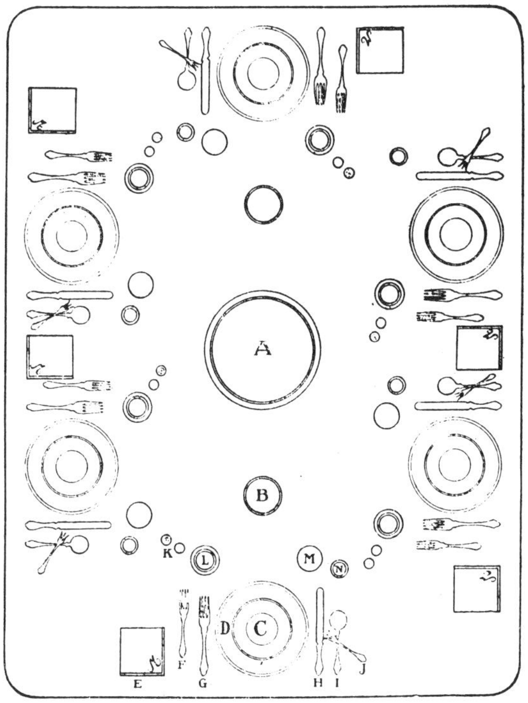

MENU

Raw Oysters

Consommé à la Royal

Breaded Turbans of Fish — Rolls

Cucumbers — French Dressing

Roast Leg of Lamb — Mint Sauce

Peas — Scalloped Potatoes

Strawberry Ice Cream

Cake — Bonbons

Coffee

A	Flowers.	H	Knife for Lamb.
B	Bonbons.	I	Soup Spoon.
C	Raw Oysters.	J	Oyster Fork.
D	Service Plate.	K	Salt and Pepper Shakers
E	Napkin.	L	Plate for Salad.
F	Fork for Fish.	M	Individual Butter Plate.
G	Fork for Lamb.	N	Glass for Water.

[54] Rigid rules governed the placement of every [55] item of "table furniture," for the formal dinner. Illustrations as detailed as this appeared in cook books, household hint books, and women's magazines.

there are some differences of opinion or custom. At the strictest houses, there is always a plate in front of each guest; but that rule is not followed rigidly in many careful establishments. Anything very ornate in the way of napkin arranging, placing of glasses, knives, forks, etc. belongs to cheap hotels, and not to any sort of private establishment.

A napkin squarely folded and lying flat at each place, a row of forks at its left, oyster fork on the outside, then fork for fish, and a large and small ordinary fork, making four, are usually arranged for a simple dinner. At the right of the napkin are knives; a fish knife at the extreme right, a steel bladed large knife, and a silver bladed knife inside, making three. A soup spoon next to the napkin is all that is required in that line; it is laid squarely across the upper side of the place. Dessert and ice spoons are brought in later, and so (usually) are salad forks and dessert forks.

Silver knives for cutting meat are obsolete, thank heaven; no one knows why they were introduced except in the interest of dishwashers at hotels. There should be a small steel knife for game; always a silver knife for fish or fruit.

A small knife and fork are placed for anchovy toast, or *caviare* or whatever is eaten as a relish before oysters at a formal dinner; but a fork will almost always be found to be sufficient. Indeed the fingers are usually employed. Soup, it may not be necessary to state, is taken up by the spoon and turned away from the eater, and sipped from the side of the implement with as little sound as possible. Fish is taken with a silver knife like the old fashioned butter knife, and with a small fork; but as there are many old fashioned American houses where fish knives are still considered a superfluity, the "fork and a bit of bread" are to be called into requisition in these establishments. Cucumbers are passed and put on the same plate as fish. An entree follows the fish; and, unless it is a fillet of beef or some such unforkable food, is to be eaten with a fork alone. There is no bread and butter plate, or butter spreader, because butter is not eaten at dinner. Game is hot, and salad cold, but the two are often put on one plate. Cheese is passed with this course in most American homes, but it is really not quite the thing. Cheese should come last on the menu. Never cut a salad, nor take cheese in your fingers. Eat it with a knife.

The seeds of grapes should be removed with a silver knife; pears, peaches and oranges should be seeded or stoned in the same manner.

The rules went on and on, and with each new rule, there came a need for even greater variety among the knives, the forks, the spoons, the tongs, the servers. But the manufacturers prepared for each new onslaught; in service after service, pattern after pattern, grade after grade—from the thinnest electroplate to the heaviest sterling—special forks

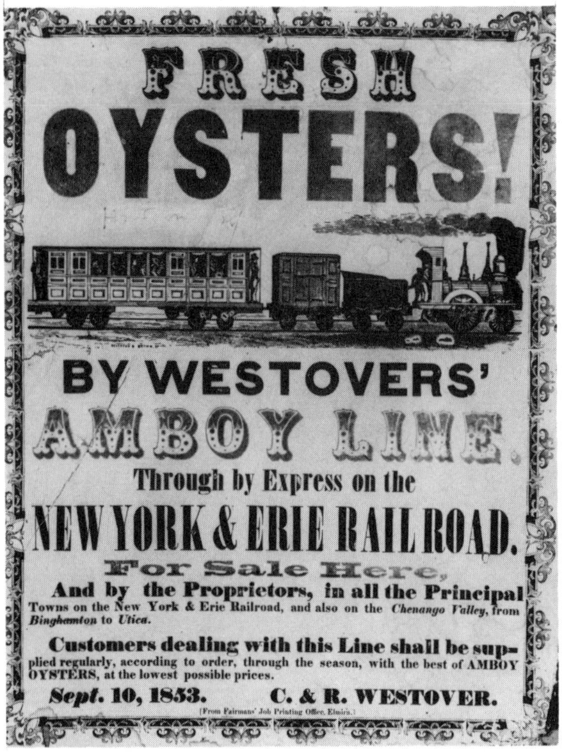

As rails and refrigeration brought oysters and seafood to inland areas, specialized pieces of silver flatware became necessary throughout the country. This 1853 announcement heralded regular sales of oysters in Upstate New York; local jewelers and silversmiths soon found a market for oyster forks. *Courtesy of The New York Historical Society, New York City.*

spewed forth from the factories; medium forks, dinner forks, dessert forks; fish forks, oyster forks, lobster forks, terrapin forks; salad forks, lettuce forks, berry forks, pie forks, ice cream forks, fruit forks, all for individual place settings, or, in terms of the trade, "Dozens Work." Among the serving pieces, called "Fancy Pieces" by the trade, forks for beef and forks for cold meat vied with forks for sardines, bread, olives, asparagus, chow-chow, pickles. There were scoops for bon-bons and almonds, crackers and cheese; special servers for toast and tomatoes, for croquettes and for cucumbers. To the sugar tongs, which had been introduced in the 18th century, the late 19th century added tongs for olives, ice, sardines, and asparagus. At least two lines included individual asparagus tongs, and individual carving sets—complete with steel—were introduced to facilitate the serving of woodcock, quail, and passenger pigeons—the seemingly endless bounty that market hunters continued to ship from field and forest to every city market.

Although frowned upon as an eating implement, the knife, too turned up in many new guises as a serving tool. As early as 1878, an American social reporter announced that:

> Queen Victoria has set the fashion for placing the whole loaf of bread upon the table with a knife by its side, leaving the bread to be cut as desired. However, the old style of having the bread already cut when it is placed upon the table will still recommend itself to many.

In the same year, bread knives with silver handles, ready to join other solid and plated ware on the table, were made available by American silversmiths. These frequently joined the bread fork which had earlier been included in some lines. Among other items, a single catalog at about the turn of the century lists butter knives, jelly knives, pie knives, cheese knives, cake knives, ice cream knives, fish knives, and bread knives, along with individual bird carvers and breakfast-carving sets.

Pierced serving pieces, which had earlier included ice spoons, sugar sifters, and tea strainers, now included servers for tomatoes, cucumbers, and peas, for pickles and beets, nuts and mints. Completely new forms were developed, too, as travelers brought home tales of exotic dining, and improved shipping facilities made a wider range of new foods available. Macaroni and spaghetti servers, resembling nothing ever seen before—except, perhaps, a cross between the familiar fish knife and a comb—made the serving of these delectable festoons, with all their foreign glamour, a new experience in dining. The popularity of the chafing dish in the 1890s brought forth chafing dish sets—a large fork and spoon, with handles of bone or stag horn as a protection against the heat generated by the open burner. The crumb knife and "crumber sets"—sometimes consisting of a crumb knife and tray, sometimes of a silver-mounted brush and receiver—made quick work of clearing the heavy damask cloths with which the dining table was usually draped.

Nor were regional foods and individual food requirements overlooked. One manufacturer added a mango fork to his selection of fruit accessories; an early Boardman catalog featured a buckwheat cake lifter; a crawfish knife for individual service was readily available from another catalog. Pap spoons, for the invalid or food faddist, were produced by several firms. At the other extreme, a number of firms, from the 1860s on, catered to those who felt the need for toddy spoons, toddy strainers, and claret spoons. The same customers probably represented the bulk of the market for such items as orange peelers and lemon knives, as distinguished from the more widely distributed conventional orange and fruit knives.

Services grew in complexity. An 1859 catalog of Mulford, Wendell & Co. of Albany, listed table, oyster and dessert fork, tea, table and dessert spoons, and dessert knives among the place pieces; serving pieces including butter and cake knives, sugar spoons and pickle forks—all in the "Olive" pattern. Sets of marrow spoons were still offered through the 1860s, and the marrow scoop continued to be listed well into the '90s. By 1877, a catalog of Reed & Barton showed, as its most complete service, a chest containing a dozen each of tablespoons, dessert spoons, teaspoons, coffee spoons, medium knives (with hollow handles), and dessert knives (with flat handles), supplemented by two butter knives, two salt spoons, a pair of sugar tongs, plus a sugar shell, and one each of soup, gravy, and cream ladles, a berry and a mustard spoon, and a fish knife, fish fork and a pie knife. By 1881, Gorham had added to the company's "List of Spoon and Fork Work," bread, cheese, cake, crumb, ice cream, jelly, macaroni, melon, pudding, salad, tea and waffle knives, as well as a knife designed for handling fried oysters. Forks for beef, melon, pastry, sardines, salmon, strawberries, toast and vegetables were listed, along with individual salad forks, and serving forks for salad *and* for chicken salad. Large and small berry spoons, egg spoons, individual fruit spoons, spoons for honey, horseradish, jelly and preserves had taken their places beside the earlier forks and spoons. Scoops for berries and cheese, sifters for sugar, and tongs for asparagus, salad, bon-bons, and beef completed the pieces made of sterling silver. Six years later, in 1887, Rogers & Smith offered, in a fine black walnut chest with drawer, all of the pieces considered standard in 1877, further enforced by ice tongs, salad serving fork and spoon, and a carving knife, fork, and steel. By 1898, these 110 pieces had grown to 297 in a mahogany chest with a deck and four drawers, offered by the Towle Manufacturing Company. The list of fancy pieces included a pair of salt spoons, and a mustard spoon, horse radish spoon, sugar spoon, jelly spoon, berry spoon, lettuce spoon, lettuce fork, pickle fork, sardine fork, cold-meat fork, butter knife, chocolate muddler, sugar tongs, tete-a-tete tongs (small sugar tongs), salad fork, salad spoon, fish knife, fish fork, cream ladle, gravy ladle, soup ladle, roast holder, an Ideal olive fork and spoon, a three-piece bird carving set and a five-piece carving set. Place pieces included dozens each of chocolate spoons, orange spoons, iced tea spoons, butter spreaders, ice cream forks, oyster forks, salad forks, soup spoons, afternoon teaspoons, teaspoons, tablespoons, dessert spoons, dessert forks, table forks, coffee spoons, bouillon spoons, tea knives, fruit knives, duck knives, fish knives, dessert knives and medium knives. Shortly after 1900, Reed & Barton featured a deck-and-four-drawer chest containing 404 pieces; the service for 18 included sherbet spoons and orange knives with saw edges, and an asparagus server, sugar sifter, macaroni server, pea spoon, cheese scoop, and vegetable fork among the additions to the earlier lists.

Some services included matching napkin rings and sets of individual butter plates or chips, along with salt shakers. Their use and placement was carefully spelled out, even for those who did not buy etiquette books. A little cook book, distributed free by the makers of Rumford Baking Powder late in the 90s, and called *Rumford Dainties and Household Helps,* carefully diagrammed the formal dinner table, and included in directions the following instructions for the placement of silver:

> Knives, forks, and spoons are set in the order of their use, the first used farthest from the plate. The knives are set on the right of the plate, the forks on the left, the soup spoon

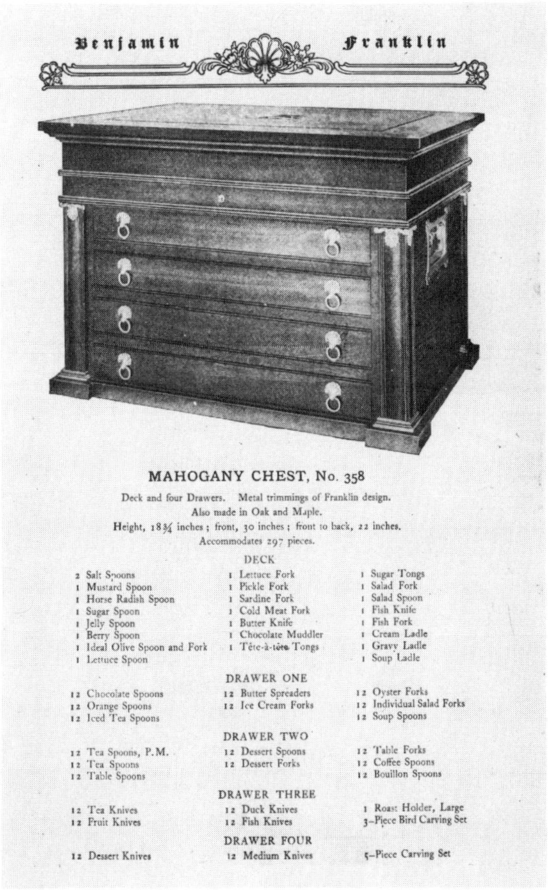

Benjamin Franklin

MAHOGANY CHEST, No. 358

Deck and four Drawers. Metal trimmings of Franklin design.
Also made in Oak and Maple.
Height, 18¾ inches; front, 30 inches; front to back, 22 inches.
Accommodates 297 pieces.

DECK

2 Salt Spoons	1 Lettuce Fork	1 Sugar Tongs
1 Mustard Spoon	1 Pickle Fork	1 Salad Fork
1 Horse Radish Spoon	1 Sardine Fork	1 Salad Spoon
1 Sugar Spoon	1 Cold Meat Fork	1 Fish Knife
1 Jelly Spoon	1 Butter Knife	1 Fish Fork
1 Berry Spoon	1 Chocolate Muddler	1 Cream Ladle
1 Ideal Olive Spoon and Fork	1 Tête-à-tête Tongs	1 Gravy Ladle
1 Lettuce Spoon		1 Soup Ladle

DRAWER ONE

12 Chocolate Spoons	12 Butter Spreaders	12 Oyster Forks
12 Orange Spoons	12 Ice Cream Forks	12 Individual Salad Forks
12 Iced Tea Spoons		12 Soup Spoons

DRAWER TWO

12 Tea Spoons, P.M.	12 Dessert Spoons	12 Table Forks
12 Tea Spoons	12 Dessert Forks	12 Coffee Spoons
12 Table Spoons		12 Bouillon Spoons

DRAWER THREE

12 Tea Knives	12 Duck Knives	1 Roast Holder, Large
12 Fruit Knives	12 Fish Knives	3-Piece Bird Carving Set

DRAWER FOUR

12 Dessert Knives	12 Medium Knives	5-Piece Carving Set

A complete service for 12, with appropriate serving pieces, could be stored in this four-drawer-and-deck chest.

beyond the knives. The oyster fork is laid diagonally across the soup spoon or on a line with it and beyond it. Silver for entrees and dessert is set in place at time of use. The cutting edges of knives are towards the plate, the tines of forks and the edge of the soup spoon upwards. The glass for water is set at the tip of the knife, the tiny butter plate when used is set to the left of the glass for water. Bread and butter plates with "spreaders" are reserved for home use and less formal meals than dinner. A salad served with the fish or meat course is eaten with the fork provided for the fish or meat. Salt and pepper shakers are set between each two individuals at table, on a line with the upper edge of each cover.

The menu suggested for this *simple* formal dinner started with Raw Oysters, continued with Consomme a la Royal, Breaded Turbans of Fish, accompanied by rolls since no fish knives were provided, Cucumbers and French Dressing, followed by Roast Leg of Lamb, Mint Sauce, Peas, and Scalloped Potatoes. Strawberry ice cream was recommended for dessert, with Cake, Bon-Bons, and Coffee. It was suggested that complicated menus and service be reserved for those households with adequate staffs!

That an adequate silver service would be available was apparently assumed. Production—and acceptance—of these complex services continued for many years. It was not until 1926 that a simplified list of 55 items was adopted as the maximum number of separate pieces to be made in any pattern introduced after that time. This program was recommended by Herbert Hoover, then Secretary of Commerce, to the members of The Sterling Silverware Manufacturers Association—a predecessor of The Sterling Silver Guild,—as one of the "Simplification Systems" suggested for all American industry.

Place and Serving Pieces

Place and Serving Pieces

Place knives for individual service. Where size or design varied in different patterns, several examples are shown. Illustrations are approximately one-third scale. *Top row (l. to r.)*: Medium or Dinner Knife, Dessert Knife, Tea Knife, Child's Knife, Duck Knife, Fish Knife, Orange Knife, Butter Spreader, Hollow Handle, Butter Spreader (Large), Butter Spreader (Small), Tea Knife, Fish Knife. *Middle row (l. to r.)*: Fruit Knives (6 styles), Orange Knives (5 styles), Individual Carving Set, Crawfish Knife, Fish Knife. *Horizontal illustrations at bottom*: *left, above*: Orange Peeler; *left, below*: Melon Fork-knife. *Right*: Fruit or Melon Set.

Place and Serving Pieces

Place forks for individual service. Where size or design varied in different patterns, several examples are shown. Illustrations are approximately one-third scale. *Top row (l. to r.)*: Medium or Dinner Fork, Dessert Fork, Pie Fork, Fish Fork, Salad Fork, Pastry Fork, Oyster Fork, Lobster Fork, Terrapin Fork, Ice Cream Fork, Berry Fork, Mango Fork. *Middle row (l. to r.)*: Oyster Cocktail Fork, Fish Fork, Lobster Fork, Terrapin Fork, Fruit Fork (hollow handle), Oyster Cocktail Fork, Oyster Fork, Lobster Fork, Child's Fork, Salad Fork (small), Salad Fork (large). *Bottom row (l. to r.)*: Ramekin Fork, Lettuce Fork, Terrapin Fork, Berry Forks (4 styles), Oyster Forks (4 styles), Oyster Fork-Spoon.

Place and Serving Pieces

Spoons and tongs for individual service. Where size or design varied in different patterns, several examples are shown. Illustrations are approximately one-third scale. *Top row (l. to r.)*: Iced Tea Spoon, Egg Spoon, Soup Spoon, Bouillon Spoon, Chocolate Spoon, Pap Spoon, Coffee Spoon, Breakfast Spoon, P.M. Tea Spoon, Dessert Spoon, Tea Spoon, Table Spoon. *Middle row (l. to r.)*: Chocolate Spoon (Large), Chocolate Spoon (Small), Coffee Spoon (Large), Coffee Spoon (Small), P.M. Tea Spoon, Child's Spoon, Bouillon Spoon, Egg or Ice Cream Spoon, Ice Cream Spoon, Ice Cream Spoon, Salt Spoon, Salt Spoon, Bar Spoon, Toddy Spoon. *Bottom row (l. to r.)*: Individual Asparagus Tongs, Grapefruit Spoons (2 styles), Orange Spoons (6 styles), Iced Tea Spoon, Sherbet Spoon, Soda Spoon, Lemonade Spoon-Sipper, Claret Spoon.

Place and Serving Pieces

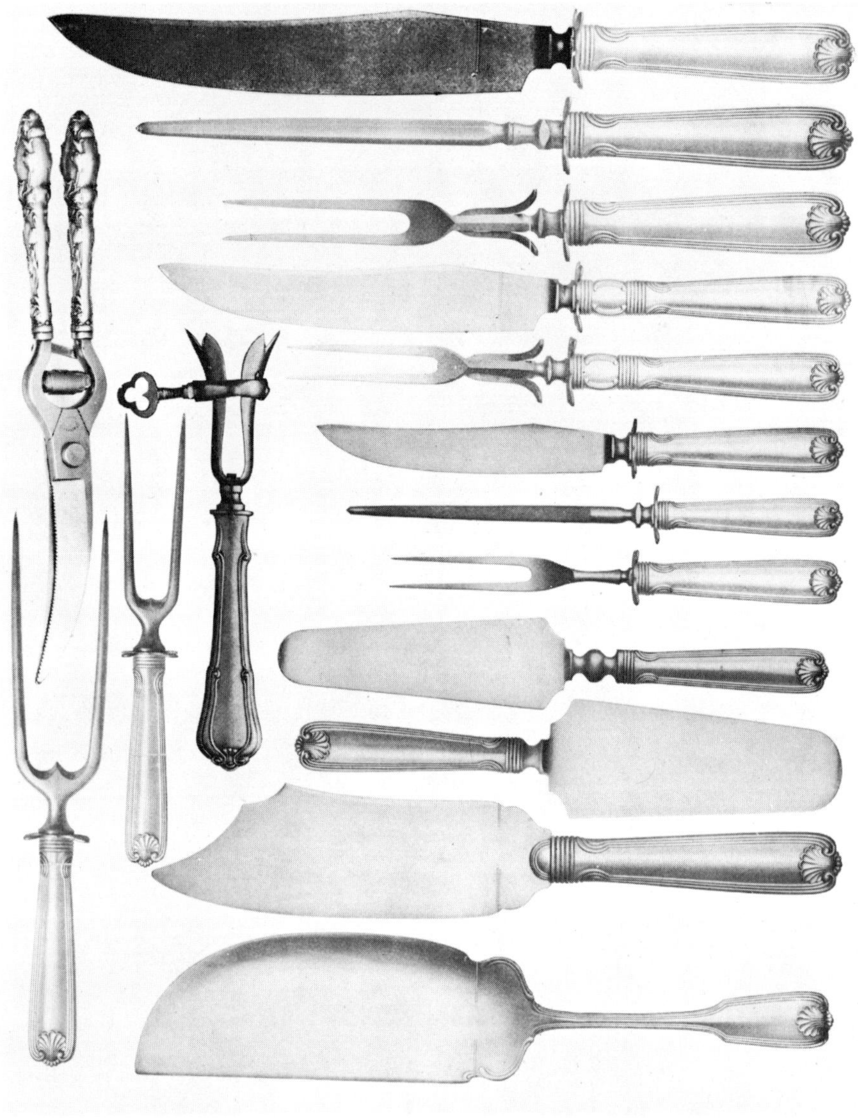

Serving pieces, carving aids and knives. Illustrations are approximately one-third scale. *Left (top to bottom)*: Duck Shears, Roast Holder (Large). *Left Center*: Roast Holder (Small), Bone Holder. *Right (Top to bottom)*: 3-piece Roast Carving Set with Steel, 2-piece Game Carving Set, 3-piece Bird Carving Set with Steel, Cake Server or Knife, Ice Cream Server or Knife, Ice Cream Slicer, Crumb Knife.

Place and Serving Pieces

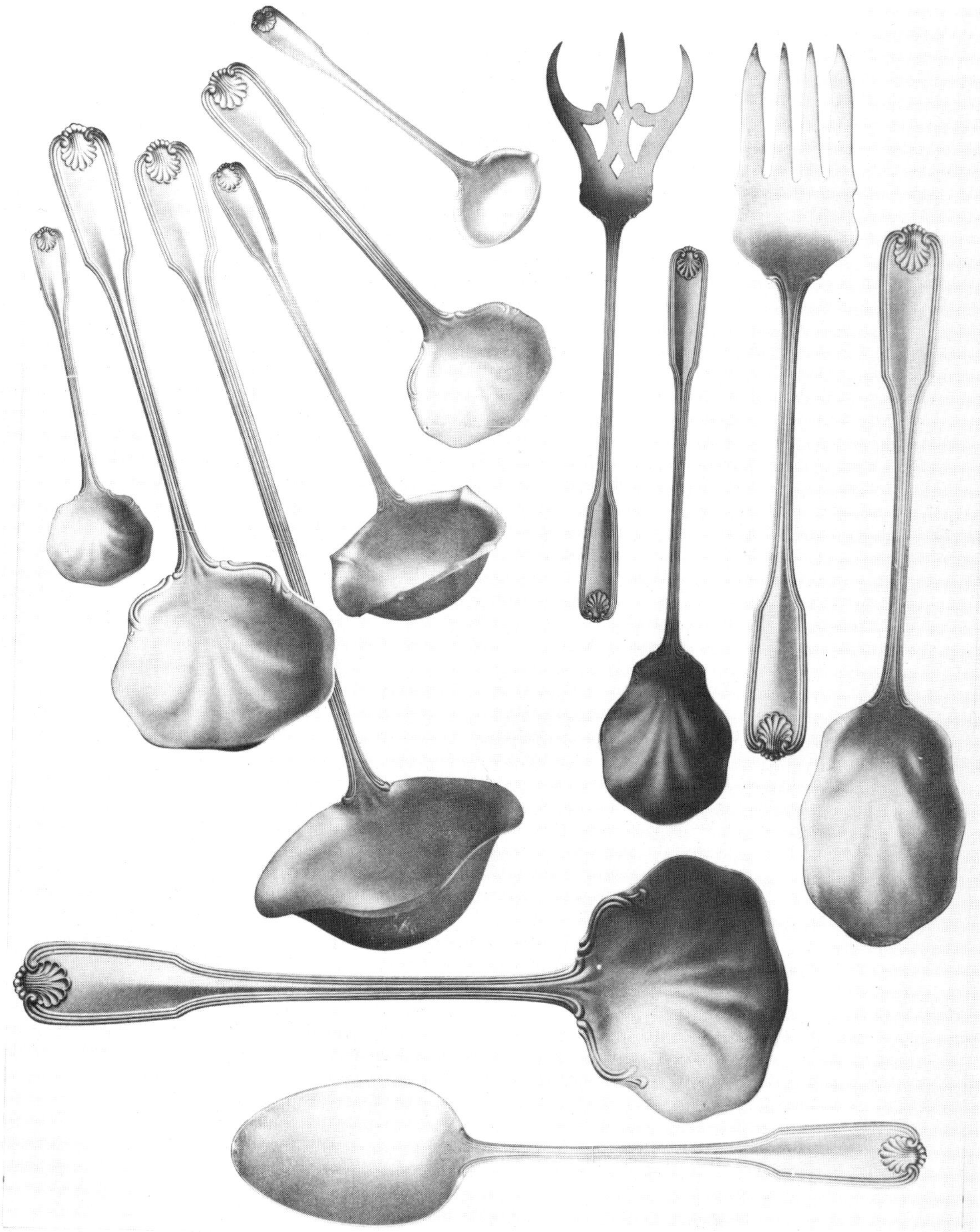

Serving spoons, forks and ladles. Illustrations are approximately one-third scale. *Upper left, counter-clockwise*: Cream Ladle, Oyster Ladle, Punch Ladle, Bouillon Ladle, Gravy Ladle, Mayonnaise Ladle. *Right, top row*: Lettuce Fork, Salad Fork (Large). *Middle row*: Lettuce Spoon, Salad Spoon (Large). *Horizontal illustrations at bottom of page*: *(Top)*: Soup Ladle. *(Bottom)*: Platter or Gravy Spoon.

Place and Serving Pieces

Serving pieces. Illustrations are approximately one-third scale. *Top row (l. to r.)*: Spinach Fork, Bread Fork, Beef Fork, Cold Meat Fork, Tomato Server, Waffle Server, Croquette Server, Cracker Scoop, Cucumber Server. *Lower left*: Fried Oyster or Entree Server, Cake Server. *Lower Right (top to bottom)*: Asparagus Server, Ice Cream Server, Fish Fork, Fish Knife.

Place and Serving Pieces

Size and design sometimes varied widely among pieces offered for the same purpose by different manufacturers. Illustrations are approximately one-third scale. *Top row (l. to r.)*: Sardine Forks (3 styles), Sardine Fork and Helper, Jelly Knives (5 styles). *Middle row (l. to r.)*: Tomato Servers (3 styles), Tomato Fork. *Lower left, top to bottom*: Butter Knife, Butter Knife (Twist), Butter Knife (Hollow Handle), Butter Knife (Bent). *Lower right, top to bottom*: Cheese Servers (2 styles), Cheese Knife, Cheese Scoops (4 styles). Handles of the Sardine Fork and Helper and the Cheese Scoop at lower right are sterling silver, *not* stag.

Place and Serving Pieces

Serving and accessory pieces were frequently highly specialized, but offered in standard production patterns. Illustrations are approximately one-third scale. *Top row (l. to r.)*: Chocolate Muddler, Tea Strainer, Tea Strainer, Tea Infuser, Tea Strainer, Brandy Burner, Toddy Strainer, Julep Strainer. *Middle row (l. to r.)*: Tea Caddy Spoons (2 styles), Lemon Fork, Lemon Servers (2 styles), Lemon Knife, Butter Pick, Butter Pick (Large), Butter Pick (Small), Nut Spoon, Nut Pick, Nut Cracker. *Bottom row (l. to r.)*: Bon Bon Scoops (2 styles), Bon Bon Spoons (3 styles, with Bon Bon Tongs above), Almond Scoops (2 styles), Nut Picks (2 styles), Nut Cracker.

Place and Serving Pieces

A similar name did not necessarily mean the same design among serving pieces, as the spoons and tongs shown here indicate. Illustrations are approximately one-third scale. *Upper left, horizontal illustrations, top to bottom*: Serving Spoon, Preserve Spoon, Preserve Spoon, Bon Bon Tongs (2 styles). *Right, top row*: Honey Spoon, Jelly Spoon, Jelly Spoon. *Right, immediately below honey and jelly spoons*: Sugar Shells (5 styles). *Right, below sugar shells*: Sugar Sifters (3 styles). *Immediately left of sugar shells*: Sugar Shaker. *Bottom row*: Ice Tongs, Ice Tongs, Asparagus Tongs (with Individual Asparagus Tongs and Olive Tongs above), Sardine Tongs, Tete-a-tete Sugar Tongs, Sugar Tongs.

Place and Serving Pieces

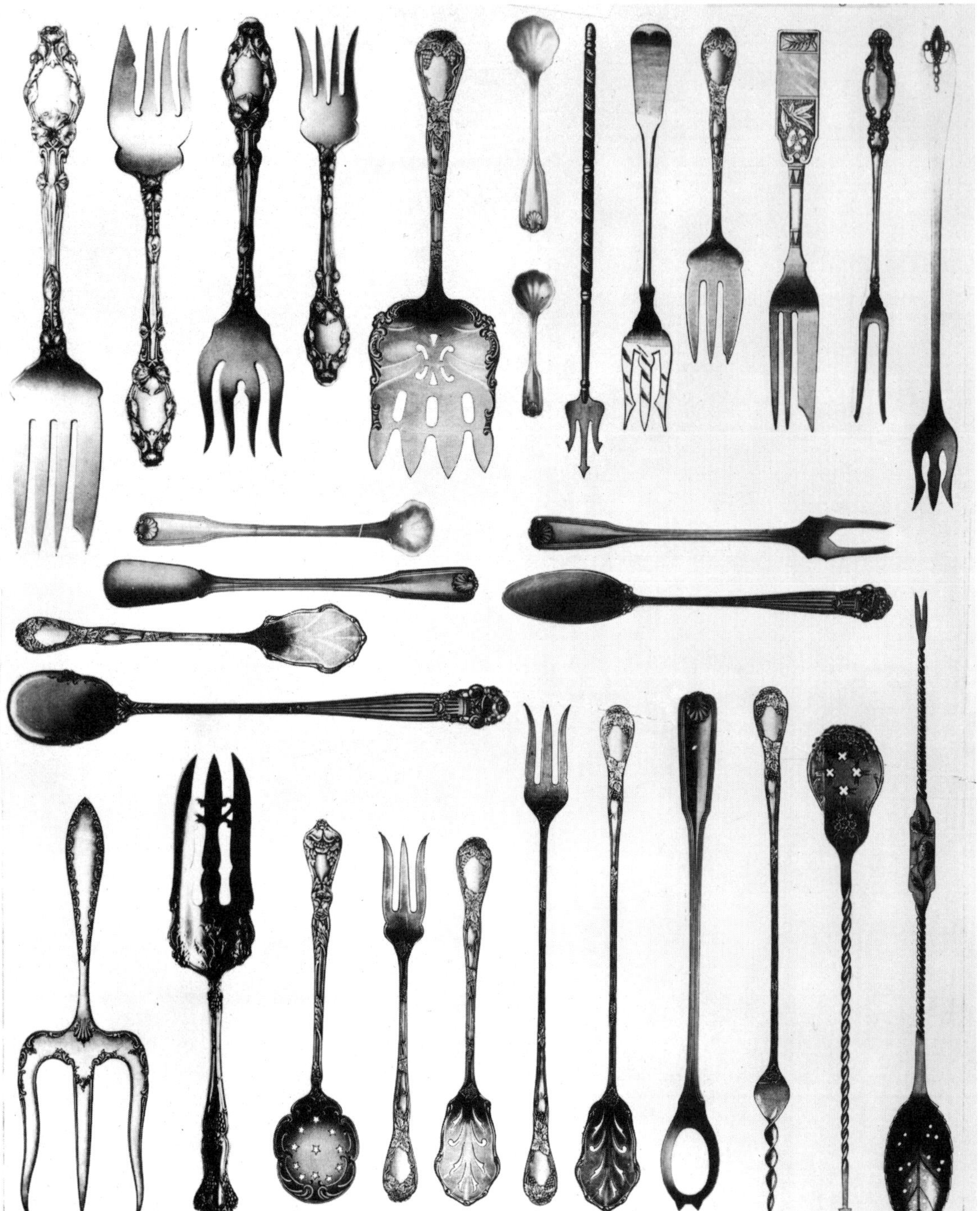

Many serving pieces were offered in two sizes. Pickles, relishes, and condiments were important adjuncts to Victorian menus, and special serving pieces were devised for many of them. Illustrations are approximately one-third scale.
Top row (l. to r.): Cold Meat Fork (Large), Cold Meat Fork (Small), Beef Fork (Large), Beef Fork (Small), Salad Fork (Small), Salt Spoon (Master), Salt Spoon (Ind.), Pickle Spear, Pickle Forks (5 styles). *Middle, horizontal illustrations (left, top to bottom)*: Mustard Spoon, Horseradish Spoons (2 styles), Piccalilli Spoon. *Right*: Chow Chow Fork, Chow Chow Spoon. *Bottom row (l. to r.)*: Toast Fork, Pastry Fork, Olive Spoon, Olive Fork and Spoon (4–5), Olive Fork and Spoon (6–7), Ideal Olive Spoon, Olive Spear, Olive Spoon-Spear, Olive Spoon-Fork.

Place and Serving Pieces

The variety of place and serving pieces was equally large in both sterling and electroplate. Throughout these pages, both types of products are represented. Illustrations are approximately one-third scale. *Top row (l. to r.)*: Salad Spoon, Oyster Ladle, Fried Oyster Server, Medium Ladle, Ice Cream Ladle, Soup Ladle. *Bottom row (l. to r.)*: Pie Knife, Cracker and Saratoga Chips Server, Pie Server, Gravy Ladle, Mustard Ladle, Cream Ladle (Large), Salt Spoon, Cream Ladle, Sauce Ladle.

Place and Serving Pieces

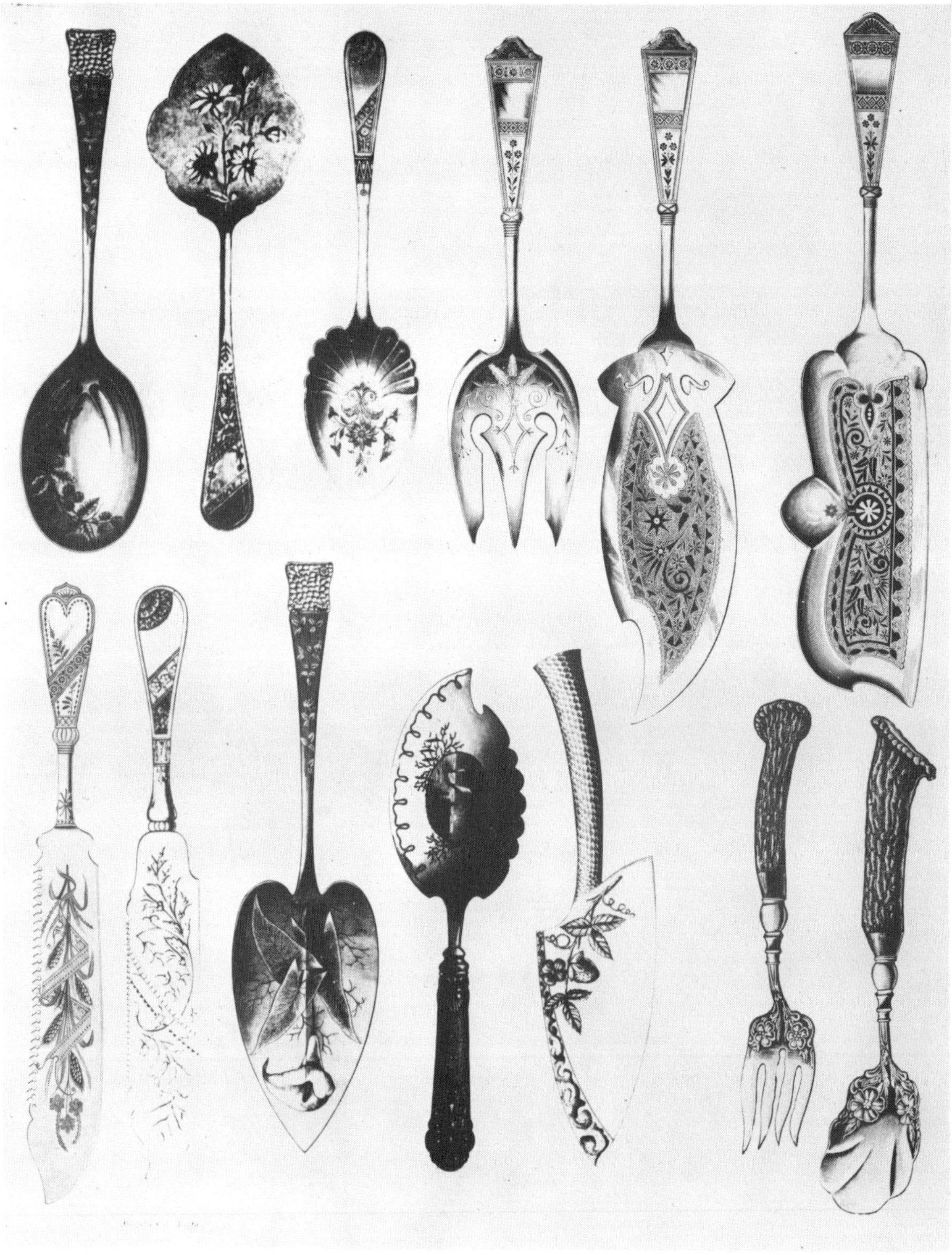

Ornately engraved blades, bowls, and tines decorated many of the serving pieces. In some lines and patterns, gold inlays were offered; in most lines, gold bowls or tines were available at a premium price. Illustrations are approximately one-third scale. *Top row (l to r.)*: Berry Shell, Buckwheat Cake Lifter, Table Spoon, Fish Fork, Fish Knife, Crumb Knife. *Bottom row (l. to r.)*: Cake Knife, Cake Knife, Pie Knife, Ice Cream Knife, Pie Knife, Chafing Dish Set (Stag Handles).

Place and Serving Pieces

Pierced serving pieces were popular, and were offered in great variety. Illustrations are approximately one-third scale. *Top row (l. to r.)*: Berry Spoon (Small), Macaroni Server, Pea Server, Ice Spoon. *Middle row (l. to r.)*: Pudding Spoon, Vegetable Spoon, Vegetable Fork. *Bottom row (l. to r.)*: Berry Spoon, Macaroni Spoon, Pea Spoon, Ice Spoon.

Place and Serving Pieces

Patent knife sharpeners frequently were offered as supplements to the standard carving steel, with handles matching other pieces in a complete service. Illustrations are approximately one-third scale. *Far left*: Bread Knife, Grape or Flower Shears. *Top row (l. to r.)*: Cream Ladle, Soup Ladle, Ice Spoon, Punch Ladle, Gravy Ladle. *Horizontal illustrations, bottom of page*: *left*: Fruit and Nut Set (knife, cracker and pick); *right*: Patent Knife Sharpeners (2 styles).

Place and Serving Pieces

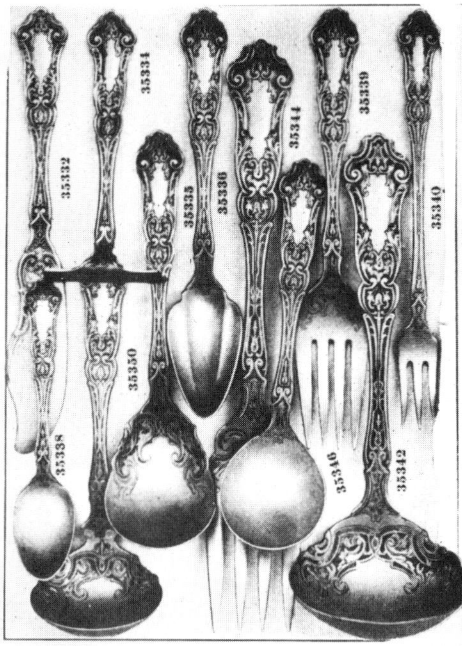

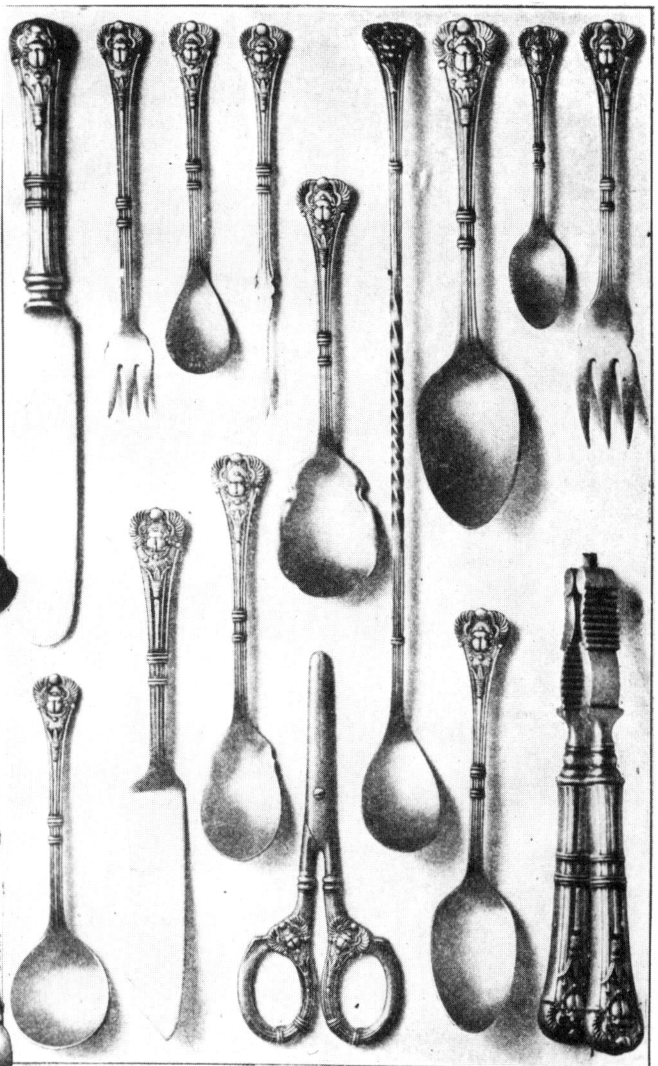

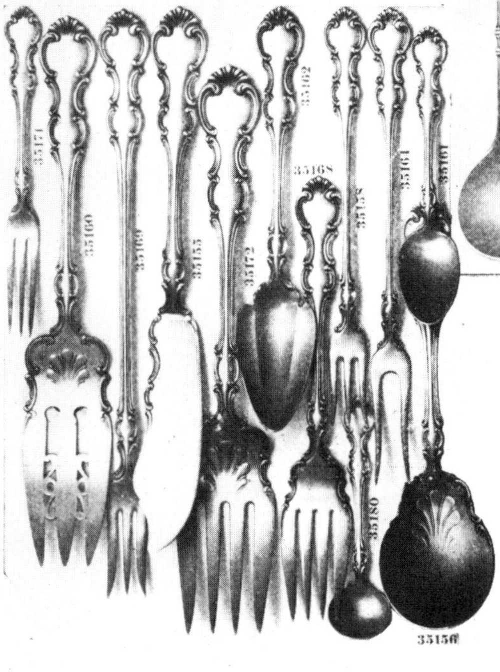

Examples of the various place and serving pieces made in both sterling and electroplate patterns. Illustrations are approximately one-third scale. *Left (top group)*: CARDINAL: 35332 Butter Spreader, 35334 Food Pusher, 35335 Sugar Spoon, 35336 Orange Spoon, 35338 Coffee Spoon, 35339 Ind. Salad Fork, 35340 Oyster Fork, 35342 Gravy Ladle, 35344 Cold Meat Fork (Large), 35346 Bouillon Spoon, 35350 Cream Ladle. *Left (bottom group)*: TROY: 35155 Butter Knife, 35156 Sugar Spoon, 35158 Oyster Fork, 35160 Cake Fork, 35161 Coffee Spoon, 35162 Orange Spoon, 35164 Olive Fork, 35168 Ind. Salad Fork, 35169 Pickle Fork, 35171 Berry Fork, 35172 Cold Meat Fork (Large), 35180 Salt Spoon. *Right (group)* ANTIQUE EGYPTIAN: *Top row (l. to r.)*: Dessert Knife, Oyster Fork, Egg Spoon, Nut Pick, Sugar Shell, Claret Spoon, Dessert Spoon, Coffee Spoon, Ind. Fish Fork, *Bottom row (l. to r.)*: Bouillon Spoon, Butter Knife, Ice Cręam Spoon, Grape Shears, Tea Spoon, Nut Cracker.

Place and Serving Pieces

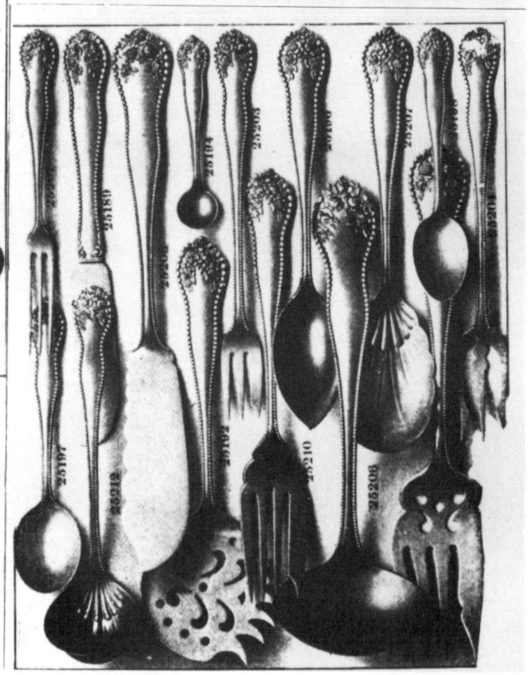

R. Wallace & Sons' "Rose" was made in both sterling and electroplate, and the same pieces were offered in both grades. Any of the spoons and forks shown in Gorham's "Lancaster" could be ordered with gilt bowls or tines. *Left Group*: ROSE: 10708 Bouillon Spoon, 10709 Bon Bon Tongs, 10710 Cold Meat Fork (Large), 10711 Child's Spoon, 10712 Child's Fork, 10713 Child's Knife, 10714 Fruit Knife, 10715 Oyster Fork, 10716 Cheese Scoop, 10717 Salt Spoon (Large), 10718 Butter Knife, 10719 Pickle Fork, 10720 Butter Pick, 10721 Olive Fork, 10722 Olive Spoon, 10723 Pie Server, 10724 Soup Spoon, 10725 Sugar Spoon, 10726 Bon Bon Spoon, 10728 Sugar Tongs, 10729 Mustard Spoon, 10730 Preserve Spoon, 10731 Ind. Salad Fork, 10732 Cream Ladle, 10733 Jelly Knife, 10734 Lettuce Fork, 10735 Gravy Ladle, 10736 Berry Spoon, 10737 Butter Spreader.

Right (top group): LOUIS XV: 10671 Baby Spoon, 10674 Oyster Fork, 10675 Ind. Salt Spoon, 10676 Cold Meat Fork (Small), 10677 Butter Knife, 10678 Coffee Spoon, 10685 Cheese Scoop, 10688 Pickle Fork, 10689 Gravy Ladle, 10690 Orange Spoon, 10696 Cream Ladle, 10698 Mustard Spoon, 10699 Olive Spoon. *Right (bottom group)*: LANCASTER: 25189 Butter Spreader, 25192 Cucumber Server, 25194 Ind. Salt Spoon, 25196 Orange Spoon, 25197 Chocolate Spoon, 25198 Coffee Spoon, 25201 Berry Fork, 25203 Oyster Fork, 25204 Olive Fork, 25205 Butter Knife, 25206 Gravy Ladle, 25207 Sugar Spoon, 25208 Cold Meat Fork (Large), 25210 Ind. Salad Fork, 25212 Cream Ladle.

Place and Serving Pieces

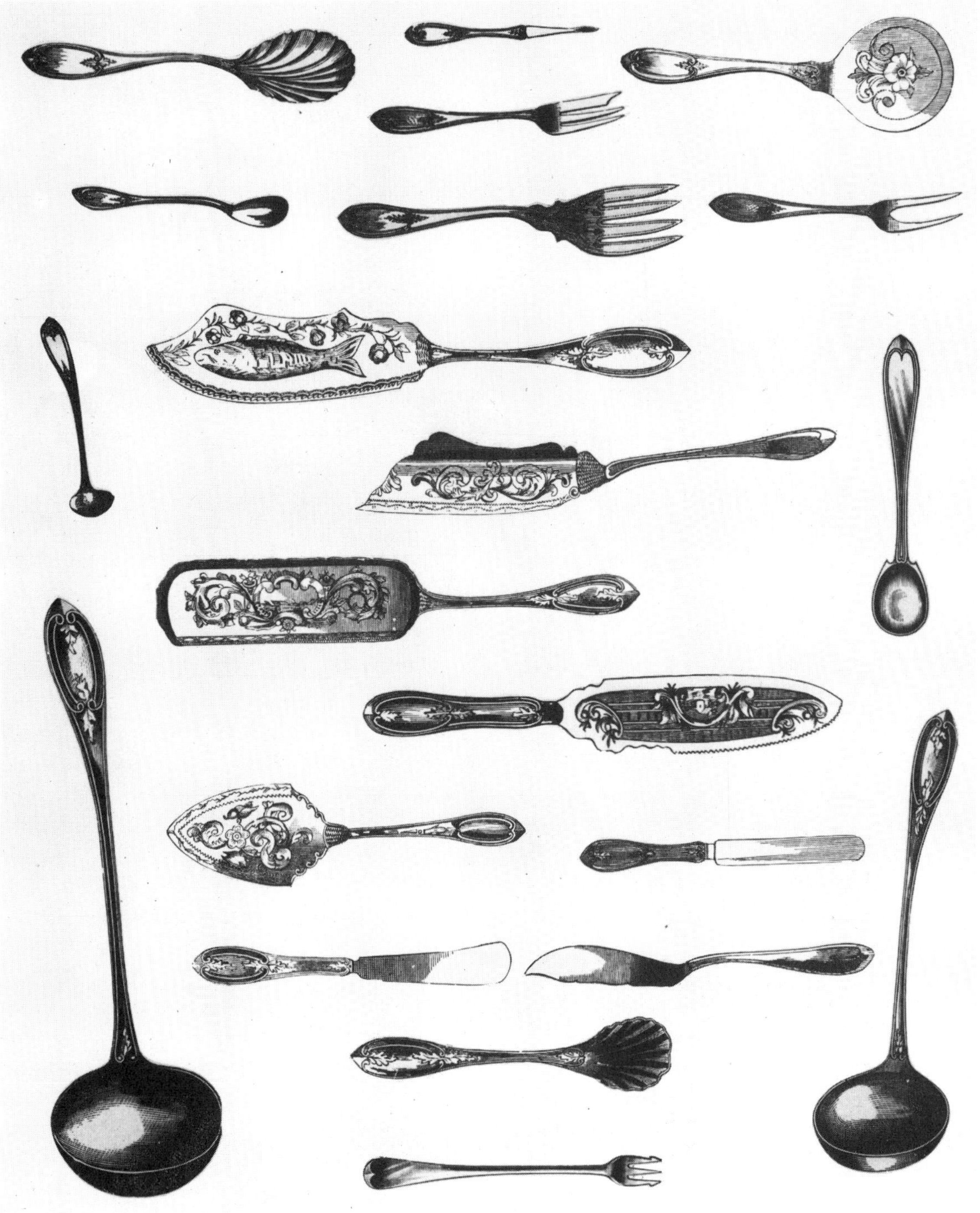

Serving and other "Fancy Pieces" offered in "Olive," "Tipped" and "Oval" patterns by 1880. Illustrations, about one-third size, are the same as those used in the Price List and Catalog of L. Boardman & Son. *Horizontal illustrations*: *Top left*: Berry Shell, *Top center*: Nut Pick, Pickle Fork, *Top right*: Buckwheat Cake Lifter. *Second row (l. to r.)*: Mustard, Egg or Bar Spoon, Fish Fork, Oyster Fork. *Third row*: Fish Knife (Engraved Blade). *Fourth Row*: Ice Cream Knife. *Fifth row*: Crumb knife. *Sixth row*: Cake cutter (Engraved Blade, saw edge). *Seventh row, left*: Pie Knife (Engraved Blade), *right*: Tea Knife (Solid or Flat Handle). *Eighth row, left*: Butter Knife, *right*: Butter Knife (Bent). *Ninth row*: Sugar Shell. *Bottom*: Oyster Fork (may be used for Pickle). *Vertical illustrations, left*: *(top)*: Mustard Ladle, *(bottom)*: Soup Ladle. *Vertical illustrations, right*: *(Top)*: Gravy Ladle (Silver Bowl), *bottom*: Medium Ladle (Old Style Bowl).

9

Presentation Sets

In *The Unbearable Bassington,* Hector Hugh Munro, better known by his pseudonym of Saki, related a post-party post-mortem:

> "It was their Silver Wedding; such lots of silver presents, quite a show."
>
> "We must not grudge them their show of presents after twenty-five years of married life; it is the silver lining to their cloud."

But even before 25 years of married life, the housewife whose dowry did not include a service of 300 or more matched pieces had no reason to despair of setting a proper table. "Combination sets" of highly specialized silver were being turned out by the thousands, and rapidly became favored Christmas, wedding, anniversary, and birthday gifts. They covered any conceivable course, food, or occasion. Among the more common were berry sets, with a berry serving spoon and six berry forks; ice cream sets, consisting of an ice cream knife or slicer and sets of individual ice cream forks or ice cream spoons; chocolate sets, a muddler for the pot, and six chocolate spoons for the cups. There were fish sets—sometimes including only the serving knife and fork, but often with these essentials as well as individual fish knives and forks; there were salad sets, sometimes, again, including only the two serving pieces, but often supplemented by a set of individual salad forks. Coffee sets usually included demi-tasse spoons and sugar tongs, although a cream ladle was sometimes added. Tea sets generally offered a choice of the regular teaspoon, or the slightly smaller size, variously called Afternoon, P.M., or Five O'Clock Tea. The combinations sometimes included a butter knife and sugar shell, and, less frequently, tea knives and tea forks, both items slightly smaller than the dessert sizes, and with knives often made with flat handles. But whether the sets were simple or elaborate, the additional teaspoons were always welcome, for the favored afternoon social events required vast numbers of these implements. Started in the 1870s, and popular throughout the next 20 years, the afternoon teas or receptions called "Kettle Drums" afforded the easiest means of repaying social obligations, and were a worthy forerunner of the cocktail party. Whether the name was derived from a British Colonial custom of serving tea from the top of a regimental drum at gatherings in remote outposts (as one source has it), or from the drumming sound of conversation when upwards of 50 guests were gathered in double parlors and the kettle for tea represented the refreshment, as another authority claims, the Kettle Drum made numerical demands on the silver chest equalled by few other social events in the average household.

Pastry sets, featuring a cake knife or cake fork, and individual pastry forks and pie sets, with a pie knife and individual pie forks, were equally popular in that calorie-unconscious age. Soup sets frequently included a ladle and set of soup spoons; oyster sets, a ladle and oyster forks; butter sets, a butter knife and individual spreaders.

What the jewelry trade termed "gift sets" were made up of innumerable combinations; sometimes a cream ladle, butter knife and sugar shell; a jelly knife and cold-meat fork; a gravy ladle and a cream ladle. Still other sets were specifically named: a "Condiment Set" included two salt spoons and a mustard spoon; a "Bon-Bon Set," tongs and a scoop; a "Cheese Set," a scoop and a knife.

Orange sets, with a serrated-blade knife for slicing and seeding, and sharply pointed spoons for the individual segments, shared the popularity of "Cold-Meat Sets," which featured a cold-meat fork, a jelly knife and a set of medium table forks. The usual jeweler's display abounded in carving sets; those in standard size, with steel, knife, and fork, flanked by matching game sets, bird sets, and chop sets, slightly smaller in size, and varying only minutely from the meat carvers. At least one manufacturer carried this specialization to the extreme of including a special duck set, adding to the carver and fork a duck shears and individual duck knives. Fruit sets, sometimes consisting of six knives, sometimes of knives and forks, sometimes of knives, forks *and* orange spoons, were, like the other sets, packaged in fitted, satin-lined presentation boxes.

A list of "Case Combinations" compiled by the Gorham Manufacturing Company in 1881, included most of these combinations, and added, for further variety, a set consisting of a butter knife, pickle knife and fork, two salt spoons and a mustard spoon; others, to prepare the hostess for any dessert contingency, consisted of a cake knife, an ice cream knife and a berry spoon; a cake knife, pie knife, and berry spoon; or a cake knife, waffle knife, and berry spoon. A berry spoon and sugar sifter were added to a set of ice cream knife and 12 ice cream spoons, while a fried-oyster knife joined a set of 12 oyster forks in another combination. Salad sets, in addition to those consisting of individual salad forks for 6 or 12, included a salad spoon and fork as well as a *chicken* salad spoon and fork. Including the children's sets, some 153 combinations were available in this single catalog.

Individual serving pieces too, were elaborately packaged for gift purposes. Single pieces might begin with a ladle—and the full range included punch ladles, soup ladles, medium ladles (intended for either soup or oysters), oyster ladles, gravy ladles, cream ladles and mayonnaise ladles, in a descending order of size—to a wide variety of forks, for cold meat, fish, beef, cake, salad, bread, asparagus, sardines, pickles and olives. The latter originally appeared in sets consisting of a fork and a pierced spoon. Late in the 1890s, these were generally superseded by the patented "Ideal" olive server—an ingenious device consisting of the outer rim of a spoon the size of an olive, with the bowl cut away to permit the brine to drip off, and equipped with a pair of prongs for spearing the elusive fruit of the glamorous olive tree. Glamour was reflected, too, in the Italian spelling of the "Maccaroni Knife," offered in a leatherette-covered, satin-lined case.

Despite the names borrowed from European sources, the multiplicity of highly specialized place and serving pieces was an American development. English silversmiths made little effort to proliferate their services, and, during the early 1890s, when the competitive rage was at its height in this country, correspondents for the jewelry trade press reported from Paris that there was no similar elaboration in the Continental market. Consequently, the reporters added, it was "unnecessary for a European bride, after being presented with a gift of silver, to ask her jeweler the purpose for which it had been designed."

That these extravagantly designed and elaborately packaged "presentation sets" achieved a wide distribution in America is attested by the social columns of the day, where, frequently, gifts were listed, along with their donors. It was probably such an item that caught the eye of David Macrae, the visitor from Scotland who wrote *The Americans at Home* after his trip to the United States in the '60s. He commented that "A Miss Whitney was married in Boston shortly before my first visit. The invitations issued for the ceremony and reception numbered 3000, and her wedding gifts in silver alone were valued at $10,000. There is a golden circle in New York in which even that would probably be reckoned a 'one-horse wedding.'"

Macrae found aniversary celebrations worthy of note, too. He wrote:

> The celebration of marriage anniversaries on the fifth, twenty-fifth, and fiftieth return of the wedding day, is very common in New England . . . friends assemble at the house, and generally bring presents with them—the presents increasing in the value of their material according to the length of time elapsed since the knot was tied. The twenty-fifth anniversary is the silver wedding, when silver toothpicks, forks, spoons, fruit-knives, cake baskets, and so forth are in demand.

He particularly commented on the festivities attendant on this anniversary of the Goughs, of Hillside, Massachusetts; the published report of "The Committee" for the silver wedding anniversary of John B. and Mary E. Gough provides more details on this 1868 celebration: Mr. Gough, a noted lecturer on temperance, and his wife were presented with a "solid-silver epergne, designed to hold either fruit or flowers, and an ice cream set of fourteen pieces, lined with gold. The value of both the above was a thousand dollars."

Other listed gifts included silver grape shears, sent from admirers in Dubuque, Iowa, silver butter knives "from the Reverend George H. Duffield and lady," of Galesburg, Illinois, a set of silver salt cellars and spoons from a couple in Ypsilanti, Michigan, and—proving that gift duplication is not a recent problem—a set of ice cream spoons and ladle, from W. H. Piper and Company of Boston *and* a set of ice cream spoons and ladle from the Newark Clayonian Society.

Anyone who has inherited or helped to clear almost any Victorian household need not be reminded that the donors of gift pieces were not always careful to match a previously selected pattern. So it may have been some bright young bride, finding herself with a fish set that failed to match her soup spoons, and a salad set that matched neither, who first started the custom of having the silver for a specific course brought in with that serving. At any rate, in 1898, one of the current social arbiters wrote that:

> Lately, some ultra people have changed the mode of putting all the knives, forks and spoon required for a dinner on at once, and have them brought in for each course, as required. This makes more work for the servants, and can only be done with a very complete service.

But the days of the "very complete service" were numbered; in a single generation, a new cycle in manners would be under way, with the cocktail party beginning to replace the "kettle drum," and the oysters-fish-and-lamb bowing to what Mary McCarthy describes in *The Group*: "one hot dish in a Pyrex, no soup, and a fresh green salad."

Presentation Sets

Presentation Sets

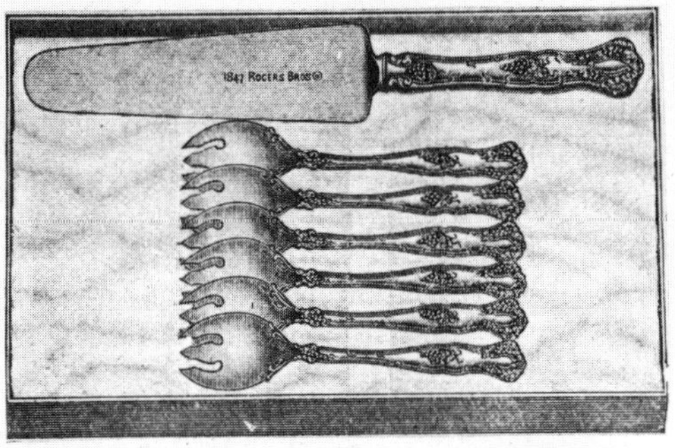

ICE CREAM SET. Vintage French gray pattern. Set contains 6 ice cream forks and 1 ice cream knife.

ICE OR VEGETABLE SPOON. Wm. Rogers Eagle Brand, York Pattern.

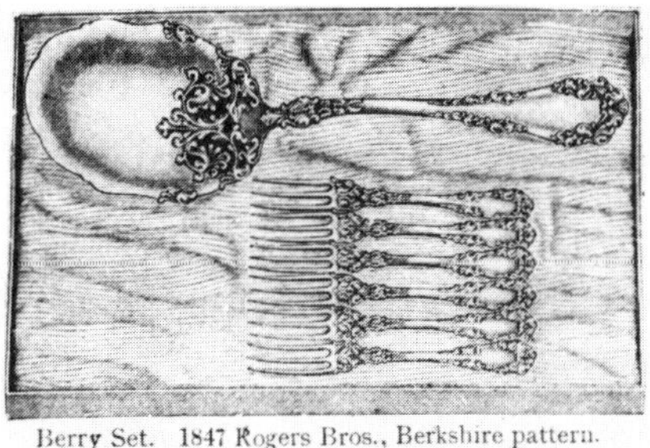

Berry Set. 1847 Rogers Bros., Berkshire pattern. Set contains 1 berry spoon and 6 berry forks.

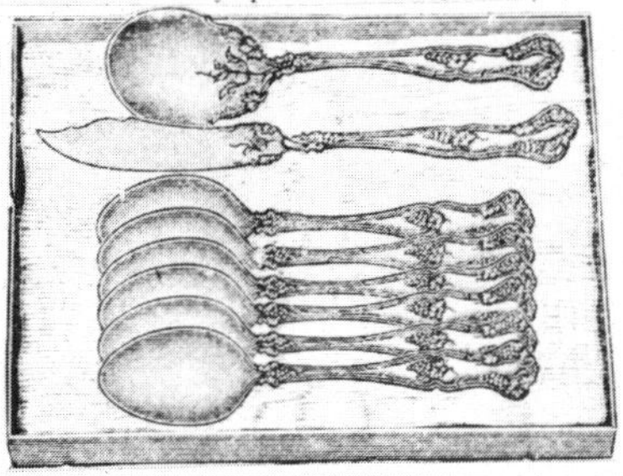

COMBINATION SET. Vintage French gray pattern. 1847 Rogers Bros. Set contains 1 butter knife, 1 sugar shell and 6 tea spoons.

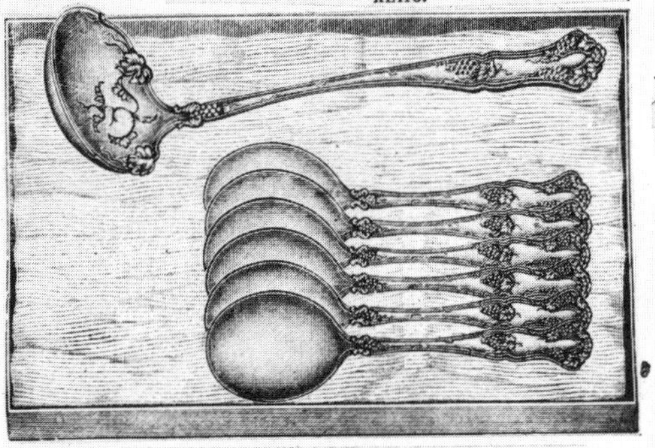

SOUP SET. 1847 Rogers Bros. Vintage French gray pattern. Set contains 1 oyster ladle and 6 round bowl soup spoons.

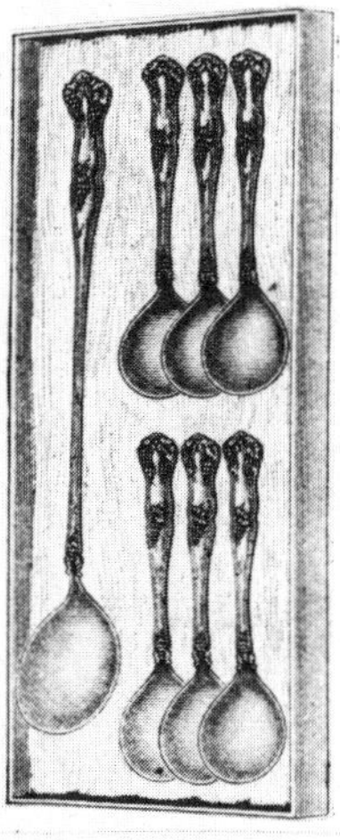

Chocolate Set. 1847 Rogers Bros., Vintage French gray pattern. Set contains one chocolate muddler and 6 chocolate spoons.

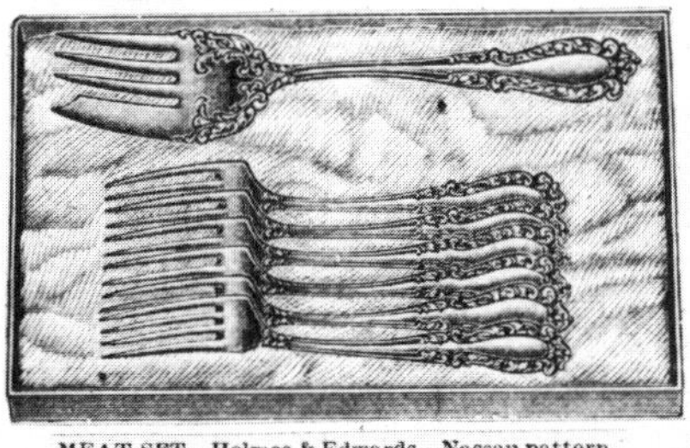

MEAT SET. Holmes & Edwards. Nassau pattern. Set contains 1 cold meat fork and 6 dessert forks.

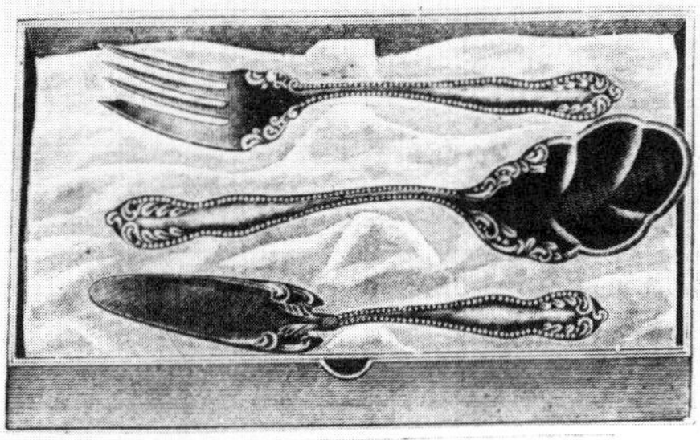

Berry Spoon, Meat Fork and Jelly Knife Set. Holmes & Edwards, Pearl pattern.

BOUILLON SPOONS. 1847 Rogers Bros., Vintage French Gray Pattern.

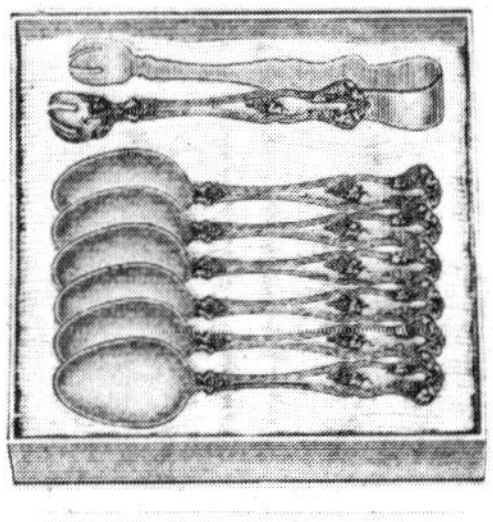

COFFEE SET. 1847 Rogers Bros. Vintage French gray pattern. Set contains 1 sugar tong and 6 coffee spoons.

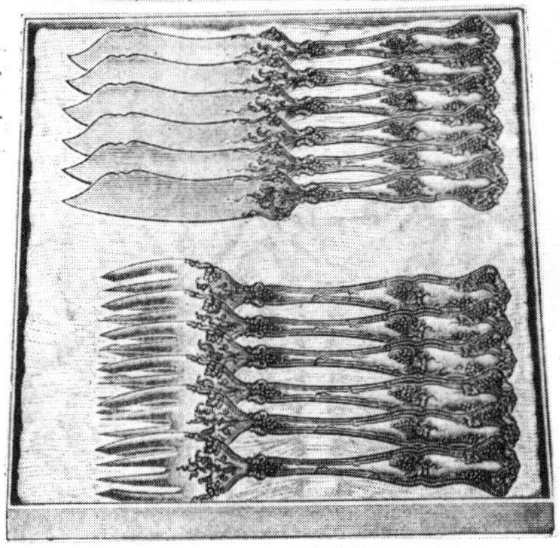

Fish Set. 1847 Rogers Bros., Vintage French gray pattern. Set contains one-half dozen each individual fish knives and forks.

Presentation sets ranged from a single boxed serving piece to a service for a complete course. Sets shown here are electroplate; similar gift packages were offered by makers of sterling ware.

Presentation Sets

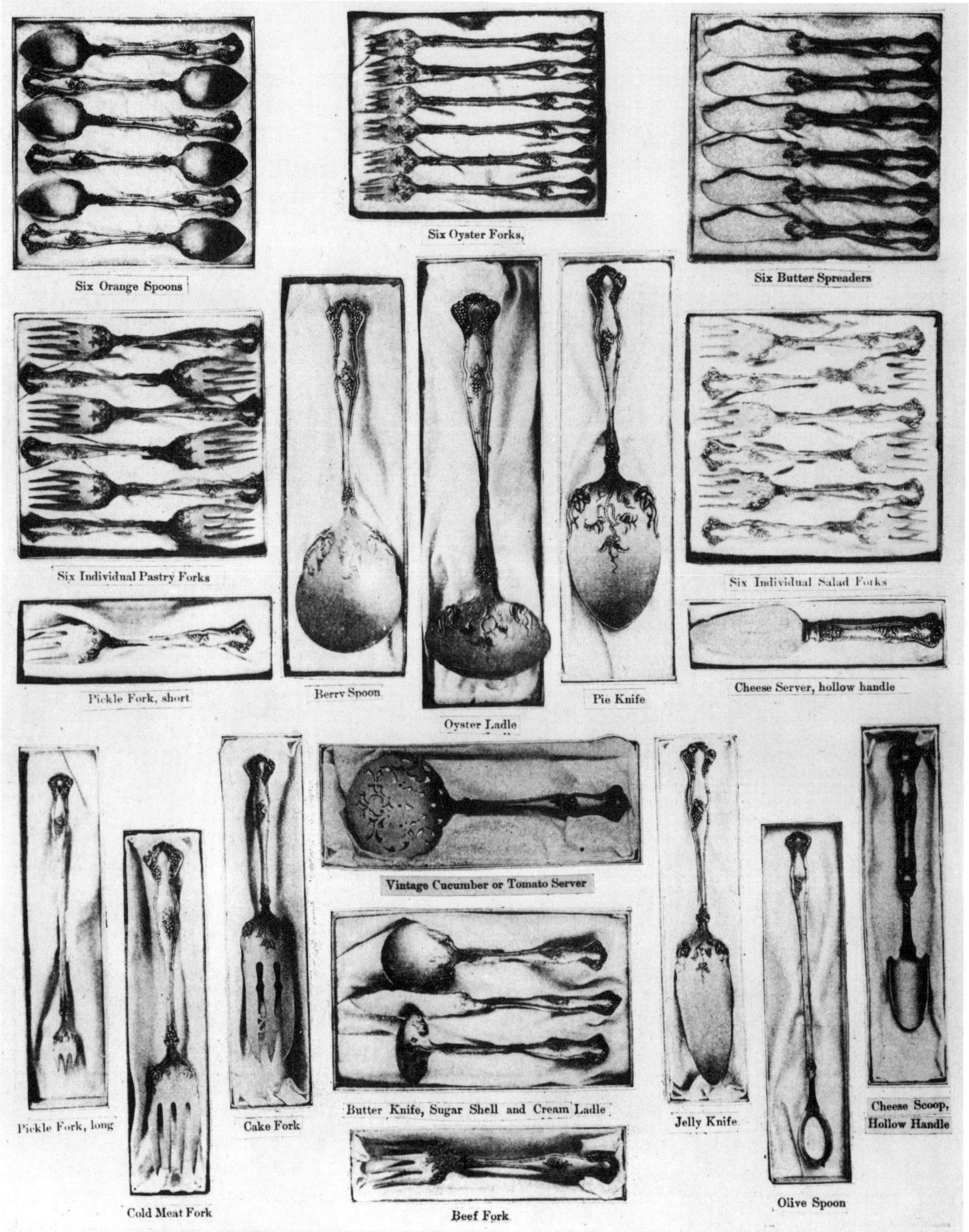

Presentations sets offered a wide choice of wedding, birthday, and holiday gifts. All shown here are 1847 ROGERS BROS.' "Vintage" pattern, active between 1904, when it was introduced, and 1918.

Presentation Sets

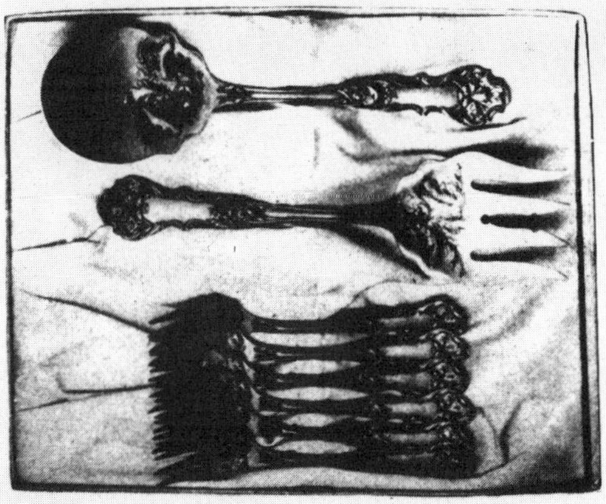

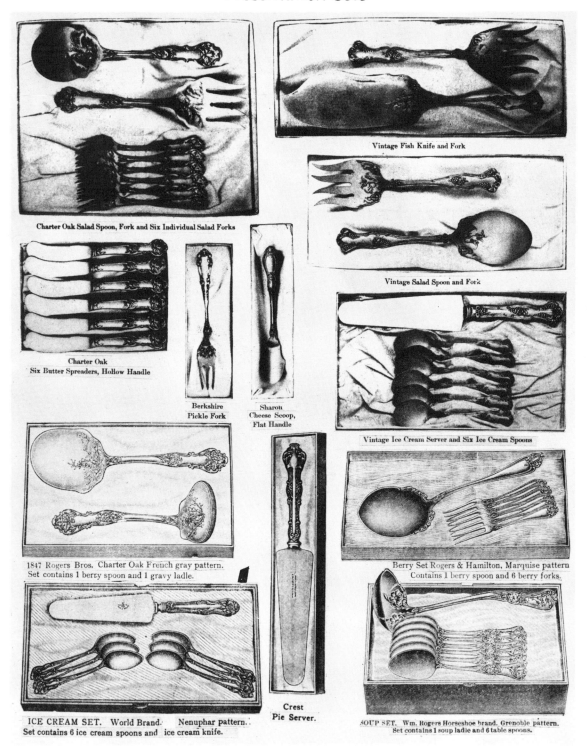

Charter Oak Salad Spoon, Fork and Six Individual Salad Forks

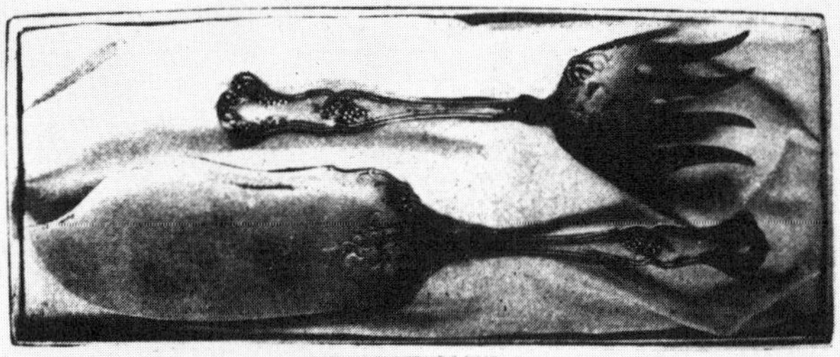

Vintage Fish Knife and Fork

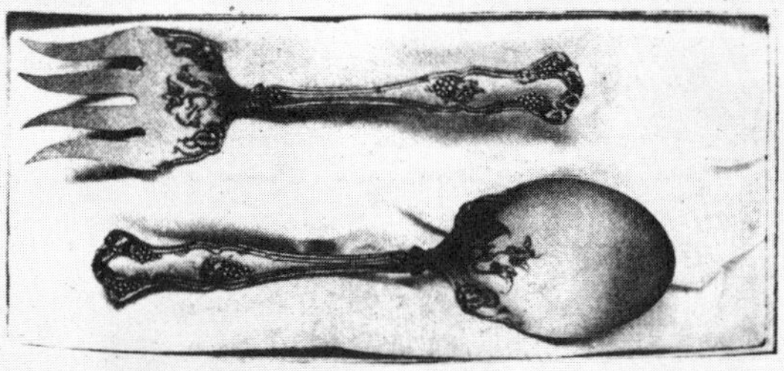

Vintage Salad Spoon and Fork

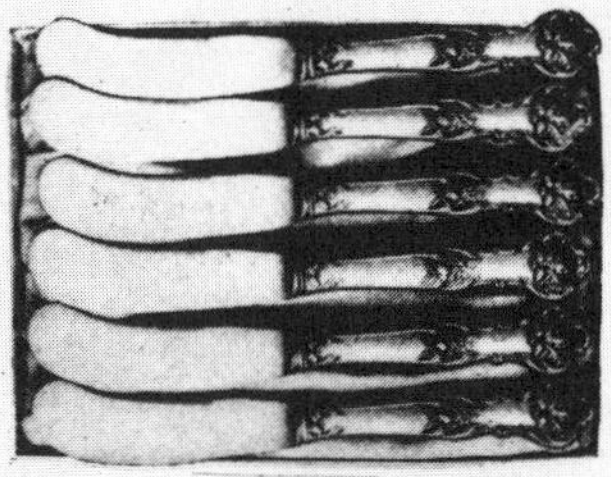

Charter Oak
Six Butter Spreaders, Hollow Handle

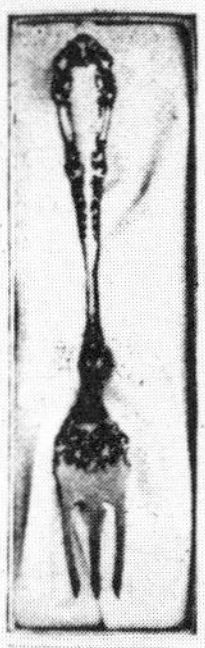

Berkshire
Pickle Fork

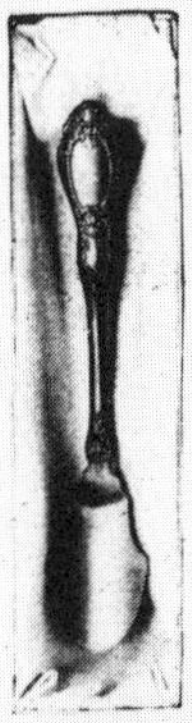

Sharon
Cheese Scoop,
Flat Handle

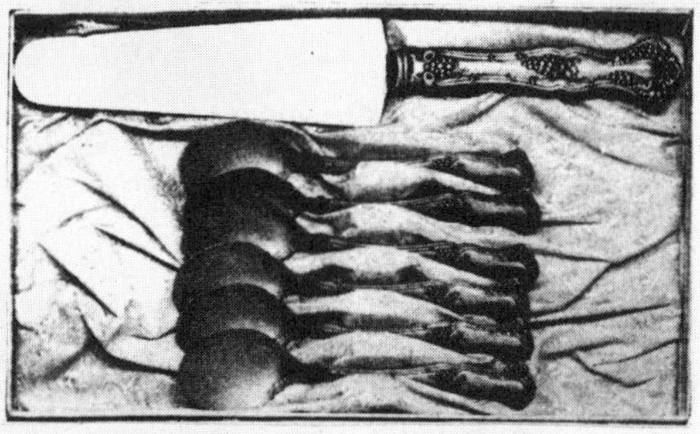

Vintage Ice Cream Server and Six Ice Cream Spoons

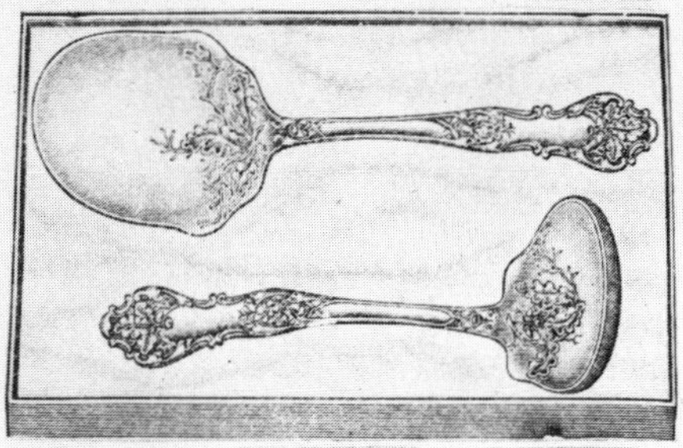

1847 Rogers Bros. Charter Oak French gray pattern.
Set contains 1 berry spoon and 1 gravy ladle.

Berry Set Rogers & Hamilton, Marquise pattern
Contains 1 berry spoon and 6 berry forks.

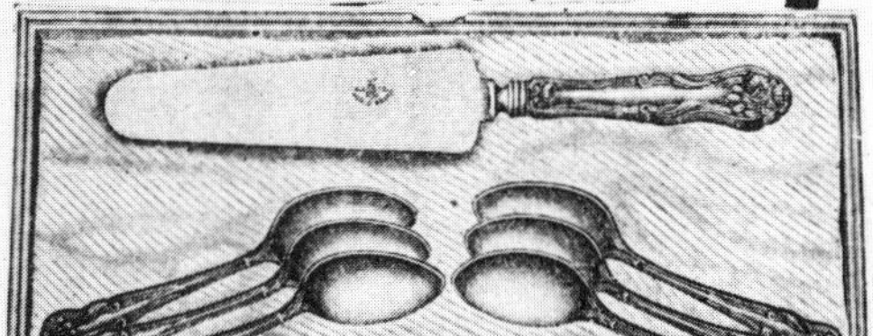

ICE CREAM SET. World Brand. Nenuphar pattern.
Set contains 6 ice cream spoons and ice cream knife.

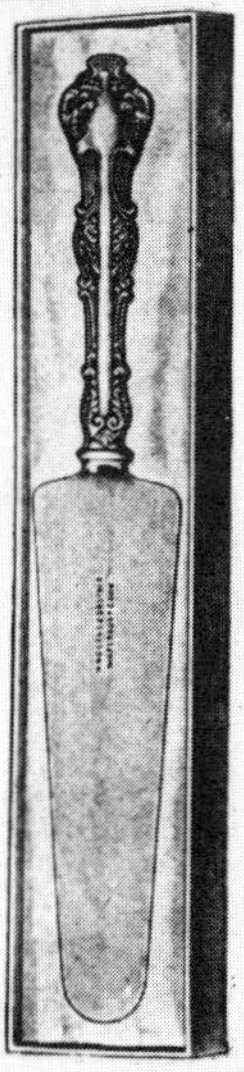

Crest
Pie Server.

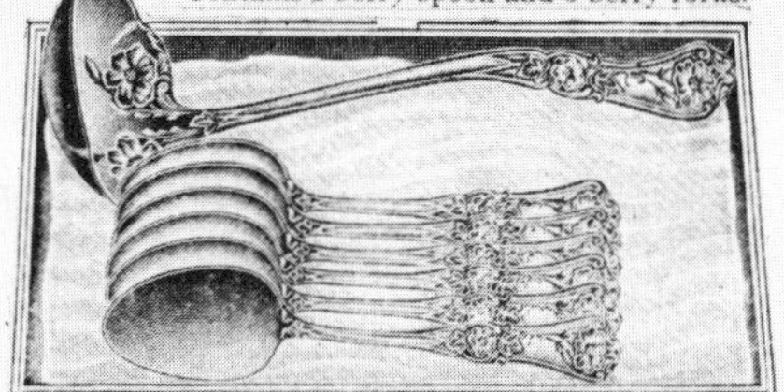

SOUP SET. Wm. Rogers Horseshoe brand. Grenoble pattern.
Set contains 1 soup ladle and 6 table spoons.

Presentation sets permitted a selection of gifts in flatware for every purse and every purpose. Similar pieces sometimes carried several designations, depending on the pattern and the maker.

Presentation Sets

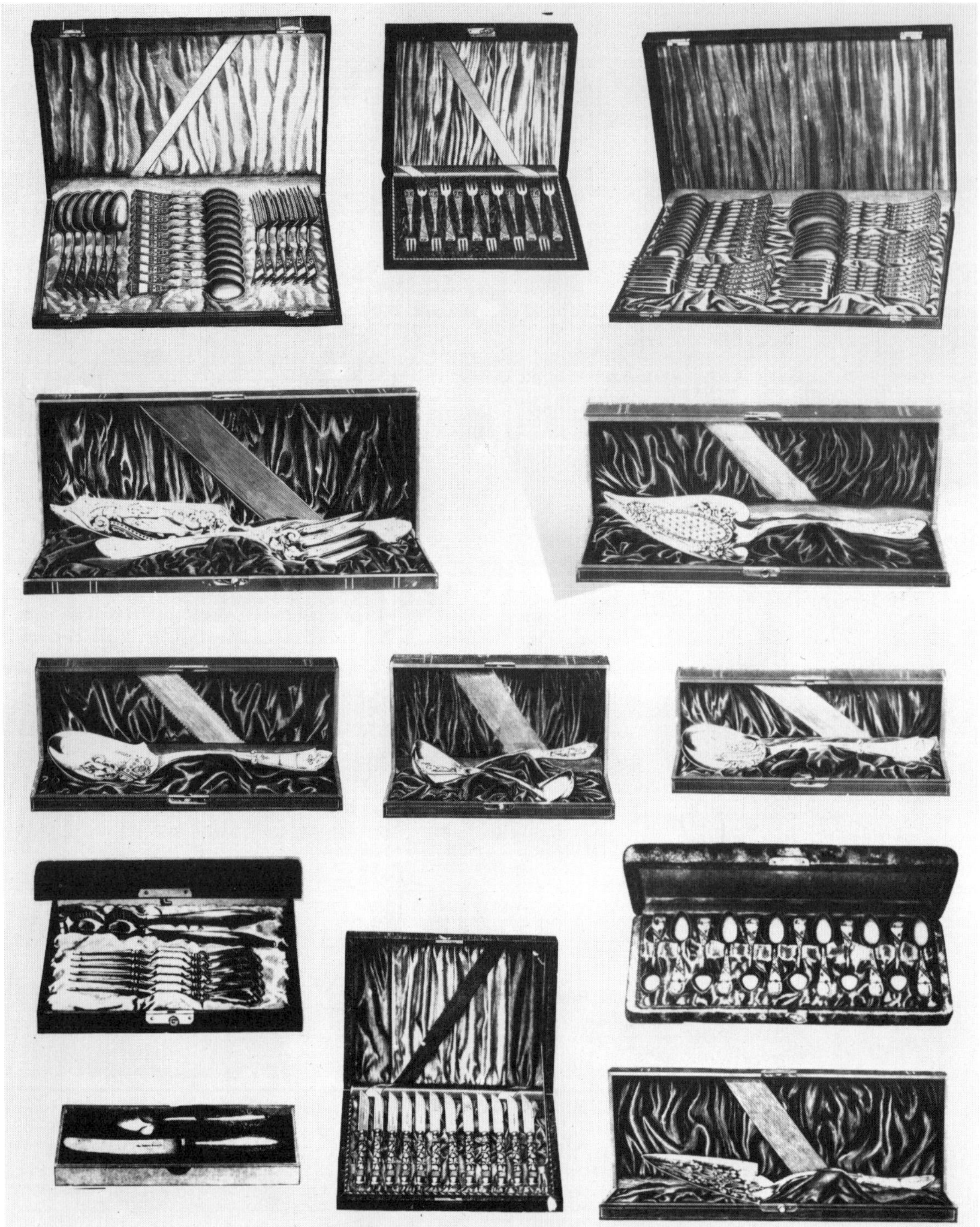

Cases for Presentation sets might be simple cardboard boxes lined with fabric or fine Morocco leather equipped with quality hardware and locks. *First row (l. to r.)*: 12 Laurel Tea Spoons, 6 Table Spoons, 6 Medium Forks; 6 each, Owl and Daisy Oyster Forks; 12 Crown Tea Spoons, 6 Table Spoons, 6 Dessert Spoons, 12 Medium Forks. *Second row*: Gem Fish Knife and Fork, Engraved, in Case; Pearl Pie Knife in Case. *Third row*: Gem Berry Spoon, Engraved, in Case; Pearl Gravy and Cream Ladles; Gem Preserve Spoon, Engraved, in Case. *Fourth row*: Half Dozen Nut Picks, with Nut Cracker, in Morocco Case; 12 Hand Engraved Coffee Spoons, Morocco Case. *Fifth row*: Savoy Orange Set; 12 No. 32 Arabesque Old Silver Fruit Knives; Gem Pie Knife, Engraved, in Case.

Presentation Sets

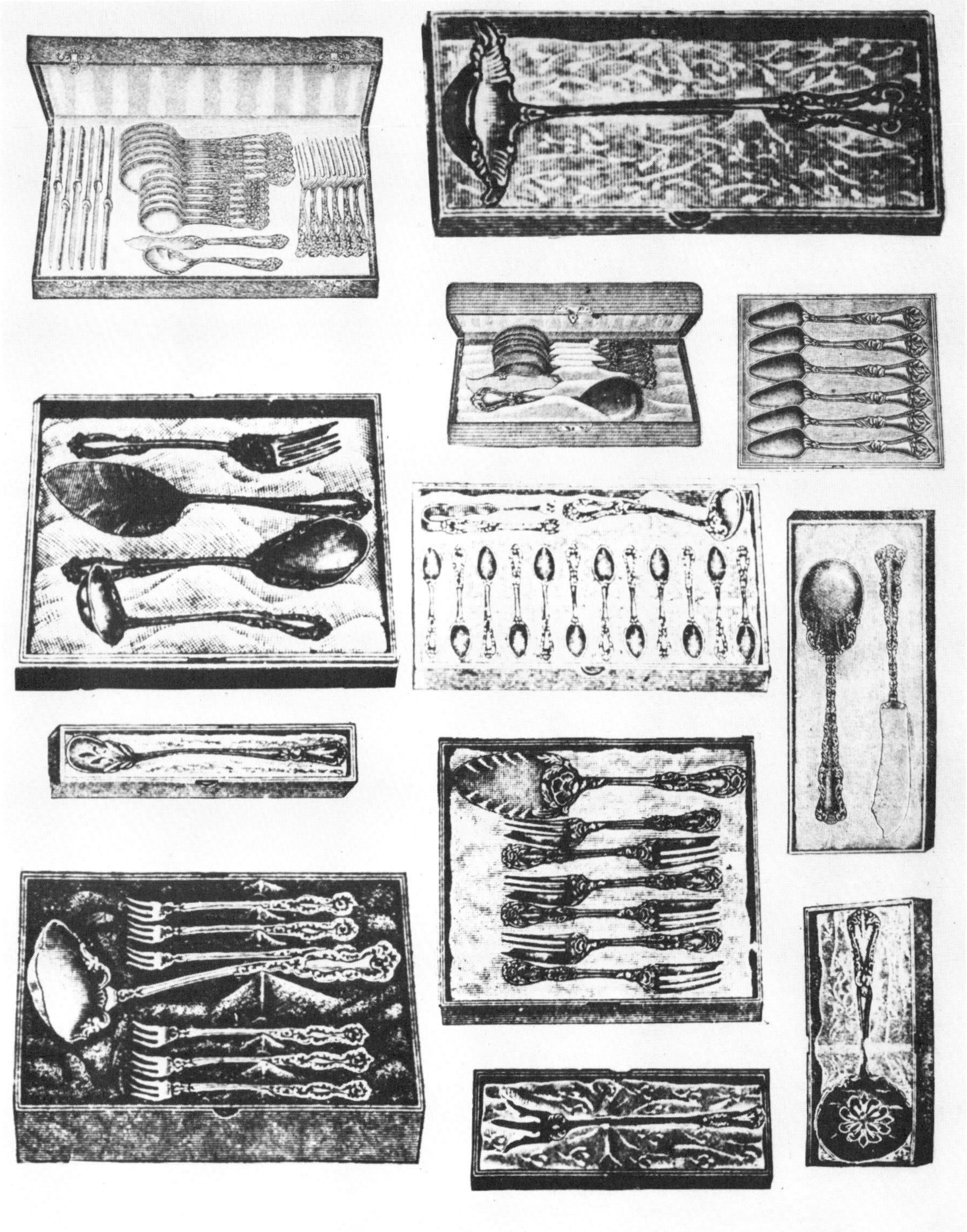

Presentation sets included every possible combination, from a basic service for six in an inexpensive grade of electroplate, to single pieces in heavy weight sterling. *First row*: 26-Piece Complete Dinner set in Presentation Case (Lilyta Pattern: 6 Teaspoons, 6 Tablespoons, 6 Medium Forks, 6 Plain Medium Knives, 1 Sugar Shell, 1 Butter Knife. Put up in lined leatherette case.); Punch Ladle, Arundel Pattern, 15 inches long. *Second row*: Set of 6 Jefferson 8-oz. Tea Spoons, 1 Butter Knife, and 1 Sugar Shell, in silk-lined cloth case: Orange Spoons, Sweet Pea Pattern. *Third row*: Four-Piece Combination set (Cold Meat Fork, Pie Knife, Berry Spoon, Gravy Ladle); Coffee Set, Arundel Pattern (12 Coffee Spoons, 1 pair Sugar Tongs, Cream Ladle); St. Louis Butter Knife and Sugar Shell, in satin-lined case. *Fourth row*: Olive Spoon, Marcella Pattern; Hanover Pie Set (1 Pie Knife and 6 individual Pie Forks). *Fifth row*: Oyster Set, Oxford Pattern (Oyster Ladle, 6 Oyster Forks); Lettuce Fork, Marcella Pattern; Tomato, Cucumber, or Poached Egg Server, Marcella Pattern.

10

Patented Pieces

Horatio's "Purposes mistook, fall'n on the inventors' heads," appeared in Shakespeare's *Hamlet* long before the first Victorian inventors turned their imaginations loose on silver flatware, but there can be no doubt that their purposes might be mistaken when some of the patents are reviewed. The inventor of a *detachable* knife and fork handle in the 1860s, for example, failed to specify what advantages the device offered to the user, but the many inventors who offered improved methods of *attaching* the handles to knives and forks found a receptive audience in the manufacturers who were always alert to gaining an advantage for their goods. There were many of these improved methods, as there were many new systems for manufacturing and attaching bolsters to knives and forks, particularly for handles of shaped hollow design.

Even before the patented pattern became standard in the silver business, ingenious combinations of various pieces of silver flatware occupied the attention of inventors. Through the early 1860s, combinations of the knife, fork, and spoon were patented in several dozen variations—most of them inspired by the mess-kit needs of both Union and Confederate soldiers. The devices, like the travelers' sets of several centuries before, sometimes featured blades and tines and bowls that would fold into the handle; utensils with a fork at one end and a spoon at the other, not unlike the early sucket fork-and-spoon; and jack-knife-like contrivances where a single handle concealed all three basic eating implements. Other variations of the single handle idea permitted the user to change implements at will, assisted by a spring or screw arrangement in the shaft of the implement or concealed in the handle.

It was perhaps the numbers of home remedies, and a Victorian pre-occupation with tonics, that led to the patenting of the first medicine spoon in 1852. New models and improved features appeared regularly each decade through the Edwardian years. One turn-of-the-century patented design was called the Red Cross Medicine Spoon. The patentees and sole manufacturers, the J. B. & S. M. Knowles Co., explained its advantages under the headline, "Reasons for Use":

> It sets level without tipping. It can be held firmly. Hands free to drop medicine. Its curved edges prevent spilling. It measures exact teaspoonful. It can be kept absolutely clean. It protects the teeth. It lasts a life-time. It saves Family Silver from medicinal use. It is endorsed by leading Physicians and Nurses.

The strange looking device had evidently developed a loyal following, for the advertisement concluded with the note that "Every jeweler is vitally interested in the Red Cross

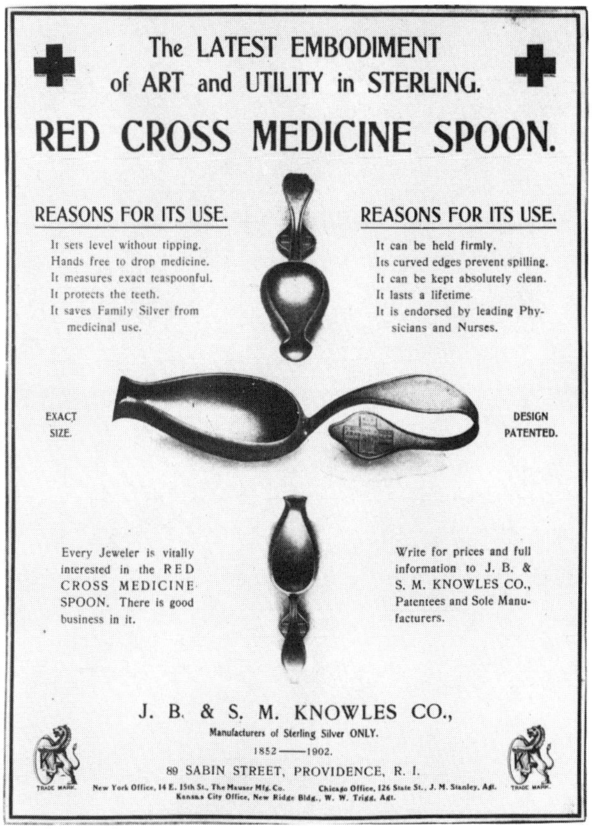

Home treatment and home remedies made the medicine spoon an essential part of the silver service in a well-equipped house. Patented designs were offered by almost all silver manufacturers.

Medicine Spoon. There is good business in it." Another model, patented in 1897, not only measured the medicine, but reminded the patient or nurse when the next dose was due. Called the "Time Medicine Spoon," the device featured a clock face with a single movable hand, so that the time for the next treatment might be set as each dose was administered.

"Invalid" spoons, too, are well represented in the older files of the U.S. Patent Office. These were sometimes called "Pap Spoons," named for the bland concoction frequently prescribed for Victorian invalids or infants. Pap spoons were often made in the same pattern as the family's standard flatware service.

In addition to the "Ideal Olive Fork and Spoon," and the cutting fork which had been patented when good manners dictated that nothing that might be cut with a fork should ever be cut with a knife, the decades following the Civil War saw many other ingenious combinations and pieces patented—although the dearth of these devices today suggests that few of them were ever manufactured in great numbers.

A "Fork and Cake Lifter" was patented in 1866 by a man from Shirleysburgh, Pennsyl-

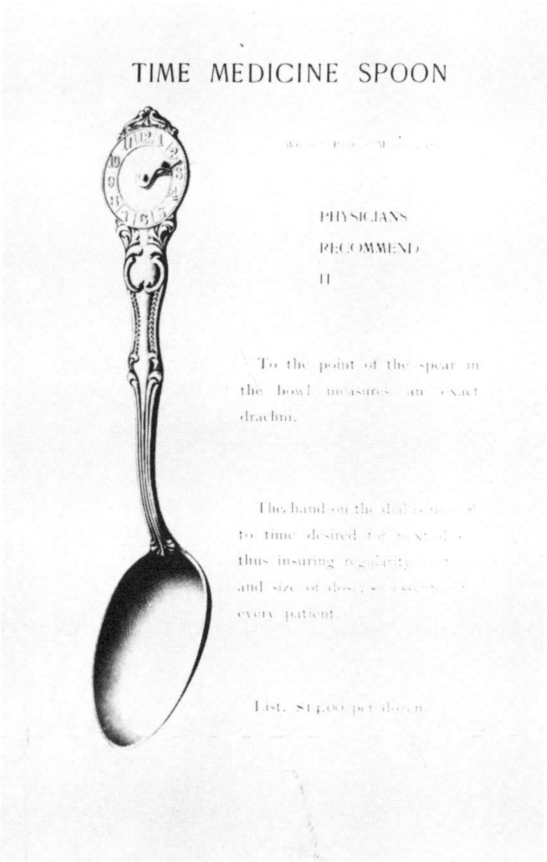

The "Time Medicine Spoon," an 1897 patent, had a movable hand on the handle clock face to remind nurse and patient of the correct time for the next dose. Its makers boasted, too, that the bowl measured an exact drachm. *Courtesy of International Silver Company.*

vania, and in 1870, a Hartford man registered a combination "Knife, Nutcracker, and Pick." The problem of keeping a keen edge on the carving knife occupied many inventors, and various patented knife sharpeners, in a great variety of sizes and styles, supplemented the standard carving steel in many flatware lines.

But it was not until 1873 that the already established moustache cup was joined by the moustache spoon, for which a patent was granted to Mr. E. B. A. Mitcheson of Philadelphia. It featured a pierced, engraved guard over the left side of the large, oval bowl, so designed that its owner might safely and politely sip from the side, with no danger to—or from—his facial decorations. The Mitcheson patent was only one of the many that continued to be registered until after 1900. *The Jewelers' Weekly* in 1891 described another model, this one patented by Mrs. Horace Goodwin and shown by Shreve, Crump & Low in Boston:

> The spoon is made on the same principle as the moustache cup. A guard of silver over the tip of the spoon, connects at the heel, leaving an aperture three-eighths of an inch wide at the back and also at the front of the spoon. Through the aperture at the back, the spoon is filled, and from that in front one may sip his soup or whatever he may be eating without the slightest danger of contact with the hirsute growth on his upper lip.

Early models of the moustache spoon were made in the soup or table spoon size; later models, such as the "Etiquette Spoon," an 1890 patented model of the Meriden Britannia Company, were offered in tea and dessert sizes as well.

Moustache spoon made by Maltby, Stevens & Curtiss Co. The shield at the side of the bowl performed the same function as the guard on a moustache cup. *Collection of Clara Price, Breezewood, Pa.; Brodton Studio photo.*

Models for left-handed sippers were not always emphasized, but it was perhaps felt that this problem had been eliminated at the source by a baby spoon designed and marketed by R. Blackinton & Company. It was heralded as "A New Idea in Baby Spoons—Something that will automatically teach the children to use their right hands when eating." The baby spoons carried, on the right edge of the bowl, realistic representations of various animals—monkeys, dogs and cats among them—which acted as a barrier to taking food from the right side if the spoon was held in the left hand. "The figure on edge

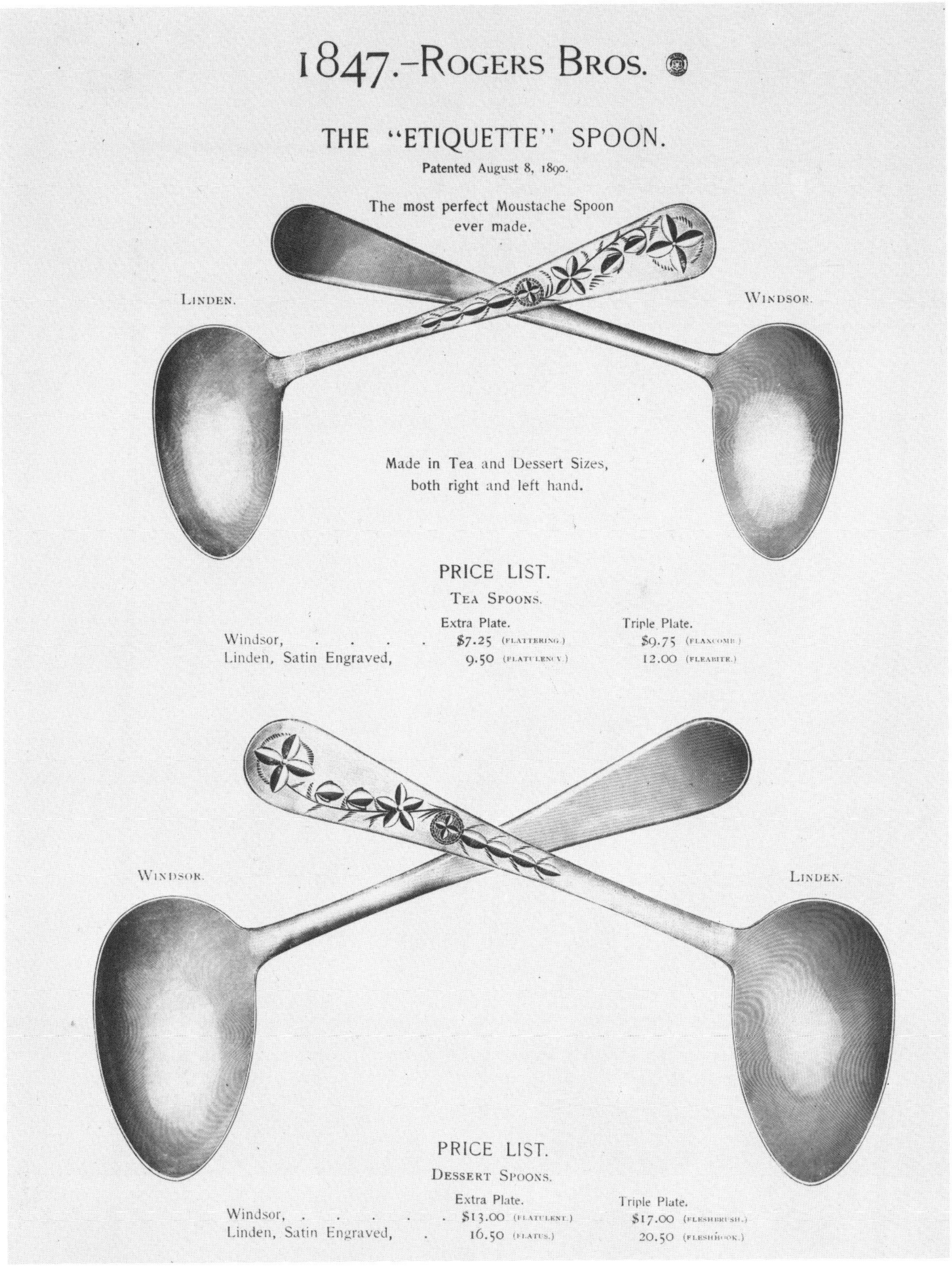
1847.-ROGERS BROS.
THE "ETIQUETTE" SPOON.
Patented August 8, 1890.
The most perfect Moustache Spoon ever made.
LINDEN.
WINDSOR.
Made in Tea and Dessert Sizes, both right and left hand.
PRICE LIST.
TEA SPOONS.
Extra Plate.
Triple Plate.
Windsor, ... $7.25 (FLATTERING.) $9.75 (FLAXCOMB.)
Linden, Satin Engraved, 9.50 (FLATULENCY.) 12.00 (FLEABITE.)
WINDSOR.
LINDEN.
PRICE LIST.
DESSERT SPOONS.
Extra Plate.
Triple Plate.
Windsor, ... $13.00 (FLATULENT.) $17.00 (FLESHBRUSH.)
Linden, Satin Engraved, . 16.50 (FLATUS.) 20.50 (FLESHHOOK.)

An 1890 patent covered the "Etiquette" Moustache Spoon, offered by The Meriden Britannia Company in two patterns, two sizes, and in models for both right and left hand. *Courtesy International Silver Co.*

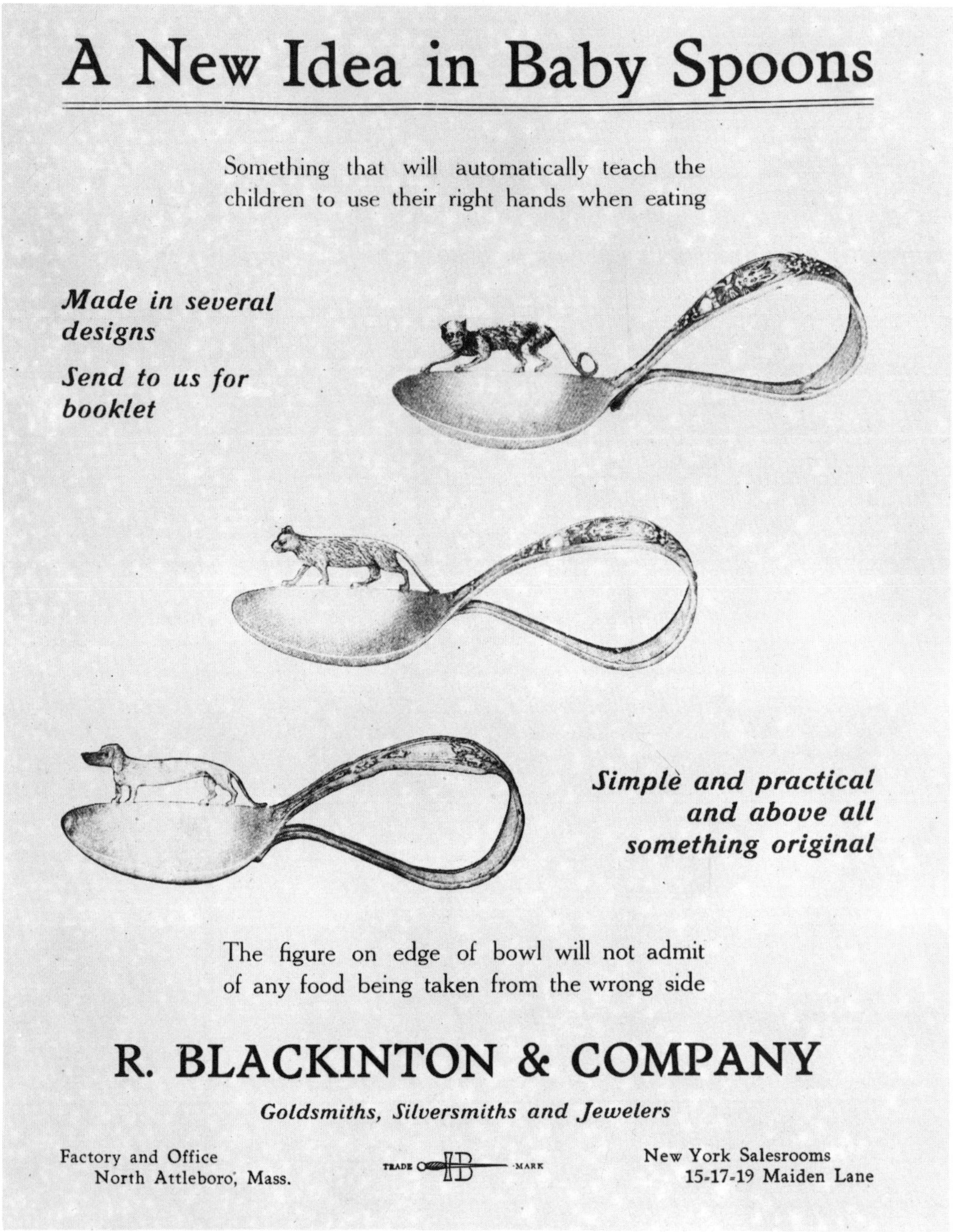
A New Idea in Baby Spoons
Something that will automatically teach the children to use their right hands when eating
Made in several designs
Send to us for booklet
Simple and practical and above all something original
The figure on edge of bowl will not admit of any food being taken from the wrong side
R. BLACKINTON & COMPANY
Goldsmiths, Silversmiths and Jewelers
Factory and Office North Attleboro, Mass.
TRADE MARK
New York Salesrooms 15-17-19 Maiden Lane

A barrier at one side of the bowl of baby training spoons supposedly frustrated the child who wanted to use his left hand at the table. The manufacturer offered a variety of appealing animal barriers.

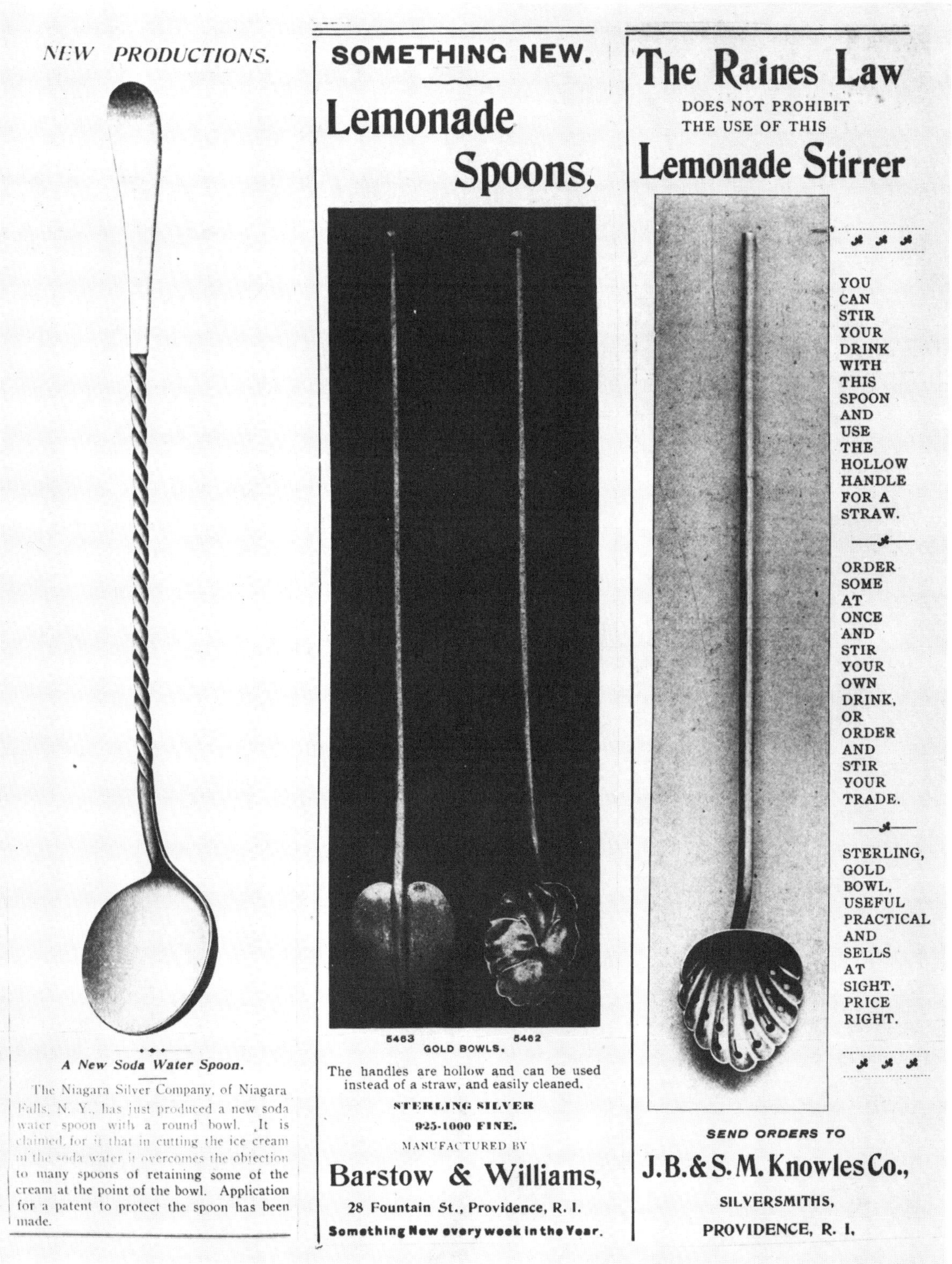

Patented items for the newly popular soda fountains as well as for home use were offered by most silverware manufacturers.

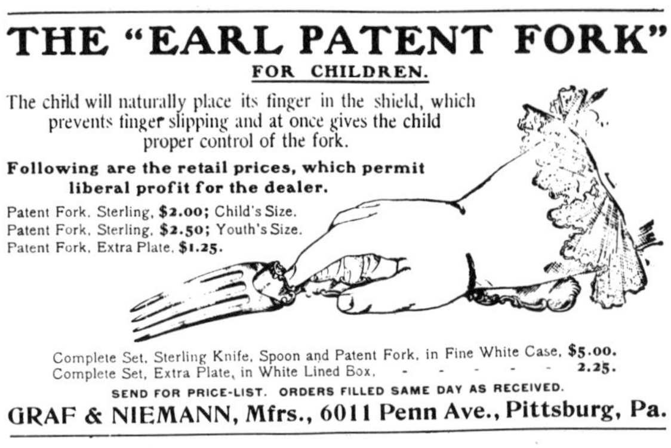

Training children the proper use of silverware occupied many inventors; with this fork, the child's finger was firmly wedged to prevent slipping.

of bowl will not admit of any food being taken from the wrong side," an advertisement for the spoon pointed out, continuing, "Simple and Practical and above all something original."

While the device may have frustrated the left-handed child, it must have encouraged the inventor, for contemporary evidence would indicate that this early training spoon was one of the few of these many inventions to find its way into more than the most limited production.

Table training devices for children were not limited to spoons. The Graf & Niemann Company offered the "Earl Patent Fork," designed to permit proper control of the implement while the youngster learned to handle the tined tool. In theory, a shield at the back of the fork held the tip of the child's finger and prevented finger slipping. These were offered in two sizes, for the child and for the youth, and could be ordered in sterling or electroplate. Matching knives and spoons were available, for those who desired a complete junior place setting.

Comparatively few of these patented novelties survived long past their introductions. Production of most of them was extremely limited, so, when an example appears today, its identification most often is another case of "the inventor's purposes mistook."

11

Pre-School Pieces

"Every man was not born with a silver spoon in his mouth" has been a common explanation for uneven economic progress ever since Miguel de Cervantes wrote the line in *Don Quixote* in the 15th century, but it was left to the mid-Victorian silver manufacturers to reduce the statement to a mathematical formula. In an advertisement featuring Sterling Birthday Spoons, addressed to the jewelry trade at the turn of the century, R. Wallace & Son pointed out that "6000 babies are born each day—15% get silver spoons at birth."

Silverware for children was not new to America; in a will dated April 18, 1726, the Reverend Timothy Stevens of Glastonbury, Connecticut, bequeathed ". . . to my son Joseph . . . three silver spoons, one of them to be a small or babe spoon, as it is called," and to his son Benjamin, among other things, ". . . three silver spoons, one of them to be a child's spoon." But it was only after the mid-1800s that plated and solid silver became common for the perambulator-to-prep-school set.

Practically every manufacturer has made "Child's Sets" in all of the standard silverware patterns. Consisting, at first, of a small knife, fork, and spoon, the sets were available in almost every price range after the late 1860s. Some were elaborately packaged in satin-lined boxes; the less expensive plated sets were often mounted on lithographed cards, the cards themselves rivaling early Valentines in elaborate depictions of decorous childhood.

By the 1880s, a cup or mug, and a matching napkin ring, had been added to many of these sets, and it was an under-privileged child who had not received his own silverware by the time he joined the rest of the family at the dinner table. As the family service increased in complexity, these smaller versions of the knife, the fork, and the spoon sometimes assumed dual roles in the catalogs and price lists of the silver firms, for, with no additional investment in dies, a separate listing enabled the manufacturer to increase the number of pieces he offered. Thus the child-size spoon was sometimes listed also as a "Five o'Clock Tea," an "Egg Spoon," or an "English Tea"; the child's fork as a "Tea Fork," "Beef Fork," or "Fruit Fork"; and the knife with a flat, solid handle as a "Tea Knife" as well as a juvenile piece. In the electroplated lines of better quality, a choice of a solid-handle knife or one with a hollow handle was usually offered; in the solid-silver lines, the hollow-handle knife was generally standard, although sets in which a flat-handled knife was mated with a small fork and spoon were offered by some companies.

During the early 1880s, one of the catalogs of the Gorham Manufacturing Company listed no less than 12 possible combinations under

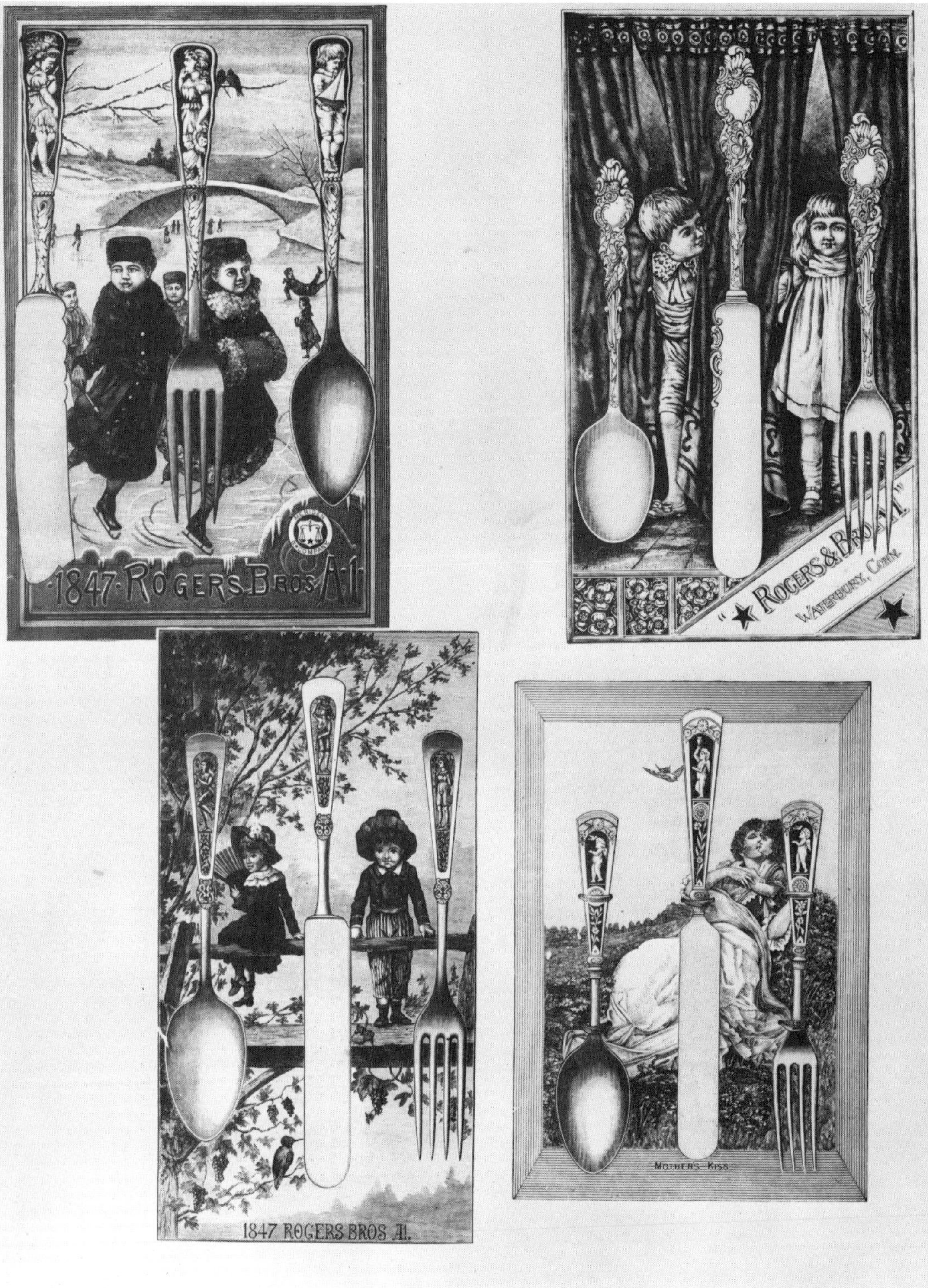

Children's sets of silver-plated flatware were frequently mounted on bright chromo cards to provide a colorful display in the store. Elastic cord threaded through holes punched in the card held utensils firmly.

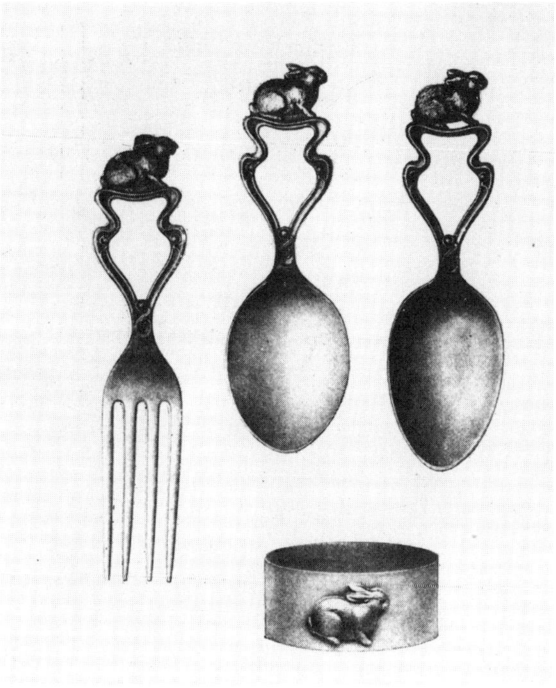

The multiplicity of pieces on parents' dining tables was matched by some of the more complex baby sets, like this Rogers, Lunt & Bowlen setting, called the "Benjamin Bunny."

the general heading of "Children's Sets"; starting with a child's knife and fork, knife, fork, and spoon, or fork and spoon, the sets matched growth by moving to combinations of tea knives, forks, and spoons, then to dessert knives, forks, and spoons. Each size could be supplemented by a matching napkin ring.

The 1890s and early 20th century saw the development of special patterns featuring the childhood heroes of the time. "Buster Brown" sets of juvenile knives and forks and spoons were manufactured by the William A. Rogers Company, as were the "Peter Possum" sets. Other manufacturers selected the names being chosen for children; "Gladys" and "Raymond" and "Mabel" might appear with equal facility on the lists of newly enrolled kindergarten pupils, or in the catalogs of such companies as The Niagara Silver Company or McGlashan, Clarke & Company.

The birthday spoon had already made its appearance in jewelry stores throughout the country. Akin to the familiar commemorative spoon, the handles were intricately wrought with the signs of the Zodiac, or a naturalistic presentation of the "birth flower," so that a design appropriate to the month in which the child was born might be selected. The bowl, like that of the commemorative spoon, was engraved with the name, date of the month, and sometimes the name of the donor. Like the child's sets, these were manufactured by most of the silver companies, in both electroplate and sterling.

During the early 90s, a new type of baby spoon made its appearance. Designed and patented by Reed & Barton, the infant spoon differed from the scaled-down teaspoon (that had previously been labeled a child's spoon) in two important respects; the handle was curved back to form a loop, with the tip curved under until it almost touched the back of the bowl, and the bowl itself was deeper than that of the conventional spoon. A few years after its introduction, it was described in a Reed & Barton catalog:

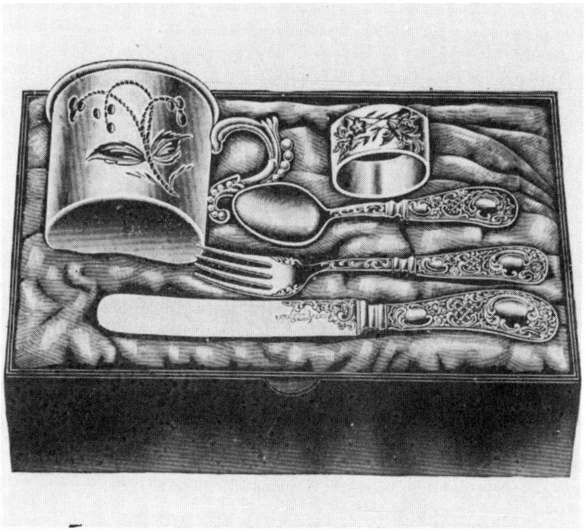

Some sets of junior flatware were supplemented by mugs and napkin rings. Children's tableware was made in both sterling and electroplate.

Favorite characters in children's books also appeared on juvenile silverware, along with personalities familiar in nursery rhymes and fairy tales.

> The first baby spoon was designed and patented several years ago by Reed & Barton, to be sold as a novelty. It proved a necessity. Its popularity became almost universal. To the little tot learning to eat it is practically indispensable. Nothing has ever been found which the chubby fist can grasp so conveniently or which carries the food so safely. The deep bowl safeguards the contents from being easily spilled. In after years it takes its place with the tiny rattle and slippers as a treasured memento of childhood. Unquestionably it is the most popular and useful baby present ever offered for sale. Baby spoons are made only in sterling silver and gold.

Variations of the original soon made their appearance; one model, patented in 1899, topped the curved handle with a short, straight tip which carried the decorative design, usually a popular flatware pattern. But it was the slightly altered versions of the Reed & Barton spoon that were sold in great volume during the first decade of the 20th century. They were made in almost every grade of plate and every weight of sterling; no silverware line was complete without a baby spoon in every flatware pattern, and special children's designs embellished a number of them. In a short time, the baby spoon was mated with the "Food Pusher," an implement resembling a miniature garden hoe, with a short handle terminating in a dull, vertical blade set at right angles to the shaft. Like the baby spoons, these were made in most household flatware patterns, so the am-

Floral baby spoons, featuring the flower designated for the birth-month of the child, were popular birth and christening gifts.

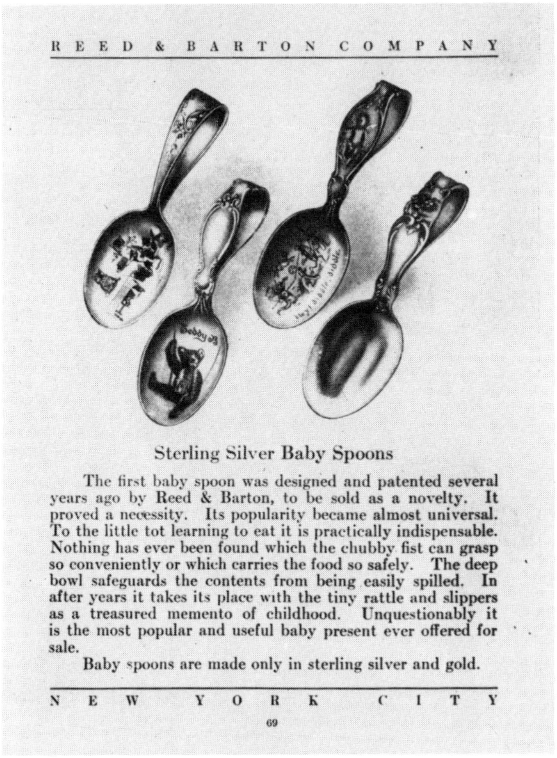
REED & BARTON COMPANY

Sterling Silver Baby Spoons

The first baby spoon was designed and patented several years ago by Reed & Barton, to be sold as a novelty. It proved a necessity. Its popularity became almost universal. To the little tot learning to eat it is practically indispensable. Nothing has ever been found which the chubby fist can grasp so conveniently or which carries the food so safely. The deep bowl safeguards the contents from being easily spilled. In after years it takes its place with the tiny rattle and slippers as a treasured memento of childhood. Unquestionably it is the most popular and useful baby present ever offered for sale.

Baby spoons are made only in sterling silver and gold.

NEW YORK CITY

69

The introduction of the bent-handle baby spoon, a design originated by Reed & Barton, opened a whole new market for silver manufacturers. Within a few years, hundreds of designs in these spoons were available.

bitious grandparent or godmother could present a complete five piece set of flatware—baby set, and the three conventional juvenile pieces—to every newborn infant, plus, in many cases, a cup and napkin ring.

Late in the 90s, when the vogue for souvenir spoons was at its height, David Howe of Reed & Barton developed and patented a new system of etching upon metal. Originally conceived as a time-and-labor saving device for the production of souvenir and commemorative spoons, the new system was rapidly adapted to the production of another line for children—spoons etched with appropriate scenes and verses. Little Miss Muffet, Little Jack Horner, and the Little Pig Who Went to Market, along with portraits of cats and dogs, carried nursery themes over to mealtime. Within a few years, other factories were producing similarly decorated spoons for children and babies, and excerpts from almost every acceptable literary effort for the late Victorian child could be found imperishably etched or engraved on the bowl of his cereal spoon. In a somewhat related vein were the Mother Goose spoons marketed by R. Wallace & Son; these carried engraved representations of the most popular nursery rhymes of the day, and included, in the ten designs manufactured, Margery Daw, The Song of Sleepyland, The Cat and the Fiddle, The Dish Ran Away with the Spoon, The Cow Jumped Over the Moon, Brushing Cobwebs from the Sky, Baa-Baa Black Sheep, Little Dog Laughed, and Mother Goose herself. Equally ornate in the treatment of the

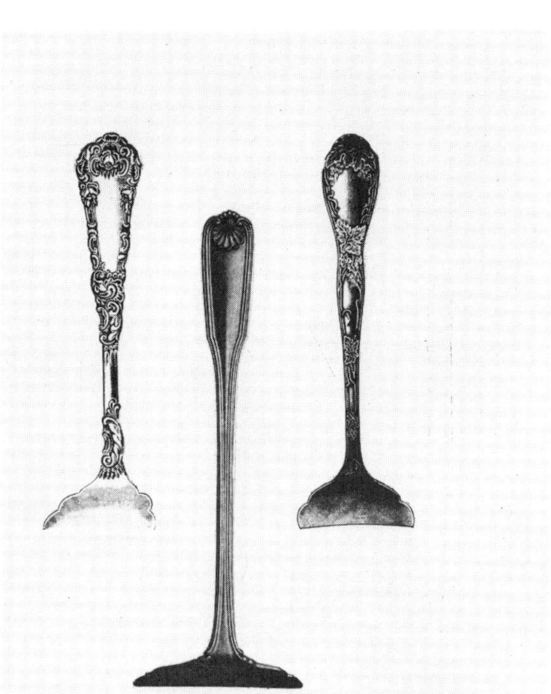

Food pushers for baby were essential in a day when "cleaning the plate" was a rule observed by every child. These pieces were available in almost every popular flatware pattern.

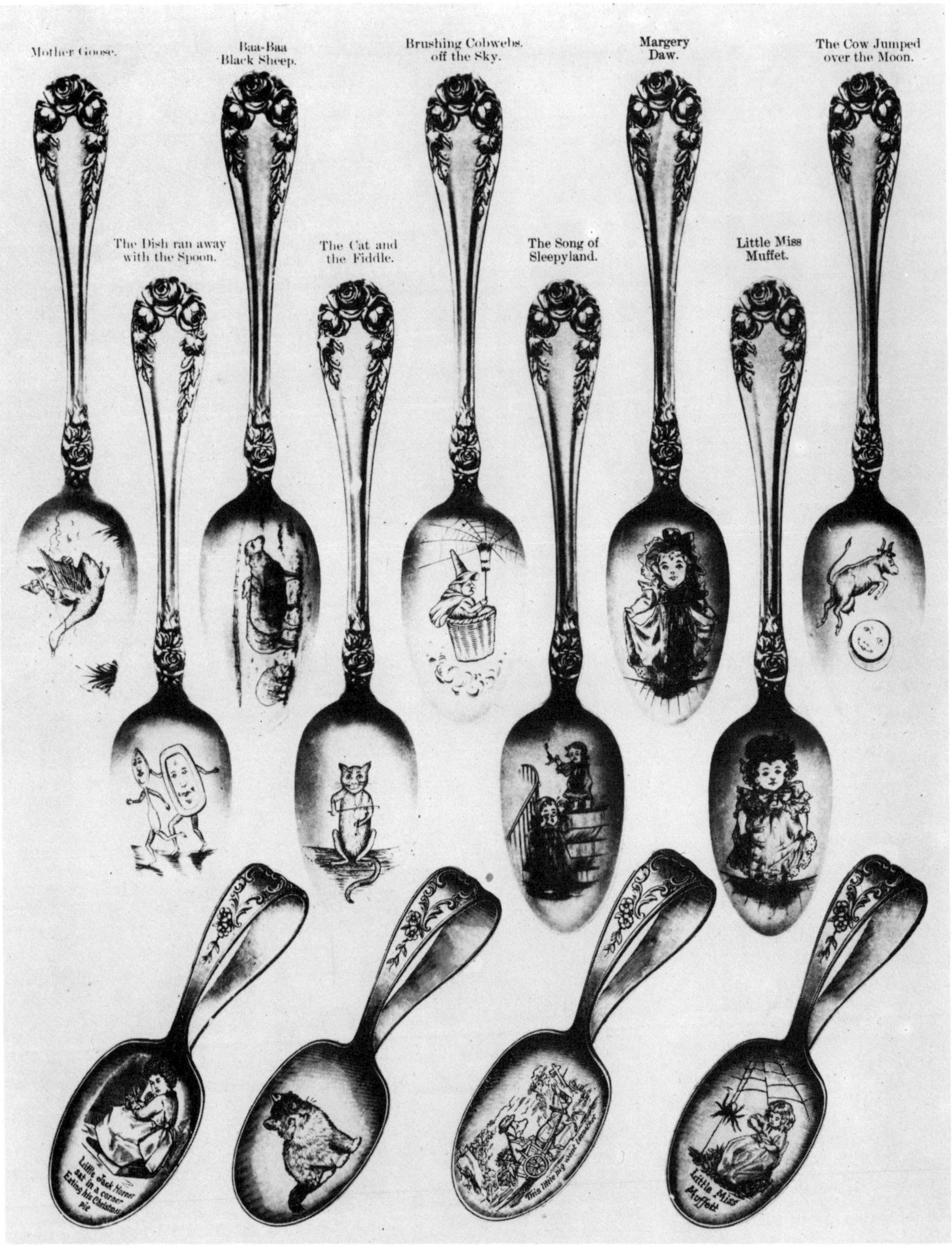

New methods of etching designs on spoon bowls developed late in the 19th century, were first used for making souvenir spoons, but rapidly brought forth novelty spoons for children and infants.

engraving, and embellished with the cupids who had early endeared themselves to the Victorians, were the Cupid Initial spoons marketed by the same firm, and adapted to use as personalized gifts for any child, from Aaron to Zelda, without requiring additional engraving on the part of the local jeweler. They were a far cry from the simple "babe spoon, as it is called," of the 18th century, but lasting reminders of the tender, loving care lavished on the 19th-century child.

"Cupid Initials" etched in spoon bowls were a romantically personal touch for birthdays and other gift occasions. The complete alphabet was available.

12

Pointers for Collectors

Collectors of Victoriana would probably have qualified as true sportsmen in the eyes of Alexander Pope, for he pointed out that the latter's "whole delight is in the pursuit." On another occasion, he reminded his readers that:

> . . . he lives twice who can at once employ
> the present well, and ev'n the past enjoy.

For those who would "the past enjoy" in a collection of American silver flatware, the present might well be employed in its pursuit. Like glass and china, or any collectible form of Victoriana, it is a nostalgic reminder of the day when manners and modes differed in many respects from our own. In its range of patterns, every decorative trend and every art form that achieved popular acceptance in the 19th century can be found. In its range of pieces, there is tangible evidence of bountiful living, and, frequently, a useful supplement to the more casual entertaining of our own day. And, unlike many collections, silver flatware may be used and enjoyed every day, for it is virtually indestructible with normal care. But despite its durability, much Victorian and Edwardian silver flatware has already disappeared. Periods of rising silver prices have seen much old sterling, in what were considered out-moded patterns, melted down. And two world wars, with premiums on nickel and copper and zinc, have seen silver-plated flatware go back to the secondary smelters by the barrelful, as scrap drives collected what was considered "kitchen silver." The same great conflicts were responsible for the destruction of many of the original dies, greatly reducing, if not eliminating entirely, the possibility of reproductions being made at some later date, as has become fairly common in such collector's fields as pattern glass. Some pieces, particularly in electroplate, have suffered what might be termed natural attrition; demotion from dining room to kitchen, as the pattern became "old-fashioned," and hard use as mixing spoons and cooking forks and paring knives that could also serve as jar-openers and screw-drivers. Tablespoons have been lost, after use in children's sand boxes and at the beach; "kitchen tableware" that could be taken on a picnic often was not returned to the house. Present supplies of Victorian flatware are probably ample enough to assure eventual completion of a goal—but they are still limited enough to provide a challenge for the collector!

Unless a piece has been marked with an engraved date, fixing a specific year is sometimes difficult; the approximate time when the pattern was introduced may be checked in this volume, but many patterns remained popular—and in production—for many years. A few manufacturers—notably the firms of Tiffany & Company and Samuel Kirk & Son—

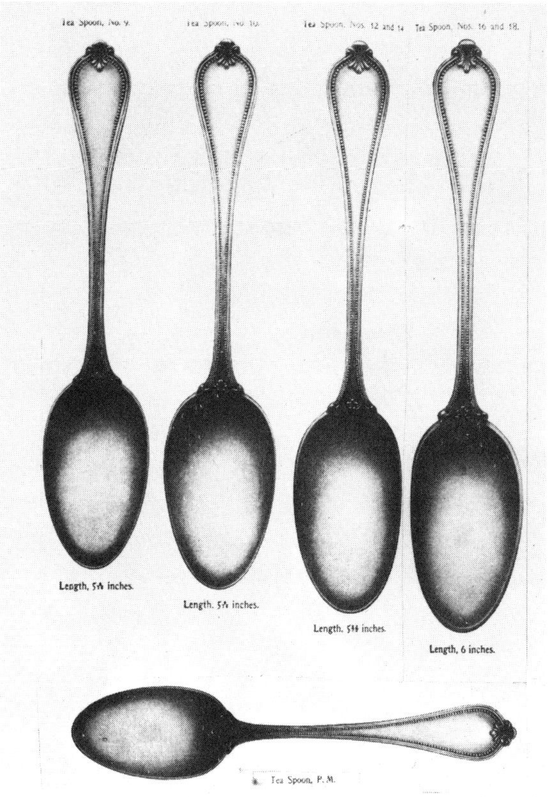

Many late Victorian silver manufacturers offered a variety of weights and grades; some even provided a choice of four sizes in standard teaspoons, in addition to the smaller afternoon tea size.

varied their sterling silver marks during different periods; these are indicated in the trade mark section of this book. In the case of Tiffany & Company, from the time of its incorporation in 1868 until the death of Edward C. Moore in 1891, the silverware bore not only the mark "Tiffany & Co.," but also the letter "M." Ever since then, the initial of the current company president has appeared on all Tiffany-made silver, along with the company mark. The products of the firms of Kirk & Smith and Samuel Kirk carried the Baltimore hallmarks from 1814 to 1830; the various marks carried after that time have been carefully documented, so that Kirk silver can be dated within a few years with reasonable accuracy.

The products of William Gale & Son included the date of manufacture in the diamond that formed part of the firm's trade-mark. Dominick & Haff, a successor company whose trademark closely resembled that of the Gale firm, continued the practice of impressing the year of production in the diamond.

While The Gorham Company used year markings on hollow ware made between 1868 and 1933 (and resumed this marking, by decades, in 1941), such a system has never been used on Gorham flatware.

In the years since 1910, a few other firms have established systems for dating flatware. The products of the Old Newbury Crafters, for example, are stamped with the personal signature mark of the individual craftsman, and thus may be dated, but this fine group was not established until 1916. The Tuttle Silver Company, during the administration of Calvin Coolidge, began marking pieces with the initials of the incumbent President of the United States, and this dating has been continued by the firm's present owners.

In some cases, a range of years may be determined by changes in the trademark used by the manufacturer. As an example, from 1847 until 1853, Rogers Brothers' merchandise was stamped "Rogers Brothers" and "Rogers Bros. 1"; from 1853 to 1862, their products bore the "Rogers Bros. Mfg. Co." or "Rogers Bros. A 1" stamp. After 1862, the founding year was added, to make the familiar "1847 Rogers Bros." mark. On the other hand, the Hartford Rogers' firm seems to have used the "1865 Wm. Rogers Mfg. Co." trademark from the time the company was started, in 1865.

One of the best guides to age is information about a pattern's obsolescence. In terms of the silver trade, a pattern may be *active, inactive, or obsolete.* An active pattern is one still being produced on a regular basis. An inactive pattern is not in production, but the dies are still available, and some manufacturers offer pieces in an inactive pattern on a made-to-order basis. Under these circumstances, the customer pays an additional charge to partially cover the costs involved in "tooling-up" for production, and minimum number of similar pieces may have to be ordered at one time. Other manufacturers may specify certain periods of the year when inactive patterns may be reordered, or, at somewhat irregular intervals, announce "revivals" of certain patterns. The final category, that of obsolete patterns, means that the dies have been destroyed, and, in all likelihood, the pattern will never again be manufactured. In the alphabetical listing of patterns in this volume, those patterns that have been obsolete since the early 1920s, are indicated by an "O" following the pattern name. This device is used merely to help establish possible relative ages for specific patterns; the absence of the "O" following the pattern name should *not be interpreted as meaning that the pattern is either active or inactive at the present time.* Many other patterns have become obsolete during the last four decades.

On the other hand, some of the earliest sterling patterns are still active, and there are a number of patterns introduced during the 1870s, '80s and '90s which are still obtainable through regular trade channels. Most of these no longer offer as wide a range of pieces as were originally made, but modern 7 to 10-piece place settings (contrasted with the original 25 or more pieces) are usually available. The variety of serving pieces has, of course, been reduced too, but such a service, supplemented perhaps by some of the unusual pieces offered in earlier years, provides an appropriate and handsome addition to a dining room furnished with Victorian tables, chairs, and chests.

Many collectors have assembled flatware services of electroplate or sterling to complement a collection of china or glassware; the varied motifs available in silver flatware make it relatively easy to select a pattern closely related to many of the collectible designs in the more fragile tableware. Others choose to match silver or silver-plated hollow ware; although the exactly matched services of this type were not generally manufactured until the late 1890s and after, similar decorative themes were applied to both flatware and hollow ware from the earliest Victorian years.

The popularity of buffet service has led other collectors to assemble a matched set of serving pieces in one of the early patterns; these are often used with modern place-setting pieces. The serving pieces—or "Fancy Work," as the Victorian catalogs sometimes

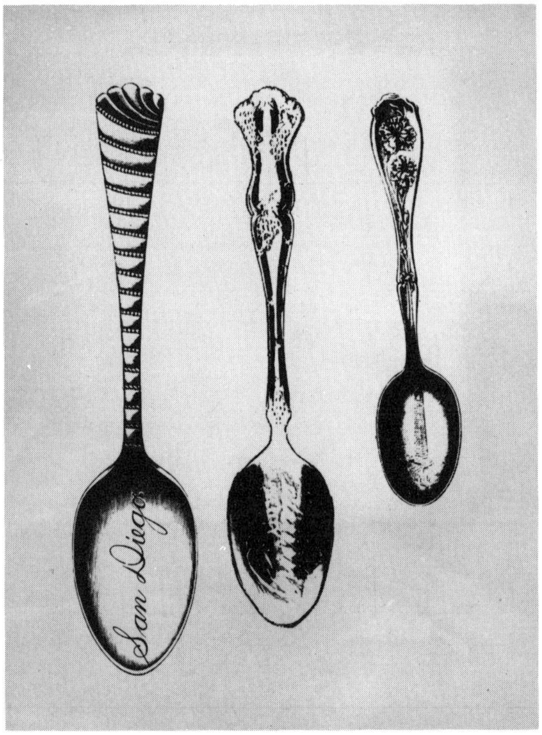

Standard production spoon patterns in tea, afternoon tea and coffee sizes often were engraved locally and sold as souvenir spoons.

called them—are readily adaptable to present-day menus. Large jelly knives and fish knives facilitate the serving of molded salads or desserts; the berry spoon is ideally adapted to the serving of such party favorites as *Stroganoff* and *Boeuf Bourguignon.* Original cheese knives and cheese scoops may be supplemented by individual tea knives or fish knives for spreads, or berry forks used for hors-d'oeuvre. And, of course, most serving pieces are ideally adapted to the purposes for which they were originally designed!

In assembling a more complete service, the collection of knives and forks, tea and dessert spoons should pose no particular problem. The very complexity of the late Victorian services simplifies the problem of adding salad forks; these were made in many patterns after 1880, and in most patterns after 1895, but fish forks, pastry forks, or pie forks serve very well; in most of the patterns of the 60s and 70s, dessert forks effectively take the place of salad forks for today's use. Butter spreaders were also made in most patterns after 1890, and the flat-handled child's knife may be substituted if your choice is one of the earliest patterns, and you *must* have butter spreaders. Oval soup spoons or dessert spoons were made in practically every pattern; they may be used for every purpose that the modern "place spoon" serves.

In collecting electroplated flatware, pieces that may require re-plating need not be passed over. There are good plating services in almost every city, and some manufacturers also offer replating service on goods of their own manufacture. Prices are generally reasonable; there may be some additional economy in having a number of pieces from the same service replated at the same time. This practice also assures *uniform* plating on the different pieces in the same service. Before placing an order for replating, try to examine some of the work that has been done by the firm you select; unless it is expertly handled, some of the detail in the more ornate patterns may be lost in the redeposit of silver.

While the collector thrills to the acquisition of a piece or a set in "mint" condition, there is no historical precedent to hinder replating; it was a procedure anticipated and encouraged by the early manufacturers. Most of the catalogs of the 1860s, 70s and 80s devoted a section to the replating services offered by the silver firms, but the modern collector should not expect to find costs as reasonable as those advertised in 1880 by L. Boardman & Son, whose catalog for that year quoted charges of $1.75 *a dozen* for replating tea, egg, mustard, and salt spoons, with an extra charge of 30¢ a dozen for refinishing before plating, "when they are scratched." Unlike old Sheffield, which should never be replated, or furniture which may suffer devaluation from "over-restoration," electroplate may safely be returned to prime condition by replating, when the work is done with care.

Plating plants for home and hobby use are available, but unless you are willing to make it a life-time project, replating of treasured old flatware is best left to professionals, for there are many pitfalls in the preparation of the ware as well as in the plating.

If the base metal has been badly damaged, you will probably find that it is not worthwhile to attempt refinishing, but some imperfections can be corrected without extravagance. Badly worn knife blades can be replaced and fitted into the original hollow handles; worn tines on forks can be ground down evenly, and sometimes minor damage to the lips of spoon bowls can be repaired in the same way. Worn and pitted base metal surfaces can sometimes be smoothed out before replating. But it is always advisable to get the opinion of a reliable plating firm *before* making a commitment.

Certain acid foods are prime enemies of flatware; vinegar, mustard, sauerkraut, mayonnaise, and ordinary table salt are among the worst offenders, and the cause of most staining and pitting. The tablespoon that has seen years of service as a mixing spoon, in frequent contact with these acid foods, will bear the marks in a deeply pitted bowl, and it becomes a poor candidate for replating. But in ordinary use, even these foods will do no harm, if the piece is washed immediately after use.

Care is no problem. The tarnished appearance that so many housewives dread is caused by sulphur and its compounds, found in coal, gas, sooty atmosphere, rubber, and the moisture from the hands. One manufacturer points out that the best way to keep silver bright can be summed up in two simple words: *use it,* for use means that it is kept clean. Frequent use and frequent washing—with hot water and soap—followed by careful rinsing in hot water, will keep silver shining. The rinsing is important, for silverware that is dried immediately after leaving soapy water will tarnish faster than will the carefully rinsed ware. An occasional cleaning, using a reputable polish (many silver manufacturers make or distribute their own brands) is all that is needed to maintain the silvery sheen. A discarded toothbrush, softened in hot water, with a little polish added to the bristles, is helpful in cleaning heavily ornamented Victorian pieces. Remember, though, that oxidation was sometimes used to emphasize the intricacies of a design; too heavy a hand with the brush and polish may destroy some of the charm of a particular pattern. Abrasive cleansers and polishes should of course be avoided. Gold finished surfaces help retard the formation of tarnish, and can generally be cleaned with a soft cloth and mild soap and water; the French formula for cleaning Vermeil—washing in white wine or champagne—need not necessarily be followed!

As a collection grows, pieces which are used only occasionally should be wrapped in sulphur-free tissue or a cloth, and kept in a chest or drawer which is as nearly air-tight as possible. In addition to the customary chests for flatware, most of which are now lined with tarnish-retardant cloth, the same fabric can be found on ready-made trays. These come in a wide range of sizes, making it easy to custom-fit drawers in sideboards, servers or antique cupboards for silver storage. Tarnish-retardant cloth may also be purchased by-the-yard, so that many unusual old

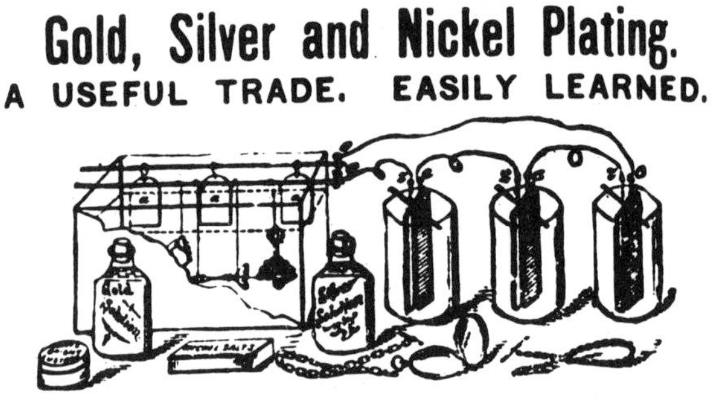

Electroplating outfits for home use were once widely advertised; few hobbyists or handymen ever mastered the art despite the claims that the "useful art was easily learned."

pieces of furniture may be customized to hold a silver collection.

While there is no reason for avoiding the use of silverware, those who choose only to display pieces—perhaps a collection of spoons in an open rack—will find satisfactory polishes that also retard the development of tarnish, even in city atmosphere. Those same products are particularly useful for dealers who may choose to display stocks of silver flatware in their shops or at antique shows.

Establishments specializing in the matching of inactive and obsolete sterling flatware have been in business in many areas for many years. Of necessity, these services are not cheap, for large stocks must be carried, and certain items may have to be held for long periods of time. In recent years, as interest in earlier electro-plated patterns has increased, some of those firms have begun to stock some plated patterns, too. While some of those companies advertise their services nationally, others rely largely on representation at antique shows.

For many years, correct identification of older flatware patterns has posed problems, both for those who would buy and those wishing to sell. "Popular" names have been applied to many of the patterns first sought by collectors; "Columbia" has often been called "Dolphin"; "Grenoble" has been referred to as "Lazy Daisy," and the term "Vintage" applied to any pattern showing a grape motif, even though that name correctly identifies only the electroplated pattern by 1847 Rogers Bros., and the sterling design made by William Durgin. This confusion is sometimes compounded by the appearance of isolated examples of older catalogs; pattern names were not always used consistently by all dealers, nor were manufacturers' choices always respected.

The large mail-order houses, perhaps in an effort to make it appear that certain patterns were their own exclusive property, frequently applied their own names to certain standard patterns. As examples, Sears, Roebuck & Company's Catalog No. 117 identified the Watson, Newell & Company "Bridal Flower" as "Orange Blossom;" a Montgomery Ward & Company catalog of 1904 presented R. Wallace & Sons' "Somerset" as "Samoset," and the Williams Brothers Company's "Norma" as "Mignon," and "Como" as "Norma." Wholesale jewelers, in particular, seem to have used a free hand in renaming standard patterns. The 1895 catalog of the Otto Young Co. identified the Towle Mfg. Company's "No. 43" as "Wild Rose" and the same firm's "Old English" as "Rococo." The S. F. Myers Co.—"The New York Jeweler"—was among the worst offenders; during a few brief years around the turn of the century, Alvin's "Raleigh," "Orient," and "Florentine" were identified in this company's catalogs as "Colon," "Irvington," and "Larchmont" respectively; the Fessenden Company's "Alice" was rechristened "Consuelo," Gorham's "Cherry Blossom" became "Montague," and four popular patterns of Simpson, Hall, Miller & Co.—"Winchester," "Warwick," "Mille Fleurs," and "Frontenac" appeared as "Richelieu," "Lucerne," "Floral," and "Monaco." Such lists might be continued almost indefinitely, and each list compounded confusion!

Increasingly, in recent years, more and more "general line" antique dealers have handled Victorian flatware, although stocks have tended to consist of only the few patterns which were among the first to attract the attention of collectors. Many dealers admit that the lack of a reliable guide to earlier flatware patterns and pieces has delayed the development of this type of collecting; this work may help remedy that deficiency.

Postscript

AMERICAN SILVERSMITHS

The following list includes the names of silversmiths who worked in the United States after 1837. There is naturally some over-lapping with earlier periods; during the first years of Victoria's reign, some of the smiths who had worked during the 18th century were still active. The number of silversmiths decreased sharply after 1860; factory-produced ware largely displaced the hand-crafted products. However, many of the skilled craftsmen continued to produce coin silver and sterling tableware, and a revival of interest in hand work about the turn of the century added some new names to the list.

In checking individual pieces, it should be recalled that during the Victorian years in America, comparatively few "marks" were used; most smiths impressed their names or initials. In names involving the prefixes "Mac," "Mc," and "M'"; "La," "Le," and "L'," early recorders often interpreted freely, and some of the smiths themselves used two forms of the same prefix. Capital "I" and "J," and lower case "s" and "f" were used interchangeably by 18th-and early 19th-century typographers, and the same practice was observed by many silversmiths when names were impressed.

Where an individual was a member of more than one firm or partnership, a chronological sequence has been used whenever possible; where an individual smith is known to have worked in more than one locality, the original location is listed first. In a few cases, where records in different cities show a time lapse of many years, the same name is listed twice, with different locations and working years. This has been done only where positive identification of the individual is lacking. Where wares are known to have been marked with only an initial or initials, the symbol is indicated following the name of the silversmith.

Bibliographical reference numbers indicate the sources of information, and, in some cases, may provide more detailed information about a particular silversmith.

John W. Abbott
c. 1839
Portsmouth, N.H.
(37, 39, 50, 90, 106)

Robert K. Abel
c. 1840–1850
Philadelphia, Pa.
(10)

John D. Abercrombie
c. 1823–1843
Philadelphia, Pa.
(10)

Henry Abraham
c. 1844
New York, N.Y.
(37)

Thad Ackley
c. 1840
Warren, Ohio
(78)

Charles Adam
c. 1860
Alexandria, Va.
(123)

Robert L. Adam
c. 1846–1898
Alexandria, Va.
(123)

William W. Adam
c. 1846
Alexandria, Va.
(23)

Benjamin F. Adams
c. 1845
Troy, N.Y.
(37)

C. J. Adams
c. 1840–1870
Frankfort, Ky.
Bowling Green, Ky.
(63)

H. B. Adams
Adams & Buttrc
Hamilton & Adams (?)
c. 1836–1842
Elmira, N.Y.
(24)

Henry B. Adams
c. 1848
Philadelphia, Pa.
(10, 37)

Nathaniel W. Adams
Sibley & Adams
c. 1842–1848
Buffalo, N.Y.
(24)

Wesley Adams
c. 1850
Philadelphia, Pa.
(10)

William Adams
c. 1829–1859
New York, N.Y.
(20, 36, 37, 50, 90, 106 161, 168)

William L. Adams
c. 1842–1850
Troy, N.Y.
(24, 37, 106)

William Addison
c. 1845–1850
Philadelphia, Pa.
(10)

Duff Adolph
c. 1837
Philadelphia, Pa.
(10)

Charles P. Adriance (CPA)
c. 1816–1874
Richmond, Va.,
Poughkeepsie, N.Y.
(23, 106, 133)

Edwin Adriance
Mead, Adriance & Co.
Mead & Adriance
c. 1832–1870
Ithaca, N.Y.
St. Louis, Mo.
(24, 37, 39, 50, 90, 133)

John Adriance
c. 1795–1873
Poughkeepsie N.Y.
(134)

Adolph Aherns
c. 1837
Philadelphia, Pa.
(10)

Charles G. Aiken
c. 1850
Cleveland, Ohio
(123)

John Brent Akin
c. 1820–1860
Danville, Ky.
(39, 63, 106, 127)

Samuel Akins
c. 1841
Philadelphia, Pa.
(10)

Anthony Albertson
c. 1848
Philadelphia, Pa.
(10)

Joseph P. Albertson
Cowles & Albertson
c. 1849–1858
New York, N.Y.
Cleveland, Ohio
(123)

Thomas F. Albright
c. 1835–1847
Philadelphia, Pa.
(10)

Isaac Alexander
c. 1850
New York, N.Y.
(18, 37, 39, 106)

Robert Alexander
c. 1847–1850
Rochester, N.Y.
(24, 100)

Samuel P. Alexander
Trotter & Alexander
Brem & Alexander
c. 1837–1848
Charlotte, N.C.
(22)

Samuel Alford
c. 1840
Philadelphia, Pa.
(106)

A. C. Allen
c. 1837
Cincinnati, Ohio
(77)

Alexander Allen
c. 1850
Rochester, N.Y.
(24)

Cairns Allen
c. 1837–1848
Philadelphia, Pa.
(10)

Caleb Allen
c. 1837
Cincinnati, Ohio
(123)

G. W. Allen
c. 1836
Batavia, N.Y.
(24)

Jared T. Allen
c. 1844–1846
Rochester, N.Y.
(24, 100, 106)
(possibly same as J. T. Allen, Batavia, N.Y.)

L. C. Allen
c. 1850
Utica, N.Y.
(24, 25)

Luther A. Allen
c. 1844–1850
Rochester, N.Y.
(24)

Philo Allen
Chedell & Allen
c. 1850
Buffalo, N.Y.
(24)

Richard Allen
c. 1850
Auburn, N.Y.
(24)

William Allison
c. 1839
Philadelphia, Pa.
(10)

William N. Allison
c. 1831–1837
Albany, N.Y.
New York, N.Y.
(18, 24)

Jacob N. Alrich
J. N. Alrich & S. W. Warriner
c. 1848
Louisville, Ky.
(63)

Thomas Alsop
c. 1842–1850
Philadelphia, Pa.
(10)

Philo G. Alvord
c. 1837–1848
Buffalo, N.Y.
(24)

H. R. Ames
H. R. Ames & Co.
c. 1850
Potsdam, N.Y.
(24)

Cornelius Amos (Armiss ?)
c. 1840
Louisville, Ky.
(63)

Albert A. Anderson
c. 1837
Philadelphia, Pa.
(10)

Alex Anderson
c. 1860–1868
Danville, Ky.
(123)

Alexander J. Anderson
c. 1848
Philadelphia, Pa.
(10)

Andrew Anderson
c. 1814–1844
Danville, Ky.
(63, 127)

David Rush Anderson
c. 1825–1855
Cincinnati, Ohio
Marietta, Ohio
(77)

Edward Anderson
c. 1854–1888
Laurens, S.C.
(14)

Henry C. Anderson
Anderson & Whittacker
H. C. Anderson & Co.
c. 1823–1839
Charleston, W.Va.
(23)

William S. Anderson
Brown & Anderson
c. 1850–1871
Wilmington, N.C.
(22)

Elon Andrews
Murdock & Andrews
before 1855
Utica, N.Y.
(24, 25)

Henry Andrews (H A)
Haddock & Andrews
c. 1830–1847
Boston, Mass.
(36, 37, 50, 106)

Nelson Andrus
N. Andrus & Co.
c. 1834–1837
New York, N.Y.
(18, 39, 106)

James Angram
c. 1837
Albany, N.Y.
(24)

William J. Angus
c. 1841
New York, N.Y.
(18)

William F. Annelly
c. 1850
Philadelphia, Pa.
(10, 37)

John Annin
Annin & Dreer
c. 1837–1841
Philadelphia, Pa.
(10)

George Ansbey
Ansbey & McEuen
c. 1837–1850
Philadelphia, Pa.
(10)

——— Anthony
Anthony & Carey
c. 1837
Cincinnati, Ohio
(77)

Edwin Anthony
c. 1837
Troy, N.Y.
(24)

Charles Antrim
c. 1837–1847
Philadelphia, Pa.
(10)

Samuel App
c. 1837–1850
Philadelphia, Pa.
(10)

George B. Appleton
c. 1850
Salem, Mass.
(39, 106)

William Applewhite
c. 1824–1837
Columbia, S.C.
Camden, S.C.
(14)

John Arbuckle
c. 1843
Philadelphia, Pa.
(10)

Joseph Arbuckle
c. 1847–1848
Philadelphia, Pa.
(10)

Dumm Archibald
c. 1843
Philadelphia, Pa.
(10)

John Archibald
c. 1843
Philadelphia, Pa.
(10)

D. P. Armer
c. 1850
Richmond, Ky.
(63)

Nelson T. Arms
c. 1837–1850
Albany, N.Y.
(24, 106)

Thomas S. Armstrong
c. 1839–1840
New York, N.Y.
(18)

John Arnault
c. 1850
New York, N.Y.
(37)

H. B. Arnold
c. 1840–1844
Rome, N.Y.
(24)

Jacob Arnold
c. 1848
Philadelphia, Pa.
(10)

John Arrison
c. 1837
Philadelphia, Pa.
(10)

William Arwin
c. 1837–1838
Albany, N.Y.
(24)

James C. Ashburn
Ashburn & Shannon
c. 1841
Philadelphia, Pa.
(10)

John Ashburner
c. 1840–1841
Philadelphia, Pa.
(10)

James Ashman
c. 1831–1841
Philadelphia, Pa.
(10)

William Ashton
c. 1845–1873
Charleston, S.C.
(14)

Matthew Atherton
c. 1837–1840
Philadelphia, Pa.
(10)

Nathan Atherton, Jr.
c. 1825–1850
Philadelphia, Pa.
(10, 36, 37, 50, 90, 106)

John A. Atkin
Hinsdale & Atkin
c. 1830–1838
New York, N.Y.
(18)

John H. Atkin
c. 1850
Chicago, Ill.
(46, 175)

Alvin S. Atkins
c. 1850
Rochester, N.Y.
(24)

William O. Atkinson
c. 1843
Louisville, Ky.
(63)

Charles Atlee
c. 1837
Philadelphia, Pa.
(10, 37, 90, 106)

Edward W. Atmore
c. 1840–1850
Philadelphia, Pa.
(10)

Marshall Atmore
c. 1821–1837
Philadelphia, Pa.
(10)

George E. Atwell
c. 1830–1838
Charleston, S.C.
(14)

David Austen
c. 1837–1839
Philadelphia, Pa.
(10, 37, 90, 106)

______ Ayers
Ayers & Dunning
c. 1839
Penn Yan, N.Y.
(24)

Socrates Ayers
Ayers & Badger
c. 1835–after 1850
Elmira, N.Y.
(24)

Elias Ayres
Ayres & Beard
before 1842
Louisville, Ky.
(63)

Thomas R. J. Ayres
c. 1823–1861
Danville, Ky.
(63)

James A. Babcock
c. 1875–1885
New York, N.Y.
(165, 175)

Thomas Bacall
Pear & Bacall
c. 1836–1850
Boston, Mass.
(37, 90, 106)

A. Bachman
c. 1848
New York State
(39, 106)

John Peter Francis Backes
c. 1852–1858
Charleston, S.C.
(14)

A. M. Badger
Badger & Lillie
Ayers & Badger
c. 1836–1837
Elmira, N.Y.
(24)

John Baen
c. 1849–1850
Philadelphia, Pa.
(10)

William Baggs
c. 1850
Philadelphia, Pa.
(10, 37)

Abbott G. Bagley
c. 1840
Buffalo, N.Y.
(24)

______ Bailey
Bailey & Parker
c. 1845
Owen, Vt.
(37)

______ Bailey
Bailey & Parmenter
c. 1849
Rutland, Vt.
(37)

Bradbury M. Bailey
c. 1852–1878
New York, N.Y.
Ludlow, Vt.
Rutland, Vt.
(37, 39, 91, 106)

Charles Bailey
c. 1830–1840
Claremont, N.H
(91)

Ebenezer Eaton Bailey
E. E. Bailey & Co.
c. 1830–1850
Claremont, N.H.
(91, 165)

Edward S. Bailey
Bailey & Owen
E. S. Bailey & Co.
c. 1848–1850
Abbeville, S.C.
Newberry, S.C.
(14)

Hugh Bailey
Bailey & Brothers
c. 1846–1852
Utica, N.Y.
(24, 25)

James Bailey
Bailey & Brothers
c. 1846–1852
Utica, N. Y.
(24, 25)

J. T. Bailey
Bailey & Kitchen (B & K)
Bailey & Co.
c. 1835–1850
Philadelphia, Pa.
(10)

Roswell H. Bailey
c. 1831–1872
Claremont, N.H.
Woodstock, Vt.
(91)

Samuel Bailey
c. 1840–1872
Rutland, Vt.
(91)

Samuel Chase Bailey
c. 1830–1840
Claremont, N.H.
(91)

Samuel G. Bailey
c. 1849–1850
Poughkeepsie, N.Y.
(134)

S. P. Bailey
c. 1822–1863
Woodstock, Vt.
(37)

T. A. Bailey
c. 1843–1845
Philadelphia, Pa.
(10)

Thomas Bailey
Bailey & Brothers
c. 1826–1852
Utica, N.Y.
(24, 25)

Westcott E. J. Bailey
c. 1842
Philadelphia, Pa.
(10)

William Bailey
Bailey & Brothers
c. 1846–1852
Utica, N.Y.
(24, 25, 39, 106)

William Bailey (Baily ?)
c. 1820–1850
Philadelphia, Pa.
New York, N.Y.
(10, 18, 90, 106)

Henry Bain
c. 1849
Philadelphia, Pa.
(10)

Pleasant H. Baird
c. 1813–1838
Paris, Ky.
Maysville, Ky.
(63, 123, 127)

Anson Baker
c. 1820–1837
New York, N.Y.
(18, 36, 37, 90, 106)

Edwin G. A. Baker
Baker & Shriver
c. 1837–1850
Philadelphia, Pa.
(10)

Eleazer Baker (E B)
before 1849
Ashford, Conn.
(37, 39, 50, 90)

Elias Baker
c. 1840
New Brunswick, N.J.
(117)

George A. Baker
c. 1841–1843
Philadelphia, Pa.
(10)

George M. Baker
c. 1842
Philadelphia, Pa.
(10)

James M. Baker
c. 1842
Philadelphia, Pa.
(10)

S. Baker
c. 1830–1840
Location unknown
(78)

Edgar Baldwin
c. 1848–1850
Troy, N.Y.
(24)

Jedediah Baldwin
c. 1791–1844
Northampton, Mass.
Norwich, Conn.
Hanover, N.H.
Fairfield, Conn.
Morrisville, N.Y.
Rochester, N.Y.
(24, 36, 37, 39, 50, 90, 106)

Stanley S. Baldwin
c. 1820–1837
New York, N.Y.
(18, 37, 39, 90, 106)

Albert Ball
c. 1811–1875
Poughkeepsie, N.Y.
(134)

Calvin S. Ball, Jr.
Stone & Ball
c. 1850
Syracuse, N.Y.
(24)

Charles Ball
c. 1840–1842
Poughkeepsie, N.Y.
(24)

David Ball
c. 1845–1846
Rochester, N.Y.
(24, 106)

Henry Ball
Marquand & Co.
Ball, Tompkins & Black
Ball, Black & Co.
c. 1833–1876
New York, N.Y.
(18, 37, 90, 106)

S. S. Ball
John B. Jones & Co.
Jones, Ball & Poor
Boston, Mass.
(50, 106)

True M. Ball
c. 1815–before 1890
Boston, Mass.
(50, 106)

Benjamin B. Banker
c. 1836
Albany, N.Y.
(24)

Edward Baptista
c. 1840
New York, N.Y.
(18)

J. C. Barber
c. 1844–1846
Philadelphia, Pa.
(10)

James Barber
c. 1842–1850
Philadelphia, Pa.
(10)

Lemuel D. Barber
c. 1850
Syracuse, N.Y.
(24, 37)

William Barber
c. 1843
Hartford, Conn.
(37)

Stephen Barbere
c. 1841
Philadelphia, Pa.
(10)

G. Barbiere
c. 1847
Philadelphia, Pa.
(10)

Stephen P. Barbiere
c. 1810–1843
Philadelphia, Pa.
(10)

James Barclay
c. 1848
Philadelphia, Pa.
(10)

Orin Barclay
c. 1849
Philadelphia, Pa.
(10)

Conrad Bard (Bird ?)
Bard & Hoffman
Bard & Lamont
C. Bard & Son (?)
c. 1825–1850
Philadelphia, Pa.
(10, 37, 39, 90)

Thomas Barge
c. 1848
Philadelphia, Pa.
(10)

George Barger
c. 1848
Philadelphia, Pa.
(10)

Edward C. Barlow
c. 1850
Georgetown, Ky.
(63, 123, 127)

S. S. Barnaby
c. 1852–1853
Utica, N.Y.
(25)

Samuel Barnard
c. 1844–1845
Utica, N.Y.
(24, 25)

James Barnes
c. 1841–1844
Philadelphia, Pa.
(10)

James M. Barnes
c. 1845–1850
Philadelphia, Pa.
(10)

James P. Barnes
c. 1848–1869
Louisville, Ky.
(63, 127)

Moses D. Barnes
before 1858
Macon, Ga.
(21)

George Barney
Barney & Valentine (?)
c. 1850
Syracuse, N.Y.
(24)

James Barney
c. 1840
Syracuse, N.Y.
(24)

Laurent Baron
c. 1841–1850
Rochester, N.Y.
(24)

Louis (Lewis ?) Baron
c. 1841–1867
Rochester, N.Y.
(24, 106)

Joseph J. Barras
c. 1833–1850
Philadelphia, Pa.
(10)

Joshua L. Barras
c. 1837
Philadelphia, Pa.
(10)

George Barringer
c. 1842
St. Louis, Mo.
(123)

T. Barrington
c. 1839
Tarboro, N.C.
(22)

Henry Barrow
c. 1833–1841
New York, N.Y.
(18)

Standish Barry
c. 1773–1844
Baltimore, Md.
(50, 119)

Charles Bartholomew
c. 1843–1846
Philadelphia, Pa.
(10)

John Bartholomew
c. 1846–1848
Philadelphia, Pa.
(10)

Israel Bartlet
(Bartlett ?)
before 1838
Haverhill, Mass.
Newbury, Mass.
(39, 106)

Edward M. Bartlett
c. 1843–1850
Philadelphia, Pa.
(10, 106)

S. Bartley
c. 1841
Philadelphia, Pa.
(10, 37)

Benjamin Barton II
c. 1821–1841
Alexandria, Va.
(23)

Hiram B. Bascom
c. 1838–1842
St. Louis, Mo.
(123)

Augustine Baton, Jr.
c. 1837
Philadelphia, Pa.
(10)

Albert T. Battel
Davies & Battel
A. T. Battel & Co.
c. 1844–1850
Utica, N.Y.
(24, 25)

Joseph Batting
c. 1850
Philadelphia, Pa.
(10)

Louis Bauman
Bauman & Kurtzborn
c. 1850–before 1870
St. Louis, Mo.
(123)

DeWitt Baxter
c. 1850
Philadelphia, Pa.
(10)

Henry F. Bayeaux
Bayeaux & Co.
c. 1833–1839
Troy, N.Y.
(24)

John J. Beal
c. 1845–1846
Louisville, Ky.
(63)

Theodore L. Beal
c. 1845–1846
Louisville, Ky.
(63)

H. L. Bean
Smith & Bean
H. L. Bean & Co.
c. 1847–1850
Skaneatelis, N.Y.
(24)

Henry Bean
c. 1848
Philadelphia, Pa.
(10)

David S. Bear
c. 1847–1857
Staunton, Va.
(23)

Jacob Bear
c. 1839
Lexington, Va.
Philadelphia, Pa.
(23)

Jehu W. Bear
Bear & Conrad
Harry & Bear
c. 1842–1852
Harrisonburg, Va.
Charlottesville, Va.
Luray, Va.
(23)

Evans C. Beard
Beard & Ayres
E. C. Beard & Co.
c. 1824–1875
Louisville, Ky.
(63, 123)

Benjamin Franklin
Beasley
Beasley & Houston
c. 1886–1890
Fayetteville, N.C.
(22)

John M. Beasley
c. 1838–1889
Fayetteville, N.C.
(22)

J. Beauchamp
c. 1840–1850
Bowling Green, Ky.
(63)

Samuel Beauchamp
c. 1840–1844
Buffalo, N.Y.
(24)

Augustus Beauvais
c. 1850
St. Louis, Mo.
(123)

E. A. Beauvais
c. 1840
St. Louis, Mo.
(39, 106)

Rene Beauvais
R. & A. Beauvais
c. 1838–1898
St. Louis, Mo.
(39, 106)

Augustus Bechtler
before 1846
Rutherfordton, N.C.
(22)

Christopher Bechtler
c. 1830–1842
Philadelphia, Pa.
Rutherfordton, N.C.
(10, 22)

Christopher Bechtler,
Jr.
C. Bechtler & Son
c. 1830–1857
Rutherfordton, N.C.
Spartanburg, S.C.
(14, 22)

Henry Beck
c. 1837–1839
Philadelphia, Pa.
(10)

John O. Beck
c. 1847
Philadelphia, Pa.
(10)

Moses Beckel
c. 1848–1853
Albany, N.Y.
(24)

Albert Becker
c. 1850
Syracuse, N.Y.
(24)

Daniel Becker
D. Becker & Co. (?)
c. 1850
Syracuse, N.Y.
(24)

Robert W. Beckwith
Ramsay & Beckwith
Thomson & Beckwith
Beckwith & Brittain
c. 1840–1868
Raleigh, N.C.
New Bern, N.C.
Tarboro, N.C.
Charlotte, N.C.
(22)

James W. Beebe
James W. & L. Beebe
J. W. Beebe & Co.
(James W. Beebe
& Co.)
c. 1835–1844
New York, N.Y.
(18, 37, 39, 55, 106)

Lemuel D. Beebe
c. 1850
Syracuse, N.Y.
(24)

William Beebe
c. 1850
New York, N.Y.
(37, 39, 106)

Clement Beecher
(C B)
before 1869
Berlin, Conn.
Cheshire, Conn.
Meriden, Conn.
(20, 36, 37, 39, 50, 106)

J. B. Beers
c. 1838–1839
Honeoye Falls, N.Y.
(24)

John Beesleyhaven
c. 1839–1840
Philadelphia, Pa.
(10)

William Beggs
Beggs & Smith (?)
McGrew & Beggs
c. 1841–1850
Louisville, Ky.
(63, 127)

George B. Beiderhase
c. 1890
New York, N.Y.
(71, 175)

Julius Beidt
c. 1848
Philadelphia, Pa.
(10)

Maxim Belgord
c. 1848
Philadelphia, Pa.
(10)

Stephen Belknap
(Belnap ?)
c. 1818–1850
Philadelphia, Pa.
(10)

S. Bell
J. & S. Bell
c. 1846–1850
San Antonio, Texas
(123)

S. W. Bell
c. 1837
Philadelphia, Pa.
(10, 39, 106)

Thomas W. Bell
c. 1837–1848
Philadelphia, Pa.
Petersburg, Va.
(10, 23)

Butler Bement
c. 1788–1869
Pittsfield, Mass.
(59)

A. Benedict
c. 1835
Syracuse, N.Y.
(24)

Andrew C. Benedict
Benedict & Scudder
Benedict & Son (?)
c. 1827–1840
New York, N.Y.
(18, 37, 39, 55, 90, 106)

Isaac H. Benedict
c. 1837–1854
Greenville, S.C.
(14)

J. H. Benedict
Munger & Benedict
after 1838
Auburn, N.Y.
(133)

Martin Benedict
Benedict & Squire
c. 1823–1839
New York, N.Y.
(18)

Samuel Benedict
c. 1845
New York, N.Y.
(161)

Barzillai Benjamin
(B B)
Benjamin & Co.
c. 1799–1844
New Haven, Conn.
Bridgeport, Conn.
Milford, Conn.
New York, N.Y.
(18, 20, 37, 39, 50, 90, 106)

Everard Benjamin
Benjamin & Ford
Everard Benjamin & Co. (EB & Co.)
E. Benjamin Co.
c. 1828–1874
New Haven, Conn.
(20, 37, 39, 55, 90, 106)

______ Bennett
Bennett & Caldwell
c. 1843–1848
Philadelphia, Pa.
(10)

______ Bennett
Bennett & Fletcher
(Fletcher & Bennett)
Bennett, Fletcher & Co.
c. 1830–1894
Louisville, Ky.
(63, 123)

Alfred Bennett
c. 1837–1847
location unknown
(29, 78)

Charles Fletcher Bennett
c. 1843–before 1876
Louisville, Ky.
(63, 123)

J. D. Bennett
J. D. Bennett & Co.
c. 1847–1849
Petersburg, Va.
(23)

Jacob Bennett
c. 1825–1850
Philadelphia, Pa.
(10)

James Bennett
c. 1839
Philadelphia, Pa.
(10)

Jordan Bennett
Bennett, Lewis & Co.
Bennett, Wilson & Co.
c. 1824–1856
York, S.C.
Chester, S.C.
(14)

L. M. Bennett
Leach & Bennett
c. 1856–1860
Utica, N.Y.
(25)

Purden Bennett
c. 1837–1839
Philadelphia, Pa.
(10)

Purnell Bennett
c. 1835–1843
Philadelphia, Pa.
(10)

Robert H. Bennett
c. 1849–1850
Philadelphia, Pa.
(10)

Lucius Benton
c. 1850
Cleveland, Ohio
(78, 123)

Peter Bentson
(Bentzon ?)
c. 1817–1849
Philadelphia, Pa.
(10, 37, 90, 106)

Eugene C. Benyard
c. 1839–1849
Philadelphia, Pa.
(10)

Hugh G. Benyard
c. 1841
Philadelphia, Pa.
(10)

Ferdinand Bera
(Bero ?)
c. 1839–1850
Philadelphia, Pa.
(10)

Samuel Berd
c. 1840
Philadelphia, Pa.
(10)

Frederick Berenbroick
Frederick Berenbroick & Co.
c. 1839–1841
New York, N.Y.
(18)

Peter W. Bergantz
c. 1848–1852
Louisville, Ky.
(63)

Jacob Berringer
A. & J. Berringer (?)
c. 1835–1843
Albany, N.Y.
(24)

Ferdinand Berstardus (Besterdes ?)
1836–1840
New York, N.Y.
(18)

A. Besselievre
c. 1837
Philadelphia, Pa.
(10, 37, 90, 106)

John Besselievre
c. 1825–1840
Philadelphia, Pa.
(10)

John A. Besselievre
c. 1841–1850
Philadelphia, Pa.
(10)

B. Best
B. Best & Co.
after 1850
Louisville, Ky.
(63, 123)

W. J. Bettinger
c. 1853–1854
Utica, N.Y.
(25)

Charles Betton
c. 1850
Philadelphia, Pa.
(10)

G. Bichler (Bechler ?)
c. 1858–1860)
Utica, N.Y.
(25)

Henry Biershing (H B)
c. 1815–1843
Hagerstown, Md.
(39, 55, 92, 106)

Abram O. Bigelow
Bigelow & Bros.
c. 1830(?)–1850
Boston, Mass.
(37)

Alanson Bigelow
Bigelow & Bros.
c. 1832–1850
Boston, Mass.
(37)

John Bigelow
Bigelow & Bros.
Bigelow Bros. & Kennard
Bigelow, Kennard & Co.
c. 1830–1863
Boston, Mass.
(36, 39, 55)

Joseph Biggs
c. 1835
New York, N.Y.
(18, 37, 90, 106)

Charles Billon
c. 1860
St. Louis, Mo.
(39, 106, 123)

James Bingham
c. 1839–1850
Philadelphia, Pa.
(10)

Albert G. Bird
c. 1829–1850
Philadelphia, Pa.
(10)

John Stiles Bird (J S B)
c. 1820–1861
Charleston, S.C.
(14, 39, 106)

William Bird
c. 1848–1850
Philadelphia, Pa.
(10)

Benjamin F. Bishop
c. 1846–1847
Philadelphia, Pa.
(10)

Edward Bishop
c. 1839
Philadelphia, Pa.
(10)

Erwin Bishop
c. 1835–1837
Philadelphia, Pa.
(10)

Joaquim Bishop
c. 1837
Philadelphia, Pa.
(10)

John Bishop
c. 1839–1851
Wheeling, W. Va.
(23)

Peter S. Bishop
c. 1837
Philadelphia, Pa.
(10)

John Black, (J B)
c. 1839–1850
Philadelphia, Pa.
(10)

William Black
Ball, Tompkins & Black
Ball, Black & Co.
c. 1833–1876
New York, N.Y.
(18, 37, 90, 106)

Frederick Starr Blackman
F. S. Blackman & Co. (FSB & Co.)
c. 1832–before 1898
Danbury, Conn.
Bridgeport, Conn.
(20, 37, 39, 55, 90)

John Clark Blackman
J. C. Blackman & Co. (J C B & Co.)
c. 1829–before 1872
Danbury, Conn.
Bridgeport, Conn.
(20, 37, 39, 90, 106)

John Starr Blackman
before 1851
Danbury, Conn.
(20, 37, 39, 50, 55, 90, 106)

William Blackwood
Blackwood & Brooks
c. 1828–1850
Utica, N.Y.
(24, 25)

Frederick Blake
c. 1840–1844
Albany, N.Y.
(24)

George H. Blake
before 1849
Troy, N.Y.
(24)

Isaac Blake
c. 1846–1850
Troy, N.Y.
(24)

Collins Blakley
c. 1845
Troy, N.Y.
(37)

William Blakslee (Blackslee ?)
before 1879
Newtown, Conn.
(20, 37, 50, 90, 106)

Asa Blanchard (A B)
c. 1808–1838
Lexington, Ky.
(37, 39, 50, 55, 63, 90, 106, 123)

Peter Blancjour
c. 1838
Richmond, Va.
(23)

Samuel Bland
c. 1837–1850
Philadelphia, Pa.
(10)

William Bland
c. 1845–1848
St. Louis, Mo.
(123)

Charles Blank
c. 1850
Philadelphia, Pa.
(10)

John Blank
c. 1837–1839
Philadelphia, Pa.
(10)

John Blatt
c. 1841
Philadelphia, Pa.
(10)

John W. Blauvelt
c. 1831–1844
New York, N.Y.
(18, 37, 90, 106)

Spencer Blauvelt
c. 1839–1840
New York, N.Y.
(18)

Joseph Block
c. 1859–1891
Charleston, S.C.
(14, 106)

George Blome
c. 1845
Philadelphia, Pa.
(10)

Charles Bloomer
c. 1850
Syracuse, N.Y.
(24)

George Blowe
c. 1837–1850
Philadelphia, Pa.
(10)

Charles L. Boehme
(CLB)
c. 1774–1868
Baltimore, Md.
(119)

Charles Bofenchen
c. 1854–1857
Camden, S.C.
(14)

William Bogart
c. 1839–1847
Albany, N.Y.
(24)

John E. Boger
Boger & Wilson
c. 1845–1853
Salisbury, N.C.
(22)

William Bogert
c. 1842
Albany, N.Y.
(37)

Thomas Boggs
c. 1849
Philadelphia, Pa.
(10)

Thomas H. Bogue
Thomas H. Bogue
& Co.
c. 1844
Philadelphia, Pa.
(10)

L. T. Boland
c. 1844
Columbia, S.C.
(14)

______ Bolles
Bolles & Hasting
c. 1840
Location unknown
(78)

C. Bond
c. 1840
Location unknown
(50)

William Boning
Boning & Co.
Holden & Boning
c. 1843–1850
Philadelphia, Pa.
(10)

Edmund C. Bonsall
Bonsall & Jacot
Bonsall & Scheer
c. 1844–1850
Philadelphia, Pa.
(10)

Edward C. Bonsall
c. 1839–1840
Philadelphia, Pa.
(10)

Michael Boon
c. 1840
Philadelphia, Pa.
(10)

Sanford Boon
c. 1822–1844
Hamilton, N.Y.
(24)

Ezra B. Booth
c. 1838–1888
Vergennes, Vt.
Rochester, N.Y.
(24, 39, 100, 106)

Thomas Booth
c. 1841
Philadelphia, Pa.
(10)

Christian Borderson
c. 1850
Russellville, Ky.
(63, 123)

Edward Borhek
c. 1835–1850
Philadelphia, Pa.
(10)

Frederick Bosardet
(Boshardt ?,
Bussarec ?)
c. 1840–1847
Philadelphia, Pa.
(10)

James Boss
c. 1846–1847
Philadelphia, Pa.
(10)

Philip Boss
Boss & Peterman
c. 1841
Rochester, N.Y.
(24)

Peter Bossordet
c. 1847–1849
Philadelphia, Pa.
(10)

Zalmon Bostwick
(Z B)
c. 1846–1852
New York, N.Y.
(18, 37, 99, 55, 106)

Samuel Bosworth
c. 1816–1837
Buffalo, N.Y.
(24, 37, 39, 55, 90)

Gideon B. Botsford
c. 1840–1849
Schenectady, N.Y.
Troy, N.Y.
(37, 39, 50, 55,
90, 106)

J. S. Botsford
c. 1840–1849
Schenectady, N.Y.
Troy, N.Y.
(24)

Samuel N. Botsford
c. 1839–1842
Norfolk, Va.
(23)

Heloise Boudo
c. 1827–1837
Charleston, S.C.
(14, 39, 106)

Joseph Boujou
c. 1812–1849
St. Louis, Mo.
(123)

Lewis Charles Boute
c. 1839
Philadelphia, Pa.
(10)

George Bowers
c. 1850
Philadelphia, Pa.
(10)

Gerardus Boyce
c. 1814–1841
New York, N.Y.
(166)

James Boyce
James Boyce & Co.
c. 1825–1841
New York, N.Y.
(18, 37, 90)

James Boyce
c. 1849
Philadelphia, Pa.
(10)

William Boyd
Shephard & Boyd
Boyd & Hoyt
Boyd & Mulford
c. 1809–1842
Albany, N.Y.
(24, 37, 50, 90, 106)

Jeffrey R. Brackett
Brackett, Crosby & Brown
c. 1815–1876
Boston, Mass.
(50)

Joseph Bradford
c. 1842–1843
Philadelphia, Pa.
(10)

O. C. Bradford
c. 1841
Binghamton, N.Y.
(24)

G. C. Bradley
c. 1841–1843
Binghamton, N.Y.
Kingston, N.Y.
(24)

Gustavus Bradley
Zebul Bradley & Son
c. 1848
New Haven, Conn.
(20, 37)

Horace P. Bradley
c. 1832–1842
Utica, N.Y.
(24, 25)

Horace S. Bradley
Leach & Bradley
H. S. Bradley & Co.
c. 1828–1850
Utica, N.Y.
(25)

Zebul Bradley
Bradley & Merriman (B & M)
Zebul Bradley & Son
c. 1806–1848
New Haven, Conn.
(20, 37, 39, 50, 55, 90, 106)

William V. Brady
c. 1834–1841
New York, N.Y.
(18, 37, 90, 106)

Frederick Augustus Brahe
before 1892
Albany, N.Y.
Augusta, Ga.
(21)

Charles Brainard
Ward, Bartholomew & Brainard
C. Brainard & Son
before 1850
Hartford, Conn.
(20, 37, 50, 90, 106)

Barnet Brakman
c. 1840
Philadelphia, Pa.
(10)

S. Bramhall
c. 1863
Plymouth, Mass.
(37, 39, 50, 55, 90, 106)

Thomas Brand
c. 1837–1842
Troy, N.Y.
(24)

Barnet Brannan
c. 1840
Philadelphia, Pa.
(10)

Bernard Brannan
c. 1842–1848
Philadelphia, Pa.
(10)

Amable Brasher
before 1840
New York, N.Y.
(37, 39, 55, 90, 106)

Louis Brechémin
c. 1816–1850
Philadelphia, Pa.
(10)

Lamon Brees
c. 1837
Wellsburg, Va.
(23)

______ Brem
Brem & Alexander
c. 1848
Charlotte, N.C.
(22)

Barnabas Brennan
c. 1843
Philadelphia, Pa.
(10)

Alexander Brewer
Lawing & Brewer
c. 1842–1847
Charlotte, N.C.
(14, 22)

Charles Brewer (C B)
Moore & Brewer
c. 1824–1844
New York, N.Y.
(18, 106)

Thomas A. Brewer
c. 1830–1850
Philadelphia, Pa.
(10)

Joseph Brier
c. 1849–1850
Philadelphia, Pa.
(10, 37)

Robert Brier
c. 1848
Philadelphia, Pa.
(10, 37)

Daniel Briggs
c. 1836–1837
New York, N.Y.
(18)

William Briggs
c. 1836–1837
New York, N.Y.
(18)

______ Bringhurst
c. 1850
Maine or New Hampshire
(50)

Henry Brinsmaid
c. 1847–1850
Rochester, N.Y.
(24)

Jacob Britton (Brittin ?)
c. 1807–1850
Philadelphia, Pa.
(10, 37, 90, 94, 106)

Thomas Britton (Brittin ?)
c. 1848–1850
Philadelphia, Pa.
(10)

John Brock
c. 1831–1841
New York, N.Y.
(11, 18, 37, 39, 50, 55, 90, 106)

F. C. Brockman
c. 1821–1844
Cincinnati, Ohio
(77)

Benjamin Franklin Brooks
Blackwood & Brooks
B. F. Brooks & Co.
Brooks & Griswold
Brooks & Van Voorhis
B. F. Brooks & Son
Brooks & Hone
c. 1828–1858
Utica, N.Y.
(24, 25)

Charles V. Brooks
B. F. Brooks & Co.
c. 1834–1838
Utica, N.Y.
(24, 25)

William Broom
Broom & Clement
c. 1837
Philadelphia, Pa.
(10)

Lewis R. Broomall
c. 1846–1850
Philadelphia, Pa.
(10)

William Broome
c. 1825–1850
Philadelphia, Pa.
(10)

B. Brower
S. & B. Brower
c. 1810–1850
Albany, N.Y.
(37, 39, 55, 90, 106)

B. D. Brower
B. D. Brower & Son
c. 1850
Albany, N.Y.
(24)

J. H. Brower
c. 1848–1849
Albany, N.Y.
(24)

S. Brower
S. & B. Brower
c. 1810–1850
Albany, N.Y.
(37, 39, 55, 90, 106)

S. Douglas Brower
Brower & Rusher
Hall, Brower & Co.
Hall, Hewson & Brower
Hall & Brower
c. 1832–1854
Troy, N.Y.
New York, N.Y.
Albany, N.Y.
(24, 37, 39, 50, 90, 106)

Walter S. Brower
c. 1850–1898
Albany, N.Y.
(37, 55, 106)

______ Brown
Brown & Kirby
c. 1850
New Haven, Conn.
(39, 106)

______ Brown
Clark & Brown
c. 1843
Norwalk, Conn.
(38, 39, 90, 106)

Alexander Brown
c. 1840–1847
Philadelphia, Pa.
(10, 37, 90, 106)

Charles C. Brown
before 1871
Rochester, N.Y.
(24, 100, 106)

Chauncey Brown
c. 1845
Philadelphia, Pa.
(10)

Francis Brown
c. 1837–1844
New York, N.Y.
(18)

Henry S. Brown
c. 1850
New York, N.Y.
(37)

Henry S. Brown
c. 1851–1860
Syracuse, N.Y.
Utica, N.Y.
(24, 25)

Isaac S. Brown
c. 1844
Philadelphia, Pa.
(10, 37)

Jacob Brown
c. 1866
Mobile, Ala.
(170)

John J. Brown
c. 1848–1852
Utica, N.Y.
(24, 25)

L. Brown
c. 1838
Rochester, N.Y.
(24, 100, 106)

L. S. F. Brown
T. W. Brown & Sons
c. 1872
Wilmington, N.C.
(22)

Lester Brown
Clark & Brown
c. 1843
Cazenovia, N.Y.
(24)

Levi Brown
c. 1840–1866
Detroit, Mich.
(136)

Martin S. Brown
c. 1827–1838
Winchester, Va.
Shepherdstown, W. Va.
(23)

Philip Brown
c. 1841
Philadelphia, Pa.
(10)

Samuel C. Brown
c. 1820–1850
New York, N.Y.
(18, 37, 38, 39, 55, 90, 106)

Seth E. Brown
c. 1844–1845
Concord, N.H.
(133)

T. J. Brown
c. 1835–1840
Location unknown
(50)

Theodore G. Brown
Theodore G. Brown & Son
c. 1825–1840
New York, N.Y.
(37)

Thomas William Brown
Brown & Anderson
T. W. Brown & Sons
c. 1850–1872
Wilmington, N.C.
(22)

William Brown
c. 1845–1849
Albany, N.Y.
(37, 39, 50, 106)

William Brown
c. 1823–1847
Philadelphia, Pa.
(10)

William H. Brown
c. 1848–1849
Philadelphia, Pa.
(10)

William S. Brown
c. 1849–1850
Philadelphia, Pa.
(10)

Hiram Brownson
c. 1841–1842
Troy, N.Y.
(24)

Thaddeus Bruder
c. 1837
Philadelphia, Pa.
(10)

______ Bruno
Bruno & Virgins
c. 1840–1849
Columbus, Ga.
Macon, Ga.
(21)

George Bruns
c. 1855–1914
Columbia, S.C.
(14)

Butler Bryant
c. 1838–1848
Louisville, Ky.
Frankfort, Ky.
(63)

Edward (Edmund ?) A. Bryson
c. 1841–1848
Louisville, Ky.
(63)

Charles W. Buard
c. 1849
Philadelphia, Pa.
(10)

Azariah Buck
c. 1847–1850
Rochester, N.Y.
(24, 100, 106)

C. I. Buel
c. 1846
Saratoga Springs, N.Y.
(24)

Charles I. Buel
c. 1849
Schenectady, N.Y.
(24)

G. W. Bull
c. 1840
Farmington, Conn.
(37, 39, 55, 90, 106)

John S. Bumm
c. 1837–1850
Philadelphia, Pa.
(10)

Benjamin Bunker
(B B)
before 1842
Nantucket Island, Mass.
(17, 39, 106)

Francis Bunnell
c. 1850
Syracuse, N.Y.
(24)

Daniel Bunting
c. 1844
Philadelphia, Pa.
(10)

A. F. Burbank
c. 1845
Worcester, Mass.
(39, 106)

Charles Burd
c. 1850
Philadelphia, Pa.
(10)

Leonard G. Burgess
c. 1831–1850
Rochester, N.Y.
(24)

Charles Burk
c. 1848
Philadelphia, Pa.
(10)

E. K. Burke
c. 1842
St. Louis, Mo.
(123)

Edmund K. Burke
c. 1841
Louisville, Ky.
(63)

Thomas F. Burkhand
c. 1837–1843
Philadelphia, Pa.
(10)

Trubert Burkhart
c. 1839–1846
Philadelphia, Pa.
(10)

Daniel Burnap
c. 1779–1838
East Windsor Hill, Conn.
Andover, Conn.
(20, 50, 59, 90, 106)

Ela Burnap
c. 1827–1844
Rochester, N.Y.
New York, N.Y.
Hartford, Conn.
Eatonton, Ga.
(18, 21, 24, 100)

B. L. Burnett
c. 1847–1857
Milledgeville, Ga.
Macon, Ga.
Lexington, Ky.
(21, 63, 123, 127)

Charles A. Burnett
(C A B)
c. 1785–1849
Georgetown, D.C.
Alexandria, Va.
(23, 37, 38, 39, 50, 55, 90, 106, 117)

Charles E. Burnham
c. 1853–1857
Utica, N.Y.
Binghamton, N.Y.
(24, 25)

P. B. Burnham
P. B. Burnham & Co.
c. 1856–1860
Greenville, S.C.
(14)

——— Burns
c. 1837–1854
Greenville, S.C.
(14)

John H. Burns
c. 1834–1838
Rochester, N.Y.
(24, 37, 90, 106)

Alexander Jay Burr
c. 1832–1838
Rochester, N.Y.
(24, 100, 106, 133)

Cornelius A. Burr
C. A. Burr & Co.
c. 1857–1864
Rochester, N.Y.
Brooklyn, N.Y.
(24, 39, 100, 106, 133)

Ezekiel Burr (E B)
Ezekiel & Wm. Burr
c. 1786–1846
Providence, R.I.
(133)

William C. Burr
Ezekiel & Wm. Burr
Burr & Lee
c. 1815–1846
Providence, R.I.
(133)

George Burrill
Burrill & Beebe
c. 1836–1837
New York, N.Y.
(18)

Joseph Curtiss Burritt
J. Burritt & Son
c. 1838–1862
Ithaca, N.Y.
(24)

William Burrows
c. 1829–1837
Philadelphia, Pa.
(10, 37, 90, 106)

M. Burt
c. 1860
Cleveland, Ohio
(78)

Jacob Burton
c. 1839
Philadelphia, Pa.
(10, 37, 90)

F. W. Burwell
Burwell & Winship
c. 1846–1855
Norfolk, Va.
(23)

Fitch Burwell
c. 1841–1844
Norfolk, Va.
Portsmouth, Va.
(23)

Francis A. Bush
c. 1852–1857
Utica, N.Y.
(25)

Benjamin Bussey
(B B)
before 1842
Dedham, Mass.
(7, 37, 38, 39, 50, 55, 90, 106)

Jason Buswell
c. 1839
Portsmouth, N.H.
(37, 90, 106)

——— Butler
Butler & McCarty
(McCarthy ?)
c. 1850
Philadelphia, Pa.
(11, 37, 39, 50, 106)

Courtland Butler
c. 1843–1845
Philadelphia, Pa.
(10)

Franklin Butler
c. 1846–1850
Philadelphia, Pa.
(10)

Henry W. Butler
c. 1833–1850
Philadelphia, Pa.
(10)

James F. Butler
c. 1850
Utica, N.Y.
(24, 25)

Lewis A. Butler
c. 1850
Binghamton, N.Y.
(24)

N. H. Butler
c. 1837
Philadelphia, Pa.
(37, 90, 106)

William H. Butler
Butler & Keim
Butler, Wise & Keim
Butler, Wise & Co.
c. 1842–1850
Philadelphia, Pa.
(10, 37)

Henry Buttercase
c. 1853–1854
Utica, N.Y.
(25)

_______ Buttre
Adams & Buttre
c. 1836–1842
Elmira, N.Y.
(24)

Columbus Buzzel
c. 1837
Philadelphia, Pa.
(10)

_______ Bwistrand
Van Ness & Bwistrand
c. 1844
New York, N.Y.
(37)

John Byrne
c. 1846–1859
Lexington, Ky.
(63)

Walter D. Cable
c. 1847
Poughkeepsie, N.Y.
(134)

Felix Ferjeux Cachot
c. 1813–1839
Bardstown, Ky.
(63, 127)

Michael Cagger
Finch & Cagger
c. 1832–1838
Albany, N.Y.
(24)

Abraham Cahn
c. 1850
Philadelphia, Pa.
(10)

Jay Caldwell
c. 1850
Philadelphia, Pa.
(10)

James E. Caldwell
Bennett & Caldwell
Caldwell & Co.
Filley, Mead & Caldwell (?)
J. E. Caldwell & Co.
c. 1840–1850
Philadelphia, Pa.
(10, 38, 106)

T. G. Calvert
c. 1815–1842
Lexington, Ky.
(123, 127)

William Cammer
c. 1839–1842
Philadelphia, Pa.
(10)

Andrew Campbell
R. & A. Campbell
c. 1835–1854
Baltimore, Md.
(37)

Andrew Campbell
c. 1829–1842
Philadelphia, Pa.
(10)

Archibald Campbell
c. 1827–1837
Baltimore, Md.
(93)

Robert Campbell (R C)
R. & A. Campbell
Richards & Campbell
c. 1819–1854–before 1872
Baltimore, Md.
(11, 37, 38, 39, 50, 55, 90, 106)

Thomas Boyle Campbell (TBC)
Campbell & Polk
Campbell & Meredith
c. 1815–1858
Winchester, Va.
(23)

_______ Candee
Candee & McEwan
c. 1858
Edgefield, S.C.
(14)

Lewis Burton Candee
Curtis & Candee
L. B. Candee & Co.
Curtis, Candee & Stiles (C C & S)
c. 1825–before 1861
Woodbury, Conn.
(20, 37, 39, 50, 90, 106)

Ira B. Canfield
Canfield & Bro.
Canfield Bro. & Co.
c. 1834–1850
Baltimore, Md.
North Haddam, Conn.
(11, 37, 50, 90, 106)

L. Canfield
c. 1849
Binghamton, N.Y.
(24)

Lewis Canfield
c. 1845
Rochester, N.Y.
(24)

William B. Canfield
Canfield & Bro.
Canfield Bro. & Co.
c. 1830–1850
Baltimore, Md.
(11, 37, 50, 90, 106)

William Canfield
c. 1843–1846
Troy, N.Y.
(24)

John Cann
Dunn & Cann
Charters, Cann & Dunn (C C & D)
Kidney, Cann & Johnson (?) (K C & J)
c. 1834–1850
New York, N.Y.
(11, 18, 37, 50, 90, 106)

James Canoll
c. 1839–1845
Albany, N.Y.
(24)

John W. H. Canoll
c. 1824–1848
Albany, N.Y.
(24)

John Porter Capelle
c. 1848–1868
Wilmington, Del.
St. Louis, Mo.
(38, 39, 106, 123)

Marcus Eugene Capelle
c. 1875–1879
St. Louis, Mo.
(123)

_______ Carey
Carey & Anthony
c. 1837
Cincinnati, Ohio
(77)

Hugh Carland
c. 1840
Macon, Ga.
(21)

J. Carmichael
c. 1840
Owego, N.Y.
(24)

Benjamin R. Carpenter
c. 1850
Syracuse, N.Y.
(24)

Lumen Carpenter
c. 1845–1847
Oswego, N.Y.
(24)

B. D. Carr
c. 1845–1846
Philadelphia, Pa.
(10)

David S. Carr
c. 1841–1845
Troy, N.Y.
(24)

John Carrow
Dubosq & Carrow
Dubosq, Carrow & Co.
c. 1839–1850
Philadelphia, Pa.
(10)

John Carrows
c. 1837
Philadelphia, Pa.
(10)

Allen Carson
c. 1849
Philadelphia, Pa.
(10, 37)

David Carson
c. 1842–1850
Albany, N.Y.
(24, 37, 50, 106)

Jane Carson
c. 1906
Cleveland, Ohio
(128, 175)

Thomas H. Carson
c. 1838–1843
Albany, N.Y.
(24)

C. W. Carter
c. 1840
Location unknown
(78)

George M. Carter
c. 1839
Philadelphia, Pa.
(10)

William Carter
c. 1844–1847
Philadelphia, Pa.
(10)

George Cartier
c. 1845–1850
Philadelphia, Pa.
(10)

D. N. Carvalks
c. 1846
Philadelphia, Pa.
(10)

Philemon N. Case
c. 1849–1852
Hamilton, N.Y.
(24)

Samuel Caskell
19th century
Louisville, Ky.
(63, 123)

William Cassaday
(Cassiday ?)
c. 1846–1850
Philadelphia, Pa.
(10)

Abraham Cassal
c. 1840
Philadelphia, Pa.
(10)

Andrew Cassedy
c. 1840
Philadelphia, Pa.
(10, 37, 90, 106)

Daniel B. Castle
Castle & Morrell
c. 1837–1844
Buffalo, N.Y.
(24)

Samuel Caswell
c. 1838–1850–
before 1878
Louisville, Ky.
(63, 127)

Charles Catlin
c. 1841
Athens, Ga.
Augusta, Ga.
(21)

Joseph Cave
c. 1837–1847
Philadelphia, Pa.
(10)

Samuel Chadwick, Jr.
c. 1839
Buffalo, N.Y.
(24)

Charles Chamberlain
c. 1833–1839
Philadelphia, Pa.
(10)

Edgar Chamberlain
c. 1850
Mobile, Ala.
(170)

Lewis Chamberlain
c. 1824–1842
Elkton, Md.
Philadelphia, Pa.
(10, 93)

Lewis C. Champney
Fisher & Champney
c. 1845–1850
Troy, N.Y.
(24)

______ Chandler
Chandler & Darrow
c. 1843–1861
New York, N.Y.
(161)

William Chandless
c. 1836–1838
New York, N.Y.
(11, 18, 37, 50, 106)

H. Chapel
c. 1845–1846
Louisville, Ky.
(63)

Henry Chapell
c. 1848
St. Louis, Mo.
(123)

Hiram F. Chapell
Chapell & Roberts
c. 1845–1850
Hartford, Conn.
(37)

Aaron Chapin
before 1838
Hartford, Conn.
(20, 37, 50, 90, 106)

Alexander Chapin
c. 1846
Hartford, Conn.
(37, 90, 106)

E. Chapin
c. 1850
Perry, N.Y.
(24)

Edwin G. Chapin
c. 1836–1839
Buffalo, N.Y.
Little Falls, N.Y.
(24)

Alonzo Chapman
c. 1836
Troy, N.Y.
(24)

Charles Chapman
c. 1838–1839
Troy, N.Y.
(24)

David W. Chapman
c. 1834–1841
Rochester, N.Y.
(24, 100)

William Chapman
c. 1849
Charleston, S.C.
(14)

Lewis Charles
c. 1837
Philadelphia, Pa.
(10)

James Charters
Charters, Cann &
Dunn (C C & D)
c. 1844–1850
New York, N.Y.
(11, 37, 50, 106)

______ Chase
Chase & Easton
c. 1837
Brooklyn, N.Y.
(37, 90, 106)

George W. Chase
c. 1842–1847
Utica, N.Y.
Troy, N.Y.
(24, 25, 37)

Thomas B. Chase
Chase & Vaughn
c. 1839–1848
Buffalo, N.Y.
(24)

Charles H. Chedell
Chedell & Allen
c. 1844
Buffalo, N.Y.
(24)

John Hatch Chedell
(Cheadell ?)
Chedell & Co.
c. 1827–before 1875
Auburn, N.Y.
(24)

______ Chelius
Location unknown
c. 1840
(50)

James Cherry
c. 1849–1850
Philadelphia, Pa.
(10, 106)

Henry T. Child
c. 1840–1842
Philadelphia, Pa.
(10)

John Child
c. 1813–1847
Philadelphia, Pa.
(10)

Samuel T. Child
S. T. & T. T. Child
c. 1843–1850
Philadelphia, Pa.
(10)

Thomas T. Child
S. T. & T. T. Child
c. 1845–1850
Philadelphia, Pa.
(10)

Asaph King Childs
O. & A. K. Childs
Childs & Chamberlain
c. 1847–1861
Athens, Ga.
(21)

George K. Childs
c. 1828–1850
Philadelphia, Pa.
(10, 11, 37, 39, 50, 90, 106)

Otis Childs
O. & A. K. Childs
Childs & Chamberlain
c. 1836–1872–before 1899
Milledgeville, Ga.
Athens, Ga.
Newton, Mass.
(21)

F. Chitry
c. 1840
Owego, N.Y.
(24)

Robert W. Choate
c. 1829–1838
Philadelphia, Pa.
(10)

Stephen G. Choate
c. 1841–1852
Louisville, Ky.
(63, 127)

George W. Christian
c. 1850
Utica, N.Y.
(24, 25)

Nathan M. Christian
c. 1840–1851
Utica, N.Y.
(24, 25)

William N. Christian
c. 1846–1847
Utica, N.Y.
(24, 25)

E. Chubbuck
E. Chubbuck & Son
c. 1850
Lockport, N.Y.
(24)

Samuel W. Chubbuck
Storrs & Chubbuck
c. 1847–1849
Utica, N.Y.
Morrisville, N.Y.
(24, 25, 133)

Charles L. Chur
c. 1837
Staunton, Va.
(23)

______ Church
Church & Metcalf
c. 1842
Providence, R.I.
(37)

Joseph Church
Church & Rogers
c. 1825–before 1876
Hartford, Conn.
New Haven, Conn.
(37, 38, 39, 50, 86, 90, 106)

Ralph Church
c. 1832–1848
Buffalo, N.Y.
(24, 37, 90, 106)

Andrew S. Clackner
c. 1847–1850
Rochester, N.Y.
(24)

John S. Clackner
c. 1833–1848
Troy, N.Y.
Rochester, N.Y.
(24)

______ Clark
c. 1837
Circleville, Ohio
(77)

______ Clark
Clark & Brown
c. 1843
Norwalk, Conn.
(38, 39, 90, 106)

______ Clark
Clark & Hartley
c. 1839–1841
Philadelphia, Pa.
(10)

Alexander G. Clark
c. 1850
Syracuse, N.Y.
(24)

Benjamin W. Clark
Benjamin & Ellis Clark
c. 1791–1848
Philadelphia, Pa.
(10)

Ellis Clark
Benjamin & Ellis Clark
c. 1816–1848
Philadelphia, Pa.
(10)

F. H. Clark
F. H. Clark & Co.
c. 1850
Memphis, Tenn.
(39, 106)

Francis C. Clark
F. Clark & Co.

F. & H. Clark
c. 1816–1860
Augusta, Ga.
(21)

Gabriel D. Clark
Foxcroft & Clark
c. 1830–1896
Baltimore, Md.
(37, 38, 39, 93, 106)

George Clark
c. 1842–1843
Philadelphia, Pa.
(10)

George R. Clark
c. 1827–1846
Auburn, N.Y.
Rome, N.Y.
Utica, N.Y.
(24, 25)

Horace Clark
F. & H. Clark
Clark, Rackett & Co.
c. 1830–1854
Augusta, Ga.
(21)

Jehiel Clark, Jr.
Clark & Brown
c. 1843
Cazenovia, N.Y.
(24)

John Clark
c. 1837–1840
Philadelphia, Pa.
(10)

John J. Clark
c. 1833–1845
Cambridge, Md.
Portsmouth, Va.
(23)

John L. Clark
c. 1837–1838
Utica, N.Y.
(24, 25)

John L. Clark
c. 1856–1857
Laurens, S.C.
Hodges Depot, S.C.
(14)

Jonas C. Clark
L. W. & J. C. Clark
c. 1836–after 1840
Watertown, N.Y.
Utica, N.Y.
Albany, .NY.
(24)

Levi Clark
before 1875
Norwalk, Conn.
(20, 38, 39, 55, 90, 106)

Lewis W. Clark
L. W. & J. C. Clark
c. 1832–1838
Watertown, N.Y.
Utica, N.Y.
(24, 25, 39, 106)

Patrick F. Clark
c. 1842–1843
Philadelphia, Pa.
(10, 37)

Philip Clark
c. 1837–1843
Albany, N.Y.
(24)

Thomas W. Clark
c. 1830–1850
Philadelphia, Pa.
(10)

Barns Clayton
c. 1850
Philadelphia, Pa.
(10)

Elias P. Clayton
c. 1848–1850
Philadelphia, Pa.
(10)

Richard Clayton
c. 1821–1844
Cincinnati, Ohio
(77)

James W. Clement
Broom & Clement (?)
c. 1833–1850
Philadelphia, Pa.
(10)

James Clements
Clements & Ashburn
c. 1847
Philadelphia, Pa.
(10)

William Cleveland
(W C)
c. 1770–1837
New London, Conn.
(119)

Josiah Clift
Silverthorn & Clift
c. 1818–1860–
before 1893
Portsmouth, Va.
Easton, Md.
Centerville, Md.
Norfolk, Va.
Baltimore, Md.
Lynchburg, Va.
(23, 123)

B. Cline
c. 1858–1859
Utica, N.Y.
(25)

Charles Cline
C. & P. Cline (?)
c. 1829–1850
Philadelphia, Pa.
(10, 37, 90, 106)

Charles Cline, Jr.
c. 1849
Philadelphia, Pa.
(10)

J. Cline
W. & J. Cline
c. 1857–1865
Utica, N.Y.
(25)

Philip Cline
C. & P. Cline (?)
c. 1819–1847 (?)
Philadelphia, Pa.
(10)

Walter Cline
W. & J. Cline
c. 1857–1861
Utica, N.Y.
(25)

Thomas B. Cloutman
c. 1837
Buffalo, N.Y.
(24)

Isaac D. Cluster
c. 1850
St. Louis, Mo.
(38, 39, 106)

A. L. Coan
c. 1857
Mobile, Ala.
(170)

Isaac Coates
c. 1835–1839
Philadelphia, Pa.
(10)

William Coates
c. 1835–1839
Buffalo, N.Y.
(24)

A. W. Coats
Coats & Boyd
c. 1831–1837
Philadelphia, Pa.
(10)

William D. Cochran
c. 1830–1841
Albany, N.Y.
Troy, N.Y.
Schenactady, N.Y.
(24)

James Cockrell
c. 1843–1850
Philadelphia, Pa.
(10)

Willard Codman
c. 1839
Boston, Mass.
(37, 90, 106)

______ Coe
Coe & Upton
c. 1840
New York, N.Y.
(37, 38, 39, 50, 55, 90,
106)

H. H. Coe
c. 1840
Location unknown
(38)

William Coffman
c. 1839–1850
Philadelphia, Pa.
(10, 37, 90,106)

Henry Cogswell
c. 1846–1853
Salem, Mass.
(39, 106)

Albert Cohen
c. 1848
St. Louis, Mo.
(123)

M. A. Cohen
c. 1840–1843
Philadelphia, Pa.
(10)

William Cohen
c. 1833–1838
Alexandria, Va.
(23, 37, 90, 106)

E. Coit
c. 1825–1839
Norwich, Conn.
(37, 38, 39, 55, 90,
106)

Albert Cole (Coles ?)
(A C)
c. 1840–1847
New York, N.Y.
(10, 37, 38, 39, 50, 55,
106, 161, 166)

John A. Cole
c. 1844
New York, N.Y.
(37)

William Groat Cole
before 1898
Utica, N.Y.
(24, 25)

______ Coleman
Decker & Coleman
c. 1847–1849
Troy, N.Y.
(24)

Alvan Coleman
c. 1847–1849
Troy, N.Y.
(24)

John Coleman
c. 1848
Philadelphia, Pa.
(10)

John F. Coleman
c. 1848
Philadelphia, Pa.
(10)

Joseph Coleman
after 1839–before 1900
Massilon, Ohio
(77)

Nathaniel Coleman
(N C)
before 1842
Burlington, N.J.
(37, 38, 39, 50, 55, 90, 95, 106, 117)

Albert Coles
Albert Coles & Co. (?)
c. 1836–1875 (?)
New York, N.Y.
(18, 50, 106)

John A. Coles (C)
Albert Coles & Co. (?)
c. 1850
New York, N.Y.
(50, 55, 106)

Lambert Collette
(Colette ?)
c. 1835–1848
Buffalo, N.Y.
(24, 37, 90, 106)

Peleg Collings
(Peley Collins ?)
c. 1836–1850
Cincinnati, Ohio
(123)

Francis Collingwood
c. 1817–1845
Elmira, N.Y.
(24)

Blakely Collins
c. 1846–1850
Troy, N.Y.
(24)

Patrick Collins
c. 1839–1844
Albany, N.Y.
(24)

Selden Collins, Jr.
Murdock & Collins
c. 1837–before 1885
Utica, N.Y.
(25, 38, 39, 106)

W. A. Collins
c. 1840–1841
Troy, N.Y.
(24)

David W. Collom
c. 1846–1850
Philadelphia, Pa.
(10)

Abraham Colser
c. 1845–1846
Albany, N.Y.
(24, 37)

——— Colwell
Colwell & Lawrence
c. 1850
Albany, N.Y.
(11, 37, 50, 106)

William Commel
c. 1837
Philadelphia, Pa.
(10)

William Compton
c. 1844–1846
Rochester, N.Y.
(24)

A. Conery
c. 1838–1854
Frankfort, Ky.
(63)

James Conning
c. 1840–1873
Mobile, Ala.
(170)

Patrick Connolly
c. 1837–1848
Buffalo, N.Y.
(24)

——— Connor
Connor & Stickles
c. 1837
New York, N.Y.
(18)

John H. Connor
(J H C)
Eoff & Connor
c. 1833–1838
New York, N.Y.
(18, 37, 38, 39, 50, 90, 106)

William J. Connor
(Conner ?)
c. 1855
Charleston, S.C.
(14)

George Conrad
c. 1839–1843
Philadelphia, Pa.
(10)

George Oliver Conrad
Bear & Conrad
c. 1846–1854
Charlottesville, Va.
Harrisonburg, Va.
Luray, Va.
(23)

Godfrey Conrad
c. 1831–1850
Philadelphia, Pa.
(10)

Osborn Conrad
c. 1841–1850
Philadelphia, Pa.
(10)

——— Cook
Cook & Co.
c. 1849
Syracuse, N.Y.
(24, 37)

A. H. Cook
c. 1838
Hudson, N.Y.
(24)

Benjamin E. Cook
Storrs & Cook
B. E. Cook
B. E. Cook & Son
c. 1827–1885
Amherst, Mass.
Northampton, Mass.
Troy, N.Y.
(24, 39, 106, 133)

Charles L. Cook
c. 1843–1850
Philadelphia, Pa.
(10)

Erastus Cook
Cook & Stillwell
c. 1815–1864
Rochester, N.Y.
Madison, Wis.
(24, 39, 100, 106)

H. T. Cook
c. 1840
Location unknown
(78)

John B. Cooke
c. 1838–1843
Petersburg, Va.
(23)

William Cooke
Cooke & Son
c. 1833–1838
Petersburg, Va.
(23)

William A. Cooke
Cooke & White
White & Cooke
William A. Cooke & Co.
Cooke & Son
c. 1826–1838
Petersburg, Va.
(23)

Henry P. Cooley
c. 1842–1846
Troy, N.Y.
Cooperstown, N.Y.
(24)

Oliver B. Cooley
Storrs & Cooley
Tanner & Cooley
c. 1831–1844
Utica, N.Y.
(24, 25, 39, 106, 133)

John W. Coon
(Coom ?)
c. 1840–1846
Cleveland, Ohio
(37, 77)

Cooper & Fisher
c. 1850
New York, N.Y.
(38, 39, 106)

Archibald Cooper
William & Archibald Cooper
c. 1838–1848
Louisville, Ky.
Frankfort, Ky.
(63, 127)

Francis W. Cooper
(F W C)
c. 1846–1851
New York, N.Y.
(11, 18, 37, 39, 50, 106)

Joseph Cooper
Cooper & Gaither
Cooper & Yongue
c. 1843–1860
Columbia, S.C.
Greenville, S.C.
(14)

Joseph B. Cooper
c. 1842–1846
Philadelphia, Pa.
(10)

Robert H. Cooper
c. 1850
Philadelphia, Pa.
(10)

Samuel B. Cooper
c. 1840
Philadelphia, Pa.
(10)

William Cooper
William & Archibald Cooper
W. & A. Cooper
c. 1838–1844
Louisville, Ky.
Frankfcrt, Ky.
(63)

William Cooper
c. 1844
Philadelphia, Pa.
(10, 37)

Robert Copeland
c. 1850
New York, N.Y.
(37)

Nathaniel P. Copp
c. 1832–1845
Troy, N.Y.
Albany, N.Y.
(11, 24, 37, 50, 90, 106)

George F. Coppock
c. 1847–1848
Utica, N.Y.
(24, 25)

George Washington Coppock
before 1882
Mount Holly, N.J.
(117)

Ferdinand Corew
c. 1837
Philadelphia, Pa.
(10)

John Cork
c. 1837–1850
Philadelphia, Pa.
(10)

Edward Corvazier
c. 1846
Philadelphia, Pa.
(10)

Thomas E. Cosby
T. E. Cosby & Co.
Cosby & Hopkins
Cosby, Hopkins & Co.
c. 1815–1858
Petersburg, Va.
(23)

Ezekiel Costen
c. 1845–1850
Philadelphia, Pa.
(10)

William W. Covell
Covell & Higgins (?)
c. 1850
Syracuse, N.Y.
(24)

Charles Cowdrick
c. 1833–1839
Philadelphia, Pa.
(10)

Charles H. Cowdrick
c. 1840–1850
Philadelphia, Pa.
(10)

Ralph Cowles
c. 1840–1850
Cleveland, Ohio
(37, 38, 39, 55, 77, 106)

Royal Cowles
Cowles & Albertson
c. 1849–1858
Cleveland, Ohio
(123)

C. J. Cowperthwait
c. 1846–1849
Philadelphia, Pa.
(10)

James Cox
John & James Cox
c. 1817–1853
New York, N.Y.
(166)

John Cox
John & James Cox
c. 1817–1853
New York, N.Y.
(166)

William Cox
c. 1825–1837
Fredericksburg, Va.
(23)

Richard Cram
c. 1845–1848
Rochester, N.Y.
(24)

Benjamin Crandall
c. 1839
Portsmouth, N.H.
(37, 90)

Benjamin F. Crane
Benjamin F. Crane & Co.
c. 1842–1861
St. Louis, Mo.
(123)

Alfred Craven
c. 1843
Philadelphia, Pa.
(10)

Alfred Craven
c. 1851
York, S.C.
(14)

John Crawford
c. 1837–1843
New York, N.Y.
Philadelphia, Pa.
(10, 11, 18, 37, 38, 39, 50, 55, 106, 161)

George Creamer
c. 1843–1869
Poughkeepsie, N.Y.
(24, 134)

S. J. Creswell
c. 1840
Philadelphia, Pa.
(10)

John T. Crew
c. 1830–1850
Albany, N.Y.
(24)

Peter Crider (Krider ?)
c. 1845
Philadelphia, Pa.
(10)

Elnathan F. Crissey
Dunning & Crissey
c. 1847
Rochester, N.Y.
(24)

Newton E. Crittenden
c. 1826–1872
Leroy, N.Y.
Cleveland, Ohio
(24, 37, 39, 77, 90, 106)

William Crocker
c. 1837
Philadelphia, Pa.
(10)

Frederick Crocks (Crox ?) (Croix ?) (Crooks ?)
c. 1835–1850
Philadelphia, Pa.
(10)

William S. Croker
c. 1839
Harpers Ferry, W. Va.
(23)

______ Cromwell
Van Vliet & Cromwell
c. 1844
Poughkeepsie, N.Y.
(24)

T. Cronsberry
c. 1848
Location unknown
(78)

C. A. W. Crosby
c. 1850
Location unknown
(78)

Samuel T. Crosby
Crosby & Brown
Brackett, Crosby & Brown
Crosby & Foss
c. 1849–1877
Boston, Mass.
(37, 50, 106, 165, 175)

David B. Crowell
c. 1849–1850
Philadelphia, Pa.
(10)

Henry Crump
c. 1848
Philadelphia, Pa.
(10)

John Cullen
c. 1840–1841
Leesburg, Va.
(23)

Hugh Cullin
c. 1844
Louisa Court House, Va.
(23)

George Cummings
c. 1843
Hartford, Conn.
(37)

Henry Cummings
c. 1849–1850
Philadelphia, Pa.
(10)

John B. Cummings
c. 1841–1850
Philadelphia, Pa.
(10)

William Cummings
c. 1841–1850
Philadelphia, Pa.
(10)

Robert Cunningham
c. 1844–1845
Louisville, Ky.
(63)

Jule F. Cure
c. 1839–1840
Philadelphia, Pa.
(10)

I. B. Curran
I. B. Curran & Co.
c. 1835–1839
Ithaca, N.Y.
(24, 39)

James Curran
c. 1843–1850
Philadelphia, Pa.
(10)

James W. Currin
Owens & Currin
c. 1843–1850
Philadelphia, Pa.
(10)

______ Curry
Curry & Preston
c. 1849
Newburgh, N.Y.
(24)

John Curry
Curry & Preston
c. 1835–1850
Philadelphia, Pa.
(10, 11, 37, 38, 39, 50, 55)

Francis Curtis
c. 1845
Woodbury, Conn.
(37)

Lewis Curtis
c. 1790–1845
Farmington, Conn.
St. Charles, Mo.
Hazel Green, Wis.
(20, 37, 39, 50, 55, 90, 106)

Thomas Curtis
c. 1831–1837
New York, N.Y.
(18, 37, 90, 106)

Isaac D. Custer
c. 1847–1854
St. Louis, Mo.
(123)

A. Cutler
c. 1820–1850
Boston, Mass.
(37, 38, 39, 50, 55, 90, 106)

Eben Cutler
c. 1820–1846
New Haven, Conn.
Boston, Mass.
(37, 38, 39, 55, 90, 106)

John N. Cutler
c. 1829–1850
Albany, N.Y.
(24, 37, 50, 106)

J. Cutter
after 1857
Newburyport, Mass.
(19)

Louis H. Dadin
c. 1849–1852
Charleston, S.C.
(14)

Henry Dagon
c. 1847–1850
Philadelphia, Pa.
(10)

Henry Dagon
c. 1847–1850
Philadelphia, Pa.
(10)

______ Dana
Dana & Maynard
c. 1841
Utica, N.Y.
(25)

Peyton Dana (P D)
before 1849
Providence, R.I.
(39, 50, 106)

James H. Daniel
c. 1830–1850
Philadelphia, Pa.
(10)

Joshua Daniel
c. 1830–1850
Philadelphia, Pa.
(10)

Charles W. Daniels
c. 1836–1838
Troy, N.Y.
(24, 37, 90, 106)

G. L. Daniels
c. 1840–1843
Rome, N.Y.
(24)

Frederick Darrigrand
c. 1854–1865
Utica, N.Y.
(25)

Edmund Darrow
c. 1843–1861
New York, N.Y.
(18, 106, 161, 162)

Edmund J. Daumont
E. J. Daumont & Co.
c. 1820–1861
Louisville, Ky.
(63)

Peter Daumont
c. 1843–1846
Louisville, Ky.
(63)

Jules D'Autel
c. 1841–1845
Augusta, Ga.
Athens, Ga.
(21)

Henry David
c. 1844
New York, N.Y.
(37)

Lewis A. David
c. 1823–1840
Philadelphia, Pa.
(10, 11, 37, 90, 106)

Marquis David
c. 1855–1859
Charleston, S.C.
(14)

Benjamin F. Davies
Thomas Davies & Sons
B. F. & T. M. Davies
c. 1853–1858
Utica, N.Y.
(24, 25)

F. L. Davies
F. L. Davies & Bro.
c. 1863–1882
Nashville, Tenn.
(89, 175)

Thomas Davies
Storrs & Davies
Leach & Davies
Davies & Battel
Davies & Taylor
Thomas Davies & Sons
c. 1823–1858
Utica, N.Y.
(24, 25, 133)

Thomas M. Davies
Thomas Davies & Sons
B. F. & T. M. Davies
c. 1856–before 1882
Utica, N.Y.
(25)

William A. Davies
Davies & Battel
c. 1844–1847
Utica, N.Y.
(24, 25)

W. H. Davies
F. L. Davies & Bro.
c. 1863–1882
Nashville, Tenn.
(89, 175)

Joshua G. Davis
c. 1796–1840
Boston, Mass.
(11, 37, 38, 39, 50, 90, 106)

M. C. Davis
c. 1871–1888
Indianapolis, Ind.
(70, 175)

Richard Davis
c. 1837
Philadelphia, Pa.
(10)

Riley A. Davis
c. 1850
New Bern, N.C.
(36)

Samuel Davis
Davis & Babbitt
Davis & Watson (D & W)
Davis, Watson & Co.
c. 1801–1842
Boston, Mass.
Plymouth, Mass.
Providence, R.I.
(37, 38, 39, 50, 55, 106)

Samuel B. Davis
c. 1837–1850
Philadelphia, Pa.
(10)

T. W. Davis
c. 1857
Greenville, S.C.
(14)

William Davis
c. 1843
Boston, Mass.
Philadelphia, Pa.
(10, 37, 50, 90)

______ Davison
c. 1883
Farmland, Ind.
(175)

Clement Davison
c. 1819–1838
New York, N.Y.
(18, 50, 106)

Jesse G. Davison
c. 1849–1850
Richmond, Va.
(23)

John G. Davison
c. 1842–1843
Utica, N.Y.
(24, 25)

Peter I. Davison
c. 1815–1860
Sherburne, N.Y.
(24)

Sidney B. Day
c. 1847–1850
Macon, Ga.
(21)

Edward Deacon
c. 1836–1838
New York, N.Y.
(18)

D. Deardorff
c. 1840
Dayton, Ohio
(77)

Philip Deas
c. 1837
Philadelphia, Pa.
(10)

James Decker
c. 1830–1848
New York, N.Y.
Troy, N.Y.
(24, 37, 38, 39, 90, 106)

Leonard Decker
Decker & Coleman (?)
c. 1845–1849
Troy, N.Y.
(24)

William C. Defrees (Defriez ?)
c. 1848
St. Louis, Mo.
(123)

Godfrey DeGilse
c. 1837
Columbus, Ga.
(21)

Jebez Delano
before 1848
New Bedford, Mass.
(37, 39, 50, 90, 106)

John Delarue (Delaroux ?)
c. 1882
New Orleans, La.
(37, 38, 39, 90, 106)

Francis Deloste
Suire & Deloste
c. 1812–1851
Baltimore, Md.
(93)

John Denham
c. 1848
Philadelphia, Pa.
(10)

______ Dennis
Dennis & Fitch
c. 1835–1839
Troy, N.Y.
(24, 37, 39, 90, 106)

Stephen A. Dennis
Dennis & Fitch (?)
c. 1839–1845
Troy, N.Y.
(24)

Conway Dentz
c. 1850
Philadelphia, Pa.
(10)

Cornelius Brower DeRiemer
DeRiemer & Mead
C. B. DeRiemer & Co.
c. 1820–1872
Auburn, N.Y.
Ithaca, N.Y.
Alton, Ill.
Fox Lake, Wis.
(24, 37, 90, 106, 133)

Jacob DeRiemer
c. 1821–1863
Auburn, N.Y.
New York, N.Y.
Alton, Ill.
Fox Lake, Wis.
Berlin, Wis.
(37, 90, 106, 133)

John Derr
c. 1825–1848
Philadelphia, Pa.
(10)

Francis Deschamps
c. 1846–1849
Philadelphia, Pa.
(10)

Jean Desnoyer
c. 1772–1846
Gallipolis, Ohio
Detroit, Mich.
(136)

Augustus Deuschler
c. 1858–1859
Utica, N.Y.
(25)

J. Develin (Devlin ?)
J. & M. Develin (Devlin ?)
c. 1848–1850
Philadelphia, Pa.
(10)

M. Develin (Devlin ?)
J. & M. Develin (Devlin ?)
c. 1848–1850
Philadelphia, Pa.
(10)

James Devine
c. 1848–1849
Philadelphia, Pa.
(10)

Charles Devit
(Devitt ?)
(Dewitt ?)
c. 1844–1846
Philadelphia, Pa.
(10, 37)

Dwight Dewey
c. 1840
Ravenna, Ohio
(77)

Abraham Henry Dewitt
c. 1847
Columbus, Ga.
(21)

W. W. Dexter
c. 1843–1846
Earlville, N.Y.
(10)

John Dey
c. 1846
Philadelphia, Pa.
(10)

Elias DeYoung
Elias DeYoung & Co.
E. DeYoung & Co.
c. 1836–1839
Louisville, Ky.
(63, 123)

Henry E. Dibble
c. 1847
Columbus, Ga.
(21)

Oscar J. H. Dibble
Dibble & Jacks
c. 1835–1849
Savannah, Ga.
Columbus, Ga.
(21)

Pliny Dickinson
Dickinson & Hannum
P. Dickinson & Co.
c. 1828–1847
Syracuse, N.Y.
(24, 133)

William Dickinson
c. 1843–1845
Philadelphia, Pa.
(10)

——— Dickson
Dickson, White & Co.
c. 1837
Philadelphia, Pa.
(10)

Henry Dickson
before 1854
Paintsville, Ky.
(63, 127)

Philip Diehr
c. 1840–1850
Philadelphia, Pa.
(10)

Gerhard Diercks
c. 1855–1880
Columbia, S.C.
(14)

C. Dietrichs
c. 1854–1883
Indianapolis, Ind.
(70, 175)

Bernard Gregory Dietz
c. 1848
Cleveland, Ohio
(77)

Aaron Dikeman
c. 1824–1837
New York, N.Y.
(18, 39, 106)

Burr Dikeman
c. 1845–1855
St. Louis, Mo.
(123)

Henry A. Dikeman
c. 1845–1855
St. Louis, Mo.
(123)

Rene Dikeman
c. 1845–1855
St. Louis, Mo.
(123)

Isaac M. Dimond
c. 1828–1838
New York, N.Y.
(18, 37, 90, 106)

James Dinwiddie
c. 1840–1868
Lynchburg, Va.
(23)

Gerriet Dirksen
c. 1856–1893
Winnebago Co., Ill.
Freeport, Ill.
(175)

Isaac Dixon
c. 1843–1850
Philadelphia, Pa.
(10, 39, 106)

Alexander M. Dobbie
c. 1844–1849
Utica, N.Y.
Troy, N.Y.
(24, 25, 37)

E. S. Dodge
c. 1840
New York State
(78)

Joseph Doerflinger
c. 1845–1850
Richmond, Va.
(23)

Philip Doflein
c. 1845–1850
Philadelphia, Pa.
(10)

Jacob Dolfinger
Dolfinger & Hudson
Hudson & Dolfinger
Hirshbuhl & Dolfinger
c. 1848–1861–
before 1892
Louisville, Ky.
(63)

W. H. Doll
c. 1845–1850
New York, N.Y.
(18, 90)

Charles Donnelly
c. 1847–1848
Philadelphia, Pa.
(10, 37)

Joseph Dorflinger
(Doerflinger ?)
c. 1837
Philadelphia, Pa.
(10)

George Dorie
c. 1845
Philadelphia, Pa.
(10, 37)

C. W. Dorn
c. 1847–1848
Philadelphia, Pa.
(10)

Henry C. Dorsey
c. 1845–1846
Louisville, Ky.
(63, 123, 127)

Michael Doster
c. 1831–1850
Philadelphia, Pa.
(10, 37, 90, 106)

John W. Doty
c. 1844
Rochester, N.Y.
(24)

William Gaylord Doud
Stephens & Doud
c. 1839–1841
Middletown, Conn.
Utica, N.Y.
(24, 25)

Henry Douglas
c. 1837–1838
New York, N.Y.
(18)

John Douglass
Douglass & Heckman
(?)
c. 1840–1842
Philadelphia, Pa.
(10, 37, 90, 106)

James Doull
c. 1823–1849
Philadelphia, Pa.
(10)

George G. Dowell
Dunlevy & Dowell
c. 1843–1847
Philadelphia, Pa.
(10, 37)

_______ Downing
Downing & Baldwin
c. 1832–1837
New York, N.Y.
(18, 39, 106)

John Draper
c. 1844
Cincinnati, Ohio
(77)

Joseph Draper
c. 1849
Cincinnati, Ohio
Hopkinsville, Ky.
(38, 39, 63, 90)

J. Dray
c. 1846
Portsmouth, Va.
(23)

R. Dreden
c. 1839
Philadelphia, Pa.
(10)

Ferdinand J. Dreer
Annin & Dreer
Dreer & Hayes
c. 1837–1850
Philadelphia, Pa.
(10)

Simon Dreyfous
c. 1825–1837
Philadelphia, Pa.
(10)

John Drinker
c. 1835–1838
New York, N.Y.
(18, 37, 90, 106)

M. A. Dropsie
c. 1842–1849
Philadelphia, Pa.
(10)

Charles A. Droz
(Dross ?)
c. 1811–1841
Philadelphia, Pa.
(10)

Hannah Droz
(Dross?)
c. 1842–1850
Philadelphia, Pa.
(10)

Arnold Druding
c. 1843–1850
Philadelphia, Pa.
(10)

Arnold Drunnin
c. 1837
Philadelphia, Pa.
(10)

William Drysdale, Jr.
c. 1842–1845
Philadelphia, Pa.
(10)

Edward Dubasee
c. 1847–1850
Philadelphia, Pa.
(10)

Peter Dubois
c. 1841–1843
Philadelphia, Pa.
(10)

Philo Dubois
c. 1842–1848
Buffalo, N.Y.
(24, 39, 106)

Thomas Dubois
c. 1849
Philadelphia, Pa.
(10)

Francis P. Dubosq
Dubosq & Baton (?)
Dubosq, Baton & Co.
(?)
Dubosq & Scheer (?)
c. 1837–1850
Philadelphia, Pa.
(10)

George Dubosq
Dubosq & Carrow (?)
Dubosq, Carrow & Co.
(?)
c. 1839–1850
Philadelphia, Pa.
(10)

Henry Dubosq, Jr.
H. & W. Dubosq (?)
c. 1818–1850
Philadelphia, Pa.
(10)

Peter Dubosq
c. 1835–1850
Philadelphia, Pa.
(10)

Philip L. Dubosq
c. 1837–1850
Philadelphia, Pa.
(10)

Theodore Dubosq
c. 1829–1850
Philadelphia, Pa.
(10)

William Dubosq
H. & W. Dubosq (?)
c. 1835–1837
Philadelphia, Pa.
(10)

William A. Dubosq
H. & W. Dubosq (?)
c. 1839
Philadelphia, Pa.
(10)

Henry Ducommun
Henry Ducommun Jr.
& Co. (?)
c. 1818–1850
Philadelphia, Pa.
(10)

George Duff
c. 1837
Philadelphia, Pa.
(10)

George C. Duff
c. 1846
New Bern, N.C.
(36)

George Hurd Duffey
before 1855
Alexandria, Va.
(23)

Major George Nelson
Duffey
after 1840-before 1896
Alexandria, Va.
(23)

_______ Duhme
Duhme & Co.
c. 1839–1887
Cincinnati, Ohio
(38, 39, 106)

_______ Dunbar
Dunbar & Bangs
c. 1850
Worcester, Mass.
(39, 106)

William Henry
Duncan
c. 1850
Shelby Co., Ky.
Springfield, Ky.
Washington Co., Ky.
(63)

Pratt Dundas
c. 1850
Philadelphia, Pa.
(10, 37, 90, 106)

George Dunkerley
c. 1844–1847
Philadelphia, Pa.
(10)

Robert Dunlevy
(Donleavey?)
(Dunlevey?)
Dunlevy & Dowell (?)
Dunlevy & Wise (?)
c. 1839–1850
Philadelphia, Pa.
(10, 37, 90, 106)

David Dunn
Dunn & Cann
Charters, Cann &
Dunn (C C & D)
Kidney & Dunn (?)
(K & D)
c. 1834–1850
New York, N.Y.
(18, 37, 90, 106)

_______ Dunning
Ayers & Dunning
Penn Yan, N.Y.
(24)

Edward Dunning
Dunning & Knapp
c. 1828–1837
Mobile, Ala.
(170)

Julius N. Dunning
Dunning & Crissey
c. 1847
Rochester, N.Y.
(24)

Bernard Dupuy
c. 1828–1844
Raleigh, N.C.
(22, 39, 106)

Freeman A. Durgin
Durgin & Burtt
c. 1859–1911
St. Louis, Mo.
(123)

William B. Durgin
c. 1850
Concord, N.H.
(38, 39, 106)

Samuel Eakins
c. 1837
Philadelphia, Pa.
(10)

Joseph Ealer
c. 1838–1842
St. Louis, Mo.
(123)

Alfred Earnshaw
c. 1846–1849
Troy, N.Y.
(24)

George Easley
c. 1838
Lexington, Ky.
(63, 127)

Moses Eastman
before 1850
Savannah, Ga.
(21)

James Easton II
Easton & Sanford
(E & S)
c. 1830–1838
Nantucket Island,
(17, 37, 38, 39, 50
90, 106)

W. Eaves
W. Eaves & A. Falize
c. 1842
Lexington, Ky.
(63)

W. T. Eaves
c. 1845–1848
St. Louis, Mo.
(123)

John Eckart
c. 1845
Philadelphia, Pa.
(10)

Alexander Perry Eckel
c. 1845–before 1906
Greensboro, N.C.
Front Royal, Va. (?)
Jefferson Co., Tenn
(?)
(36)

Andrew Eckel
c. 1837–1840
Philadelphia, Pa.
(10)

Valentine Eckert
c. 1839
Philadelphia, Pa.
(10)

Adam Eckfeldt
c. 1800–1850
Philadelphia, Pa.
(10)

Charles Eckfeldt
c. 1839–1843
Philadelphia, Pa.
(10)

John Eckhart
c. 1848–1850
Camden, N.J.
(10)

Lewis Ecuyer
c. 1851–1854
Utica, N.Y.
(25)

Charles Edler
c. 1844–1846
Philadelphia, Pa.
(10)

J. C. Edler
c. 1841
Philadelphia, Pa.
(10)

William Edmond
c. 1848
Philadelphia, Pa.
(10)

Peter Edwards
c. 1850
Philadelphia, Pa.
(10)

Edward Egg
c. 1860–1880
Columbia, S.C.
(14)

William Elder
c. 1841
Philadelphia, Pa.
(10)

H. P. Elias
c. 1840
Location unknown
(78)

George Elliot
(Elliott ?)
c. 1810–1852
Wilmington, Del.
(39, 60, 106)

Benjamin P. Elliott
c. 1843–1850
Philadelphia, Pa.
(10)

James Elliott (J E)
before 1865
Winnsboro, S.C.
(14, 106)

John Aaron Elliott
(A E)
Before 1857
Sharon, Conn.
Michigan State
New York State
(20, 37, 39, 50, 90)

George Ellis
c. 1850
Philadelphia, Pa.
(10)

Lewis W. Ellis
c. 1837
Philadelphia, Pa.
(10, 37, 90, 106)

Samuel O. Ellis
c. 1839–1847
Philadelphia, Pa.
(10)

Thomas Elmes
c. 1841
Philadelphia, Pa.
(10)

Hermann Elson
c. 1843–1848
Philadelphia, Pa.
(10)

Julius Elson
c. 1842–1844
Philadelphia, Pa.
(10)

A. D. Elton
Hall & Elton
c. 1841
Geneva, N.Y.
(24)

William D. Eltonhead
c. 1849–1850
Philadelphia, Pa.
(10)

Albert Emerick
c. 1847–1850
Philadelphia, Pa.
(10, 37)

Samuel Engard
c. 1837–1842
Philadelphia, Pa.
(10)

C. W. Engelbert
c. 1839
Philadelphia, Pa.
(10)

Charles M. Englehart
c. 1839–1850
Philadelphia, Pa.
(10)

Charles Ensign
c. 1842–1850
Troy, N.Y.
(24)

Edgar M. Eoff
(EME)
c. 1850
New York, N.Y.
(18, 37, 38, 39, 106)

Garret Eoff
Eoff & Howell
(E & H)
Eoff & Connor
Eoff & Moore
Eoff & Phyfe (E & P)
Eoff & Shepherd (?)
(E & S)
c. 1779–1858
New York, N.Y.
(11, 37, 38, 39, 50, 55, 90, 95, 161)

Mortimer E. Eoff
c. 1850
New York, N.Y.
(37, 39)

John Eppelsheimer
c. 1845
Philadelphia, Pa.
(10)

Ashman Epps
c. 1848
Philadelphia, Pa.
(10)

John Erens
c. 1845–1846
Louisville, Ky.
(63)

Henry B. Ernst
c. 1830–1845
Cooperstown, N.Y.
(24)

Andrew Erwin
c. 1837
Philadelphia, Pa.
(10, 37, 90, 106)

Henry Erwin
c. 1795–1842
Philadelphia, Pa.
(10, 37, 38, 55, 90, 95, 106)

Thomas M. Erwin
c. 1845–1846
Louisville, Ky.
(63)

William C. Erwin
c. 1850
Rochester, N.Y.
(24)

Charles Esslinger
c. 1840–1848
Buffalo, N.Y.
(24)

Jacob R. Esterle
Esterle Sons (?)
c. 1832–1868
Louisville, Ky.
(63)

George Eter (Etter ?)
c. 1833–1850
Philadelphia, Pa.
(10)

John E. Ethridge
c. 1838–1848
Louisville, Ky.
(63)

——— Ettenheimer
c. 1850
Location unknown, probably Ohio
(78)

——— Eubank
Eubank & Jeffries
(Jeffries & Eubank ?)
c. 1805–1841
Glasgow, Ky.
(63, 127)

James Eubank
Savage & Eubank
James & Joseph Eubank
c. 1829–1855
Glasgow, Ky.
(63)

Joseph Eubank
James & Joseph Eubank
c. 1829–1855
Glasgow, Ky.
(63, 127)

——— Evans
Evans & Allen
c. 1850
Binghamton, N.Y.
(24)

——— Evans
Evans & Manning
c. 1850
New York, N.Y.
(78)

Alfred J. Evans
H. & A. J. Evans
c. 1831–1854
Binghamton, N.Y.
(24)

Edwin T. Evans
c. 1836–1841
Binghamton, N.Y.
(24)

Horatio Evans
H. & A. J. Evans
c. 1836–1841
Binghamton, N.Y.
(24)

W. R. Evans
c. 1850
Covington, Ky.
(63)

William M. Evans
c. 1813–1848
Philadelphia, Pa.
(10)

Charles A. Evard
c. 1847–1849
Lynchburg, Va.
(23)

Charles C. Evard
c. 1837
Philadelphia, Pa.
(10)

Charles Edward Evard
(C E E)
C. E. Evard & Brother
c. 1849–before 1906
Leesburg, Va.
Staunton, Va.
(23)

Charles Eugene Evard
C. E. Evard & Brother
c. 1837–1857
Philadelphia, Pa.
Lynchburg, Va.
Winchester, Va.
Staunton, Va.
(23)

Cornelius Everest
c. 1847–1850
Philadelphia, Pa.
(10)

John Ewan
before 1852
Charleston, S.C.
(14, 37, 39, 50, 55, 90, 95, 106)

Warren B. Ewing
Sharrard & Ewing
c. 1840–1876
Shelbyville, Ky.
(63, 106, 127)

William Faber
Faber & Hoover
c. 1828–1850
Philadelphia, Pa.
(10, 11, 50, 90, 106)

H. Fabian
c. 1853
Chester, S.C.
Lancaster, S.C.
(14)

Augustus P. Faff
c. 1837
Philadelphia, Pa.
(10)

B. Fagan
c. 1845
Cassville, Ga.
(21)

——— Fairbanks
Fairbanks & Paul
c. 1857
Newburyport, Mass.
(19)

Artemus O. Fairchild
Fairchild & Taylor
c. 1838–1851
Wheeling, W. Va.
(23)

James L. Fairchild
c. 1824–1838
New York, N.Y.
(18, 37, 90, 106)

A. Falize
W. Eaves & A. Falize
c. 1842
Lexington, Ky.
(63)

Samuel E. Farnham
c. 1840–1845
Oxford, N.Y.
(24)

——— Farr
Farr & Co.
c. 1837–1850
Philadelphia, Pa.
(10)

John C. Farr
c. 1824–1840
Philadelphia, Pa.
(10, 39, 90, 106)

John S. Farr
c. 1834–1849
Elmira, N.Y.
Norwich, N.Y.
(24)

Joseph Farr
Farr & Gilbert
c. 1813–1844
Manlius, N.Y.
(24)

John Farrington
Farrington & Hunnewell (F & H)
c. 1833–1850
Boston, Mass.
(10, 11, 50, 106)

——— Fatman
Fatman Brothers
c. 1843
Philadelphia, Pa.
(10)

——— Fatton
Fatton & Co.
c. 1840–1841
Philadelphia, Pa.
(10)

Frederick Fatton
c. 1830–1839
Philadelphia, Pa.
(10)

George H. Fay
c. 1853–1857
Utica, N.Y.
(25)

Henry C. Fay
Fay & Fisher
c. 1841–1843
Troy, N.Y.
(24)

August Feckhart
c. 1849–1850
Rochester, N.Y.
(24, 100, 106)

Abraham VanBenschoten Fellows
c. 1810–1851
Troy, N.Y.
Montreal, Que. Can.
Newport, R.I.
Waterford, N.Y.
New York, N.Y.
Albany, N.Y.
Buffalo, N.Y.
(18, 24, 25, 38, 39, 50, 55, 90, 106, 133)

Ignatius W. Fellows
I. W. & J. K. Fellows
after 1834
Lowell, Mass.
(39, 106, 133)

James Fellows
J. Fellows & Co.
Fellows & Young
Fellows & Read
Fellows, Read & Co.
Fellows, Wadsworth & Co.
c. 1796–1867
Troy, N.Y.
New York, N.Y.
New Haven, Conn.
(133)

James K. Fellows
I. W. & J. K. Fellows
after 1834
Lowell, Mass.
(39, 106, 133)

Jermiah Chichester Fellows
c. 1844–1879
Troy, N.Y.
Albany, N.Y.
Buffalo, N.Y.
Brooklyn, N.Y.
(24, 133)

Jesse Fellows
c. 1844–1845
Concord, N.H.
(133)

John F. Fellows
Warner & Fellows
c. 1837
Salem, Mass.
(133)

Louis Strite Fellows
Fellows & Storm
Fellows, Storm & Cargill
Fellows, Cargill & Co.
Louis S. Fellows & Schell
c. 1814–1866
New York State
(133)

Philip M. Fellows
c. 1839–1841
Troy, N.Y.
(24, 133)

——— Fenno
Fenno & Hale
c. 1825–1840
Bangor, Me.
(39, 106)

Elijah Ferguson
c. 1833–1850
New Bern, N.C.
(22)

Lewis Ferrey
c. 1837
Philadelphia, Pa.
(10)

Edward B. Ferris
c. 1846–1848
Philadelphia, Pa.
(10)

R. Ferris
c. 1850
Location unknown
(106)

William Ferris
c. 1836–1839
Buffalo, N.Y.
(24)

Ziba Ferris
c. 1810–1860
Wilmington, Del.
(39, 60, 106)

——— Fessenden
c. 1845
Newport, R.I.
(37, 38, 106)

Alfred Fest
Fest & Bro. (?)
c. 1850
Philadelphia, Pa.
(10)

Edwy Fest
Fest & Bro. (?)
c. 1842–1850
Philadelphia, Pa.
(10)

James B. Fidler
c. 1850
Philadelphia, Pa.
(10)

Charles Field
c. 1835–1850
Philadelphia, Pa.
(10)

David E. Field
c. 1840–1848
Cleveland, Ohio
(77)

George Field
c. 1840
Philadelphia,Pa.
(10)

Peter Field
c. 1808–1837
New York, N.Y.
(106)

Francis Fillette
(Fellette?)
c. 1807–1838
Charleston, S.C.
(14)

——— Filley
Filley, Mead & Caldwell
c. 1850
Philadelphia, Pa.
(10)

Hiram Finch
Finch & Cagger
c. 1829–1840
Albany, N.Y.
(11, 24, 37, 50, 90, 106)

Samuel Finefield
c. 1834–1838
Troy, N.Y.
Buffalo, N.Y.
(24, 37)

Francis Finney
c. 1844
Philadelphia, Pa.
(10, 37)

Jean B. Fischesser
c. 1857
Walhalla, S.C.
(14)

Isaac Fish, Jr.
c. 1843–1850
Utica, N.Y.
(24, 25)

Willson Fish
c. 1838
Rochester, N.Y.
(24)

George Fisher
Fay & Fisher
George Fisher & Co.
Fisher & Champney
c. 1837–1847
Troy, N.Y.
(24)

Henry Fisher
c. 1849–1850
Philadelphia, Pa.
(10)

William Fisher
c. 1841–1845
Charleston, W. Va.
(23)

Dennis M. (W ?) Fitch
c. 1840–1850
Troy, N.Y.
(24, 37, 38, 78, 90, 106)

James Fitzer
c. 1849
Camden, N.J.
(10)

George G. K. Fitzgerald
c. 1841–1848
Philadelphia, Pa.
(10, 37)

James Fitzgerald
c. 1841–1846
Philadelphia, Pa.
(10, 37)

George W. Flach
c. 1840–1870
Charleston, S.C.
(14)

L. H. Flersheim
c. 1839
Buffalo, N.Y.
(24)

Henry Fletcher
Fletcher & Bennett
Fletcher, Bennett & Co.
c. 1818–1866
Louisville, Ky.
Lexington, Ky.
(63, 127)

John Flexion
c. 1837
Philadelphia, Pa.
(10)

James Flood
c. 1839–1850
Philadelphia, Pa.
(10)

William Flood
c. 1837
Philadelphia, Pa.
(10)

Simon Flootron
c. 1838
St. Louis, Mo.
(123)

William Floto
c. 1849
Philadelphia, Pa.
(10)

Joseph Flower
c. 1844
Philadelphia, Pa.
(10, 37)

Charles Fobes
c. 1850
Philadelphia, Pa.
(10)

Jacob Fogle
Foster & Fogle
c. 1825–1867
Milledgeville, Ga.
Columbus, Ga.
(21)

William Folkrod
c. 1849–1850
Philadelphia, Pa.
(10)

Godfrey G. Folwell
c. 1832–1845
Philadelphia, Pa.
(10)

John T. Folwell
Folwell & Haines (?)
c. 1844–1850
Philadelphia, Pa.
(10)

Louis H. Fontenay
c. 1840
Charleston, S.C.
(14)

Benjamin G. Forbes
Fordham & Forbes
c. 1817–1837
New York, N.Y.
(11, 18, 37, 50, 90, 106)

Colin V. G. Forbes
(C U G F)
Colin & John W. Forbes
Colin V. G. Forbes & Son
c. 1808–1838
New York, N.Y.
(11, 18, 37, 39, 50, 55, 90, 106)

Garret Forbes
c. 1808–1837
New York, N.Y.
(106)

John W. Forbes
(I W F)
Colin & John W. Forbes
J. W. Forbes & Co.
c. 1808–1838
New York, N.Y.
(7, 11, 18, 37, 38, 39, 50, 95, 161, 162)

Joseph R. Forbes
c. 1858(?)–1875
Indianapolis, Ind.
(70, 175)

Leonard Forbes
L. Forbes & Co.
c. 1845–1865
St. Louis, Mo.
(123)

William Forbes
c. 1827–1850
New York, N.Y.
(164)

Jabez W. Force
Wood & Force
c. 1819–1841
New York, N.Y.
(18, 37, 38, 39, 55, 90, 106)

——— Ford
c. 1879
New Haven, Conn.
(7)

——— Ford
Ford & Brother
c. 1847
Oswego, N.Y.
(24)

George H. Ford
Benjamin & Ford
c. 1834–1884
New Haven, Conn.
(50, 165)

James M. Ford
19th century
Location unknown
(50)

William Ford
c. 1848
Philadelphia, Pa.
(10)

J. Silas Fors
Wheeling, W. Va.
c. 1839–1851
(23)

George H. Forsythe
c. 1843–1848
Louisville, Ky.
(63, 127)

——— Foss
Lincoln & Foss
Haddock, Lincoln & Foss
c. 1850–1865
Boston, Mass.
(11, 37, 50, 106)

Charles M. Foss
Crosby & Foss
c. 1875–1877
Boston, Mass.
(165, 175)

Chandler Foster
c. 1832–1840
Albany, N.Y.
(24)

Elliott K. Foster
Foster & Talbott
(Talbott & Foster ?)
c. 1833–1870
Indianapolis, Ind.
(175)

George B. Foster
c. 1838–1854
Boston, Mass.
(37, 39, 50, 90, 106)

Henry Foster
c. 1841
Savannah, Ga.
(21)

Joseph Foster
before 1839
Boston, Mass.
(7, 11, 37, 38, 39, 50, 90, 106)

Nathaniel Foster
Nathaniel & Thomas Foster
c. 1820–1860
Newburyport, Mass.
(19, 37, 39, 50, 90, 106)

Thomas Foster
Nathaniel & Thomas Foster
c. 1823–1860
Newburyport, Mass.
(19, 37, 39, 50, 55, 90, 106)

W. Foster
Foster & Fogle
Foster & Ward
Foster & Purple
c. 1835–1845
Columbus, Ga.
(21)

Nathaniel Fowle
Fowle & Kirkland
c. 1819–1850
Northampton, Mass.
(132)

Andrew W. Fox
c. 1843
Hartford, Conn.
(37)

DeForest Fox
c. 1846–1850
Troy, N.Y.
(24)

John T. Fox
C. A. Burr & Co.
c. 1841–1864
Rochester, N.Y.
(24, 100, 133)

James A. Foxcroft
Foxcroft & Clark
c. 1822–1839
Baltimore, Md.
(93)

G. F. Foy
G. F. Foy & Co.
c. 1850
Location unknown
(78)

Edward Francis
c. 1828–1837
Leesburg, Va.
(23, 106)

Justus Francis
c. 1850
Hartford, Conn.
(37)

Thomas Francis
c. 1841–1848
Philadelphia, Pa.
(10)

S. Franks
J. & S. Franks
c. 1850
Philadelphia, Pa.
(10)

Jacob Franks
J. & S. Franks (?)
c. 1845–1849
Philadelphia, Pa.
(10)

William Franks
c. 1839
Philadelphia, Pa.
(10, 90, 106)

William Franks
(Francks ?)
c. 1839–1840
Philadelphia, Pa.
(10, 37)

H. N. Frazer
c. 1839
Vienna, N.Y.
(24)

Robert Frazer
(Frazier ?)
Phillips & Frazer
c. 1799–1851
Paris, Ky.
Lexington, Ky.
(63, 127)

Robert Frazer, Jr.
c. 1838–1851
Lexington, Ky.
(63)

Daniel Frederick
c. 1847–1850
Philadelphia, Pa.
(10)

John H. Frederick
c. 1823–1850
Philadelphia, Pa.
(10)

Daniel Fredericks
c. 1841
Philadelphia, Pa.
(10)

Joseph M. Freeman
Freeman & Pollard
J. M. Freeman & Co.
c. 1831–before 1882
Norfolk, Va.
(23, 38)

J. N. Freeman
c. 1860
Augusta, Ga
(21)

N. A. Freeman
c. 1850
Richmond, Va.
(78)

Thomas W. Freeman
before 1853
Augusta, Ga.
(21)

William Freeman
c. 1839–1840
Philadelphia, Pa.
(10, 37, 90, 106)

Meyer Freide
c. 1848
St. Louis, Mo.
(123)

Henry Freideberg
c. 1849–1850
Philadelphia, Pa.
(10)

John L. Friedlein
c. 1835–1850
Philadelphia, Pa.
(10)

J. Fries
c. 1850
Location unknown
(38, 106)

John Fries
J. & P. Fries (?)
c. 1830–1850
Philadelphia, Pa.
(10)

P. Fries
J. & P. Fries (?)
c. 1837
Philadelphia, Pa.
(10)

James Frith (Frinth ?)
c. 1840–1850
Philadelphia, Pa.
(10, 37, 90, 106)

C. Fritz
c. 1848–1850
Philadelphia, Pa.
(10)

Benjamin C. Frobisher
Stodder & Frobisher (?)
before 1862
Boston, Mass.
(11, 37, 38, 39, 50, 55, 90, 106)

James Frodsham
c. 1845
St. Louis, Mo.
(123)

Charles Froligh
c. 1857–1860
Utica, N.Y.
(25)

C. Fry
c. 1837–1857
Canton, Ohio
(77)

N. L. Fry
Titlow & Fry
c. 1844–1847
Philadelphia, Pa.
(10, 37)

Rudolph Fuchs
c. 1890
New York, N.Y.
(71, 175)

David Fuller
c. 1854–1855
Utica, N.Y.
(25)

F. A. Fuller
c. 1850
Jamestown, N.Y.
(24)

George W. Fuller
c. 1829–1844
Lewisburg, Va.
(23)

David C. Fulton
c. 1838–1841
Louisville, Ky.
(63)

James Fulton
c. 1838–1861
Louisville, Ky.
(63)

Thomas G. Funston
c. 1850
Philadelphia, Pa.
(10, 37)

Philip H. Furman
c. 1821–1842
Schenectady, N.Y.
(24)

Charles Furnace
c. 1837–1838
Albany, N.Y.
(24)

John W. Fury
c. 1850
Philadelphia, Pa.
(10)

Peter Fuselli
Fuselli & Valenti
McLure & Fuselli
Fuselli & Hilburn
Fuselli & McGoodwin
c. 1850–1885
Bowling Green, Ky.
(123)

W. B. Gainey
c. 1859
Pendleton, S.C.
(14)

J. W. Gaither
Cooper & Gaither
c. 1855
Greenville, S.C.
(14)

John L. Gale (J L G)
Heyer & Gale
J. L. & O. W. Gale
c. 1816–1837
New York, N.Y.
(11, 37, 50, 55, 90, 106)

William Gale (W G) (W. G.)
Gale & Stickler (G & S)
Gale & Mosely (G & M)
Gale, Wood & Hughes
Gale & Willis
Gale & Hayden (G & H)
William Gale & Son (G & S) (W G & S)
c. 1823–before 1867
New York, N.Y.
(11, 18, 37, 39, 50, 55, 90, 106, 161)

William Gale, Jr.
William Gale & Son
William Gale Jr. & Co.
c. 1844–1850
New York, N.Y.
(37, 39, 55, 90, 106, 165)

Christopher Gallup
(Gallop ?)
(Gullup ?)
before 1849
North Groton, Conn.
(20, 37, 50, 90, 106)

James Galt
c. 1802–1847
Georgetown, Va.
Alexandria, Va.
(148, 150, 175)

M. W. Galt
Galt & Bro.
c. 1840–1880
Washington, D.C.
(148, 150, 175)

Norman Galt
Galt & Bro.
c. 1880–1908
Washington, D.C.
(148, 150, 175)

William Galt
Galt & Bro.
c. 1840–1880
Washington, D.C.
(148, 150, 175)

J. A. Galtz
c. 1852–1863
Nashville, Tenn.
(89, 175)

Charles Gamble
c. 1847–1849
Philadelphia, Pa.
(10)

James Gamble
James Gamble & Son
Gamble & Son
c. 1852
Charleston, S.C.
(14)

Richard J. Gamble
James Gamble & Son
Gamble & Son
c. 1849–1852
Charleston, S.C.
(14)

William A. Gamble
Walker & Gamble
c. 1846–1847
Chicago, Ill.
(45, 175)

Hugh Ganley
c. 1842–1847
Utica, N.Y.
(24, 25)

Aaron Gannet
c. 1842–1844
Troy, N.Y.
(24)

John Garde
c. 1849–1850
Philadelphia, Pa.
(10, 37)

A. Gardiner
J. & A. Gardiner
c. 1853–1861
St. Louis, Mo.
(123)

Baldwin Gardiner
(B G)
Fletcher & Gardiner
B. Gardiner & Co. (?)
(B G & Co.)
c. 1814–1840
Philadelphia, Pa.
New York, N.Y.
(10, 11, 18, 37, 38, 50, 55, 106, 161)

J. Gardiner
J. & A. Gardiner
c. 1853–1861
St. Louis, Mo.
(123)

George Gardner
c. 1841–1842
Philadelphia, Pa.
(10)

Samuel Gardner
c. 1826–1840
Syracuse, N.Y.
(24)

William W. Gardner
c. 1858–1859
Utica, N.Y.
(25)

John R. Garland
Garland & Menard
Rockwell & Garland
c. 1826–1843
Greenville, S.C.
Macon, Ga.
Greensboro, N.C.
Charlotte, N.C.
(14, 21, 22)

Edwin T. Garner
c. 1842–1843
Utica, N.Y.
(24, 25)

Eli C. Garner
Garner & Winchester
Garner & Stewart
c. 1838–1864
Lexington, Ky.
(63, 127)

George Garner
c. 1850
Lexington, Ky.
(63)

——— Garrett
Garrett & Hartley
c. 1837
Philadelphia, Pa.
(10, 37)

——— Garrett
Garrett & Haydock
c. 1837–1840
Philadelphia, Pa.
(10)

Philip Garrett
Philip Garrett & Son
c. 1828–1837
Philadelphia, Pa.
(10)

Thomas C. Garrett
Thomas C. Garrett & Co.
c. 1829–1850
Philadelphia, Pa.
(10, 37, 55, 90, 106)

Jacob J. Garrigues
c. 1837
Philadelphia, Pa.
(10)

Joseph Garrison
c. 1836–1838
New York, N.Y.
(18)

Gotlieb Gause
c. 1840–1841
Philadelphia, Pa.
(10)

Charles H. Gay
c. 1837
Athens, Ga.
(21)

S. Gayhart
c. 1846–1849
Camden, N.J.
(10)

James Gaymare
c. 1837
Mobile, Ala.
(170)

Nicholas Geffoy
before 1839
Newport, R.I.
(38, 39, 50, 55, 90, 96, 106)

George S. Gelston
Gelston & Treadwell
Gelston & Co.
Gelston, Ladd & Co.
c. 1833–1840
New York, N.Y.
(11, 37, 38, 50, 55, 90, 106)

Hugh Gelston
Gelston & Gould
before 1873
Baltimore, Md.
(39, 50, 55, 93, 106)

T. V. Gendar
W. T. & T. V. Gendar
c. 1850
Location unknown
(106)

W. T. Gendar
W. T. & T. V. Gendar
c. 1850
Location unknown
(106)

A. Gennet
c. 1850
Binghamton, N.Y.
(24)

Charles Gennet, Jr.
Gennet & James
c. 1837–1866
Richmond, Va.
(23)

W. Gennett
c. 1850
Watertown, N.Y.
(24)

Herman Gery
(Gerg ?)
c. 1848–1850
Philadelphia, Pa.
(10)

Christian Gessler
c. 1841–1850
Philadelphia, Pa.
(10)

James Gibbs
c. 1847
Philadelphia, Pa.
(10)

Michael Gibney
(M G)
Gibney & Reade
c. 1836–1845
New York, N.Y.
(18, 37, 39, 50, 106)

Luther R. Gibson
c. 1851
Norfolk, Va.
(23)

William Gibson
c. 1845–1849
Philadelphia, Pa.
(10, 37, 38, 39, 106)

Clifton C. Gifford
c. 1850
Rochester, N.Y.
(24)

C. Gigon
C. Gigon & Bros.
c. 1839
Philadelphia, Pa.
(10)

Gustavus Gigon
Z. & G. Gigon (?)
c. 1845–1847
Philadelphia, Pa.
(10)

Z. Gigon
Z. & G. Gigon
c. 1842–1850
Philadelphia, Pa.
(10)

——— Gilbert
Gilbert & Cunningham
c. 1839–1840
New York, N.Y.
(11, 18, 37, 50, 90, 106)

Charles Gilbert
c. 1835–1837
Philadelphia, Pa.
(10)

Henry Gilbert
c. 1850
Mount Morris, N.Y.
(24)

Philo B. Gilbert
c. 1839
New York, N.Y.
(18, 37)

Edward Giles
c. 1841
Philadelphia, Pa.
(10)

Caleb Gill
before 1855
Hingham, Mass.
(37, 38, 39, 50, 55, 90, 106)

John Gill
c. 1814–1843
New Bern, N.C.
(22)

Leavitt Gill
before 1855
Hingham, Mass.
(50, 90, 106)

John Gillaspie
(Gillespie?)
(Gillispie?)
c. 1845–1846
Louisville, Ky.
(63, 127)

Samuel Gillespie
c. 1848–1849
Louisville, Ky.
(63)

A. B. Gillett
Gillett & Jenison
c. 1850–1883
Warren, Ohio
Adrian, Mich.
Bloomington, Ill.
Indianapolis, Ind.
(70, 175)

——— Gilpin
Gilpin & Taylor
c. 1837–1842
Philadelphia, Pa.
(10)

Vincent C. Gilpin
c. 1837–1843
Philadelphia, Pa.
(10)

John B. Ginochio
c. 1837–1854
New York, N.Y.
(18, 36, 39, 106)

A. Givan (Given?)
c. 1849
Albany, N.Y.
(24)

David Glass
Glass & Baird
c. 1803–1856
Raleigh, N.C.
(22)

Schenck Glass
c. 1847
Poughkeepsie, N.Y.
(134)

William Glaze
Veal & Glaze
Glaze & Radcliffe
c. 1838–1882
Columbia, S.C.
(14)

F. A. Gleason
Gleason & Hovey
c. 1846–1848
Rome, N.Y.
(24)

John W. Gleaves
c. 1850
Philadelphia, Pa.
(10)

George Glenford
c. 1848
Philadelphia, Pa.
(10)

Edwin Glover
c. 1843–1869
Fayetteville, N.C.
(22)

Christian Gobrecht
(Gobright?)
c. 1819–1844
Philadelphia, Pa.
(10)

D. Goddard
D. Goddard & Son
D. Goddard & Co.
c. 1845–1850
Worcester, Mass.
(37, 38, 39, 55, 106)

M. T. Godfrey
c. 1845
Cambridge, Mass.
(37)

Richard Godley
Godley & Johnson
(Johnson & Godley?)
c. 1843–1849
Albany, N.Y.
(24)

Peter Goetes (Gates?)
c. 1813–1844
Bardstown, Ky.
(63, 127)

Thomas Goldsmith
c. 1842–1850
Troy, N.Y.
(24)

B. Goldstone
c. 1839
Philadelphia, Pa.
(10)

James L. Goman
c. 1847–1848
Utica, N.Y.
(24, 25)

——— Gooch
Gooch & Hequembourg
c. 1845
St. Louis, Mo.
(123)

D. T. Goodhue
(DTG)
c. 1840
Boston, Mass.
(39, 106)

John Goodhue
c. 1822–1855
Salem, Mass.
(37, 38, 39, 50, 55, 90, 106)

Henry Gooding
c. 1820–1854
Boston, Mass.
(11, 37, 38, 39, 50, 55, 90, 106)

Joseph Gooding
c. 1861
Boston, Mass.
(37, 39, 90, 106)

Josiah Gooding
c. 1841–1859
Boston, Mass.
(39, 50, 55, 106)

——— Goodrich
Smith & Goodrich
c. 1850
Philadelphia, Pa.
(10)

C. W. Goodrich
Hyde & Goodrich
c. 1816–1866
New Orleans, La.
(123)

Erastus H. Goodrich
c. 1837–1848
Buffalo, N.Y.
(24)

Allyn Goodwin
H. & A. Goodwin
c. 1811–before 1869
Hartford, Conn.
(20, 37, 50, 90, 106)

Homer Goodwin
c. 1857
Cleveland, Ohio
(69)

Horace Goodwin
H. & A. Goodwin
Goodwin & Dodd
(G & D)
c. 1811–before 1864
Hartford, Conn.
New Britain, Conn.
Vermont State
(20, 37, 50, 90, 106)

Ralph Goodwin
before 1856
Hartford, Conn.
(20, 37, 50, 90, 106)

——— Gordon
Gordon & Co.
c. 1849
Boston, Mass.
(11, 37, 50, 106)

George Gordon
c. 1795–1840
Newburgh, N.Y.
(24, 37, 38, 39, 55, 90)

George Gordon
c. 1847–1850
Philadelphia, Pa.
(10)

George Clinton Gordon
c. 1847
Augusta, Ga.
(21)

G. C. Gordon
c. 1845
Edgefield, S.C.
(14)

Jabez Gorham
Gorham & Beebe
Gorham & Webster
Gorham, Webster & Price
Gorham & Son
J. Gorham & Son
Gorham Mfg. Co.
c. 1813–1868
Providence, R.I.
(37, 38, 39, 50, 51, 86, 90, 106, 138)

John Gorham
Gorham & Son
J. Gorham & Son
Gorham Mfg. Co.
c. 1842
Providence, R.I.
(37, 50, 51, 86, 106, 138)

Miles Gorham (M G)
before 1847
New Haven, Conn.
(20, 37, 38, 39, 50, 55, 90, 106)

Richard Gorham
Shethear & Gorham
before 1841
New Haven, Conn.
(20, 37, 50, 90, 106)

——— Gottschalk
Gottschalk & Bolland
c. 1848
St. Louis, Mo.
(123)

Edwin F. Gould
c. 1842–1847
Utica, N.Y.
Cortland, N.Y.
(24, 25)

Ezra B. Gould
c. 1841
Rochester, N.Y.
(24)

James Gould
Gelston & Gould
Gould, Stowell & Ward
Gould & Ward
c. 1816–before 1874
Baltimore, Md.
(37, 38, 39, 55, 90, 93, 106)

John H. Gould
c. 1840–1850
Philadelphia, Pa.
(10, 37, 90, 106)

George Govett
c. 1811–1850
Philadelphia, Pa.
(10)

John Graham
c. 1837–1840
Philadelphia, Pa.
(10)

Mitchell Graham
c. 1837
Philadelphia, Pa.
(10)

George B. Graves
Graves & Thompson
c. 1827–1844
Winchester, Va.
(23)

George W. Graves
c. 1848
Winchester, Va.
(23)

Jesse Graves
c. 1804–1847
Cooperstown, N.Y.
(24)

——— Gray
c. 1850
Cleveland, Ohio
(69)

G. Gray
c. 1839
Portsmouth, N.H.
(37, 38, 39, 50, 55, 90, 106)

Henry A. Gray
c. 1854
Edgefield, S.C.
(14)

Robert Gray (RG)
before 1850
Portsmouth, N.H.
(37, 38, 39, 50, 90, 106)

William H. Gray
c. 1845–1846
Philadelphia, Pa.
(10)

——— Green
c. 1843
Hartford, Conn.
(37)

Glover Green
c. 1844
Philadelphia, Pa.
(10)

John N. Green
c. 1822–1842
Baltimore, Md.
(93)

Josiah B. Green
c. 1847–1850
Leesburg, Va.
(23)

——— Greene
Greene & Bros.
c. 1835–1837
Philadelphia, Pa.
(10)

William Greene
c. 1837–1841
Philadelphia, Pa.
(10)

George Greenleaf
before 1849–1850
Newburyport, Mass.
(19, 123)

Charles F. Greenwood
C. F. Greenwood & Bro.
after 1858–before 1904
Norfolk, Va.
(23)

Frederick Greenwood
C. F. Greenwood & Bro.
after 1851
Norfolk, Va.
(23)

William Gregg
Gregg & Hayden
(Hayden & Gregg ?)
Gregg, Hayden & Co.
Gregg, Hayden & Whilden
c. 1838–1855
Lexington, Ky.
Petersburg, Va.
Columbia, S.C.
Charleston, S.C.
(14, 23, 63, 106)

James Gregory
Gregory & Shuber
c. 1837
Philadelphia, Pa.
(10)

George W. Greiner
c. 1837–1843
Waynesboro, Va.
(23)

Michael Gretter
before 1869
Richmond, Va.
Lynchburg, Va.
Baltimore, Md.
(23)

George M. Griffen
G. M. & C. B. Griffen
c. 1827–1855
Troy, N.Y.
Athens, Ga.
Savannah, Ga.
(21, 24)

Peter Griffen
Griffen & Hoyt
Griffen & Son
c. 1815–1840
Albany, N.Y.
New York, N.Y.
(37, 38, 39, 90, 106)

George Griffin
c. 1841–1852
Louisville, Ky.
(63)

Edward Griffith
c. 1847
Albany, N.Y.
(24)

George F. Griffith (Griffee?)
c. 1841–1850
Philadelphia, Pa.
(10)

Greenberry Griffith (G G)
before 1848
Alexandria, Va.
(23)

L. Griffith
c. 1842–1843
Philadelphia, Pa.
(10)

Samuel Griffith
c. 1847
Philadelphia, Pa.
(10)

John Griffiths
c. 1855
Greenville, S.C.
(14)

A. B. Griswold
A. B. Griswold & Co.
c. 1866
New Orleans, La.
(123)

Chauncey D. Griswold
c. 1838–1839
Troy, N.Y.
(24)

Francis A. Griswold
c. 1838–1839
Louisville, Ky.
(63)

H. A. Griswold
c. 1850
Whitehall, N.Y.
(24)

J. R. Groff
c. 1841–1850
Philadelphia, Pa.
(10, 37)

J. L. Gropengiesser
c. 1841–1850
Philadelphia, Pa.
(10)

——— Grosjean
Woodward & Grosjean (W & G)
c. 1847–1852
Boston, Mass.
Hartford, Conn.
(11, 37, 38, 39, 50, 55, 106)

Francis J. Gross
c. 1841–1850
Philadelphia, Pa.
(10)

George Gruber
c. 1840
Berryville, Va.
(23)

A. Guelberth
c. 1838–1848
St. Louis, Mo.
(123)

Theodore Guesnard
c. 1837–1852
Mobile, Ala.
(170)

James S. Guignard
Radcliffe & Guignard
c. 1856–1858
Columbia, S.C.
(14)

Joseph Guingan
c. 1837–1838
Albany, N.Y.
(24)

Jacob Guinguigner
c. 1840–1853
Utica, N.Y.
(24, 25)

——— Guion
Howe & Guion
c. 1839–1840
New York, N.Y.
(18, 38)

Calvin Guiteau
c. 1828–1845
Watertown, N.Y.
(24)

——— Gunn
Gunn & Mitchell
c. 1832–1841
New York, N.Y.
(18)

Benjamin Gurnee
Benjamin Gurnee & Co.
Gurnee & Co.
Gurnee & Stephen (?)
B. & S. Gurnee (?)
c. 1824–1840
New York, N.Y.
(18, 37, 39, 90, 106)

Daniel Gurnee
c. 1850
New York, N.Y.
(37)

James Guthre
Guthre & Jefferis
c. 1840–before 1877
Wilmington, Del.
Philadelphia, Pa.
(39, 60, 106)

Benjamin Guyer
c. 1848
Philadelphia, Pa.
(10)

James A. Haas
c. 1846–1850
Philadelphia, Pa.
(10)

N. Haas
c. 1846–1850
Philadelphia, Pa.
(10)

Joseph Hacker
c. 1831–1850
Philadelphia, Pa.
(10)

William Hacker
c. 1848–1849
Philadelphia, Pa.
(10)

William Hadder
c. 1837
Philadelphia, Pa.
(10)

Henry Haddock
Haddock & Andrews
Haddock, Lincoln & Foss
c. 1836–1865
Boston, Mass.
(11, 37, 50, 106)

William Hadwen
before 1862
Nantucket Island, Mass.
Providence, R.I.
(17, 37, 38, 39, 50, 90, 106)

Elias Hager
c. 1841–1844
Rochester, N.Y.
(24, 100, 106)

John W. Haight
Haight & Leach
c. 1838–1850
Auburn, N.Y.
(24)

Nelson Haight
Haight & Sterling
Haight & Leonard
c. 1839–1852
Newburgh, N.Y.
(24, 39, 106)

Holme Haike
(Haikes ?)
(Hakes ?)
c. 1840
Paris, Ky.
(63, 127)

Joshua J. Hair
c. 1848
Louisville, Ky.
(63)

G. W. Haley
Haley & Haley
c. 1850
Paris, Ky.
(63)

P. Haley
Haley & Haley
c. 1850
Paris, Ky.
(63)

Abraham B. Hall
c. 1806–1839
Geneva, N.Y.
(24, 106)

George Hall
c. 1823–1842
Philadelphia, Pa.
(10)

George W. Hall
Ayers & Hall (?)
Hall & Bennett (?)
c. 1840
Newburgh, N.Y.
(24)

Green Hall
Carson & Hall
Hall & Brower
Hall, Brower & Co.
Hall, Hewson & Merrifield
Hall & Hewson (H & H)
Hall, Hewson & Brower
Hall, Hewson & Co.
c. 1810–1863
Albany, N.Y.
(24, 37, 50, 90, 106)

Ivory Hall
before 1870
Concord, Conn.
(37, 90, 106)

John Hall
c. 1804–1840
Philadelphia, Pa.
(10)

John Hall
c. 1848
Louisville, Ky.
(63)

Ranson E. Hall
Hall & Snow
c. 1829–1837
Cleveland, Ohio
Detroit, Mich.
Geneva, N.Y.
(24, 69, 123)

——— Hall
Hughes & Hall
c. 1840
Location unknown
(38, 106)

Alonzo Corwin Halleck (Hallack ?)
c. 1840–1853
Paris, Ky.
(63)

——— Haller
(Hiller ?)
c. 1837
Circleville, Ohio
(77)

Hiram Halliday
c. 1834–1844
Albany, N.Y.
(24)

James H. Halliday
c. 1841–1843
Philadelphia, Pa.
(10, 37)

George William Halliwell
c. 1811–1875
Poughkeepsie, N.Y.
(134)

Charles Halsel
c. 1839
Philadelphia, Pa.
(10)

Joseph Halstrick
Stanwood & Halstrick
c. 1850–before 1886
Boston, Mass.
(11, 37, 106)

Daniel S. Hamilton
Hamilton & Adams
c. 1837–1848
Elmira, N.Y.
(24)

James Hamilton
c. 1848
Philadelphia, Pa.
(10)

R. J. Hamilton
c. 1837–1846
Philadelphia, Pa.
(10)

Samuel Hamilton
c. 1837
Philadelphia, Pa.
(10)

Cyrus Hamlin
c. 1831–1900
Portland, Me.
(37, 50, 90, 106)

William Hamlin
before 1869
Middletown, Conn.
Providence, R.I.
(20, 37, 38, 39, 50, 55, 90, 106)

Richard Hammett
c. 1844–1845
Troy, N.Y.
(24)

J. Hand
c. 1837
Philadelphia, Pa.
(10)

Joseph S. K. Hand
Spencer & Hand
c. 1833–1850
Philadelphia, Pa.
(10)

John Handle
c. 1839–1848
Philadelphia, Pa.
(10, 37, 90, 106)

Abraham Hanis
c. 1840
Charleston, S.C.
(14)

William W. Hannah
c. 1840–1850
Albany, N.Y.
Hudson, N.Y.
(24, 37, 39, 50, 55, 90, 106)

John Hannum
Dickinson & Hannum
c. 1837–1849
Northampton, Mass.
Syracuse, N.Y.
(24, 132)

L. Hano
Hano & Co .
c. 1848–1849
Philadelphia, Pa.
(10)

Hamlet Hansbrough
c. 1800–1839
Lexington, Ky.
(63)

James Hansell
c. 1816–1850
Philadelphia, Pa.
Valley Forge, Pa.
(10, 39, 106)

Benjamin Hanson
c. 1822–1840
Albany, N.Y.
(24)

George Harbottle
Harbottle & Smith
c. 1850
Auburn, N.Y.
(24)

W. Hardeman
c. 1838
Lexington, Ky.
(123)

C. H. Harding
c. 1850
Location unknown
(50)

Newell Harding
N. Harding & Co.
(N.H.&Co.)
c. 1830–1862
Boston, Mass.
(11, 37, 38, 39, 50, 55, 90, 106)

Jacob N. Hardman
c. 1845–1849
Louisville, Ky.
(63, 127)

William Hardman
c. 1838–1840
Lexington, Ky.
(63, 127)

Stephen Hardy (S.H.)
before 1843
Portsmouth, N.H.
(37, 38, 39, 50, 55, 90, 106)

William Harker
c. 1850
Philadelphia, Pa.
(10)

Willis Harker
c. 1845
Philadelphia, Pa.
(10)

James Harkins
c. 1840–1847
Philadelphia, Pa.
(10)

Benjamin Harper
c. 1843
Philadelphia, Pa.
(10)

John M. Harper
c. 1841–1850
Philadelphia, Pa.
(10)

Thomas E. Harper
c. 1847–1850
Philadelphia, Pa.
(10)

William W. Harpur
c. 1839–1850
Philadelphia, Pa.
(10)

Samuel Harrington
Prevear & Harrington
c. 1841–1845
Amherst, Mass.
(132)

William Harrington
c. 1849–1850
Philadelphia, Pa.
(10)

——— Harris
Harris & Wilcox
c. 1844–1850
Albany, N.Y.
Troy, N.Y.
(11, 24, 39, 50, 55)

Edward Harris
c. 1848
Philadelphia, Pa.
(10, 37)

Edwin Harris
Harris & Shafer
c. 1831–after 1900
Washington, D.C.
(148, 150, 175)

George Harris
Harris & Co.
c. 1850
Pittsburgh, Pa.
New York, N.Y.
(37, 90, 106)

Herman Harris
c. 1833–1847
Troy, N.Y.
(24)

——— Harry
Harry & Bear
c. 1842
Harrisonburg, Va.
(23)

Eliphaz Hart (EH)
before 1866
New Britain, Conn.
Norwich, Conn.
(20, 37, 38, 39, 50, 55, 90, 106)

Walter Hart
c. 1849–1850
Philadelphia, Pa.
(10, 37)

Jeremiah Hartley
c. 1837–1850
Philadelphia, Pa.
(10)

Samuel Hartley
Garrett & Hartley
Clark & Hartley
c. 1818–1850
New York, N.Y.
Albany, N.Y.
Philadelphia, Pa.
(10, 24, 37, 90, 106)

Samuel S. Hartwell
c. 1842
Philadelphia, Pa.
(10)

Alexander R. Hascy
(Hasey ?)
c. 1831–1850
Albany, N.Y.
(24, 39, 50, 106)

Nelson Hascy
Hasey ?)
c. 1843–1849
Albany, N.Y.
(24, 37, 50, 106)

George W. Haselwood
c. 1848–1850
Philadelphia, Pa.
(10)

William Haselwood
c. 1848–1850
Philadelphia, Pa.
(10)

Moses Hassan
(Hessen ?)
c. 1848–1852
Louisville, Ky.
(63)

Charles Hassell
(Hassan ?)
c. 1837–1842
Philadelphia, Pa.
(10)

——— Hastings
Bolles & Hastings
Location Unknown
(78)

B. B. Hastings
c. 1830–1846
Cleveland, Ohio
(37, 38, 39, 50, 77, 90, 106)

B. B. Hatch
c. 1836–1840
Cleveland, Ohio
(77)

Israel A. Hatch
c. 1844–1845
Philadelphia, Pa.
(10)

James L. Hathaway
c. 1842
Norfolk, Va.
(23)

James R. Hattrick
(Haterick ?)
Hattrick & Smith
Hattrick & Shannon
c. 1837–1850
Philadelphia, Pa.
(10)

——— Hawes
Hawes & Co.
c. 1851
Location unknown
(38)

James Hawkins
c. 1841
Philadelphia, Pa.
(10)

Horace H. Hawley
H. H. Hawley & Co.
Hawley, Fuller & Co.
H. & H. H. Hawley
Hawley & Leach
c. 1837–1856
Utica, N.Y.
(25)

John Dean Hawley
Willard & Hawley
c. 1844–1851–before 1913
Syracuse, N.Y.
Cazenovia, N.Y.
(24)

O. A. Hawley
c. 1850
Cazenovia, N.Y.
(24)

T. S. Hawley
c. 1837
Canajoharie, N.Y.
(24)

John Haws
c. 1837
Philadelphia, Pa.
(10, 37, 90, 106)

John Hay
c. 1830–1850 (?)
New York State (?)
(78)

H. Sidney Hayden
Hayden, Gregg & Co.
Gregg, Hayden & Whilden
Hayden & Whilden
Hayden Bros. & Co.
c. 1846–1863
Charleston, S.C.
(14, 106, 166)

William H. Hayden
c. 1845–1851
Martinsburg, W. Va.
(23)

Eden Haydock
c. 1839–1850
Philadelphia, Pa.
(10)

James B. Haydock
c. 1846–1849
Location unknown
(78)

Thomas O. Haydock
c. 1850
Philadelphia, Pa.
(10)

Charles B. Hayes
C. B. Hayes & Co.
c. 1844–1845
Poughkeepsie, N.Y.
(24, 134)

Edmund M. Hayes
c. 1842–1857
Poughkeepsie, N.Y.
(24, 134)

George Hayes
Dreer & Hayes
c. 1842–1850
Philadelphia, Pa.
(10)

Peter P. Hayes
Peter P. Hayes & Son
Hayes & Adriance
before 1842
Poughkeepsie, N.Y.
(24, 39, 106, 133)

David Haynes
D. Haynes & Son (?)
c. 1835–1850
Troy, N.Y.
(24)

J. R. Haynes
c. 1851
Cincinnati, Ohio
(123)

Lafayette Haynes
c. 1836–1837
Troy, N.Y.
(24)

George Hays (Haes ?)
c. 1849–1859
Utica, N.Y.
(25)

N. L. Hazen
Hazen & Collins
c. 1836–1850
Troy, N.Y. (?)
Cincinnati, Ohio
(123)

William Headman
c. 1828–1850
Philadelphia, Pa.
(10)

Samuel Heasley
c. 1847–1852
Winchester, Ky.
(63)

——— Hebbard
Hebbard & Co.
c. 1850
New York, N.Y.
(37)

H. Hebberd
c. 1847–1850
New York, N.Y.
(11, 37, 50, 106)

Archimedes Heckman
Douglas & Heckman (?)
c. 1839–1840
Philadelphia, Pa.
(106)

George Hedge (Hedges? Hedger?)
c. 1819–1848
Waterford, N.Y.
Buffalo, N.Y.
(24, 50, 106)

David (Daniel ?) Hedges
c. 1779–1856
Easthampton, N.Y.
(59)

Daniel Hedges, Jr.
before 1856
Easthampton, N.Y.
(24, 37, 38, 39, 55, 90, 106)

A. Judson Heffron
c. 1859–1860
Utica, N.Y.
(25)

James Hegeman
c. 1829–1850
Troy, N.Y.
(24)

John Heilig
c. 1829–1850
Troy, N.Y.
(24)

Gottlieb Heimberg
c. 1842–1847
St. Louis, Mo.
(123)

Daniel Heineman
c. 1837
Philadelphia, Pa.
(10)

L. C. (G. ?) Heineman
c. 1849–1850
Philadelphia, Pa.
(10)

James P. Heiss
c. 1849–1850
Philadelphia, Pa.
(10)

Henry Helgefort (Helgerfort?)
c. 1849
Philadelphia, Pa.
(10, 37)

Jacob Heller
c. 1837
Philadelphia, Pa.
(10)

Thomas Helm
c. 1835–1850
Philadelphia, Pa.
(10)

George Hemburgh
c. 1845
St. Louis, Mo.
(123)

Thomas J. Hemphill
c. 1836–1841
Philadelphia, Pa.
(10)

Daniel B. Hempsted
D. Hempsted & Co.
before 1852
Eatonton, Ga.
(106)

A. A. Henderson
c. 1835–1837
Philadelphia, Pa.
(10, 38, 39, 106)

Adam Henderson
Henderson &
Lossing (?)
c. 1794–1859
Poughkeepsie, N.Y.
(24, 39, 106, 134)

John Hendricks
c. 1848
Philadelphia, Pa.
(10, 37)

William Hendrickson
c. 1848–1850
Philadelphia, Pa.
(10, 37)

John A. Henneman
c. 1854–1889
Chester, Pa.
Spartanburg, S.C.
Norfolk, Va.
(14)

Charles Hequembourg, Jr. (C H)
c. 1804–1851
New Haven, Conn.
New York, N.Y.
Buffalo, N.Y.
Hartford, Conn.
(18, 20, 24, 32, 37, 38, 39, 50, 90, 106)

Charles Louis Hequembourg
Gooch & Hequembourg (?)
c. 1845–1856
St. Louis, Mo.
(123)

Theodore Hequembourg (?)
Gooch & Hequembourg (?)
c. 1835–1856
Buffalo, N.Y.
St. Louis, Mo.
(123)

A. Herbel
c. 1821–1853
St. Louis, Mo.
(123)

Charles Heringer
c. 1844–1850
Philadelphia, Pa.
(10)

John C. Heringer
c. 1849–1850
Philadelphia. Pa.
(10)

William Herrington
c. 1850
Syracuse, N.Y.
Philadelphia, Pa.
(10, 24)

C. W. Hewit
c. 1850
Utica, N.Y.
(24, 25)

A. Hews, Jr.
c. 1823–1850
Boston, Mass.
(37, 38, 39, 50, 55, 90, 106)

John D. Hewson
Hall, Hewson & Co.
Hall, Brower & Co.
Hall, Hewson & Merrifield
Hall & Hewson (H & H)
Hall, Hewson & Brower
c. 1816–1850
Albany, N.Y.
(24, 37, 50, 90, 106)

Charles Heyde
c. 1839–1840
Philadelphia, Pa.
(10)

Charles W. Heydon
c. 1841–1845
Portsmouth, Va.
(23)

John Hickman
c. 1832–1862
Louisville, Ky.
Taylorsville, Ky.
(63, 127)

George E. Higgins
Covell & Higgins
c. 1850
Syracuse, N.Y.
(24)

Jonas Jacob Hilburn
Fuselli & Hilburn
c. 1857–1877
Bowling Green, Ky.
(123)

——— Hildeburn
Hildeburn & Bros.
Hildeburn & Watson (?)
c. 1833(?)–1850
Philadelphia, Pa.
(10)

Samuel Hildeburn
c. 1810–1837
Philadelphia, Pa.
(10, 90, 106)

E. Hill
c. 1821–1844
Cincinnati, Ohio
(77)

John Hill
Hill & Johnson
c. 1818–1850
Richmond, Va.
(23)

William Hill
c. 1843
Chicago, Ill.
(43, 175)

Christopher Hilliard
before 1871
Hagerstown, Md.
(93)

C. F. Hills
c. 1850
Hartford, Conn.
(37)

Frederick Hillworth
c. 1844–1849
Philadelphia, Pa.
(10)

Philip Hillyartiner
c. 1844
Philadelphia, Pa.
(10)

Richard Hinckley
c. 1839–1841
Philadelphia, Pa.
(10)

Robert H. Hinckley
c. 1839–1841
Philadelphia, Pa.
(10)

D. B. Hindman (Hinman ?)
D. B. Hindman & Co. (D B H & Co.)
c. 1833–1837
Philadelphia, Pa.
(10, 39, 106)

Robert Hines
c. 1848–1850
Philadelphia, Pa.
(10)

Benjamin Hinkin
c. 1837
Philadelphia, Pa.
(10)

Benjamin Hinkle
Thirion & Hinkle
c. 1840–1850
Philadelphia, Pa.
(10)

Horace Hinsdale
Palmer & Hinsdale
Hinsdale & Atkin
c. 1815–1842
Newark, N.J.
New York, N.Y.
(18, 37, 39, 50, 106)

William M. Hinton
c. 1844–1854
Paris, Ky.
Shelbyville, Ky.
(63, 127)

——— Hirshbuhl
Hirshbuhl & Dolfinger
c. 1859–1861
Louisville, Ky.
(63)

Nathan Hobbs
before 1868
Boston, Mass.
(11, 37, 38, 39, 50, 55, 90, 106)

Willis Hocker
c. 1846–1849
Philadelphia, Pa.
(10)

J. F. Hodgkins
after 1857
Newburyport, Mass.
(19)

Daniel Hodkins
c. 1840–1841
Albany, N.Y.
(24)

Edward Hoell
c. 1830–1873
New Bern, N.C.
Greenville, N.C.
Washington, N.C.
Pitt Co., N.C.
(22)

Augustus E. Hofer
c. 1841–1843
Albany, N.Y.
(24)

George W. Hoff
Hyde & Hoff
c. 1850
(24)

Frederick Hoffman
Bard (Bird ?) & Hoffman
c. 1820–1849
New York, N.Y.
Philadelphia, Pa.
(10, 37, 90, 106)

John H. Hoffman
c. 1848–1850
Philadelphia, Pa.
(10)

——— Hogan
Hogan & Wade
c. 1850
Cleveland, Ohio
(78)

Eli Holden
Holden & Boning
c. 1843–1850
Philadelphia, Pa.
(10)

A. A. Holdredge
c. 1841
Glens Falls, N.Y.
(24)

Julius Holister (Hollister ?)
Seymour & Holister (Hollister) (S & H)
c. 1843
Hartford, Conn.
(37)

Littleton Holland (L H)
c. 1800–1847
Baltimore, Md.
(37, 38, 39, 50, 55, 90, 93, 95, 106)

A. Hollinger
c. 1839
Philadelphia, Pa.
(10)

Julius Hollister
before 1905
Oswego, N.Y.
(24, 39, 106)

——— Holmes
Holmes & Rowan
c. 1847–1850
Philadelphia, Pa.
(10)

Adrian B. Holmes
c. 1801–1849
New York, N.Y.
(18, 37, 38, 39, 55, 90, 106)

George H. Holmes
c. 1840–1850
Philadelphia, Pa.
(10)

J. Holmes
c. 1842
Philadelphia, Pa.
(10)

Charles Holzapel
c. 1846
New York, N.Y.
(37)

Samuel D. Honeyman
c. 1841
Charleston, W. Va.
(23)

——— Hood
Hood & Tobey
c. 1848–1849
(24, 37, 38, 39, 50, 55, 90)

Benjamin L. Hood
c. 1841–1844
Buffalo, N.Y.
Rochester, N.Y.
(24)

Harry O. Hood
c. 1842–1844
Buffalo, N.Y.
(24)

Henry O. Hood
c. 1841
Rochester, N.Y.
(24)

Joseph E. Hoover
Faber & Hoover
c. 1837–1841
Philadelphia, Pa.
(10, 37, 90, 106)

Lawrence Hopkins
c. 1836–1837
New York, N.Y.
(18)

Thomas R. Hopkins
Cosby & Hopkins
c. 1846–before 1869
Petersburg, Va.
(23)

Benjamin C. Hopper
c. 1844–1850
Philadelphia, Pa.
(10)

Joseph M. Hopper
c. 1835–1850
Philadelphia, Pa.
(10, 37, 90, 106)

James Horah
c. 1849
Salisbury, N.C.
(22)

William Henry Horah
before 1863
Salisbury, N.C.
(22)

E. B. Horn
c. 1847
Boston, Mass.
(37, 50, 106)

Henry Horn
Bolton & Horn
Horn & Kneass
c. 1809–1840
Philadelphia, Pa.
(10)

George Horner
c. 1848
Camden, N.J.
(10)

H. P. Horton
Horton & Rikeman
c. 1850–1856
Savannah, Ga.
(21)

H. V. Horton
c. 1848
Louisville, Ky.
(63)

David Hotchkiss
Hotchkiss & Norton (Norton & Hotchkiss)
Hotchkiss & Schreuder (H & S)
c. 1841–1855
Palmyra, N.Y.
Syracuse, N.Y.
(24, 39)

John Hotchkiss
c. 1850
Syracuse, N.Y.
(24)

John W. Hotchkiss
Hotchkiss & Co.
c. 1847–1848
Buffalo, N.Y.
(24)

Frederick Houck
Harpers Ferry, W. Va.
c. 1834–1839
(23)

John E. S. Hough
c. 1846–1852
Leesburg, Va.
(23)

J. C. Houston
Beasley & Houston
c. 1886–1890
Fayetteville, N.C.
(22)

J. S. Hovey
Gleason & Hovey
c. 1846–1848
Rome, N.Y.
(24)

William How
(Howe ?)
c. 1842–1846
Philadelphia, Pa.
(10, 37)

——— Howard
Howard & Co.
c. 1866
New York, N.Y.
(123, 161, 162)

George C. Howe
George C. Howe & Co.
Howe & Guion
Stebbins & Howe (?)
c. 1810–1843
New York, N.Y.
(18, 37, 38, 39, 55, 90, 106, 161, 162)

Benjamin H. Howell
(Howells ?)
c. 1835–1848
Buffalo, N.Y.
(24)

Benoni H. Howell
(Howells ?)
c. 1835–1848
Buffalo, N.Y.
Newburgh, N.Y.
(24, 106)

William Howell
c. 1841
Philadelphia, Pa.
(10)

Freeman Hoyt
F. Hoyt & Co.
c. 1831–1869
Sumter, S.C.
(14)

George A. Hoyt
George A. Hoyt & Co.
George A. Hoyt & Son
c. 1822–1846
Albany, N.Y.
(24)

George B. Hoyt
Hoyt & Kippen
Boyd & Hoyt
c. 1827–1850
Albany, N.Y.
(24, 37, 38, 39, 50, 55, 106)

James A. Hoyt
c. 1838–1850
Troy, N.Y.
(24)

Jonathan Perkins Hoyt
c. 1847–1871
Clarkesville, Ga.
Laurens, S.C.
(14, 21)

Seymour Hoyt
S. Hoyt & Co.
c. 1817–1850
New York, N.Y.
(18, 37, 38, 39, 55, 90, 106)

Addison T. Hubbard
c. 1870
Cleveland, Ohio
(69)

John Hubbs
c. 1830–1837
Philadelphia, Pa.
(10)

John L. Hubert
c. 1848
Philadelphia, Pa.
(10)

Lafayette Hubert
c. 1846–1850
Philadelphia, Pa.
(10)

Henry Huddy
c. 1843–1844
Philadelphia, Pa.
(10)

Henry Hudson
Hudson & Dolfinger
c. 1841–1858–before 1888
Louisville, Ky.
(63, 127)

Joseph Huggins
c. 1837
Philadelphia, Pa.
(10)

——— Hughes
Hughes & Hall
c. 1840
Location unknown
(38, 106)

Charles Hughes
c. 1849
Philadelphia, Pa.
(10, 37)

Jasper W. Hughes
Gale, Wood & Hughes
Wood & Hughes
(W & H)
c. 1827–1845
New York, N.Y.
(18)

Jeremiah Hughes
before 1848
Annapolis, Md.
(39, 55, 93, 106)

Daniel S. Hulett
c. 1833–1849
Schenectady, N.Y.
(24)

Alexander Huling
c. 1837
Philadelphia, Pa.
(10)

Thomas B. Humphreys
Thomas B. Humphreys & Son
c. 1831–1850
Philadelphia, Pa.
Baltimore, Md.
Louisa Court House, Va.
(10, 11, 23, 37, 50, 90, 93, 106)

Thomas F. Humphreys
Thomas F. Humphreys & Son
c. 1849–1869
Richmond, Va.
(23)

George W. Hunnewell
Farrington & Hunnewell (F & H)
c. 1835–1850
Boston, Mass.
(37, 90, 106)

John T. Hunt
c. 1819–1840
Lynchburg, Va.
(23)

John Hunter
c. 1835–1847
Albany, N.Y.
(24, 38)

Asa Huntington
c. 1821–1857
Rochester, N.Y.
Pittsford, N.Y.
(24, 100)

John Huntington
William & John Huntington
Huntington & Wynne
Trotter & Huntington
Huntington & Lynch
c. 1824–before 1855
Oxford, N.C.
Salisbury, N.C.
Charlotte, N.C.
Hillsboro, N.C.
(22)

Richard Huntington
c. 1823–1850
Utica, N.Y.
(24, 38, 39, 106)

S. Huntington
c. 1850
Portland, Me.
(38, 39, 50, 106)

William Huntington
William Huntington & Co.
W. P. Huntington & Co.
William & John Huntington
c. 1815–before 1874
Oxford, N.C.
Hillsboro, N.C.
Milton, N.C.
(22)

John B. Huquenele
c. 1839–1842
Philadelphia, Pa.
(10)

John Hurt (Hurtt ?)
c. 1839–1842
Philadelphia, Pa.
(10)

Charles Hutchinson
c. 1847
Warrenton, Va.
(23)

J. Hutchinson
c. 1820–1850
Location unknown
(50)

Samuel Hutchinson
c. 1828–1839
Philadelphia, Pa.
(10, 39, 106)

Isaac Hutton
before 1855
Albany, N.Y.
Utica, N.Y.
(24, 32, 37, 38, 39, 50, 55)

Samuel Hutton
c. 1850
Philadelphia, Pa.
(10, 37)

Charles L. Hyde
c. 1842
Philadelphia, Pa.
(10)

James Hyde
Hyde & Hoff
c. 1850
Auburn, N.Y.
(24)

James N. Hyde
Hyde & Goodrich
c. 1816–1866
New Orleans, La.
(123)

Henry W. Hyman
c. 1800–1846
Lexington, Ky.
Richmond, Va.
(23, 39, 63, 106, 127)

Lewis Hyman
Hyman & Co.
c. 1845–1846
Richmond, Va.
(23)

Charles Inglehart
c. 1840
Philadelphia, Pa.
(10)

James Ingram
c. 1837–1850
Albany, N.Y.
Troy, N.Y.
(24)

W. K. Ingram
c. 1862
Chicago, Ill.
(175)

David Irving
c. 1848–1850
Philadelphia, Pa.
(10)

Mason T. Irwin
c. 1838–1859
Louisville, Ky.
(63)

Thomas M. Irwin
c. 1832–1850
Louisville, Ky.
(127)

D. C. Jaccard
Jaccard & Co.
D. C. Jaccard & Co.
Mermod & Jaccard
Mermod, Jaccard & King
c. 1847–1860
St. Louis, Mo.
(123, 175)

Eugene Jaccard
E. Jaccard & Co.
Jaccard & Co.
c. 1837–1901
St. Louis, Mo.
(123, 175)

Louis Jaccard
c. 1829–1837
St. Louis, Mo.
(123, 175)

Pulaski Jacks
Dibble & Jacks
c. 1842
Savannah, Ga.
(106)

A. Jackson
c. 1840
Norwalk, Conn.
(39, 106)

James Jackson
c. 1840–1850
Troy, N.Y.
Syracuse, N.Y.
(24)

Thomas Jackson
c. 1837–1849
Philadelphia, Pa.
(10)

Celestin Jacob
c. 1840
Philadelphia, Pa.
(10)

George Jacob (Jacobs ?)
c. 1802–1846
Baltimore, Md.
(11, 37, 38, 50, 55, 90, 93, 106)

A. Jacobi
c. 1879
Baltimore, Md.
(78)

William F. Jacobi
Jacobi & Jenkins
c. 1894–1908
Baltimore, Md.
(78)

D. Jacobs
c. 1852
Charleston, S.C.
(14)

George W. Jacobs
c. 1839–1846
Philadelphia, Pa.
(10)

John M. Jacobs
c. 1839–1844
Warrenton, Va.
(23)

Henry W. Jacot
c. 1841–1850
Philadelphia, Pa.
(10)

Julius Jacot
Bonsall & Jacot
c. 1848–1850
Philadelphia, Pa.
(10)

Jacob S. James
c. 1837
Philadelphia, Pa.
(10)

Joseph H. James
Gennet & James
c. 1849–1866
Richmond, Va.
(23)

Henry J. Javain
c. 1835–1838
Charleston, S.C.
(14, 39, 106)

Thomas Jeanes
c. 1835–1837
Philadelphia, Pa.
(10)

——— Jeannert
Sleeper & Jeannert
c. 1850
Philadelphia, Pa.
(10)

David H. Jefferies
c. 1846–1850
Philadelphia, Pa.
(10)

E. Jefferies
c. 1837–1839
Philadelphia, Pa.
(10)

Emmor Jefferis
Guthre & Jefferis
c. 1840–before 1892
Wilmington, Del.
(39, 60, 106)

Ephraim Jefferson
before 1844
Smyrna, Del.
(39, 60, 106)

James Jeffries
Jeffries & Eubank
c. 1820–1860
Glasgow, Ky.
(63, 106)

George M. Jenison
Gillett & Jenison
c. 1858–after 1883
Indianapolis, Ind.
(70, 175)

——— Jenkins
Jenkins & Jenkins
c. 1850
Baltimore, Md.
(37)

Edward J. Jenkins
c. 1843–1850
Philadelphia, Pa.
(10)

John Jenkins (I J)
c. 1844–1848
Philadelphia, Pa.
(10)

Martin J. Jenkins
c. 1847–1848
Troy, N.Y.
(24)

B. Jenner
c. 1846
Philadelphia, Pa.
(10)

——— Jenning
Jenning & Lander
c. 1848–1851
New York, N.Y.
(18, 39, 106)

Thomas Jennings
c. 1837
Philadelphia, Pa.
(10)

Chauncey Jerome
c. 1846–1849
Philadelphia, Pa.
(10)

Stephen C. Jett
c. 1848–1860
St. Louis, Mo.
(123)

John M. Johannes
c. 1828–1850–
before 1883
Baltimore, Md.
(37, 90, 93, 106)

——— Johnson
Johnson & Godley
c. 1843–1849
Albany, N.Y.
(11, 24, 37, 50, 106)

——— Johnson
Johnson & Lewis
c. 1837–1842
Philadelphia, Pa.
(10)

——— Johnson
Kidney, Cann &
Johnson (K C & J)
c. 1850–1853
New York, N.Y.
(11, 37, 38, 55, 106)

Alonzo W. Johnson
C. & A. W. Johnson
c. 1831–1838
Albany, N.Y.
(24)

B. Johnson
c. 1840
Richmond, Va.
(23)

Chauncey Johnson
C. & A. W. Johnson
c. 1824–1841
Albany, N.Y.
(24, 37, 39, 50, 90,
106)

Daniel B. Johnson
c. 1834–1850
Utica, N.Y.
(24, 25)

Elisha Johnson
c. 1841
Greensboro, N.C.
(22)

James R. Johnson
c. 1829–1846–
before 1855
Fredericksburg, Va.
Norfolk, Va.
Richmond, Va.
Clarksburg, W. Va.
(23)

N. B. Johnson
c. 1838
Watertown, N.Y.
(24)

Robert Johnson
(Johnston ?)
c. 1823–1850
Philadelphia, Pa.
(10)

Samuel W. Johnson
(Simeon W. Johnson ?)
c. 1836–1844
Louisville, Ky.
(63)

W. M. Johnson
Hill & Johnson
c. 1849
Richmond, Va.
(23)

William E. Johnson
c. 1841
Philadelphia, Pa.
(10)

Edmund J. Johnston
W. B. Johnston & Bros.
c. 1845–1849–
before 1870
Macon, Ga.
(21)

James Johnston
c. 1812–1843
Louisville, Ky.
(63, 127)

William Blackstone
Johnston
William B. Johnston
& Co.
W. B. Johnston & Bros.
c. 1839–1849–
before 1881
Macon, Ga.
(21)

William B. Johonnot
(W J)
Johonnot & Tuells
before 1849
Middletown, Conn.
Windsor, Vt.
(20, 37, 38, 39, 50, 90,
106)

John Jolineth
c. 1829–1850
Philadelphia, Pa.
(10)

John Jolivet
c. 1829–1850
Philadelphia, Pa.
(10)

——— Jones
Newland & Jones
c. 1824–1847
Albany, N.Y.
(24)

C. H. Jones
C. H. Jones & Co.
c. 1854
Georgetown, S.C.
(14)

Christopher Jones
c. 1847
St. Louis, Mo.
(123)

George B. Jones
before 1875
Boston, Mass.
(37, 50, 90, 106)

G. W. Jones
c. 1838
Savannah, Ga.
(21)

George W. Jones
c. 1840–1841
Philadelphia, Pa.
(10)

J. F. Jones
Jones & Wood (?)
c. 1846–1850
Syracuse, N.Y.
(24)

J. Walter Jones
c. 1842
Troy, N.Y.
(24)

James M. Jones
Spear & Jones
c. 1825–1850
Savannah, Ga.
(21)

John B. Jones
Jones & Ward
Baldwin & Jones
John B. Jones & Co.
Jones, Low & Ball
Jones, Ball & Poor
Jones, Ball & Co.
Jones, Shreve, Brown & Co.
c. 1809–1854
Boston, Mass.
(11, 37, 38, 39, 50, 55, 90, 106)

John W. Jones
John W. Jones & Son
19th century
Mount Sterling, Ky.
(63)

Levi Jones
c. 1845–1846
Philadelphia, Pa.
(10)

Philip Jones
Jones & Hutton (?)
c. 1840–1860 (?)
Wilmington, Del.
(39, 106)

Prince H. Jones
c. 1842–1861
St. Louis, Mo.
(123)

Robert E. Jones
c. 1837–1838
Utica, N.Y.
(24)

Rowland Jones
c. 1837–1839
Utica, N.Y.
(24, 25)

Samuel S. Jones
c. 1844
Philadelphia, Pa.
(10)

William E. Jones
c. 1847
Rochester, N.Y.
(24, 100, 106)

William G. Jones
c. 1837
Philadelphia, Pa.
(10)

William H. Jones
c. 1837–1841
Charleston, S.C.
(14)

William P. Jones
Towle & Jones
c. 1857
Newburyport, Mass.
(19, 172, 175)

C. H. Judson
c. 1846
Syracuse, N.Y.
(24)

Hiram Judson
c. 1824–1854
Syracuse, N.Y.
(24, 39, 106)

Thomas W. Judson
c. 1850
Syracuse, N.Y.
(24)

Cadmus Julian
c. 1840
Philadelphia, Pa.
(10)

Joseph J. Justice
c. 1844–1848
Philadelphia, Pa.
(10)

J. Kadmus
c. 1839
St. Louis, Mo.
(123)

William Kahmar
c. 1843–1850
Philadelphia, Pa.
(10)

H. Q. Kakle
c. 1838–1848
St. Louis, Mo.
(123)

B. Kayton
c. 1847
Fredericksburg, Va.
(23)

John W. Kean
c. 1837–1850
Philadelphia, Pa.
(10)

John Kearsing
c. 1843
Poughkeepsie, N.Y.
(134)

——— Keating
Warner & Keating
c. 1840–1843
Philadelphia, Pa.
(10)

Lambert Keatting, Jr.
c. 1831–1843
Philadelphia, Pa.
(10)

John Kedzie
J. Kedzie & Co.
c. 1838–1868
Rochester, N.Y.
(24, 39, 100, 106)

John Keel
c. 1835–1837
Philadelphia, Pa.
(10)

George Keesee
c. 1831–1846
Richmond, Va.
(23)

G. H. Keeve
c. 1848–1849
Louisville, Ky.
(63)

Alexander Keim
Butler & Keim
Butler, Wise & Keim
c. 1841–1850
Philadelphia, Pa.
(10, 37)

Charles Keller
c. 1841
Philadelphia, Pa.
(10)

George Keller
c. 1846
Philadelphia, Pa.
(10)

Edward G. Kelley
E. G. & J. S. Kelley
H. A. & E. G. Kelley
c. 1840–1842
Nantucket Island, Mass.
(17)

Henry A. Kelley
H. A. & E. G. Kelley
c. 1815–1869
Nantucket Island, Mass.
(17)

James S. Kelley
E. G. & J. S. Kelley
c. 1838–1856–
before 1900
Nantucket Island,
Mass.
(17)

John V. Kellinger
c. 1857
Philadelphia, Pa.
(10)

Robert Kelly
c. 1843–1844
Philadelphia, Pa.
(10)

William Kendrick
Harris & Kendrick
Lemon & Kendrick
c. 1824–1880
Louisville, Ky.
(37, 38, 39, 55, 63, 90, 106, 127)

Hugh Kennedy
c. 1837–1850
Philadelphia, Pa.
(10)

John Kennedy
c. 1839
Charleston, S.C.
(14)

Luke Kent
c. 1817–1841
Cincinnati, Ohio
(77)

Thomas Kent
c. 1822–1844
Cincinnati, Ohio
(77)

Samuel Keplinger
c. 1812–1849
Baltimore, Md.
(39, 55, 93, 106)

Robert M. Kerrison
c. 1842–1850
Philadelphia, Pa.
(10)

Edward Kersey
Kersey & Pearce
c. 1845–1878
Richmond, Va.
(23)

James Ketchum
(Ketcham ?)
c. 1807–1849
New York, N.Y.
Utica, N.Y.
(24, 25, 37, 38, 39, 90, 106)

Lewis A. Ketchum
L. A. Ketchum & Co.
c. 1837–1842
Buffalo, N.Y.
(24)

Thomas Kettel
(Kettell ?) (T K)
before 1850
Charlestown, Mass.
(37, 39, 50, 55, 90, 106)

George Kew
c. 1840
Philadelphia, Pa.
(10)

F. C. Key
Key & Sons
c. 1848–1850
Camden, N.J.
Philadelphia, Pa.
(10)

William Keyser
c. 1850
Philadelphia, Pa.
(10, 37)

John Keywood
c. 1851
Wheeling, W.Va.
(23)

——— Kidney
Kidney, Cann &
Johnson (K C & J)
c. 1850–1853
New York, N.Y.
(11, 37, 38, 39, 50, 55, 106)

——— Kidney
Kidney & Dunn
(K & D)
c. 1844
New York, N.Y.
(37, 38, 39, 55, 106)

——— Kimball
Woodford & Kimball
c. 1850
Dunkirk, N.Y.
(24)

Lewis A. Kimball
c. 1837–1842
Buffalo, N.Y.
(39, 106)

O. Kimball
Yates & Kimball
c. 1842–1843
Elmira, N.Y.
(24)

William H. Kimberly
(W K)
c. 1842
St. Louis, Mo.
(123)

George King
c. 1834–1844
New York, N.Y.
(18, 37)

Gilbert King
c. 1845
Rochester, N.Y.
(24)

Thomas King
c. 1840
Leesburg, Va.
(23)

William King
c. 1838
Charleston, S.C.
(14)

A. Kinley
c. 1841
Philadelphia, Pa.
(10, 37)

Jesse Kinsel
William & Jesse Kinsel
c. 1837–1839
Philadelphia, Pa.
(10)

William Kinsel
William & Jesse Kinsel
c. 1837–1839
Philadelphia, Pa.
(10)

David R. (I. ?)
Kinsey
Edward & David
Kinsey
c. 1817–1860
Newport, Ky.
Cincinnati, Ohio
(37, 38, 39, 55, 63, 106)

Edmund Kinsey
c. 1845
Jamaica, N.Y.
(24)

Edward Kinsey
Edward & David
Kinsey
c. 1834–1850
Newport, Ky.
Cincinnati, Ohio
(63, 77)

F. Kinsey
c. 1837
Cincinnati, Ohio
(77)

William Kip
c. 1825–1850
Kinderhook, N.Y.
(24)

George Kippen
G. Kippen & Hoyt
(Hoyt & Kippen ?)
before 1845
Bridgeport, Conn.
Albany, N.Y.
Middletown, Conn.
(20, 37, 38, 39, 50, 55, 90, 106, 108)

——— Kirby
Brown & Kirby
c. 1850
New Haven, Conn.
(39, 106)

Henry Child Kirk
Samuel Kirk & Son
Samuel Kirk & Sons
c. 1846–before 1894
Baltimore, Md.
(37, 155)

Henry Child Kirk, Jr.
c. 1900–1901
Samuel Kirk & Sons, Inc.
(155)

Joshua Kirk
c. 1848–1849
Philadelphia, Pa.
(10)

Samuel Kirk (S K)
Kirk & Smith (K & S)
Samuel Kirk & Son
Samuel Kirk & Sons
Samuel Kirk & Son Co.
c. 1815–1872
Baltimore, Md.
(11, 37, 38, 39, 50, 55, 90, 106, 155)

J. Kirkham
c. 1840
Location unknown
(39)

E. M. Kirkpatrick
c. 1856–1861
York, S.C.
(14)

Andrew B. Kitchen
Bailey & Kitchen
c. 1835–1846
Philadelphia, Pa.
(10, 37, 90, 106)

John Kitts
Smith & Kitts
Kitts & Stoy
John Kitts & Co.
Kitts & Werne
c. 1836–1878
Louisville, Ky.
(39, 63, 106, 127)

John Klauer
c. 1842
St. Louis, Mo.
(123)

John Klein
c. 1828–1850
Philadelphia, Pa.
(10)

John A. Klein
c. 1833–1837
Leesburg, Va.
(23)

Bartholomew Kline
B. Kline & Co.
c. 1837–1850
Philadelphia, Pa.
(10, 37, 90)

Foster S. Kline
F. S. Kline & Co. (?)
c. 1850
Lyons, N.Y.
(24)

John J. Klink
c. 1841–1859–before 1900
Louisville, Ky.
(63)

John Kloebner
c. 1845–1850
Richmond, Va.
(23)

B. T. Kluth
c. 1850
Louisville, Ky.
(63)

Alanson Knapp
Dunning & Knapp
Knapp & Leslie
c. 1828–after 1850
Mobile, Ala.
(170)

Philip Knappe
c. 1839–1841
Philadelphia, Pa.
(10)

Christian Kneass
c. 1811–1837
Philadelphia, Pa.
(10)

William Kneass
Horn & Kneass
c. 1805–1842
Philadelphia, Pa.
(10)

John W. Knight
c. 1845
Rochester, N.Y.
(24)

Julius Knock
c. 1845–1850
Philadelphia, Pa.
(10)

——— Knowles
Knowles & Ladd
c. 1850
Providence, R.I.
(38, 147, 175)

Ebenezer B. Knowlton
c. 1848
Cazenovia, N.Y.
(24)

Henry Knox
c. 1848
Louisville, Ky.
(63)

Augustus Koch
c. 1850
Philadelphia, Pa.
(10)

Carl Koch
c. 1846–1848
Philadelphia, Pa.
(10)

H. Koch
c. 1838–1845
St. Louis, Mo.
(123)

Henry Kocksperger
c. 1837
Philadelphia, Pa.
(10)

Peter Kolb
c. 1829–1850
Philadelphia, Pa.
(10)

F. Koldewey
c. 1850
Location unknown—probably southern Ohio
(175)

Abraham I. Kolster
c. 1850
Syracuse, N.Y.
(24)

Henry Kopke
c. 1850
New York, N.Y.
(37)

William Kramer
c. 1848
Philadelphia, Pa.
(10)

Peter Krebs
c. 1844
New York, N.Y.
(37)

Peter L. Krider (PLK)
Krider & Biddle
Peter L. Krider Co.
c. 1850–1900
Philadelphia, Pa.
(11, 37, 38, 39, 50, 55, 106)

O. Kuchler
c. 1850
New Orleans, La.
(39, 106)

Jacob Ladomus
c. 1843–1850
Philadelphia, Pa.
(10, 39, 106)

Lewis Ladomus
c. 1830–1850
Philadelphia, Pa.
(10, 38)

John Joseph Lafar
c. 1805–1849
Charleston, S.C.
(14, 39, 106)

——— Laforme
Laforme & Brother
c. 1850
Boston, Mass.
(37)

Vincent Laforme
Vincent Laforme & Brother (VL&B)
Laforme & Brother (?)
c. 1850–1855
Boston, Mass.
(39, 106)

J. C. LaGrange
c. 1839–1842
Charlottesville, Va.
Staunton, Va.
(78)

Ebenezer Knowlton Lakeman
Stevens & Lakeman
before 1857
Salem, Mass.
(37, 38, 39, 50, 55, 90, 95, 106)

John Lalande (Lalarde ?)
c. 1844–1850
Philadelphia, Pa.
(10)

Lewis Lammel
c. 1843–1850
Philadelphia, Pa.
(10)

Robert Lamont
Bard & Lamont
c. 1841–1845
Philadelphia, Pa.
(10, 37)

Americus Lancaster
c. 1842–1850
Philadelphia, Pa.
(10)

Arman Lancaster
c. 1837
Philadelphia, Pa.
(10)

M. Lancaster
c. 1839
Philadelphia, Pa.
(10)

——— Lander
Jenning & Lander
c. 1848–1851
Philadelphia, Pa.
(10)

——— Lane
Lane, Bailey & Co.
Madison, N.Y.
(24)

——— Lane
Lane & Bros.
c. 1840
Clarks Mills, N.Y.
(24)

Abraham Lang
c. 1850
Philadelphia, Pa.
(10)

Lewis W. Lang
c. 1837–1844
Philadelphia, Pa.
(10)

William Lange
c. 1844
New York, N.Y.
(37, 38, 39, 55, 106)

Lyman Barker Langworthy
Burwill & Langworthy
c. 1808–1880
Ballston Spa, N.Y.
Quebec, Que. Can.
Rochester, N.Y.
(133)

William Andrews Langworthy
c. 1814–1868
Ballston Spa, N.Y.
Saratoga Springs, N.Y.
Rochester, N.Y.
(133)

Gerrit Lansing
c. 1838
Albany, N.Y.
(24)

Jacob H. Lansing
c. 1847
Rochester, N.Y.
(24)

Alexander E. Larer
c. 1846–1850
Philadelphia, Pa.
(10)

Elias Larson
c. 1850
Rochester, N.Y.
(24)

William LaRue
c. 1847–1849
Philadelphia, Pa.
(10)

James E. Lasell
c. 1844–1846
Troy, N.Y.
(24)

Luther R. Lasell
c. 1831–1846
Troy, N.Y.
(24)

A. Lauder
c. 1840
Location unknown
(38)

George Laval
c. 1842–1843
Philadelphia, Pa.
(10)

Peter Laval
c. 1842
Philadelphia, Pa.
(10)

William P. Law
c. 1837–1850
Philadelphia, Pa.
(10)

——— Lawrence
Colwell & Lawrence
c. 1850
Albany, N.Y.
(11, 37, 50, 90)

Martin M. Lawrence
c. 1832–1840
New York, N.Y.
(18, 39, 106)

Robert D. Lawrie
Taylor & Lawrie
Taylor, Lawrie & Wood
c. 1837–1850
Philadelphia, Pa.
(10, 11, 50)

Robert O. Lawrie
c. 1840
Philadelphia, Pa.
(37, 90, 106)

Almon Leach
Hawley & Leach
Leach & Bennett
c. 1845–1858
Utica, N.Y.
(24, 25)

Charles B. Leach
c. 1843–1847
Utica, N.Y.
(24, 25)

Ebenezer Leach
Leach & Bradley
Leach & Davies
c. 1832–1840
Utica, N.Y.
(24, 25)

George Leach
Hawley & Leach
c. 1853–1857
Utica, N.Y.
(25)

Leonard D. Leach
Haight & Leach
c. 1850
Auburn, N.Y.
(24)

Sewell Jones Leach
c. 1857
Mobile, Ala.
(170)

John Lebeau
c. 1848
St. Louis, Mo.
(123)

George Lee
c. 1837–1850
Philadelphia, Pa.
(10)

John A. Lee
c. 1840–1850
Mansfield, Ohio
(77)

Samuel W. Lee
(SWL)
Burr & Lee
c. 1840–1846
Providence, R.I.
(133)

Samuel W. Lee, Jr.
c. 1849–1850
Rochester, N.Y.
(24, 100)

Gideon H. Leeds
c. 1841–1842
Philadelphia, Pa.
(10)

Howard G. Leeds
c. 1840
Philadelphia, Pa.
(10)

Peter Leevell
c. 1841
Philadelphia, Pa.
(10)

Louis, Andrew Legay
c. 1842–1845
Columbus, Ga.
(21)

John A. L'Hommedieu
c. 1843–1859
Mobile, Ala.
(170)

William L. L'Hommedieu
c. 1843–1850
Mobile, Ala.
(170)

Nicholas J. LeHuray, Jr.
c. 1821–1846
Philadelphia, Pa.
(10, 39, 106)

Theodore LeHuray
c. 1843–1850
Philadelphia, Pa.
(10)

Nathaniel Augustine Leinbach
c. 1850–1860
Salem, N.C.
(22)

Traugott Leinbach
c. 1821–1860
Salem, N.C.
(22)

Joseph Leland
c. 1845
Philadelphia, Pa.
(10)

James Innes Lemon
Lemon & Kendrick
James I. Lemon & Co.
Lemon & Son
c. 1828–1869
Louisville, Ky.
(63, 127)

William Lenoir
(Lenon ?)
c. 1843–1850
Philadelphia, Pa.
(10)

Allen Leonard
Leonard & Rogers
c. 1827–1840
New York, N.Y.
(18, 37, 39, 106)

Allen Leonard
Leonard & Wilson
(L & W)
c. 1844–1850
Philadelphia, Pa.
(10, 90)

D. Gillis Leonard
Haight & Leonard
c. 1841–1847
Newburgh, N.Y.
(24)

Samuel T. Leonard
Lynch & Leonard
c. 1805–1848
Baltimore, Md.
Chestertown, Md.
(38, 39, 55, 93)

Edward Leppleman
c. 1836–1839
Buffalo, N.Y.
(24)

Edward P. Lescare
(Lescure ?) (EPL)
c. 1822–1850
Philadelphia, Pa.
(10, 37, 38, 39, 80, 106)

Louis Leschot
c. 1836–1838
Charlottesville, Va.
(23)

Franklin A. Leslie
Knapp & Leslie
c. 1850
Mobile, Ala.
(170)

William Lesser
c. 1859
Orangeburg, S.C.
(14)

J. U. Lester
c. 1843–1845
Oswego, N.Y.
(24)

Talbot G. Lester
c. 1831–1840
Portsmouth, Va.
(23)

Garretson Levi
c. 1840–1843
Philadelphia, Pa.
(10)

Henry A. Levy
c. 1841–1850
Philadelphia, Pa.
(10)

Jonas Levy
c. 1835–1838
New York, N.Y.
(18, 39, 106)

Lewis B. Levy
c. 1841–1845
Philadelphia, Pa.
(10)

C. C. Lewis
c. 1844–1847
Staunton, Va.
(23)

Frederick H. Lewis
c. 1850
Rochester, N.Y.
(24)

Isaac Lewis
before 1860
Huntington, Conn.
Ridgefield, Conn.
(20, 37, 38, 39, 50, 55, 90, 106)

J. N. Lewis
J. N. Lewis & Co.
Lewis & Co.
c. 1854–1856
York, S.C.
(14)

John M. (I. ?) Lewis
Johnson & Lewis (?)
c. 1830–1850
Philadelphia, Pa.
(10)

John V. Lewis
c. 1847–1852
Utica, N.Y.
(24, 25)

Cassimir Lhulier
(Luhlier ?)
(Lunier ?)
c. 1825–1850
Philadelphia, Pa.
(10)

Lewis Lhulier
(Luhlier ?)
(Lunier ?)
c. 1829–1849
Philadelphia, Pa.
(10)

Jacob G. L. Libby
c. 1820–1846
Boston, Mass.
(38, 39, 50, 55, 106)

John Lidden
c. 1850
St. Louis, Mo.
(38, 39, 106)

J. H. Lillie
Badger & Lillie
c. 1837
Elmira, N.Y.
(24)

A. L. Lincoln
Lincoln & Foss
Haddock, Lincoln & Foss
c. 1820–1865
Boston, Mass.
St. Louis, Mo.
(38, 39, 106)

George Lindner (Lendner ?) (Lentner ?)
c. 1837–1850
Philadelphia, Pa.
(10, 37, 90, 106)

William Lindsay
c. 1839–1841
Portsmouth, Ohio
(77)

William K. Lindsay
c. 1839
Wheeling, W. Va.
(23)

Clark Lindsley
c. 1843–1850
Hartford, Conn.
(37, 39, 106)

James Lines
c. 1839
Charleston, S.C.
(14)

Robert Lisenbee
c. 1860
Abbeville, S.C.
(14)

John List
List & Smith
c. 1837–1850
Philadelphia, Pa.
(10)

Archibald Little
c. 1839–1840
Camden, N.J.
Philadelphia, Pa.
(10)

John Little
c. 1823–1838
Martinsburg, W. Va.
(23)

John Little
c. 1830–1837
Mobile, Ala.
(170)

H. Lloyd
c. 1836–1842
Cooperstown, N.Y.
(24)

——— Lockwood
Pratt & Lockwood
c. 1841
Newburgh, N.Y.
(24)

Alfred Lockwood
c. 1817–1837
New York, N.Y.
(18, 37, 38, 39, 55, 90, 106)

Frederick Lockwood
c. 1828–1845
New York, N.Y.
(11, 37, 38, 39, 50, 55, 106)

James Lockwood
c. 1799–1838
New York, N.Y.
(18, 37, 38, 39, 90, 106)

Lewis Lodds
c. 1836–1837
Buffalo, N.Y.
(24)

John J. Loew
c. 1846–1848
Philadelphia, Pa.
(10)

Richard Logan
c. 1837
Albany, N.Y.
(24)

Andrew K. Long
c. 1837–1844
Philadelphia, Pa.
(10, 37, 90, 106)

George W. Long
c. 1837–1850
Philadelphia, Pa.
(10)

Robert M. Long
c. 1832–1837
Buffalo, N.Y.
(24)

Samuel R. Long
c. 1842–1846
Philadelphia, Pa.
(10)

——— Loomis
Loomis & Ralph
c. 1819–1838
Frankfort, Ky.
(63, 127)

G. Loomis
G. Loomis & Co.
c. 1850
Erie, Pa.
(38, 39, 106)

Worham P. Loomis
Loomis & Ralph (?)
c. 1819–1854
Frankfort, Ky.
(63)

John Lorange
c. 1837–1850
Philadelphia, Pa.
(10)

Benjamin B. Lord
B. B. Lord & Co.
c. 1770–1843
Pittsfield, Mass.
Rutland, Vt.
Athens, Ga.
Norwich, Conn.
(21, 37, 38, 39, 59, 90, 106)

Ebenezer Lord
B. B. Lord & Co.
c. 1801–1838
Athens, Ga.
(21)

Jabez C. Lord
Lord & Smith
c. 1825–1840
New York, N.Y.
(18, 37, 38, 39, 55, 90, 106)

Benson John Lossing
Henderson & Lossing
c. 1835–before 1891
Poughkeepsie, N.Y.
(7, 24, 50)

Benjamin C. Lotier
c. 1846–1847
Philadelphia, Pa.
(10, 37)

Benjamin Louderback
c. 1830–1845
Philadelphia, Pa.
(10)

George Loughlin
c. 1849–1850
Philadelphia, Pa.
(10)

Lawrence Loughlin
c. 1848
Philadelphia, Pa.
(10)

Daniel Love
c. 1817–1840
Bedford, Va.
Lynchburg, Va.
(23)

——— Lovell
Lovell & Smith
c. 1841–1843
Philadelphia, Pa.
(10)

A. E. Lovell
c. 1844–1849
Philadelphia, Pa.
(10)

Peter Lovell
c. 1837
Philadelphia, Pa.
(10)

Robert Lovett
c. 1818–1838
New York, N.Y.
Philadelphia, Pa.
(10, 18, 39, 106)

Robert Lovett, Jr.
c. 1840–1850
Philadelphia, Pa.
(10)

——— Low
Low, Ball & Co.
c. 1840
Boston, Mass.
(7, 37, 39, 50, 90, 106)

Francis Low
John J. Low & Co.
before 1855
Boston, Mass.
(37, 39, 50, 55, 90, 106)

John J. Low
John J. Low & Co.
before 1876
Boston, Mass.
Salem, Mass.
(37, 39, 50, 106)

Joseph J. Low
c. 1845–1850
Philadelphia, Pa.
(10)

Mark Low
c. 1847–1850
Philadelphia, Pa.
(10)

Peter Low
c. 1832–1837
Buffalo, N.Y.
(24)

Isaac Lower
c. 1844–1846
Philadelphia, Pa.
(10)

Jacob Lower
c. 1833–1850
Philadelphia, Pa.
(10)

Theodore O. Lower
c. 1844
Philadelphia, Pa.
(10)

William Lower
c. 1837–1848
Philadelphia, Pa.
(10)

Isaac Lowner
c. 1844
Philadelphia, Pa.
(37)

William Lowner
c. 1837
Philadelphia, Pa.
(37, 90, 106)

J. J. Lowrey
c. 1840–1844
Pendleton, S.C.
(14)

R. B. Lowrie
c. 1847–1849
Philadelphia, Pa.
(10, 37)

John P. Lucke
c. 1849
Philadelphia, Pa.
(10)

J. Lukens
c. 1837
Philadelphia, Pa.
(10)

William Lukens
c. 1847
Philadelphia, Pa.
(10)

John M. Lunquest
c. 1835–1846
Charleston, S.C.
Edgefield, S.C.
(14)

George C. Lunt
c. 1882–after 1902
Newburyport, Mass.
Greenfield, Mass.
(175)

Henry Lupp
c. 1790–1845
New Brunswick, N.J.
(123)

William Lupp
before 1845
New Brunswick, N.J.
(117, 123)

——— Lynch
Lynch & Leonard
c. 1805–1840
Baltimore, Md.
Chestertown, Md.
(55, 93, 106)

John Lynch (I L)
c. 1786–1848
Baltimore, Md.
(37, 38, 39, 50, 55, 90, 93, 95, 106)

L. George Lynch
c. 1840
Hillsboro, N.C.
(22)

Lemuel Lynch
Huntington & Lynch
c. 1828–1893
Hillsboro, N.C.
Greensboro, N.C.
Concord, N.H.
(22)

Seaborn Lynch
c. 1840
Hillsboro, N.C.
(22)

Thomas M. Lynch
c. 1840
Oxford, N.C.
(22)

William Lyndahl
c. 1844
Philadelphia, Pa.
(10)

George Lyon
c. 1819–1844
Wilmington, N.C.
(22)

Alexander Mac Harey
c. 1842
Albany, N.Y.
(37)

John Mackey
c. 1841–1842
Philadelphia, Pa.
(10, 37)

Edward Mackinder
c. 1839
St. Louis, Mo.
(123)

F. W. Maffit
c. 1846
Syracuse, N.Y.
(24)

Simon M. Magnus
c. 1849
Albany, N.Y.
(24)

Thomas S. Mahin
before 1880
Franklin, Ky.
(63, 127)

John Mahony
c. 1847–1849
Utica, N.Y.
(25)

William A. Mahony
c. 1837–1849
Philadelphia, Pa.
(10)

August Mai
c. 1868–1883
Indianapolis, Ind.
(70, 175)

David Main
c. 1765–1843
Stonington, Conn.
(20, 32, 37, 50, 90, 106)

John A. Mallory
c. 1839
Delhi, N.Y.
(24)

Samuel Mallory
c. 1842
Catskill, N.Y.
(24)

Henry Mander
c. 1848–1850
Philadelphia, Pa.
(10, 37)

Matthew Manley
c. 1843
Philadelphia, Pa.
(10)

Ezra L. Manning
c. 1858–1860
Utica, N.Y.
(25)

Joseph Manning
c. 1823–1840
New York, N.Y.
(18, 37)

Samuel A. Mansfield
c. 1848–1850
Philadelphia, Pa.
(10)

John Mansure
c. 1844–1850
Philadelphia, Pa.
(10)

Jules Manuel
c. 1849–1850
Philadelphia, Pa.
(10)

Benjamin Marble
c. 1840–1850
Albany, N.Y.
(39, 106)

Simeon Marble
before 1856
New Haven, Conn.
(20, 37, 38, 39, 50, 55, 90, 106)

Frank W. W. Marchisi
c. 1855–1860
Utica, N.Y.
(25)

Joseph Marchisi
c. 1845–1868
Chittenango, N.Y.
Utica, N.Y.
(24, 25)

Henry Maree (Marce ?)
c. 1845–1850
Philadelphia, Pa.
(10)

Frederick Marquand (F M)
Marquand & Brother
Marquand & Company
before 1838–before 1880
Savannah, Ga.
New York, N.Y.
(18, 21, 37, 90, 106)

Isaac Marquand
Marquand & Brother
Marquand, Harriman & Co.
before 1838
Fairfield, Conn.
Edenton, N.C.
Savannah, Ga.
New York, N.Y.
(18, 21, 22, 37, 90, 106)

Josiah P. Marquand
Marquand & Company
c. 1834–1839
New York, N.Y.
(18)

Benedict Beal Marsh
before 1875
Flemingsburg, Ky.
Paris, Ky.
Richmond, Ky.
(63, 127)

Benjamin Marsh
c. 1840–1850
Albany, N.Y.
(24, 32, 50)

Edwin A. Marsh
c. 1847–1850
Rochester, N.Y.
(24)

Edwin A. Marsh
c. 1832–1840
Buffalo, N.Y.
(24)

Eli P. Marsh
c. 1858–1859
Utica, N.Y.
(25)

Thomas King Marsh
c. 1831–1850
Paris, Ky.
(38, 39, 63, 106, 127)

——— Marshall
Marshall & Smith
c. 1837
Philadelphia, Pa.
(10)

Alexander D. Marshall
c. 1847–1848
Philadelphia, Pa.
(10)

John Marshall
c. 1838–1840
Troy, N.Y.
(24)

John C. Marshall
c. 1836–1849
Louisville, Ky.
(63)

Joseph Marshall
c. 1818–1850
Philadelphia, Pa.
(10, 11, 37, 50, 90, 106)

Thomas Henry Marshall
c. 1832–1852
Albany, N.Y.
Troy, N.Y.
Rochester, N.Y.
(24, 37, 39, 90, 100, 106)

Abraham W. Martin
c. 1835–1840
New York, N.Y.
(18, 37, 38, 90, 106)

Ambrose Martin
c. 1835–1840
Philadelphia, Pa.
(10)

John L. Martin
c. 1844–1850
Philadelphia, Pa.
(10)

Valentine Martin
c. 1842–1859
Boston, Mass.
(39, 50, 55, 106)

John Martini
c. 1859
Charleston, S.C.
(14)

John F. Mascher
c. 1845–1850
Philadelphia, Pa.
(10)

Charles T. Mason
c. 1851–before 1893
Sumter, S.C.
(14)

Levant L. Mason
c. 1847–1850
Rochester, N.Y.
Jamestown, N.Y.
(24)

Charles R. Massey
c. 1837–1839
Philadelphia, Pa.
(10)

Charles A. Masson
c. 1829–1850
Philadelphia, Pa.
(10)

William Masterman
Masterman & Son
c. 1852–1870
Charleston, S.C.
(14)

Theodore Mather
Mather & Pitkin
c. 1844–1848
Buffalo, N.Y.
(24)

F. V. Mathew
c. 1850–1855
Mobile, Ala.
(170)

Harriet Mathews
c. 1850
Charlottesville, Va.
(23)

Richard Mathews
c. 1836–1848
Charlottesville, Va.
(23)

Thomas Mathews
before 1852
Charles Town, W. Va.
(23)

Peter Mathiew
c. 1837–1843
Philadelphia, Pa.
(10)

Newell Matson
c. 1845
Oswego, N.Y.
(24, 39, 106)

H. E. Matteson
c. 1840
Location unknown
(78)

L. Matthews
c. 1852
Paris, Ky.
(63, 127)

Peter Matthews
c. 1845
Philadelphia, Pa.
(10)

Charles Matthias
c. 1849
Philadelphia, Pa.
(10)

John Maull
c. 1848–1849
Philadelphia, Pa.
(10)

Joseph E. Maull
c. 1830–1837
Philadelphia, Pa.
(10)

E. Maussenet
c. 1841–1845
Macon, Ga.
(21)

John Mautz
c. 1841
Philadelphia, Pa.
(10)

John Mawdsley
c. 1846–1847
Philadelphia, Pa.
(10)

Gotlieb A. Mayer
Minton & Mayer
c. 1840–1868
Norfolk, Va.
(23)

Jacob Mayer
(Meier ?) (Myre ?)
(Myers ?)
c. 1830–1846
Cleveland, Ohio
(37, 77)

Thomas Maynard
Dana & Maynard
Maynard & Taylor
c. 1841–1860
Utica, N.Y.
Cleveland, Ohio
(25)

William McAdams
c. 1846–1850
Philadelphia, Pa.
(10)

James McAllister
c. 1840–1850
Philadelphia, Pa.
(10)

Daniel McCalvey
c. 1837
Philadelphia, Pa.
(10)

Michael McCann
c. 1839–1845
Philadelphia, Pa.
(10)

John McCarter
(McCarty ?)
c. 1845–1850
Philadelphia, Pa.
(10)

——— McCarty
(McCarthy ?)
Butler & McCarty
Butler & McCarthy (?)
c. 1850
Philadelphia, Pa.
(11, 37, 39, 50, 106)

Edward McCarty
c. 1845–1850
Philadelphia, Pa.
(10, 37)

John A. McCaulley
c. 1840
Lexington, Ky.
Richmond, Ky.
(63, 127)

William McClain
c. 1848
Philadelphia, Pa.
(10)

James McClanahan
Myer & McClanahan
c. 1836–1837
Buffalo, N.Y.
(24)

W. S. McClean, Jr.
c. 1837
Philadelphia, Pa.
(10)

Daniel McCleary
c. 1837–1841
Philadelphia, Pa.
(10)

F. McCloskey
c. 1850
Philadelphia, Pa.
(10)

John McClymon
(McClymoan ?)
(McClyman ?)
c. 1805–1840
New York, N.Y.
(11, 18, 37, 38, 39, 50, 55, 90, 106)

Patrick McCocker
c. 1842–1846
Philadelphia, Pa.
(10)

——— McConnaghy
before 1850
Wayne Co., Ky.
(63, 127)

John McConnell
c. 1827–before 1858
Richmond, Va.
(23)

Milton McConothy
c. 1843–1848
Louisville, Ky.
(63, 127)

Bernard McCormick
c. 1844–1850
Philadelphia, Pa.
(10)

John McCormick
c. 1837
Philadelphia, Pa.
(10, 37, 90, 106)

Coles McCoun
c. 1840–1841
Whitehall, N.Y.
(24)

Henry T. McCoun
c. 1837–1840
Troy, N.Y.
(24)

George W. McCoy
c. 1837–1850
Philadelphia, Pa.
(10)

R. A. McCredie
before 1839
Savannah, Ga.
(21)

George H. McCulley
c. 1829–1850
Philadelphia, Pa.
(10)

William McCulley
c. 1841–1850
Philadelphia, Pa.
(10)

Francis McCutchen
c. 1844–1846
Philadelphia, Pa.
(10)

John McDaniel
c. 1848–1849
Philadelphia, Pa.
(10, 37)

Charles C. McDermott
c. 1850
Philadelphia, Pa.
(10)

Edward McDermott
c. 1848
Philadelphia, Pa.
(10)

Charles McDonald
19th Century
Lexington, Ky.
(63)

Daniel McDonald
(McDonell)
c. 1828–1837
Philadelphia, Pa.
(10, 37, 90, 106)

William T. McDonald
c. 1845–1850
Shepherdstown, W. Va.
Alexandria, Va.
Harpers Ferry, W. Va.
(23)

William Hanse
McDowell
before 1842
Philadelphia, Pa.
(39, 106)

J. B. McFadden
c. 1840
Pittsburgh, Pa.
(38, 39, 106)

John McGlensey
c. 1845–1850
Philadelphia, Pa.
(10)

I. D. McGoodwin
Fuselli & McGoodwin
c. 1870–1885
Bowling Green, Ky.
(123)

——— McGrew
McGrew & Beggs
c. 1850
Louisville, Ky.
(63)

Wilson McGrew
W. McGrew & Son (?)
c. 1824–1864
Cincinnati, Ohio
(77)

Alexander McHarg
McHarg & Selkirk
c. 1815–1849
Albany, N.Y.
(24, 50, 106)

John K. McIlvaine
(McIlWaine ?)
c. 1823–1837
Philadelphia, Pa.
(10)

James McIntire
c. 1840
Philadelphia, Pa.
(10, 37, 90, 106)

Murdo McIvor
c. 1844
Rochester, N.Y.
(24)

J. R. McKay
c. 1837
New York, N.Y.
(18)

Henry McKeen
c. 1823–1850
Philadelphia, Pa.
(10, 38, 39, 106)

James McKeever
c. 1829–1850
Philadelphia, Pa.
(10)

Edward McKinley
c. 1830–1837
Philadelphia, Pa.
(10)

Daniel J. McLean
c. 1850
Philadelphia, Pa.
(10)

O. P. McLean
c. 1840
Columbus, Ga.
(21)

William S. McLean
c. 1845–1850
Philadelphia, Pa.
(10)

James McLure
McLure & Fuselli
McLure & Valenti
c. 1840–1881
Bowling Green, Ky.
(63)

John McManus
c. 1840
Philadelphia, Pa.
(10)

Michael McManus
c. 1839
New York, N.Y.
(18)

Hugh A. McMasters
c. 1839–1850
Philadelphia, Pa.
(10)

James McMinn
c. 1846–1850
Philadelphia, Pa.
(10)

Edward McMullen
c. 1846–1848
Philadelphia, Pa.
(10)

John McMullin
(McMullen ?) (IM)
c. 1765–1843
Philadelphia, Pa.
(10, 11, 37, 38, 39, 50,
55, 59, 90, 106)

E. McNeil
c. 1813–1839
Binghamton, N.Y.
Troy, N.Y.
(24, 39, 106)

William McNeir
c. 1835–1848
Philadelphia, Pa.
(10)

Ezra McNutt
c. 1848
Philadelphia, Pa.
(10)

William McParlin
(WMcP)
c. 1803–1850
Annapolis, Md.
(38, 39, 55, 93, 106)

John McPherson
c. 1846–1850
Philadelphia, Pa.
(10)

Robert McPherson
c. 1828–1850
Philadelphia, Pa.
(10, 37, 90, 106)

William McQuilkin
c. 1845–1853
Philadelphia, Pa.
(123)

Solomon McQuivey
c. 1832–1841
Utica, N.Y.
(24, 25)

Francis McStocker
c. 1831–1850
Philadelphia, Pa.
(10)

Daniel Mead
c. 1845–1848
Louisville, Ky.
(63, 127)

Edward Edmund
Mead
Mead, Adriance &
Co.
Mead & Adriance
c. 1831–1832
Ithaca, N.Y.
St. Louis, Mo.
(24, 38, 39, 106, 133)

John O. Mead
c. 1837–1850
Rogers & Mead
Filley, Mead &
Caldwell
Philadelphia, Pa.
(10, 86, 91)

Lewis Mears
c. 1848
Philadelphia, Pa.
(10)

Lewis J. Mears
c. 1839
Philadelphia, Pa.
(10)

John Mecke
c. 1837–1850
Philadelphia, Pa.
(10)

John Medenhall
c. 1841–1846
Philadelphia, Pa.
(10)

Andrew G. Medley
c. 1832–1850
Louisville, Ky.
(63, 127)

Benjamin F. Meek
J. F. & B. F. Meek
Meek & Milam
c. 1832–1901
Danville, Ky.
Frankfort, Ky.
Louisville, Ky.
(63)

Jonathan Fleming Meek
J. F. & B. F. Meek
J. F. Meek & Co.
Meek & Milam
c. 1837–1852
Frankfort, Ky.
Louisville, Ky.
(63)

Thomas J. Megear
c. 1830–1850
Philadelphia, Pa.
Wilmington, Del.
(10, 39, 60, 106)

F. Megonegal
c. 1841–1842
Philadelphia, Pa.
(10)

W. H. Megonegal
c. 1842
Philadelphia, Pa.
(10)

John Mendenhall
c. 1841
Philadelphia, Pa.
(37)

——— Menkens
Menkens & Recordon
c. 1842
St. Louis, Mo.
(38, 123)

John Menzies
c. 1804–1850
Philadelphia, Pa.
(10)

John Menzies, Jr.
c. 1835–1850
Philadelphia, Pa.
(10)

James Meredith
Meredith & Johnston
J. Meredith & Son
c. 1827–before 1860
Winchester, Va.
(23)

Joseph P. Meredith
c. 1824–1848
Baltimore, Md.
(38, 39, 93, 106)

Perry Merkle (Parry Merkle ?)
c. 1840–1850
Philadelphia, Pa.
(10)

A. S. Mermod
Mermod & Jaccard
Mermod, Jaccard & King
c. 1845–1901
St. Louis, Mo.
(175)

James Merrifield
c. 1850
New York, N.Y.
(37)

Thomas V. F. Merrifield
Hall, Hewson & Merrifield
c. 1817–1845
Albany, N.Y.
(24, 25, 37, 50, 90, 106)

Marcus Merriman (M M)
before 1850
New Haven, Conn.
Cheshire, Conn.
(20, 37, 38, 39, 50, 90, 106)

Marcus Merriman, Jr.
Bradley & Merriman (B & M)
c. 1826–1847
New Haven, Conn.
(37, 50)

Reuben Merriman (R M)
before 1866
Cheshire, Conn.
Litchfield, Conn.
(20, 38, 39, 50, 90, 106)

——— Metten
Metten & Muller
c. 1839
St. Louis, Mo.
(123)

Godfrey Mexter (Mesker ?)
c. 1837–1840
Philadelphia, Pa.
(10)

Joseph Meyer
c. 1840
Canton, Ohio
(77, 106)

Matthew Meyer
c. 1858–1859
Utica, N.Y.
(25)

Maurice Meyer
c. 1849
Philadelphia, Pa.
(10)

Albert G. Meyers
c. 1837–1846
Philadelphia, Pa.
(10)

Adrian L. Michel
c. 1820–1858
Charleston, S.C.
(14)

John E.Michel
c. 1819–1844
Charleston, S.C.
(14)

William B. Middlebrook
c. 1842
Middletown, N.Y.
(24)

Thomas F. Midlam
c. 1850–1860
Utica, N.Y.
(24, 25)

P. Miedzielski
c. 1837
Columbus, Ga.
(21)

James Mikles
c. 1828–1841
New York, N.Y.
(18)

Benjamin Cave Milam
Meek & Milam
c. 1850–1852
Frankfort, Ky.
(63)

John Miler
19th century
Cincinnati, Ohio
(77)

Robert Miles
c. 1828–1850
Philadelphia, Pa.
(10)

John Miley
c. 1829–1850
Philadelphia, Pa.
(10)

R. P. Milks
c. 1840
Mansfield, Ohio
(77)

A. H. Miller
c. 1856–1862
Chicago, Ill.
(175)

D. B. Miller
c. 1850
Boston, Mass.
(38, 39, 106)

George Miller
c. 1829–1853
Philadelphia, Pa.
(10)

John Miller
c. 1840–1841
New York, N.Y.
(18)

Joseph Miller
c. 1837
Milledgeville, Ga.
(21)

Julius Miller
c. 1850
Prattsville, N.Y.
(24)

L. H. Miller
L. H. Miller & Co.
c. 1840
Baltimore, Md.
(39, 106)

Matthew Miller
c. 1805–1840
Charleston, S.C.
(14, 39, 106)

S. W. Miller
c. 1843
Philadelphia, Pa.
(10)

Thomas Miller
c. 1819–1841
Philadelphia, Pa.
(10)

William Miller
Ward & Miller
c. 1810–1847
Philadelphia, Pa.
(10, 37, 38, 39, 55, 90, 106)

William S. Miller
c. 1844–1848
Philadelphia, Pa.
(10)

George F. Mills
c. 1834–1837
New York, N.Y.
(18)

Gustavus Mindel
c. 1850
Philadelphia, Pa.
(10)

Joseph Miner
c. 1840
Burton, Ohio
(77)

Joseph B. Minton
Minton & Mayer
c. 1840–1847
Norfolk, Va.
(23, 106)

Charles Missing
c. 1847
Philadelphia, Pa.
(10)

Henry Mitchell
Gunn & Mitchell (?)
c. 1837–1841
New York, N.Y.
(18)

Henry Mitchell
c. 1844–1850
Philadelphia, Pa.
(10, 37, 38, 39, 106)

James Mitchell
c. 1845–1846
Philadelphia, Pa.
(10)

Samuel Philips Mitchell
Mitchell & Tyler
c. 1845–1866
Richmond, Va.
(23)

William Mitchell, Jr. (W M Jr.)
Taft & Mitchell
before 1852
Richmond, Va.
(23, 106)

James Mix, Jr.
c. 1846
Albany, N.Y.
(11, 24, 37, 50, 90, 106)

Vischer Mix
c. 1840–1849
Albany, N.Y.
(24, 32, 37, 50, 106)

William Mobbs
c. 1835–1838
Albany, N.Y.
Buffalo, N.Y.
(24, 37, 90, 106, 119)

Peter Moeller
c. 1849
Cleveland, Ohio
(123)

——— Moffat
Moffat & Chase
c. 1839
Buffalo, N.Y.
(24)

F. W. Moffat
c. 1853
Albany, N.Y.
(11, 50)

William Moffat
Larzalere & Moffat
c. 1832–1848
Buffalo, N.Y.
(24)

Benjamin Moffett
c. 1839
Philadelphia, Pa.
(10)

David Molan
c. 1835–1841
Troy, N.Y.
Albany, N.Y.
(24)

Daniel Monier
c. 1825–1850
Philadelphia, Pa.
(10)

E. P. Monroe
c. 1830–1840
Mogadore, Ohio
(77)

James F. Monroe
c. 1848
St. Louis, Mo.
(123)

Nathaniel Monroe
c. 1842–1850
Mobile, Ala.
Selma, Ala.
(170)

William R. Montcastle
c. 1844–1856
Warrenton, Va.
(23)

Benjamin Monteith
Monteith & Co (?)
c. 1847–1848
Philadelphia, Pa.
(10)

Charles Monteith
Monteith & Co. (?)
c. 1847–1848
Philadelphia, Pa.
(10)

John Monteith
J. & R. Monteith
c. 1814–1849
Baltimore, Md.
(106, 160)

Edwin Montgomery
c. 1850
Syracuse, N.Y.
(24)

Summerfield Montgomery
c. 1856–1872
Newberry, S.C.
(14)

Christian Adam Mood
before 1858
Charleston, S.C.
(14)

John Mood
Peter Mood & Son
Peter Mood & Sons
J. & P. Mood
c. 1816–1864
Charleston, S.C.
Athens, Ga.
(14, 21, 39, 50, 106)

Peter Mood, Jr.
Peter Mood & Sons
P. Mood & Co.
J. & P. Mood
c. 1819–1879
Charleston, S.C.
(14)

Thomas S. Mood
c. 1821–1871
Athens, Ga.
Charleston, S.C.
Orangeburg, S.C.
Sumter, S.C.
Columbia, S.C.
Augusta, Ga.
(14, 21)

Apollos Moore
c. 1842
Albany, N.Y.
(24)

E. C. Moore
c. 1850
New York, N.Y.
(37, 50)

Jared (John ?) L. Moore
Moore & Brewer
Jared L. Moore & Co.
c. 1825–1844
New York, N.Y.
(11, 18, 37, 38, 39, 106, 161, 162)

John C. Moore
(J C M)
Eoff & Moore
c. 1832–1844
New York, N.Y.
(18, 37, 38, 50, 90, 106)

John Moore
John Moore & Son
c. 1845–1869
New York, N.Y.
(171, 175)

Robert Moore
c. 1829–1840
Philadelphia, Pa.
(10)

Sylvanus Moore
c. 1847
Oxford, N.Y.
(24)

William V. Moore
c. 1850–1859
Mobile, Ala.
(170)

Thomas F. Moreland
c. 1850
Philadelphia, Pa.
(10, 37)

——— Morgan
c. 1860
Location unknown
(50, 106)

Aaron Morgan
c. 1842–1850
Philadelphia, Pa.
(10)

Arthur Morgan
c. 1849
Philadelphia, Pa.
(10)

Chauncey Morgan
c. 1850
Hartford, Conn.
(37)

Elijah Morgan
Sadd & Morgan
Morgan & Cook
Morgan & Kennedy
E. Morgan & Son
c. 1797–1857
Poughkeepsie, N.Y.
(24, 38, 39, 106, 133)

John Morgan
Morgan & Gibson
c. 1844–1848
Camden, N.J.
(10)

Lewis Morgan
c. 1847
Hartford, Conn.
(37)

William S. Morgan
E. Morgan & Son
c. 1832–1886
Poughkeepsie, N.Y.
(24, 133)

Alexander C. Morin
c. 1813–1850
Philadelphia, Pa.
(10)

Anthony Morin
c. 1849–1850
Philadelphia, Pa.
(10)

Angelo Morozzi
c. 1839–1842
Philadelphia, Pa.
(10)

Joseph Morrell
Castle & Morrell
c. 1840–1844
Buffalo, N.Y.
(24)

S. S. Morrill
c. 1850
Fulton, N.Y.
(24)

James Morris
c. 1844
Philadelphia, Pa.
(10)

John Morris
c. 1817–1842
Philadelphia, Pa.
(37, 50, 90, 106)

William Morris
c. 1837–1850
Philadelphia, Pa.
(10)

William Morris, Jr.
c. 1844–1850
Philadelphia, Pa.
(10)

William C. Morris
c. 1850
Penn Yan, N.Y.
(24)

C. R. Morrissey
c. 1837
Philadelphia, Pa.
(10)

George Morton
c. 1829–1850
Philadelphia, Pa.
(10)

Joseph Mosely
Gale & Mosely
(G & M)
c. 1828–1838
New York, N.Y.
(18, 37, 90, 106)

Barnet Moss
c. 1840
Warrenton, Va.
(23)

Isaac Nichols Moss
before 1840
Derby, Conn.
(20, 32, 37, 50, 90)

George Moton
c. 1849–1850
Philadelphia, Pa.
(10)

——— Mott
Mott Bros.
c. 1840
New York, N.Y.
(18)

E. L. Mottley
E. L. Mottley & Co.
c. 1857
Bowling Green, Ky.
(123)

Abel Moulton
Moulton & Davis
(M & D)
c. 1824–1840
Newburyport, Mass.
(19, 37, 38, 39, 50, 55, 90)

Edward Moulton
c. 1862–1907
Newburyport, Mass.
(50)

Edward S. Moulton
before 1855
Rochester, N.H.
(39, 106)

Joseph Moulton IV
c. 1830–1903
Newburyport, Mass.
(19, 37, 38, 39, 50, 55, 90, 106)

William Moulton IV
(W M)
before 1861
Newburyport, Mass.
(19, 37, 50, 55, 90)

William Moulton V
Moulton & Lunt
c. 1870
Newburyport, Mass.
(19, 50)

Samuel P. Mountain
c. 1842
Philadelphia, Pa.
(10)

John Hugan
Moyston
before 1844
Schenectady, N.Y.
(24)

——— Mudge
Mudge & Co.
c. 1848
New York, N.Y.
(37)

George A. Mudge
George A. Mudge
& Co.
c. 1858–1866
New York, N.Y.
(165, 175)

M. A. Mudge
c. 1837
Philadelphia, Pa.
(10)

Edward H. Mulford
James & Edward
Mulford
c. 1839–before 1843
Chicago, Ill.
(42, 43, 175)

James H. Mulford
James & Edward
Mulford
c. 1839–before 1843
Chicago, Illinois
(42, 43, 175)

John H. Mulford
Boyd & Mulford
Mulford & Wendell
c. 1832–1850
Albany, N.Y.
(24, 32, 37, 38, 39, 50,
106)

William Mulholland
c. 1837–1844
Philadelphia, Pa.
(10)

Charles Muller
19th century
Winnsboro, S.C.
(14)

Ferdinand Muller
c. 1844
New York, N.Y.
(37)

H. Mulligan
c. 1840
Philadelphia, Pa.
(38, 39, 106)

J. T. Munds
c. 1855–1859
Sumter, S.C.
(14)

Asa Munger
Munger & Benedict
A. Munger & Son (?)
c. 1800–1851
Ludlow, Mass.
Parish, N.Y.
Herkimer, N.Y.
Auburn, N.Y.
(24, 106, 133, 151)

Austin E. Munger
c. 1830–1892
Herkimer, N.Y.
Syracuse, N.Y.
(24, 133)

James E. Munger
c. 1839–after 1845
Ithaca, N.Y.
New York, N.Y.
(24, 133)

Sylvester Munger
Munger & Dodge
Munger & Pratt
c. 1816–1857
Onondaga, N.Y.
Clinton, N.Y.
Ithaca, N.Y.
Elmira, N.Y.
(24, 133)

James Munroe
before 1879
Barnstable, Mass.
(37, 38, 39, 50, 55, 90,
106)

Nathaniel Munroe
Munroe & Holman
c. 1815–before 1861
Norfolk, Va.
(Massachusetts ?)
Baltimore, Md.
(23, 38, 39, 55, 93,
106)

A. H. Munyan
c. 1848
Northampton, Mass.
(132)

James Murdock
Murdock & Andrews
James Murdock & Co.
Murdock & Collins
c. 1822–1850
Utica, N.Y.
(24, 25)

John B. Murphy
c. 1830–1845
Norfolk, Va.
Augusta, Ga.
(21, 23)

Robert E. Murphy
c. 1849–1850
Philadelphia, Pa.
(10)

William Murray
c. 1850
Louisville, Ky.
(63)

Perry Murtel
c. 1839
Philadelphia, Pa.
(10)

S. Musgrove
c. 1800–1850
Location unknown
(125)

Henry B. Myer
H. B. Myer & Co.
Myer & McClanahan
c. 1818–1848
Newburgh, N.Y.
Buffalo, N.Y.
(24, 39, 55, 106)

Albert G. Myers
Myers & Jacob
c. 1837–1847
Philadelphia, Pa.
Camden, N.J.
(10, 37, 90, 106)

Christalar Myers
c. 1844
Philadelphia, Pa.
(10)

J. P. Mylius
c. 1838
St. Louis, Mo.
(123)

Jacob Mytinger
c. 1827–1860
Newtown, Va.
Warrenton, Va.
(23)

William Nagel
c. 1865
Paducah, Ky.
(123)

George P. Nagle
c. 1823–1850
Philadelphia, Pa.
(10)

Martin Nangle
c. 1842
Philadelphia, Pa.
(10, 37)

William Nangle
c. 1833–1837
Philadelphia, Pa.
(10)

Daniel Neall (D N)
before 1846
Milford, Del.
(39, 60, 106)

Samuel Neely
c. 1842
Philadelphia, Pa.
(10)

George B. Neisser
c. 1829–1839
Philadelphia, Pa.
(10)

J. Nelson
R. & J. Nelson
c. 1850
Dunkirk, N.Y.
(24)

R. Nelson
R. & J. Nelson
c. 1850
Dunkirk, N.Y.
(24)

Richard W. Nelson
c. 1829–1837
Philadelphia, Pa.
(10)

James W. Newberry
c. 1819–1850
Philadelphia, Pa.
(10)

H. K. Newcomb
c. 1821–1850
Philadelphia, Pa.
(10)

Henry Newcomb
c. 1842–1843
Cooperstown, N.Y.
(24)

Norman Newell
c. 1844
Rochester, N.Y.
(24)

Luke F. Newland
Newland & Jones
c. 1824–1847
Albany, N.Y.
(24)

Edward G. Newlin
Warner & Newlin
c. 1848–1850
Philadelphia, Pa.
(10)

John Newman
c. 1833–1837
Philadelphia, Pa.
(10)

John A. Newman
Witham & Newman
c. 1833–1850
Philadelphia, Pa.
(10)

William Newth
c. 1832–1843
Little Falls, N.Y.
Schenectady, N.Y.
Utica, N.Y.
(24, 25)

——— Newton
Newton & Reed
c. 1850
Location unknown
(78)

William S. Nichol
(W S N)
c. 1785–1871
Newport, R.I.
(37, 38, 39, 50)

Casper Nicholas
c. 1837
Philadelphia, Pa.
(10)

——— Nichols
c. 1840
Albany, N.Y. (?)
(32, 50)

——— Nichols
Nichols & Salisbury
(N & S)
c. 1844–1846
Charleston, S.C.
(14, 106)

David B. Nichols
D. B. Nichols & Co.
c. 1815–before 1860
Savannah, Ga.
(21)

H. M. (?) Nichols
c. 1840–1850
Location unknown
(39, 106, 125)

Julian Nicolet
c. 1842–1848
St. Louis, Mo.
(123)

George Noble
c. 1846–1850
Philadelphia, Pa.
(10)

Alpheus (Alpherrs ?) Noe
c. 1850
Philadelphia, Pa.
(10, 37)

Beverly Noel
c. 1838–1839
Louisville, Ky.
(63)

Charles Nordmeyer
c. 1845–1850
Richmond, Va.
(23)

James S. Norman
c. 1840
Lincolnton, N.C.
(22)

Patrick Norris
c. 1844–1845
Philadelphia, Pa.
(10)

William B. North
(W B N)
William B. North & Co.
Mather & North
c. 1810–1838
New Haven, Conn.
New York, N.Y.
New Britain, Conn.
(37, 38, 39, 50, 55, 90, 106)

Elijah Northey
c. 1844–1850
Philadelphia, Pa.
(10)

Andrew Norton
before 1838
Goshen, Conn.
(20, 37, 39, 50, 90, 106)

Benjamin R. Norton
Hotchkiss & Norton
B. R. Norton & Co.
Norton & Seymour
Norton, Seymour & Co.
c. 1841–1850
Palmyra, N.Y.
Syracuse, N.Y.
(24, 39, 106)

Thomas Nowlan
Nowlan & Co.
c. 1848–1908
Petersburg, Va.
Richmond, Va.
(23)

John Oathret
c. 1843
Philadelphia, Pa.
(10)

James O'Brien
c. 1850
Philadelphia, Pa.
(10)

John O'Brien
c. 1844–1849
Philadelphia, Pa.
(10)

Patrick O'Brien
c. 1848–1850
Philadelphia, Pa.
(10)

Perry O'Daniel
c. 1837–1850
Philadelphia, Pa.
(10)

Andrew Oehler
c. 1858–1883
Indianapolis, Ind.
(70, 175)

Charles E. Oertelt
(O'Ertell ?)
c. 1830–1850
Philadelphia, Pa.
(10, 37, 90, 106)

Charles G. Oertelt
c. 1847–1849
Philadelphia, Pa.
(10, 106)

John O'Hara
c. 1844–1849
Philadelphia, Pa.
(10)

Franklin Olds
c. 1842
Providence, R.I.
(37)

D. F. Olendorf
c. 1849
Cooperstown, N.Y.
(24)

Frederick Oliver
c. 1840–1842
Buffalo, N.Y.
(24)

William G. Oliver
c. 1839–1848
Buffalo, N.Y.
(24)

Nathaniel Olmstead
N. Olmstead & Son
c. 1808–before 1860
Farmington, Conn.
New Haven, Conn.
(20, 37, 38, 39, 50, 55, 90, 106)

Henry Olwine
c. 1840–1850
Philadelphia, Pa.
(10)

Thomas O'Neil
c. 1837–1842
Philadelphia, Pa.
(10)

John O'Neil
c. 1841
Philadelphia, Pa.
(10)

——— Ordway
c. 1840
Location unknown
(78)

Henry Ormsby
c. 1839–1850
Philadelphia, Pa.
(10)

Thomas Orr
c. 1848–1849
Louisville, Ky.
(63, 127)

Robert Osborn
c. 1847
Rochester, N.Y.
(24)

Henry J. Osborne
c. 1848–1860
Milledgeville, Ga.
Augusta, Ga.
(21)

A. Osgood
c. 1857
Newburyport, Mass.
(19)

Clement Oskamp
c. 1849–1865
Cincinnati, Ohio
(227, 175)

Ralph Ostrom
c. 1830–1842
Troy, N.Y.
Schenectady, N.Y.
(24)

Henry Ott
H. & S. M. Ott (?)
c. 1837–1850
Harrisonburg, Va.
(23)

S. M. Ott
H. & S. M. Ott
c. 1845–1848
Harrisonburg, Va.
(23)

A. T. Otto
c. 1843
Chicago, Ill.
(43, 175)

——— Owen
Owen & Reed (Read ?)
c. 1840
Cincinnati, Ohio
(77)

Ann Owen
c. 1837
Philadelphia, Pa.
(10)

J. T. Owen
M. T. & J. T. Owen
c. 1859–1860
Abbeville, S.C.
(14)

Jesse Owen
J. Owen & Co.
c. 1841–1848
Philadelphia, Pa.
(10)

M. T. Owen
M. T. & J. T. Owen
Bailey & Owen
c. 1848–1860
Abbeville, S.C.
(14)

Samuel H. Owens
c. 1857
Anderson, S.C.
(14)

Samuel W. Owens
Owens & Currin
c. 1846–1850
Philadelphia, Pa.
(10)

William Owens
c. 1839–1860
Utica, N.Y.
(24)

F. W. Pachman
c. 1850–1865
Location unknown
(78)

William Pack
c. 1850–1860
Utica, N.Y.
(24, 25)

Jonathan Packard
Huntington & Packard
Packard & Brown
Packard & Scofield
c. 1811–1854
Springfield, Mass.
Albany, N.Y.
Rochester, N.Y.
(24, 100)

L. H. Packard
c. 1847
Potsdam, N.Y.
(24)

Lewis Pagaud
c. 1815–1846
Norfolk, Va.
Petersburg, Va.
(23)

Washington Paine
c. 1841–1850
Philadelphia, Pa.
(10)

Isaac Painter
c. 1837–1842
Philadelphia, Pa.
(10)

Isaac Painter, Jr.
c. 1845–1850
Philadelphia, Pa.
(10)

John S. Painter
c. 1835–1848
Philadelphia, Pa.
(10)

Abraham Palmer
Palmer & Owen (?)
c. 1849
Cincinnati, Ohio
(123)

E. H. P. Palmer
c. 1865
Richmond, Va.
(123)

James Palmer
Palmer & Hinsdale
Palmer & Clapp
Palmer & Batchelder
c. 1815–1850
New York, N.Y.
Boston, Mass.
(37, 90, 106)

John C. Palmer
Hampton & Palmer
Palmer & Ramsay
c. 1830–1850–before 1893
Salisbury, N.C.
Raleigh, N.C.
(22)

Thomas Palmer
c. 1845
Rochester, N.Y.
(24)

William H. Palmer
c. 1837–1840
Philadelphia, Pa.
(10)

John Park
c. 1848–before 1858
Louisville, Ky.
(63)

Isaac Parker
Parker & Co.
c. 1818–1850
Philadelphia, Pa.
(10)

T. E. Parker
c. 1840 (?)
Location unknown
(78)

William H. Parker
c. 1835–1843
New York, N.Y.
Brooklyn, N.Y.
(37, 90)

Nelson Parkes
c. 1846–1847
Utica, N.Y.
(25)

Joseph Parkins
c. 1837
Philadelphia, Pa.
(10)

A. Parks
c. 1845
Oswego, N.Y.
(24)

Frederick W. Parrot
(Perrot ?)
c. 1847–1850
Philadelphia, Pa.
(10)

Joseph Parrot
(Perrot ?)
c. 1835–1843
Philadelphia, Pa.
(10)

Francis Parry
c. 1846–1850
Philadelphia, Pa.
(10, 37)

Thomas Parry
c. 1848–1850
Philadelphia, Pa.
(10)

Henry R. Parsons
c. 1840–1850
Philadelphia, Pa.
(10)

T. A. Patchin
c. 1846
Syracuse, N.Y.
(24)

A. Paton
c. 1850
Boston, Mass.
(11, 37, 50, 106)

James Patterson (I P)
c. 1837–1848
Philadelphia, Pa.
(10)

Wilson M. Patterson
c. 1840
Mansfield, Ohio
(77)

——— Paul
Fairbanks & Paul
c. 1857
Newburyport, Mass.
(19)

Philip Paul
S. & P. Paul
c. 1835–1840
Philadelphia, Pa.
(10)

Simon Paul
S. & P. Paul
c. 1839–1840
Philadelphia, Pa.
(10)

Chauncey S. Payne
c. 1815–before 1877
Detroit, Mich.
(136)

Nathaniel Prentiss
Peabody
c. 1830–1870–
before 1883
Bennettsville, S.C.
(14)

Thomas Peacock
c. 1845–1879
Lancaster, Ky.
Louisville, Ky.
(63)

Daniel Peake
c. 1837–1840
Philadelphia, Pa.
(10)

Daniel Peake, Jr.
c. 1839–1850
Philadelphia, Pa.
(10)

Edward Peake
c. 1829–1850
Philadelphia, Pa.
(10)

Thomas Peake
c. 1850
Philadelphia, Pa.
(10)

Edward Pear (E P)
Pear & Bacall
c. 1836–1850
Boston, Mass.
(11, 37, 38, 39, 50, 55,
90)

Hamett A. Pearce
Kersey & Pearce
c. 1845–1850
Richmond, Va.
(23)

J. G. Pearson
c. 1849
Newburyport, Mass.
(19)

George Peck, Jr.
c. 1850
New York, N.Y.
(37)

Lawrence M. Peck
c. 1837
Philadelphia, Pa.
(10, 37, 90, 106)

James Peckham
Peckham & George
c. 1830–1847
Charleston, S.C.
(14)

Allen T. Peebles
c. 1837–1857
Charlottesville, Va.
Staunton, Va.
Leesburg, Va.
Richmond, Va.
(23)

William S. Peirce
c. 1841
Philadelphia, Pa.
(10)

H. G. Peirson
c. 1890
Troy, N.Y.
(263, 175)

William Pelham
c. 1841
Fishkill, N.Y.
(24)

Emmett (Emmet ?)
T. Pell
c. 1824–1841
New York, N.Y.
(18, 39, 106)

Maltby Pelletreau
Pelletreau, Bennet &
Cooke
Clark & Pelletreau
Pelletreau, Bennet &
Co.
c. 1815–1840
Charleston, S.C.
New York, N.Y.
(18, 37, 39, 90, 106)

William Smith
Pelletreau (W S P)
Pelletreau &
Van Wyck
Pelletreau & Upson
(P & U)
Pelletreau & Richards
(Richards &
Pelletreau ?)
c. 1815–before 1842
Southampton, N.Y.
(24, 25, 38, 39, 50, 55,
90, 106)

James S. Pemberton
c. 1842
Albany, N.Y.
(24)

William F. Pendrell
(Pendren ?)
c. 1843–1846
Philadelphia, Pa.
(10, 37)

Charles D. Pennell
c. 1847
Providence, R.I.
(37)

A. C. Pennington
c. 1849
Wellsburg, W. Va.
(23)

H. S. Pepper
c. 1837
Philadelphia, Pa.
(10)

Henry J. Pepper
Henry J. Pepper & Son
c. 1828–1850
Philadelphia, Pa.
(10, 37, 38, 39, 60, 90, 106)

Joel S. Pepper
c. 1850
Philadelphia, Pa.
(10)

S. W. Pepper
c. 1848–1850
Philadelphia, Pa.
(10)

Thomas Percival
c. 1840
Albany, N.Y.
(24)

Jacob Perkins
c. 1766–1849
Newburyport, Mass.
(37, 38, 39, 50)

Jacob Perkins (I P)
before 1841
Philadelphia, Pa.
(37, 38, 39, 50, 55, 90, 106)

W. D. Perrine
c. 1850
Lyons, N.Y.
(24)

Thomas Perry
c. 1828–1865
Westerly, R.I.
(50, 90, 106)

Jefferson Peterman
Boss & Peterman
c. 1841
Rochester, N.Y.
(24)

William Peterman
c. 1837
Philadelphia, Pa.
(10)

James Peters
J. Peters & Co.
c. 1821–1850
Philadelphia, Pa.
(10, 37, 39, 90, 106)

William S. Peters
c. 1833–1850
Philadelphia, Pa.
(10)

Peter Pezant
c. 1815–before 1843
Charleston, S.C.
(14)

F. Pfeiffer
c. 1839–1847
St. Louis, Mo.
(123)

Hermann Pfluefer
c. 1849–1850
Philadelphia, Pa.
(10)

Samuel F. Phelps
c. 1834–1838
Troy, N.Y.
(24)

James Philip
c. 1850
Poughkeepsie, N.Y.
(134)

Edward Philley
c. 1846
Philadelphia, Pa.
(10)

James Phillips
c. 1839
Philadelphia, Pa.
(10)

John W. Phillips
(J W P)
c. 1842–1850
Philadelphia, Pa.
(10)

Augustus Philobad
(Philibert ?)
c. 1839
St. Louis, Mo.
(123)

William H. C. Philpot
c. 1846–1849
Philadelphia, Pa.
(10, 37)

William Phyfe
Eoff & Phyfe (E & P)
c. 1830–1850
Boston, Mass.
New York, N.Y.
(18, 37, 90, 106)

W. A. Piatt
W. A. Piatt & Co.
c. 1840–1847
Columbus, Ohio
(77)

Joseph Pickering
c. 1816–1846
Philadelphia, Pa.
(10)

J. L. Pickrell
c. 1851
Greenville, S.C.
(14)

George P. Pilling
c. 1845
Philadelphia, Pa.
(10, 37)

Charles Pine
c. 1844–1850
Philadelphia, Pa.
(10)

Edwin Pine
c. 1850
Philadelphia, Pa.
(10)

H. S. Pine
c. 1849
Philadelphia, Pa.
(10)

Edward Pink
c. 1843
Philadelphia, Pa.
(10)

George Pinney
c. 1849
Philadelphia, Pa.
(10)

E. J. Pinson
c. 1856
Greenville, S.C.
(14)

Jean Baptiste Piquet
(Piquette ?)
c. 1809–1851
Detroit, Mich.
(136)

Joseph N. Piquet
c. 1835–1850
Philadelphia, Pa.
(10)

Charles Piquette
c. 1813–1859
Detroit, Mich.
(136)

Jean Baptiste Piquette
(Piquet ?)
c. 1809–1851
Detroit, Mich.
(136)

John O. Pitkin
J. O. & W. Pitkin
East Hartford, Conn.
Vicksburg, Tenn.
(20, 38, 39, 50, 90, 106)

Joseph F. Pitkin
c. 1844–1848
Mather & Pitkin
Buffalo, N.Y.
(24)

Walter M. Pitkin
Pitkin & Norton
(Norton & Pitkin ?)
J. O. & W. Pitkin
c. 1825–before 1885
East Hartford, Conn.
Vicksburg, Tenn.
(20, 37, 38, 39, 50, 55, 90, 106)

Benjamin Pitman
c. 1810–1840
Providence, R.I.
(38, 39, 50, 55, 90, 106)

Daniel Place
c. 1837–1845
Rochester, N.Y.
Ithaca, N.Y.
(24, 100, 106)

Edward Plain
c. 1836–1850
New York, N.Y.
Philadelphia, Pa.
(10, 37, 90, 106)

James Platt
c. 1834–1837
New York, N.Y.
(18, 37, 90, 106)

John Platt
c. 1843
Philadelphia, Pa.
(10)

John Frederick Plint
c. 1839
Philadelphia, Pa.
(10)

P. S. Plowman
c. 1838
Wheeling, W.Va.
(23)

William A. Poindexter
W. Poindexter & Son (?)
c. 1820–1859
Lexington, Ky.
(63)

D. R. Poland
c. 1837
Philadelphia, Pa.
(10)

John Polhemus (Polhamus ?)
c. 1833–1837–before 1876
New York, N.Y.
(11, 37, 50, 90, 106)

Albert Isaac Watts Polk
Campbell & Polk
c. 1850–before 1861
Winchester, Va.
(23)

Hyman Pollock
c. 1841–1850
Philadelphia, Pa.
(10)

David L. Pool
before 1861
Philadelphia, Pa.
Salisbury, N.C.
(22)

James Pool
c. 1837–1844
Philadelphia, Pa.
(10)

James M. Pool
c. 1846
Washington, N.C.
(22)

Thomas Pool
c. 1848–1850
Philadelphia, Pa.
(10)

J. Poole
c. 1850
Leesburg, Va.
(23)

William Poole (W P)
before 1846
Wilmington, Del.
(39, 60, 106)

William W. Poole
c. 1828–1843
Philadelphia, Pa.
(10)

Nathaniel C. Poor
before 1895
Boston, Mass.
(37, 50, 90, 106)

George E. Porter
c. 1834–1841
Utica, N.Y.
Syracuse, N.Y.
(24, 25)

John Porter
c. 1842
Philadelphia, Pa.
(10)

Joseph S. Porter
Barton & Porter
c. 1805–1849
Utica, N.Y.
(24, 25, 39, 50, 106)

Frederick J. Posey
c. 1820–1842
Hagerstown, Md.
Shepherdstown, W. Va.
(23, 39, 55, 93, 106)

John B. Powell
c. 1850
Philadelphia, Pa.
(10)

W. S. Powell
c. 1839
Honeoye Falls, N.Y.
(24)

Charles Powelson
c. 1841
Albany, N.Y.
(24)

Henry Power
c. 1822–1867
Poughkeepsie, N.Y.
(134)

Daniel Pratt
Munger & Pratt
c. 1832–1839
Ithaca, N.Y.
(24)

George W. Pratt
Pratt & Lockwood
c. 1839–1845
Newburgh, N.Y.
(24)

Nathan Pratt
before 1842
Essex, Conn.
(20, 32, 37, 38, 39, 50, 55, 90, 106)

Alonzo T. Prentice
c. 1826–1850
Lockport, N.Y.
(24)

John H. Prentiss
c. 1838
Little Falls, N.Y.
(24, 25)

Stephen L. Preston
c. 1849
Newburgh, N.Y.
(24, 25, 106)

Edward Prevear
Prevear & Harrington
c. 1841–1842
Amherst, Mass.
(132)

John N. Prior
Warren Prior & Son
after 1887
Fayetteville, N.C.
(22)

Warren Prior
Campbell & Prior
Warren Prior & Son
c. 1833–1887–before 1909
Fayetteville, N.C.
Northfield, Mass.
(22)

Jonathan H. Pugh
c. 1845–1850
Philadelphia, Pa.
(10)

Richard Pugh
c. 1845
Cleveland, Ohio
(69)

Samuel B. Purple
Foster & Purple
c. 1844–1857
Columbus, Ga.
(21)

William Purse
before 1844
Charleston, S.C.
(14, 39, 106)

John S. Putnam
Wright & Putnam
c. 1836–1848
Buffalo, N.Y.
(24)

Benjamin Pyle II
Selph & Pyle
c. 1837–1841
Fayetteville, N.C.
(22)

George Pyle
c. 1850
Philadelphia, Pa.
(10)

Lewis Quandale
c. 1813–1845
Philadelphia, Pa.
(10)

J. V. D. Quereau
(Quercau ?)
c. 1841–1845
Philadelphia, Pa.
(10)

Joseph Quinn
c. 1849–1850
Philadelphia, Pa.
(10)

F. F. Quintard
c. 1843
New York, N.Y.
(37)

James Rabbeth
(Rabeth ?)
c. 1836–1838
New York, N.Y.
(37, 90, 106)

George Rackett
Clark, Rackett & Co.
c. 1840–1852
Augusta, Ga.
(21)

Thomas W. Radcliffe
Glaze & Radcliffe
Thomas W. Radcliffe & Co.
Radcliffe & Guignard
c. 1827–1870
Columbia, S.C.
Camden, S.C.
(14)

David Rait
c. 1835–1850
New York, N.Y.
(37, 90, 106)

Robert Rait
c. 1830–1855
New York, N.Y.
(18, 37, 38, 39, 55, 90, 161, 162)

William Ralston
c. 1840–1850
Ashland, Ohio
(77)

John Rambo
c. 1837
Philadelphia, Pa.
(10)

Peter Rambo
c. 1837–1841
Philadelphia, Pa.
(10)

William Rambo
c. 1837
Philadelphia, Pa.
(10)

John Ramp
c. 1848–1859
Louisville, Ky.
(63)

William Ramp
c. 1848–1859
Louisville, Ky.
(63)

Walter J. Ramsay
W. J. Ramsay & Co.
Ramsay & Beckwith
Palmer & Ramsay
c. 1826–1856
Raleigh, N.C.
New Bern, N.C.
(22)

C. A. Rand
c. 1846
Haverstraw, N.Y.
(24)

James H. Randolph
c. 1827–1857
Greenville, S.C.
(14)

Asa Ransom
c. 1837
Buffalo, N.Y.
(24)

William D. Rapp
c. 1828–1850
Philadelphia, Pa.
(10, 39, 106)

Frederick Rath
c. 1840
New York, N.Y.
(18, 39, 106)

Benjamin Rawls
c. 1816–1866
Columbia, S.C.
(14)

Newton Rawson
c. 1850–1854
Utica, N.Y.
(25)

Henry Raymond
c. 1833–1840
Albany, N.Y.
(24)

——— Read (Reed ?)
Read & Owen (?)
c. 1840
Cincinnati, Ohio
(77)

John Read
c. 1835–1848
Buffalo, N.Y.
(24)

William H. J. Read
c. 1831–1850
Philadelphia, Pa.
(10)

——— Reade
Gibney & Reade
c. 1847
New York, N.Y.
(37)

John Reasnors
c. 1841
Rochester, N.Y.
(24)

G. F. Reber
c. 1858–1883
Indianapolis, Ind.
(70, 175)

——— Recordon
Menckens & Recordon
c. 1838–1842
St. Louis, Mo.
(38, 123)

Jacob Redifer
c. 1844–1850
Philadelphia, Pa.
(10)

Henry H. Redman
Redman & Potter
before 1840
Norfolk, Va.
(23)

G. Washington Reed
c. 1839–1850
Philadelphia, Pa.
(10)

Isaac Reed
Isaac Reed & Son
(IR & S)
c. 1820–1850
Philadelphia, Pa.
(10)

John W. Reed
Isaac Reed & Son (?)
c. 1846–1847
Philadelphia, Pa.
(10)

Joseph Reed
c. 1847
St. Louis, Mo.
(123)

Osmon Reed
Reed & Co.
Osmon Reed & Co.
c. 1831–1850
Philadelphia, Pa.
(10, 37, 38, 39, 50, 55, 90, 106)

Robert W. Reed
c. 1837–1852
Winchester, Va.
Baltimore, Md.
(23)

Stephen Reed
c. 1846–1850
Philadelphia, Pa.
(10, 37, 38, 39, 106)

Elisha Reed
c. 1836–1837
Columbus, Ga.
(21)

Templeton Reed
T. &. E. Reed
c. 1813–1851
Milledgeville, Ga.
Columbus, Ga.
(21)

Abner Reeder
before 1841
Philadelphia, Pa.
Trenton, N.J.
(10, 11, 37, 38, 39, 50, 55, 90, 106)

P. L. Reese
c. 1857–1897
Mount Sterling, Ky.
(123)

Charles Reeve
Charles Reeve & Co.
c. 1826–1840
Newburgh, N.Y.
(24)

Abner Reeves
c. 1832–1838
Louisville, Ky.
(63)

J. F. Reeves
c. 1836–1840
Baltimore, Md.
(39, 106)

James Reeves
c. 1837–1838
New York, N.Y.
(18, 106)

Joseph James Reeves
c. 1831–1837
New York, N.Y.
(18)

Joseph Reibley (Rively ?)
c. 1845–1846
Philadelphia, Pa.
(10)

John Reinhardt
c. 1839
Buffalo, N.Y.
(24)

J. H. Relay
J. H. & R. J. Relay
c. 1848
Albany, N.Y.
(24)

William Renville
c. 1837
New York, N.Y.
(18)

Henry Reymond
c. 1842
St. Louis, Mo.
(123)

George W. Reynolds
c. 1837–1843
Philadelphia, Pa.
(10)

Henry A. Reynolds
c. 1847
Rochester, N.Y.
(24)

Theodore J. Reynolds
c. 1837
New York, N.Y.
(18)

Theodore J. Reynolds
c. 1850–1851
Utica, N.Y.
(24, 25)

——— Rhodes
c. 1837
Cincinnati, Ohio
(77)

——— Rice
Rice & Burnett
c. 1860
Cleveland, Ohio
(78)

A. W. Rice
c. 1850
Hamilton, N.Y.
(24)

Joseph T. Rice (JTR)
c. 1813–1850
Albany, N.Y.
(11, 24, 37, 38, 39, 50, 55, 106)

William C. Rice
c. 1835–1850
Philadelphia, Pa.
(10)

William H. Rice
c. 1839
Albany, N.Y.
(24)

Obadiah Rich
Ward & Rich
c. 1832–1850
Boston, Mass.
(11, 37, 38, 39, 50, 55, 90, 106)

George Richards
c. 1829–1840
Philadelphia, Pa.
(10)

Hervey M. Richards
c. 1839–1842
Philadelphia, Pa.
(10)

William Richards
c. 1842–1843
Utica, N.Y.
(24, 25)

George Richardson
c. 1845–1848
Louisville, Ky.
(63)

James Richardson
c. 1840–1850
Mansfield, Ohio
(77)

Martin Richardson
c. 1837–1839
Little Falls, N.Y.
(24)

Isaac Richman
c. 1850
Philadelphia, Pa.
(10)

William Richmond
c. 1835–1848
Philadelphia, Pa.
(10)

Charles William Richter
c. 1842–1867
Madison, Ga.
(21)

——— Rickards
Rickards & Snyder
c. 1842
Philadelphia, Pa.
(10)

John Rickards (Richards ?)
c. 1841–1850
Philadelphia, Pa.
(10)

Nutter Rickards (Rickett ?)
c. 1829–1850
Philadelphia, Pa.
(10)

William Rickards
William Rickards & Son
c. 1841–1850
Philadelphia, Pa.
(10)

Israel Ricksecker
c. 1834–1872
Dover, Ohio
(77)

John Ridgway
before 1851
Boston, Mass.
Groton, Mass.
Worcester, Mass.
(37, 38, 39, 50, 55, 90, 95, 106)

John Ridgway, Jr.
c. 1813–1869
Boston, Mass.
(50)

Benjamin McKenny Riggs
before 1839
Paris, Ky.
(39, 63, 106, 127)

David H. Riggs
c. 1840
Paris, Ky.
(63, 127)

George W. Riggs (GR)
Riggs & Griffith (R & G)
before 1864
Baltimore, Md.
Georgetown, D.C.
Washington, D.C.
(55, 93, 106, 127)

William H. C. Riggs
c. 1819–1850
Philadelphia, Pa.
(10)

Albert M. Rihl
c. 1849–1850
Philadelphia, Pa.
(10)

——— Rikeman
Horton & Rikeman
c. 1850–1856
Savannah, Ga.
(21)

Bernard Riley
c. 1845–1850
Philadelphia, Pa.
(10, 37)

Conrad Riley
c. 1837–1841
Philadelphia, Pa.
(10)

Amos Robbins
c. 1846–1849
Philadelphia, Pa.
(10)

E. Robbins
c. 1846–1848
Camden, N.J.
(10)

Elisha Robbins
c. 1831–1843
Philadelphia, Pa.
(10, 37, 90, 106)

George Robbins
c. 1833–1850
Philadelphia, Pa.
(10)

Jeremiah Robbins (Robins ?)
c. 1847–1850
Philadelphia, Pa.
(10)

Daniel F. Roberts
Daniel F. Roberts & Co.
c. 1840–1850
Philadelphia, Pa.
(10)

George Roberts
c. 1835–1843
Philadelphia, Pa.
(10)

John Roberts
c. 1841–1849
Philadelphia, Pa.
(10)

L. D. Roberts
Chapell & Roberts
c. 1850
Hartford, Conn.
(37, 78)

N. H. Roberts
c. 1848–1850
Philadelphia, Pa.
(10)

Samuel Roberts
c. 1833–1850
Fredericksburg, Va.
(23)

Thomas Roberts
c. 1842
Philadelphia, Pa.
(10)

Alexander Robinson
A. Robinson & Co.
c. 1839–1842
Charlottesville, Va.
Staunton, Va.
(23)

Andrew Robinson
Robinson & Dixon
c. 1845–1846
Portsmouth, Va.
(23)

Benjamin Robinson
c. 1818–1844
Philadelphia, Pa.
(10, 37, 90, 106)

G. E. Robinson
c. 1850
Nashua, N.H.
(78)

Hannah Robinson
c. 1865
Wilmington, Del.
(39, 60, 106)

Israel Robinson
c. 1840
Philadelphia, Pa.
(37, 90, 106)

John F. Robinson
before 1867
Wilmington, Del.
(39, 60)

William Robinson
c. 1840–1844
Portsmouth, Va.
Baltimore, Md.
(23)

William D. Robinson
c. 1846–1850
Philadelphia, Pa.
(10)

William F. Robinson
c. 1850
Wilmington, Del.
(60)

William Rochead
c. 1833–1844
Albany, N.Y.
(24)

William B. Rock
c. 1850
Philadelphia, Pa.
(10, 37)

——— Rockwell
c. 1839
Bridgeport, Conn. (?)
(32, 50)

Edward Rockwell
Edward & Samuel Rockwell
c. 1807–1841
New York, N.Y.
(18, 37, 38, 39, 55, 90, 106, 161, 162)

Samuel D. Rockwell
Edward & Samuel Rockwell
c. 1815–1841
New York, N.Y.
(18, 38, 39, 106)

——— Rogers
Leonard & Rogers
c. 1827–1840
New York, N.Y.
(18, 37, 39, 106)

——— Rogers
Rogers & Wendt
c. 1850
Boston, Mass.
(11, 37, 50, 106)

Asa Rogers
Church & Rogers
Rogers & Cole
William Rogers & Co.
c. 1840–1858
Hartford, Conn.
(86, 97)

Augustus Rogers
c. 1840–1850
Boston, Mass.
(11, 37, 50, 90, 106)

Henry Rogers
c. 1838–1850
Troy, N.Y.
(24)

James M. Rogers
c. 1836–1840
Troy, N.Y.
(24)

Simeon Rogers
William Rogers & Co.
c. 1845
Hartford, Conn.
(86, 97)

S. B. Rogers
c. 1840–1855
Charleston, S.C.
(14)

William Rogers
Church & Rogers
Rogers & Cole
Rogers & Mead
Wm. Rogers & Co.
c. 1823–1873
Hartford, Conn.
(20, 37, 39, 50, 55, 86, 90, 97, 106)

William Rollinson
(Rollingson ?)
before 1842
New York, N.Y.
(37, 50, 90, 106)

——— Root
Root & Chaffee
c. 1826–1880
Hartford, Conn.
(125)

Charles Boudinot Root
before 1903
Raleigh, N.C.
(39, 106)

W. M. Root
c. 1840
Pittsfield, Mass.
(39)

W. N. Root
W. N. Root & Brother
c. 1850
New Haven, Conn.
(39, 106)

William E. Rose
c. 1844
New York, N.Y.
(37)

William Ross
c. 1838–1839
Troy, N.Y.
(24)

Nelson Roth
c. 1837–1853
Utica, N.Y.
(24, 25, 39, 106)

Volkert Roth
c. 1846–1847
Utica, N.Y.
(24, 25)

Sidney Rouse
c. 1849–1850
Rochester, N.Y.
(24, 100, 106)

William Madison
Rouse
before 1888
Charleston, S.C.
(14, 39, 106)

——— Rowan
Holmes & Rowan
c. 1847–1850
Philadelphia, Pa.
(10)

David S. Rowland
c. 1831–1839
Utica, N.Y.
(24, 25)

Harvey Royce
c. 1834–1850
Morrisville, N.Y.
(24)

J. Rudd
J. Rudd & Co.
c. 1831–1841
New York, N.Y.
(18, 39, 106)

William Rudell
c. 1844–1848
Buffalo, N.Y.
(24)

Alexander Rumrill, Jr.
c. 1840
New York, N.Y.
(18)

R. Rumrill
c. 1839
Chicago, Ill.
(42, 175)

Charles Rumsey
before 1841
Salem, N.J.
(106, 117)

Arthur Russell
19th Century
Bardstown, Ky.
(63)

George Russell
c. 1831–1850
Philadelphia, Pa.
(10, 50, 106)

Thomas Russell
c. 1855–1856
Charleston, S.C.
Columbia, S.C.
(14)

William Russell
William Russell
& Son (?)
c. 1840–1865 (?)
Bardstown, Ky.
(63)

William A. Russell
c. 1842–1843
Utica, N.Y.
(24, 25)

Peter Rutter
c. 1837–1850
Philadelphia, Pa.
(10)

Low Ryerson
before 1855
Manchester, N.J.
York, Pa.
(37, 38, 39, 50, 55, 90)

Philip Benjamin
Sadtler
Sadtler & Pfaltz
Philip Sadtler & Son
before 1860
Baltimore, Md.
(11, 37, 38, 39, 50, 55, 90, 93, 106)

H. Sage
c. 1840
Location unknown
(78)

William P. Sage
c. 1833–1852
Athens, Ga.
(21)

Charles Grandison
St. John
c. 1811–1846
Macon, Ga.
(21)

Henry Salisbury
(Salsbury ?)
Salisbury & Co.
c. 1830–1838
New York, N.Y.
(18, 37, 39, 50, 106)

Owen Salisbury
c. 1847
Providence, R.I.
(37)

William H. Salmon
c. 1830–1850
Cazenovia, N.Y.
Morrisville, N.Y.
Troy, N.Y.
(24)

A. Sanborn
c. 1850
Lowell, Mass.
(37, 38, 39, 50, 106)

Jacob Sandbuhler
(Jacobi
Cembuhler ?)
c. 1854–1860
Utica, N.Y.
(25)

Charles Sanders
c. 1833–1845
Schenectady, N.Y.
(24)

Louis Sandoz
c. 1845
Philadelphia, Pa.
(10)

D. Sands
c. 1840
Location unknown
(78)

Abel Sanford
before 1843
Hamilton, N.Y.
(24)

Edward N. Sanford
c. 1855–1859
Utica, N.Y.
(25)

Frederick Sanford
(Sandford ?)
Easton & Sanford
(E & S)
c. 1828–1838–before 1890
Nantucket, Island, Mass.
(17, 37, 38, 39, 50, 90, 106)

Judson Sanford
c. 1843–1844
Hamilton, N.Y.
(24)

Ensign Sargeant
before 1843
Hartford, Conn.
Mansfield Depot, Conn.
Boston, Mass.
(37, 38, 39, 50, 55, 90, 106)

Jacob Sargeant
c. 1785–1838
Hartford, Conn.
Mansfield Depot, Conn.
Springfield, Mass.
(7, 20, 37, 38, 39, 50, 55, 90, 106, 133, 180)

A. G. Sargent
c. 1830–1840
Milan, Ohio
(77)

William Savil
(Saville ?)
c. 1820–1837
Philadelphia, Pa.
(10)

Silas W. Sawin (S S)
c. 1825–1838
New York, N.Y.
(37, 38, 90, 106)

H. L. Sawyer
c. 1840
New York, N.Y.
Hartford, Conn.
(37, 38, 39, 50, 55, 90, 106)

David A. (E. ?) Sayre
before 1870
Lexington, Ky.
(63, 127)

John Sayre
Sayre & Richards
(S & R)
before 1852
New York, N.Y.
(7, 10, 11, 18, 37, 38, 39, 90, 161)

L. Sayre
19th century
Lexington, Ky.
(63, 127)

M. Schafer
c. 1840
Location unknown
(78)

Bernard Scheer
c. 1855
Charleston, S.C.
(14)

John C. Scheer
Bonsall & Scheer
Dubosq & Scheer
c. 1835–1850
Philadelphia, Pa.
(10, 37)

Frederick Schern
c. 1848–1850
Philadelphia, Pa.
(10, 37)

Lewis Scherr
c. 1843–1850
Philadelphia, Pa.
(10)

John G. Schmid
c. 1850
Philadelphia, Pa.
(10)

Christian Schmid
(Smith ?)
c. 1819–1840
New Philadelphia, Ohio
(77)

John Schmitt
(Smith ?)
c. 1846–1850
Philadelphia, Pa.
(10, 37)

——— Schoolfield
c. 1855
Location unknown
(106)

F. V. Schrader
F. V. Schrader & Co.
c. 1837
Philadelphia, Pa.
(10)

Andrew B. Schreuder
(Schroeder?)
Hotchkiss & Schreuder
(H & S)
c. 1850
Utica, N.Y.
Syracuse, N.Y.
(24, 25)

A. Schroeder
Schroeder & Wangelin
c. 1844–1850
Cleveland, Ohio
(123)

J. Schuller
c. 1845–1846
Philadelphia, Pa.
(10)

Gottlieb Schultz
(Shultz ?)
c. 1821–1844
Philadelphia, Pa.
(10)

John G. Schwing
before 1868
Louisville, Ky.
(63, 127)

Charles Scott
c. 1839
Penn Yan, N.Y.
(24)

David Scott
before 1875
Greensboro, N.C.
(22)

John Scott
c. 1838–1847
St. Louis, Mo.
(123)

John B. Scott
c. 1820–1850
New York, N.Y.
(37, 38, 39, 50, 106)

William D. Scott
Scott & Kitts
W. D. Scott & Co.
c. 1841–1849
Louisville, Ky.
(63)

——— Scovil
Scovil & Kinsey (?)
Scovil & Co.
c. 1830–1840
Cincinnati, Ohio
(39, 55, 106)

Edward Scranton
c. 1847
Philadelphia, Pa.
(10)

Andrew Scudder
c. 1850–1851
Utica, N.Y.
(24, 25)

Egbert Scudder
c. 1827–1837
New York, N.Y.
(18)

Charles Seager
c. 1840–1841
Utica, N.Y.
(24, 25)

J. W. Sealey
(Suley ?)
c. 1846–1849
Charleston, S.C.
(14)

J. M. Seamans
c. 1848–1850
Troy, N.Y.
(24)

Joseph Searl
c. 1840–1850
Philadelphia, Pa.
(10)

Samuel Sears
c. 1839–1850
Philadelphia, Pa.
(10)

John Seccombe
c. 1850
Cobleskill, N.Y.
(24)

John D. Seckle
c. 1837–1850
Philadelphia, Pa.
(10)

Margaret Seddinger
c. 1846
Philadelphia, Pa.
(10)

Matthias Seddinger
c. 1812–1850
Philadelphia, Pa.
(10)

Conrad Frederick
Seeger
c. 1823–1850
Philadelphia, Pa.
(10)

Philip B. Segee
c. 1840
Location unknown
(38)

Lawrence Sekel
c. 1841
Philadelphia, Pa.
(10, 37)

Samuel Selby
c. 1841
Philadelphia, Pa.
(10)

John Selph
Selph & Pyle
c. 1807–1838
Fayetteville, N.C.
(22)

E. Sepes
c. 1851–1852
Utica, N.Y.
(24, 25)

John Serad (Scerad ?)
c. 1835–1850
Philadelphia, Pa.
(10)

Charles Servoss
c. 1849
Philadelphia, Pa.
(10)

Joseph S. Servoss
c. 1850
Philadelphia, Pa.
(10)

Benjamin Settle
c. 1867
Russellville, Ky.
(123)

Lewis Sevrin
(Sivrin ?)
c. 1837–1840
Philadelphia, Pa.
(10, 37, 90, 106)

Joseph Seydell
c. 1848–1849
Philadelphia, Pa.
(10)

Edward Seymour
c. 1839–1850
Philadelphia, Pa.
(10)

H. P. Seymour
c. 1840
Location unknown
(106)

Joseph Seymour
Joseph Seymour & Co
(JS & Co.)
Norton & Seymour
Norton, Seymour
& Co.
c. 1835–1863
New York, N.Y.
Syracuse, N.Y.
Utica, N.Y.
(24, 25, 37, 90, 106)

Oliver D. Seymour
Seymour & Hollister
(S & H)
Hollister &
Seymour (?)
c. 1850
Hartford, Conn.
(37, 39, 55, 106)

John V. Shade
c. 1845–1847
Philadelphia, Pa.
(10)

Charles A. Shafer
Harris & Shafer
c. 1850–after 1896
Washington, D.C.
(148, 150, 175)

J. Shakespeare
c. 1850
Nyack, N.Y.
(24)

Robert Shannon
Ashburn & Shannon
Hattrick & Shannon
c. 1841–1844
Philadelphia, Pa.
(10)

George Sharp
(Sharpe ?) (GS)
c. 1850–1870
Danville, Ky.
(63, 127)

George B. Sharp (S)
William & George
Sharp
c. 1844–1850
Philadelphia, Pa.
(10, 37, 39, 50, 55, 106)

William Sharp
William & George
Sharp
c. 1835–1850
Philadelphia, Pa.
(10, 37, 39, 50, 55, 90,
106)

William H. Sharpe
c. 1843
Philadelphia, Pa.
(10)

R. Sharpley
c. 1855
Location unknown
(106)

James S. Sharrard
Sharrard & Ewing
c. 1836–1861
Scott Co., Ky.
Paris, Ky.
Henderson, Ky.
Paducah, Ky.
(38, 39, 63, 106, 127)

Judson Sharrard
c. 1848
Shelbyville, Ky.
(39, 63)

William M. Sharrard
c. 1839–1850
Harrodsburg, Ky.
(63)

Jacob A. Shartle
c. 1844
Philadelphia, Pa.
(10)

Charles C. Shaver
(C C S)
c. 1854–before 1900
Utica, N.Y.
(24, 25, 106)

Michael Shaver
before 1859
Abingdon, Va.
(23)

Edward Shaw
c. 1837
Philadelphia, Pa.
(10)

James Shaw
c. 1839–1841
Philadelphia, Pa.
(10)

James W. Shaw
c. 1854
Winnsboro, S.C.
(14)

John Shaw
John Shaw & Co.
c. 1842–1851
St. Louis, Mo.
(123)

William W. Sheed
c. 1840
Philadelphia, Pa.
(10)

Alonzo D. Sheldon
c. 1851–1852
Utica, N.Y.
(24, 25)

Thomas Jefferson
Shepard
c. 1817–1875
Georgetown, Ky.
Louisville, Ky.
(63, 127)

Cumberland Shepherd
c. 1850
Philadelphia, Pa.
(10)

Ephraim Shepherd
c. 1834–1837
Newport, Ky.
(63)

George L. Sheppard
c. 1846–1848
Philadelphia, Pa.
(10, 37)

George M. Sheppard
c. 1837
Philadelphia, Pa.
(10)

Edward Sherman
c. 1850
Hartford, Conn.
(37)

Smith J. Sherwood
Sherwood & Whatley
c. 1839–after 1854
Chicago, Ill.
(42, 47, 175)

William Sherwood, Jr.
c. 1843–1846
Chicago, Ill.
(43, 44, 175)

Walter D. Shewell
c. 1829–1840
Philadelphia, Pa.
(10)

Jesse C. Shields
c. 1845
Philadelphia, Pa.
(10)

Anthony Shimer
c. 1850
Auburn, N.Y.
(24)

——— Shinn
Shinn & Baldwin
c. 1840
Location unknown
(168)

Nathaniel Shipman
(NS)
c. 1764–1853
Norwich, Conn.
(37, 38, 39, 50)

——— Shipp
Shipp & Collins
c. 1850
Cincinnati, Ohio
(39, 106)

——— Shipp
Shipp & Woodbridge
c. 1842
St. Louis, Mo.
(123)

Abraham Shoemaker
c. 1846
Philadelphia, Pa.
(10)

Joseph Shoemaker
(JS)
c. 1793–1839
Philadelphia, Pa.
(10, 11, 37, 38, 39, 50, 55, 90, 106)

Benjamin Shreve
Jones, Shreve, Brown
& Co.
Shreve, Brown & Co.
Shreve, Stanwood
& Co.
Shreve, Crump & Low
c. 1834–1896
Boston, Mass.
Salem, Mass.
(37, 50, 90, 106)

George C. Shreve
Shreve & Co.
c. 1852–1912
San Francisco, Cal.
(175)

Samuel S. Shreve
Shreve & Co.
c. 1852–1892
San Francisco, Cal.
(175)

Thomas H. Shriver
Baker & Shriver
c. 1837–1843
Philadelphia, Pa.
(10)

——— Shuber
Gregory & Shuber
c. 1837
Philadelphia, Pa.
(10)

John Shuler
c. 1849
Philadelphia, Pa.
(10)

John Shuman
c. 1818–1837
Philadelphia, Pa.
(10)

John Shurley
c. 1839–1840
Albany, N.Y.
(24)

James Sibley
c. 1799–1865
Great Barrington,
Mass.
Albany, N.Y.
Canandaigua, N.Y.
Ann Arbor, Mich.
Detroit, Mich. (?)
Rochester, N.Y.
(24, 90)

O. E. Sibley
Sibley & Adams
c. 1836–1848
Buffalo, N.Y.
Canandaigua, N.Y.
(24)

R. J. Sibley
c. 1850
Genesee, N.Y.
(24)

Joseph Sidall
c. 1846–1847
Philadelphia, Pa.
(10)

John Siddons
c. 1841–1850
Philadelphia, Pa.
(10)

Josiah C. Siddons
c. 1835–1837
Philadelphia, Pa.
(10)

Lawrence L. Siddons
c. 1853–1855
Charleston, S.C.
(14)

Michael Siebenlist
c. 1846–1850
Camden, N.J.
(10)

Amos Sigler
c. 1847–1850
Philadelphia, Pa.
(10, 37)

Alanson P. Sigourney
W. H. & A. P.
Sigourney
Sigourney &
Turner (?)
c. 1839
Watertown, N.Y.
(24)

William H.
Sigourney
W. H. & A. P.
Sigourney
W. H. Sigourney
& Co.
Sigourney &
Turner (?)
Sigourney &
Hitchcock (?)
c. 1839–after 1850
Watertown, N.Y.
(24)

William Sikler
c. 1850
Philadelphia, Pa.
(10)

H. Sill
H. & R. W. Sill
c. 1840
New York, N.Y.
(18, 39, 106)

Henry T. (?) Silverthorn
Silverthorn & Clift
c. 1832–1897
Baltimore, Md.
Lynchburg, Va.
(23)

F. W. Sim
F. W. Sim & Co.
c. 1847–after 1897
Troy, N.Y.
(263, 175)

Robert H. Simmons
c. 1837–1850
Philadelphia, Pa.
(10)

——— Simons
c. 1857
Chicago, Ill.
(175)

George W. Simons
c. 1844–1850
Philadelphia, Pa.
(10)

James Simpkins
c. 1845–1846
Louisville, Ky.
(63)

David Simpson
Simpson & Bro. (?)
c. 1807–1850
Philadelphia, Pa.
(10)

J. Alexander Simpson
Simpson & Bro. (?)
c. 1848–1850
Philadelphia, Pa.
(10)

James Simpson
Simpson & Bro. (?)
c. 1840
Philadelphia, Pa.
(10)

John W. Simpson
Simpson & Bro. (?)
c. 1839–1850
Philadelphia, Pa.
(10)

Jonathan Simpson
c. 1830–1863
Bardstown, Ky.
Madison, Ind.
(63, 127)

Moses Simpson
Simpson & Beckel
c. 1848–1849
Albany, N.Y.
(24, 25)

S. Simpson
19th century
Hopkinsville, Ky.
(63)

Thomas W. Simpson
c. 1839–1841
Philadelphia, Pa.
(10)

William Simpson
c. 1830–1844
Philadelphia, Pa.
(10)

William Sinclair
c. 1837
Philadelphia, Pa.
(10)

Louis Singer
c. 1846
New York, N.Y.
(37)

Robert Singleton
c. 1839
Greensboro, N.C.
(22)

Joseph A. Sixte
c. 1837–1850
Philadelphia, Pa.
(10, 37, 90, 106)

Vincent B. Sixte
c. 1837–1840
Philadelphia, Pa.
(10, 37, 90, 106)

Joseph Skerret (Scarret ?)
c. 1804–1850
Philadelphia, Pa.
(10, 50, 106)

George W. Skerry
c. 1837
Boston, Mass.
(37, 50, 90, 106)

Elizer Skinner
before 1858
Hartford, Conn.
(37, 50, 90, 106)

Josiah U. Slack
c. 1837–1839
Norfolk, Va.
(23)

William Slack
c. 1850
Philadelphia, Pa.
(10)

John Slattery
c. 1850
Hartford, Conn.
(37)

——— Sleeper
Sleeper & Jeannert
c. 1850
Philadelphia, Pa.
(10)

John Smart
c. 1839–1850
Philadelphia, Pa.
(10)

——— Smith
Marshall & Smith
c. 1837
Philadelphia, Pa.
(10)

——— Smith
Smith & Beggs
c. 1840
Louisville, Ky.
(63)

——— Smith
Smith & Bro.
c. 1843–1844
Philadelphia, Pa.
(10)

——— Smith
Smith & Goodrich
c. 1850
Philadelphia, Pa.
(10)

——— Smith
Smith & Kitts
c. 1844–1845
Louisville, Ky.
(63)

——— Smith
Smith & List
c. 1848–1850
Philadelphia, Pa.
(10)

——— Smith
Smith & Patterson
c. 1860
Boston, Mass.
(78)

A. Smith
19th century
Location unknown
(78)

Allen Smith
c. 1841
Philadelphia, Pa.
(10)

Alvin Smith
c. 1846
Port Chester, N.Y.
(24)

Benjamin C. Smith
c. 1850
Philadelphia, Pa.
(10)

Benjamin H. Smith
B. H. Smith & Co.
c. 1834–1838
Fredericksburg, Va.
(23)

C. C. Smith
c. 1841–1843
Fayetteville, N.C.
(22)

Charles Smith
c. 1848–1850
Philadelphia, Pa.
(10)

Charles Smith
c. 1848–1853
Pendleton, S.C.
Laurens, S.C.
Spartanburg, S.C.
Greenville, S.C.
Lancaster, S.C.
(14)

Charles A. Smith
Harbottle & Smith
c. 1850
Auburn, N.Y.
(24)

Charles R. Smith
c. 1837–1850
Philadelphia, Pa.
(10, 37)

Edwin Smith
c. 1837
Albany, N.Y.
(24)

F. C. Smith
c. 1844
Philadelphia, Pa.
(10)

Francis W. Smith
c. 1837
Philadelphia, Pa.
(10)

George Smith
c. 1823–1849
Philadelphia, Pa.
(10, 37, 90, 106)

George C. Smith
c. 1839–1845
Philadelphia, Pa.
(10)

George E. Smith
c. 1848–1849
Louisville, Ky.
(63)

George H. Smith
c. 1850
Watertown, N.Y.
(24)

George M. Smith
c. 1845–1849
Philadelphia, Pa.
(10)

George O. Smith
c. 1825–1850
New York, N.Y.
(37, 90)

Gerrit Smith
c. 1840
New York, N.Y.
(18)

Hartley T. Smith
c. 1850–1860
Bowling Green, Ky.
(63)

Hezekiah Smith
c. 1845
Philadelphia, Pa.
(10)

I. Smith (I S)
c. 1842
Boston, Mass.
(11, 37, 39)

Isaac Smith
c. 1840–1843
Philadelphia, Pa.
(10)

J. W. W. Smith
c. 1847
Shelbyville, Ky.
(63, 127)

Jacob C. Smith
c. 1839–1850
Philadelphia, Pa.
(10, 37, 90, 106)

James E. Smith
c. 1839
Albany, N.Y.
(24)

James S. Smith
c. 1837–1850
Philadelphia, Pa.
(10)

John Smith
c. 1835–1850
Philadelphia, Pa.
(10)

John Smith
(Schmitt ?)
c. 1846–1850
Philadelphia, Pa.
(10)

John Smith
c. 1850
Camden, N.J.
(10)

John Creagh Smith
c. 1839–1850
Philadelphia, Pa.
(10)

John Leonard Smith
c. 1850–1855
Syracuse, N.Y.
(24, 39, 106)

Joseph E. Smith
c. 1839–1850
Philadelphia, Pa.
(10)

Levin H. Smith
c. 1837–1843
Philadelphia, Pa.
(10, 37, 90, 106)

Nathaniel W. Smith
c. 1829–1845
Wheeling, W.Va.
Clarksburg, W.Va.
(23)

Philip Smith
c. 1847–1850
Philadelphia, Pa.
(10)

Richard Ewing Smith
Smith & Grant
c. 1821–1849
Louisville, Ky.
(39, 63, 106, 127)

Roderick D. Smith
c. 1846–1850
Philadelphia, Pa.
(10)

S. Smith
Smith & Bean
c. 1844
Skaneateles, N.Y.
(24)

Samuel Smith
c. 1845
Philadelphia, Pa.
(10, 37, 90, 106)

S. Smith
c. 1846
Saratoga Springs, N.Y.
(24)

Thomas Smith
before 1850
Lexington, Ky.
(63, 127)

W. C. Smith
c. 1850–1860
Bowling Green, Ky.
(63, 127)

William Smith
c. 1817–1840
New York, N.Y.
(18, 106)

William Smith
c. 1857
Philadelphia, Pa.
(10)

William Smith
William Smith & Co.
c. 1837
Wellsburg, W. Va.
(23)

William A. Smith
c. 1840
Leesburg, Va.
(23)

William K. Smith
B. H. Smith & Co.
c. 1836–1838
Fredericksburg, Va.
(23)

Zebulon Smith (Z S)
c. 1820–1830–
before 1865
Maine State
(39, 106)

R. T. Smitten
c. 1844–1847
Philadelphia, Pa.
(10)

John Smoker
c. 1846–1847
Philadelphia, Pa.
(10)

John L. Snedecker
c. 1837–1841
New York, N.Y.
(18)

William H. Snow
Hall & Snow
c. 1833–1842
Cleveland, Ohio
Troy, N.Y.
(24)

——— Snyder
Snyder & Bros.
c. 1847–1850
Philadelphia, Pa.
(10)

George W. Snyder, Jr.
J. C. & G. W. Snyder
c. 1821–1848
Paris, Ky.
(63, 127)

Joseph H. Snyder
c. 1848–1850
Philadelphia, Pa.
(10)

——— Snyder
Rickards & Snyder
c. 1842
Philadelphia, Pa.
(10)

Robert Snyder
c. 1850
Philadelphia, Pa.
(10)

Daniel H. Solliday
c. 1829–1850
Philadelphia, Pa.
(10)

Lewis Solomon
c. 1840–1841
Philadelphia, Pa.
(10)

William Somerdike
c. 1848–1850
Philadelphia, Pa.
(10)

Albertus Somers
before 1863
Woodstown, N.J.
Gloucester Co., N.J.
(117)

John Somerville
(Sommerville ?)
c. 1844–1846
Philadelphia, Pa.
(10)

William South
c. 1828–1850
Philadelphia, Pa.
(10)

——— Spear
Spear & Jones
c. 1841
Savannah, Ga.
(21)

Isaac Spear (Speer ?)
c. 1836–1837
Boston, Mass.
Newark, N.J.
(7, 37, 39, 90, 106)

James E. Spear
Spear & Co.
c. 1846–1871
Charleston, S.C.
(14)

Thomas S. Spear
c. 1858
Columbus, Ga.
(21)

David H. Spears
before 1850
Washington Co., Ky.
Springfield, Ky. (?)
(63, 127)

Isaac Spears (Spear ?)
c. 1850
Chicago, Ill.
(46, 175)

I. Speer (Spear ?)
(Spears ?)
c. 1845–1846
Chicago, Ill.
(44, 175)

Ferdinand
Speigelhalder
Speigelhalder & Werne
c. 1836–1858
Louisville, Ky.
(63, 127)

John F. Speigelhalder
Speigelhalder & Sons
c. 1844–1867
Louisville, Ky.
(63)

G. Spence
c. 1830–1840
Newark, N.J.
(39, 106)

George Spencer
before 1878
Essex, Conn.
(20, 32, 37, 50, 106)

George W. Spencer
c. 1860
Charleston, S.C.
(14)

James Spencer, Jr.
c. 1843
Hartford, Conn.
(37, 106)

Julius A. Spencer
before 1874
Utica, N.Y.
(24, 25)

Oliver Spencer
Spencer & Marshall
Spencer & Hand
c. 1829–1843
Philadelphia, Pa.
(10)

William Sperry
c. 1843–1849
Philadelphia, Pa.
(10)

David M. Spurgin
c. 1829–1852
Mount Sterling, Ky.
Carlisle, Ky.
Winchester, Ky.
Greencastle, Ind.
(63, 127)

——— Squire
Squire & Bros.
c. 1846
New York, N.Y.
(37, 39, 50, 106)

——— Squire
Squire & Landers
c. 1840
New York, N.Y.
(37, 39, 55, 90, 106)

Bela S. Squire
Benedict & Squire
c. 1839
New York, N.Y.
(18)

R. Squires
c. 1845
Binghamton, N.Y.
(24)

Richard M. Stainer
c. 1843
Poughkeepsie, N.Y.
(134)

Joseph M. Stanley
c. 1804–1848
Zanesville, Ohio
Cleveland, Ohio
(77)

Henry Stanton
W. P. & H. Stanton
Stanton & Brother
c. 1825–1872
Providence, R.I.
Rochester, N.Y.
(24, 100, 133)

William P. Stanton
W. P. & H. Stanton
Stanton & Brother
c. 1818–1878
Providence, R.I.
Rochester, N.Y.
(24, 100, 133)

——— Stanwood
Stanwood & Halstrick
c. 1850
Boston, Mass.
(11, 37, 50, 106)

Henry B. Stanwood
Harris & Stanwood
c. 1835–1869
Boston, Mass.
(37, 38, 39, 50, 55, 90, 106)

J. E. Stanwood
c. 1850
Philadelphia, Pa.
(37, 38, 39, 106)

James D. Stanwood
c. 1846
Boston, Mass.
(11, 37, 50, 106)

George Staple (Staples ?)
c. 1848–1850
Philadelphia, Pa.
(10, 37)

E. F. Starbuck
before 1848
Nantucket Island, Mass.
(17)

Erastus Charles Starin
c. 1832–1839
Utica, N.Y.
(24, 25)

Theodore B. Starr
c. 1890–1900 (?)
New York, N.Y.
(51)

P. M. Statzell
c. 1845–1850
Philadelphia, Pa.
(10)

A. Lewis Staub
c. 1852
Mobile, Ala.
(170)

Edwin Stebbins
E. Stebbins & Co. (?)
Stebbins & Co.
c. 1810–1841
New York, N.Y.
(18, 37, 38, 50, 44, 106)

N. W. Stebbins
c. 1848
Seneca Co., Ohio
Huron Co., Ohio
Muskingum Co., Ohio
(77)

James P. Steele
c. 1838–1855
Rochester, N.Y.
(24, 100, 106)

Robert Steele
c. 1832–1848
Louisville, Ky.
(63)

Samuel Steele
c. 1829–1850
Baltimore, Md.
(93)

The Rev. William Steele
c. 1780–1844
Henderson Co., Ky.
(63, 127)

Haldor S. Steen
c. 1844–1850
Rochester, N.Y.
(24)

Ole S. Steen
c. 1847
Rochester, N.Y.
(24)

Charles K. Stellwagen
c. 1840–1848
Philadelphia, Pa.
(10)

David Stephens
T. C. & D. Stephens
Stephens & Doud
c. 1840–1841
Utica, N.Y.
(24, 25)

Joseph Lawrence Stephens
before 1848
Paris, Ky.
(63)

Thomas C. Stephens
T. C. & D. Stephens
c. 1840–1841
Utica, N.Y.
(24, 25)

William Stephens
c. 1840–1842
Albany, N.Y.
(24)

Thomas Stephenson
Thomas Stephenson & Co.
c. 1835–1848
Buffalo, N.Y.
(24, 39, 106)

——— Sterling
Haight & Sterling
c. 1841–1843
Newburgh, N.Y.
(24)

Abraham Sterne
Sterne Brothers
c. 1850
Syracuse, N.Y.
(24)

Baruch Sterne
Sterne Brothers
c. 1850
Syracuse, N.Y.
(24)

T. W. Sters
c. 1850
Location unknown
(78)

George Stevens
c. 1845–1848
Philadelphia, Pa.
(10)

J. C. Stevens
c. 1837–1838
Utica, N.Y.
(24, 25)

Thomas H. Stevens (Stephens ?)
c. 1839–1846
Philadelphia, Pa.
(10, 37, 106)

John Stevenson
c. 1850
Location unknown
(78)

Aaron Steward
c. 1843
Philadelphia, Pa.
(10)

Alexander Stewart
c. 1850
New York, N.Y.
(37)

C. W. Stewart
c. 1840
New York, N.Y.
(37, 90)

C. W. Stewart
c. 1850
Lexington, Ky.
(123)

C. Stewart
19th century
Location unknown
(168)

Charles Stewart
c. 1837–1851
Albany, N.Y.
Utica, N.Y.
(24, 25)

Charles G. Stewart
Charles G. Stewart & Son
c. 1847–1849
Charles Town, W. Va.
(23)

George W. Stewart
Garner & Stewart
c. 1846–1852
Lexington, Ky.
(63, 127)

James D. Stewart
c. 1836–1841
New York, N.Y.
(18)

Warner W. Stewart
c. 1837–1838
Utica, N.Y.
(24, 25)

William Stewart
c. 1790–1851
Russellville, Ky.
(63)

William Stewart
c. 1845
St. Louis, Mo.
(123)

Worthington Stewart
c. 1842–1847
St. Louis, Mo.
(123)

——— Stickles
Connor & Stickles
c. 1837
New York, N.Y.
(18)

B. H. Stief
c. 1863–1882
Nashville, Tenn.
(89, 175)

Benjamin Stiles
Curtis, Candee & Stiles
Curtis & Stiles
c. 1830–1840
Woodbury, Conn.
(20, 37, 50, 90, 106, 133)

George Keith Stiles
c. 1834–1873
Cortland, N.Y.
Brooklyn, N.Y.
(24, 133)

Joseph Stiles
John & Joseph Stiles
before 1838
Augusta, Ga.
(21)

William James Stiles
c. 1837
Rhinebeck, N.Y.
(133)

Barton Stillman
before 1858
Westerly, R.I.
(50, 106)

Samuel W. Stillman
c. 1850
Hartford, Conn.
(37, 106)

Mortimer F. Stillwell
Cook & Stillwell
c. 1845–1859
Rochester, N.Y.
(24, 100)

William Stilman
before 1858
Hopkinton, R.I.
(7, 50, 90, 106)

George F. (A. ?) Stinger
c. 1845
Cincinnati, Ohio
(77)

S. J. Stinger
c. 1850
Cincinnati, Ohio
(77)

Philo W. Stocking
Stocking & Kipp
c. 1833–1839
Wheeling, W.Va.
(23)

Jacob Stockman
c. 1828–1850
Philadelphia, Pa.
(10, 37, 39, 90, 106)

S. Stockman
c. 1837
Philadelphia, Pa.
(10)

George Stokeberry
c. 1837
Philadelphia, Pa.
(10)

Seymour H. Stone
Stone & Ball
c. 1850
Syracuse, N.Y.
(24)

William R. Stone
c. 1845–1846
Louisville, Ky.
(63)

John Adriance Storm
A. G. Storm & Son
c. 1836–1837
Poughkeepsie, N.Y.
(133)

Charles Storrs
Storrs & Parker
Storrs & Davies
Storrs & Cooley
(S & C)
c. 1820–1839
Utica, N.Y.
(24, 25, 133)

Henry Southworth Storrs
Storrs & Chubbuck
c. 1832–1862
Utica, N.Y.
(24, 25, 133)

Nathan Storrs
Storrs & Baldwin
Storrs & Cook
c. 1791–1839
Amherst, Mass. (?)
Northampton, Mass.
Troy, N.Y.
(37, 38, 39, 50, 55, 106, 133)

Shubael Storrs
c. 1803–1847
Utica, N.Y.
(24, 25, 133)

E. F. Story
c. 1872
Wilmington, N.C.
(22)

S. N. Story
c. 1845
Worcester, Mass.
(39, 106)

Edwin Stott
c. 1850
Philadelphia, Pa.
(10)

A. Stowell, Jr.
Gould, Stowell & Ward
c. 1855–1858
Baltimore, Md.
Charlestown, Mass.
(38, 50, 106)

Avery W. Stowell
before 1844
Syracuse, N.Y.
(24)

David C. Stoy
Kitts & Stoy
c. 1844–1852
Louisville, Ky.
(63)

C. Strade
c. 1838
Richmond, Va.
(23)

Samuel Stradley
c. 1857
Greenville, S.C.
(14)

George A. Stringer
(Stinger ?)
c. 1849
Cincinnati, Ohio
(123)

Samuel Stringfellow
c. 1816–1837
Augusta, Ga.
(21)

Edmund Strock
c. 1850
Philadelphia, Pa.
(10)

A. Strub (Staub ?)
c. 1847
St. Louis, Mo.
(123)

Alexander C. Stuart
c. 1834–1841
New York, N.Y.
(18)

James Stuart
(Stewart ?)
(Steward ?)
c. 1839–1850
Philadelphia, Pa.
(10)

L. Studley
19th century
Location unknown
(78)

James Stutson
c. 1838
Rochester, N.Y.
(24)

Cornelius D. Sullivan
c. 1842–1848
St. Louis, Mo.
(123)

——— Sunderlin
Sunderlin & Weaver
after 1864
Rochester, N.Y.
(100, 133)

Amos B. Swift
c. 1846
Earlville, N.Y.
(24)

George J. Swortfinger
c. 1840–1842
Schenectady, N.Y.
(24)

J. Sylvester
c. 1838–1881
St. Louis, Mo.
(123)

William Sylvester
19th century
Nixonton, N.C.
(22)

R. Taft
19th century
Location unknown
(106)

Thomas E. Taggart
c. 1839
Columbus, Ga.
(21)

A. G. Talbot
c. 1840
Oswego, N.Y.
(24)

W. H. Talbot
c. 1850–1865
Indianapolis, Ind.
Kentucky
(63, 70)

William H. Talbott
c. 1833–1865
Indianapolis, Ind.
(70, 175)

C. Talcott
19th century
Location unknown
(78)

Theodore Tankey
c. 1859–1860
Utica, N.Y.
(25)

Perry G. Tanner
Tanner & Cooley
c. 1840–1844
Utica, N.Y.
Cooperstown, N.Y.
(24, 25, 27, 29, 106)

Richard Tape
c. 1844
Rochester, N.Y.
(24)

John Targee (I T)
John & Peter Targee
(I & P T)
c. 1797–1841
New York, N.Y.
(37, 38, 39, 50, 90, 106)

——— Taylor
Taylor & Lawrie
Taylor, Lawrie & Wood
c. 1837–1850
Philadelphia, Pa.
(10, 37, 38, 39, 50, 90, 106)

Edward Taylor
c. 1828–1837
New York, N.Y.
(18)

George Taylor
c. 1825–1852
Mobile, Ala.
(170)

George W. Taylor
c. 1823–1850
Philadelphia, Pa.
(10, 37, 90, 106)

John G. Taylor
c. 1837–1843
Philadelphia, Pa.
(10)

Noah C. Taylor
c. 1844
Salisbury, N.C.
(22)

Richard Taylor
c. 1834–1841
New York, N.Y.
(18)

Robert Taylor
c. 1839–1850
Philadelphia, Pa.
(10)

W. S. Taylor
(William S. ?)
c. 1847–1849
Troy, N.Y.
(24)

William Taylor (W T)
c. 1829–1850
Philadelphia, Pa.
(10)

William S. Taylor
Davics & Taylor
Maynard & Taylor
W. S. Taylor & Co.
c. 1829–1858
Utica, N.Y.
(24, 25)

Robert Tempest
c. 1814–1850
Philadelphia, Pa.
(10, 50)

William I. Tenney
c. 1831–1852
New York, N.Y.
(18, 37, 38, 39, 55, 90)

Geer Terry
before 1858
Enfield, Conn.
Worcester, Mass.
(20, 37, 38, 39, 50, 90, 106)

Joseph Blake Thaxter
before 1863
Hingham, Mass.
(37, 39, 50, 90, 106)

Felix Thibault
c. 1814–1837
Philadelphia, Pa.
(10, 37, 90, 106)

Francis Thibault
c. 1816–1850
Philadelphia, Pa.
(10)

John Thiels
c. 1847
St. Louis, Mo.
(123)

Lewis Thirion
Thirion & Hinkle
c. 1828–1850
Philadelphia, Pa.
(10)

August Thomas
c. 1838
Piqua, Ohio
(77)

Benjamin Thomas
c. 1813–1850
Philadelphia, Pa.
(10)

Henry Thompson
c. 1847–1850
Philadelphia, Pa.
(10)

Isaac P. Thompson
c. 1857
Orangeburg, S.C.
(14)

Jeremiah Thompson
c. 1840–1841
Philadelphia, Pa.
(10)

Peter Thompson
c. 1835–1850
Philadelphia, Pa.
(10, 37)

Robert Thompson
c. 1840–1841
Philadelphia, Pa.
(10)

James Thomson
c. 1834–1841
New York, N.Y.
(11, 18, 37, 38, 39, 50, 90, 106)

John L. Thomson
c. 1849
Philadelphia, Pa.
(10)

William Thomson
Thomson & Beckwith
c. 1834–1850
Raleigh, N.C.
Wilmington, N.C.
(22)

John Thorn
c. 1837
Philadelphia, Pa.
(10)

William N. Tibbets
c. 1837–1838
Utica, N.Y.
(24, 25)

William Tibbits
c. 1842
Buffalo, N.Y.
(24)

Foster Tinkham
F. Tinkham & Co.
c. 1840–1850
New York, N.Y.
(18, 39)

William Tisdale II
before 1861
New Bern, N.C.
(22)

J. Titlow
Titlow & Fry
c. 1844–1850
Philadelphia, Pa.
(10, 37)

Charles T. Tittle
c. 1841–1847
Philadelphia, Pa.
(10, 37)

Peter N. Titus
c. 1843
Albany, N.Y.
(24)

Erastus O. Tompkins
Ball, Tompkins & Black
c. 1836–1851
New York, N.Y.
(18)

James Took
c. 1842–1847
St. Louis, Mo.
(123)

Anthony F. Towle
Towle & Jones
Anthony F. Towle & Son
A. F. Towle & Son
A. F. Towle & Son Mfg. Co.
A. F. Towle & Son Co.
c. 1855–1902
Newburyport, Mass.
Greenfield, Mass.
(175)

Edward Towle
Anthony F. Towle & Son
A. F. Towle & Son
A. F. Towle & Son Mfg. Co.
A. F. Towle & Son Co.
c. 1879–1902
Newburyport, Mass.
Greenfield, Mass.
(175)

Charles Townsend
c. 1799–1850
Philadelphia, Pa.
(10)

Charles Townsend, Jr.
c. 1829–1850
Philadelphia, Pa.
(10)

John Townsend
c. 1849
Philadelphia, Pa.
(10)

Philemon Towson
before 1843
Baltimore, Md.
(93)

J. F. Tozer
c. 1850
Binghamton, N.Y.
(24)

Junius F. Tozer
c. 1847–1850
Binghamton, N.Y.
Rochester, N.Y.
(24, 100, 106)

A. Fayette Tracy
Tracy & Hawley
c. 1844–1848
Oswego, N.Y.
Cazenovia, N.Y.
(24)

Charles Tracy
C. & E. Tracy
c. 1842–1850
Philadelphia, Pa.
(10)

E. Tracy
C. & E. Tracy
c. 1842–1850
Philadelphia, Pa.
(10)

William Tracy
c. 1843–1850
Philadelphia, Pa.
(10)

Peter C. Trahn (Thran ?)
c. 1843–1849
Philadelphia, Pa.
(10)

J. Trast
c. 1850
Syracuse, N.Y.
(24)

Samuel Treadway
c. 1848
St. Louis, Mo.
(123)

Oren B. Treadwell
c. 1847–1849
Philadelphia, Pa.
(10)

Arthur Trench
c. 1833–1839
Raleigh, N.C.
(22)

Peter Trone
c. 1844
Philadelphia, Pa.
(10)

John Proctor Trott (J P T)
Trott & Cleveland (T & C)
Trott & Brooks (T & B)
John P. Trott & Son (J P T & Son)
Currier & Trott
c. 1798–1852
New London, Conn.
(7, 37, 38, 39, 50, 55, 90, 106)

Jeremiah Trotter
c. 1821–1844
Cincinnati, Ohio
(77)

Thomas Trotter
Thomas Trotter & Co.
Trotter & Huntington
Trotter & Alexander
c. 1827–1865
Charlotte, N.C.
(22)

A. W. Trou
c. 1846–1854
Charleston, S.C.
(14)

George Trout
c. 1837–1843
Philadelphia, Pa.
(10)

Dewitt Truax
c. 1842–1843
Utica, N.Y.
(25)

M. Tucker
c. 1840
Location unknown
(38)

Alonzo B. Turner
Sigourney & Turner
c. 1838–1844
Watertown, N.Y.
(24)

William Turner
c. 1847–1850
Philadelphia, Pa.
(10)

William Tuttle
c. 1800–1849
New Haven, Conn.
Suffield, Conn.
(20, 32, 37, 50, 90, 106)

Weston Weed Tuxford
c. 1837
Clarkesville, Ga.
(21)

William Twybill
c. 1841
Philadelphia, Pa.
(10)

John Henry Tyler
John H. Tyler & Co.
Mitchell & Tyler
c. 1840–1866
Richmond, Va.
Boston, Mass. (?)
(23, 38, 39, 106)

Jacob Ulman
A. & J. Ulman (?)
c. 1843
Philadelphia, Pa.
(10)

George M. Updike
c. 1848
Philadelphia, Pa.
(10)

George Urwiler
c. 1814–1844
Philadelphia, Pa.
(10)

Austin Usher
c. 1842
Philadelphia, Pa.
(10)

Elijah M. Vail
c. 1835–1850
Albany, N.Y.
Troy, N.Y.
(24, 37, 50, 106)

Philip Valenti
Fuselli & Valenti
McLure & Valenti
c. 1860–1879
Bowling Green, Ky.
(123)

Dennis Valentine
Barney & Valentine
c. 1850
Syracuse, N.Y.
(24)

Benjamin F. Vallet
c. 1833–1850
Kingston, N.Y.
(24)

James Vanarsdale
c. 1849
Philadelphia, Pa.
(10)

Peter Van Bomell
c. 1792–1848
Poughkeepsie, N.Y.
(134)

James S. Vancourt
c. 1855
New York, N.Y.
(165, 175)

John G. Vanderleyden
c. 1842–1845
Utica, N.Y.
(24, 25)

——— Vanderslice
Vanderslice & Co.
c. 1860–1906
San Francisco, Cal.
(123)

W. Vanderslice
c. 1840
Philadelphia, Pa.
(10)

Shelby Van Hoy
19th century
Shelbyville, Ky.
(123)

Peter Van Ness
Van Ness & Waterman
(V & W)
Van Ness & Bwistrand
Van Ness, Wood & Co.
c. 1833–1846
New York, N.Y.
(18, 37, 38, 39, 50, 55, 90, 106)

——— Vansant
Vansant & Co.
(V & Co.)
c. 1850–1880
Philadelphia, Pa.
(39, 106)

G. Van Schaik
c. 1800–1840
Albany, N.Y.
(39, 50, 55, 106)

John L. Vantine
c. 1828–1847
Philadelphia, Pa.
(10)

Benjamin Cromwell VanVliet
VanVliet & Cromwell
c. 1830–1851
Poughkeepsie, N.Y.
(24, 37, 55, 90)

——— Van Voorhis
Brooks & Van Voorhis
c. 1843
Utica, N.Y.
(24, 25)

John Van Zandt
c. 1842–1848
Albany, N.Y.
(24)

Joseph Varley
c. 1858–1860
Utica, N.Y.
(25)

Robert Varrick
c. 1844–1845
Philadelphia, Pa.
(10, 37)

George C. Vaughn
Chase & Vaughn
c. 1840–1844
Buffalo, N.Y.
(24)

——— Vautroit
Vautroit & Meyers
c. 1860
Warren, Ohio
(78)

John Veal
Veal & Glaze
c. 1827–1857
Columbia, S.C.
(14, 106)

Joseph E. Veal
c. 1848–1853
Madison, Ga.
(21)

Bordo Vensal
c. 1850
Philadelphia, Pa.
(10)

Nathaniel Vernon
(N V)
N. Vernon & Co.
Nathaniel Vernon & Co.
Vernon & Co.
before 1843
Charleston, S.C.
(14, 32, 37, 38, 39, 50, 55, 90, 106)

Edward William Victor
c. 1844–1850
Lynchburg, Va.
(23)

John Victor
Williams & Victor
(W & V)
c. 1814–1845
Lynchburg, Va.
(23)

L. Villenjur
c. 1845
St. Louis, Mo.
(123)

Jonathan Ambrose Virgin (Virgins ?)
J. A. & S. S. Virgin
c. 1834–before 1881
Macon, Ga.
(21)

Samuel Stanley Virgin (Virgins ?)
J. A. & S. S. Virgin
Bruno & Virgin
Virgins & Stringfellow
c. 1833–1849–before 1889
Macon, Ga.
(21)

——— Virney
c. 1844–1845
Louisville, Ky.
(63)

Elias Alexander Vogler
before 1876
Salem, N.C.
(22)

John Utzmann Vogler
c. 1812–1856
Salem, N.C. (?)
Salisbury, N.C.
(22)

Frederick C. von Borstel
c. 1848–1875
Anderson, S.C.
Athens, Ga.
(14, 21)

Jacob Vonneide
c. 1837–1840
Philadelphia, Pa.
(10)

Abraham Voorhees
c. 1840
New Brunswick, N.J.
(106, 117)

John O. Vorse
c. 1841
Palmyra, N.Y.
(24)

John Hobart Vosburgh
c. 1852–1860
Utica, N.Y.
(25)

Louis C. Voute (Vouty ?)
c. 1826–1850
Bridgeton, N.J.
Philadelphia, Pa.
(10, 117)

——— Wade
Hogan & Wade
c. 1850
Cleveland, Ohio
(78)

——— Wait
Wait & Wright
c. 1837
Philadelphia, Pa.
(10, 37, 90, 106)

Edgar S. Wait
c. 1848
Louisville, Ky.
(63)

L. D. Wait
c. 1838–1847
Skaneateles, N.Y.
(24)

Alva Waite
c. 1840
Ravenna, Ohio
(77)

Edwin F. Waite
c. 1840
Ravenna, Ohio
(77)

George Waite
c. 1847–1850
Philadelphia, Pa.
(10)

Frederick Waitt
c. 1843–1850
Philadelphia, Pa.
(10)

Thomas Wakefield
c. 1837
Philadelphia, Pa.
(10)

——— Walker
Walker & Peak
c. 1843
Philadelphia, Pa.
(10)

Julius Walker
c. 1840–1848
Buffalo, N.Y.
(24)

Richard Walker
c. 1837–1846
Philadelphia, Pa.
(10)

Robert Wallin
Freeman & Wallin
c. 1845–1850
Philadelphia, Pa.
(10)

Richard Waln
c. 1837
Philadelphia, Pa.
(10)

Abraham Walter
c. 1849–1850
Philadelphia, Pa.
(10)

H. N. Walter
c. 1833–1850
Norwich, N.Y.
(24)

Jacob Walter
c. 1815–before 1865
Baltimore, Md.
(38, 39, 55, 93)

John J. Walter
c. 1837
Canton, Ohio
(77)

Edward Walters
c. 1847
Philadelphia, Pa.
(10)

John J. Walto
c. 1849–1850
Philadelphia, Pa.
(10)

Edward Wangelin
Schroeder & Wangelin
c. 1844–1850
Cleveland, Ohio
(123)

Benjamin Ward
c. 1845–1846
Troy, N.Y.
(24)

Charles Ward
c. 1839–1840
Philadelphia, Pa.
(10)

Edward H. Ward
c. 1839–1842
Philadelphia, Pa.
(10)

J. Ward
J. Ward & Co.
c. 1843
Philadelphia, Pa.
(10)

James Ward (I W) (J W)
before 1856
Guilford, Conn.
Hartford, Conn.
(20, 37, 38, 39, 50, 55, 90, 106, 180)

Jehu Ward
Jehu & W. L. Ward
Jehu & W. L. Ward & Co.
c. 1808–1850
Philadelphia, Pa.
(10, 39, 168)

John Ward
Ward & Cox
Ward & Govett
Ward & Miller
c. 1803–1839
Philadelphia, Pa.
(10, 37, 50, 55, 90, 95, 106)

W. W. Ward
c. 1841
Winnsboro, S.C.
(14)

William H. Ward
Gould & Ward
Gould, Stowell & Ward
c. 1850–1858
Baltimore, Md.
(37, 90, 93, 106)

William L. Ward
c. 1831–1850
Philadelphia, Pa.
(10)

Abijah B. Warden
c. 1842–1850
Philadelphia, Pa.
(10, 39, 106)

G. Waring
c. 1848
Hudson, N.Y.
(24)

William Wark
c. 1848–1850
Philadelphia, Pa.
(10)

——— Warner
Warner & Keating
Warner & Newlin
c. 1840–1850
Philadelphia, Pa.
(10)

Andrew Ellicott Warner (A E W)
c. 1837–1870
Baltimore, Md.
(11, 32, 37, 38, 39, 50, 55, 90, 93, 106)

Caleb Warner
Warner & Fellows
c. 1824–1861
Portsmouth, N.H.
Portland, Me.
Salem, Mass.
(37, 38, 39, 50, 55, 106, 133)

Cuthbert Warner
before 1838
Baltimore, Md.
(93)

John S. Warner
c. 1825–1846
Philadelphia, Pa.
(10)

Joseph Warner (I W)
c. 1811–1850
Philadelphia, Pa.
(10)

Joseph P. Warner (J P W)
c. 1830–1862
Baltimore, Md.
(38, 39, 50, 93, 106)

Joseph P. Warner
c. 1839
Philadelphia, Pa.
(10)

Robert P. Warner
c. 1839–1850
Philadelphia, Pa.
(10)

William Warner
William Warner & Co.
c. 1814–1850
Philadelphia, Pa.
(10)

S. W. Warriner
J. N. Aldrich & S. W. Warriner
c. 1845–1848
Louisville, Ky.
(63, 127)

John Warrington
John Warrington & Co. (?)
John & S. R. Warrington
c. 1811–1850
Philadelphia, Pa.
(10)

Samuel R. Warrington
John & S. R. Warrington
Samuel R. Warrington & Co. (?)
c. 1841–1850
Philadelphia, Pa.
(10)

F. A. Wart
c. 1841
Philadelphia, Pa.
(10)

William Warwick
c. 1837
Philadelphia, Pa.
(10)

Charles Washburn
c. 1844–1850
Rochester, N.Y.
(24)

Charles H. Waterhouse
c. 1847
Providence, R.I.
(37)

George Waterman
Waterman & Whalen
c. 1848–1850
Albany, N.Y.
(24, 32, 37, 50, 106)

John Watkins
c. 1831–1837
Philadelphia, Pa.
(10, 106)

Mildred Watkins
c. 1906
Cleveland, Ohio
(128, 175)

O. C. Watkins
c. 1850
Unadilla, N.Y.
(24)

James Watling
c. 1837–1850
Philadelphia, Pa.
(10, 37, 90)

——— Watson
Hildeburn & Watson
c. 1833–1849
Philadelphia, Pa.
(10)

Edward E. (J. ?) Watson
Davis & Watson
Davis, Watson & Co.
before 1839
Boston, Mass.
(7, 37, 38, 39, 50, 55, 90)

Isaac S. Watson
c. 1843–1846
Philadelphia, Pa.
(10, 37)

James Watson
c. 1820–1850
Philadelphia, Pa.
(10, 37, 38, 39, 55, 90, 106)

Joseph H. Watson
c. 1844–1878
Warrenton, Va.
(23)

Robert Watson
c. 1842–1850
Philadelphia, Pa.
(10)

Charles Watts
c. 1844–1850
Rochester, N.Y.
(24)

James Watts
J. & W. Watts
c. 1835–1850
Philadelphia, Pa.
(10, 37, 90, 106)

William Watts
J. & W. Watts
c. 1839–1850
Philadelphia, Pa.
(10, 37)

David Weatherly
c. 1805–1850
Philadelphia, Pa.
(10)

——— Weaver
Sunderlin & Weaver
after 1864
Rochester, N.Y.
(133)

Emmor T. Weaver
before 1860
Philadelphia, Pa.
(10)

Joseph S. Weaver
N. N. Weaver & Son
c. 1846–1849
Utica, N.Y.
(24, 25)

Nicholas N. Weaver
N. N. & W. Weaver
N. N. Weaver & Son
c. 1817–1853
Utica, N.Y.
Cleveland, Ohio
(24, 25, 39, 106)

William N. Weaver
N. N. Weaver & Son
c. 1846–1847
Utica, N.Y.
(24, 25)

Charles Webb
c. 1850
Philadelphia, Pa.
(10)

Daniel A. Webb
c. 1830–1860
Indianapolis, Ind.
(175)

George W. Webb
c. 1817–before 1890
Baltimore, Md.
(11, 32, 37, 38, 39, 50, 93, 106)

James Webb
Webb & Johannes
James Webb & Son
c. 1817–1844
Baltimore, Md.
(37, 38, 39, 50, 55, 106)

John Webb
c. 1827–1842
Baltimore, Md.
(93)

Henry L. Webster
Gorham, Webster & Price
Henry L. Webster & Co.
Gorham & Webster
c. 1831–1841
Providence, R.I.
Boston, Mass.
(32, 37, 38, 39, 50, 55, 90, 106)

P. M. Weddell
c. 1845
Cleveland, Ohio
(78)

Simon Wedge, Jr.
c. 1823–1869
Baltimore, Md.
(93)

Solomon Weida
c. 1847
Rochester, N.Y.
(24)

George Weiss
c. 1847
Philadelphia, Pa.
(10, 37)

——— Welles
Welles & Gelston
c. 1840
New York, N.Y.
(38, 39, 50)

A. Welles
before 1860
Hebron, Conn.
(20, 39, 50, 90, 106)

David Welsh
c. 1848–1851
Lincolnton, N.C.
(22)

Charles Wendell
Wendell & Co.
c. 1850–1880
Chicago, Ill.
(175)

Maurice Wendell
Wendell & Co.
c. 1870–1900
Chicago, Ill.
(175)

William Wendell
Mulford & Wendell
Wendell & Roberts
c. 1839–1850
Albany, N.Y.
(24, 37)

Cyrus King Wentworth
C. K. Wentworth & Co.
c. 1816–1850
Milledgeville, Ga.
Macon, Ga.
(21)

Jason Wentworth
c. 1846
Boston, Mass.
(39, 106)

Benjamin Wenzell
(Winzel ?)
(Winson ?)
c. 1839–1850
Philadelphia, Pa.
(10)

Joseph Werne
Werne & Speiglehalder
c. 1808–1858
Louisville, Ky.
(63, 127)

Joseph Werne, Jr.
Kitts & Werne
c. 1857–1903
Louisville, Ky.
(63, 127)

S. W. West
c. 1859
Laurens, S.C.
(14)

William E. West
19th century
Lexington, Ky.
(123)

John L. Westervelt
(Westervell ?)
(J L W)
c. 1826–1850
Newburgh, N.Y.
(24, 37, 38, 39, 50, 55, 106)

Edward A. Wetmore
c. 1839–1843
Troy, N.Y.
(24)

Jacob G. Weyman
c. 1844–1846
Philadelphia, Pa.
(10)

James Whalen
Waterman & Whalen
c. 1849
Albany, N.Y.
(24)

James Whartenby
c. 1847–1848
Philadelphia, Pa.
(10, 37)

Thomas Whartenby
(T W)
Whartenby & Bumm
Thomas Whartenby & Co.
c. 1811–1850
Philadelphia, Pa.
(10, 11, 37, 38, 39, 50, 55, 90, 95, 106)

William Whartenby
c. 1844
Philadelphia, Pa.
(10, 37)

Eli Whatley
Sherwood & Whatley
c. 1850–after 1854
Chicago, Ill.
(46, 47, 175)

Ralph Wheeler
c. 1838
Hudson, N.Y.
(24)

Samuel Wheeler, Jr.
c. 1844
Rochester, N.Y.
(24)

Samuel H. Wheritt
c. 1860
Richmond, Va.
(123)

William G. Whilden
Gregg, Hayden & Whilden
Hayden & Whilden
c. 1855–1863
Charleston, S.C.
(123)

——— White
Dickson, White & Co.
c. 1837
Philadelphia, Pa.
(10)

Charles White
c. 1830–1848
Mobile, Ala.
(170)

Francis White
c. 1849
Philadelphia, Pa.
(10)

George L. (A. ?) White
Woodruff & White
c. 1822–1843
Cincinnati, Ohio
(77)

Philo White
c. 1843–1844
Utica, N.Y.
(24, 25)

William H. White
H. White & Son
William H. White & Co.
c. 1822–1839–before 1859
Fredericksburg, Va.
(23)

William J. White
c. 1833–1838
New York, N.Y.
(18, 37, 90, 106)

William Wilson White
c. 1827–1841
Philadelphia, Pa.
New York, N.Y.
(10, 37, 38, 39, 55, 90, 106)

John Whitehead
c. 1821–before 1875
Haddonfield, N.J.
(117)

John Whitehead
c. 1848–1849
Philadelphia, Pa.
(10)

William W. Whitehead
c. 1850
Philadelphia, Pa.
(10)

Frederick A. Whitlock
Woodstock & Whitlock
c. 1850–1851
Augusta, Ga.
(21)

——— Whitnery
c. 1846
New York, N.Y.
(78)

Edward T. Whitney
c. 1847
Rochester, N.Y.
(24)

Ezra (Ebed ?) Whitney
before 1879
Boston, Mass.
(11, 37, 38, 39, 50, 55, 90, 106)

John Whitney
c. 1839–1845
Albany, N.Y.
(24)

Lemuel Whitney
c. 1785–1847
Newfane, Vt.
Brattleboro, Vt.
(123)

Leonard Whitney
c. 1841–1842
Philadelphia, Pa.
(10)

William H. Whitney
c. 1845
Rochester, N.Y.
Binghamton, N.Y.
(24)

Daniel H. Wickham, Jr.
c. 1832–1841
New York, N.Y.
(18, 37, 90, 106)

Frederick W. Widman
c. 1817–1848
Philadelphia, Pa.
(10)

Frederick Wieland
c. 1848
Philadelphia, Pa.
(10)

John Wilbank
c. 1839–1841
Philadelphia, Pa.
(10)

Alanson D. Wilcox
Harris & Wilcox (?)
c. 1843–1850
Albany, N.Y.
Troy, N.Y.
(24, 39, 106)

Alvan Wilcox (Willcox ?)
c. 1805–1870
Norwich, Conn.
Fayetteville, N.C.
New Haven, Conn.
(20, 22, 37, 50, 90, 106)

Cyprian Wilcox
Wilcox & Perkins
c. 1818–1875
Sparta, Ga.
Berlin, Conn.
New Haven, Conn.
(20, 21, 37, 50, 90, 106)

L. H. Wilder
L. H. Wilder & Co.
c. 1845
Philadelphia, Pa.
(10)

E. Wilkinson
c. 1840
Mansfield, Ohio
(77)

Wilson Wilkinson
c. 1840
Mansfield, Ohio
(77)

B. Willard
c. 1838
Schenectady, N.Y.
(24, 106)

William W. Willard
Willard & Stokes
Willard & Hawley
c. 1833–1851
Cazenovia, N.Y.
Syracuse, N.Y.
(24)

Bushnell Willey
Willey & Co.
Willey & Blakesley (?)
c. 1836–1837
Cincinnati, Ohio
(55, 106)

George William (Williams ?)
c. 1843–1848
Philadelphia, Pa.
(10)

Charles M. Williams
Monell & Williams
c. 1825–1837
New York, N.Y.
(37, 106)

Jehu Williams
Williams & Victor (W & V)
Williams & Son
c. 1814–1859
Lynchburg, Va.
(23)

John Williams
c. 1858–1860
Utica, N.Y.
(25)

Oliver S. Williams
c. 1850
Hartford, Conn.
(37)

W. H. Williams
c. 1839–1844
Hamilton, N.Y.
(24)

William A. Williams
c. 1809–1846
Alexandria, Va.
Washington, D.C.
(23, 38, 39, 50, 90, 106)

Andrew Willis
c. 1842
Boston, Mass.
(39, 106)

J. Wilmer
c. 1849
Philadelphia, Pa.
(10)

Samuel Wilmot
Wilmot & Richmond
Samuel & Thomas T. Wilmot
c. 1800–1846
New Haven, Conn.
Georgetown, S.C.
Charleston, S.C.
(14, 37, 38, 39, 50, 55, 90, 106, 130, 180)

Thomas T. Wilmot
Samuel & Thomas T. Wilmot
c. 1810–1850
New Haven, Conn.
Charleston, S.C.
Savannah, Ga.
Columbus, Ga.
(14, 21, 39, 106)

——— Wilson
Leonard & Wilson
c. 1844–1850
Philadelphia, Pa.
(10, 90)

Albert Wilson
c. 1833–1850
Albany, N.Y.
Troy, N.Y.
(24, 37, 50, 90, 106)

Alfred Wilson
c. 1842
St. Louis, Mo.
(123)

Andrew Wilson
c. 1844–1847
Philadelphia, Pa.
(10)

D. W. Wilson
c. 1854
York, S.C.
(39)

Edwin Franklin Wilson
c. 1838–1904
Rochester, N.Y.
(24, 100)

George Wilson
c. 1848–1850
Philadelphia, Pa.
(10, 11, 37, 50, 106)

J. Wilson
c. 1838–1839–before 1889
Lexington, Ky.
(63)

John Sylvester Wilson
c. 1837–before 1919
Rochester, N.Y.
(100)

P. G. Wilson
c. 1840
Philadelphia, Pa.
(10)

Robert Wilson (R W)
Robert & William Wilson
c. 1805–1846
New York, N.Y.
Philadelphia, Pa.
(10, 11, 38, 39, 50, 55, 90)

Thomas Wilson
c. 1837–1839
Philadelphia, Pa.
(10, 37, 90, 106)

William Wilson (W W)
Robert & William Wilson
c. 1829–1850
Philadelphia, Pa.
(10, 11, 50, 90)

William Rowan Wilson
Roger & Wilson
c. 1846–1866
Salisbury, N.C.
(22)

Christian Wiltberger (Wiltburger ?) (Jr. ?) (C W)
Wiltberger & Alexander
c. 1793–1851
Philadelphia, Pa.
(10, 11, 38, 39, 50, 55, 90)

Francis Wilte
c. 1839
St. Louis, Mo.
(123)

——— Winchester
Garner & Winchester
c. 1813–1861
Lexington, Ky.
(63)

Daniel F. Winchester
c. 1841
Louisville, Ky.
(63)

Phineas Wing
c. 1850
Poughkeepsie, N.Y.
(134)

Stephen Wing
S. Wing & Co.
c. 1845–1851
Utica, N.Y.
(24, 25)

Isaac Winslow
c. 1847–1848
Philadelphia, Pa.
(10)

Isaac Winters
c. 1844–1848
Philadelphia, Pa.
(10)

William Wirth
c. 1839
St. Louis, Mo.
(123)

George K. Wise
Butler, Wise & Keim
Dunlevy & Wise (?)
c. 1842–1850
Philadelphia, Pa.
(10, 37)

B. Wishart
c. 1839–1840
Philadelphia, Pa.
(10)

——— Witham
Witham & Newman
c. 1837–1850
Philadelphia, Pa.
(10)

Ebenezer Witham
c. 1833–1850
Philadelphia, Pa.
(10)

William Witham
c. 1846–1850
Philadelphia, Pa.
(10)

Daniel Withington
c. 1840
Ashland, Ohio
(77)

Samuel Withington
c. 1820–1841
Philadelphia, Pa.
(10)

S. B. Wolcott
c. 1840
Massachusetts (?)
(106)

——— Wolf (Wolfe ?)
Wolf & Wriggins
c. 1837
Philadelphia, Pa.
(10, 37, 38, 39, 55, 90, 106)

Francis H. Wolf (Wolfe ?)
c. 1829–1849
Philadelphia, Pa.
(10, 37, 38, 39, 90)

George Wolfe
c. 1870–1895
Louisville, Ky.
(123)

——— Wood
Wood & Force
c. 1839–1841
New York, N.Y.
(18)

A. Wood
A. & W. Wood
c. 1850
New York, N.Y.
(37, 38, 39, 106)

Benjamin B. Wood
c. 1794–1846
New York, N.Y.
(18, 37, 38, 39, 50, 55, 90, 106)

J. Charles Wood
c. 1849
Charleston, S.C.
(14)

J. (Jacob ?) E. Wood
c. 1845
New York, N.Y.
(11, 18, 38, 39, 50, 55, 106)

Jacob Wood
Gale, Wood & Hughes
Wood & Hughes (W & H)
c. 1834–1845
New York, N.Y.
(11, 18, 37, 38, 39, 50, 55, 90, 106)

T. S. Wood
c. 1845
Laurens, S.C.
(14)

Thomas Wood
c. 1837–1848
Philadelphia, Pa.
(10)

——— Woodbridge
Shipp & Woodbridge
c. 1842
St. Louis, Mo.
(123)

——— Woodford
Woodford & Kimball
c. 1850
Dunkirk, N.Y.
(24)

S. D. Woodhill
c. 1852–1853
Utica, N.Y.
(24, 25)

L. Woodruff
c. 1843
Cincinnati, Ohio
(77)

William G. Woodstock
Woodstock & Whitlock
c. 1840–1853
Augusta, Ga.
(21)

Eli Woodward
Woodward & Grosjean (W & G)
c. 1812–1852
Boston, Mass.
Hartford, Conn.
(37, 50, 106)

Charles Wooley
c. 1848–1849
Philadelphia, Pa.
(10)

Aaron Woolworth
Woolworth & Anderson
c. 1825–1856
Salisbury, N.C.
Greensboro, N.C.
(22)

Richard Woolworth
c. 1830–1839
Philadelphia, Pa.
(10)

W. W. Wormwood
c. 1850
Lyons, N.Y.
(24)

James W. Worn
c. 1849–1850
Philadelphia, Pa.
(10)

Goodwin Worrell
c. 1837–1849
Philadelphia, Pa.
(10)

John Worrell
c. 1837
Philadelphia, Pa.
(10)

Robert Worton
c. 1849
Philadelphia, Pa.
(10)

Thomas Wriggins
Wriggins & Co.
T. Wriggins & Co.
Wolf & Wriggins (?)
c. 1831–1846
Philadelphia, Pa.
(10, 11, 37, 50, 90, 106)

George B. Wright
c. 1849
Staunton, Va.
(23)

H. C. Wright
c. 1850
Cleveland, Ohio
(78)

James Wright
c. 1841–1844
Philadelphia, Pa.
(10)

James R. Wright
c. 1846–1856
Lynchburg, Va.
Lexington, Va.
(23)

John Wright
c. 1845–1850
Philadelphia, Pa.
(10)

John Auston Wright
c. 1844–1846
Leesburg, Va.
(23)

John F. Wright
c. 1841–1848
Louisville, Ky.
(63)

Mary Ann Wright
c. 1847–1850
Leesburg, Va.
(23)

John Wyand
c. 1847
Philadelphia, Pa.
(10)

Eleazer Wyer
Wyer & Noble
Wyer & Farley
c. 1772–1848
Charlestown, Mass.
Boston, Mass.
Portland, Me.
(37, 38, 39, 50, 55, 90, 106)

Eleazer Wyer, Jr.
Wyer & Noble
Wyer & Farley
c. 1823–1848
Portland, Me.
(38, 39, 50, 55, 90, 106)

Christopher Wynn
before 1883
Baltimore, Md.
(38, 39, 55, 93, 106)

William P. Yates
Yates & Kimball
c. 1841–1850
Elmira, N.Y.
(24)

Edward Yeager
c. 1844–1850
Philadelphia, Pa.
(10)

J. M. Yeager
c. 1839–1846
Philadelphia, Pa.
(10)

Joseph Yeager
c. 1816–1847
Philadelphia, Pa.
(10)

William Yeager
c. 1837
Philadelphia, Pa.
(10)

Frederick Yeiser
c. 1814–1857
Danville, Ky.
Lexington, Ky.
(63)

Alexander Yeoman
c. 1837
Philadelphia, Pa.
(10)

Robert A. Yongue
Cooper & Yongue
c. 1852–1857
Columbia, S.C.
(14)

William Yost
c. 1846–1847
Wheeling, W.Va.
(23)

Alexander Young
A. Young & Co.
Young & Co.
A. Young & Son
c. 1807–1856
Baltimore, Md.
Camden, S.C.
(14, 37, 38, 39, 55, 90, 106)

Daniel D. Young
c. 1841
Schenectady, N.Y.
(24)

Edward Young
A. Young & Co.
Young & Co.
A. Young & Son
c. 1848
Camden, S.C.
Columbia, S.C.
(14)

J. T. Young
c. 1855
Petersburg, Va.
(23)

James Young
c. 1829–1838
Troy, N.Y.
(24)

James H. Young
c. 1817–1850
Philadelphia, Pa.
(10)

Nicholas E. Young
c. 1839–1846
Saratoga Springs, N.Y.
(24)

S. E. Young
c. 1840
Laconia, N.H.
(11, 39, 106)

Walter Young
c. 1831–1839
Albany, N.Y.
Rochester, N.Y.
(24)

G. M. Zahn
c. 1840
Lancaster, Pa.
(38, 39, 106)

Jacob Zane
c. 1837–1846
Philadelphia, Pa.
(10)

John Zeibler
c. 1848
St. Louis, Mo.
(123)

G. A. Zeissler
c. 1848
Philadelphia, Pa.
(10)

William Zeller
c. 1835–1850
Philadelphia, Pa.
(10)

Samuel Zepp
c. 1842–1850
Philadelphia, Pa.
(10)

George A. Zumar
(Zuma ?)
(Zumer ?)
(Zeuma ?)
(Zeumer ?)
(Zoomer ?)
c. 1831–1849
Louisville, Ky.
(63)

MANUFACTURERS, TRADE MARKS AND TRADE NAMES

In this section, the names of those firms producing flatware between 1837 and 1910 are arranged alphabetically under sterling and electroplate headings; trade names, other than firm names, are arranged in the same order in each classification. Each manufacturer's name is followed by the years during which the firm is known to have operated, the location of the company, the names of successor companies, and the trade mark or marks used. Many of the manufacturers made both sterling and electroplate; these are listed in both sections, with appropriate trade marks.

Some of the listed firms made only limited lines of flatware; others made only coffee, afternoon tea and teaspoons; a few manufactured only "fancy pieces" to complement hollow ware products. These trade marks and trade names are included to facilitate identification of such pieces, even though complete flatware services in matching patterns were not made. The names and marks of companies known to have produced only hollow ware or toilet goods are not included, nor are those of jobbers, wholesalers or retailers who did not maintain their own design or manufacturing facilities.

Some of the firm names listed also appear in the preceding silversmith list; this duplication is a natural result of the 19th-century transition from crafts shop to factory production. The list has been made as complete as available records will permit, and any omissions are not necessarily those defined in the following statement, which originally appeared in the 1915 edition of *Trade Marks of the Jewelry and Kindred Trades*:

> There is an amount of cheap plated ware on the market stamped with the names of fictitious companies, such as "Quadruple Silver Plate Co.," "Royal Sterling Plate Co.," etc. These goods are furnished, bearing no stamp, to certain types of storekeepers, conductors of gift enterprises and jobbers of cheap merchandise, who stamp the goods themselves with such names as suit their fancy. It is, therefore, practically impossible to trace these stamps.

STERLING FLATWARE MANUFACTURERS, TRADE MARKS AND TRADE NAMES

A
(See Alvin Mfg. Co.)

ADAMS & SHAW CO.
c. 1870–1879
New York, N.Y.
Flatware patterns and dies acquired from John R. Wendt & Co. were sold to Dominick & Haff in 1879, when the firm went out of business. Electroplate discontinued, 1879.
(147, 150, 175)

LDA
(See L. D. Anderson Co.)

ADELPHI SILVER PLATE CO.
c. 1890–before 1915
New York, N.Y.
(73, 167)

ALVIN MFG. CO.
ALVIN SILVER CO.
ALVIN CORPORATION
c. 1886–present
Newark, N.J.
Irvington, N.J.
Sag Harbor, N.Y.
New York, N.Y.
Providence, R.I.
Operated as a branch of the Fahy Watch Case Co., Sag Harbor, N.Y. c. 1898–1910; flatware pattern patents were issued to the parent company. The Gorham Company, successor, c. 1928. Marks still in use.
(73, 105, 147, 148, 150, 163, 167, 182)

ALVIN STERLING

AMERICAN SILVER CO.
c. 1901–1935
Bristol, Conn.
Made sterling flatware c. 1907. International Silver Co., Successor, c. 1935.
(73, 86, 105, 147, 148, 150, 183)

L. D. ANDERSON CO.
c. 1910–after 1922
Reading, Pa.
(73)

L. D. A.

Apollo Sterling
(See Bernard Rice's Sons)

B
(See E. & J. Bass)
(See Battin & Co.)
(See R. Blackinton & Co.)
(See Thomas G. Brown & Sons)

BAILEY, BANKS & BIDDLE CO.
c. 1833–1910
Philadelphia, Pa.
(83)

BAKER-MANCHESTER CO.
c. 1914–1915–before 1920
Providence, R.I.
Succeeded Manchester Mfg. Co.; Manchester Silver Co., Successor.
(73, 175)

BALTIMORE SILVERSMITHS MFG. CO.
before 1910
Baltimore, Md.
Heer-Schofield Co., successor
(147, 148, 150)

BALTIMORE STERLING SILVER CO.
c. 1892–1904
Baltimore, Md.
The Stieff Co., successor
(73, 147, 148, 150, 267)

BARBOUR SILVER CO.
c. 1892–1898
Meriden, Conn.
International Silver Co., successor
(73, 86, 147, 150, 152)

B. S. C.
SOUTHINGTON CO.

E. & J. BASS
c. 1890–after 1922
New York, N.Y.
(73, 105, 147, 148, 163)

BATTIN & CO.
before 1907–after 1922
Newark, N.J.
(73, 148, 150, 163)

STERLING B.

BAY STATE
SILVER CO.
after 1887–before 1907
Boston, Mass.
(73, 105, 163)

SAMUEL E.
BERNSTEIN
c. 1890–1928
New York, N.Y.
National Silver Co., successor
(147, 148)

JAMES BINGHAM
c. 1850–before 1887
Philadelphia, Pa.
(10, 73)

BIXBY SILVER CO.
c. 1895–1905
Providence, R.I.
(73, 105, 163)

BLACK, STARR &
FROST, INC.
c. 1876–present
New York, N.Y.
(51, 73)

R. BLACKINTON
& CO.
c. 1862–present
North Attleboro, Mass.
(3, 73, 105, 147, 175)

JAMES E. BLAKE
CO.
c. 1900–before 1936
Attleboro, Mass.
(105)

Boston Silver
(See Tuttle Silver Co.)

S. D. BROWER &
SON
WALTER S.
BROWER
c. 1850–1898
Albany, N.Y.
(37, 55, 73, 105)

THOMAS G.
BROWN & SONS
c. 1840
New York, N.Y.
(37, 73)

C
(See Frederick H. Clark)

CB & H
(See Codding & Heilborn Co.)

CMR
(See Charles M. Robbins Co.)

CAMPBELL-
METCALF
SILVER CO.
c. 1893–1904
Providence, R.I.
(73, 105, 147, 150)

CARTER, HOWE
& CO.
c. before 1907–1915
New York, N.Y.
(105)

FREDERICK H.
CLARK
c. 1900–1918
Newark, N.J.
(73, 105)

COBB, GOULD
& CO.
c. 1874–1894
Attleboro, Mass.
Watson & Newell, successor
(147, 150)

CODDING &
HEILBORN CO.
INC.
after 1887–1918
North Attleboro, Mass.
(73, 105, 147, 150)

ALBERT COLES
c. 1840–1847
New York, N.Y.
(147, 150)

ALBERT COLES
& CO.
c. 1847–1868
New York, N.Y.
M. Morgan, Successor
(147, 150)

COLES & REYNOLDS
c. 1868–1875
New York, N.Y.
George W. Shiebler, Successor
(147, 150, 175)

COMMONWEALTH
SILVER CO.
before 1907
Los Angeles, Cal.
(73, 105)

H. H. CURTIS
CO., INC.
after 1887–1915
North Attleboro, Mass.
(73, 105)

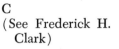

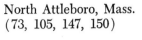

D
(See Deitsch Bros.)
(See Wm. B. Durgin Co.)
(See Hamilton & Diesinger)
(See The Dorst Co.)

D & H
(See Dominick & Haff)

DS
(See The Dorst Co.)

DSF
(See Dirksen Silver Co.)

DAVIS & GALT
before 1887–after 1915
Philadelphia, Pa.
(73, 105)

DEITSCH BROS.
before 1907–after 1920
New York, N.Y.
(73, 105)

DIRKSEN SILVER FILIGREE CO.
DIRKSEN SILVER CO.
c. 1892–1910
Freeport, Ill.
During later years, sterling spoon and fork blanks were purchased from other companies, notably A. F. Towle & Son Co. Marks of these companies sometimes appear on pieces with Dirksen filigree handles.
(73, 175)

D. S. F. CO.

DOMINICK & HAFF
c. 1873–1927
New York, N.Y.
Newark, N.J.
Taunton, Mass.
Reed & Barton, successor c. 1927. Year of Manufacture impressed in diamond; note resemblance to the mark of Wm. Gale & Sons, a predecessor firm.
(73, 147, 150, 163, 167)

D. & H.

(Production date impressed in diamond)

DORST CO.
after 1887–after 1922
Cincinnati, Ohio
(73, 105)

DUHME & CO.
DUHME JEWELRY CO.
c. 1840–after 1887
Cincinnati, Ohio
(38, 39, 73, 105, 106)

F. A. DURGIN
c. 1865–1888
St. Louis, Mo.
(123, 175)

WM. B. DURGIN CO.
c. 1853–1935
Concord, N.H.
The Gorham Co. acquired financial interest in 1905; operated as independent firm by The Silversmiths Co. and Silversmiths Stocks Co. 1906–1923. Merged with Gorham in 1923; moved to Providence, R.I. in 1931. Mark used by successor company.
(73, 105, 138, 139)

TE & Co.
(See Theodore Evans & Co.)

EAGLE STERLING CO.
c. 1894–1900
Glastonbury, Conn.
New Haven, Conn.
Eagle Spoon Co., successors
(130, 131)

EAGLE SPOON CO.
c. 1900–1905
New Haven, Conn.
(130, 131)

EVANS & COOK
c. 1855–1865
New York, N.Y.
Theo. Evans & Co., successor
(147, 150, 175)

THEODORE EVANS & CO.
c. 1865–1875
New York, N.Y.
George W. Shiebler & Co., successor
(73, 147, 150, 167)

F
(See L. W. Fairchield & Co.)
(See Ferdinand Fuchs & Bros.)

FCo.
(See Fessenden & Co.)

OTTO G. FABER
after 1887–before 1922
Baltimore, Md.
(73, 105)

L. W. FAIRCHILD & CO.
after 1887–before 1907
New York, N.Y.
(73, 105)

F

FARRINGTON & HUNNEWELL
before 1850–after 1887
Boston, Mass.
(3, 50, 106)

FESSENDEN & CO., INC.
c. 1858–before 1922
Providence, R.I.
Patterns and dies sold to the Manchester Silver Co., Mount Vernon Co., Roger Williams Silver Co. and others c. 1920.
(3, 73, 105)

F 925 STERLING 1000 CO

925
STERLING
1000

F STERLING CO

WILLIAM C. FINCK CO.
c. 1905–before 1915
Elizabeth, N.J.
(73, 105)

925/1000 STERLING

THEO. W. FOSTER & BROS.
c. 1898–after 1910
Providence, R.I.
(73, 105)

F&B

F. & B.

CHESTER FROST & CO.
c. 1875–1895
Chicago, Ill.
(196)

FERDINAND FUCHS & BROS.
c. 1910–1920
New York, N.Y.
(73, 105, 147)

F

FUCHS & CO.
FUCHS & BEIDERHASE
c. 1890–before 1907
New York, N.Y.
(73, 105)

G
(See The Gorham Co.)
(See F. S. Gilbert)

G J
(See Goodnow & Jenks)

GALE & NORTH
c. 1860–1867
New York, N.Y.
Gale, North & Dominick, successor
(147, 151)

GALE, NORTH & DOMINICK
c. 1868–1873
New York, N.Y.
Dominick & Haff, successor
(147)

WILLIAM GALE
c. 1821–1840
New York, N.Y.
William Gale & Sons, successor
(147)

WILLIAM GALE & SON
c. 1840–1860
New York, N.Y.
Year of manufacture impressed in diamond.
Gale & North; Gale, Wood & Hughes, successors
(19, 37, 39, 42, 147)

WM GALE & SON
G&S 1850

(Before 1856)

WM. GALE & SON
NEW YORK
925 STERLING

(After 1856)

GALE, WOOD & HUGHES
c. 1833–1845
New York, N.Y.
Wood & Hughes, successor
(73, 147)

F. S. GILBERT
before 1907
North Attleboro, Mass.
(73, 105)

STERLING G

Gilbert
(See George W. Shiebler & Co.)

W. H. GLENNY SONS & CO.
c. 1840–1900
Buffalo, N.Y.
(71)

W H GLENNY SONS & CO 1840

GOODNOW & JENKS
after 1887–before 1900
Boston, Mass.
(73, 105)

G TRADE MARK J

GORHAM & CO.
c. 1852–1865
Providence, R.I.
Gorham Mfg. Co., successor
(138, 139, 147)

GORHAM & THURBER
c. 1850–1852
Providence, R.I.

Gorham & Co., successor
(138, 139, 147)

GORHAM & WEBSTER
c. 1831–1837
Providence, R.I.
Gorham, Webster & Price, successor
(138, 139, 147, 150)

GORHAM, WEBSTER & PRICE
c. 1837–1841
Providence, R.I.
Jabez Gorham & Son, successor
(138, 139, 147)

JABEZ GORHAM & SON
c. 1841–1850
Providence, R.I.
Gorham & Thurber, successor
(138, 139, 147)

GORHAM MFG. CO.
THE GORHAM CO.
c. 1865–present
Providence, R.I.
Acquired by The Textron Corp., 1968
(73, 105, 138, 139)

GRAF & NIEMANN
c. 1900
Pittsburgh, Pa.
(147)

GRAFF, WASHBOURNE & DUNN
c. 1899–1961
New York, N.Y.
The Gorham Co., successor, 1961.
(73, 105, 147, 148, 167)

(Initials "G" "W" and "B" sometimes inside trademark)

H
(See Hayden Mfg. Co.)
(See Watson & Newell Co.)

HD
(See Hamilton & Diesinger)

HE
(See Holmes & Edwards Silver Co.)

HM
(See Hayes & McFarland)

HS
(See Hartford Sterling Co.)
(See Heer-Schofield Co.)

HALL, HEWSON & BROWER
HALL & BROWER
HALL, BROWER & CO.
c. 1849–1854
Albany, N.Y.
S. D. Brower & Son, successor
(73, 147, 148, 150)

HAMILTON & DIESINGER
before 1887–before 1907
Philadelphia, Pa.
M. F. Hamilton & Son, successor
(73, 105)

HAYDEN MFG. CO.
before 1907
Providence, R.I.
G. W. Parks Co., successor
(73, 105, 175)

HAYES & McFARLAND
HAYES, McFARLAND & CO.
H. A. McFARLAND CO.
after 1887–before 1914
Mount Vernon, N.Y.
The Mount Vernon Co.; The Gorham Co., successors
(73, 147, 148, 167)

W. A. HEATH & CO.
c. 1890
Newport, R.I.
(71)

HEER-SCHOFIELD CO.
c. 1903–1927
Baltimore, Md.
Frank M. Schofield Co., successor
(73, 105, 147, 150, 167)

HOLMES & EDWARDS SILVER CO.
c. 1882–1898
Bridgeport, Conn.
International Silver Co., successor
(73, 86, 105, 147, 148)

GEORGE E. HOMER
c. 1890–1900
Boston, Mass.
(73, 105)

H. HOWARD & CO.
c. 1878–1891
Providence, R.I.
Started flatware production in 1886, in a division called The Sterling Co. Howard & Son Co., successor.
(147, 150, 175)

HOWARD & SON CO.
1891
Providence, R.I.
Howard Sterling Co., successor
(147, 150, 175)

HOWARD STERLING CO.
c. 1891–1904
Providence, R.I.
Company went into receivership c. 1901–1902. Some patterns and dies were sold to the Roger Williams Silver Co. and others.
(73, 147, 150, 175)

INTERNATIONAL SILVER CO.
c. 1898–present
Meriden, Conn.
Continued marks of predecessor companies after 1898; International Silver Co. mark not used until after 1928 on sterling flatware.
(86, 175)

A. JACOBI
c. 1878–1890
Baltimore, Md.
Jacobi & Co., successor
(105, 175)

JACOBI & CO.
c. 1890–1894
Baltimore, Md.
Jacobi & Jenkins, successor
(105)

JACOBI & JENKINS
c. 1894–1908
Baltimore, Md.
Jenkins & Jenkins, successor
(73, 105)

JENKINS & JENKINS
c. 1908–1915
Baltimore, Md.
Continued use of Jacobi & Jenkins mark. Schofield Co., successor
(73, 105, 147, 163)

JENNINGS BROS. CO.
c. 1907
Bridgeport, Conn.
(105)

J. H. JOHNSTON
c. 1890
New York, N.Y.
(71)

K
(See Wm. Knoll & Co.)

(See Simons Bros. Co.)

KB
(See Krider & Biddle)

K & O COMPANY
c. 1908–1910
Brooklyn, N.Y.
(147)

THE KINNEY CO.
c. 1905
Providence, R.I.
(147)

KIRK & SMITH
c. 1814–1820
Baltimore, Md.
Samuel Kirk, successor
(154, 155)

B. 1814

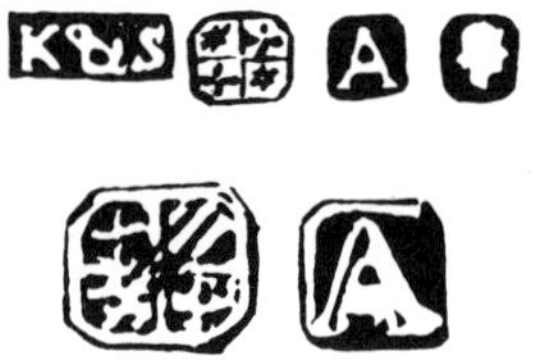

A. 1815

G.F. 1816

E. 1817

D. 1818

C. 1819

A. or B. 1820

SAMUEL KIRK
c. 1821–1846
Baltimore, Md.
Samuel Kirk & Son, successor
(154, 155)

G. 1821

F. 1822

E. 1823

D. or C. 1824

In the absence of any example of the assayer's marks for the years 1825 through 1827, and because of the great number of examples in existence bearing the 1824 marks, it is generally conceded that the 1824 marks were continued through the years 1825, 1826 and 1827.

F

SAM^L KIRK

SK 11OZ

2011 X S F

F. or E. 1828

S·KIRK

D

D. 1829

S·KIRK

KIRK

C. 1830

10.15 S KIRK

10 S·KIRK

SAM^L KIRK 10.15

S·K 11OZ

SK 11 S·K 11OZ

1830 to 1846

SAMUEL KIRK & SON
c. 1846–1861
Baltimore, Md.
Samuel Kirk & Sons, successor
(154, 155)

S.KIRK&SON 11OZ

S KIRK & SON 1015

10.15 S.KIRK&SON

S·K·&SON

(1846–1861)

SAMUEL KIRK & SONS
c. 1861–1868
Baltimore, Md.
Samuel Kirk & Son, successor
(154, 155)

S.KIRK&SONS11OZ.

S.KIRK& SONS 10.15

(1861–1868)

SAMUEL KIRK & SON
c. 1868–1896
Baltimore, Md.
Samuel Kirk & Son Co., successor
(3, 154, 155)

S KIRK & SON 925/1000

10.15 S.KIRK&SON

S.KIRK & SON 10.15

S.KIRK&SON

1868 to 1896

S.Kirk & Son 11OZ

10.15 S.KIRK&SON

1880 to 1890

SAMUEL KIRK & SON CO.
c. 1896–1924
Baltimore, Md.
became Samuel Kirk & Son, Inc., 1924–present
(73, 105, 147, 154, 155, 175)

S KIRK & SON Co 925/1000

S. KIRK & SON CO. 925/1000

S.KIRK & SON CO 925/1000

S.KIRK & SON 925/1000

1896 to 1907

S.KIRK&SON CO 925/1000

S.KIRK&SON Co 0001/926

1907 to 1924

WM. KNOLL & CO.
after 1887–before 1907
New York, N.Y.
(73, 105)

J. B. & S. M. KNOWLES
c. 1875–1891
Providence, R.I.
J. B. & S. M. Knowles Co., successor
(147, 175)

J. B. & S. M. KNOWLES CO.
c. 1891–1906
Providence, R.I.
Succeeded firm founded in 1852 by J. B. Knowles and H. L. Webster
(73, 105, 147, 167, 175)

RED CROSS

KNOWLES & LADD
c. 1865–1875
Providence, R.I.
J. B. & S. M. Knowles, successor
(147, 175)

KRIDER & BIDDLE
c. 1859–1869
Philadelphia, Pa.
Peter L. Krider Co., successor
(11, 37, 38, 39, 50, 55, 73, 90, 175)

PETER L. KRIDER CO.
c. 1869–1903
Philadelphia, Pa.
Simons Bros. Co., successor

(11, 37, 38, 39, 50, 55, 73, 90, 147, 175)

PETER L. KRIDER CO.,

L
(See LeBolt & Co.)
(See Lebkuecher & Co.)
(See Warwick Sterling Co.)

L'Aiglon
(See Bernard Rice's Sons)

FERDINAND C. LAMY
after 1887–before 1922
Saranac Lake, N.Y.
(73)

LANDERS, FRARY & CLARK
c. 1865–present
New Britain, Conn.
New York, N.Y.
(*Flatware production discontinued c. 1950*)
(73, 105, 175, 195, 281)

LEBKUECHER & CO.
before 1905–1918
Newark, N.J.
Became F. A. Lester; The Eleder Co., successor in 1918
(73, 105)

LEBOLT & CO.
c. 1899–present
Chicago, Ill.
(73, 105, 175)

F. A. LESTER
(See Lebkuecher & Co.)

CHARLES J. LEWARD
c. 1890–1900
New York, N.Y.
(73, 147)

Little Men–Little Women
(See Rogers, Lunt & Bowlen Co.)

Lunt Silversmiths
(See Rogers, Lunt & Bowlen Co.)

M
(See Maltby, Stevens & Curtiss Co.)
(See Manchester Mfg. Co.)
(See Manchester Silver Co.)
(See Mauser Mfg. Co.)

MB
(See Joseph Mayer, Inc.)

MCo.
(See The McChesney Co.)

MSC
(See Maltby, Stevens & Curtiss Co.)

MALTBY, STEVENS & CURTISS CO.
c. 1879–1890
Wallingford, Conn.
Watrous Mfg. Co.; International Silver Co., successors
(33, 73, 86, 147, 175)

W. H. MANCHESTER & CO.
c. 1877–1904
Providence, R.I.
Started flatware production in 1895. Manchester Mfg. Co., successor
(105, 147, 175)

MANCHESTER MFG. CO.
c. 1904–1914–15
Providence, R.I.
Baker-Manchester Mfg. Co., successor
(73, 105, 147, 175)

MANCHESTER SILVER CO.
c. 1914–present
Providence, R.I.
(73, 105, 147, 150, 175)

MAUSER MFG. CO.
before 1896–after 1914
Mount Vernon, N.Y.
The Mount Vernon Co.; Gorham Mfg. Co., successors. Some flatware patterns and dies acquired by Wendell Mfg. Co., c. 1896–1897.
(73, 105, 175)

JOSEPH MAYER & BROS.
JOSEPH MAYER, INC.
c. 1897–after 1922
Seattle, Washington
E. J. Towle Co., successor; pick-and-shovel mark, without initials MB, used by successor company.
(73, 167, 175)

MAYO & CO.
before 1890–after 1905
Chicago, Ill.
(73, 105)

MERIDEN BRITANNIA CO.
c. 1852–1898
Meriden, Conn.
International Silver Co., successor. Produced sterling flatware under 1847 Rogers Bros. and Rogers, Smith & Co. brands. c. 1878–1880. Meriden Sterling was promoted by The International Silver Co., successor firm, c. 1911–12. Patterns marketed under this brand were the same as those produced by Simpson, Hall, Miller & Co., Watrous Mfg. Co., and Wilcox & Evertsen, all subsidiaries of International.
(73, 86, 105, 147, 150, 175)

MERIDEN CUTLERY CO.
c. 1825–1866
Meriden, Conn.
Made some sterling silver handle carving knives and sets; Landers, Frary & Clark, successors. Mark used by successor company on some sterling ware.
(73, 105, 175)

MERIDEN STERLING CO.
after 1887–before 1907
Meriden, Conn.
(73, 105)

MERRILL BROS. & CO.
c. 1895–1920
Newark, N.J.
The Merrill Co., Inc., successor
(73, 105, 147)

THE MERRILL CO., INC.
c. 1920–1930
Newark, N.J.
The Merrill Shop, successor
(73, 147)

MONTGOMERY BROS.
c. 1890–after 1915
Los Angeles, Cal.
(73, 175)

JOHN MOORE & SON
c. 1848–1869
New York, N.Y.
Supplied Tiffany, Young & Ellis, Tiffany & Co.; Merged with Tiffany & Co. in 1869.
(171, 175)

M. MORGAN
c. 1847–1877
New York, N.Y.
George W. Shiebler, successor
(147, 150, 175)

THE MOUNT VERNON COMPANY
c. 1910–1923
Mount Vernon, N.Y.
Formed by merger of Hayes & McFarland, Mauser Mfg. Co., Roger Williams Silver Co. The Gorham Company, successor, 1923.
(73, 105, 139, 167)

N
(See E. Newton & Co.)
(See William Nost, Inc.)

N. & D. O.
(See N. & D. Onderdonk)

NSCo.
(See Newburyport Silver Co.)

NATIONAL SILVER CO.
c. 1890–present
New York, N.Y.
Flatware production discontinued c. 1955.
(105, 175)

E. NEWTON & CO.
c. 1896–1900
New York, N.Y.
(73, 105)

STERLING N

NEWBURYPORT SILVER CO.
c. 1907–1913
Keene, N.H.
(73, 154, 175)

NSCO
N. S. C.

NIAGARA SILVER CO.
c. 1890–1905
Niagara Falls, N.Y.
Wm. A. Rogers, Ltd., successor
(33, 73, 167, 224)

Sterling $\frac{925}{1000}$ Fine

NORTON & SEYMOUR
NORTON, SEYMOUR & CO.
c. 1850–1855
Syracuse, N.Y.
Joseph Seymour, successor
(147)

WILLIAM NOST CO., INC.
after 1887–after 1922
New York, N.Y.
(73, 105)

N & D O
(See N. & D. Onderdonk)

N. & D. ONDERDONK
c. 1890–1900
New York, N.Y.
(73, 105)

N. & D. O.

ONEIDA COMMUNITY, LTD.
ONEIDA, LTD.
c. 1846–present
Sterling flatware not manufactured until after 1946.
(33, 73, 147, 167, 175)

P
(See Philadelphia Silversmithing Co.)

PR
(See Towle Mfg. Co.)

P & B
(See Paye & Baker Mfg. Co.)

G. W. PARKS CO.
c. 1907–after 1920
Providence, R.I.
(73, 105, 175)

PAYE & BAKER MFG. CO.
after 1887–1934–35
North Attleboro, Mass.
Flatware production discontinued c. 1920.
(73, 105)

PHILADELPHIA SILVERSMITHING CO.
after 1887–after 1922
Philadelphia, Pa.
(73)

JOHN POLHEMUS
c. 1839–1876
New York, N.Y.
George W. Shiebler, successor
(147, 175)

S. C. POWELL
before 1907
New York, N.Y.
(73, 105)

R
(See Reed & Barton)

RBCo.
(See R. Blackinton & Co.)

RCo.
(See Redlich & Co.)

R & B
(See Charles M. Robbins Co.)

RLB
(See Rogers, Lunt & Bowlen Co.)

RW
(See Roger Williams Silver Co.)

CMR
(See Charles M. Robbins Co.)

Red Cross
(See J. B. & S. M. Knowles Co.)

REDLICH & CO.
c. 1890–1946
New York, N.Y.
Elgin Silversmiths Co., successors
(73, 105)

REED & BARTON
c. 1836–present
Taunton, Mass.
Began manufacture of sterling silver flatware in 1889. See electroplate manufacturers list for predecessor companies.
(51, 73, 105, 147, 148, 150, 175)

BERNARD RICES' SONS
c. 1867–after 1950
New York, N.Y.
(73, 105)

CHAS. M. ROBBINS CO.
c. 1900–after 1915
Attleboro, Mass.
The Robbins Co., Inc., successor. Flatware production discontinued before 1920.
(73, 105)

ROCKFORD SILVER PLATE CO.
c. 1882–1925
Rockford, Ill.
See electroplate manufacturers' list for sequence of corporate names.
(73, 105, 147, 150, 175)

STERLING

Rogers Bros.
1847 Sterling
(See Meriden Britannia Co.)

ROGERS, LUNT & BOWLEN CO.
c. 1902–present
Greenfield, Mass.
Now called Lunt Silversmiths; succeeded A. F. Towle & Son Co.
(73, 105, 147, 150, 175)

TRADE MARK R & L B Co STERLING

Little Men & Little Women
STERLING SILVER TABLEWARE

Trade Treasure Mark

Rogers, Smith & Co. Sterling
(See Meriden Britannia Co.)

S
(See Joseph Seymour Mfg. Co.)
(See George W. Shiebler Co.)
(See Simons Bros. Co.)
(See Frank W. Smith Co.)

SH
(See Silberstein, Hecht & Co.)

SS
(See Syracuse Sterling Silver Co.)

SSS
(See Sterling Silver Souvenir Co.)
(See Stone Sterling Silver Co.)

GEORGE A. SCHLECHTER
c. 1890
Reading, Pa.
(71)

FRANK M. SCHOFIELD CO.
c. 1927–1930
Baltimore, Md.
The Schofield Co., successor
(73, 147, 148, 150, 175)

THE SCHOFIELD CO.
c. 1930–1965
Baltimore, Md.
Oscar Caplan & Sons, successor, 1965; The Stieff Company, successor, 1967.
(73, 105, 147, 148, 150, 175)

HENRY SEARS & SON
c. 1865–1895
Chicago, Ill.
(175, 185)

HENRY SEARS & SON 1865 WARRANTED

JOSEPH SEYMOUR, SONS & CO.
JOSEPH SEYMOUR MFG. CO.
c. 1882–1905
Syracuse, N.Y.
(3, 73, 105, 147)

★ S ★

Trade ★ S ★ Mark
STERLING

JOSEPH SEYMOUR
c. 1855–1882
Syracuse, N.Y.
Joseph Seymour, Sons & Co., successor
(147, 175)

CHARLES C. SHAVER
c. 1854–1900
Utica, N.Y.
(24, 25, 73, 79)

C.C.S

GEORGE E. SHAW
before 1885–after 1922
Putnam, Conn.
(73, 105)

GEN. PUTNAM

GEORGE W. SHIEBLER
c. 1875–1892
Brooklyn, N.Y.
New York, N.Y.
George W. Shiebler Co., successor
(73, 147, 150, 167, 175)

GEORGE W. SHIEBLER CO.
c. 1892–1915
New York, N.Y.
(73, 105, 147, 150, 175)

GILBERT

TRADE MARK

GEORGE C. SHREVE
SHREVE & CO.
c. 1852–present
San Francisco, Cal.
Manufactured first flatware in 1904.
(73, 105, 175)

GEO. C. SHREVE & CO.

(1852–1892)

(1892–present)

SILBERSTEIN, HECHT & CO.
after 1887–before 1907
New York, N.Y.
A. L. Silberstein; Griffon Cutlery Works, successors
(73, 105)

THE SILVERSMITHS CO.
SILVERSMITHS STOCKS CO.
1906–1923
Holding companies chartered in New York 1906–1907; held The Gorham Company's interests in William B. Durgin Co., Wm. B. Kerr Co., The Mount Vernon Co. and Whiting Mfg. Co. Dissolved in 1923, when these companies were merged into The Gorham Co.
(138, 139)

F. W. SIM & CO.
c. 1847–after 1897
Troy, N.Y.
(175, 263)

SIMMONS & PAYE
c. 1890–after 1910
Providence, R.I.
Some patterns and dies sold to Wendell Mfg. Co.
(147, 167)

SIMONS, BRO. & CO.
SIMONS BROS. CO.
c. 1839–present
Philadelphia, Pa.
Sterling silver flatware discontinued c. 1908; Simons Bros. & Peter L. Krider Co. patterns and dies sold to the Alvin Mfg. Co.
(73, 105, 147, 167, 175)

TRADE MARK

S. B. & Co.

SIMPSON, HALL, MILLER & CO.
c. 1866–1898
Wallingford, Conn.
Sterling silver flatware produced after 1895. International Silver Co., successor; mark used by successor company.
(73, 86, 105, 147, 150, 175)

FRANK W. SMITH CO.
c. 1882–present
Gardner, Mass.
North Attleboro, Mass.
The Webster Co.; Reed & Barton, successors
(51, 73, 147, 163, 167, 175)

W. D. SMITH SILVER CO.
c. 1910–after 1922
Chicago, Ill.
(73, 105)

THEODORE B. STARR
c. 1900–1924
New York, N.Y.
Reed & Barton, successors
(51, 73, 105, 175)

THE STERLING CO.
(See H. Howard & Co.)

THE STERLING SILVER MFG. CO., INC.
c. 1900–after 1915
Providence, R.I.
(73, 105)

STERLING SILVER SOUVENIR COMPANY
c. 1890–1900
Boston, Mass.
(73, 105)

THE STIEFF CO.
1904–present
Baltimore, Md.
Succeeded Baltimore Sterling Silver Co. c. 1892–1904.
(73, 105, 147, 175, 267)

STIEFF STERLING

STONE STERLING SILVER CO.
after 1887–before 1904
New York, N.Y.
(73, 105)

STROBEL & CRANE
c. 1907
Newark, N.J.
(105)

SYRACUSE SILVER MFG. CO.
after 1887–before 1900
Syracuse, N.Y.
(73, 105)

T
(See Edward Todd & Co.)
(See Towle Mfg. Co.)
(See Tuttle Silver Co.)

TPCo.
(See Tucker & Parkhurst Co.)

TS
(See A. F. Towle & Son Co.)

TIFFANY & CO.
c. 1852–present
New York, N.Y.
(73, 105, 171, 175)

TIFFANY & Co 271 BROADWAY J.C.M. TIFFANY & COMPY M TIFFANY & Co G&W TIFFANY & Co 271 BROADWAY M

(*Used* 1852-53.)

2 TIFFANY & CO M LATE M TIFFANY, YOUNG & ELLIS 550 BROADWAY TIFFANY & Co 6601 G&W • G&W ENGLISH STERLING 925-1000 4 550 BROADWAY. N.Y.

(*Used* 1854-55.)

TIFFANY & CO 295 M ENGLISH STERLING M 925-1000 • 550 BROADWAY

TIFFANY & CO 657 M M 2712 GOLD & SILVERSMITHS 550 BROADWAY

(*Used* 1854-70.)

TIFFANY & Co. TIFFANY

TIFFANY & CO 1824 QUALITY 925-1000 M 5731 UNION SQUARE

TIFFANY & Co 1063 STERLING M 1100 UNION SQUARE TIFFANY & CO. UNION SQ.

Marks in use 1870-75

TIFFANY & Co MAKERS STERLING-SILVER 925-1000 M

(*Used* 1875-91.)

TIFFANY & Co 9074 MAKERS 7184 STERLING SILVER 925-1000 T

(*Used* 1891-1902.)

TIFFANY & Co 14786 MAKERS 5885 STERLING SILVER 925-1000 C

Mark in use 1902-07

TIFFANY & Co 12345 MAKERS 67890 STERLING SILVER 925-1000 M

Mark in use 1907-38

TIFFANY & WALES
c. 1898
Boston, Mass.
(147, 167)

TIFFANY & YOUNG
c. 1837–1848
New York, N.Y.
(73, 105, 171)

TIFFANY, YOUNG & ELLIS
c. 1848–1852
New York, N.Y.
(73, 105, 171, 175)

TIFFANY YOUNG & ELLIS J.C.M 20

TIFFT & WHITING
c. 1840–1866
North Attleboro, Mass.
Whiting Mfg. Co., successor
(147, 148)

EDWARD TODD & CO.
c. 1869–after 1922
New York, N.Y.
(73, 105)

TOWLE & JONES
c. 1857–1873
Newburyport, Mass.
A. F. Towle & Son, successors
(19, 174, 175)

TOWLE & JONES

A. F. TOWLE & SON
c. 1873–1879
Newburyport, Mass.
A. F. Towle & Son Mfg. Co., successor
(19, 174, 175)

A F TOWLE & SON

A. F. TOWLE & SON CO.
c. 1883–1902
Newburyport, Mass.
Greenfield, Mass.
Rogers, Lunt & Bowlen Co., successor
(3, 73, 147, 148, 105, 175)

TRADE MARK STERLING

A. F. TOWLE & SON MFG. CO.
c. 1879–1883
Newburyport, Mass.
A. F. Towle & Son Co.; The Towle Mfg. Co., successors
(147, 148, 175)

TOWLE MFG. CO.
c. 1883–present
Newburyport, Mass.
(3, 73, 147, 148, 150, 172, 174, 175)

(Paul Revere Silverware.)

(La Fayette Silverware.)

TOWNSEND, DESMOND & VOORHIS CO.
c. 1890–before 1904
New York, N.Y.
(73, 105)

T. D. & V. CO.
STERLING

TUCKER & PARKHURST CO.
before 1907
Ogdensburg, N.Y.
(73, 105)

TIMOTHY TUTTLE
c. 1890–1909
Boston, Mass.
Tuttle Silver Co., successor
(150)

TUTTLE SILVER CO.
c. 1909–1955
Boston, Mass.
Wallace Silversmiths, successors
(73, 105, 150, 177)

BOSTON SILVER

U
(See Unger Brothers)

UB
(See Unger Brothers)

UNGER BROTHERS
after 1887–c. 1920
Newark, N.J.
New York, N.Y.
Manufactured no complete flatware line. Made some fancy pieces, spoons.
(73, 105, 147, 148)

U

UPSON & HART CO.
c. 1895
Unionville, Conn.
(150)

V & Co.
(See W. K. Vanderslice Co.)
(See Vansant & Co.)

W. K. VANDERSLICE CO.
c. 1860–1900
San Francisco, Cal.
(3, 73, 105, 175)

JOHN T. VANSANT MFG. CO.
c. 1887–before 1907
Philadelphia, Pa.
Succeeded Vansant & Co.
(3, 39, 105)

W
(See Watrous Mfg. Co.)
(See The Watson Co.)
(See E. G. Webster & Son)
(See Weidlich Sterling Spoon Co.)
(See The Wendell Co.)
(See Frank M. Whiting & Co.)
(See Whiting Mfg. Co.)

W & H
(See Wood & Hughes)

WCo.
(See The Wallingford Co.)
(See Wendell Mfg. Co.)

WR (RW)
(See Roger Williams Silver Co.)

WS
(See Warwick Sterling Co.)
(See Wayne Silver Co.)

WV
(See Wortz & Voorhis)

WW
(See Wilcox & Wagoner Co.)

WWH
(See William W. Hayden Co.)

Wallace Silversmiths
(See R. Wallace & Sons Mfg. Co.)

R. WALLACE & SONS MFG. CO.
1871–present
Wallingford, Conn.
Lancaster, Pa.
Hamilton Watch Co., successors since 1959. Name changed to Wallace Silversmiths c. 1955. Sterling silver flatware made after 1875. See electroplate manufacturers list for

predecessor companies.
73, 105, 147, 148, 150, 175, 177, 273)

THE WALLINGFORD CO., INC.
after 1887–1955
Wallingford, Conn.
Wallace Silversmiths, successors
(73, 105, 177)

WARWICK STERLING CO.
c. 1906–1910–after 1914
Providence, R.I.
(73, 175)

WATROUS MFG. CO.
c. 1896–1898
Wallingford, Conn.
International Silver Co., successor. Mark used by successor company after 1898.
(73, 86, 105, 148, 167, 175)

THE WATSON CO.
c. 1910–1955
Attleboro, Mass.
Wallace Silversmiths, successor
(73, 105, 148, 175, 177)

WATSON, NEWELL & CO.
c. 1894–1919
Attleboro, Mass.
The Watson Co.; Wallace Silversmiths, successors
(73, 105, 147, 148, 150, 167, 175, 177)

WAYNE SILVER CO.
before 1905
Honesdale, Pa.
(73, 105)

A. A. WEBSTER & CO.
c. 1890–1899
Brooklyn, N.Y.
(165)

WEBSTER & KNOWLES
c. 1852–1865
Providence, R.I.
Knowles & Ladd, successor
(147, 150, 175)

E. G. WEBSTER & SON
c. 1883–1923
New York, N.Y.
Brooklyn, N.Y.
International Silver Co., successor. See electroplate manufacturers list for predecessor companies.
(73, 86, 147, 150, 175)

G. K. WEBSTER
c. 1869–before 1915
North Attleboro, Mass.
The Webster Co., successor
(73, 105)

THE WEBSTER CO.
c. 1910 (?)–present
North Attleboro, Mass.
Reed & Barton, successor
(73, 105)

WEIDLICH BROS. MFG. CO.
WEIDLICH STERLING SPOON CO.
c. 1901–after 1950
Bridgeport, Conn.
Firm did not make flatware prior to 1910, according to the Web Silver Co., present owner of Weidlich patterns and dies.
(73, 148, 163, 175)

WILLIAM WEIDLICH & BRO.
c. 1900–1905
St. Louis, Mo.
(147, 175)

WENDELL MFG. CO.
WENDELL & CO.
c. 1890–present
Chicago, Ill.
Founded by Charles Wendell c. 1850. Made sterling wares

for Marshall Field & Co.; some pieces bear both store mark and trademark. Flatware production discontinued c. 1900.
(73, 105, 163, 175)

JOHN R. WENDT & CO.
c. 1855–1870
New York, N.Y.
Made silver for Ball, Black & Co. Flatware patterns and dies were sold in two lots, c. 1870; one lot to Whiting Mfg. Co., second lot to Adams & Shaw Co.
(147, 175)

WHITE & FOSTER
WHITE, FOSTER & CO.
c. 1873–1898
Providence, R.I.
Theo. Foster & Bro. Co., successor
(147, 175)

H. L. WHITE & CO.
c. 1852–1891
Providence, R.I.
J. B. & S. M. Knowles, successor
(147, 148, 175)

FRANK M. WHITING & CO.
F. M. WHITING & CO.
c. 1840–present
North Attleboro, Mass.
Ellmore Silver Co.; Crown Silver, Inc., successors.
(73, 147, 150, 167, 175)

WHITING MFG. CO.
c. 1866–1923
New York, N.Y.
Bridgeport, Conn.
Providence, R.I.
The Gorham Company acquired financial interest in 1905; operated as independent firm by The Silversmiths Co. and Silversmiths Stocks Co. 1906–1923. Plant moved to Bridgeport, Conn. 1910. Merged with The Gorham Company in 1923; moved to Providence, R.I. 1925. Some flatware patterns produced by successor company.
(73, 105, 138, 139, 167, 175)

F. M. WHITNEY & CO.
c. 1887
Attleboro, Mass.
(3)

WILCOX & EVERTSEN
c. 1892–1898
Meriden, Conn.
International Silver Co. successor. Mark used by successor company after 1898.
(73, 86, 147, 148, 150, 175)

WILCOX & WAGONER
after 1887–c. 1910
Attleboro, Mass.
The Watson Co.; Wallace Silversmiths, successors
(73, 105, 177)

ROGER WILLIAMS SILVER CO.
c. 1900–1910
Providence, R.I.
The Mount Vernon Co.; The Gorham Co., successors.
(73, 105, 147, 150, 175)

WILLIAM WISE & SONS
c. 1890–1899
Brooklyn, N.Y.
(71, 165)

A. & W. WOOD
c. 1850–1860
New York, N.Y.
Coles & Reynolds, successor
(73, 147, 150, 175)

WOOD & HUGHES
c. 1845–1899
New York, N.Y.
Graff, Washbourne & Dunn, successor
(73, 147, 167, 175)

to 1871

1871–1899

ELECTROPLATE FLATWARE MANUFACTURERS,
TRADE MARKS AND TRADE NAMES

A. L. Nickel Silver 210
(See Oneida, Ltd.)

A.S.Co.
ASCo.
(See American
Silver Co.)

ACME SILVER
PLATE CO.
c. 1887
Boston, Mass.
(3)

ADAMS & SHAW CO.
(See Sterling entry)

ADELPHI SILVER
PLATE CO.
c. 1890–before 1915
New York, N.Y.
(73, 167)

Albany Silver Plate Co.
(See Barbour
Silver Co.)

Aetna Works
(See Landers,
Frary & Clark)

Alpha Plate
(See Oneida, Ltd.)

Alvin Long Life Plate
(See Alvin Mfg. Co.)

Alvin Patent
(See Alvin Mfg. Co.)

ALVIN MFG. CO.
ALVIN SILVER CO.
ALVIN
CORPORATION
c. 1886–present
Newark, N.J.
Irvington, N.J.
Sag Harbor, N.Y.
New York, N.Y.
Providence, R.I.
Electroplate flatware introduced in 1908. Also see Sterling entry. The Gorham Co., successor, c. 1926.
(73, 105, 147, 148, 150, 175)

ALVIN PATENT

LONG LIFE SILVER PLATE

AMERICAN
SILVER CO.
c. 1901–1935
Bristol, Conn.
Succeeded Holmes & Tuttle; Bristol Brass & Clock Co., c. 1853–1901. International Silver Co., successor.
(73, 86, 147, 150, 167, 175)

1857 STANDARD OF THE WORLD TRADE MARK "WORLD BRAND"

NICKEL ASCo SILVER

A. S. CO. 1857

Windsor Table Spoons.

1857 STANDARD OF THE WORLD TRADE MARK WORLD BRAND

A S Co #1 INDEPENDENCE BRAND

THE AMERICAN SILVER CO.
A. S. CO.
ATLAS SILVER CO.
BEACON SILVER CO.
CROWN SILVER PLATE CO.
CROWN SILVER CO.
EASTERN SILVER CO.
H. & T. MFG. CO.
NEW ENGLAND SILVER PLATE
NEW ENGLAND CUTLERY CO.
OLD ENGLISH BRAND
OLD ENGLISH BRAND, B.
PEQUABUCK MFG. CO.
ROYAL PLATE CO.
STERLING PLATE ◁B▷
WELCH SILVER
1857 WELCH-ATKINS

ANCHOR SILVER
PLATE CO.
c. 1900–before 1920
St. Paul, Minn.
Muncie, Ind. (?)
(73, 105)

TRADE MARK S. P. REGISTERED

S. P. TRADE MARK REGISTERED

ANCHOR BRAND
INDIANA BRAND
(On Triple Plate.)

ANCHOR SILVER PLATE CO.
(On Quadruple Plate.)

A. T. ANDERSON
c. 1884
Chicago, Ill.
(3, 175)

Arrow Plate
Arrow Silver Plate Co.
(See Glastonbury
Silver Co.)

ASSOCIATED
SILVER CO.
before 1907–after 1920
Chicago, Ill.
(73, 105, 163, 175)

Yourex

Astec Coin Metal
(See Holmes &
Edwards Silver Co.)

Atlas Silver Co.
(See American Silver Co.)

EDGAR ATWATER
c. 1849–1854
Wallingford, Conn.
(177)

AURORA SILVER PLATE CO.
c. 1869–1907
Aurora, Ill.
Mulholland Bros., successor
(3, 73, 105, 175)

1869
AURORA SILVER PLATE MFG. CO.
12 Dwt.

1869 AURORA SILVER PLATE M'F'G. CO.

B
(See C. E. Barker Mfg. Co.)

B.S.Co.
(See Holmes & Edwards Silver Co.)

M.S.B.
(See Benedict Silver Co.)

JAMES A. BABCOCK
c. 1880–1890
New York, N.Y.
(165)

Banquet Plate
(See Gorham Mfg. Co.)

BARBOUR SILVER CO.
c. 1882–1898
Hartford, Conn.
Meriden, Conn.
International Silver Co., successor
(73, 86, 147, 150, 175)

ALBANY SILVER PLATE CO.

C. E. BARKER MFG. CO.
before 1907
New York, N.Y.
(73, 105)

DUCIMUS
TRADE MARK

E. & J. BASS
c. 1900–after 1922
New York, N.Y.
(73, 105, 147, 150)

SILVER PLATED

Beacon Silver Co.
(See American Silver Co.)

BEAVER FALLS CUTLERY CO.
c. 1880–1890
Beaver Falls, Pa.
(165)

BENEDICT-CLARKE SILVER CO.
c. 1883–1902
East Syracuse, N.Y.
M. S. Benedict Mfg. Co., successor
(105, 147, 150)

BENEDICT-DUNN CO.
c. 1880–1902
East Syracuse, N.Y.
M. S. Benedict Mfg. Co., successor
(105, 147)

M. S. BENEDICT MFG. CO.
c. 1902–1909
East Syracuse, N.Y.
Firm made Benedict and Hamilton Brands of electroplated flatware.

Benedict Mfg. Co., successor
(105, 147, 167)

TRADE MARK

BENEDICT SHEFFIELD PLATE NICKEL SILVER

M. S. BENEDICT MFG. CO.

T. N. BENEDICT MFG. CO.
c. 1890–1904
East Syracuse, N.Y.
M. S. Benedict Mfg. Co., successor
(73, 105, 147, 150)

BENEDICT MFG. CO.
c. 1909–1927
East Syracuse, N.Y.
Benedict Silver Co., successor
(147)

BENEDICT

BENEDICT
TABARD SILVER

BENEDICT

QUADRUPLE PLATE

BENEDICT & BURNHAM MFG. CO.
c. 1905–1915
Waterbury, Conn.
(105)

JACOB BIESCH
c. 1910
New York, N.Y.
(147)

BIGGINS-RODGERS CO.
c. 1900–1920
Wallingford, Conn.
Dowd-Rodgers Co., successor
(73, 105)

D

E. A. BLISS CO.
BLISS SILVER CO.
c. 1883–1920
Attleboro, Mass.
Meriden, Conn.
Napier Co., successor
(105, 147, 150, 175)

B. S. CO. A I

B. S. CO.
12

Bliss Silver Plate
(See E. A. Bliss Co.)

LUTHER BOARDMAN
c. 1820–1840
East Haddam, Conn.
L. Boardman & Son, successor
(147, 188)

L. BOARDMAN & SON
c. 1840–1908
East Haddam, Conn.
(105, 147, 148, 150, 188)

L. BOARDMAN & SON

"G. S. RICHMOND."

"S. J. FRANCONIA."

BRIDGEPORT SILVER CO.
before 1880–after 1882
Bridgeport, Conn.
Possibly merged with F. B. Rogers Silver Co.
(130, 131, 167)

BRIDGEPORT SILVER PLATE CO.
c. 1891–1898
Bridgeport, Conn.
MacFarlane Bros. Mfg. Co., successor; moved to Norfolk, Va., in 1898.
(130, 131, 167, 175)

BRISTOL BRASS & CLOCK CO.
c. 1857–1902
Bristol, Conn.
American Silver Co., successor; marks used by successor company.
(86, 130, 131, 175)

Trade Mark 1850 BRISTOL 1857 Diamond Brand

BRISTOL CUTLERY CO.

NEW ENGLAND SILVER PLATE CO.
1857 WELCH-ATKINS WELCH SILVER
H. & T. MFG. CO. ROYAL PLATE CO.

Bristol Cutlery Co.
(See American Silver Co.)
(See Bristol Brass & Clock Co.)

Bristol Plate Co.
(See Pairpoint Mfg. Co.)

BROWN & BROS.
c. 1875–1905
Waterbury, Conn.
(73)

J. E. CALDWELL & CO.
c. 1900–1912
Philadelphia, Pa.
(83)

CALIFORNIA SILVER MFG. CO.
c. 1905–1915
San Francisco, Cal.
(105)

CAMBRIDGE SILVER CO.
CAMBRIDGE SILVER PLATE
c. 1900–1910
location unknown
Possibly secondary trade name.
(260)

C S P

CARPENTER & BLISS
c. 1875–1883
North Attleboro, Mass.
E. A. Bliss Co., successor
(147, 148)

CATTARAUGUS CUTLERY CO.
c. 1876–present
Little Valley, N.Y.
(73, 105)

YUKON SILVER
96-100 Fine

Columbia
(See Middletown Plate Co.)
(See G. I. Mix Co.)

Colonial Plate Co.
(See Melrose Silver Co.)

Community
(See Oneida, Ltd.)

Community Plate
(See Oneida, Ltd.)

COWLES MFG. CO.
c. 1842–1850
Granby, Conn.
(86)

Crescent Silver Co.
(See Albert G. Finn Silver Co.)

CROMWELL PLATE CO.
c. 1887
Boston, Mass.
(3)

Crown Guild
(See Rockford Silver Plate Co.)

Crown Prince
(See G. I. Mix & Co.)

Crown Silver Co.
(See American Silver Co.)

Crown Silver Plate Co.
(See American Silver Co.)

Croydon
(Trade name used by Silverware Wholesalers Association, New York, N.Y., c. 1910–1920)

FRED R. CURTIS CO.
c. 1848–1854
Waterbury, Conn.
(177)

H. H. CURTIS CO.
c. 1900–1915
North Attleboro, Mass.
(73, 105)

CURTIS & ROWLEY
c. 1880–1890
New York, N.Y.
(73, 165)

D
(See Biggins-Rodgers Co.)
(See Dorst Co.)

A. DAVIS & CO.
c. 1900–before 1915
Chicago, Ill.
M. C. Eppenstein, successor
(73, 105)

R. COIN
R. SPECIAL

JAMES J. DAWSON CO.
c. 1904–before 1915
New York, N.Y.
(73, 105)

NORTH AMERICA

DERBY SILVER PLATE CO.
c. 1873–1898
Birmingham (later Derby), Conn.

Shelton, Conn.
Meriden, Conn.
International Silver Co., successor
(73, 86, 192, 193)

Dolly Varden
(See Middletown Silver Co.)

DORST CO.
c. 1900–after 1922
Cincinnati, Ohio
(73, 105)

Duro Plate
(See Oneida, Ltd.)

E. S. CO.
(See Benedict Mfg. Co.)
(See Empire Silver Co.)

EASTERN CAROLINA SILVER CO.
c. 1907–1908
Hartsville, S.C.
(105)

Eastern Silver Co.
(See American Silver Co.)

Elmwood Plate
(See Gorham Mfg. Co.)

Empire Silver Co.
(See Benedict Mfg. Co.)

EMPIRE SILVER CO.
c. 1890–before 1909
Brooklyn, N.Y.
Benedict Mfg. Co., successor. Marks used by successor company.
(73, 105, 167)

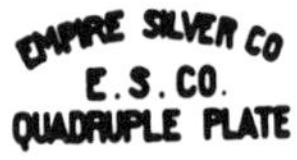

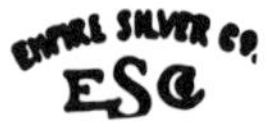

Eureka Silver Plate Co.
(See Meriden Silver Plate Co.)

Extra Coin Silver Plate
(See Niagara Silver Co.)
(See Wm. A. Rogers, Ltd.)

WILLIAM FABER & SONS
c. 1887
Philadelphia, Pa.
Wm. B. Faber, successor
(3, 105)

FILLEY, MEAD & CALDWELL
c. 1850
Philadelphia, Pa.
(10, 86)

HARVEY FILLEY & SONS
c. 1859–after 1887
Philadelphia, Pa.
(3, 10)

ALBERT G. FINN SILVER CO.
c. 1900–before 1915
Syracuse, N.Y.
P. A. Coon Silver Mfg. Co., successor
(73, 105)

CRESCENT SILVER CO.

FLORENCE SILVER PLATE CO.
c. 1907–present
Baltimore, Md.
(105)

FORBES SILVER CO.
c. 1894–1898
Meriden, Conn.
International Silver Co., successor
(73, 86, 147, 148, 150)

FRANKLIN SILVER PLATE CO.
c. 1905–1917
Greenfield, Mass.
Rogers, Lunt & Bowlen Co., successor
(73, 105, 163)

WEE FOLK'S

FRARY & CLARK & SMITH
c. 1850–1865
Meriden, Conn.
Merged with Landers & Smith in 1865 to form Landers, Frary & Clark.
(175)

F. FULMER
c. 1870
Indianapolis, Ind.
(70)

GALE MFG. CO.
c. 1905–after 1920
Syracuse, N.Y.
(105)

Gee-Esco
(See Glastonbury Silver Co.)

German Silver
(See Holmes & Edwards Silver Co.)

GLASTONBURY SILVER CO.
c. 1906–c. 1950
Glastonbury, Conn.
Chicago, Ill.
Glastonbury, Inc., successor
(57, 78, 85, 105, 163)

GEE-ESCO

GORHAM MFG. CO.
THE GORHAM CO.
c. 1865–present
Providence, R.I.
Electro-plated flatware first manufactured in 1865; See sterling flatware manufacturers list for predecessor companies.
(51, 73, 86, 138, 139, 147, 150, 179)
Banquet Plate
Elmwood Plate

GORHAM

G M Co
E P

GRIFFON CUTLERY WORKS
c. 1905–present
New York, N.Y.
(73, 105, 175)

"Griffon"

TRADE-MARK
GRIFFON

L. B. GRUM
c. 1868–1870
Richmond, Ind.
c. 1877–after 1883
Indianapolis, Ind.
(70)

H & E S Co.
(See Holmes & Edwards Silver Co.)

H & T MFG. CO.
(See American Silver Co.)
(See Holmes & Tuttle Mfg. Co.)

H. B. & H. A 1
(See Holmes, Booth & Haydens)

HE
(See Holmes & Edwards Silver Co.)

HALL, BOARDMAN & CO.
c. 1830–1850
New York, N.Y.
(33, 86)

HALL, ELTON & CO.
c. 1837–1852
Wallingford, Conn.
Meriden Britannia Co.; International Silver Co., successors.
(3, 33, 86, 147, 148, 177)

HAMILTON MFG. CO.
before 1902
location unknown
Merged with M. S. Benedict Mfg. Co., Syracuse, N.Y. in February 1902. Benedict Mfg. Co. continued to market Hamilton Brand flatware after 1902.
(147, 150, 175)

Hampton Plate Co.
(See Meriden Britannia Co.)

HARTFORD SILVER PLATE CO.
c. 1887
Hartford, Conn.
(105)

HAYES & Mc FARLAND
HAYES, Mc FARLAND & CO.
H. A. Mc FARLAND CO.
after 1887–before 1914
Mount Vernon, N.Y.
The Mount Vernon Co,. The Gorham Co., successors
(73, 105, 147, 148, 150)

HM

W. A. HENDRIE
c. 1850–1860
Chicago, Ill.
(16)

GEORGE A. HERRING
c. 1900
Chicago, Ill.
Associated Silver Co., successor
(73, 105, 175)

Hexco Mexican
(See Holmes & Edwards Silver Co.)

WILLIAM D. HIGGINS
c. 1870
Indianapolis, Ind.
(70)

HOLMES, BOOTH & HAYDENS
c. 1853–1886
New York, N.Y.
Rogers & Hamilton, successor
(73, 86, 147, 148, 175)

H. B. & H. A. 1.

SHEFFIELD PLATED CO.
STERLING SILVER PLATE CO.
UNION SILVER PLATE CO.

HOLMES & EDWARDS SILVER CO.
c. 1882–present
Bridgeport, Conn.
Stratford, Conn.
Meriden, Conn.
International Silver Co., successor, 1898. Marks used by successor company.
(73, 86, 105, 147, 148, 150, 167, 175)

HOLMES 14 EDWARDS

HE

HOLMES & EDWARDS XIV

STERLING INLAID

GERMAN SILVER

MEXICAN SILVER

LASHAR ▭ SILVER

HOLMES & EDWARDS SILVER-INLAID HE

+ HOLMES & EDWARDS HE

HOLMES & EDWARDS 12

HOLMES & EDWARDS XIV HE

HE

ASTEC COIN METAL
EDWARDS
B. S. CO.
HEXCO MEXICAN
HESCO
▭ LASHAR
H. & E. S. CO.
MEXICAN CRAIG
ORIENTAL
STRATFORD SILVER CO.
STRATFORD PLATE
STRATFORD SILVER PLATE CO

HOLMES & GRIGGS
before 1850
Waterbury, Conn.
Holmes & Tuttle; American Silver Co.; International Silver Co., successors.
(86)

HOLMES & HOTCHKISS
before 1850
Waterbury, Conn.
Holmes & Tuttle; American Silver Co.; International Silver Co., successors.
(86)

Holmes Silver Co.
(See Holmes & Edwards Silver Co.)

HOLMES & TUTTLE MFG. CO.
c. 1851–1857
Boston, Mass.
Bristol, Conn.
Bristol Brass & Clock Co.; American Silver Co.; International Silver Co., successors. Marks used by successor companies.
(86, 147, 167, 175, 179)

HOLMES & TUTTLE

H. & T. MFG. CO.

HOUSATONIC MFG. CO.
c. 1900
New Haven, Conn.
Succeeded Eagle Spoon Co.
(130, 131, 175)

HOWARD CUTLERY CO.
c. 1904–before 1920
New York, N.Y.
(73, 105)

HOWARD'S NICKEL SILVER WARRANTED

H. HOWARD & CO.
HOWARD & SON CO.
1878–1891
Providence, R.I.
Made electroplated flatware c. 1886–1891; plating division sold in 1891. Sterling flatware production continued under the Howard Sterling Co. name.
(147, 150)

JOHN HURLY SILVER CO.
c. 1890–1894
Scriba, N.Y.
M. S. Benedict Mfg. Co., successor
(147)

Illinois Silver Co.
(See Associated Silver Co.)

Indiana Brand
(See Anchor Silver Plate Co.)

W. K. INGRAM
c. 1862
Chicago, Ill.
(16)

INTERNATIONAL SILVER CO.
1898–present
Meriden, Conn.
International Silver Co. mark rarely used on flatware before 1928.
(73, 86, 147, 148, 175)

J. W. JOHNSON
c. 1869–1910
New York, N.Y.
American Silver Co., successor
(73, 175)
Royal Plate Co.
Crown Silver Plate Co.

KNICKERBOCKER SILVER CO.
c. 1900–after 1922
Port Jervis, N.Y.
Niagara Falls, N.Y.
(73, 105)

K S C

Lakeside
(Montgomery Ward & Co. private label; some electroplated flatware made by E. H. H. Smith Silver Co., other patterns by Williams Bros. Co.)

LANDERS, FRARY & CLARK
c. 1865–present
New Britain, Conn.
New York, N.Y.
Cutlery and silver flatware production discontinued c. 1950.
(73, 175)

UNIVERSAL

RESISTAIN
SILVADIUM

Lashar
Lashar Silver
(See Holmes & Edwards Silver Co.)

H. LEONARD
c. 1847–1882
Nashville, Tenn.
(89)

LEONARD, REED & BARTON
c. 1837–1847
Taunton, Mass.
Reed & Barton, successor. Made unplated Britannia metal spoons; began silver-plating spoons c. 1848.
(51, 175)

L. A. LITTLEFIELD SILVER CO.
c. 1905–1915
New Bedford, Mass.
(105)

Lion Brand
(See Williams Bros. Mfg. Co.)

Long Life Silver Plate
(See Alvin Silver Co.)

M
(See Melrose Silver Co.)

MB
(See Joseph Mayer, Inc.)

M B Co.
(See Meriden Britannia Co.)

M S B
(See Benedict Mfg. Co.)

M S C
(See Maltby, Stevens & Curtiss Co.)

MAC FARLANE BROS. MFG. CO.
MAC FARLANE MFG. CO.
c. 1898–1913
Bridgeport, Conn.
Norfolk, Va.
Bridgeport plant sold to Newfield Silver Co., c. 1913.
(130, 131)

MADISON SILVER PLATE CO.
c. 1887
Madison, Ind.
(3)

E. MAGNUS
c. 1890–before 1904
New York, N.Y.
Howard Cutlery Co., successor
(73)

Malacca Plated
(See G. I. Mix & Co.)

MALTBY, STEVENS & CO.
c. 1870–1879
Wallingford, Conn.
Maltby, Stevens & Curtiss, successor
(86, 175)

MALTBY, STEVENS & CURTISS CO.
c. 1879–1890
Wallingford, Conn.
Watrous Mfg. Co., successor. Made some plated and sterling flatware; most production was unplated, sold to Wm. Rogers Mfg. Co. and others for plating.
(73, 86, 147, 148, 150)

MANHATTAN SILVER PLATE CO.
c. 1877–1898
Brooklyn, N.Y.
International Silver Co., successor
(73, 86, 147, 148)

Marion Plate Co.
(See Bernard Rice's Sons)

JOSEPH MAYER, INC.
c. 1897–after 1922
Seattle, Wash.
(73, 105, 147, 150, 175)

DAVID H. McCONNELL
c. 1890–1910
New York, N.Y.
(73)

SO. AM.

McGLASHAN, CLARKE & CO.
c. 1900–1910
Niagara Falls, Ont., Can.
Muncie, Ind.
Wm. A. Rogers, Ltd.; Oneida, Ltd., successors
(167)

JOHN O. MEAD
c. 1837–1859
Philadelphia, Pa.
J. O. Mead & Sons; Filley, Mead & Caldwell, successors
(86)

MEAD & ROGERS (ROGERS & MEAD)
c. 1845–1847
Hartford, Conn.
Rogers Brothers, successors
(86)

J. W. MELLISH
c. 1870
Indianapolis, Ind.
(70)

THE MELROSE SILVER CO.
before 1903–before 1922
Hartford, Conn.
Manufactured low-priced electroplated flatware c. 1903–1905.
(73, 147, 150)

COLONIAL PLATE CO.

MERIDEN BRITANNIA CO.
c. 1852–1898
Meriden, Conn.
International Silver Co., successor
(73, 86, 105, 147, 148, 150, 175)

MERIDEN BRIT^A Co.

1847 ROGERS BROS.

1847 ROGERS BROS (TRADE MARK)

1847 ROGERS BROS.

1847 ROGERS BROS

MERIDEN CUTLERY CO.
c. 1825–1866
Meriden, Conn.
Landers, Frary & Clark, successor.

Mark used by Landers, Frary & Clark after 1866.
(73, 105, 175)

MERIDEN CUTLERY CO.
1855
12

M C Co
12

MERIDEN SILVER PLATE CO.
c. 1869–1898
Meriden, Conn.
International Silver Co., successor
(73, 86)

EUREKA SILVER PLATE CO.

MERRY & PELTON SILVER CO.
c. 1901–1906
St. Louis, Mo.
(73, 105)

TRIPLE PLATE 12

SECTIONAL PLATE XII
STANDARD PLATE 4

METROPOLITAN MFG. CO.
c. 1907
Boston, Mass.
(105)

Mexican Craig
(See Holmes & Edwards Silver Co.)

Mexican Silver
(See Holmes & Edwards Silver Co.)

Middlesex Silver Co.
(See Middletown Silver Co.)

MIDDLETOWN PLATE CO.
c. 1864–1898
Middletown, Conn.
Meriden, Conn.
International Silver Co., successor
(73, 86, 175)

COLUMBIA
SUPERIOR

MIDDLETOWN SILVER CO.
before 1907–1945
Middletown, Conn.
R. Wallace & Sons Mfg. Co., successor
(73, 105, 177)

MIDDLETOWN
SILVERWARE

MIDDLESEX SILVER CO.

Middletown Silverware
(See Middletown Silver Co.)

G. I. MIX & CO.
c. 1860–before 1904
Yalesville, Conn.
(73, 86)

CROWN PRINCE
MALACCA PLATED
THE COLUMBIA

MONTGOMERY WARD & CO.
c. 1872–present
Chicago, Illinois
Private label flatware made by E. H. H. Smith Co. Williams Bros. and others.
(175, 276)

MONTGOMERY WARD & CO.
LAKESIDE.

MONTGOMERY WARD & CO

MULFORD, WENDELL & CO.
c. 1855–1865
Albany, N.Y.
(179, 219)

MULHOLLAND BROS., INC.
c. 1904–after 1922
Aurora, Ill.
(73, 175)

MultiSilver
(See E. H. H. Smith Silver Co.)

NSCo.
(See National Silver Co.)

N.S.Co.
(See Newburyport Silver Co.)

NATIONAL SILVER CO.
c. 1890–present
New York, N.Y.
Flatware production facilities sold c. 1956.
(105, 175)

National Cutlery Co.
(See Rockford Silver Plate Co.)

210 Nearsilver
(See Oneida, Ltd.)

NEWBURYPORT SILVER CO.
c. 1907–1913
Keene, N.H.
(73, 175)

N. S. CO.

NEW AMSTERDAM SILVER CO.
c. 1890
New York, N.Y.
Knickerbocker Silver Co., successor.
Mark used by successor company
(73, 105, 147)

New England Cutlery Co.
(See American Silver Co.)

New England Silver Plate Co.
(See American Silver Co.)

N. F. Nickel Silver
(See Oneida, Ltd.)

N. F. Silver Co. 1877
(See Oneida, Ltd.)

Niagara Falls Co. 1877
(See Oneida, Ltd.)

NIAGARA FALLS SILVER CO.
c. 1877–1902
Niagara Falls, N.Y.
Oneida Community Ltd., successors
(33, 167, 175)

N. F. SILVER CO. 1877

NIAGARA SILVER CO.
c. 1890–1905
Niagara Falls, N.Y.
Wm. A. Rogers, Ltd.; Oneida, Ltd., successors
(33, 73, 167, 175, 224)

NIAGARA SILVER CO.

NIAGARA SILVER CO.

Extra { COIN SILVER } Plate

R. S. Mfg. Co. A 1
Coin Silver Metal
Pure Aluminum
X-XX-XXX

North America
(See James J. Dawson Co.)

NORWICH CUTLERY CO.
c. 1890–1898
Norwich, Conn.
International Silver Co., successor
(86, 148)

O.C.
(See Oneida Community, Ltd.)

O. C. Lustra
(See Oneida Community, Ltd.)

Old English Brand
Old English Brand B
(See American Silver Co.)

Old Home Plate
(See Wm. Rogers Mfg. Co.)

Oneida
(See Oneida, Ltd.)

Oneida Community Diamond Plate
(See Oneida, Ltd.)

Oneida Community Par Plate
(See Oneida, Ltd.)

Oneida Community Reliance Plate
(See Oneida, Ltd.)

Oneida Community Silver Plate
(See Oneida, Ltd.)

ONEIDA COMMUNITY SILVER CO.
ONEIDA COMMUNITY, LTD.
ONEIDA, LTD.
1846–present
Wallingford, Conn.
Niagara Falls, N.Y.
Oneida, N.Y.
Name changed to Oneida, Ltd. in 1935
(33, 163, 147, 148, 150, 167, 175, 226)

ONEIDA

W SILVER PLATE

REX PLATE
RELIANCE
RELIANCE PLATE
J. ROGERS & CO.
SILVER METAL
TRIPLE PLUS
TUDOR PLATE
U. S. SILVER CO.
ALPHA PLATE
CARBON
COMMUNITY
DURO PLATE
210 NEARSILVER
O. C.
O. C. LUSTRA

ONEIDA COMMUNITY SILVER PLATE

A. 1. NICKEL SILVER NO. 210

COMMUNITY PLATE

N. F. NICKEL SILVER
NIAGARA FALLS CO. 1877
N. F. SILVER CO., 1877
ONEIDA COMMUNITY DIAMOND PLATE
ONEIDA COMMUNITY PAR PLATE
ONEIDA COMMUNITY RELIANCE PLATE

ONTARIO SILVER CO.
c. 1907–1915
Muncie, Ind.
(105)

Oriental
(See Holmes & Edwards Silver Co.

Our Very Best
(See Williams Bros. Mfg. Co.)

Oxford Cutlery Co.
(See Wm. A. Rogers, Ltd.)

Oxford Silver Plate Co.
(See Wm. A. Rogers, Ltd.)

PAIRPOINT MFG. CO.
PAIRPOINT CORPORATION
c. 1880–1958
New Bedford, Mass.
Flatware department purchased by Niagara Silver Co., c. 1900.
Some patterns and dies sold to the Rockford S.P.Co.
(73, 105, 147, 148, 150, 167, 175, 224)

PAIRPOINT MFG. CO. NEW BEDFORD MASS. QUADRUPLE PLATE P

BRISTOL PLATE CO

PAIRPOINT
FLAT 1880 WARE
BEST

TRADE P MARK.

Panama
(Montgomery Ward & Co. private label; manufacturer unknown)

Paragon Plate
(See McGlashan Clarke Co., Ltd.)

Paragon Plate
(Private mail order company label, produced by International Silver Co. Bridgeport plant c. 1910)
(175, 260)

CHAS. PARKER CO.
c. 1887–1907
Meriden, Conn.
(3, 105)

PARKER & CASPER
c. 1867–1870
Meriden, Conn.
Wilcox Silver Plate Co.; International Silver Co., successors
(86, 147, 148, 150)

G. W. PARKS CO.
before 1909–before 1922
Providence, R.I.
(73, 105)

HOPE SILVER CO.

PELTON BROS. & CO.
PELTON BROS. SILVER CO.
c. 1884–1901
St. Louis, Mo.

Merry & Pelton Silver Co., successor
(3, 73, 105)

Pequabeck Mfg. Co.
(See American Silver Co.)

ALBERT PICK CO.
c. 1857–1965
Chicago, Ill.
(73, 175, 229)
Acorn Brand
Everwear
Sterlinguard

PIX

Puritan Silver Co.
(See Wm. A. Rogers, Ltd.)

R
(See Wm. A. Rogers, Ltd.)

R Co.
(See Wm. A. Rogers, Ltd.)

RSPCo.
(See Rockford Silver Plate Co.)

R. Coin
(See A. Davis & Co.)

RACINE SILVER PLATE CO.
c. 1875–1882
Racine, Wisconsin
Rockford Silver Plate Co., successor
(150)

REDFIELD & RICE
c. 1867–before 1900
New York, N.Y.
Bernard Rice's Sons, successor
(73, 147, 148, 150, 175)

REED & BARTON
c. 1835–present
Taunton, Mass.
Succeeded Babbitt & Crossman (1824)
Babbitt, Crossman & Co. (1828)
Crossman, West & Leonard (1829)
Taunton Britannia Mfg. Co. (1830)
Crossman & Pratt (1833)
Production of electroplated flatware began in 1848
(51, 73, 105, 147, 148, 150, 175)

REED & BARTON

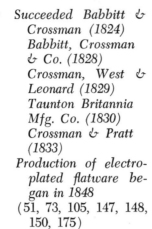

GOLDYN-BRONZ
REED & BARTON

REED & BARTON

REED & BARTON
TRADE MARK

REGAL SILVER MFG. CO.
c. 1905–after 1922
New Haven, Conn.
(73)

REGAL

REGAL SILVER MFG. CO.
WARRANTED 12 DWT
NEW HAVEN CONN

Reliance Plate
Reliance
(See Oneida, Ltd.)

Rex Plate
(See Oneida, Ltd.)

BERNARD RICE'S SONS
c. 1900–after 1946
New York, N.Y.
(73, 105, 147, 148, 150)

QUADRUPLE PLATE R

APOLLO

B R S
NICKEL SILVER
TRADE MARK

G. S. Richmond
(See L. Boardman & Son)

CHARLES M. ROBBINS CO.
before 1904–1920
Attleboro, Mass.
Plated flatware discontinued before 1915
The Robbins Co., successor
(73, 105, 147)

CMR

ROBESON CUTLERY WORKS
c. 1907–present
Rochester, N.Y.
(105)

ROCKFORD SILVER PLATE CO.
c. 1882–1925
Rockford, Ill.
Sheets-Rockford Co., successor
Flatware patterns, patents and dies purchased by Oneida, Ltd. in 1925.
(73, 105, 147, 150, 148, 175)

ROCKFORD S.P. CO.
1875
WARRANTED 12 DWT.

ROCKFORD

CROWN GUILD

CROWN GUILD
3

ROCKFORD S.P.CO.

CUSTOM
NATIONAL CUTLERY CO.
SUPERIOR

ROCKFORD S. P. Co
1875
WARRANTED 12DWT

ROCKFORD S P Co
N. S.
WARRANTED 16DWT.

ROGERS & BRITTIN
before 1904
West Stratford, Conn.
(73)

UNXLD

ROGERS & BRO.
c. 1858–1898
Waterbury, Conn.
International Silver Co., successor; marks used by successor company after 1898.
(73, 86, 147, 148, 150, 167, 175, 179)

Rogers & Bro.

STAR (★) BRAND

★ROGERS & BRO. A-1.
(*Best Quality Flatware.*)

R. & B.
(*Medium Quality Flatware.*)

★ ROGERS & BRO.
(*H. H. Cutlery.*)

ROGERS & BRO.
No. 12
(*Steel Knives.*)

ROGERS & BRO. NICKEL SILVER
(*Nickel Silver Flatware, Unplated*)

ROGERS & HAMILTON CO.
c. 1886–1898
Waterbury, Conn.
International Silver Co., successor; marks used by successor company after 1898.
(73, 86, 147, 148, 150, 167, 175)

HAMILTON

ROGERS & HAMILTON 12

ROGERS & HAMILTON

ROGERS & HAMILTON. A 1

ROGERS & MEAD
c. 1845–1847
Hartford, Conn.
Rogers Brothers, successors
(86)

ROGERS BROTHERS
c. 1847–1853
Hartford, Conn.
Rogers Bros. Mfg. Co., successor
(86)

ROGERS BROS. MFG. CO.
c. 1853–1861
Hartford, Conn.
c. 1862–1898
Meriden, Conn.
Merged with Rogers, Smith & Co. in 1861; merged with Meriden Britannia Co. in 1862; International Silver Co., successor; marks used by successor company after 1898.
(86, 147, 148, 150, 175, 212–216)

Rogers Bros. A 1

Rogers Bros. Mfg. Co

ROGERS BROS. MFG. CO. HARTFORD CONN. EXTRA HEAVY PLATE

C. B. ROGERS & CO.
C. ROGERS
C. ROGERS & BROS.
c. 1866–1902
Meriden, Conn.
International Silver Co., successor
(73, 147, 150)

C-B-ROGERS-&-CO

C. ROGERS & BROS. MERIDEN, CONN. 12 DWT.

C. ROGERS & BROS. A1.

C. ROGERS & BROS., A 1.

ROGERS CUTLERY CO.
c. 1871–1898
Hartford, Conn.
International Silver Co., successor
(86, 147, 150, 175)

ROGERS (CO)

ROGERS CUTLERY CO.

R.C. CO.

R. C. CO. AI PLUS

1881 Rogers
(See Wm. A. Rogers, Ltd.)

1847 Rogers Bros.
(See Meriden Britannia Co. Mark used 1862–present)

1865 Wm. Rogers
(See Wm. Rogers' Mfg. Co. Mark used from 1865.)

F. B. ROGERS SILVER & CUTLERY CO.
c. 1883–1890
Shelbourne Falls, Mass.
Hartford, Conn.
F. B. Rogers Silver Co., successor
(3, 105)

FRANK W. ROGERS
c. 1900–before 1915
Hartford, Conn.
(73, 105)

WM ROGERS SON

J. ROGERS SILVER CO.
J. ROGERS & CO.
c. 1901–1929
Wallingford, Conn.
Oneida Community, Ltd., successor
(33, 73, 105, 167, 175)
1901 Rogers

ROGERS, LUNT & BOWLEN CO.
c. 1902–present
Greenfield, Mass.
Succeeded A. F. Towle & Son Co.; known as Lunt Silversmiths since c. 1930.
(73, 105, 147, 150, 175)

1901 Rogers
(See J. Rogers Silver Co.)

ROGERS SILVER PLATE CO.
c. 1905–1920
Danbury, Conn.
Meriden, Conn.
(105)

R.S.P.Co. MERIDEN

ROGERS SILVER PLATE
NB
TRADE MARK
CONN.

SIMEON L. & GEORGE H. ROGERS CO.
c. 1900–1929
Hartford, Conn.
Wm. A. Rogers, Ltd.; Oneida Community, Ltd., successors
(33, 147, 167, 146)

Trade-Mark:
ROGERS

ACORN

SL&GHR CO
EPNS

Trade-Mark:
ROGERS BROS.

R Rogers R

The S. L. and G. H. Rogers Co.

S. L. & G. H. Rogers
(See Simeon L. & George H. Rogers Co.)

ROGERS, SMITH & CO.
c. 1856–1861
Hartford, Conn.
Merged with Rogers Bros. Mfg. Co. in 1861; merged with Meriden Britannia Co., in 1862; International Silver Co., successor, 1898. Marks used by successor companies.
(73, 86, 147, 148, 247)

ROGERS SMITH & CO. MERIDEN CT.

R. S. & CO.

GUARANTEED BY ROGERS SMITH & CO. MERIDEN CT.

ROGERS SMITH & CO. WARRANTED 12 DWT.

ROGERS & SPURR MFG. CO.
c. 1881–1885
Greenfield, Mass.
(147, 150, 165, 175)

W. A. Rogers
(See Wm. A. Rogers, Ltd.)

WILLIAM A. ROGERS, LTD.
c. 1903–1929
New York, N.Y.
Niagara Falls, N.Y.
Wallingford, Conn.
Northampton, Mass.
Toronto, Ont. Can.
Oneida Community, Ltd., successor. Marks used by successor company after 1929.
(33, 73, 105, 147, 148, 150, 167, 248–255)
Puritan Silver Co.

WM. A. ROGERS

HEIRLOOM PLATE

1881 ROGERS NEW YORK

TRADE MARK

WM. A. ROGERS 16 DWT SPECIAL

Wm. A. Rogers Spotless

WM. A. ROGERS NEW YORK

ROGERS 1881 Warranted 12 Dwt

W R BURNISHED No 12

WM. A. ROGERS SILVER NICKEL R

WM. A. ROGERS Warranted 12 Dwt

Wm. A. Rogers Warranted

WM. A. ROGERS SPOTLESS

Wm A Rogers Damascus Steel

W R

OXFORD CUTLERY CO WARRANTED No 12

WM. A. ROGERS Special 16 Dwt.

OXFORD CUTLERY CO. WARRANTED No. 12
(Light Plate Knives and Forks.)

Wm. A. Rogers
(12Dwt. Knives and Forks.)

ROGERS
(12 Dwt. Knives and Forks.)

W. R.
(Half Plate Flatware.)

R. S. MFG. CO.
(Half Plate Flatware.)

BUSTER BROWN
(Silver Plate on Brass.)

BILLY POSSUM
(Silver Plate on Brass Base.)

Extra { COIN SILVER } Plate

W. A. Rogers

OXFORD SILVER PLATE CO.

WM. A. ROGERS
NEW YORK

1881 ROGERS A 1

NIAGARA SILVER CO.

WILLIAM ROGERS & CO.
c. 1841–1855
Hartford, Conn.
Wm. Rogers & Son, successor
(86)

WILLIAM ROGERS & SON
c. 1855–1865
Hartford, Conn.
Wm. Rogers Mfg. Co., successor
(86)

Wm. Rogers & Son
(See Wm. Rogers Mfg. Co.)

Wm. Rogers Eagle Brand
(See Simpson, Hall, Miller & Co.)

WILLIAM ROGERS MFG. CO.
c. 1865–1898
Hartford, Conn.
Meriden Britannia Co.; International Silver Co., successors. Marks used by successor companies.
(73, 86, 147, 148, 150, 175, 179, 256–259)

1865 WM. ROGERS MFG. CO.
WM. ROGERS MFG. CO.
ROGERS CUTLERY CO

WM. ROGERS & SON

TRADE MARK:
WM. ROGERS & SON.

TRADE MARK:
WM. ROGERS MFG. CO.

ROGERS

W. F. Rogers
(See C. Rogers & Bros.)

WILLIAM G. ROGERS
c. 1904–before 1922
New York, N.Y.
(73)

WILLIAM H. ROGERS
c. 1904
Hartford, Conn.
(73)

ROGERS A1

WILLIAM H. ROGERS CORP.
after 1904–before 1918
Plainfield, N.J.
(73, 105)

R TRADE MARK

SEAL BRAND WM. H. ROGERS CORPORATION PLAINFIELD N.J.

Royal Brand
(See National Silver Co.)

ROYAL MFG. CO.
c. 1894–1908
Detroit, Mich.
(147)

Royal Plate Co.
(See American Silver Co.)

JOHN RUSSELL CUTLERY CO.
c. 1834–after 1922
Turners Falls, Mass.
(73)

RUSSELL

RUSSELL

1834 J RUSSELL & CO

1834
J RUSSELL & CO

J. RUSSELL & CO.
GREEN RIVER WORKS

RUSSELL
GREEN RIVER WORKS

S
(See E. H. H. Smith Silver Co.)
(See Stevens Silver Co.)

SSCo.
(See W. D. Smith Silver Co.)

SSP
(See Salem Silver Plate)

ST. LOUIS SILVER CO.
c. 1880–1913
St. Louis, Mo.
(73, 105, 175)

SALEM SILVER PLATE CO.
c. 1910
location unknown
Possibly secondary trade name
(260)

SSP

SCHADE & CO.
c. 1885–1905
Brooklyn, N.Y.
Harry M. Schade, successor
(73)

BROOKLYN PLATE CO.

HARRY M. SCHADE
c. 1887–before 1922
Brooklyn, N.Y.
(73, 105)

SCHULTZ & FISHER
c. 1868–after 1887
San Francisco, Cal.
(3)

Sears Silver Filled
(Private label of Sears, Roebuck & Co. Goods apparently manufactured by Fahy Watch Case Co.)
(175, 160)

Sears
Seroco
Sears Triple Plate
(Private labels of Sears, Roebuck & Co.; manufacturer unknown. Some goods made by Bridgeport Silver Co., some by Holmes & Edwards.)
(175, 160)

SEARS ROEBUCK & CO.

HENRY SEARS & SON
c. 1865–1895
Chicago, Ill.

Sectional Plate XII
(See Merry & Pelton Silver Co.)

Sheffield Plated Co.
(See Holmes, Booth & Haydens)

SILBERSTEIN, HECHT & CO.
c. 1900–1905
New York, N.Y.
Griffon Cutlery Co., successor
(73, 105)

Silver Applied
(See Holmes & Edwards Silver Co.)

Silver Metal
(See Oneida Community, Ltd.)

SILVER PLATE CUTLERY CO.
c. 1907–1918
Shelton, Conn.
(105)

SILVER PLATE CUTLERY WORKS
c. 1907
Derby, Conn.
(105)

Silverweld
(See Holmes & Edwards Silver Co.)

SIMPSON-BRAINERD CO.
c. 1905–after 1920
Providence, R.I.
(73, 105)

ENGLISH SILVER

SIMPSON, HALL, MILLER & CO.
c. 1866–1898
Wallingford, Conn.
International Silver Co., successor.
Marks used after 1898 by successor company.
(73, 86, 105, 147, 148, 150, 167, 175)

SHM&Co

Wm Rogers

SIMPSON NICKEL SILVER CO.
c. 1871–1898
Wallingford, Conn.
International Silver Co., successor
(147, 150)

E. H. H. SMITH KNIFE CO.
before 1899–1904
Bridgeport, Conn.
E. H. H. Smith Silver Co., successor
(73, 105, 147)

E. H. H. SMITH SILVER CO.
c. 1900–1910
Bridgeport, Conn.
Stratford, Conn.
Albert Pick Co., successor before 1910
(73, 105, 147, 175, 229)

MULTISILVER

STERLINGUARD

LAWRENCE B. SMITH CO.
c. 1887–after 1946
Boston, Mass.
(73, 105)

W. D. SMITH SILVER CO.
c. 1900–1920
Chicago, Ill.
(73, 105)

So. Am.
(See David H. McConnell)

SOUTHINGTON CUTLERY CO.
c. 1887–before 1907
Southington, Conn.
(3, 105)

GEORGE W. SPURR & CO.
c. 1873–1881
Greenfield, Mass.
Rogers & Spurr, successor
(147, 165)

Stag Brand
(See Williams Bros. Mfg. Co.)

Standard Plate 4
(See Merry & Pelton Silver Co.)

STANDARD SILVER WARE CO.
c. 1887
Boston, Mass.
(105)

Sterling Inlaid
(See Holmes & Edwards Silver Co.)

Sterling Silver Plate Co.
(See Holmes, Booth & Haydens)

Sterlinguard
(See Albert Pick & Co.)

STEVENS SILVER CO.
before 1904
Portland, Me.
(73, 105)

Stratford Silver Co.
Stratford Silver Plate Co.
(See Holmes & Edwards Silver Co.)

Superior
(See Middletown Plate Co.)

T
(See Towle Mfg. Co.)

TE
(See A. F. Towle & Son Co.)

A. F. TOWLE & SON CO.
c. 1883–1902
Newburyport, Mass.
Greenfield, Mass.
Rogers, Lunt & Bowlen Co. (Lunt Silversmiths) successor.
(73, 105, 147, 148, 150, 175)

A. F. TOWLE & SON MFG. CO.
c. 1880–1883
Newburyport, Mass.
Succeeded Anthony F. Towle & Son (1855–1880). A. F. Towle

& Son Co. and the Towle Mfg. Co., successors.
(73, 147, 148, 150, 174, 175)

TOWLE MFG. CO.
c. 1883–present
Newburyport, Mass.
Electroplated flatware discontinued before 1920.
(73, 147, 148, 150, 174, 175)

Triple Plate 12
(See Merry & Pelton Silver Co.)

Triple Plus
(See Oneida Community, Ltd.)

Tudor Plate
(See Oneida Community, Ltd.)

JAMES W. TUFTS
c. 1883–1902
Boston, Mass.
(73, 147, 148, 150)

Union Silver Plate Co.
(See Holmes, Booth & Haydens)

U.S. Silver Co.
(See Oneida Community, Ltd.)

Universal
(See Landers, Frary & Clark)

WALDO FOUNDRY
c. 1895–1905
Bridgeport, Conn.
Made gold finished and aluminum flatware.
(73, 105)

Waldorf
(See Woodman-Cook Co.)

WALLACE & POMEROY
c. 1849–1854
Wallingford, Conn.
R. Wallace & Co., successor. Made unplated German Silver flatware for Hall, Elton & Co., Edgar Atwater, Fred H. Curtis Co. and other plating firms.
(177)

Wallace Bros. Silver Co.
(See The Wallingford Co.)

Wallace Mfg. Co.
(See R. Wallace & Sons Mfg. Co.)

Wallace Silversmiths
(See R. Wallace & Sons Mfg. Co.)

WALLACE, SIMPSON & CO.
c. 1865–1871
Wallingford, Conn.
R. Wallace & Sons Mfg. Co., successor. Made unplated German Silver flatware for Meriden Britannia Co. and others.
(177)

1835 R. Wallace
(See R. Wallace & Sons Mfg. Co.)

R. WALLACE
c. 1833–1849
Cheshire, Conn.
Wallingford, Conn.
Wallace & Pomeroy, successor. Made unplated Britannia and German Silver spoons for Hall, Elton & Co. and other platers.
(177)

R. WALLACE & CO.
c. 1855–1865
Wallingford, Conn.
Wallace, Simpson & Co., successor
(177)

R. WALLACE & SONS MFG. CO. (WALLACE SILVERSMITHS)
c. 1871–present
Wallingford, Conn.
Lancaster, Pa.
Name changed to Wallace Silversmiths in 1956. Hamilton Watch Co., successor (1959). Made electroplated flatware from 1877 to 1941; electroplated hotel flatware until 1953.
(73, 105, 147, 148, 150, 167, 175, 177, 273, 274, 275)

TRADE 1835 MARK
R. WALLACE

TRADE R. WALLACE SILVER SOLDERED MARK

TRADE "R. WALLACE" MARK

THE WALLINGFORD CO.
after 1887–1955
Wallingford, Conn.
Wallace silversmiths, successors
(73, 105, 177)

WALLACE BROS. SILVER CO.

Wallingford Ware
(See Simpson, Hall, Miller & Co.)

The Warner Silver Co.
(See Weidlich Bros. Mfg. Co.)

WARNER MFG. CO.
c. 1905–1909
Greenfield, Mass.
Among the first manufacturers to offer retail dealers private brand etched on electroplated flatware.
(147, 150, 175)

WARNER SILVER MFG. CO.
c. 1904–before 1910
Chicago, Ill.
(73, 105)

WATERBURY MFG. CO.
c. 1900–1910
Waterbury, Conn.
Patented flatware patterns c. 1908.
(147, 148)

WATROUS MFG. CO.
c. 1896–1898

Wallingford, Conn.
International Silver Co., successor
(73, 86, 105, 147, 148, 150, 175)

W M CO

E. G. WEBSTER
c. 1859–1873
Brooklyn, N.Y.
E. G. Webster & Bro., successor
(86, 175)

E. G. WEBSTER & BRO.
c. 1873–1886
Brooklyn, N.Y.
E. G. Webster & Son, successor
(3, 147)

E. G. WEBSTER & SON
c. 1886–1923
Brooklyn, N.Y.
International Silver Co., successor
(73, 86, 147, 148, 175)

E G W & S

EPBM
E G W & S

E G W & S
E P N S

Wearever
(See National Silver Co.)

THE WEIDLICH BROS. MFG. CO.
c. 1901–after 1946
Bridgeport, Conn.
(73, 163, 148)

W-B
MFG CO

POMPEIAN GOLD

THE WARNER SILVER CO.

Welch Silver
(See American Silver Co.)

1857 Welch-Atkins
(See American Silver Co.)

WILCOX SILVER PLATE CO.
c. 1865–1898
Meriden, Conn.
International Silver Co., successor. Marks used by successor company after 1898.
(3, 73, 86, 147, 148, 150)

GEM SILVER CO.

S SP C

WILLIAMS BROS. MFG. CO.
before 1887–1950
Naubuc, Conn.
Glastonbury, Conn.
(3, 73, 105, 175, 280)

Williams TRIPLE PLATE

STAG BRAND

OUR VERY BEST

Williams

Lion Brand

Williams Plate

WILLIAM WILSON & SON
c. 1900–before 1920
Philadelphia, Pa.
(73, 105)

WILMORT MFG. CO.
c. 1905–after 1920
Chicago, Ill.
(73, 105)

Wilmort

WOODMAN-COOK CO.
c. 1905–1910
Portland, Me.
(73, 105)

WALDORF SILVER CO.

World Brand
(See American Silver Co.)

YALE & CURTIS
before 1880
New York, N.Y.
Curtis & Rowley, successor
(147, 150, 165)

Yourex
(See Associated Silver Co.)

ENGLISH AND CANADIAN SILVER AND ELECTROPLATE

The following marks are included to facilitate the identification of English and Canadian silver and electroplate.

The condensed tables of Assay Office and Dominical or Date Marks show the cycle of letters used during the Victorian and Edwardian years. Complete cycles are shown for London; the tables for other Assay Offices illustrate the device and letter style for each cycle with the letter "A."

The examples of makers' marks shown for both silver and electroplate makers are not complete; this selection is based on a series of articles in *The Jewelers' Weekly* during the late 1890s, in which the reporter discussed those English and Canadian firms most active in the export of their wares to the United States. Consequently, the products of the firms listed here are probably those most frequently found in American homes.

Many of the English electroplate producers made Sheffield Plate during the 18th and early 19th centuries; some of them later used marks resembling their Sheffield Plate marks on the electroplated ware they produced. No other Sheffield Plate marks are shown; flatware was seldom made of this plate, and only isolated examples, now generally in poor condition, have survived.

Canadian manufacturers, like those in the United States, used the sterling designation for solid silver, as their marks indicate.

While several United States manufacturers operated factories in Great Britain and in Canada, their products were marked with the same trade marks and trade names used on ware made for sale in the United States; therefore, these marks are not included in this compilation.

The help of the office of the British Consulate General in Chicago, in obtaining marks not included in the original series of articles in *Jewelers' Weekly*, is gratefully acknowledged.

ENGLISH SILVER MARKS

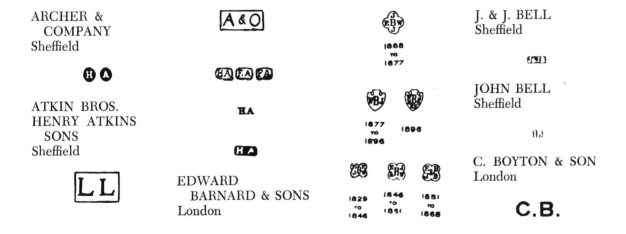

ARCHER & COMPANY
Sheffield

ATKIN BROS.
HENRY ATKINS SONS
Sheffield

EDWARD BARNARD & SONS
London

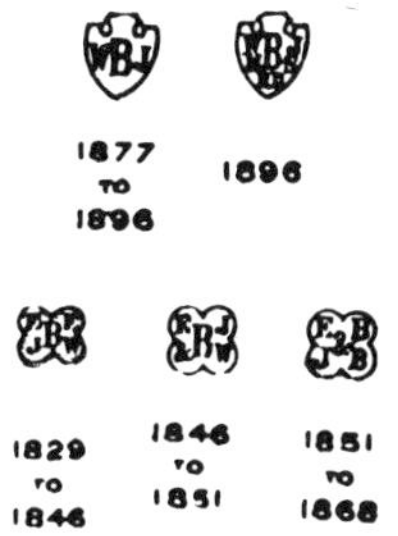

J. & J. BELL
Sheffield

JOHN BELL
Sheffield

C. BOYTON & SON
London

WM. COMYNS
& SONS
London

COOPER BROS.
& SONS, LTD.
Sheffield

CRESWICK
& COMPANY
Sheffield
(*William Hutton & Sons, successor*)

JAS. DEAKIN
& SONS, LTD
Sheffield

WM. DEVENPORT
Birmingham

W.D.

JAMES DIXON
& SONS
Sheffield

ELKINGTON
& CO., LTD.
Birmingham

ELKINGTON,
MASON & CO.
Birmingham & London

W. GALLIMORE
& SONS
Sheffield

R & S GARRARD
& CO.
London

James Garrard
Reg. 1881

Robert Garrard, 2d.
Reg. 1822

C. S. HARRIS
& SONS, LTD.
London

Spoon Work

1817—1850

1850 to date

HARRISON BROS.
& HOWSON
Sheffield

1870—1893
(only) Silver

or

HAWKSWORTH,
EYRE & CO.
Sheffield

F. HIGGINS & SON
London

HOLLAND,
ALDWINKLE &
SLATER
London

R. Hennell's Mark, 1791 (or earlier) to 1887

H. Chawner's Mark, about 1786 and onwards

G. Adams's Mark up to 1883

H. Holland's Mark, 1840 to 1880

Slater & Aldwinckle, about 1880 to 1848

Holland, Aldwinckle & Slater, 1884 to 1893

1893 to present date.

HOULE BROS.
Sheffield

DH
CH

HUNT &
ROSKELL, LTD.
London

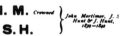

I. M. *Crowned* } *John Mortimer, J. S Hunt & J. Hunt, 1839–1842*
I. S. H.

I. S. H. *J. S. Hunt & J. Hunt, 1842 1865*

I. H. } *Crowned* *J. Hunt & R. Roskell, 1865 1882*
R. R.

R. R. } *R. & A. Roskell & J. M. Hunt, 1882—*
A. R.
I. M. H.

WM. HUTTON
& SONS, LTD.
Sheffield

RH WH

EH 

LEVI & SALAMAN
Birmingham

L&S

MAPPIN & WEBB
Sheffield & London

MAPPIN & WEBB
SILVERSMITHS
LONDON
(or in a small circle.)

JNM

M&W

MAPPIN BROS.
Sheffield

MB

EM JM EM JM MB

S. MORDAN
& CO., LTD.
London

Registered Trade Mark.
"S. MORDAN & CO."

Old marks

S.M. S.M. & G.R.
S.M. & CO.

R. PRINGLE & SONS
London

RP

ROBERTS & BELK
Sheffield & London

TRADE MARK

R&B

Silver Marked in Sheffield.

CB

Silver Marked in London.

JOSEPH RODGERS
& SONS, LTD.
Sheffield

J R

JR JR JR

JOHN ROUND
& SON, LTD.
Sheffield

JR & S

HENRY
STRATFORD
Sheffield

H.S.

TAYLOR & PERRY
Birmingham
(J. Thomason & Nephews, successors)

T. & P.

J. THOMASON
& NEPHEWS
Birmingham

H. & T.

J. H.

Before 18[illegible]

JOSIAH WILLIAMS
& CO.
Bristol

R. W.
J. W.
J. W.

Robert Williams and his two sons—James and Josiah.

J. W.
J. W.

James and Josiah Williams.

J. W.
&
Co.

Josiah Williams and partners. (After 1877.)

G. M. J.

George M. Jackson—1879-1883.

G. J.

G. M. Jackson (London Hall)—1883-1896.

D. F.

G. M. Jackson and D. L. Fullerton. (Present Mark.)

A. & J. ZIMMERMAN
Birmingham

A & J Z

A&JZ

TABLES OF DATE LETTERS

London Assay Marks

A	1836	a	1856	A	1876	a	1896
B	VICTA 1837	b	1857	B	1877	b	1897
C	1838	c	1858	C	1878	c	1898
D	1839	d	1859	D	1879	d	1899
E	1840	e	1860	E	1880	e	1900
F	1841	f	1861	F	1881	f	1901
G	1842	g	1862	G	1882	g	1902
H	1843	h	1863	H	1883	h	1903
I	1844	j	1864	I	1884	i	1904
K	1845	k	1865	K	1885	k	1905
L	1846	l	1866	L	1886	l	1906
M	1847	m	1867	M	1887	m	1907
N	1848	n	1868	N	1888	n	1908
O	1849	o	1869	O	1889	o	1909
P	1850	p	1870	P	1890	p	1910
Q	1851	q	1871	Q	1891	q	1911
R	1852	r	1872	R	1892	r	1912
S	1853	s	1873	S	1893	s	1913
T	1854	t	1874	T	1894	t	1914
U	1855	u	1875	U	1895	u	1915

Sheffield

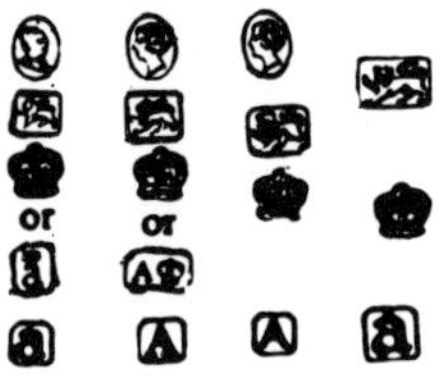

A	1824	1844	1868	1893
B	1825	1845	1869	1894
C	1826	1846	1870	1895
D	1827	1847	1871	1896
E	1828	1848	1872	1897
F	1829	1849	1873	1898
G	1830	1850	1874	1899
H	1831	1851	1875	1900
I	——	1852	——	1901
J	——	——	1876	——
K	1832	1853	1877	1902
L	1833	1854	1878	1903
M	1834	1855	1879	1904
N	——	1856	1880	1905
O	——	1857	1881	1906
P	1835	1858	1882	1907
Q	1836	——	1883	1908
R	1837	1859	1884	1909
S	1838	1860	1885	1910
T	1839	1861	1886	1911
U	1840	1862	1887	1912
V	1841	1863	1888	1913
W	——	1864	1889	1914
X	1842	1865	1890	1915
Y	——	1866	1891	1916
Z	1843	1867	1892	1917

Birmingham

A	1824	1849	1875	1900
B	1825	1850	1876	1901
D	1826	1851	1877	1902
C	1827	1852	1878	1903
E	1828	1853	1879	1904
F	1829	1854	1880	1905
G	1830	1855	1881	1906
H	1831	1856	1882	1907
I	1832	1857	1883	1908
J	——	1858	——	——
K	1833	1859	1884	1909
L	1834	1860	1885	1910
M	1835	1861	1886	1911
N	1836	1862	1887	1912
O	1837	1863	1888	1913
P	1838	1864	1889	1914
Q	1839	1865	1890	1915
R	1840	1866	1891	1916
S	1841	1867	1892	1917
T	1842	1868	1893	1918
U	1843	1869	1894	1919
V	1844	1870	1895	1920
W	1845	1871	1896	1921
X	1846	1872	1897	1922
Y	1847	1873	1898	1923
Z	1848	1874	1899	1924

Chester

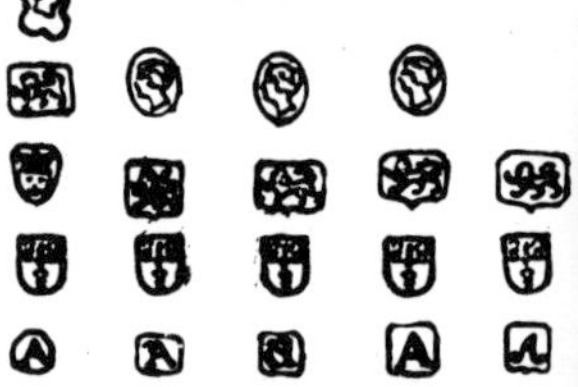

A	1818	1839	1864	1884	1901
B	1819	1840	1865	1885	1902
C	1820	1841	1866	1886	1903
D	1821-2	1842	1867	1887	1904
E	1823	1843	1868	1888	1905
F	1824	1844	1869	1889	1906
G	1825	1845	1870	1890	1907
H	1826	1846	1871	1891	1908
I	1827	1847	1872	1892	1909
J	——	——	——	——	——
K	1828	1848	1873	1893	1910
L	1829	1849	1874	1894	1911
M	1830	1850	1875	1895	1912
N	1831	1851	1876	1896	1913
O	1832	1852	1877	1897	1914
P	1833	1853	1878	1898	1915
Q	1834	1854	1879	1899	1916
R	1835	1855	1880	1900	1917
S	1836	1856	1881	——	1918
T	1837	1857	1882	——	1919
U	1838	1858	1883	——	1920
V	——	1859	——	——	1921
W	——	1860	——	——	1922
X	——	1861	——	——	1923
Y	——	1862	——	——	1924
Z	——	1863	——	——	1925

Edinburgh

A	1832	1857	1882	1906
B	1833	1858	1883	1907
C	1834	1859	1884	1908
D	1835	1860	1885	1909
E	1836	1861	1886	1910
F	1837	1862	1887	1911
G	1838	1863	1888	1912
H	1839	1864	1889	1913
I	1840	1865	1890	1914
J	——	——	——	——
K	1841	1866	1891	1915
L	1842	1867	1892	1916
M	1843	1868	1893	1917
N	1844	1869	1894	1918
O	1845	1870	1895	1919
P	1846	1871	1896	1920
Q	1847	1872	1897	1921
R	1848	1873	1898	1922
S	1849	1874	1899	1923
T	1850	1875	1900	1924
U	1851	1876	1901	1925
V	1852	1877	1901	1926
W	1853	1878	1902	1927
X	1854	1879	1903	1928
Y	1855	1880	1904	1929
Z	1856	1881	1905	1930

Glasgow

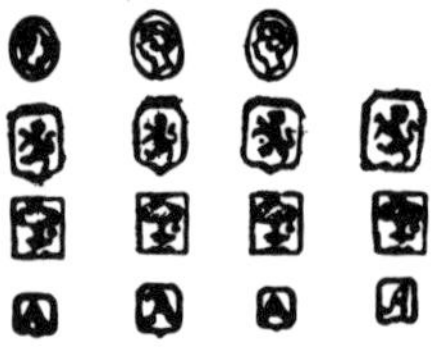

A	1819	1845	1871	1897
B	1820	1846	1872	1898
C	1821	1847	1873	1899
D	1822	1848	1874	1900
E	1823	1849	1875	1901
F	1824	1850	1876	1902
G	1825	1851	1877	1903
H	1826	1852	1878	1904
I	1827	1853	1879	1905
J	1828	1854	1880	1906
K	1829	1855	1881	1907
L	1830	1856	1882	1908
M	1831	1857	1883	1909
N	1832	1858	1884	1910
O	1833	1859	1885	1911
P	1834	1860	1886	1912
Q	1835	1861	1887	1913
R	1836	1862	1888	1814
S	1837	1863	1889	1915
T	1838	1864	1890	1916
U	1839	1865	1891	1917
V	1840	1866	1892	1918
W	1841	1867	1893	1919
X	1842	1868	1894	1920
Y	1843	1869	1895	1921
Z	1844	1870	1896	1922

York

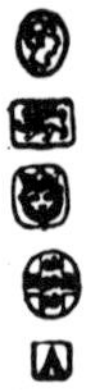

A	1837
B	1838
C	1839
D	1840
E	1841
F	1842
G	1843
H	1844
I	1845
J	——
K	1846
L	1847
M	1848
N	1849
O	1850
P	1851
Q	1852
R	1853
S	1854
T	1855
U	——
V	1856
W	
X	*closed*
Y	*in*
Z	*1857*

Exeter

A	1837	1857	1877
B	1838	1858	1878
C	1839	1859	1879
D	1840	1860	1880
E	1841	1861	1881
F	1842	1862	1882
G	1843	1863	
H	1844	1864	
I	1845	1865	
—	——	——	
K	1846	1866	
L	1847	1867	
M	1848	1868	
N	1849	1869	
O	1850	1870	
P	1851	1871	
Q	1852	1872	
R	1853	1873	
S	1854	1874	
T	1855	1875	
U	1856	1876	
V	——	——	
W	——	——	
X	——	——	*closed*
Y	——	——	*in*
Z	——	——	*1883*

Newcastle

A	1815	1839	1864
B	1816	1840	1865
C	1817	1841	1866
D	1818	1842	1867
E	1819	1843	1868
F	1820	1844	1869
G	1821	1845	1870
H	1822	1846	1871
I	1823	1847	1872
J	——	1848	——
K	1824	1849	1873
L	1825	1850	1874
M	1826	1851	1875
N	1827	1852	1876
O	1828	1853	1877
P	1829	1854	1878
Q	1830	1855	1879
R	1831	1856	1880
S	1832	1857	1881
T	1833	1858	1882
U	1834	1859	1883
—	——	——	
W	1835	1860	
X	1836	1861	*closed*
Y	1837	1862	*in*
Z	1838	1863	*1884*

Dublin

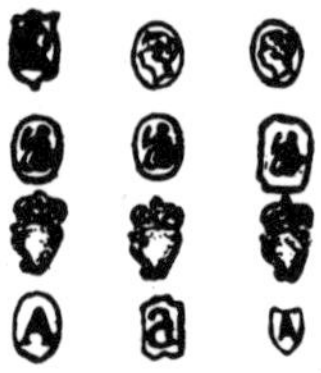

A	1821	1846	1871
B	1822	1847	1872
C	1823	1848	1873
D	1824	1849	1874
E	1825	1850	1875
F	1826	1851	1876
G	1827	1852	1877
H	1828	1853	1858
I	1829	1854	1879
K	1830	1855	1880
L	1831	1856	1881
M	1832	1857	1882
N	1833	1858	1883
O	1834	1859	1884
P	1835	1860	1885
Q	1836	1861	1886
R	1837	1862	1887
S	1838	1863	1888
T	1839	1864	1889
U	1840	1865	1890
V	1841	1866	1891
W	1842	1867	1892
X	1843	1868	1893
Y	1844	1869	1894
Z	1845	1870	8951

The Sovereign's Head mark was not used after 1890

Examples of Complete Marks

CANADIAN STERLING
MANUFACTURERS TRADE MARKS

P. W. ELLIS
& CO. LTD.
Toronto, Ont.

E
(See P. W. Ellis
& Co., Ltd.)

HC
(See The Hemming
Mfg. Co.)

THE HEMMING
MFG. CO.
Montreal, Que.

K
(See Ambrose Kent
& Sons)

AMBROSE KENT
& SONS, LTD.
Toronto, Ont.

R
(See Roden Bros.,
Ltd.)

STERLING

RODEN BROS., LTD.
Toronto, Ont.

STERLING SILVER

S
(See Sterling Craft)

STERLING CRAFT
Toronto, Ont.

TSF
(See Toronto Silver
Plate Co.)

TORONTO SILVER
PLATE CO.
Toronto, Ont.

T. S. P.
STERLING

TRADE MARK

STERLING

STERLING T.S.P.

ENGLISH ELECTROPLATE MANUFACTURERS, TRADE MARKS AND TRADE NAMES

EDGAR ALLEN & CO.
Sheffield

K 9

£ s d

ATKIN BROS.
Sheffield

TRADE MARK

General Mark

ATKIN BROTHERS,
SHEFFIELD

A B * S

A B * S
E. P. on Britannia Metal

HA EA FA EPNS

E. P. on Nickel Silver*

BARKER BROS.
Birmingham

REGISTERED
TRADE MARK

GRIEL NICKEL SILVER

JOHN BATT & CO.
London

SPHINX BRAND

WILLIAM BATT & SONS
Sheffield

W B & S

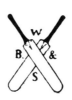

MAURICE BAUM
Sheffield

SILVERINE

BOARDMAN, GLOSSUP & CO.
Sheffield

B & G

GS

EP

THOMAS BRADBURY & SONS
Sheffield

TB&S

S. BRIGHT & CO.
Sheffield

ALFRED BROWETT
Birmingham

COLLINGS & WALLIS
Birmingham

MONTANA SILVER.

Collings & Wallis

COOPER BROS. & SONS, LTD.
Sheffield

COOPER

C Bros

CRESWICK & CO.
Sheffield
William Hutton & Sons, successor

CRESWICK & Co

JAMES DEAKIN & SONS
Sheffield

AND TRADE MARK S F REGISTERED

JAMES DEAKIN & SONS. LTD. SHAW & FISHER.

FREDERICK DERRY
Birmingham
Succeeded Derry & Jones

"ROYAL STANDARD"

"ROYAL STANDARD"
VICTORIA
SILVER

"STANDARD"
VICTORIA
SILVER

THE "STANDARD" ELECTRO PLATE SPOONS, FORKS, &c.

JAMES DIXON & SONS
Sheffield

DIXON

DIXON

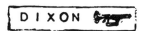

ELKINGTON & CO., LTD.
Birmingham

ELKINGTON & C°

ELKINGTON
ELKINGTON & C°

TRADE MARKS
E&C°
E & C°
ELKINGTON & C°
ELKINGTON.

ELKINGTON.

CHARLES ELLIS & CO.
Sheffield

C E & C°

ISAAC ELLIS & SON
Sheffield

PRIMUS ISAAC ELLIS & SONS. SHEFFIELD.

ELLIS & CO.
Birmingham

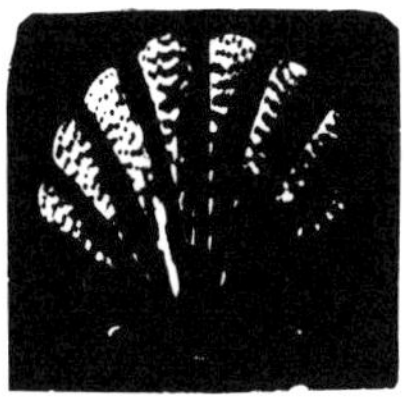

ALFRED FIELD & CO.
Birmingham & Sheffield

G B

W. GALLIMORE & SONS
Sheffield

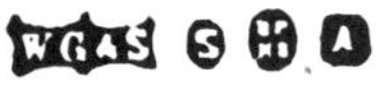

E. P. Mark

Nickel Mark

Special "Norwegian"

NORWEGIAN SILVER

Silver

Occasional Mark

ALMADA SILVER

JOSEPH GILBERT
Birmingham

ARGENTINA SILVER
Joseph Gilbert

JG

JOHN GOODE & SONS
Birmingham

GRINSELL & SONS
GRINSELL & BOURNE (?)
London & Birmingham

J.G.&SONS

Silver and E. P.

General Mark

HANDS & SONS
THOMAS HANDS
Birmingham

HARRISON BROTHERS & HOWSON
Sheffield

ALPHA

HAWKSWORTH, EYRE & CO.
Sheffield

E. P. Goods

WILLIAM HAY
Sheffield

EUREKA

WILLIAM HUTTON & SONS
Sheffield & London
Succeeded Creswick & Co.

W & R DOUBLE SHEAR

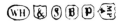

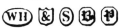

Steel Cutlery

Nickel Spoons and Forks

Various Quality Marks. The first is best work

R. M. JOHNSON & CO.
Sheffield

BMJ & CO

LEVI & SALAMAN
Birmingham

TRADE MARK

JAMES McEWAN & CO., LTD.
London

McLEAN BROS. & RIGG
London

MAPPIN BROS.
London & Sheffield

MAPPIN BROS

CORPORATE TRADE MARK GRANTED BY THE CUTLERS COMPANY JUNE 1835.

MAPPIN, WEBB & CO.
MAPPIN & WEBB, LTD.
MAPPIN & WEBB
London & Sheffield

MAPPIN & WEBB'S PRINCE'S PLATE.

TUSCA

M TRUSTWORTHY

E. P. Mark

WILLIAM MARPLES & SON
Sheffield

"HIBERNIA"

HIBERNIA

JOHN NEAL & CO.
London

NEAL'S PYRO SILVER

PYRO GOLD

PYRO

WILLIAM PADLEY & SON
Sheffield

WILLIAM PAGE & CO.
Birmingham

TRADE MARK WP

WP SILVERITE & Co

THE POTOSI COMPANY
Birmingham
(112, 222)
Barker Bros., Silversmiths successor.
Marks used by successor company.

TRADE MARK

ELECTRO-POTOSI

POTOSI SILVER

THOMAS PRIME
& SON
Birmingham
(153, 212, 222)

PRIME

R. PRINGLE
& SONS
London

REGISTERED TRADE MARK

Nickel Silver Goods

E. P. Goods

JOSEPH RODGERS
& SONS
Sheffield
(112, 153, 212, 222)

JOSEPH RODGERS & SONS SHEFFIELD

E P

REGISTERED TRADE MARK.
GRANTED 1682.

J RODGERS & SONS

RODGERS EP

RODGERS EP

RODGERSINE

RODGERS

JOSEPH RODGERS

V R

JOSEPH RODGERS & SONS
CUTLERS TO HER MAJESTY.

JOSEPH RODGERS & SONS
CUTLERS TO THEIR MAJESTIES
No 6 NORFOLK STREET
SHEFFIELD

JOSEPH RODGERS & SONS

RODGERS' ORIGINAL
& GENUINE PLATE

HENRY ROGERS,
SONS & CO.
Sheffield
(112, 212, 222)
Also see Canadian list

JOHN ROUND
& SON
Sheffield

J.R & S World

VALARIUM

KENDULAM

JOHN ROUND & SON
SHEFFIELD

TRADE ALL THE ROUND MARK

E. P. Goods.

Britannia Goods.

HENRY RUSSELL
& CO.
Sheffield
(222)

VICTORY

HENRY RUSSELL & CO
SHEFFIELD

JOHN SHERWOOD
& SONS
Sheffield

REGENT SILVER

HENRY
STRATFORD
Sheffield

E. P. Mark

SUCKLING, LTD.
Birmingham

BURMESE

REGIS PLATE REG'D
E.P.N.S

W.S&S EPNS A1

KINGSWAY PLATE

W.S&S EPNS A1

THOMAS TURNER
THOMAS TURNER
& CO.
Sheffield

T.T

T.T

FREDERICK
WHITEHOUSE
Birmingham

Imperial
F.W.

Electro-Imperial.
F.W.

Imperial Silver
F.W.

HENRY
WILKINSON
& CO.
London & Sheffield

HW &CO

WILKINSON
SWORD CO.
London & Sheffield

T. WILKINSON
& SONS
Birmingham

WILSON & DAVIS
London & Sheffeld

FW
WD

W & D L & S

W & D S EP

JOHN YATES
& SONS
Birmingham

YATES'S
VIRGINIAN

J YATES & SONS

SILVER ASH.

NICKELOID

YATES

Y

V S

YATES & SONS

Y & S

J Y & S

JOHN YATES & SONS

J. YATES & SONS

VIRGINIAN SILVER

A. & J. ZIMMERMAN
Birmingham

EP

A&JZ

CANADIAN ELECTROPLATE MANUFACTURERS, TRADE MARKS AND TRADE NAMES

BENEDICT-PROCTOR MFG. CO.
Trenton, Ont.

J. D. CAMIRAND & CO.
Montreal, Que.

CROWN SILVER PLATE CO.
Toronto, Ont.

P. W. ELLIS & CO., LTD.
Toronto, Ont.

SOVEREIGN PLATE

Essay Canada
(See Stanley & Aylward, Ltd.)

GOLDSMITHS CO. OF CANADA, LTD.
Toronto, Ont.

NICKELITE SILVER
SHEFFIELD CUTLERY

H R S & Co.
(See Henry Rogers, Sons & Co.)

Monarch Silver Co.
(See Standard Silver Co. of Toronto, Ltd.)

Nickelite Silver
(See Goldsmiths Co. of Canada)

Norman Plate
(See Stanley & Aylward, Ltd.)

RODEN BROS., LTD.
Toronto, Ont.

G. Rodgers
(See Standard Silver Co. of Toronto)

HENRY ROGERS, SONS & CO.
Montreal, Que.

Sheffield Cutlery
(See Goldsmiths Co. of Canada, Ltd.)

Sovereign Plate
(See P. W. Ellis, Ltd.)

S S Co.
(See Standard Silver Co. of Toronto, Ltd.)

STANDARD SILVER CO. OF TORONTO, LTD.
Toronto, Ont.

MONARCH SILVER CO.

STANLEY & AYLWARD, LTD.
Toronto, Ont.

BEDFORD
BRAUMONT

BERKELEY
BERKSHIRE

TORONTO SILVER PLATE CO.
Toronto, Ont.

Torsil
Torsil Steel
(See Toronto Silver Plate Co.)

WINNIPEG SILVER PLATE CO.
Winnipeg, Man.

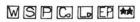

FLATWARE PATTERNS

In the following pages, sterling and electroplate flatware patterns produced by American manufacturers before 1910 have been arranged alphabetically, followed by the name of the manufacturer, the year in which the pattern was patented or introduced, a key to obsolescence, and the number of the page on which the pattern is illustrated.

Pattern Names are the original manufacturers' designations; where a pattern name was changed while the design remained active, the alternate name is listed in parenthesis. Pattern names sometimes used regionally by wholesalers and retailers selling standard production designs have been deleted; in a few instances, where the original manufacturer's designation could not be traced, the manufacturer's firm name and a number have been listed. Since some pattern names were used by more than one company and applied to different designs, both the firm name and the pattern should be checked when identifying a particular piece of flatware.

The Manufacturer listed generally is the firm that introduced the pattern; in many cases, the same pattern was continued in production by a successor. Such corporate transitions through purchase or merger are indicated in the Flatware Manufacturers section of this book. Because patterns, patents, and dies were sometimes purchased by other companies, occasional pieces may appear stamped with a name other than that of the original maker or a listed successor company. Where identical patterns made by different firms are listed, the earliest introduction date indicates the originator of the design.

Introduction Dates have been determined by manufacturers' records, where these are still in existence, Patent Office records, or by the patent date sometimes stamped on flatware. Where such records are not available, the date of the earliest reference to the pattern in catalogs, trade journals or other printed materials is used.

The letter "O" following the introduction date indicates that the pattern was obsolete by 1929; this is intended only as a guide to the period of time a particular pattern remained active, and does not indicate its present status. The absence of this symbol following the introduction date does *not* signify that the listed pattern is active or available on special order; your own jeweler can give you this information.

Illustrations of the listed patterns will be found on the page or pages indicated in the last column; if no illustration is available, the letters "NIA" appear. Where an *identical* pattern was made by more than one manufacturer, as was the case with much early electroplate, the listed illustration reference may be to an identical design made by another firm. Where a manufacturer made identical patterns in both sterling and electroplate, only one of these patterns may be shown; accordingly, the page reference for an electroplate pattern may be to an illustration in the sterling section, or vice-versa.

An asterisk (*) preceding a pattern name indicates that the pattern was not made in a complete line. In some instances, the pattern may have been made only in teaspoons; in others, in tea, afternoon tea or coffee spoons; other manufacturers may have offered the asterisked patterns only in "fancy pieces" for place setting or serving use.

STERLING FLATWARE PATTERNS

Pattern	Brand or Manufacturer	Introduction Date and Obsolescence		Page
Abbotsford	Simpson, Hall, Miller & Co.	1906	O	112
Aberdeen	Tuttle Silver Co.	c. 1905		119
Acanthus	Dominick & Haff	c. 1890	O	92
Acanthus	Gorham Mfg. Co.	1891	O	96
Acanthus	George W. Shiebler	1890	O	110
Acorn	Gorham Mfg. Co.	1894		96
Adam	Shreve & Co.	c. 1906	O	NIA
Adam	Whiting Mfg. Co.	1906		127
Aeolian	J. B. & S. M. Knowles	1882	O	103
Agate	J. B. & S. M. Knowles (Co.)	1878	O	103
*Albany	Towle Mfg. Co.	c. 1885	O	118
Albion	Wm. B. Durgin Co.	c. 1880	O	NIA
Alcazar	Wm. B. Durgin Co.	c. 1885	O	NIA
*Alden	R. Blackinton & Co.	c. 1900	O	NIA
Alden (Fiddle Shell)	Frank W. Smith Co.	c. 1910		114
Alexander	Newburyport Silver Co.	c. 1907	O	NIA
*Alexander	Unger Bros.	c. 1905	O	NIA
Alexandra	Dominick & Haff	1902	O	92
*Alhambra	Whiting Mfg. Co.	c. 1880	O	129
*Alice	Fessenden & Co.	c. 1900	O	94
Altair	Watson, Newell & Co.	1904	O	122
Althea	Watrous Mfg. Co.	c. 1910	O	121
Amaranth	Joseph Seymour Mfg. Co.	c. 1900	O	NIA
Amaryllis	George W. Shiebler	c. 1880	O	111
American Beauty	George W. Shiebler	1896	O	110
Angelo	Gorham Mfg. Co.	1870	O	97
Angelo	J. B. & S. M. Knowles Co.	c. 1900	O	103
Angelo	Wood & Hughes	c. 1870-1875	O	131
Antique	Alvin Mfg. Co.	1907	O	85
Antique	Dominick & Haff	c. 1870	O	85
Antique	Wm. B. Durgin Co.	c. 1880	O	85
Antique	Wm. Gale & Son	c. 1850	O	85
Antique	Gorham Mfg. Co.	1880		85
Antique	Knowles & Ladd	1865	O	104
Antique	J. B. & S. M. Knowles	1875	O	104
Antique	Merrill Bros. Co.	1903	O	NIA
Antique	John Polhemus	c. 1840-1850	O	85
Antique	1847 Rogers Bros.	c. 1879	O	147
Antique	George W. Shiebler	1876	O	85
Antique	Shreve & Co.	c. 1904		111
Antique	Frank W. Smith Co.	c. 1895	O	85
*Antique	Towle Mfg. Co.	c. 1885	O	117
Antique	Webster & Knowles	c. 1852	O	85
Antique	John R. Wendt & Co.	before 1870	O	85
Antique	F. M. Whiting Co.	c. 1880	O	85
Antique	Whiting Mfg. Co.	c. 1870	O	85
Antique B	F. M. Whiting Co.	c. 1885	O	125
Antique Chased	Whiting Mfg. Co.	c. 1885	O	127
Antique Engraved	Whiting Mfg. Co.	c. 1880	O	126
Antique Eng. M-2	Whiting Mfg. Co.	c. 1885	O	127
Antique Hammered	Gorham Mfg. Co.	1880		101
Antique Hammered	Shreve & Co.	c. 1904		111
Antique Hammered Applied	Gorham Mfg. Co.	c. 1880		101

STERLING FLATWARE PATTERNS (*Cont'd*)

Pattern	Brand or Manufacturer	Introduction Date and Obsolescence		Page
Antique Hammered Applied # 2	Gorham Mfg. Co.	c. 1880		101
Antique Lily Eng.	Whiting Mfg. Co.	c. 1885	O	127
Antique No. 3	Alvin Mfg. Co.	c. 1900		89
Antique No. 6	Alvin Mfg. Co.	c. 1900		89
Antique No. 8	Gorham Mfg. Co.	1880		96
Antique No. 15	Gorham Mfg. Co.	1890		96
Antique No. 45	Gorham Mfg. Co.	1891		NIA
Antique Rosette	Whiting Mfg. Co.	c. 1880	O	127
Antique Sheaf	Wm. B. Durgin Co.	c. 1895	O	93
Antique Tip	Whiting Mfg. Co.	c. 1880	O	127
Antique Twist	Whiting Mfg. Co.	c. 1880	O	126
Antoinette	Wm. B. Durgin Co.	c. 1890	O	NIA
Apollo	Alvin Mfg. Co.	c. 1900		89
Apollo	J. B. & S. M. Knowles Co.	1892	O	103
Apollo	John R. Wendt & Co.	before 1870	O	NIA
*Apostle Large	Gorham Mfg. Co.	1887		168
*Apostle Small	Gorham Mfg. Co.	c. 1890		168
*Aquilla	Towle Mfg. Co.	c. 1900	O	118
*Arabesque	John R. Wendt & Co.	before 1870	O	127
*Arabesque	Whiting Mfg. Co.	c. 1880	O	127
Arcadian	1847 Rogers Bros.	1884	O	150, 170
Arcadian	Rogers, Smith & Co.	1884	O	150, 170
Argo	J. B. & S. M. Knowles Co.	1892	O	103
Argyl	Newburyport Silver Co.	c. 1905	O	NIA
Argyll	Towle Mfg. Co.	c. 1885	O	117
Ariel	Mauser Mfg. Co.	c. 1900	O	NIA
Arkeba	Watson, Newell & Co.	c. 1900	O	NIA
Arlington	Towle Mfg. Co.	c. 1890	O	117
Armenian	1847 Rogers Bros.	1884	O	148, 170
Armenian	Rogers, Smith & Co.	1884	O	148, 170
Armor	John Polhemus	c. 1845-1855	O	105
Armor	George W. Shiebler	1876	O	105
*Armor	Whiting Mfg. Co.	c. 1875	O	127
Arts & Crafts	Wm. B. Durgin Co.	c. 1910		93
*Astor	Gorham Mfg. Co.	c. 1910	O	97
Atalanta	R. Wallace & Sons	1895	O	120
Athene	F. M. Whiting & Co.	c. 1890	O	124
Athenian	Wm. B. Durgin Co.	c. 1875	O	NIA
Athenian	Reed & Barton	1891	O	106
*Athenian	Whiting Mfg. Co.	c. 1890	O	127
Athenian Engraved	Reed & Barton	1891	O	106
Athens	Mauser Mfg. Co.	c. 1900	O	NIA
Atlanta	Gorham Mfg. Co.	c. 1910	O	98
Audubon (Japanese)	Tiffany & Co.	1871		115, 173
Aurora	Gorham Mfg. Co.	c. 1870	O	97
Autumn	F. M. Whiting & Co.	1888	O	125
Auvergne	Towle Mfg. Co.	c. 1885	O	116
Avalon	Wilcox & Evertson	1900	O	130
Avon	Fessenden & Co.	c. 1900	O	94
*Azalea	R. Blackinton & Co.	c. 1910	O	NIA
Ball Twist	A. F. Towle & Son Co.	1892	O	116
Baltimore Rose	Baltimore Silversmiths Mfg. Co.	c. 1903	O	102

STERLING FLATWARE PATTERNS (*Cont'd*)

Pattern	Brand or Manufacturer	Introduction Date and Obsolescence		Page
Baltimore Rose	Heer-Schofield Co.	c. 1905		102
Baltimore Scroll	Baltimore Silversmiths Mfg. Co.	c. 1904	O	NIA
*Balzac	Gorham Mfg. Co.	c. 1910	O	98
Bamboo	Gorham Mfg. Co.	1880		97
*Bamboo	Henry Sears & Son	c. 1890	O	108
Baronial	Gorham Mfg. Co.	1896		98
Baronial	Frank W. Smith Co.	c. 1890		114
Basket of Flowers	Tuttle Silver Co.	c. 1905	O	119
Bead	Alvin Mfg. Co.	c. 1908		104
Bead (Original Bead)	Wm. B. Durgin Co.	1886	O	93
Bead	Peter L. Krider Co.	c. 1900	O	104
Bead	John Polhemus	c. 1840-1850	O	106
Bead	George W. Shiebler	1876	O	106
Bead	Frank W. Smith Co.	c. 1900		114
Bead	Whiting Mfg. Co.	c. 1880	O	126
Beaded (Bead)	Alvin Mfg. Co.	c. 1908	O	104
Beaded	Gorham Mfg. Co.	c. 1855		99
Beaded	1847 Rogers Bros. (Meriden Ba. Co.)	c. 1879	O	147
Bedford	Gorham Mfg. Co.	1895	O	99
Beekman (Tiffany)	Tiffany & Co.	1869		115
Benjamin Franklin	Towle Mfg. Co.	1904		118
Berain	R. Wallace & Sons	1907		120
Berlin	Gorham Mfg. Co.	1885	O	101
*Berry	Whiting Mfg. Co.	c. 1885	O	127
*Bessie	R. Wallace & Sons	before 1893	O	120
Betsy Ross	Newburyport Silver Co.	1903	O	105
Beverly	Frank W. Smith Co.	c. 1905		113
Beverly	Wilcox & Evertson	1910		130
Bird	Adams & Shaw Co.	before 1879	O	124
Bird	Dominick & Haff	1884	O	124
*Bird	Mauser Mfg. Co.	c. 1896		NIA
Bird	John R. Wendt & Co.	before 1870	O	124
Bird	F. M. Whiting Co.	c. 1884-1891	O	125
*Birds Nest	Gorham Mfg. Co.	1885	O	97
*Birthday (Zodiac)	Gorham Mfg. Co.	c. 1890		97, 168
Bizarre	Frank W. Smith Co.	c. 1890	O	NIA
Blenheim	Joseph Mayer & Bro.	c. 1905	O	NIA
Blossom	Dominick & Haff	1905	O	92
Blossom	The Sterling Silver Mfg. Co.	c. 1900	O	NIA
Bostonia	Frank W. Smith Co.	c. 1905	O	113
Bouquet	Wm. B. Durgin Co.	c. 1900	O	NIA
*Bow Knot	F. M. Whiting & Co.	1890		125
Bradford	Wm. B. Durgin Co.	c. 1909		93
Bridal	Wm. B. Durgin Co.	c. 1880	O	NIA
Bridal Flower	Watson, Newell & Co.	c. 1910		121
Bridal Rose	Alvin Mfg. Co.	1900		89
Bridal Wreath (Southern Rose)	Manchester Mfg. Co.	c. 1910		104
*Bristol	Gorham Mfg. Co.	1885	O	98
Broom Corn	Tiffany & Co.	1890		NIA
Buckingham	Gorham Mfg. Co.	c. 1890		99
*Bug	Wm. B. Durgin Co.	c. 1880	O	NIA
Burlington	Whiting Mfg. Co.	c. 1900	O	128
Buttercup	Gorham Mfg. Co.	1900		98
Byzantine	Gorham Mfg. Co.	1875	O	101

STERLING FLATWARE PATTERNS *(Cont'd)*

Pattern	Brand or Manufacturer	Introduction Date and Obsolescence		Page
Byzantine	Wood & Hughes	c. 1875-1885	O	130
Cairo	Gorham Mfg. Co.	1880		96
Cairo	R. Wallace & Sons	c. 1908	O	119
Cambodia	Frank W. Smith Co.	c. 1900		114
Cambridge	Gorham Mfg. Co.	1899		98
Cambridge	Simpson, Hall, Miller & Co.	1899	O	111
*Cambridge	Towle Mfg. Co.	c. 1895	O	118
*Camden	R. Blackinton & Co.	c. 1900	O	NIA
Canterbury	Towle Mfg. Co.	1895	O	118
*Carnation	Alvin Mfg. Co.	1906	O	90
Carnation	Gorham Mfg. Co.	1894		96
*Carnation	Simpson, Hall, Miller & Co.	1908	O	112
Carnation	R. Wallace & Sons	1909	O	120
*Carnation (Pink)	Watson, Newell & Co.	1910	O	121
Cashmere	Wood & Hughes	c. 1875-1885	O	131
*Cat Tail	Wm. B. Durgin Co.	c. 1890	O	NIA
Cedric	Simpson, Hall, Miller & Co.	1903	O	113
Celestial	Wood & Hughes	c. 1865-1875	O	131
Cellini	Frank W. Smith Co.	c. 1890	O	NIA
Cellini	Wood & Hughes	c. 1875-1885	O	131
Celtic	Rogers, Lunt & Bowlen Co.	1909	O	108
Century	Dominick & Haff	1899	O	92
Century	Shreve & Co.	c. 1904	O	NIA
*Century	Frank W. Smith Co.	c. 1900	O	114
Chambord	Reed & Barton	c. 1900		107
Chantilly	Gorham Mfg. Co.	1895		99
Charles II	Dominick & Haff	1894	O	92
Charles II	Tuttle Silver Co.	c. 1900-1910		119
Chatelaine (Enid)	A. F. Towle & Son Co.	1894	O	116
Chatham	Wm. B. Durgin Co.	c. 1910		94
*Cherry Blossom	R. Blackinton & Co.	c. 1900	O	NIA
Cherry Blossom	Gorham Mfg. Co.	1894		96
*Cherub	Watson, Newell & Co.	c. 1895	O	122, 174
Chester	Gorham Mfg. Co.	c. 1900	O	100
Chesterfield	Gorham Mfg. Co.	1908		99
Chippendale (Old)	Alvin Mfg. Co.	c. 1900		89
Chippendale	Dominick & Haff	c. 1890	O	NIA
Chippendale	Gorham Mfg. Co.	1890		100
Chippendale	Frank W. Smith Co.	1908		114
*Chrysanthemum	Alvin Mfg. Co.	1906	O	90
Chrysanthemum	Wm. B. Durgin Co.	c. 1890		93
Chrysanthemum	Gorham Mfg. Co.	1885		96
Chrysanthemum	George W. Shiebler	1885	O	110
*Chrysanthemum	Simpson, Hall, Miller & Co.	1908	O	112
Chrysanthemum	The Stieff Co.	c. 1904	O	115
Chrysanthemum (Indian Chrysanthemum)	Tiffany & Co.	1880	O	115
*Claremont	R. Blackinton & Co.	c. 1900	O	NIA
Clematis	Coles & Reynolds	c. 1870	O	110
Clematis	Gorham Mfg. Co.	1885		96
Clematis	George W. Shiebler	c. 1875	O	110
Clematis	A. & W. Wood	c. 1860-1865	O	130
Clifton	Towle Mfg. Co.	c. 1885	O	117

STERLING FLATWARE PATTERNS (*Cont'd*)

Pattern	Brand or Manufacturer	Introduction Date and Obsolescence		Page
Clinton	J. B. & S. M. Knowles (Co.)	1876	O	103
Cloeta	Wilcox & Evertson	1905		130
Clover	Towle Mfg. Co.	c. 1885	O	117
Clover Blossom	Jos. Mayer & Bros.	c. 1897	O	105
Cluny	Gorham Mfg. Co.	1880		95, 165
Cobweb	Jos. Seymour Mfg. Co.	c. 1900	O	NIA
Coeur de Lion (Lion)	Frank W. Smith Co.	c. 1904	O	114
Colbert	Frank W. Smith Co.	c. 1900	O	114
Colfax	Wm. B. Durgin Co.	c. 1910		94
Coligni	Gorham Mfg. Co.	1887		97
Colonial	Campbell-Metcalf Silver Co.	1895	O	91
Colonial	Gorham Mfg. Co.	1880		101
Colonial	Tiffany & Co.	1895		115
Colonial (Old Colonial)	Towle Mfg. Co.	1895		118
Colonial	Whiting Mfg. Co.	c. 1900	O	127
Columbine	Watson, Newell & Co.	c. 1900	O	123
Commonwealth	Watson, Newell & Co.	c. 1910		122
Commonwealth Eng.	Watson, Newell & Co.	c. 1910		122
Connecticut	J. B. & S. M. Knowles (Co.)	1876	O	124
Connecticut	Knowles & Ladd	1865	O	124
Connecticut	Webster & Knowles	c. 1852	O	124
Cook (Saratoga)	Tiffany & Co.	1870		115
Copley	Simpson, Hall, Miller & Co.	1910	O	111
Cordova	Towle Mfg. Co.	1902	O	116
Corinthian	Baltimore Silversmiths Mfg. Co.	c. 1900	O	NIA
Corinthian	Gorham Mfg. Co.	1870	O	95
Corinthian	John Polhemus	c. 1855-1865	O	106
Corinthian	George W. Shiebler	1876		106
Corinthian	R. Wallace & Sons	c. 1910		121
Corinthian	Roger Williams Silver Co.	1902	O	130
Corona	Dominick & Haff	c. 1885	O	92
Coronet	J. B. & S. M. Knowles	1879	O	103
*Cosmos	Alvin Mfg. Co.	1906	O	90
*Cosmos	Simpson, Hall, Miller & Co.	1908	O	112
Cottage	Adams & Shaw Co.	before 1870	O	124
Cottage	Dominick & Haff	1884	O	124
Cottage	Gorham Mfg. Co.	1860		95
Cottage	John Polhemus	c. 1840-1850	O	105
Cottage	Jos. Seymour, Sons & Co.	c. 1846-1850	O	109
Cottage	George W. Shiebler	1876	O	105
Cottage	John R. Wendt & Co.	before 1870	O	124
Countess	Frank W. Smith Co.	c. 1900	O	114
*Cox	Whiting Mfg. Co.	c. 1870	O	126
Crescent	J. B. & S. M. Knowles (Co.)	1878	O	103
Cromwell	Wm. B. Durgin Co.	c. 1890		93
Cromwell	Gorham Mfg. Co.	c. 1900		99
Crystal	Frank W. Smith Co.	c. 1895	O	114
Crystal	F. M. Whiting & Co.	c. 1910	O	NIA
Cupid	Dominick & Haff	1891	O	92
Cupid	George W. Shiebler	c. 1890	O	110
*Cupid's Nosegay	Unger Bros.	c. 1890	O	NIA
*Cupid's Sunbeam	Unger Bros.	c. 1890	O	NIA
*Daisy	Alvin Mfg. Co.	1906	O	90
*Daisy	Fessenden & Co.	c. 1900	O	94

STERLING FLATWARE PATTERNS (*Cont'd*)

Pattern	Brand or Manufacturer	Introduction Date and Obsolescence		Page
Daisy	Gorham Mfg. Co.	1882	O	101
*Daisy	Gorham Mfg. Co.	c. 1890	O	166
*Daisy	Simpson, Hall, Miller & Co.	1908	O	112
*Daisy (Victor)	Towle Mfg. Co.	c. 1885	O	117
*Daisy	Watson, Newell & Co.	c. 1900	O	123
Damascus	F. M. Whiting Co.	1894	O	125
Dauphin	Wm. B. Durgin Co.	c. 1900		93
Dauphin	Howard Sterling Co.	1892	O	102
*Dawn	Unger Bros.	c. 1910	O	NIA
*DeCoverly	R. Blackinton & Co.	c. 1900	O	NIA
*Deer Crown	Henry Sears & Son	c. 1890	O	108
*Deer Foot	Henry Sears & Son	c. 1890	O	108
Delaware	Alvin Mfg. Co.	c. 1910		89
Delhi	Gorham Mfg. Co.	1880		101
Devon	Reed & Barton	c. 1900		107
Dew Drop	Coles & Reynolds	c. 1870	O	130
Dew Drop	George W. Shiebler	1875	O	130
Dew Drop	A. & W. Wood	c. 1855-1865	O	130
Diadem	Jos. Seymour, Sons & Co.	1892	O	109
Diamond	John Polhemus	c. 1855-1865	O	106
Diamond	George W. Shiebler	1876	O	106
*Diamond	Whiting Mfg. Co.	c. 1880	O	129
Diana	Gorham Mfg. Co.	1880		96
Diana	Simpson, Hall, Miller & Co.	c. 1901	O	111
Diana	Towle Mfg. Co.	c. 1885	O	118
Dixie	Manchester Mfg. Co.	c. 1910		104
Dolly Madison	Wm. B. Durgin Co.	c. 1904		93
Dolores	Shreve & Co.	c. 1909		111
Domestic	Gorham Mfg. Co.	1880	O	95
Dorchester	Watrous Mfg. Co.	1910	O	121
Dorchester	Watson, Newell & Co.	c. 1905	O	122
Doric	Coles & Reynolds	before 1875	O	91
Doric	Manchester Mfg. Co.	c. 1910	O	104
Doric	Charles M. Robbins Co.	c. 1900	O	NIA
Doric	George W. Shiebler	1875	O	91
Dorothy Q	Rogers, Lunt & Bowlen Co.	1902		108
Dorothy Vernon	Whiting Mfg. Co.	1909		128
Douglass	Gorham Mfg. Co.	1899	O	101
*Dover	Towle Mfg. Co.	c. 1885	O	118
Dowager	Gorham Mfg. Co.	1875	O	97
Dresden	Gorham Mfg. Co.	1885	O	98
Dresden	Simpson, Hall, Miller & Co.	1901	O	111
*Dresden	Whiting Mfg. Co.	c. 1890	O	NIA
DuBarry (Madame DuBarry)	Wm. B. Durgin Co.	1904		93
*DuBarry	Towle Mfg. Co.	1900	O	118
Duchess	Jos. Seymour, Sons & Co.	1876	O	109
Duchess	Whiting Mfg. Co.	1907	O	128
Duchesse	Simpson, Hall, Miller & Co.	1907	O	112
Duke of York	Whiting Mfg. Co.	c. 1900		128
*Duvaine	Unger Bros.	c. 1900	O	NIA
Earle	Frank W. Smith Co.	c. 1890	O	NIA
East Lake	Dominick & Haff	c. 1890	O	NIA
East Lake	Whiting Mfg. Co.	c. 1880	O	NIA

STERLING FLATWARE PATTERNS (*Cont'd*)

Pattern	Brand or Manufacturer	Introduction Date and Obsolescence		Page
*Easter Lily	Alvin Mfg. Co.	1906	O	90
*Easter Lily	Simpson, Hall, Miller & Co.	1908	O	112
*Easter Lily	Watson, Newell & Co.	c. 1910	O	123
Edgewood	Simpson, Hall, Miller & Co.	1909		112
Edward VII	Frank W. Smith Co.	c. 1902		114
Eglantine	Gorham Mfg. Co.	1870		101
*Egyptian	Henry Sears & Son	c. 1890	O	108
*Egyptian	Whiting Mfg. Co.	c. 1880	O	129
Eighty-eight (88)	Gorham Mfg. Co.	1888	O	NIA
Eighty-three (83)	Gorham Mfg. Co.	1883	O	100
Elaine	A. F. Towle & Son Co.	1893	O	116
Elmwood	Gorham Mfg. Co.	1894		96
Embossed	1847 Rogers Bros.	c. 1880	O	108
Embossed	Rogers, Smith & Co.	c. 1880	O	108
Embossed	R. Wallace & Sons	1886	O	121
Emperor	J. B. & S. M. Knowles (Co.)	1875	O	104
Emperor	Knowles & Ladd	1872	O	104
Emperor	Mauser Mfg. Co.	1896	O	105
Empire	Wm. B. Durgin Co.	c. 1880		93
Empire	John Polhemus	c. 1855-1865	O	105
Empire (L'Empire)	Reed & Barton	1892	O	106
Empire	George W. Shiebler	1876	O	105
Empire (New Empire)	Towle Mfg. Co.	1894	O	118
Empire	Whiting Mfg. Co.	c. 1890	O	126
*Empress	R. Blackinton & Co.	c. 1900	O	NIA
Empress	Coles & Reynolds	c. 1870	O	91
Empress	Gorham Mfg. Co.	1885	O	95
Empress	George W. Shiebler	1875	O	91
Empress	A. & W. Wood	c. 1860-1865	O	91
English Antique	Wm. B. Durgin Co.	c. 1900		NIA
English Antique	Reed & Barton	c. 1900		107
English Antique Eng.	Reed & Barton	c. 1900		107
English Antique Etched	Reed & Barton	c. 1900		107
English King	Tiffany & Co.	1885		115
English Tip	Wm. B. Durgin Co.	c. 1900		NIA
Enid (Chatelaine)	A. F. Towle & Son Co.	1894		116
Essex	Wm. B. Durgin Co.	1904		94
Essex	J. B. & S. M. Knowles (Co.)	1889	O	103
*Essex	Towle Mfg. Co.	1890	O	116
*Esther	F. M. Whiting & Co.	1890	O	124
Eton	Campbell-Metcalf Silver Co.	1894	O	91
*Eton	R. Wallace & Sons	1904	O	120
Etruscan	George W. Shiebler	c. 1890	O	NIA
Eugenie	Watson, Newell & Co.	c. 1900	O	122
Eva	Gorham Mfg. Co.	1875	O	97
Evangeline	Alvin Mfg. Co.	1908		89
*Evangeline	Unger Bros.	c. 1900	O	NIA
Evangeline #7	Alvin Mfg. Co.	c. 1910		89
Evelyn	Newburyport Silver Co.	c. 1905	O	NIA
Fairfax	Wm. B. Durgin Co.	c. 1910		94
Fairfax Engraved	Wm. B. Durgin Co.	c. 1910		94
Fairfax Engraved #2	Wm. B. Durgin Co.	c. 1910		94
*Fairfield	Whiting Mfg. Co.	c. 1910	O	127

STERLING FLATWARE PATTERNS (*Cont'd*)

Pattern	Brand or Manufacturer	Introduction Date and Obsolescence		Page
Fancy Tip	Whiting Mfg. Co.	c. 1890	O	126
Faneuil	Tiffany & Co.	1910		115
Faneuil No. 95 (Feather Edge)	Tiffany & Co.	1901		115
Feather Edge (Faneuil No. 95)	Tiffany & Co.	1901		115
*Fiddle	Wm. B. Durgin Co.	c. 1855	O	85
Fiddle	Theo. Evans & Co.	c. 1855-1860	O	85
Fiddle	Gorham Mfg. Co.	c. 1855	O	85
Fiddle	1847 Rogers Bros. (Meriden Ba. Co.)	1879	O	85
Fiddle	Rogers, Smith & Co.	c. 1880	O	85
Fiddle	Frank W. Smith Co.	c. 1895	O	114
*Fiddle	Towle Mfg. Co.	c. 1883	O	85
Fiddle	R. Wallace & Sons	c. 1890	O	85
Fiddle	Wendell Mfg. Co.	c. 1880		85
*Fiddle	Whiting Mfg. Co.	c. 1890	O	85
Fiddle	Wood & Hughes	c. 1845-1855	O	85
Fiddle, Old	Gorham Mfg. Co.	c. 1855	O	96
Fiddle Shell (Alden)	Frank W. Smith Co.	c. 1910		114
Fiddle Tip	Whiting Mfg. Co.	c. 1866		85
Fiddle Tipped	Dominick & Haff	c. 1870	O	85
Fiddle Tipped	Wm. Gale & Son	before 1870	O	85
Fiddle Tipped	J. B. & S. M. Knowles (Co.)	1875	O	85
Fiddle Tipped	Knowles & Ladd	c. 1865	O	85
Fiddle Tipped	Webster & Knowles	c. 1852	O	85
Fiddle Tipped	Whiting Mfg. Co.	c. 1880	O	85
Fiddle Tip't	Jos. Seymour, Sons & Co.	1852	O	109
Figured French	1847 Rogers Bros. (Meriden Ba. Co.)	c. 1879	O	108
Figured French	Rogers, Smith & Co.	c. 1880	O	108
Figured Shell	R. Wallace & Sons	1874	O	121
Figured Tipped	R. Wallace & Sons	1891	O	121
Filigree (8 patterns)	Dirksen Silver Co.	c. 1880-1900	O	91
Fiorito	George W. Shiebler & Co.	c. 1902	O	110, 172
First Empire	Howard Sterling Co.	1892	O	102
Flanders	Alvin Mfg. Co.	1908		111
Flanders	Simons Bros Co.	1903	O	111
Flemish	F. M. Whiting & Co.	c. 1897	O	124
Fleur de Lis	Alvin Mfg. Co.	1907		89
*Fleur de Lis	Wm. B. Durgin Co.	c. 1890	O	93
Fleur de Lis	Gorham Mfg. Co.	1865		100
Fleur de Lis	Newburyport Silver Co.	c. 1905	O	105
Fleury	Gorham Mfg. Co.	c. 1909		100
Flora	Reed & Barton	1890	O	106
*Flora (12 designs)	George W. Shiebler Co.	c. 1890	O	110, 172
Florac	Newburyport Silver Co.	c. 1905	O	NIA
Floral	Gorham Mfg. Co.	1865	O	101
Floral	F. M. Whiting & Co.	c. 1900	O	NIA
Floral Series #1	Watson, Newell & Co.	c. 1900-1910	O	123
Floral Series #2	Watson, Newell & Co.	c. 1900-1910	O	123
Floral Series #3	Watson, Newell & Co.	c. 1900-1910	O	123
Floral Series #4	Watson, Newell & Co.	c. 1900-1910	O	123
Florence	Gorham Mfg. Co.	1887		97
Florence	Towle Mfg. Co.	c. 1885	O	117
Florence	F. M. Whiting & Co.	c. 1900	O	124
Florence	Wilcox & Evertson	1903	O	130

STERLING FLATWARE PATTERNS (*Cont'd*)

Pattern	Brand or Manufacturer	Introduction Date and Obsolescence		Page
Florence	Roger Williams Silver Co.	1903	O	130
Florentine	Adams & Shaw Co.	before 1879	O	124
Florentine	Alvin Mfg. Co.	c. 1900	O	89
Florentine	Dominick & Haff	1884	O	124
Florentine	Tiffany & Co.	1900		NIA
Florentine	Gorham Mfg. Co.	1901		98
Florentine	John R. Wendt & Co.	before 1870	O	124
Florentine Lace	Reed & Barton (See Trianon, Pierced, Dominick & Haff)			92
Flute	J. B. & S. M. Knowles Co.	c. 1900	O	NIA
Fontainebleau	Gorham Mfg. Co.	1882		101
*Fontenay	Unger Bros.	c. 1890	O	NIA
*Forget-me-not	Gorham Mfg. Co.	c. 1890	O	166
*Four Georges	Reed & Barton	c. 1900	O	106
Francis I	Alvin Mfg. Co.	c. 1910		89
Francis I	Reed & Barton	1907		107
Franklin	Dominick & Haff	c. 1900	O	NIA
French	Gorham Mfg. Co.	1885	O	101
French	1847 Rogers Bros. (Meriden Ba. Co.)	c. 1879	O	155
French	Rogers, Smith & Co.	c. 1880	O	155
French Antique	Wm. B. Durgin Co.	c. 1870		NIA
French Antique	Reed & Barton	c. 1900		107
French Antique	Frank W. Smith Co.	1895		114
French Antique Eng.	Reed & Barton	c. 1900		107
French Antique, Watteau Engraved	Reed & Barton	c. 1900		107
French Oval	1847 Rogers Bros. (Meriden Ba. Co.)	c. 1879	O	147
French Thread	J. B. & S. M. Knowles (Co.)	1875	O	124
French Thread	Knowles & Ladd	1865	O	124
French Thread	John Polhemus	c. 1845-1855	O	85
French Thread	George W. Shiebler	1876	O	85
French Thread	Frank W. Smith Co.	1895	O	85
French Thread	Webster & Knowles	c. 1852	O	124
French Thread	Whiting Mfg. Co.	c. 1880	O	85
French Thread	Wood & Hughes	c. 1860-1870	O	85
French Tip't	Gorham Mfg. Co.	1855	O	96
French Tip't	Jos. Seymour, Sons, & Co.	c. 1846-1850	O	109
Frontenac	Simpson, Hall, Miller & Co.	1903		112
*Fruit	Whiting Mfg. Co.	c. 1880	O	129
*Fruit Series	Watson, Newell & Co.	c. 1910	O	123
*Fuchsia	Watson, Newell & Co.	c. 1910	O	123
Gadroon	Wood & Hughes	c. 1860-1870	O	131
*Gem Leaf	Whiting Mfg. Co.	c. 1880	O	127
Geneva	Campbell-Metcalf Silver Co.	1894	O	91
*Genoa	F. M. Whiting & Co.	1893	O	125
George III	F. M. Whiting & Co.	1891	O	125
Georgian	Towle Mfg. Co.	1898		118
Georgian Hand Engraved	Tuttle Silver Co.	c. 1905		119
*Georgian Hollow Handle	Towle Mfg. Co.	1898		118
*Gibney	Whiting Mfg. Co.	1870	O	126
Gilpin	Gorham Mfg. Co.	1880	O	101
Gipsy	George W. Shiebler	c. 1880	O	111
Gladstone	1847 Rogers Bros. (Meriden Ba. Co.)	1893	O	108
Gladstone	F. M. Whiting & Co.	1891	O	125

STERLING FLATWARE PATTERNS (*Cont'd*)

Pattern	Brand or Manufacturer	Introduction Date and Obsolescence		Page
Gladys	Towle Mfg. Co.	c. 1885	O	117
*Glenmore	Towle Mfg. Co.	1890	O	117
Godroon	Towle Mfg. Co.	1907		116
*Goldenrod	Watson, Newell & Co.	c. 1900	O	123
Golden Rod	Campbell-Metcalf Silver Co.	c. 1910	O	NIA
*Golden Rod	Reed & Barton	c. 1890	O	169
Gorham	Gorham Mfg. Co.	c. 1870		95
Gothic	Dominick & Haff	1899	O	92
Gothic	Charles M. Robbins Co.	c. 1900	O	NIA
Gothic	1847 Rogers Bros. (Meriden Ba. Co.)	c. 1879	O	147
Gothic (Salisbury)	George W. Shiebler Co.	c. 1890	O	110
*Gothic	F. M. Whiting & Co.	1893	O	124
Grape (Grape Vine)	Dominick & Haff	c. 1895	O	92
Grape	Gorham Mfg. Co.	1880	O	99
Grape	The Sterling Silver Mfg. Co.	c. 1910	O	NIA
*Grape	Watson, Newell & Co.	c. 1910	O	123
*Grape	Whiting Mfg. Co.	1875	O	126
Grape Vine (Grape)	Dominick & Haff	c. 1895	O	92
Grecian	Gorham Mfg. Co.	1860	O	95
Grecian	John R. Wendt & Co.	before 1870	O	127
*Grecian	Whiting Mfg. Co.	1875	O	127
Greenfield	A. F. Towle & Son Co.	1890	O	116
Greenwich	Fessenden & Co.	c. 1900	O	94
*H83	Gorham Mfg. Co.	c. 1890	O	101
*H111	Gorham Mfg. Co.	c. 1890	O	97
Hagie	F. M. Whiting & Co.	1892	O	125
Hamburg	Gorham Mfg. Co.	1880	O	101
Hamilton	Alvin Mfg. Co.	c. 1910		89
Hamilton	Gorham Mfg. Co.	c. 1905		96
Hamilton	Newburyport Silver Co.	c. 1910	O	NIA
Hamilton	R. Wallace & Sons	c. 1910		119
Hampshire	Wm. B. Durgin Co.	1907		93
*Hampton	Towle Mfg. Co.	1892	O	118
Hampton	R. Wallace & Sons	1904		120
Hand-Kraft	Charles M. Robbins Co.	c. 1900	O	NIA
Hanover	Gorham Mfg. Co.	1896		98
*Harlequin (Floral series)	Reed & Barton	c. 1890	O	169
Hawthorne	Gorham Mfg. Co.	1885		101
Hawthorn	R. Wallace & Sons	1875	O	121
*Helena	R. Blackinton & Co.	c. 1900	O	NIA
*Helena	F. M. Whiting & Co.	after 1896	O	NIA
*Helena I	F. M. Whiting & Co.	1892	O	124
Henry II	Gorham Mfg. Co.	1900		100
Hepplewhite	Reed & Barton	1907		107
Hepplewhite Eng.	Reed & Barton	1907		107
Heraldic	Wm. B. Durgin Co.	c. 1888	O	NIA
Heraldic	Whiting Mfg. Co.	c. 1885	O	127
Hereford	Wm. B. Durgin Co.	c. 1900	O	NIA
Hermitage	The Sterling Silver Mfg. Co.	c. 1910		NIA
Hindostanee (Hindustani)	Gorham Mfg. Co.	1875		95
Hizen	Gorham Mfg. Co.	1880		97
*Holly	Alvin Mfg. Co.	1906	O	90
*Holly	Simpson, Hall, Miller & Co.	1908	O	112
*Holly	Watson, Newell & Co.	c. 1910	O	123

STERLING FLATWARE PATTERNS (*Cont'd*)

Pattern	Brand or Manufacturer	Introduction Date and Obsolescence		Page
*Home	Whiting Mfg. Co.	c. 1870	O	126
Honeysuckle	Wm. B. Durgin Co.	c. 1880	O	NIA
Honeysuckle	John Polhemus	c. 1855-1865	O	105
Honeysuckle	Jos. Seymour, Sons & Co.	c. 1850	O	109
Honeysuckle	George W. Shiebler	1876	O	105
*Honeysuckle	Whiting Mfg. Co.	c. 1870	O	126
Hope	Howard Sterling Co.	1894	O	102
Hope	Roger Williams Silver Co.	1902		102
Humboldt	Wood & Hughes	c. 1875-1885	O	131
Hyperion	Whiting Mfg. Co.	c. 1890	O	127
Imperial	Dominick & Haff	1910	O	92
Imperial	Gorham Mfg. Co.	1893		98
Imperial (Imperial Queen)	Whiting Mfg. Co.	c. 1890	O	128
Imperial	Roger Williams Silver Co.	1909		130
Imperial Chrysanthemum	Gorham Mfg. Co.	1894		98
Imperial Queen (Imperial)	Whiting Mfg. Co.	c. 1890		128
Indian	Whiting Mfg. Co.	c. 1875-1880	O	126
Indian Chrysanthemum (Chrysanthemum)	Tiffany & Co.	1880		115
Intaglio	Reed & Barton	1904		107, 169
Ionic	Gorham Mfg. Co.	1865	O	99
Ionic	John Polhemus	c. 1850-1860	O	106
Ionic	George W. Shiebler	1876	O	106
Irene	Wilcox & Evertson	1902	O	130
Irian	R. Wallace & Sons	1902	O	120
*Iris	Wm. B. Durgin Co.	1904		93
Irving	R. Wallace & Sons	1900		120
Isis	Gorham Mfg. Co.	c. 1869	O	97
Isleworth	Frank W. Smith Co.	c. 1905	O	114
Italia	Campbell-Metcalf Silver Co.	c. 1895	O	NIA
Italian	Dominick & Haff	1870	O	94
Italian	Wm. Gale & Son	before 1870		94
Italian	Gorham Mfg. Co.	1865	O	97
*Italian	Whiting Mfg. Co.	c. 1875-1880	O	126, 174
*Italian J	Whiting Mfg. Co.	c. 1880	O	174
*Italian K	Whiting Mfg. Co.	c. 1880	O	174
Ivanhoe	Albert Coles	c. 1855-1865	O	91
Ivanhoe	M. Morgan	c. 1870	O	91
Ivanhoe	1847 Rogers Bros. (Meriden Ba. Co.)	1893	O	108
Ivanhoe	George W. Shiebler	1875	O	91
Ivanhoe	Frank W. Smith Co.	c. 1900	O	114
*Ivanhoe	R. Wallace & Sons	1891	O	120
Ivy	Gorham Mfg. Co.	1867	O	97
Ivy (Plain Mayflower)	J. B. & S. M. Knowles (Co.)	1875	O	103
Ivy (Plain Mayflower)	Knowles & Ladd	1869	O	103
Ivy	1847 Rogers Bros. (Meriden Ba. Co.)	c. 1879	O	150
*Ivy	Frank W. Smith Co.	c. 1900	O	114
*Ivy	Whiting Mfg. Co.	1875	O	129
Jacobean	Reed & Barton	c. 1910		107
Jac Rose	Gorham Mfg. Co.	1885		96
Jac Rose	Frank W. Smith Co.	1895		114
Japanese	Gorham Mfg. Co.	c. 1872		97, 168

STERLING FLATWARE PATTERNS (*Cont'd*)

Pattern	Brand or Manufacturer	Introduction Date and Obsolescence		Page
Japanese (Audubon)	Tiffany & Co.	1871		115, 173
*Japanese (Jap)	Whiting Mfg. Co.	c. 1880	O	127
Japanese	Wood & Hughes	c. 1865-1875	O	131
Jeanne D'Arc	Simpson, Hall, Miller & Co.	1905	O	113
Jefferson	Gorham Mfg. Co.	c. 1910		96
Jefferson	Watson, Newell & Co.	c. 1900	O	122
Jefferson Hammered	Rogers, Lunt & Bowlen Co.	1903		108
Jenny Lind	Albert Coles	c. 1850-1860	O	91
Jenny Lind	M. Morgan	c. 1870	O	91
Jenny Lind	George W. Shiebler	1877	O	91
Jenny Lind	Whiting Mfg. Co.	c. 1910	O	129
John Winthrop	Wilcox & Evertson	1910	O	130
*Jonquil	Wm. B. Durgin Co.	c. 1900	O	93
*Jonquil	Unger Bros.	c. 1910	O	NIA
Josephine	Alvin Mfg. Co.	1910	O	89
Josephine	Gorham Mfg. Co.	1855		99
Josephine	Howard Sterling Co.	1899	O	102
Josephine	F. M. Whiting Co.	c. 1890		124
Josephine	Roger Williams Silver Co.	1902		102
Juliet	A. F. Towle & Son Co.	c. 1890-1900	O	116
Junior Rococo	Mauser Mfg. Co.	1896	O	105
Karlton	The Sterling Silver Mfg. Co.	c. 1900	O	NIA
Kenilworth	Albert Coles	c. 1850-1860	O	91
Kenilworth	M. Morgan	c. 1870	O	91
Kenilworth	George W. Shiebler	1877	O	91
Kenilworth	Simpson, Hall, Miller & Co.	1897	O	113
Kensington	Gorham Mfg. Co.	1890	O	99
*Kensington	Frank W. Smith Co.	c. 1895	O	114
Kentucky Tipt	Jos. Seymour, Sons & Co.	c. 1855	O	109
*Keystone	Whiting Mfg. Co.	c. 1880	O	129
King (Kirk King)	Samuel Kirk & Son	1824		102
King	J. B. & S. M. Knowles (Co.)	1886	O	103
King Albert	Whiting Mfg. Co.	c. 1910	O	129
King Edward	Whiting Mfg. Co.	1901		128
King George	Gorham Mfg. Co.	1894		100
King George	Watson, Newell & Co.	c. 1910	O	NIA
King Philip	Watson, Newell & Co.	1904		122
King William	Tiffany & Co.	1870		115
Kings	Adams & Shaw Co.	before 1870	O	124
Kings	Dominick & Haff	1879	O	124
Kings	John Polhemus	c. 1825-1845	O	105
Kings	Reed & Barton	c. 1890		85
Kings	George W. Shiebler	1876	O	105
Kings	Towle Mfg. Co.	1905		85
Kings	R. Wallace & Sons	1903		85
Kings	John R. Wendt & Co.	before 1870	O	124
Kings I	Gorham Mfg. Co.	c. 1875		100
Kings II	Gorham Mfg. Co.	c. 1885		100
Kings III	Gorham Mfg. Co.	c. 1890		100
Kirk King (King)	Samuel Kirk & Son	1824		102
Knickerbocker	Gorham Mfg. Co.	1872		96
Knickerbocker Engraved	Gorham Mfg. Co.	1872		95

STERLING FLATWARE PATTERNS (*Cont'd*)

Pattern	Brand or Manufacturer	Introduction Date and Obsolescence		Page
Knickerbocker Etched	Gorham Mfg. Co.	1872		96
L'Elegante	Reed & Barton	1895		107
L'Empire (Empire)	Reed & Barton	c. 1890		106
LaComtesse	Reed & Barton	1897	O	107
*LaFantasie	Unger Bros.	c. 1900	O	NIA
LaFayette	Howard Sterling Co.	1898	O	102
LaFayette	W. H. Manchester Co.	1898	O	104
LaFayette	Towle Mfg. Co.	1905		116
LaFayette Engraved	Towle Mfg. Co.	1905		116
*LaFleurette	Unger Bros.	c. 1900	O	NIA
LaFrance	Dominick & Haff	c. 1900	O	NIA
LaMarquise	Reed & Barton	1884		106
LaModele	Gorham Mfg. Co.	c. 1910		99
LaParisienne	Reed & Barton	1902		107, 169
LaPerle	Reed & Barton	1902		107
LaPerle Engraved	Reed & Barton	1905		107
*LaProvence	Fessenden & Co.	c. 1900	O	94
LaReine	Reed & Barton	1893	O	106
LaRocaille	Reed & Barton	1890	O	106
LaRochelle	Wilcox & Evertson	1909		130
LaSplendide	Reed & Barton	1903		106
LaTouraine	Reed & Barton	1897	O	106
Labors of Cupid	Reed & Barton (See 1900, Dominick & Haff)			92
Lady Baltimore	Whiting Mfg. Co.	c. 1910	O	129
Lady Beatrice	Alvin Mfg. Co.	c. 1910		89
Lady Washington	Gorham Mfg. Co.	1875	O	95
Lady's	Gorham Mfg. Co.	1887	O	97
Lancaster	Gorham Mfg. Co.	1897		98
Landers #1	Landers, Frary & Clark	c. 1900	O	104
Landers #2	Landers, Frary & Clark	c. 1900	O	104
Lap-over-Edge	Tiffany & Co.	1880		NIA
Laureate	Whiting Mfg. Co.	c. 1890	O	127
Laurel	Gorham Mfg. Co.	c. 1885	O	101
Laurel	1847 Rogers Bros. (Meriden Ba. Co.)	c. 1879	O	148
Laurel	Frank W. Smith Co.	1909		113
LeBolt	LeBolt & Co.	c. 1910		104
LeCordon	Whiting Mfg. Co.	1870	O	126
*Le Secrete de Fleurs	Unger Bros.	c. 1905	O	NIA
*Leaf	Gorham Mfg. Co.	1891	O	101
Leaf (Shell)	George W. Shiebler	c. 1880	O	110
Lenox	Wm. B. Durgin Co.	c. 1910		94
Lenox	Gorham Mfg. Co.	1897	O	99
Lenox	J. B. & S. M. Knowles (Co.)	1890	O	103
*Lenox	Towle Mfg. Co.	c. 1885	O	117
*Les Ceres	Unger Bros.	c. 1900	O	NIA
Les Cinq Fleurs	Reed & Barton	1900		107, 169
Les Six Fleurs	Reed & Barton	1901		106
Lexington	Dominick & Haff	c. 1900		NIA
Lexington	J. B. & S. M. Knowles Co.	c. 1900	O	103
Lilly	Gorham Mfg. Co.	1870	O	166
Lily	Baltimore Silversmiths Mfg. Co.	c. 1900	O	NIA
Lily	Coles & Reynolds	c. 1870	O	130
Lily	Newburyport Silver Co.	c. 1905	O	NIA

STERLING FLATWARE PATTERNS (*Cont'd*)

Pattern	Brand or Manufacturer	Introduction Date and Obsolescence		Page
Lily	1847 Rogers Bros. (Meriden Ba. Co.)	c. 1879	O	85
Lily	George W. Shiebler	c. 1875	O	130
Lily (Martha Washington Lily)	Frank W. Smith Co.	c. 1895	O	113
Lily	Towle Mfg. Co.	c. 1885	O	117
Lily	Watson, Newell & Co.	1902		123
Lily	Whiting Mfg. Co.	1902		128
Lily	A. & W. Wood	c. 1860-1865	O	130
Lily Engraved	Jos. Seymour, Sons & Co.	1884	O	109
Lily Engraved	F. M. Whiting & Co.	1889	O	125
Lily Engraved Antique	Whiting Mfg. Co.	1881	O	127
*Lily of the Valley	Alvin Mfg. Co.	1906	O	90
Lily of the Valley	Gorham Mfg. Co.	c. 1880	O	97
*Lily of the Valley	Simpson, Hall, Miller & Co.	1908	O	112
*Lily of the Valley	Watson, Newell & Co.	c. 1910	O	122, 123
Lily of the Valley	F. M. Whiting & Co.	c. 1900	O	125
Lily of the Valley	Whiting Mfg. Co.	c. 1890		127
Lincoln	Frank W. Smith Co.	c. 1908		113
Lincoln Engraved	Frank W. Smith Co.	c. 1910		113
Lincoln Kraft Engraved	Frank W. Smith Co.	c. 1910		113
Lincoln Kraft	Frank W. Smith Co.	c. 1910		113
Lion (Coeur de Lion)	Frank W. Smith Co.	1904	O	114
Litchfield	Wilcox & Evertson	1898	O	130
Livingston	Whiting Mfg. Co.	c. 1910	O	129
Lombardy	Mauser Mfg. Co.	c. 1890	O	NIA
London	Gorham Mfg. Co.	1880		96
Lorne	1847 Rogers Bros.	c. 1879	O	148
Lorne	Rogers, Smith & Co.	c. 1879	O	148
Lorraine	Alvin Mfg. Co.	1904	O	89
Lorraine	Howard Sterling Co.	1892	O	102
Lotus	Gorham Mfg. Co.	c. 1867	O	97
Lotus	Frank W. Smith Co.	c. 1890	O	NIA
Louis XIV	Dominick & Haff	1888	O	92
Louis XIV	Gorham Mfg. Co.	1870	O	95
Louis XIV	John Polhemus	c. 1840-1850	O	106
Louis XIV	George W. Shiebler	1876	O	106
Louis XV	Wm. B. Durgin Co.	c. 1890		NIA
Louis XV	Whiting Mfg. Co.	c. 1890		128
Louis XV	Wood & Hughes	c. 1880	O	131
Louis XVI	Dominick & Haff	c. 1900	O	NIA
Louis XVI	Gorham Mfg. Co.	c. 1880		100
Louvre	George W. Shiebler	c. 1890	O	110
*Louvre	R. Wallace & Sons	1893	O	120
Louvre	Wood & Hughes	c. 1885	O	131
Love Disarmed	Reed & Barton	1900	O	107
*Love's Dream	Unger Bros.	c. 1900	O	NIA
Lucerne	R. Wallace & Sons	1896		120
Luxembourg	Gorham Mfg. Co.	c. 1890		98
Luxembourg	Reed & Barton	1890	O	106
Luxembourg	George W. Shiebler	1887	O	110
Luxembourg	Wood & Hughes	c. 1888	O	131
Luzon	Simpson, Hall, Miller & Co.	1903	O	111
Madame DuBarry (DuBarry)	Wm. B. Durgin Co.	c. 1904		93

STERLING FLATWARE PATTERNS (*Cont'd*)

Pattern	Brand or Manufacturer	Introduction Date and Obsolescence		Page
Madame Jumel	Whiting Mfg. Co.	1908		129
Madame LaFayette	Towle Mfg. Co.	c. 1905		116
Madame Morris	Whiting Mfg. Co.	1900		129
Madame Royale	Wm. B. Durgin Co.	c. 1897		93
*Magnolia	Wm. B. Durgin Co.	c. 1890	O	NIA
Maintenon	George W. Shiebler	c. 1895	O	110
Majestic	Alvin Mfg. Co.	1902		89, 165
Majestic	Reed & Barton	1894		106
Manchester	Manchester Mfg. Co.	c. 1910		104
Mandarin	Whiting Mfg. Co.	c. 1910		129
Marcell	Wilcox & Evertson	1907	O	130
Marechal Niel	Wm. B. Durgin Co.	c. 1896		93
Margaret	Simpson, Hall, Miller & Co.	1906	O	113
Marguerite, New	Gorham Mfg. Co.	c. 1901		98
Marguerite	Gorham Mfg. Co.	c. 1881		96
Marguerite	Wood & Hughes	c. 1880	O	130
Marie	R. Wallace & Sons Mfg. Co.	1893	O	NIA
Marie Antoinette	Alvin Mfg. Co.	c. 1900	O	90
Marie Antoinette	Dominick & Haff	c. 1895	O	92
Marie Antoinette	Gorham Mfg. Co.	1891		98, 165
Marie Antoinette	George W. Shiebler	c. 1893		110
Marie Louise	Fessenden & Co.	c. 1900	O	94
Marigold	Gorham Mfg. Co.	1880	O	96
Marlboro	1847 Rogers Bros. (Meriden Ba. Co.)	1879	O	108
Marlborough	Reed & Barton	1906		107
Marlborough	F. M. Whiting & Co.	c. 1895		124
Marquis	F. M. Whiting & Co.	1889	O	125
Marquise	Tiffany & Co.	1902		115
Marseilles	Alvin Mfg. Co.	1899	0	89
Martha Randolph	Frank W. Smith Co.	c. 1906		115
Martha Washington	Frank W. Smith Co.	c. 1905	O	113
Martha Washington Lily	Frank W. Smith Co.	c. 1905	O	113
Martha Washington Star	Frank W. Smith Co.	c. 1905	O	113
Maryland	Gorham Mfg. Co.	1896	O	98
Maryland	Baltimore Sterling Silver Co.	1892		115
Maryland (Rose)	The Stieff Co.	c. 1904		115
Mary Warren	Manchester Mfg. Co.	c. 1910		104
*Mask	Whiting Mfg. Co.	c. 1889	O	126
*Master	Gorham Mfg. Co.	1885		168
Mayfair	Dominick & Haff	c. 1900	O	NIA
Mayfair Engraved	Dominick & Haff	c. 1900	O	NIA
Mayflower	Baltimore Silversmiths Mfg. Co.	c. 1900	O	NIA
Mayflower	Albert Coles	c. 1845-1855	O	91
Mayflower	Dominick & Haff	1891	O	94
Mayflower	Wm. Gale & Son	c. 1840	O	94
Mayflower	Jacobi & Jenkins	c. 1900	O	NIA
Mayflower	Samuel Kirk & Sons	1846		102
Mayflower	J. B. & S. M. Knowles (Co.)	1878	O	103
Mayflower	M. Morgan	c. 1870	O	91
Mayflower	George W. Shiebler	1877	O	91
Mayflower	Frank W. Smith Co.	c. 1900		113
Mayflower Chased	Frank W. Smith Co.	c. 1900	O	113
Mazarin	Dominick & Haff	1892	O	92
McKinley	Fessenden & Co.	c. 1890	O	94

STERLING FLATWARE PATTERNS (*Cont'd*)

Pattern	Brand or Manufacturer	Introduction Date and Obsolescence		Page
Meadow	Gorham Mfg. Co.	1897	O	100
Meadow Rose	Watson, Newell & Co.	1907		121
Medallion	Dominick & Haff	c. 1905	O	92
Medallion	Wm. B. Durgin Co.	c. 1870	O	NIA
Medallion	Gorham Mfg. Co.	1860		97
Medallion	George W. Shiebler	c. 1870	O	110
Medallion	W. K. Vanderslice & Co.	c. 1865-1870	O	119
Medici	Gorham Mfg. Co.	1880		95, 165
Melrose	Alvin Mfg. Co.	c. 1910		90
*Melrose	Gorham Mfg. Co.	c. 1910		99
Milan	Gorham Mfg. Co.	1885	O	97
Mille Fleurs	Simpson, Hall, Miller & Co.	1904	O	112, 173
Mission	Jos. Mayer & Bros.	c. 1905		105
Monarque	Howard Sterling Co.	1899	O	102
Monroe	John R. Wendt & Co.	before 1870	O	NIA
*Montclair	Gorham Mfg. Co.	c. 1910		98
Montezuma	George W. Shiebler	1881	O	111
Monticello	Rogers, Lunt & Bowlen Co.	1908		108
Moresque	Adams & Shaw Co.	before 1879	O	124
Moresque	Dominick & Haff	1884	O	124
Moresque	John R. Wendt & Co.	before 1870	O	124
Morning Glory	Alvin Mfg. Co.	1909		89
Mothers	Gorham Mfg. Co.	1875		100
Mothers Engraved	Gorham Mfg. Co.	1875		100
Mount Vernon	Rogers, Lunt & Bowlen Co.	1905		108
Mount Vernon	Watson, Newell & Co.	1908		122
Murillo	Wood & Hughes	c. 1875-1885	O	131
M. W. Lily (Martha Washington Lily)	Frank W. Smith Co.	c. 1905	O	113
M. W. Star (Martha Washington Star)	Frank W. Smith Co.	c. 1905	O	113
Mythologique	Gorham Mfg. Co.	1899		97, 165
Napoleon	George W. Shiebler	1894	O	110
Napoleon	Wilcox & Evertson	1910		130
Napoleonic	Shreve & Co.	c. 1905		111
*Narcissus	R. Blackinton & Co.	c. 1900	O	NIA
*Narcissus	Wm. B. Durgin Co.	c. 1900	O	NIA
Narcissus	Fessenden & Co.	c. 1905	O	94
Narcissus	Rogers, Lunt & Bowlen Co.	1903	O	108
*Narcissus	Unger Bros.	c. 1900	O	NIA
Narcissus	F. M. Whiting & Co.	1886	O	125
*Nassau	R. Blackinton & Co.	c. 1900	O	NIA
*Nautilus	R. Blackinton & Co.	c. 1900	O	90
Nautilus	Albert Coles	c. 1845-1855	O	91
Nautilus	M. Morgan	c. 1870	O	91
Nautilus	George W. Shiebler	1877	O	91
Navarre	Wm. B. Durgin Co.	1909		93
Navarre	A. F. Towle & Son Co.	1895	O	116
Neapolitan	F. M. Whiting & Co.	1895	O	125
Neptune	John Polhemus	c. 1845-1855	O	105
Neptune	George W. Shiebler	c. 1876	O	105
*New Art	Wm. B. Durgin Co.	1904		93
New Empire (Empire)	Towle Mfg. Co.	1894	O	118

STERLING FLATWARE PATTERNS (*Cont'd*)

Pattern	Brand or Manufacturer	Introduction Date and Obsolescence		Page
New Empire	Whiting Mfg. Co.	c. 1895	O	128
New Honeysuckle	Whiting Mfg. Co.	c. 1875-1880	O	126
New Jap	Whiting Mfg. Co.	c. 1875-1880	O	126
New King	Wood & Hughes	c. 1890	O	131
New Kings	Dominick & Haff	1898	O	92
New Marguerite	Gorham Mfg. Co.	c. 1900		98
New Plymouth (Plymouth)	Gorham Mfg. Co.	1899		98
New Poppy	Gorham Mfg. Co.	1901		100, 168
New Queens	Wm. B. Durgin Co.	c. 1907	O	93
New Queens	Gorham Mfg. Co.	c. 1895		100
New Standish	Wm. B. Durgin Co.	1905		93
New Tip't	Gorham Mfg. Co.	c. 1870		95
Newbury (Old Newbury)	Towle Mfg. Co.	1900		116
Newcastle	Gorham Mfg. Co.	c. 1895		96
Newport (No. 88)	Fessenden & Co.	1899	O	94
Newport	1847 Rogers Bros. (Meriden Ba. Co.)	c. 1880	O	148
Newport	Rogers, Smith & Co.	c. 1880	O	148
Newport	Whiting Mfg. Co.	c. 1910	O	129
*Nightingale	Gorham Mfg. Co.	c. 1885	O	96
Nile	R. Wallace & Sons	1908		119
1900	Dominick & Haff	1900		92
1909	Jos. Mayer & Bros.	1909	O	105
"99"	F. M. Whiting Co.	c. 1893-1899	O	124
Nordica	Frank W. Smith Co.	c. 1910	O	115
Norfolk	Gorham Mfg. Co.	1904		99
No. 2	Frank W. Smith Co.	c. 1900	O	114
No. 3	Wood & Hughes	c. 1880-1890	O	131
*No. 4	Frank W. Smith Co.	c. 1910	O	114
*No. 4	R. Wallace & Sons	1896	O	120
*No. 6	Simmons & Paye	1898	O	111
*No. 8	Simmons & Paye	1898	O	111
No. 8 Chased	Wood & Hughes	c. 1880-1890	O	131
No. 9 Engraved	Frank W. Smith Co.	c. 1895	O	114
No. 10	Dominick & Haff	c. 1890	O	92
*No. 10	Frank W. Smith Co.	c. 1895	O	114
*No. 12	Frank W. Smith Co.	c. 1895	O	114
*No. 14	Frank W. Smith Co.	c. 1895	O	113
*No. 15	Frank W. Smith Co.	c. 1895	O	114
No. 30	Wood & Hughes	c. 1880-1890	O	131
No. 38	Towle Mfg. Co.	c. 1885		117
No. 39	Towle Mfg. Co.	c. 1885		117
*No. 40	R. Wallace & Sons	1910	O	119
*No. 41	R. Wallace & Sons	1910	O	119
*No. 42	R. Wallace & Sons	1910	O	119
No. 43	Towle Mfg. Co.	c. 1885		117
*No. 43	R. Wallace & Sons	1910	O	119
*No. 44	R. Wallace & Sons	1910	O	119
*No. 45	R. Wallace & Sons	1910		119
No. 45 Chased	Wood & Hughes	c. 1880-1890	O	131
No. 50	Towle Mfg. Co.	c. 1885	O	117
No. 62	Towle Mfg. Co.	c. 1885	O	117
No. 63	Towle Mfg. Co.	c. 1885	O	117
*No. 80	R. Wallace & Sons	1909	O	NIA
No. 83	Gorham Mfg. Co.	1872	O	100

STERLING FLATWARE PATTERNS (*Cont'd*)

Pattern	Brand or Manufacturer	Introduction Date and Obsolescence		Page
No. 85 (Victoria)	Wood & Hughes	c. 1885-1895	O	131
No. 88 (Newport)	Fessenden & Co.	1899	O	94
No. 90	J. B. & S. M. Knowles	1882	O	103
*No. 128	Towle Mfg. Co.	c. 1885	O	116
*No. 300	R. Wallace & Sons	1907	O	119
*No. 598	Simmons & Paye	1900	O	111
*No. 599	Simmons & Paye	1900	O	111
*No. 601	Simmons & Paye	c. 1900	O	111
No. 2159	Landers, Frary & Clark	c. 1900	O	104
No. 2160	Landers, Frary & Clark	c. 1900	O	104
*No. 6198	Simmons & Paye	1898	O	111
Nuremburg	Alvin Mfg. Co.	1903	O	90
Nuremburg	Gorham Mfg. Co.	c. 1880		97, 168
Oak	Frank W. Smith Co.	1906	O	114
Oakland	Watson, Newell & Co.	1903		122
Old Colony	Gorham Mfg. Co.	1897		100
Old Dominion	A. F. Towle & Son Co.	1897		116
*Old Empire (Empire)	Whiting Mfg. Co.	c. 1890	O	126
Old English	Gorham Mfg. Co.	1873		85
Old English	Towle Mfg. Co.	1892		117
*Old English	Whiting Mfg. Co.	c. 1890	O	85
Old Fiddle	Gorham Mfg. Co.	c. 1855	O	96
Old French	Gorham Mfg. Co.	1910		96
Old King	Whiting Mfg. Co.	c. 1890	O	128
Old Maryland Plain	Samuel Kirk & Sons	1840		102
*Old Master	Gorham Mfg. Co.	1887		97
Old Newbury (Newbury)	Towle Mfg. Co.	1900		116
Old Newport	Gorham Mfg. Co.	1878		100
*Old Rose	Fessenden & Co.	c. 1900	O	94
Olive	Wm. B. Durgin Co.	c. 1860	O	85
Olive	Theo. Evans & Co.	c. 1860	O	85
Olive	Wm. Gale & Son	c. 1850	O	94
Olive	Gorham Mfg. Co.	1867	O	85
Olive	1847 Rogers Bros. (Meriden Ba. Co.)	c. 1879	O	85
Olive	Whiting Mfg. Co.	c. 1870	O	126
Olive	Wood & Hughes	c. 1845-1855	O	85
Olympia	Watson, Newell & Co.	c. 1890	O	122
Olympian	Jos. Mayer & Bros.	c. 1898	O	105
Olympian	Tiffany & Co.	1878		115
Oneida	Mauser Mfg. Co.	1896	O	105
Orange Blossom	Alvin Mfg. Co.	1905		89
*Orange Blossom	Wm. B. Durgin Co.	c. 1890	O	NIA
Orchid	Gorham Mfg. Co.	1894		96
Orchid	Watson, Newell & Co.	c. 1903	O	121
*Orchids	Towle Mfg. Co.	c. 1885	O	118, 173
Oregon	Watson, Newell & Co.	c. 1900		NIA
Oriana	Whiting Mfg. Co.	c. 1910	O	129
Orient	Alvin Mfg. Co.	c. 1900	O	90
Oriental	John Polhemus	c. 1855-1865	O	105
Oriental	George W. Shiebler	1876	O	105
Original Bead (Bead)	Wm. B. Durgin Co.	1886	O	93
*Orleans	Towle Mfg. Co.	c. 1890	O	118
Orleans	Watson, Newell & Co.	c. 1900		122

STERLING FLATWARE PATTERNS *(Cont'd)*

Pattern	Brand or Manufacturer	Introduction Date and Obsolescence		Page
Orleans	F. M. Whiting Co.	1892	O	124
Osiris	Adams & Shaw Co.	before 1879	O	124
Osiris	Dominick & Haff	1884	O	124
Osiris	John R. Wendt & Co.	before 1870	O	124
Oval	1847 Rogers Bros. (Meriden Ba. Co.)	c. 1879	O	85
Oval Thread	Theo. Evans & Co.	c. 1855-1860	O	85
Oval Thread	John Polhemus	c. 1840-1850	O	85
*Oval Thread	Reed & Barton	c. 1890	O	85
Oval Thread	George W. Shiebler	1876	O	85
Oval Thread	John R. Wendt & Co.	before 1870	O	85
Oval Thread	Whiting Mfg. Co.	c. 1880	O	85
*Oval Twist	Whiting Mfg. Co.	c. 1880	O	NIA
Oxalis	F. M. Whiting & Co.	1887	O	125
*Oxford	Gorham Mfg. Co.	1895	O	98
Palace	Albert Coles	c. 1850-1860	O	91
Palace	M. Morgan	c. 1870	O	91
Palace	George W. Shiebler	1877	O	91
Palm	Gorham Mfg. Co.	c. 1872	O	95
Palm	Tiffany & Co.	1871		115
Palm	F. M. Whiting & Co.	1887	O	125
*Pansy	Gorham Mfg. Co.	c. 1890	O	166
Pansy	Wilcox & Evertson	c. 1909	O	130
Paris	Gorham Mfg. Co.	1901		97, 168
*Passaic	Unger Bros.	c. 1910	O	NIA
*Passion Flower	Gorham Mfg. Co.	c. 1890	O	166
Patrician	Gorham Mfg. Co.	1901		100
Patrician	Jos. Seymour, Sons & Co.	1880	O	109
Paul Revere (Engraved)	Frank W. Smith Co.	c. 1900	O	113
Paul Revere	Towle Mfg. Co.	1900		116
*Peach Blossom	Watson, Newell & Co.	c. 1910	O	121
*Pear	Watson, Newell & Co.	c. 1910	O	123
*Pearl	F. M. Whiting & Co.	1888	O	NIA
*Pembroke	Gorham Mfg. Co.	1895		99
Penn	George W. Shiebler	c. 1880	O	110
Peony	R. Wallace & Sons	1906	O	120
Persian	Gorham Mfg. Co.	1875	O	97
Persian	1847 Rogers Bros. (Meriden Ba. Co.)	c. 1879	O	148
Persian	Tiffany & Co.	1872		NIA
Persian	Whiting Mfg. Co.	c. 1880	O	127
Phoebe	Watson, Newell & Co.	c. 1895	O	122, 174
Pilgrim	Newburyport Silver Co.	c. 1905	O	NIA
Pilgrim	Frank W. Smith Co.	1906		113
Pineapple	J. B. & S. M. Knowles (Co.)	1875	O	124
Pineapple	Knowles & Ladd	c. 1865	O	124
*Pineapple	Watson, Newell & Co.	c. 1910	O	123
Pineapple	Webster & Knowles	1859	O	124
*Pine Cone	Watson, Newell & Co.	c. 1910	O	121
*Piper	Gorham Mfg. Co.	c. 1883	O	101, 165
Plain	1847 Rogers Bros. (Meriden Ba. Co.)	c. 1879	O	85
Plain	The Stieff Co.	c. 1904	O	85
Plain	Wood & Hughes	c. 1845-1855	O	85
Plain Antique (Antique)	Wood & Hughes	c. 1845-1855	O	85
Plain Thread	Dominick & Haff	c. 1870	O	85

STERLING FLATWARE PATTERNS (*Cont'd*)

Pattern	Brand or Manufacturer	Introduction Date and Obsolescence		Page
Plain Thread	Theo. Evans & Co.	c. 1855	O	85
Plain Thread	Wm. Gale & Sons	before 1870	O	85
Plain Thread	John Polhemus	c. 1840-1850	O	85
Plain Thread	George W. Shiebler	1876	O	85
Plain Thread	Whiting Mfg. Co.	c. 1870	O	85
Plain Thread	Wood & Hughes	c. 1845-1855	O	85
Plain Tip	F. M. Whiting & Co.	1880	O	85
*Plain Tip	Whiting Mfg. Co.	c. 1870	O	85
Plain Tipped	Dominick & Haff	c. 1870	O	85
Plain Tipped	Theo. Evans & Co.	c. 1860	O	85
Plain Tipped	Wm. Gale & Son	before 1870	O	85
Plain Tip't	John Polhemus	c. 1840-1850	O	85
Plain Tip't	George W. Shiebler	1876	O	85
*Play Fellow	Gorham Mfg. Co.	1885	O	96
Plymouth	Baltimore Silversmiths Mfg. Co.	c. 1900	O	NIA
Plymouth (New Plymouth)	Gorham Mfg. Co.	1899	O	98
Plymouth	Frank W. Smith Co.	c. 1900	O	NIA
Plymouth	Watson, Newell & Co.	c. 1905	O	122
Plymouth	Roger Williams Silver Co.	c. 1905	O	NIA
Pointed Antique	Jacobi & Jenkins	c. 1900	O	NIA
Pomona	Towle Mfg. Co.	c. 1885	O	118
Pompadour	Wm. B. Durgin Co.	c. 1880	O	93
Pompadour	Whiting Mfg. Co.	1895	O	128
Pompeii	Gorham Mfg. Co.	1867	O	100
Pompeiian	Whiting Mfg. Co.	c. 1905		129
*Poppy	Alvin Mfg. Co.	1906	O	90
*Poppy	Gorham Mfg. Co.	c. 1869	O	96
*Poppy	Simpson, Hall, Miller & Co.	1908	O	112
*Poppy, Series 1	Watson, Newell & Co.	c. 1900	O	123
Poppy, New	Gorham Mfg. Co.	1901		100, 168
*Poppy, Series 3	Watson, Newell & Co.	c. 1910	O	123
*Poppy, Series 4	Watson, Newell & Co.	c. 1910	O	123
*Portland	Gorham Mfg. Co.	1904		99
Portland	Whiting Mfg. Co.	c. 1905	O	129
Potomac	Sterling Silver Mfg. Co.	c. 1910	O	NIA
Prairie Flower	Jos. Seymour, Sons & Co.	1866	O	109
Prince Albert	John Polhemus	c. 1860-1870	O	105
Prince Albert	George W. Shiebler	1876	O	105
*Prince Albert	Whiting Mfg. Co.	c. 1880	O	128
Princess	Gorham Mfg. Co.	1867	O	99
Princess	Manchester Mfg. Co.	c. 1910	O	104
Princess	John Polhemus	c. 1860-1870	O	106
Princess	1847 Rogers Bros. (Meriden Ba. Co.)	c. 1879	O	155
Princess	George W. Shiebler	1876	O	106
*Princess	Towle Mfg. Co.	1892	O	118
Princess	Watson, Newell & Co.	c. 1900	O	122
Princeton	Wood & Hughes	1893	O	131
Priscilla	Campbell-Metcalf Silver Co.	1895	O	91
Priscilla	Dominick & Haff	c. 1900	O	NIA
Priscilla	Gorham Mfg. Co.	1890		100
Priscilla (Priscilla Hammered)	Manchester Mfg. Co.	c. 1910	O	104
Priscilla	Charles M. Robbins Co.	c. 1900	O	NIA
Priscilla	Frank W. Smith Co.	c. 1905		115
Priscilla	A. F. Towle & Son Co.	1897		116

STERLING FLATWARE PATTERNS (*Cont'd*)

Pattern	Brand or Manufacturer	Introduction Date and Obsolescence		Page
Priscilla	R. Wallace & Sons	1910	O	119
Priscilla Hammered (Priscilla)	Manchester Mfg. Co.	c. 1910		104
Provence	A. F. Towle & Son Co.	1896	O	116
Psyche	Watson, Newell & Co.	c. 1904	O	122
Puritan	Frank W. Smith Co.	c. 1906		114
Puritan	R. Wallace & Sons	1909		119
Puritan	F. M. Whiting & Co.	c. 1907		124
Pynchon (Ye Pynchon)	Rogers, Lunt & Bowlen Co.	1910		108
Queen	Howard Sterling Co.	1893	O	102
Queen	J. B. & S. M. Knowles (Co.)	1875	O	104
Queen	Knowles & Ladd	1870	O	104
Queen Anne	Gorham Mfg. Co.	1871	O	101
Queen Anne	Tiffany & Co.	c. 1870	O	115
Queens	Gorham Mfg. Co.	1870	O	95
Queen's	John Polhemus	c. 1845-1855	O	105
Queen's	George W. Shiebler	1876		105
Queens, New	Gorham Mfg. Co.	1899		100
Radiant	Whiting Mfg. Co.	c. 1890	O	128
Raleigh	Alvin Mfg. Co.	c. 1900		89
Ram's Head	John R. Wendt & Co.	before 1870	O	NIA
Raphael	Alvin Mfg. Co.	c. 1902		89, 165
Raphael	Gorham Mfg. Co.	1875		95
Raphael, Small	Gorham Mfg. Co.	1875		95
Regal	Newburyport Silver Co.	c. 1905	O	NIA
Regent	Wm. B. Durgin Co.	c. 1890		NIA
Regent	Gorham Mfg. Co.	1892		99
*Reine de Fleurs	Unger Bros.	c. 1910	O	NIA
Reliance	Newburyport Silver Co.	c. 1905	O	NIA
Renaissance	Dominick & Haff	1894	O	92
Renaissance	Tiffany & Co.	c. 1905		NIA
Repousse	Jacobi & Jenkins	c. 1910	O	NIA
Repousse	Samuel Kirk & Sons	1828		102
Revere	Wilcox & Evertson	1898	O	130
Ribbed Antique	Dominick & Haff	c. 1900	O	NIA
Ribbon	Adams & Shaw Co.	before 1879	O	124
Ribbon	Dominick & Haff	1884		124
Ribbon	Theo. Evans & Co.	c. 1865	O	94
Ribbon	Geo. W. Shiebler	c. 1875	O	94
Ribbon	John R. Wendt & Co.	before 1870	O	124
Richelieu	Tiffany & Co.	1892		115
Richfield	Frank W. Smith Co.	c. 1900	O	114
Richmond	Towle Mfg. Co.	1900		118
Richmond	Watrous Mfg. Co.	1910	O	121
Roanoke	Alvin Mfg. Co.	c. 1910		89
Robert Bruce	Graff, Washbourne & Dunne	c. 1910		102
Robert Fulton	Sterling Silver Mfg. Co.	c. 1910		NIA
Rococo	Campbell-Metcalf Silver Co.	1895	O	91
Rococo	Dominick & Haff	1888	O	92
Rococo	George W. Shiebler	1884	O	110
*Roderic	F. M. Whiting & Co.	c. 1888	O	125
Rodney	R. Wallace & Sons	1894	O	120
Roman	Gorham Mfg. Co.	1855	O	99

STERLING FLATWARE PATTERNS (*Cont'd*)

Pattern	Brand or Manufacturer	Introduction Date and Obsolescence		Page
Roman	J. B. & S. M. Knowles Co.	c. 1900	O	103
Roman	1847 Rogers Bros. (Meriden Ba. Co.)	c. 1879	O	147
Rosalind	Simpson, Hall, Miller & Co.	1908	O	112
*Rose	Alvin Mfg. Co.	1906	O	90
*Rose	Gorham Mfg. Co.	c. 1890	O	166
Rose	J. B. & S. M. Knowles	1881	O	103
*Rose	Simpson, Hall, Miller & Co.	1908	O	112
Rose (Maryland)	The Stieff Co.	c. 1904		115
Rose	R. Wallace & Sons	1898		120, 161
*Rose	Watson, Newell & Co.	c. 1910	O	123
Rosebud	The Sterling Silver Mfg. Co.	c. 1910	O	NIA
Rose Engraved	Jos. Seymour, Sons & Co.	c. 1880	O	109
Rose Engraved	Wendell Mfg. Co.	c. 1885	O	124
Rose Engraved	F. M. Whiting & Co.	1885	O	125
Rosemary	The Sterling Silver Mfg. Co.	c. 1910	O	NIA
Rosette	Gorham Mfg. Co.	1867		95
*Rosette	Whiting Mfg. Co.	c. 1880	O	129
Rosette, Antique	Whiting Mfg. Co.	c. 1880	O	127
Rouen	Gorham Mfg. Co.	1898	O	100
Royal Oak	Gorham Mfg. Co.	c. 1910		98
Ruby	John Polhemus	c. 1850-1860	O	105
Ruby	George W. Shiebler	1876	O	105
Rustic	Towle Mfg. Co.	1895		118
St. Charles	1847 Rogers Bros. (Meriden Ba. Co.)	c. 1879	O	147
St. Cloud	Gorham Mfg. Co.	1885		95
St. Dunstan	Tiffany & Co.	1909		115
St. George (Chased)	Reed & Barton	c. 1890	O	107
St. George	R. Wallace & Sons	1883		121
*St. Germaine	Whiting Mfg. Co.	1906		128
St. James	Tiffany & Co.	1898		NIA
St. Leon	1847 Rogers Bros. (Meriden Ba. Co.)	c. 1880	O	121
St. Leon	Rogers, Smith & Co.	c. 1880	O	121
*St. Leon	R. Wallace & Sons	1887	O	121
St. Louis	Watson, Newell & Co.	c. 1904	O	122
Salem	Dominick & Haff	c. 1910	O	NIA
Salem	Frank W. Smith Co.	c. 1905	O	113
Salisbury (Gothic)	George W. Shiebler	c. 1890	O	110
Sandringham	George W. Shiebler	c. 1895	O	110
*Sappho	R. Wallace & Sons	1895	O	120
Saratoga	1847 Rogers Bros. (Meriden Ba. Co.)	c. 1879	O	148
Saratoga	Rogers, Smith & Co.	c. 1879	O	148
Saratoga (Cook)	Tiffany & Co.	1870		115
Saxon	R. Wallace & Sons	1910		119
*Saxon Stag	Gorham Mfg. Co.	1865	O	97
Scandinavian	Gorham Mfg. Co.	1898	O	101
Scroll	Wm. B. Durgin Co.	c. 1885	O	NIA
*Scroll	Henry Sears & Son	c. 1890		108
Scroll	Towle Mfg. Co.	before 1890	O	117
1776	Dominick & Haff	c. 1907	O	92
1776	Howard Sterling Co.	c. 1898	O	102
Shell	Dominick & Haff	1906	O	85
Shell	Wm. B. Durgin Co.	c. 1890	O	NIA
Shell	J. B. & S. M. Knowles Co.	1875	O	104

STERLING FLATWARE PATTERNS (*Cont'd*)

Pattern	Brand or Manufacturer	Introduction Date and Obsolescence		Page
Shell	Knowles & Ladd	1865	O	104
Shell	John Polhemus	c. 1840-1850	O	105
*Shell	Reed & Barton	1905	O	85
Shell	1847 Rogers Bros. (Meriden Ba. Co.)	c. 1879	O	85
Shell	Rogers, Smith & Co.	c. 1879	O	85
Shell	George W. Shiebler	c. 1880	O	105
Shell	Frank W. Smith Co.	c. 1885		85
Shell	A. F. Towle & Son Co.	c. 1885	O	85
Shell	Towle Mfg. Co.	c. 1885	O	117
Shell	Webster & Knowles	c. 1852	O	104
Shell	Wendell Mfg. Co.	c. 1880		85
*Shell	F. M. Whiting & Co.	c. 1890	O	125
Shell Tipped	1847 Rogers Bros. (Meriden Ba. Co.)	c. 1879	O	148
Shell Tipped	Rogers, Smith & Co.	c. 1879	O	148
Shell Tipped, round handle	1847 Rogers Bros. (Meriden Ba. Co.)	c. 1879	O	108
Shell Tipped, round handle	Rogers, Smith & Co.	c. 1880	O	108
Shell & Thread	Tiffany & Co.	1905		115
Sheraton	Rogers, Lunt & Bowlen Co.	1908	O	108
Sheraton (Victorian)	Wm. B. Durgin Co.	c. 1910		94
Sherwood (Windsor)	R. Wallace & Sons	1893	O	119
Shirley	Simpson, Hall, Miller & Co.	1910	O	111
Silver	1847 Rogers Bros. (Meriden Ba. Co.)	c. 1879	O	147
Silver	Rogers, Smith & Co.	c. 1879	O	147
Simplicity	The Sterling Silver Mfg. Co.	c. 1910	O	NIA
Somerset	R. Wallace & Sons	c. 1904	O	120
Sorrento	Alvin Mfg. Co.	c. 1905		90
Southern Rose (Bridal Wreath)	Manchester Mfg. Co.	c. 1910	O	104
Spanish	1847 Rogers Bros. (Meriden Ba. Co.)	c. 1879	O	147
Spanish	Rogers, Smith & Co.	c. 1879	O	147
Spartan	W. H. Manchester & Co.	1898	O	104
*Springfield	Unger Bros.	c. 1910	O	NIA
Square Handle Engraved	Jos. Seymour, Sons & Co.	1885	O	109
Standish (New)	Wm. B. Durgin Co.	1905	O	93
Standish (Old)	Wm. B. Durgin Co.	c. 1895	O	93
Star (Martha Washington Star)	Frank W. Smith Co.	c. 1895	O	113
Straight Tipped	J. B. & S. M. Knowles (Co.)	c. 1875	O	124
Straight Tipped	Knowles & Ladd	c. 1865	O	124
Straight Tipped	Webster & Knowles	c. 1852	O	124
Strasbourg	Gorham Mfg. Co.	1897		99
Stratford	Simpson, Hall, Miller & Co.	1901	O	112
Stratford	Whiting Mfg. Co.	c. 1910	O	129
*Strawberry	Wm. B. Durgin Co.	c. 1900	O	NIA
*Strawberry	Watson, Newell & Co.	c. 1910	O	123
Stuart	Campbell-Metcalf Silver Co.	1894	O	91
*Stuart	Towle Mfg. Co.	1885	O	118
Stuart	Whiting Mfg. Co.	c. 1910	O	129
Suffolk	Alvin Mfg. Co.	1905		89
*Sweet Briar	R. Blackinton & Co.	c. 1910	O	NIA
*Sweet Clover	Watson, Newell & Co.	c. 1910	O	123
Sweet Pea	J. B. & S. M. Knowles Co.	1902	O	103
Swiss	Gorham Mfg. Co.	1873		95
Threaded	Gorham Mfg. Co.	1860		85

STERLING FLATWARE PATTERNS (*Cont'd*)

Pattern	Brand or Manufacturer	Introduction Date and Obsolescence		Page
Threaded	1847 Rogers Bros. (Meriden Ba. Co.)	c. 1879	O	85
Threaded	Rogers, Smith & Co.	c. 1879	O	85
Thread Shell	Peter L. Krider Co.	c. 1900	O	104
Thread Shell	Simons Bros. Co.	1903	O	104
Tiffany (Beekman)	Tiffany & Co.	1869		115
Tipped	1847 Rogers Bros. (Meriden Ba. Co.)	c. 1879	O	85
Tipped	Rogers, Smith & Co.	c. 1879	O	85
*Tipped	Simpson, Hall, Miller & Co.	1901	O	85
Tipped	A. F. Towle & Son Co.	1883		85
*Tipped	Towle Mfg. Co.	c. 1885		85
Tipped	R. Wallace & Sons	c. 1890	O	85
Tipped	Watson, Newell & Co.	c. 1880	O	85
Tipped	Wendell Mfg. Co.	c. 1880		85
Tip Sheaf	Wm. B. Durgin Co.	c. 1888	O	93
Tip't	Gorham Mfg. Co.	1855		85
Tip't	Frank W. Smith Co.	c. 1885	O	85
Trajan	Reed & Barton	1892		106
*Tremont	Fessenden & Co.	c. 1910	O	94
Trianon	J. B. & S. M. Knowles Co.	1889	O	103
Trianon, Pierced	Dominick & Haff	1892		92
Trianon, Solid	Dominick & Haff	1892		92
Triumph	Wendell Mfg. Co.	c. 1897	O	NIA
Trumbull	Simpson, Hall, Miller & Co.	1908	O	113
Tudor	Dominick & Haff	1892		92
Tudor	Gorham Mfg. Co.	c. 1885		96
Tudor	J. B. & S. M. Knowles (Co.)	1885	O	103
Tudor	A. F. Towle & Son Co.	1900		116
Tuileries	Gorham Mfg. Co.	c. 1890		98
*Tulip	Wm. B. Durgin Co.	c. 1890	O	93
Tulip	Fessenden & Co.	c. 1910	O	94
Tulip	Gorham Mfg. Co.	1889	O	101
Tulip	John R. Wendt & Co.	before 1870	O	NIA
Tuscan	Wm. Gale & Son	c. 1850		94
Tuscan	1847 Rogers Bros. (Meriden Ba. Co.)	c. 1879		147
Tuscan	John R. Wendt & Co.	before 1870	O	126
*Tuscan	Whiting Mfg. Co.	c. 1870	O	126
Tuscan	Wood & Hughes	c. 1845-1855	O	94
Twist Engraved	Jos. Seymour, Sons & Co.	1867	O	109
Tyrolean	F. M. Whiting & Co.	c. 1890	O	124
Undine	Wood & Hughes	c. 1845-1855	O	131
Union	Jos. Seymour, Sons & Co.	1867	O	109
Union	John R. Wendt & Co.	before 1870	O	NIA
V. Kraft (Vergennes Kraft)	Frank W. Smith Co.	c. 1905	O	113
Vanderslice #1	W. K. Vanderslice & Co.	c. 1895	O	119
Van Dyke	Simpson, Hall, Miller & Co.	1910	O	113
Van Dyke, Applied Initial	Simpson, Hall, Miller & Co.	1910	O	113
Venetia	The Sterling Silver Mfg. Co.	c. 1910	O	NIA
Venetian	Wood & Hughes	c. 1875-1885	O	131
Venice	Roger Williams Silver Co.	c. 1909	O	130
Venus	Simpson, Hall, Miller & Co.	1901	O	111
Vergennes	Frank W. Smith Co.	c. 1905	O	113
Vergennes Kraft	Frank W. Smith Co.	c. 1905	O	113
*Verona	R. Blackinton & Co.	c. 1910	O	90
Verona	A. F. Towle & Son Co.	1894	O	116

STERLING FLATWARE PATTERNS (*Cont'd*)

Pattern	Brand or Manufacturer	Introduction Date and Obsolescence		Page
Versailles	Dominick & Haff	1884	O	92
Versailles	Gorham Mfg. Co.	1888	O	97, 165
*Victor (Daisy)	Towle Mfg. Co.	c. 1890	O	117
Victoria	Dominick & Haff	c. 1901	O	92
Victoria	Wm. B. Durgin Co.	c. 1900	O	NIA
Victoria	George W. Shiebler	1894	O	110
Victoria	The Stieff Co.	c. 1904	O	115
Victoria (New)	Watson, Newell & Co.	c. 1900	O	122
Victoria (Old)	Watson, Newell & Co.	c. 1890	O	122
Victoria (Engraved in many patterns; No. 85 shown)	Wood & Hughes	c. 1885-1895	O	131
Victorian	Wm. B. Durgin Co.	c. 1910		94
Viking	Alvin Mfg. Co.	1906	O	89
*Villa	Whiting Mfg. Co.	c. 1895	O	127
*Vine	Gorham Mfg. Co.	c. 1900	O	98
Vintage	Wm. B. Durgin Co.	c. 1904	O	93
Viola	Wood & Hughes	c. 1875-1885	O	131
*Violet	Alvin Mfg. Co.	1906	O	90
*Violet	R. Blackinton & Co.	c. 1910	O	90
Violet	Gorham Mfg. Co.	c. 1890	O	97
*Violet	Simpson, Hall, Miller & Co.	1908	O	112
Violet	R. Wallace & Sons	1904		120
Violet	Whiting Mfg. Co.	1905		128
Virginia	Alvin Mfg. Co.	c. 1900	O	89
Virginia	Gorham Mfg. Co.	1890	O	100
Virginia	Rogers, Lunt & Bowlen Co.	1910		108
Virginia Dare	Heer-Schofield Co.	c. 1900	O	102
Virginiana	Gorham Mfg. Co.	1905		98
Wadefield	Samuel Kirk & Son	1840		102
Warren	J. B. & S. M. Knowles (Co.)	1875	O	104
Warren	Knowles & Ladd	1865	O	104
Warren	Newburyport Silver Co.	c. 1905	O	NIA
Warren	A. F. Towle & Son Co.	1883		116
Warren	Towle Mfg. Co.	c. 1885		116
Warren	Webster & Knowles	c. 1852	O	104
Warwick	Simpson, Hall, Miller & Co.	1898	O	113
Washington	Baltimore Silversmiths Mfg. Co.	c. 1910	O	NIA
Washington	Dominick & Haff	c. 1900	O	NIA
Washington	Howard Sterling Co.	1894	O	102
Washington	W. H. Manchester & Co.	1895	O	104
*Water Lily	Alvin Mfg. Co.	1906	O	90
*Water Lily	Simpson, Hall, Miller & Co.	1908	O	112
*Watson No. 1	Watson, Newell & Co.	c. 1895	O	174
Watteau	Wm. B. Durgin Co.	c. 1890	O	NIA
Watteau	Howard Sterling Co.	1893	O	102
Wave	George W. Shiebler	1904	O	110
*Wave	Unger Bros.	c. 1910	O	NIA
Wave Edge	Tiffany & Co.	1884	O	115
Waverly	R. Wallace & Sons	1892	O	120
Webster	J. B. & S. M. Knowles	1880	O	103
Webster	W. H. Manchester & Co.	1895	O	104
Wedding Rose	Watson, Newell & Co.	1908		121
Wedgwood	Whiting Mfg. Co.	1910		128

STERLING FLATWARE PATTERNS (*Cont'd*)

Pattern	Brand or Manufacturer	Introduction Date and Obsolescence		Page
Wellington	Alvin Mfg. Co.	c. 1897		90
Wellington	Wm. B. Durgin Co.	1908		93
Wendt	John R. Wendt & Co.	before 1870	O	NIA
Wentworth	A. F. Towle & Son Co.	1899		116
Wheat Engraved	Jos. Seymour, Sons & Co.	1880	O	109
Wheat Engraved	F. M. Whiting & Co.	1885	O	125
*Wild Rose	Alvin Mfg. Co.	1906	O	90
*Wild Rose	Simpson, Hall, Miller & Co.	1908	O	112
Wild Rose	Watson, Newell & Co.	c. 1905	O	121
William Penn	Alvin Mfg. Co.	1907		89
William Penn #7	Alvin Mfg. Co.	c. 1910	O	89
Winchester	Shreve & Co.	c. 1910		111
Winchester	Simpson, Hall, Miller & Co.	1902	O	112
Windsor	Wm. B. Durgin Co.	c. 1860	O	85
Windsor	1847 Rogers Bros.	c. 1879	O	85
Windsor	Rogers, Smith & Co.	c. 1879	O	85
Windsor	Simpson, Hall, Miller & Co.	c. 1880	O	85
Windsor	Frank W. Smith Co.	c. 1885	O	85
Windsor	A. F. Towle & Son Co.	1883		85
Windsor	Towle Mfg. Co.	c. 1885		85
Windsor (Sherwood)	R. Wallace & Sons	c. 1890		119
Windsor	Wendell Mfg. Co.	c. 1880		85
Windsor Engraved	Jos. Seymour, Sons & Co.	1870	O	109
Winslow	Samuel Kirk & Son	1840		102
Winthrop	Shreve & Co.	c. 1908		NIA
Winthrop	Tiffany & Co.	1909		115
Woodbine Engraved	Jos. Seymour, Sons & Co.	1885	O	109
Wreath	Gorham Mfg. Co.	c. 1910	O	100
Wreath	Jos. Seymour, Sons & Co.	1854	O	109
*York	R. Blackinton & Co.	c. 1905	O	90
York	Howard Sterling Co.	c. 1898	O	102
Zephyr	Wood & Hughes	c. 1865-1875	O	131
*Zodiac (Birthday)	Gorham Mfg. Co.	1894		97, 168

ELECTROPLATE FLATWARE PATTERNS

Pattern	Brand or Manufacturer	Introduction Date and Obsolescence		Page
Abington	Wm. A. Rogers	1907	O	154
Acanthus	Rogers & Bro.	c. 1890	O	146
Acanthus	Rogers & Hamilton	1888	O	152
Adam	W. D. Smith Silver Co.	c. 1910	O	NIA
Adams	Niagara Falls Silver Co.	c. 1905	O	142
Adell	Sears	1903	O	157
Admiral	Rogers & Bro.	c. 1910	O	NIA
Adonis	S. L. & G. H. Rogers	c. 1910		153
Alberta	Niagara Silver Co.	c. 1900	O	142
Alberta	Wm. A Rogers	c. 1900	O	142
Alden	Reed & Barton	1905	O	145
Aldine	Rogers & Bro.	1895	O	146
Aldine	Rogers & Hamilton	1897	O	146

ELECTROPLATE FLATWARE PATTERNS (*Cont'd*)

Pattern	Brand or Manufacturer	Introduction Date and Obsolescence		Page
Alhambra	Rogers & Hamilton	1908	O	156
Alhambra	Wm. Rogers Mfg. Co.	1908	O	156
Alma (Queen Helena)	Williams Bros.	c. 1905	O	162
Alton	W. F. Rogers (Rogers Cutlery Co.)	1902	O	155
American	L. Boardman & Son	c. 1880	O	137
America	Wm. Rogers Mfg. Co.	1904	O	156
American Beauty	M. S. Benedict Mfg. Co.	c. 1900	O	136
American Beauty Rose	Holmes & Edwards	1909	O	140
Anchor	Wm. Rogers Mfg. Co.	1882	O	155
Angelo	Holmes & Edwards	1883	O	140
Anjou	1835 R. Wallace	1898	O	161
Antique	Hall, Elton & Co.	1875	O	85
Antique	Reed & Barton	1877	O	85
Antique	Rogers & Bro.	c. 1885	O	147
Antique	Rogers Bros.	1849	O	147
Antique	Rogers Bros. Mfg. Co.	1853	O	155
Antique	1847 Rogers Bros.	1862	O	147
Antique	Wm. Rogers Mfg. Co.	1882	O	147
Antique	Towle Mfg. Co.	c. 1885	O	160
Antique Egyptian	E. H. H. Smith Silver Co.	1910	O	159
Arabesque	Benedict Mfg. Co.	c. 1900	O	NIA
Arbutus	Wm. Rogers Mfg. Co.	1908	O	157
Arbutus	A. F. Towle & Son Co.	1883	O	160
Arcadia	S. L. & G. H. Rogers	c. 1910	O	NIA
Arcadian	1847 Rogers Bros.	1884	O	150, 170
Arcadian	Rogers, Smith & Co.	1884	O	150, 170
*Arctic	Reed & Barton	c. 1884	O	144
Arden	Holmes & Edwards	c. 1910	O	NIA
Ardsley	Wm. A. Rogers	1905	O	154
Argent	Associated Silver Co.	c. 1910	O	NIA
Argyle	Wm. Rogers Mfg. Co.	1907	O	156
Arlington	Pairpoint Mfg. Co.	1896	O	143
Arlington	Rockford S. P. Co.	c. 1908	O	143
Armenian	1847 Rogers Bros.	1886	O	148, 170
Armenian	Rogers, Smith & Co.	1886	O	148, 170
Arundel	Wm. A. Rogers	1903	O	154
Arundel	A. F. Towle & Son Co.	1890	O	160
Arvilla	Associated Silver Co.	c. 1910	O	NIA
Ascot	Pairpoint Mfg. Co.	c. 1886	O	143
*Ashford	1847 Rogers Bros.	c. 1905	O	149
Assyrian	Rogers & Bro.	1893	O	148
Assyrian	1847 Rogers Bros.	1887	O	148
Assyrian	Rogers, Smith & Co.	1887	O	148
Assyrian Head	Rogers & Bro.	1886	O	148
Assyrian Head	1847 Rogers Bros.	1886	O	148
Assyrian Head	Rogers, Smith & Co.	1886	O	148
Astoria	1835 R. Wallace	1897	O	161
Athenian	Landers, Frary & Clark	c. 1900	O	NIA
Athens	SHMCo.; Wm. Rogers Eagle	1883	O	158
Attica	Rogers & Bro.	1895	O	146
Aumont	Benedict Mfg. Co.	c. 1910	O	NIA
Aurora #1	Aurora Silver Plate Co.	c. 1870	O	136
Avalon	Oneida Community	1901	O	142
Avon	1847 Rogers Bros.	1901	O	150

ELECTROPLATE FLATWARE PATTERNS (*Cont'd*)

Pattern	Brand or Manufacturer	Introduction Date and Obsolescence		Page
Aztec	Holmes & Edwards	c. 1900	O	NIA
B. Engraved	C. Rogers & Bro.	1896	O	151
Beaded	American Silver Co.	c. 1901	O	NIA
Beaded	L. Boardman & Son	c. 1870	O	137
Beaded	Hall, Elton & Co.	1867	O	138
Beaded	Reed & Barton	before 1868	O	147
Beaded	Rogers & Bro.	c. 1865	O	147
Beaded	Rogers Bros. Mfg. Co.	1855	O	147
Beaded	1847 Rogers Bros.	1862	O	147
Beaded	S. L. & G. H. Rogers	1901	O	NIA
Beaded	Wm. Rogers Mfg. Co.	c. 1875	O	156
Beaded	SHMCo.; Wm. Rogers Eagle	1904	O	157
Beaded	Williams Bros.	c. 1900	O	162
Beaded Cherub	Niagara Silver Co.	c. 1900	O	142
Beaumont	Gorham Mfg. Co.	c. 1910	O	NIA
Beauty	Rogers & Hamilton	1910	O	156
Beauty	Wm. Rogers Mfg. Co.	1910	O	156
Belle	Rogers & Bro.	1890	O	146
Belmont	Reed & Barton	1904	O	145
Belmont	Rogers & Bro.	1905	O	146
Belmont	C. Rogers & Bro.	c. 1895	O	151
Benedict #1	Benedict Mfg. Co.	c. 1895	O	136
Benedict #2	Benedict Mfg. Co.	c. 1900	O	136
Benedict #3	Benedict Mfg. Co.	c. 1900	O	136
Berkshire	1847 Rogers Bros.	1895	O	150
Berlin	American Silver Co.	1905	O	135
Berlin	Wm. Rogers Mfg. Co.	1882	O	155
Bernice	Wm. A. Rogers	c. 1900	O	154
Berwick	Wm. Rogers Mfg. Co.	1906	O	158
Berwick	SHMCo.; Wm. Rogers Eagle	1904	O	158
Bijou	Reed & Barton	1884	O	144
Biltmore	Wm. A. Rogers	c. 1905	O	154
Blenheim	Wm. Rogers Mfg. Co.	1886	O	158
Blenheim	SHMCo.; Wm. Rogers Eagle	1886	O	158
Blossom	1835 R. Wallace	1908	O	161
*Blue Point	SHMCo.; Wm. Rogers Eagle	1888	O	157
Boston	E. A. Bliss Co.	1891	O	136
Boston (Thread Hotel)	Holmes & Edwards	c. 1890	O	141
Bradford	American Silver Co.	c. 1910	O	NIA
Bradford	Gorham Mfg. Co.	c. 1900	O	NIA
Breton	L. Boardman & Son	c. 1880	O	137
Briar Cliff	Wm. A. Rogers	c. 1910	O	NIA
Brides Bouquet	Alvin Mfg. Co.	1908	O	135
Brighton	Pairpoint Mfg. Co.	c. 1887	O	143
Brighton	Wm. A. Rogers	c. 1900	O	154
Brilliant	Reed & Barton	1869	O	144
Broadfield	Salem Silver Plate Co.	c. 1907	O	157
Brunswick	L. Boardman & Son	c. 1880	O	137
Brunswick	Reed & Barton	c. 1884	O	144
*Brunswick	1847 Rogers Bros.	1891	O	148
*Brunswick	Rogers, Smith & Co.	c. 1886	O	148
Cambridge	Rockford S. P. Co.	c. 1900	O	NIA

ELECTROPLATE FLATWARE PATTERNS (*Cont'd*)

Pattern	Brand or Manufacturer	Introduction Date and Obsolescence		Page
Cardinal	Rogers & Hamilton	1887	O	152
Cardinal (Mikado)	SHMCo.; Wm. Rogers Eagle	1888	O	158
Cardinal	1835 R. Wallace	1907	O	161
Carlton	Reed & Barton	1896	O	145
Carlton	Wm. A. Rogers	c. 1904	O	154
Carnation	Wm. A. Rogers	1907	O	153
Carolina	Gorham Mfg. Co.	c. 1895	O	138
Carolina	Holmes & Edwards	c. 1910	O	141
Carrollton	Wm. Rogers Mfg. Co.	c. 1910	O	158
Carrollton	SHMCo.; Wm. Rogers Eagle	c. 1910	O	158
*Cascade	Niagara Silver Co.	c. 1900	O	142
Cashmere	Reed & Barton	1884	O	144
Cecil	Reed & Barton	1899	O	145
Cedric	SHMCo.; Wm. Rogers Eagle	1906	O	158
Ceres	Wm. Rogers Mfg. Co.	1892	O	156
Cereta	Oneida Community	1904	O	63, 142
Champlain	Wm. Rogers Mfg. Co.	c. 1910	O	NIA
Charter Oak	1847 Rogers Bros.	1906	O	150
Chatsworth	Holmes & Edwards	c. 1910	O	NIA
Chelsea	Wm. Rogers Mfg. Co.	1904	O	156
Cherokee Rose	1835 R. Wallace	c. 1910	O	NIA
Cherry	E. H. H. Smith Silver Co.	c. 1900	O	NIA
Chester	Towle Mfg. Co.	c. 1910	O	160
Chevalier	Wm. Rogers Mfg. Co.	1897	O	156
Chicago	Lakeside	1895	O	141
Cinderella	Niagara Silver Co.	c. 1900	O	142
Clarendon	Reed & Barton	c. 1910	O	NIA
Classic	Oneida Community	1906	O	142
Clifton	Pairpoint Mfg. Co.	1896	O	143
Climber	A. F. Towle & Son Co.	1890	O	160
Clinton	Wm. Rogers Mfg. Co.	c. 1907		157
Clovis	Forbes Silver Co.	1898	O	138
Clyde	C. Rogers & Bro.	c. 1902	O	NIA
Clyde	A. F. Towle & Son Co.	1883	O	160
Coligny	American Silver Co.	c. 1901	O	NIA
*Colonade	Rogers & Bro.	1895	O	147
Colonial	Niagara Falls Silver Co.	c. 1895	O	142
Colonial	Paragon Plate	c. 1906	O	143
Colonial	S. L. & G. H. Rogers	c. 1909	O	153
Columbia	1847 Rogers Bros.	1893	O	150
Columbia	Rogers & Bro.	1898	O	150
Columbia	Wm. A. Rogers	c. 1910	O	NIA
Columbia	Wm. H. Rogers Corp.	c. 1910	O	155
Columbia	Wm. Rogers Mfg. Co.	c. 1895	O	150
*Columbian	1847 Rogers Bros.	1891	O	149
Columbus	Wm. Rogers Mfg. Co.	1895	O	156
Commonwealth	Reed & Barton	c. 1910	O	145
Como	Williams Bros.	c. 1910	O	162
Conant	Salem Silver Plate	1907	O	157
*Concord	1847 Rogers Bros.	1905	O	149
Concord	Wm. Rogers Mfg. Co.	1910	O	158
Concord	SHMCo.; Wm. Rogers Eagle	1910	O	158
Continental	Benedict Mfg. Co.	c. 1910	O	NIA
*Coral	Rogers, Smith & Co.	c. 1885	O	153

ELECTROPLATE FLATWARE PATTERNS (*Cont'd*)

Pattern	Brand or Manufacturer	Introduction Date and Obsolescence		Page
Cordova	SHMCo.; Wm. Rogers Eagle	1896	O	158
Corinth	Holmes, Booth & Haydens	c. 1879-1886	O	139
Cornell	Rogers & Bro.	c. 1897		146
Cornell	SHMCo.; Wm. Rogers Eagle	c. 1897	O	146
Corona	American Silver Co. (H & T)	c. 1910	O	135
Corona	Holmes, Booth & Haydens	1884	O	139
Coronet	Hall, Elton & Co.	c. 1875	O	139
Coronet	Wm. Rogers Mfg. Co.	1882	O	155
Countess	Wm. Rogers Mfg. Co.	1882	O	155
Countess	SHMCo.; Wm. Rogers Eagle	1880	O	158
Crescent	Hall, Elton & Co.	c. 1875	O	139
Crest	Rogers & Bro.	1906	O	146
Cromwell	Wm. Rogers Mfg. Co.	1892	O	156
Crown	Rogers & Bro.	1876	O	146
Crown	1847 Rogers Bros.	1885	O	146
Crown	Rogers, Smith & Co.	c. 1886	O	146
Croyden	Pairpoint Mfg. Co.	c. 1887	O	143
Crystal	Rogers & Bro.	1895	O	146
Crystal	Williams Bros.	c. 1900	O	NIA
Cupid	Wm. Rogers Mfg. Co.	c. 1893	O	157
Daffodil	Rockford S. P. Co.	c. 1900	O	NIA
*Daffodil	1847 Rogers Bros.	1891	O	149
*Daisy	Rogers, Smith & Co.	c. 1886	O	153
Daisy	Wm. Rogers Mfg. Co.	1900	O	157
Daisy (New)	Wm. Rogers Mfg. Co.	c. 1908		157
Danish	Wm. Rogers Mfg. Co.	1882	O	155
Delmar	Benedict Mfg. Co.	c. 1910	O	NIA
*Delmonico	1847 Rogers Bros.	1891	O	149
Delsarte	Holmes & Edwards	1895	O	141
Derby	Derby Silver Co.	c. 1883	O	137
Derby	E. G. Webster & Bro.	1889	O	137
DeSancy	Holmes & Edwards	c. 1910	O	NIA
DeWitt	Benedict Mfg. Co.	1901	O	136
DeWitt	Williams Bros.	c. 1900	O	NIA
Diamond	Rogers & Bro.	1886	O	147
Diana	Alvin Mfg. Co.	c. 1908	O	135
Diana	1847 Rogers Bros.	1894	O	148
Dolly Madison	Holmes & Edwards	c. 1910	O	141
Doric	Rogers & Bro.	1910	O	152
Doric	Rogers & Hamilton	1909	O	152
Dorothy	C. E. Barker Mfg. Co.	c. 1910	O	NIA
Dorothy Vernon	E. H. H. Smith Silver Co.	c. 1910	O	159
Dover	Pairpoint Mfg. Co.	c. 1887	O	143
Dowager	Gorham Mfg. Co.	c. 1875		97
Dumont	American Silver Co.	c. 1910	O	NIA
Dunbar	Salem Silver Plate	c. 1907	O	157
Dundee	Rogers & Bro.	1886	O	148
Dundee	1847 Rogers Bros.	1886	O	148
Dundee	Rogers, Smith & Co.	1886	O	148
Dunster	Cambridge Silver Plate	1907	O	137
Easter Lily (Lily)	Alvin Mfg. Co.	1908	O	135
Eastlake	Hall, Elton & Co.	c. 1875	O	139

ELECTROPLATE FLATWARE PATTERNS *(Cont'd)*

Pattern	Brand or Manufacturer	Introduction Date and Obsolescence		Page
Eastlake	Holmes & Edwards	1883	O	140
Eastlake	Rogers & Bro.	1886	O	155
Eastlake	Wm. Rogers Mfg. Co.	1882	O	155
Egyptian	Hall, Elton & Co.	c. 1867	O	138
Egyptian (Antique Egyptian)	E. H. H. Smith Silver Co.	1910	O	159
*1890	1847 Rogers Bros.	1890	O	149
Elaine	E. H. Curtis Co.	c. 1900	O	NIA
Elberon	Niagara Silver Co.	c. 1900	O	154
Elberon	Wm. A. Rogers	c. 1900	O	154
Elmore	Wm. A. Rogers	c. 1905	O	154
Elmwood	Cambridge Silver Co.	1907	O	137
*Elsie	Wm. A. Rogers	c. 1898	O	154
Elsmere	McGlashan, Clarke & Co.	c. 1905	O	141
Eltham	A. F. Towle & Son Co.	1890	O	160
Elton	Rogers & Bro.	1900	O	146
Embossed	Rogers & Bro.	c. 1889	O	148
Embossed	1847 Rogers Bros.	1882	O	148, 171
Embossed	Rogers, Smith & Co.	1882	O	148, 171
Emerson	Wm. A. Rogers	c. 1910	O	NIA
Empire	Gorham Mfg. Co.	c. 1880	O	138
Empire	1847 Rogers Bros.	1896	O	150
Empress	Derby Silver Co.	c. 1883	O	137
Endicott	Salem Silver Plate	1907	O	157
Engraved '05	Towle Mfg. Co.	1905	O	160
Erminie	Pairpoint Mfg. Co.	c. 1889		143
Erminie	Rockford S. P. Co.	c. 1900	O	143
Essex	Niagara Falls Silver Co.	c. 1900	O	142
Essex	Pairpoint Mfg. Co.	c. 1887	O	143
Essex	Wm. Rogers Mfg. Co.	c. 1910	O	155
Etruscan	1847 Rogers Bros.	1891	O	150
Eucla	C. Rogers & Bro.	c. 1900	O	151
Eudora (Linden)	Wm. A. Rogers	c. 1905	O	154
Eudora	Towle Mfg. Co.	c. 1905	O	NIA
Eunice	C. E. Barker Mfg. Co.	c. 1910	O	NIA
Fairfax	Benedict Mfg. Co.	1909	O	136
*Fairie	1847 Rogers Bros.	1887	O	150, 170
Fairoaks	Rockford S. P. Co.	1909	O	145
Faneuil	1847 Rogers Bros.	1908	O	150
Farmington	Landers, Frary & Clark	c. 1910	O	141
Fiddle	Derby Silver Co.	c. 1883	O	85
Fiddle	Hall, Elton & Co.	1867	O	85
Fiddle	Holmes & Edwards	c. 1885	O	85
Fiddle	Oneida Community	c. 1900	O	85
Fiddle	Reed & Barton	1869	O	85
Fiddle	Rogers & Bro.	1872		85
Fiddle	Rogers Bros.	1850	O	85
Fiddle	Rogers Bros. Mfg. Co.	1853	O	85
Fiddle	1847 Rogers Bros.	1862	O	85
Fiddle	S. L. & G. H. Rogers	c. 1900	O	85
Fiddle	Rogers, Smith & Co.	c. 1870	O	85
Fiddle	Wm. A. Rogers	c. 1900	O	85
Fiddle	Wm. Rogers Mfg. Co.	1882	O	85
Fiddle	SHMCo.; Wm. Rogers Eagle	c. 1900	O	85

ELECTROPLATE FLATWARE PATTERNS *(Cont'd)*

Pattern	Brand or Manufacturer	Introduction Date and Obsolescence		Page
Fiddle	A. F. Towle & Son Co.	1883	O	85
Fiddle	Towle Mfg. Co.	c. 1885	O	85
Fiddle	R. Wallace; 1835 R. Wallace	1871	O	85
Fiddle	Williams Bros.	c. 1895	O	85
*Flanders	1847 Rogers Bros.	1905	O	149
Flemish	Rogers & Bro.	1893	O	146
Flemish	E. H. H. Smith Silver Co.	c. 1900	O	159
Fleur de Lis	Paragon Plate	1907	O	143
Fleur de Luce (Flower de Luce)	Oneida Community	1904		142
*Floral	1847 Rogers Bros.	1891	O	147
Floral	S. L. & G. H. Rogers	c. 1900	O	NIA
Floral	1835 R. Wallace	1901	O	161, 174
Florence	Hall, Elton & Co.	c. 1867	O	138
Florence	Redfield & Rice	c. 1870	O	143
Florence	Reed & Barton	1877	O	144
*Florentine	1847 Rogers Bros.	1891	O	149
Florentine	S. L. & G. H. Rogers	c. 1900	O	NIA
Florentine	Wm. Rogers Mfg. Co.	1895	O	157
Florette	Rogers & Bro.	1909	O	146
Florida	Wm. Rogers Mfg. Co.	1894	O	156
Flower	Holmes & Edwards	1887	O	140, 168
Flower	Wm. Rogers Mfg. Co.	1906	O	157
Flower de Luce (Fleur de Luce)	Oneida Community	1904	O	142
*Forget-me-not	1847 Rogers Bros.	1905	O	149
Franklin	S. L. & G. H. Rogers	1901	O	152
French	L. Boardman & Son	c. 1880	O	137
French	Hall, Elton & Co.	c. 1875	O	139
French	Reed & Barton	c. 1875	O	144
French	Wm. Rogers Mfg. Co.	1882	O	155
French	SHMCo.; Wm. Rogers Eagle	1883	O	158
French	E. G. Webster & Bro.	1879	O	161
French Oval	Rogers Bros.	1852	O	147
French Oval	Rogers Bros. Mfg. Co.	1853	O	147
French Oval	1847 Rogers Bros.	1862	O	147
French Oval	Rogers, Smith & Co.	c. 1880	O	147
French Tipped	L. Boardman & Son	c. 1880	O	137
French Tipped	Rogers & Bro.	c. 1898	O	85
*Fruit	1847 Rogers Bros.	1891	O	149
*Game	1847 Rogers Bros.	1891	O	149
Garland	Wm. A. Rogers	c. 1900	O	153
Garrick	SHMCo.; Wm. Rogers Eagle	1908	O	158
Geisha	Williams Bros.	c. 1895	O	162
Gem	Reed & Barton	1869	O	144
Gem	Wm. Rogers Mfg. Co.	1892	O	156
Geneva	Wm. Rogers Mfg. Co.	c. 1900	O	158
Geneva	SHMCo.; Wm. Rogers Eagle	c. 1890	O	158
Genoa	Williams Bros.	c. 1900	O	162
*Gladys	Niagara Silver Co.	c. 1900	O	142
Glasgow	Sears	1903	O	157
Glenrose	Wm. A. Rogers	1905	O	153
Gloria	Rockford S. P. Co.	c. 1900	O	NIA

ELECTROPLATE FLATWARE PATTERNS (*Cont'd*)

Pattern	Brand or Manufacturer	Introduction Date and Obsolescence		Page
Codetia	Wm. A. Rogers	c. 1910	O	NIA
Gothic	Derby Silver Co.	c. 1875	O	147
Gothic	Rogers & Bro.	c. 1885	O	147
Gothic	Rogers Bros. Mfg. Co.	1860	O	147
Gothic	1847 Rogers Bros.	1862	O	147
Grape	McGlashan, Clarke & Co.	c. 1905	O	141
Grape	Rockford S. P. Co. (See Vineyard, Williams Bros.)	c. 1908	O	162
Grape (Isabella)	Wm. Rogers Mfg. Co.	c. 1907	O	157
Grape	1835 R. Wallace	c. 1908	O	NIA
*Grecian	1847 Rogers Bros.	1895	O	149
Grecian	Wm. A. Rogers	1907	O	154
Greek	Holmes & Edwards	c. 1880	O	140
Grenada	A. F. Towle & Son Co.	1883	O	160
Grenoble	Wm. A. Rogers	c. 1905	O	153
Greylock	Wm. A. Rogers	c. 1910	O	154
*Griffon #1	Griffon Cutlery Co.	c. 1910	O	138
Halcyon	Rogers & Bro.	c. 1897	O	147
Hanover	Wm. A. Rogers	c. 1904	O	153
Hardwick	SHMCo.; Wm. Rogers Eagle	1909	O	158
*Harlequin	Rogers & Hamilton	1895	O	152
Harold	Rogers & Bro.	c. 1897	O	147
Hartford	Wm. Rogers Mfg. Co.	1879	O	155
Harvard	Derby Silver Co.	c. 1883	O	137
Harvard	Rogers & Bro.	c. 1897	O	156
*Harvard	1847 Rogers Bros.	1891	O	149
Harvard	Wm. Rogers Mfg. Co.	c. 1897	O	156
Harvard	SHMCo.; Wm. Rogers Eagle	1891	O	156
Harvard	E. G. Webster & Bro.	c. 1879	O	161
Hawthorne	Rockford S. P. Co.	c. 1908	O	145
Helena	Wm. A. Rogers	c. 1905	O	154
Helena	Wm. H. Rogers Corp.	c. 1910	O	155
Hiawatha	Holmes & Edwards	c. 1910	O	NIA
*Hoffman	1847 Rogers Bros.	1895	O	148
Holland	1835 R. Wallace	1904	O	161
Holly	E. H. H. Smith Silver Co.	c. 1905	O	159
Holyoke	Cambridge Silver Plate	1907	O	137
Ideal	Rogers & Hamilton	1897	O	152
Imperial	L. Boardman & Son	c. 1880	O	137
Imperial	Holmes & Edwards	1904	O	140
Imperial	C. Rogers & Bro.	1897	O	151
Imperial	1847 Rogers Bros.	1880	O	148
Imperial	Rogers, Smith & Co.	c. 1886	O	148
Imperial	Wm. Rogers Mfg. Co.	1882	O	155
Imperial	Williams Bros.	c. 1910	O	162
India	Holmes, Booth & Haydens	c. 1884	O	139
India	Pairpoint Mfg. Co.	c. 1887	O	143
Ionic	Rogers & Bro.	c. 1893	O	147
Ionic	A. F. Towle & Son Co.	1890	O	160
Iris	E. H. H. Smith Silver Co.	c. 1904	O	159
Iroquois	Niagara Silver Co.	c. 1900	O	142
Iroquois	Wm. A. Rogers	c. 1910	O	142
Irving	Benedict Mfg. Co.	c. 1909	O	NIA

ELECTROPLATE FLATWARE PATTERNS (*Cont'd*)

Pattern	Brand or Manufacturer	Introduction Date and Obsolescence		Page
Irving	Holmes & Edwards	c. 1903	O	140
Isabella	Williams Bros.	c. 1910	O	NIA
Isabella (Grape)	Wm. Rogers Mfg. Co.	c. 1907	O	157
Italian	Hall, Elton & Co.	c. 1867	O	139
Italian	Reed & Barton	c. 1867	O	144
Ivy	Rogers & Bro.	c. 1885	O	147
Ivy	1847 Rogers Bros.	1870	O	150
Jac Rose	Holmes & Edwards	1893	O	141
Japanese	E. A. Bliss Co.	c. 1890	O	136
Japanese	Holmes, Booth & Haydens	c. 1875	O	139
Japanese	Holmes & Edwards	1885	O	141
Japanese	Reed & Barton	c. 1877	O	144
Jefferson	S. L. & G. H. Rogers	c. 1910	O	NIA
Joan	1835 R. Wallace	1896	O	161
Kensico	Williams Bros.	c. 1890	O	162
Kensington	Wm. Rogers Mfg. Co.	c. 1890	O	NIA
Kenwood	Oneida Community (Reliance)	1909	O	142
King	Holmes & Edwards	c. 1885	O	140
King	SHMCo.; Wm. Rogers Eagle	1890		85
Kings	Gorham Mfg. Co.	c. 1890		138
Kings	Reed & Barton	c. 1890		145
Kings	1847 Rogers Bros.	1888		85
Kings	E. H. H. Smith Silver Co.	c. 1900	O	85
Kings	1835 R. Wallace	1903		85
Kirkwood	Benedict Mfg. Co.	c. 1905	O	NIA
Kremlin	A. F. Towle & Son Co.	1883	O	160
LaConcorde	Wm. A. Rogers	1910	O	153
LaFayette	Benedict Mfg. Co.	c. 1900	O	136
LaFayette	Holmes & Edwards	1907	O	141
LaFayette	Williams Bros.	c. 1900	O	NIA
LaFrance Rose	Benedict Mfg. Co.	c. 1901	O	136
LaMode	Reed & Barton	1900	O	145
LaSalle (Marquette)	1835 R. Wallace	1909	O	161
LaVigne	Wm. A. Rogers	1907	O	153
Lakewood	Benedict Mfg. Co.	c. 1910	O	NIA
Lakewood	S. L. & G. H. Rogers	1901	O	152
Lashar #1	Holmes & Edwards (Lashar Silver)	c. 1900	O	141
Laureate	S. L. & G. H. Rogers	c. 1910	O	153
Laurel	Rogers & Bro.	c. 1890	O	148
Laurel	1847 Rogers Bros.	1878	O	148
Laurel	Rogers, Smith & Co.	1878	O	148
Laurel	1835 R. Wallace	c. 1887	O	161
Laurence	American Silver Co.	c. 1903	O	135
Laurian	Pairpoint Mfg. Co.	c. 1887	O	143
Le Grand	Reed & Barton	c. 1910	O	145
Leader	Holmes & Edwards	1887	O	140
Lenora	Wm. A. Rogers	c. 1910	O	154
Lenox	1847 Rogers Bros.	c. 1891	O	148
Lenox	C. Rogers & Bro.	c. 1896	O	151
Lenox	Rogers & Hamilton	c. 1900	O	148
Lenox	1835 R. Wallace	1903	O	161

ELECTROPLATE FLATWARE PATTERNS (*Cont'd*)

Pattern	Brand or Manufacturer	Introduction Date and Obsolescence		Page
Leona	Glastonbury Silver Co.	c. 1910	O	138
Lexington	Alvin Mfg. Co.	1909	O	135
Lexington	S. L. & G. H. Rogers	c. 1910	O	153
Lexington	Wm. Rogers Mfg. Co.	1904	O	156
Leyland	Wm. A. Rogers	c. 1910	O	154
Liberty	Holmes & Edwards	c. 1895	O	140
Lilian	Wm. Rogers Mfg. Co.	1882	O	155
Lily (Easter Lily)	Alvin Mfg. Co.	1908	O	135
Lily	Benedict Mfg. Co.	c. 1900	O	NIA
Lily	Derby Silver Co.	1875	O	85
Lily	Oneida Community	c. 1877	O	85
Lily	Rogers & Bro.	1874	O	148
Lily	1847 Rogers Bros.	1874	O	148
Lily	Rogers, Smith & Co.	1874	O	148
Lily	Wm. Rogers Mfg. Co.	1882	O	148
*Lily of the Valley	1847 Rogers Bros.	1891	O	149
Lilyta	Stratford Silver Co.	c. 1910	O	159
Lincoln	Holmes & Edwards	1895	O	141
Lincoln	Wm. Rogers Mfg. Co.	c. 1907	O	157
Lincoln	E. H. H. Smith Silver Co.	1908	O	159
Linden	1847 Rogers Bros.	1891	O	148
Linden (Eudora)	Wm. A. Rogers	c. 1895	O	154
Lloyd	Benedict Mfg. Co.	c. 1900	O	NIA
Lois	S. L. & G. H. Rogers	c. 1905	O	153
Loraine	American Silver Co. (H & T)	c. 1910	O	135
Lorelei	E. H. H. Smith Silver Co.	c. 1900	O	NIA
Lorne	Rogers & Bro.	1878	O	148
Lorne	1847 Rogers Bros.	1878	O	148
Lorne	Rogers, Smith & Co.	c. 1878	O	148
*Lorraine	1847 Rogers Bros.	1891	O	149
Lotus	1847 Rogers Bros.	1895	O	150
Louis XV	1847 Rogers Bros.	1891	O	148
Louis XVI	Oneida Community	1908	O	142
Louis XVI	E. H. H. Smith Silver Co.	c. 1900	O	159
Louvre	Rockford S. P. Co.	c. 1905	O	145, 162
Louvre	Williams Bros.	c. 1900	O	145, 162
Lucerne	1847 Rogers Bros.	1886	O	148, 170
Lucerne	Rogers, Smith & Co.	1886	O	148, 170
Lucille	Glastonbury Silver Co.	c. 1910	O	138
Luxfer	Williams Bros.	c. 1895	O	162
Lyonnaise	Hall, Elton & Co.	c. 1867	O	139
Lyonnaise	Wm. Rogers Mfg. Co.	c. 1880	O	155, 171
*Mabel	Wm. A. Rogers	1895	O	154
Magnolia	SHMCo.; Wm. Rogers Eagle	1888	O	158, 171
Majestic	Rogers & Hamilton	1897	O	152
Malvern	Williams Bros.	c. 1910	O	NIA
Manchester	Wm. Rogers Mfg. Co.	c. 1907	O	157
Marathon	American Silver Co.	1910	O	135
Marcella	Wm. A. Rogers	1903	O	154
Marie Antoinette	E. H. H. Smith Silver Co.	c. 1900	O	NIA
Marina	Holmes & Edwards	1895	O	140
Marjo-Nell	Associated Silver Co.	c. 1910	O	136
Marquette (LaSalle)	1835 R. Wallace	1909	O	161

ELECTROPLATE FLATWARE PATTERNS *(Cont'd)*

Pattern	Brand or Manufacturer	Introduction Date and Obsolescence		Page
Marquise	Rogers Cutlery Co.	1904	O	151
Marquise	Rogers & Hamilton	1904	O	152
Marseilles	E. H. H. Smith Silver Co.	c. 1905	O	159
Martha Washington	E. H. H. Smith Silver Co.	c. 1910	O	159
Maybell	Benedict Mfg. Co.	c. 1910	O	NIA
Mayflower	Holmes & Edwards	1885	O	140
Mayflower	C. Rogers & Bro.	c. 1895	O	151
Mayflower	Wm. Rogers Mfg. Co.	1896	O	156
Medallion No. 1	L. Boardman & Son (Nickel Silver Base)	c. 1880	O	137
Medallion No. 2	L. Boardman & Son (Nickel Silver Base)	c. 1880	O	137
Medallion	Hall, Elton & Co.	c. 1867	O	139, 168
Medallion	SHMCo.; Wm. Rogers Eagle	c. 1875	O	157
Melrose	SHMCo.; Wm. Rogers Eagle	1896	O	158
Mikado (Cardinal)	SHMCo. (Wm. Rogers Eagle)	1888	O	158
*Milan	1847 Rogers Bros.	1900	O	149
Milton	C. Rogers & Bro.	c. 1897	O	151
Minerva	S. L. & G. H. Rogers	c. 1910	O	153
Minnehaha	Holmes & Edwards	1904	O	141
Mission	E. H. H. Smith Silver Co.	1908	O	159
Mission	1835 R. Wallace	c. 1910		NIA
Mistletoe	Pairpoint Mfg. Co.	c. 1887	O	143
Modern Art	Reed & Barton	1900	O	145
Moline	1847 Rogers Bros.	1893	O	150
Monarch	Rogers & Bro.	1891	O	152
Monarch	Rogers & Hamilton	1891	O	152
Montauk	Holmes & Edwards	1903	O	140
Monterey	Benedict Mfg. Co.	c. 1910	O	NIA
Monticello	American Silver Co.	1908	O	135
Morning Glory	Pairpoint Mfg. Co.	c. 1887	O	143
Moselle	American Silver Co.	1906	O	135
*Moselle	1847 Rogers Bros.	1891	O	149
Mothers	Glastonbury Silver Co.	c. 1910	O	NIA
Muscatel	Paragon Plate	c. 1910	O	143
Mystic	Rogers & Bro.	1903	O	146
Naples	C. Rogers & Bro.	1896	O	151
Narcissus	Wm. A. Rogers	c. 1900	O	153
Nassau	Holmes & Edwards	1899		140
Navarre	Rogers & Bro.	1896	O	146
Nenuphar	American Silver Co.	c. 1903	O	135
Nevada	Rogers & Bro.	c. 1896	O	146
Nevada	1847 Rogers Bros.	1882	O	147
New Century	Rogers & Bro.	1898	O	146
New Model (Portia)	E. H. H. Smith Silver Co.	c. 1910	O	159
New Pattern	L. Boardman & Son (Franconia)	c. 1880	O	137
Newington	Landers, Frary & Clark	c. 1910		141
Newport	Rogers & Bro.	1879	O	148
Newport	1847 Rogers Bros.	1880	O	148
Newport	Rogers & Hamilton	c. 1890	O	148
Newport	Rogers, Smith & Co.	c. 1880	O	148
Newton	C. Rogers & Bro.	c. 1900	O	151
Newtown	Cambridge Silver Plate	1907	O	137
Niagara	Hall, Elton & Co.	c. 1875	O	139
Niagara Falls No. 1	Niagara Falls Silver Co.	c. 1900	O	142

ELECTROPLATE FLATWARE PATTERNS (*Cont'd*)

Pattern	Brand or Manufacturer	Introduction Date and Obsolescence		Page
*Norfolk	Rogers & Bro.	c. 1900	O	149
*Norfolk	1847 Rogers Bros.	c. 1900	O	149
Norma	Williams Bros.	c. 1900	O	162
Normandie	Rogers & Hamilton	1887	O	152
Norwood	Towle Mfg. Co.	c. 1900	O	160
Norwood	Williams Bros.	c. 1910	O	NIA
No. 80	A. F. Towle & Son Co.	1890	O	159
No. 83	A. F. Towle & Son Co.	1883	O	160
No. 300	A. F. Towle & Son Co.	1883	O	160
No. 1731	Landers, Frary & Clark	c. 1895	O	141
Nydia	Williams Bros.	c. 1900	O	NIA
Oak	Wm. Rogers Mfg. Co.	c. 1908	O	157
Oak	E. H. H. Smith Silver Co.	c. 1905	O	159
Oak	Williams Bros.	c. 1910	O	NIA
Old English	Gorham Mfg. Co.	c. 1875		85
Olive	L. Boardman & Son	c. 1850	O	26, 85
Olive	Derby Silver Co.	c. 1873	O	85
Olive	Hall, Elton & Co.	c. 1850	O	85
Olive	Holmes, Booth & Haydens	c. 1875	O	85
Olive	J. O. Mead & Sons	c. 1850	O	43, 85
Olive	Mulford, Wendell & Co.	c. 1855	O	85
Olive	Redfield & Rice	c. 1860	O	85
Olive	Reed & Barton	before 1868	O	85
Olive	Rogers & Bro.	1878	O	85
Olive	Rogers Bros.	1848	O	85
Olive	Rogers Bros. Mfg. Co.	1853	O	59, 85
Olive	1847 Rogers Bros.	1862	O	85
Olive	Rogers, Smith & Co.	c. 1856	O	85
Olive	Wm. Rogers Mfg. Co.	c. 1865	O	85
*Olympia	1847 Rogers Bros.	1900	O	149
Opal	Wm. Rogers Mfg. Co.	c. 1900	O	NIA
Orchid	S. L. & G. H. Rogers	1903	O	152
Oregon	American Silver Co.	1902	O	135
Orient	Holmes & Edwards	1904	O	140
Orient	Reed & Barton	c. 1870	O	144
Orient	Wm. A. Rogers	c. 1898	O	154
Orleans	Hall, Elton & Co.	c. 1875	O	139
Orleans	Rogers Cutlery Co.	1904	O	151
Ormonde	Wm. Rogers Mfg. Co.	c. 1895	O	156
Oval	Derby Silver Co.	c. 1875	O	85
Oval	Hall, Elton & Co.	c. 1867	O	85
Oval	Oneida Community	c. 1877	O	85
Oval	Reed & Barton	before 1868	O	85
Oval	Rogers & Bro.	c. 1865	O	85
Oval	Rogers Bros. Mfg. Co.	1855	O	85
Oval	1847 Rogers Bros.	1862	O	85
Oval	Rogers & Hamilton	c. 1883	O	85
Oval	Rogers, Smith & Co.	c. 1870	O	85
Oval Thread	Holmes & Edwards	c. 1885	O	85
Oval Thread	Reed & Barton	c. 1870	O	85
Oval Thread	Rogers & Bro.	c. 1865	O	85
Oval Thread	Rogers Bros. Mfg. Co.	1860	O	85
Oval Thread	1847 Rogers Bros.	1862	O	85

ELECTROPLATE FLATWARE PATTERNS *(Cont'd)*

Pattern	Brand or Manufacturer	Introduction Date and Obsolescence		Page
Oval Thread	Wm. Rogers Mfg. Co.	1882	O	85
Oval Thread	R. Wallace; 1835 R. Wallace	c. 1875	O	85
Oval Thread	E. G. Webster & Bro.	c. 1879	O	85
Oval Threaded	L. Boardman & Son	c. 1860	O	85
*Owl	1847 Rogers Bros.	c. 1886	O	149
*Owl	Rogers, Smith & Co.	c. 1886	O	149
Oxford	Reed & Barton	c. 1884	O	144
Oxford	Wm. Rogers Mfg. Co.	1904	O	156
Oxford	W. F. Rogers (Rogers Cutlery Co.)	1902	O	156
Palace	Hall, Elton & Co.	c. 1875	O	139
Palace	Holmes, Booth & Haydens	c. 1879-1886	O	139
Palace	Reed & Barton	c. 1885	O	144
Pansy	S. L. & G. H. Rogers	c. 1910	O	NIA
Paragon	Williams Bros.	c. 1900	O	162
Parisian	Reed & Barton	1885	O	144
*Parisian	1847 Rogers Bros.	1891	O	149
Paul Revere	Williams Bros.	c. 1905	O	NIA
Pearl	Glastonbury Silver Co.	c. 1910		138
Pearl	Holmes & Edwards	1898	O	141
Pearl	Reed & Barton	c. 1877	O	144
Pearl	Rockford S. P. Co.	c. 1908	O	162
*Pearl	1847 Rogers Bros.	1891	O	149
Pearl	1835 R. Wallace	c. 1910	O	NIA
Pearl	Williams Bros.	c. 1900	O	162
Peerless	Wm. Rogers Mfg. Co.	1891	O	155
Peerless	Rockford S. P. Co.	c. 1908	O	162
Peerless	Williams Bros	c. 1905	O	162
Pequot	Wm. Rogers Mfg. Co.	1892	O	156
Perfect	Holmes & Edwards	1883	O	140
Persian	L. Boardman & Son	c. 1870	O	137
Persian	Rogers & Bro.	1872	O	148
Persian	1847 Rogers Bros.	1871	O	148
Persian	Wm. Rogers Mfg. Co.	1882	O	148
Pilot	Williams Bros.	c. 1900	O	NIA
Plain	Bliss Silver Co.	c. 1890	O	85
Plain	L. Boardman & Son	c. 1850	O	85
Plain	L. Boardman & Son (Franconia)	c. 1880	O	85
Plain	Pairpoint Mfg. Co.	c. 1875	O	143
Plain	Reed & Barton	before 1868	O	85
Plain	Rockford S. P. Co.	c. 1895	O	85
Plain	Rogers & Bro.	c. 1865	O	85
Plain	Rogers Bros.	1847	O	85
Plain	Rogers Bros. Mfg. Co.	1853	O	85
Plain	1847 Rogers Bros.	1862	O	85
Plain	Rogers, Smith & Co.	c. 1860	O	85
Plain	Wm. Rogers Mfg. Co.	1882	O	85
Plain	Wm. H. Rogers Corp.	c. 1910	O	85
Plastron	Williams Bros.	c. 1910	O	162
Plaza	Rogers & Bro.	c. 1896	O	147
Pluto	C. Rogers & Bro.	c. 1897	O	151
Plymouth	Wm. A. Rogers	c. 1900	O	NIA
Plymouth	Wm. Rogers Mfg. Co.	1891	O	157
Pompeiian	Derby Silver Co.	c. 1883	O	137

ELECTROPLATE FLATWARE PATTERNS (*Cont'd*)

Pattern	Brand or Manufacturer	Introduction Date and Obsolescence		Page
Pompeiian	E. H. H. Smith Silver Co.	c. 1910	O	NIA
Ponce de Leon	American Silver Co.	1903	O	135
Poppy	Rogers & Bro.	c. 1900	O	146
Portia (New Model)	E. H. H. Smith Silver Co.	c. 1910	O	159
Portland	1847 Rogers Bros.	1891	O	150
Primrose	Rogers & Bro.	1881	O	147
*Primrose	1847 Rogers Bros.	c. 1895	O	147
Princess	Derby Silver Co.	c. 1875	O	155
Princess	Rogers & Bro.	c. 1872	O	155
Princess	1847 Rogers Bros.	1874	O	155
Princess	S. L. & G. H. Rogers	1901	O	152
Princess	Rogers, Smith & Co.	c. 1886	O	155
Princess	Wm. Rogers Mfg. Co.	c. 1872	O	155
Princess	Williams Bros.	1910	O	162
Princess Louise	Gorham Mfg. Co.	c. 1880	O	138
Princeton	Rogers & Bro.	c. 1897	O	146
Priscilla	1847 Rogers Bros.	1900	O	150
Priscilla	A. F. Towle & Son Co.	1890	O	159
Priscilla	Williams Bros.	c. 1910	O	162
Providence	Gorham Mfg. Co.	c. 1910	O	NIA
Puritan	S. L. & G. H. Rogers	c. 1900	O	152
Puritan	Rogers, Smith & Co.	c. 1886	O	153
Puritan	Wm. Rogers Mfg. Co.	1907	O	157
Queen	Holmes & Edwards	c. 1885	O	140
Queen	Rogers & Bro.	1895	O	158
Queen	Wm. Rogers Mfg. Co.	1890	O	158
Queen	SHMCo.; Wm. Rogers Eagle	1890	O	158
Queen Anne	Holmes & Edwards	1885	O	139
Queen Anne	Williams Bros.	1905	O	162
Queen Bertha	Glastonbury Silver Co.	c. 1910	O	138
Queen Elizabeth	Williams Bros.	1908	O	162
Queen Helena (Alma)	Williams Bros.	c. 1905	O	162
Queen Victoria	Williams Bros.	c. 1900	O	162
*Rajah	Rogers & Bro.	c. 1893	O	147
Raleigh	A. F. Towle & Son Co.	1890	O	160
Raleigh	Wm. A. Rogers	c. 1907	O	154
Raleigh	Wm. Rogers Mfg. Co.	1904	O	156
Randolph	Wm. Rogers Mfg. Co.	c. 1905	O	158
Randolph	Simpson, Hall, Miller & Co.	c. 1905	O	158
Randolph	SHMCo.; Wm. Rogers Eagle	c. 1905	O	158
Raphael	Rogers & Hamilton	1897	O	152
*Raymond	Wm. A. Rogers	c. 1898	O	154
Regal	Wm. Rogers Mfg. Co.	1880	O	155
Regent	Gorham Mfg. Co.	c. 1880		138
Regent	Hall, Elton & Co.	c. 1875	O	139
Regent	C. Rogers & Bro.	c. 1896	O	151
Regent	Wm. Rogers Mfg. Co.	c. 1880	O	155
Revere	Wm. A. Rogers	c. 1905		154
Rex	Reed & Barton	1900	O	145
Rhinebeck (St. Elmo)	Wm. A. Rogers	c. 1900	O	154
Rialto	Holmes & Edwards	c. 1900	O	141
Richelieu	Reed & Barton	c. 1900	O	NIA

ELECTROPLATE FLATWARE PATTERNS (*Cont'd*)

Pattern	Brand or Manufacturer	Introduction Date and Obsolescence		Page
Richmond	Gorham Mfg. Co.	c. 1897	O	138
Rival	Wm. Rogers Mfg. Co.	1882	O	155
Roanoke	American Silver Co.	c. 1910	O	135
Rockford #1 (Como?)	Rockford S. P. Co.	c. 1900	O	145, 162
Roman	Derby Silver Co.	c. 1875	O	147
Roman	Gorham Mfg. Co.	c. 1865	O	138
Roman	Holmes, Booth & Haydens	c. 1884	O	139
Roman	Rogers & Bro.	c. 1880	O	147
Roman	1847 Rogers Bros.	1865	O	147
Roman Medallion	Reed & Barton	1868	O	144
Romanesque	1847 Rogers Bros.	1895	O	150
Rosalie	American Silver Co. (Royal Plate)	c. 1905	O	135
Rosalind	Williams Bros.	c. 1900	O	162
Rose	Paragon Plate	1903	O	143
Rose	Rogers Cutlery Co.	c. 1910	O	151
Rose	Wm. Rogers Mfg. Co.	c. 1910	O	151
Rose	Sears	1903	O	151
Rose (York Rose)	E. H. H. Smith Silver Co.	c. 1905	O	159
Rose	1835 R. Wallace	c. 1900	O	120, 161
Rosemary	Holmes & Edwards	c. 1910	O	NIA
Rosemary	Rockford S. P. Co.	1905	O	145
Roslyn	Gorham Mfg. Co. (Elmwood Plate)	c. 1900		NIA
Royal	Aurora S. P. Co.	c. 1880	O	136
Royal	Gorham Mfg. Co.	c. 1885	O	NIA
Royal	Reed & Barton	1899	O	145
Royal	C. Rogers & Bro.	1897	O	151
*Ruby	1847 Rogers Bros.	1891	O	149
*Russian	Reed & Barton	c. 1883	O	144
Rustic	A. F. Towle & Son Co.	c. 1883	O	160
*Saddle Rock	SHMCo.; Wm. Rogers Eagle	1888	O	157
*St. Augustine	SHMCo.; Wm. Rogers Eagle	1888	O	158
St. Charles	Rogers Bros. Mfg. Co.	1855	O	147
St. Charles	1847 Rogers Bros.	1862	O	147
St. Elmo (Rhinebeck)	Wm. A. Rogers	c. 1906		154
St. James	SHMCo.; Wm. Rogers Eagle	1880	O	158
St. James	Wm. Rogers Mfg. Co.	1880	O	158
St. Paul	American Silver Co.	c. 1907	O	135
Salem	Benedict Mfg. Co.	c. 1909	O	136
Salina	Benedict Mfg. Co.	c. 1900	O	NIA
Samoset	A. F. Towle & Son Co.	1883	O	159
San Diego	Wm. Rogers Mfg. Co.	c. 1885	O	155
Saratoga	Rogers & Bro.	c. 1891	O	148
Saratoga	C. Rogers & Bros.	c. 1896	O	148
Saratoga	1847 Rogers Bros.	1878	O	148
Saratoga	Rogers, Smith & Co.	c. 1878	O	148
Saratoga	Wm. Rogers Mfg. Co.	c. 1880	O	148
Savarin	C. Rogers & Bro.	c. 1896	O	151
Savoy	Rogers & Bro.	1893	O	150
Savoy	1847 Rogers Bros.	1893	O	150
Saxon	Benedict Mfg. Co.	c. 1900	O	NIA
Saxony	Gorham Mfg. Co.	c. 1890		138
Saybrook	Landers, Frary & Clark	c. 1910	O	141
Scroll	Wm. Rogers Mfg. Co.	c. 1910	O	NIA

ELECTROPLATE FLATWARE PATTERNS *(Cont'd)*

Pattern	Brand or Manufacturer	Introduction Date and Obsolescence		Page
*Scythian	1847 Rogers Bros.	1900	O	149
Seville	Reed & Barton	c. 1910	O	NIA
Seville	SHMCo.; Wm. Rogers Eagle	1896	O	157
Sharon	1847 Rogers Bros.	1910	O	150
Sheffield (Warwick)	Gorham Mfg. Co.	c. 1890	O	NIA
Sheffield	Reed & Barton	c. 1910	O	NIA
Sheffield	Wm. Rogers Mfg. Co.	c. 1910	O	NIA
Sheffield	Williams Bros.	c. 1910	O	NIA
Shell	American Silver Co.	c. 1902	O	85
Shell	Associated Silver Co.	c. 1910	O	85
Shell	E. A. Bliss Co.	c. 1895	O	85
Shell	Forbes Silver Co.	c. 1898	O	85
Shell	Gorham Mfg. Co.	c. 1870	O	85
Shell	Holmes & Edwards	1894	O	85
Shell	Lakeside	1895	O	141
Shell	Niagara Silver Co.	c. 1900	O	85
Shell	Paragon Plate	c. 1907	O	85
Shell (Shell #1)	Reed & Barton	before 1868	O	85
Shell	Rogers & Bro.	1895	O	85
Shell	C. Rogers & Bros.	1896	O	85
Shell	Rogers Bros. Mfg. Co.	1860	O	85
Shell	1847 Rogers Bros.	1862	O	85
Shell	Rogers & Hamilton	1897	O	85
Shell	W. F. Rogers	1902	O	85
Shell	S. L. & G. H. Rogers	1901	O	152
Shell	Wm. Rogers Mfg. Co.	1895	O	85
Shell	Wm. A. Rogers	1898	O	154
Shell	Sears	1903	O	85
Shell	SHMCo.; Wm. Rogers Eagle	1895	O	85
Shell	E. H. H. Smith Silver Co.	c. 1904	O	85
Shell	Towle Mfg. Co.	c. 1883	O	160
Shell	R. Wallace; 1835 R. Wallace	1871	O	85
Shell	Williams Bros.	c. 1900	O	85
Shell #1 (Shell)	Reed & Barton	before 1868	O	85
Shell #1	Rogers & Bro.	c. 1870	O	85
Shell #1	A. F. Towle & Son Co.	1883	O	85
Shell #2	Rogers & Bro.	1895	O	150
Shell #2	1847 Rogers Bros.	1895	O	150
Shell #2	A. F. Towle & Son Co.	1890	O	159
Shell Thread	Holmes & Edwards	c. 1885	O	140
Shell Tipped	1847 Rogers Bros.	1866	O	148
Shell Tipped	Rogers, Smith & Co.	c. 1886	O	148
Sheraton	Oneida Community	1910	O	142
*Sherwood	Rogers, Smith & Co.	c. 1886	O	153
Sherwood	Wm. A. Rogers	c. 1910	O	NIA
Shirley	Williams Bros.	c. 1900	O	162
*Shrewsbury	1847 Rogers Bros.	1891	O	149
Signet	Wm. Rogers Mfg. Co.	c. 1900	O	NIA
Silver	L. Boardman & Son	c. 1860	O	137
Silver	Rogers & Bro.	1891	O	147
Silver	Rogers Bros.	1850	O	147
Silver	Rogers Bros. Mfg. Co.	1853	O	147
Silver	1847 Rogers Bros.	1862	O	147
Silver	Wm. Rogers Mfg. Co.	c. 1880	O	157

ELECTROPLATE FLATWARE PATTERNS (*Cont'd*)

Pattern	Brand or Manufacturer	Introduction Date and Obsolescence		Page
Simeon #1	S. L. & G. H. Rogers	c. 1900	O	152
Siren	Rogers & Bro.	1891	O	150
Siren	1847 Rogers Bros.	1891	O	150
Solvay	Benedict Mfg. Co.	1901	O	136
Spanish	Holmes & Edwards	1885	O	139
Spanish	Reed & Barton	c. 1884	O	144
Spanish	Rogers Bros. Mfg. Co.	1860	O	147
Spanish	1847 Rogers Bros.	1862	O	147
Spanish	Williams Bros.	c. 1890	O	NIA
Spartan	Williams Bros.	c. 1890	O	NIA
Spray	Rogers & Bro.	c. 1887	O	146
Standard	Sears	c. 1885	O	157
Standish	Wm. A. Rogers	1907	O	154
Stanhope	Gorham Mfg. Co.	c. 1900	O	138
Stuart	Benedict Mfg. Co.	c. 1910	O	NIA
Stuart	1835 R. Wallace	1899	O	161
Suffolk	Wm. A. Rogers	1902	O	154
Sultana	Wm. Rogers Mfg. Co.	c. 1900	O	155
Sultana	SHMCo.; Wm. Rogers Eagle	c. 1902	O	155
Sweet Pea	Associated Silver Co.	c. 1910	O	136
Sweet Pea	Paragon Plate	1908	O	143
Swiss	Reed & Barton	c. 1884	O	144
Sylvan	Wm. A. Rogers	c. 1910	O	NIA
Tacoma	Niagara Silver Co.	c. 1900	O	142
Thistle	Rogers & Bro.	c. 1900	O	146
Thistle	Wm. Rogers Mfg. Co.	c. 1900	O	146
Threaded	Hall, Elton & Co.	c. 1867	O	85
Threaded	Reed & Barton	before 1868	O	85
Threaded	Rogers & Bro.	c. 1880	O	85
Threaded	Rogers Bros.	1847	O	85
Threaded	Rogers Bros. Mfg. Co.	1853	O	85
Threaded	1847 Rogers Bros.	1862	O	85
Thread Hotel (Boston)	Holmes & Edwards	1904	O	141
Tiger Lily	Reed & Barton	1901	O	145
Tiger Lily	Wm. Rogers Mfg. Co.	1895	O	156
Tipped	American Silver Co.	c. 1902	O	85
Tipped	Associated Silver Co.	c. 1910	O	85
Tipped	L. Boardman & Son	c. 1850	O	85
Tipped	Derby Silver Co.	c. 1883	O	85
Tipped	Forbes Silver Co.	1898	O	85
Tipped	Hall, Elton & Co.	c. 1867	O	85
Tipped	Holmes & Edwards	1883	O	85
Tipped	Lakeside	c. 1895	O	85
Tipped	Niagara Silver Co.	c. 1900	O	85
Tipped	Oneida Community	c. 1900	O	85
Tipped	Paragon Plate	1907	O	85
Tipped	Reed & Barton	c. 1870		85
Tipped	Rogers & Bro.	1872	O	85
Tipped	Rogers Bros.	1847	O	85
Tipped	Rogers Bros. Mfg. Co.	1853	O	85
Tipped	1847 Rogers Bros.	1862		85
Tipped	C. Rogers & Bros.	c. 1896	O	85
Tipped	Rogers Cutlery Co.	1904		85

ELECTROPLATE FLATWARE PATTERNS (*Cont'd*)

Pattern	Brand or Manufacturer	Introduction Date and Obsolescence		Page
Tipped	Rogers & Hamilton	1887		85
Tipped	Rogers, Smith & Co.	c. 1886	O	85
Tipped	S. L. & G. H. Rogers	c. 1900	O	85
Tipped	Wm. A. Rogers	c. 1900		85
Tipped	Wm. Rogers Mfg. Co.	1882		85
Tipped	W. F. Rogers	1902	O	85
Tipped	Sears	1903	O	85
Tipped	Sears Silver Filled	1910	O	85
Tipped	SHMCo.; Wm. Rogers Eagle	1880	O	85
Tipped	A. F. Towle & Son Co.	1883	O	85
Tipped	Towle Mfg. Co.	c. 1883	O	85
Tipped	R. Wallace; 1835 R. Wallace	1888	O	85
Tipped	E. G. Webster & Bro.	c. 1879	O	85
Tipped	Williams Bros.	c. 1895	O	85
*Tolland	1847 Rogers Bros.	1891	O	149
Tours	American Silver Co.	1904	O	135
Triumph	Holmes & Edwards	c. 1910	O	140
Troy	1835 R. Wallace	1896	O	161
Trumpet Vine	1835 R. Wallace	c. 1890	O	NIA
Tudor	Rogers & Bro.	1905	O	152
Tudor	Rogers & Hamilton	1905	O	152
Tufts No. 1	James W. Tufts	c. 1885	O	160
Tuscan	Rogers & Bro.	c. 1880	O	147
Tuscan	Rogers Bros.	1852	O	147
Tuscan	Rogers Bros. Mfg. Co.	1853	O	147
Tuscan	1847 Rogers Bros.	1862	O	147
*Tuxedo	Rogers & Bro.	1895	O	146
Unique	Holmes & Edwards	1897	O	141
Unique	Reed & Barton	1879	O	144
Utica	C. Rogers & Bro.	c. 1900	O	151
Valada	Williams Bros.	1897	O	162
*Vassar	1847 Rogers Bros.	1891	O	149
Vendome	Reed & Barton	1884	O	144
*Venetian	Reed & Barton	c. 1884	O	144
*Venetian	Rogers, Smith & Co.	c. 1886	O	153
Venetian	Wm. Rogers Mfg. Co.	c. 1880	O	153
Venice	Rockford S. P. Co.	c. 1900	O	NIA
Verdi	E. H. H. Smith Silver Co.	1904	O	159
*Vernon	Niagara Silver Co.	c. 1900	O	142
*Vernon	Wm. A. Rogers	c. 1910	O	142
Verona	Rogers & Bro.	c. 1910	O	146
Verona	Williams Bros.	c. 1900	O	NIA
Vesta	Rogers & Bro.	1898	O	150
Vesta	1847 Rogers Bros.	1895	O	150
Victor	C. Rogers & Bro.	c. 1896	O	151
Victor	Towle Mfg. Co.	c. 1900	O	160
Victoria	Rogers & Bro.	1896	O	146
Victoria	Wm. Rogers Mfg. Co.	c. 1895	O	156
Victoria (Queen Victoria)	Williams Bros.	c. 1900	O	162
Victory	Associated Silver Co.	c. 1910		136
Vincent	American Silver Co. (Royal)	c. 1910	O	135
Vineyard	Williams Bros.	c. 1905	O	162

ELECTROPLATE FLATWARE PATTERNS (*Cont'd*)

Pattern	Brand or Manufacturer	Introduction Date and Obsolescence		Page
Vintage	1847 Rogers Bros.	1904	O	150
Violet	S. L. & G. H. Rogers	1905	O	152
Violet	Wm. A. Rogers	c. 1905	O	153
Virginia	Wm. Rogers Mfg. Co.	c. 1907	O	NIA
Virginia	1835 R. Wallace	1898	O	161
Wadsworth	Wm. Rogers Mfg. Co.	c. 1910	O	NIA
Waldorf	Holmes & Edwards	1904	O	141
Wallingford #1	Wallingford Co.	c. 1905	O	161
Wallingford #2	Wallingford Co.	c. 1905	O	161
Warner	Holmes & Edwards	c. 1900	O	140
Warren	S. L. & G. H. Rogers	1901		152
Warren	A. F. Towle & Son Co.	1883	O	159
Warwick	L. Boardman & Son	c. 1880	O	137
Warwick (Sheffield)	Gorham Mfg. Co.	c. 1890	O	NIA
Warwick	Wm. A. Rogers	c. 1901		154
Warwick	A. F. Towle & Son Co.	1883	O	160
Warwick	E. G. Webster & Bro.	c. 1875	O	161
Washington	Holmes & Edwards	1910	O	141
Webster	S. L. & G. H. Rogers	c. 1900		153
Wellesley	Wm. A. Rogers	c. 1910	O	NIA
Westfield	Holmes & Edwards	1904	O	140
Westminster	Gorham Mfg. Co.	c. 1900	O	NIA
Westminster	C. Rogers & Bro.	c. 1896	O	151
Wildflower	American Silver Co. (H & T)	c. 1910	O	135
Wild Rose	Niagara Falls Silver Co.	c. 1900	O	142
Wildwood	Oneida Community (Reliance)	c. 1910	O	142
Windsor	American Silver Co.	c. 1900	O	85
Windsor	Associated Silver Co.	c. 1910		85
Windsor	Derby Silver Co.	c. 1883	O	85
Windsor	Glastonbury Silver Co.	c. 1910	O	85
Windsor	Holmes & Edwards	1890		85
Windsor	Lakeside	1895	O	85
Windsor	Landers, Frary & Clark	c. 1890	O	85
Windsor	Niagara Silver Co.	c. 1900	O	85
Windsor	Oneida Community	c. 1900	O	85
Windsor	Reed & Barton	c. 1880	O	85
Windsor	Rogers & Bro.	1886		85
Windsor	Rogers Bros.	1850	O	85
Windsor	Rogers Bros. Mfg. Co.	1853	O	85
Windsor	1847 Rogers Bros.	c. 1862	O	85
Windsor	Rogers, Smith & Co.	c. 1886	O	85
Windsor	S. L. & G. H. Rogers	c. 1900		85
Windsor	Wm. A. Rogers	1891		85
Windsor	Wm. Rogers Mfg. Co.	1891		85
Windsor	E. H. H. Smith Silver Co.	c. 1910		85
Windsor	A. F. Towle & Son Co.	1883	O	85
Windsor	Towle Mfg. Co.	c. 1883	O	85
Windsor	1835 R. Wallace	1895		85
Windsor	Williams Bros.	c. 1900		85
Windsor Engraved #5	A. F. Towle & Son Co.	1883	O	159
Windsor Engraved #43	A. F. Towle & Son Co.	1883	O	159
Winthrop	Gorham Mfg. Co.	1896		138
Winthrop	C. Rogers & Bro.	1896	O	151

ELECTROPLATE FLATWARE PATTERNS *(Cont'd)*

Pattern	Brand or Manufacturer	Introduction Date and Obsolescence		Page
Wistaria	E. H. H. Smith Silver Co.	c. 1904	O	159
Yale	Wm. Rogers Mfg. Co.	1891	O	156
Yale	SHMCo.; Wm. Rogers Eagle	1891	O	156
York	Wm. Rogers Mfg. Co.	1900	O	158
York	SHMCo.; Wm. Rogers Eagle	1900	O	158
York Rose (Rose)	E. H. H. Smith Silver Co.	c. 1904	O	159

DATES OF INTRODUCTION FOR DOZENS WORK AND FANCY PIECES

Obviously, space does not permit listing each of the pieces made in each of the patterns introduced between 1837 and 1910. Since this information is of interest to collectors, the following compilation will serve as a guide to the general composition of silver services sold during these years. The dates listed here were determined by the first appearance of a specific piece in available catalogs and price lists; standard reference books on earlier silver work established dates for pieces in general use before the Victorian years.

Supplementary pieces were often added to the basic pieces made in patterns that remained active over a number of years; consequently, a later introductory date for a specific piece does not necessarily imply that the piece may not have been made in a pattern introduced some years before. For example, while the "Olive" pattern was first made in 1848, new "fancy pieces" were still being introduced in this pattern as late as 1880. Another example is found in 1847 Rogers Bros. "Vintage"; the pattern was introduced in 1904, and iced tea spoons added to the line about 1910.

Names of pieces originally applied by the manufacturers are used in this listing. These designations have frequently changed in modern usage; for instance, table forks or medium forks have become dinner forks; dessert knives and forks are called luncheon knives and forks; orange spoons have become grapefruit spoons; coffee spoons are referred to as demitasse spoons. Illustrations in the "Pieces" section of this book should clarify designations appearing in this list; page numbers following each listing refer to the illustrations. Where alternate names were used by manufacturers, these are shown in parenthesis. Many of the pieces were made in both small and large sizes; the initials (S-L) following the listing, indicate this variation. The abbreviation *ind.* following a piece name indicates that it was made in dozens work, for individual place settings.

KNIVES	PAGE
Bread, c. 1880	202
Butter, c. 1830	195, 203, 204, 205
Butter Spreaders, ind. (S-L), c. 1885	189, 203, 204
Cake, c. 1875	192, 200
Carving, ind., c. 1890	189
Cheese, c. 1880	195
Child's, ind., c. 1840	189, 204, 224
Crawfish, ind., c. 1895	189
Crumb, c. 1850	192, 200
Dessert, ind., 18th century	174, 189, 203
Duck, ind., c. 1895	189
Fish (S-L), c. 1820	194, 200, 205, 211, 213
Fish, ind., c. 1830	189
Fruit, ind., c. 1860	189, 204
Fruit, pocket, c. 1850	177
Ice Cream, c. 1870	192, 200, 205, 211
Jelly, c. 1870	195, 204, 212
Lemon, c. 1900	196
Macaroni, c. 1880	201
Medium (Table), ind., 18th century	189
Melon, ind., c. 1875	189
Orange, ind., c. 1880	189
Oyster, Fried, c. 1880	199

Ice Cream Server, c. 1880 192
Jelly Server, c. 1875 195, 197, 211
Lemon Server, c. 1895 196
Macaroni Server, c. 1880 201
Nut Scoop, c. 1870 196
Oyster Scoop, c. 1875 199
Oyster Server, c. 1880 194
Oyster Server, Fried, c. 1880 194, 199
Pea Server, c. 1895 201
Pie Server, c. 1870 199, 204, 213
Saratoga Chips Server, c. 1875 199
Tomato Server, c. 1890 194

LADLES

Bouillon, c. 1895 193
Cream, Deep Bowl, c. 1880 199
Cream, Regular, c. 1870 193, 199, 202, 203, 204
Gravy, 18th century 193, 199, 202, 203, 204, 205
Ice Cream, c. 1860 199
Mayonnaise, c. 1895 193
Medium, c. 1870 199, 205
Mustard, 18th century 199, 205
Olive, c. 1880 198
Oyster, c. 1860 193, 199, 211
Punch, 18th century 193, 202, 215
Sauce, c. 1840 199, 215
Soup, 18th century 193, 199, 202, 205

TONGS

Asparagus, c. 1850 197
Asparagus, ind., c. 1895 191, 197
Bon Bon, c. 1880 196, 197, 204
Ice, c. 1875 197
Salad (See Asparagus), c. 1855 197
Sardine, c. 1885 197
Sugar (S-L), 18th century 174, 197, 204, 211
Sugar, Tete-a-tete, c. 1875 197

MISCELLANEOUS

Bone Holder, c. 1880 192
Brandy Burner, c. 1860 196
Buckwheat Cake Lifter, c. 1880 200, 205
Butter Pick (S-L), c. 1870 196
Cake Cutter, c. 1870 205
Carving Sets*
Bird (3 pieces), c. 1880 192
Breakfast (Individual) (3 pieces), c. 1890 189
Game (2 or 3 pieces), c. 1880 192
Individual (Breakfast) (3 pieces), c. 1895 189
Meat (3 pieces), c. 1840 192
Steak (2 pieces) (See Game), c. 1900 192
* Individual carving pieces have been used for centuries; the sets listed here are Victorian designations.
Chocolate Muddler, c. 1895 196, 211
Crumb Scraper and Receiver, c. 1850 192, 200, 205
Duck Shears, c. 1890 192
Food Pusher, c. 1900 174, 203, 227
Grape Shears, c. 1830 202, 203
Ice Cream Server, c. 1880 192
Ice Cream Slicer, c. 1890 192
Julep Strainer, c. 1860 196
Knife Sharpener (other than steels) 202
These patent pieces, made to match carvers and forks, came in many styles. Patent dates are usually stamped on the individual piece.
Lemonade Stirrer-Sipper, c. 1900 191, 221
Melon Fork-Knife, c. 1890 189
Nut Cracker, c. 1860 196, 202, 203
Nut Pick, c. 1860 196, 202, 203, 205
Olive Fork and Spoon (Ideal), c. 1905 198, 212
Olive Spoon-Fork, c. 1870 198
Orange Peeler, c. 1875 189
Oyster Fork and Spoon Combination, c. 1875 190
Roast Holder, c. 1880 192
Sardine Helper, c. 1880 198
Sugar Shaker (Sifter), c. 1860 197
Sugar Sifter (Shaker), c. 1850 197
Tea Infuser, c. 1870 196
Tea Strainer, 18th century 196
Toddy Strainer, 18th century 196

Glossary

Alaska Silver — See Nickel Silver.

Albata — One of the white metal alloys of nickel, copper, and zinc.

Alpacca — See Nickel Silver.

Applied — Decorative part, made separately and attached to the main body of a silver or other piece; in flatware, sometimes an initial or initials.

Argetin, Argentine — Literally, "silvery"; generally an alloy of tin and antimony sometimes used as a base metal for plating; one of the "white metals."

Assay — In metallurgy, analysis to determine quality of metal or ore; also the tabulated result of such analysis.

Base Metal — Metal or alloy to which plating is applied; generally of value inferior to that of the plating metal.

Beading — Decorative treatment consisting of half-spheres in series. Frequently used as border on flatware.

Bright Cut — Decorative treatment consisting of shallow engraving with bevelled edges to catch and reflect light.

Britannia Metal — A silver-white alloy containing the elements of tin hardened with copper and antimony.

Cast — Molded, formed in a mold. In the case of metal objects, formed of molten metal poured into a form.

Chasing — Decorative treatment of metal, similar to embossing. Usually accomplished by cutting away or hammering an ornamental design.

Coin Silver — A silver alloy containing 892–4/10 parts silver to 107–6/10 other metal for hardness, according to the U.S. Mint Act of 1792. It is generally considered 900/1000 pure silver, 100/1000 other metal. The term is applied to flatware and other pieces of silver made in the United States during the 18th and 19th centuries; these pieces were sometimes fashioned from actual coins and at other times from silver meeting the standards set by the Mint Act.

Die — One of a pair of tools, which, when moved toward each other by pressure or blow, cut, shape or impress a desired device on an object or surface. In the production of silver flatware, the dies are generally of steel.

Die-cut, Die-cast, etc. — Production methods using dies.

Dollar — Mark sometimes used to indicate Coin Silver.

Dozens Work — Silver trade term used to designate pieces of flatware ordinarily priced or sold in dozens; place pieces, as opposed to serving pieces.

Electroplate To deposit a coating of silver, nickel, or other metal by electrolysis; the term is also used to describe anything so plated, particularly tableware plated with silver.

Embossing Decorative treatment consisting of raising parts of the surface; in metal, usually by pressure against a steel roller engraved or cut with a pattern.

Engraving Decorative treatment formed by cutting or carving ornamental design into surface of object with sharp tools called *gravers.*

Etching Decorative treatment produced by reaction of a chemical agent on specially prepared metal surface.

Fancy Pieces Silver trade term used to designate pieces of flatware ordinarily sold at retail as single pieces; serving pieces.

Fancy Work See Fancy Pieces.

Feather Edge Decorative treatment for borders of metal pieces; usually parallel slanting lines engraved or embossed at edge.

Fine Silver Silver metal assayed at better than 999/1000 pure.

Flatware Articles for the table, more or less flat in form; specifically knives, forks, and spoons.

Fluting Decorative treatment consisting of a series of parallel concave grooves; reverse of *reeding.*

Gadroon Decorative border treatment consisting of a series of low broad arches or ovals, usually separated by fluted or reeded areas.

German Silver See Nickel Silver.

Hafts The two halves of hollow handles for tableware, originally soldered together to form the handle.

Holloware or *Hollow Ware* Silver pieces in the form of vessels, such as bowls, pots, trays, etc.

Ingot Mass of metal cast into a form convenient for storing or transporting, usually a rectangular bar.

Nickel Silver A composition metal of copper, nickel, and zinc; the usual proportion of metals is about 2/3 copper, with varying portions of nickel and zinc. The alloy is also called Alpacca, German Silver, etc., and was given various trade names by Victorian flatware makers—many of whom used slightly varied formulations.

Oxidizing Film formed by application of oxide or other chemical substance to darken deeper portions of a decorated metal surface, producing effect of highlights and shadows.

Pewter An alloy having tin as the principal constituent. The finest grade consists of tin hardened with a little antimony, copper, and bismuth. Inferior grades may contain much lead.

Place Pieces The pieces of flatware used for individual service at the table, as opposed to serving pieces.

Place Setting Matched pieces of flatware for individual service at the table; the basic place setting is a knife, a fork and a teaspoon.

Also used, since the 1930s, to describe a unit of sale for silver flatware consisting of three to seven individual pieces.

Plate — In England and Europe, solid silver; sometimes also used to describe articles of any precious metal.

Plated Silver — Electroplated silverware; in England, the term is used to describe the ware that is called silver plate in the United States.

Reeding — Decorative treatment consisting of a series of convex, parallel moldings; the reverse of *fluting.*

Relief — Decorative treatment consisting of ornament projected above the surrounding surface.

Repoussé — Decorative treatment in metal consisting of relief ornament in metal hammered from the reverse side.

Roped Edge; Rope Edge — Decorative border treatment consisting of spiralled reeding or fluting.

Sheffield Plate — Silver coated copper, produced by fusing with intense heat, a thin sheet of silver on one or both sides of a thicker sheet of copper, which can then be rolled to the desired density or thickness. The term is also used to describe articles made of Sheffield Plate.

Silver Plate — The term commonly used in the United States to describe ware with a layer of silver on a base metal, or electroplate. In England, the term is used for solid silver, or what is called sterling silver in the United States.

Sterling — A silver alloy, containing 925/1000 pure silver, 75/1000 added metal to give the required hardness. The standards for sterling were established in England in 1562 by Act of Queen Elizabeth; in the United States, by the Stamping Act of 1906.

Temper — To harden, toughen or strengthen metal by heat treatment, to adapt metal to a specific use or purpose.

Touch Mark — Mark of maker; in the case of silversmiths, generally impressed with a punch bearing a distinctive device or initials.

White Metal — Alloys usually containing two or more of the following elements: tin, copper, antimony, and bismuth. The color varies with the proportion of tin; the more tin, the whiter the color.

Bibliography

List of source materials consulted in the preparation of this book.

BOOKS

1. *Designs for Gold and Silversmiths.* London: Ackerman & Co., 1836.
2. Andrews, Wayne. *Architecture, Ambition and Americans.* New York: Harper & Brothers, 1955
3. *Manufacturers of the United States.* New York: Armstrong & Knauer, 1887.
4. *Industrial America; or, Manufacturers and Inventors of the United States.* New York: Atlantic Publishing Co., 1876.
5. Avery, Clara Louise. *Early American Silver.* New York & London: The Century Company, 1930.
6. Bailey, Major C. T. P. *Knives and Forks.* London: Victoria & Albert Museum; London & Boston: The Medici Society, 1927.
7. Bigelow, Francis Hill. *Historic Silver of the Colonies and its Makers.* New York: The Macmillan Company, 1941.
8. Bradbury, Frederick. *History of Old Sheffield Plate.* London: Macmillan and Co., Ltd., 1912.
9. Brillat-Savarin, Anthelme. *Physiology of Taste.* New York: Liveright, 1948.
10. Brix, Maurice. *List of Philadelphia Silversmiths and Allied Artificers.* Philadelphia: Privately Printed, 1920.
11. Buck, J. H. *Old Plate, Its Makers and Marks.* New York: Gorham Mfg. Co., 1888.
12. Bunce, Mrs. Oliver Bell. *What to do; a Companion to Don'ts.* New York: D. Appleton & Co., 1892.
13. Burgess, Frederick William. *Silver, Pewter, Sheffield Plate.* New York: Tudor Publishing Co., 1937.
14. Burton, E. Milby. *South Carolina Silversmiths 1690–1860.* Charleston, S.C.: The Charleston Museum, 1942.
15. Chapman, Robert. *The Portrait of a Scholar.* London: Oxford University Press, 1920.
16. *History of Chicago; Its Commercial and Manufacturing Interests and Industry.* Chicago: Church, Goodwin & Cushing, 1862.
17. Crosby, Everett Umberto. *Ninety-five Percent Perfect (The Spoon Primer). Silversmiths of Old Nantucket.* Nantucket, Mass.: Tataukimo Press, 1953.
18. Currier, Ernest M. *Early American Silversmiths; List of New York City Smiths 1815–1841.* Portland, Me.: Southworth—Athoenson Press, 1938.
19. Currier, Ernest M. *Early American Silversmiths; The Newbury Spoonmakers.* New York: Privately Printed, 1930.
20. Curtis, George Munson. *Early Silver of Connecticut and its Makers.* Meriden, Conn.: International Silver Co., 1913.
21. Cutten, George Barton. *Silversmiths of Georgia.* Savannah, Ga.: The Pigeonhole Press.
22. Cutten, George Barton. *Silversmiths of North Carolina.* Raleigh, N.C.: The State

Department of Archives and History, 1948.
23. Cutten, George Barton. *Silversmiths of Virginia.* Richmond, Va.: The Dietz Press, 1952.
24. Cutten, George Barton. *The Silversmiths, Watchmakers and Jewelers of the State of New York outside New York City.* Hamilton, N.Y.: Privately Printed, 1939.
25. Cutten, George Barton and Cutten, Minnie Warren. *The Silversmiths of Utica.* Hamilton, N.Y.: Privately Printed, 1936.
26. Downing, Andrew Jackson. *A Treatise on the Theory of Landscape Gardening adapted to North America.* New York & London: Wiley & Putnam; Boston: C. C. Little & Co., 1841.
27. Downing, Andrew Jackson. *Cottage Residences.* New York & London: Wiley & Putnam, 1842.
28. Downing, Andrew Jackson. *The Architecture of Country Houses.* New York: D. Appleton & Co., 1851.
29. Dyer, Walter Alden. *Early American Craftsmen.* New York: The Century Company, 1915.
30. Eastlake, Charles L. *Hints on Household Taste.* Boston: Houghton, (Sixth Edition) 1881.
31. Eberlein, Harold Donaldson and McClure, Abbot. *The Practical Book of Early American Arts and Crafts.* Philadelphia & London: J. B. Lippincott Co., 1916.
32. Eberlein, Harold Donaldson and McClure, Abbot. *The Practical Book of American Antiques.* Garden City, N.Y.: Halcyon House, by special arrangement with J. B. Lippincott Co., 1948.
33. Edmonds, Walter D. *The First Hundred Years.* Oneida, N.Y.: Oneida, Ltd., 1958.
34. *General Directory and Business Advertiser of the City of Chicago for the Year 1844,* with a Historical Sketch and statistics extending from 1837 to 1844 by J. W. Norris. Chicago: Ellis & Fergus, 1844.
35. Elwell, Newton W. *Colonial Silverware.* Boston: G. H. Palley & Co., 1899.
36. Ensko, Robert. *Makers of Early American Silver.* New York: Trow Press, 1915.
37. Ensko, Stephen G. C. *American Silversmiths and Their Marks.* New York: Privately Printed, 1927.
38. Ensko, Stephen G. C. *American Silversmiths and Their Marks II.* New York: Robert Ensko, Inc., 1937.
39. Ensko, Stephen G. C. *American Silversmiths and Their Marks III.* New York: Robert Ensko, Inc., 1948.
40. Ensko, Stephen G. C. and Wenham, Edward. *English Silver, 1675–1825.* New York: Robert Ensko, Inc., 1945.
41. Fales, Mrs. Martha Lou Gandy. *American Silver in the Henry Francis Dupont Winterthur Museum.* Winterthur, Del.: The Museum, 1958.
42. *Directory of Chicago for 1839.* Chicago: Fergus Printing Co., 1876.
43. *General Business Directory and Business Advertiser of the City of Chicago for 1844.* Chicago: Fergus Printing Co., 1843–44.
44. *General Directory and Business Advertiser of the City of Chicago for 1845–46.* Chicago: Fergus Printing Co., 1845.
45. *General Directory and Business Advertiser of the City of Chicago for 1846–47.* Chicago: Fergus Printing Co., 1853.
46. *General Directory and Business Advertiser of the City of Chicago for 1850.* Chicago: Fergus Printing Co., 1850.
47. *General Directory and Business Advertiser of the City of Chicago for 1853–54.* Chicago: Fergus Printing Co., 1853.
48. *Pattern Book for Jewelers, Gold and Silversmiths.* London: A. Fischer, 1883.
49. Franklin, Benjamin. *The Life of Ben-*

jamin Franklin, written by himself. Philadelphia: J. B. Lippincott & Co., 1875.
50. French, Hollis. *A List of Early American Silversmiths and Their Marks.* New York: Walpole Society, 1917.
51. Gibb, George Sweet. *The Whitesmiths of Taunton.* Cambridge, Mass.: Harvard University Press, 1943.
52. *Annual Report of the Commissioner of Patents.* Washington: Government Printing Office, Editions of 1847, 1849; 1850–61; 1904–06; 1907–08.
53. *Manufactures of the United States in 1860.* Washington: Government Printing Office, 1865.
54. *Official Gazette of the U. S. Patent Office.* Washington: U. S. Patent Office—Government Printing Office, Editions of 1873 through 1910.
55. Graham, James, Jr. *Early American Silver Marks.* New York: Privately Printed, 1936.
56. *The American Chesterfield,* or the Way to Wealth, Honor and Distinction, being collections from the letters of Lord Chesterfield to his son, and tracts from other eminent authors on the subject of politeness; with alterations and additions suited to the youth of the United States. By a member of the Philadelphia bar. Philadelphia: John Grigg, 1828; Grigg & Elliot, 1833.
57. *Directory of New England Manufacturers.* Boston: G. D. Hall, 18—.
58. Hall, John. *The Cabinet Makers Assistant.* Baltimore: J. D. Murphy, 1840.
59. Hammerslough, Philip H. *American Silver Collected by Philip Hammerslough.* Hartford, Conn.: Privately Printed, 1958. Vol. II, 1960.
60. Harrington, Jessie. *Silversmiths of Delaware, 1700–1850.* Delaware National Society of Colonial Dames of America, 1939.
61. Hayden, Arthur. *Chats on Old Sheffield Plate.* London: T. F. Unwin, Ltd., 1924.
62. Hayden, Arthur. *Chats on Old Silver.* New York: A. A. Wyn, 1949.
63. Hiatt, Noble W. and Lucy F. *The Silversmiths of Kentucky.* Louisville, Ky.: The Standard Printing Co., 1954.
64. Hipkiss, Edwin J. *The Philip Leffingwell Spalding Collection of Early American Silver.* Cambridge, Mass.: Harvard University Press, 1945.
65. Holland, John A. *A Treatise on the Progressive Improvement and Present State of the Manufactures in Metal.* London: Longman, Brown, Green and Longman, 1831–1834.
66. *Silver Wedding of John B. and Mary E. Hough.* Hillside, Mass.: The Committee, 1869.
67. Hughes, George Bernard. *Small Antique Silverware.* London: Batsford, 1957.
68. Hughes, George Bernard. *Three Centuries of English Domestic Silver. 1500–1820.* New York: Funk, 1952.
69. Huitsma, Muriel Cutten. *Early Cleveland Silversmiths.* Cleveland: Gates Publishing Co., 1953.
70. *Manufacturing and Mercantile Resources of Indianapolis, Indiana.* n.p., 1883.
71. James, George B., Jr. (compiled by) *Souvenir Spoons.* Boston: A. W. Fuller & Co., 1891.
72. *Sterling Flatware Pattern Index.* (First Edition) New York: The Jewelers' Circular-Keystone.
73. *Trade Marks of the Jewelry and Kindred Trades.* New York: The Jewelers' Circular-Keystone. Editions of 1898, 1904, 1910, 1915, 1922.
74. Jones, Edward Alfred. *Old Silver of Europe and America from Early Times to the 19th Century.* Philadelphia: J. B. Lippincott Co., 1928.

75. Kirkland, Mrs. Caroline Mathilda. *The Evening Book, or Fireside Talk on Morals and Manners,* with Sketches of Western Life. New York: C. Scribner, 1853.
76. Kirkland, Miss E. S. *Speech and Manners for Home and School.* Chicago: Jansen, McClurg & Co., 1878.
77. Knittle, Rhea Mansfield. *Early Ohio Silversmiths and Pewterers 1787–1847* (Ohio Frontier Series). Cleveland: Calvert-Hatch Co., 1943.
78. Kovel, Ralph M. and Terry H. *American Silver, Pewter and Silver Plate.* New York: Crown Publishers, 1961.
79. Leggett, M. D. (compiled and published under the direction of), *Subject Matter of Patents Issued by the U. S. Patent Office from 1790 to 1873.* Washington: U. S. Patent Office—Government Printing Office, 1874.
80. Lichten, Frances. *Decorative Art of Victoria's Era.* London & New York: Charles Scribner's Sons, 1950.
81. Lucas, Walter Arndt. *100 Years of Railroad Cars.* New York: Simmons-Boardman Publishing Corp., 1958.
82. Lynes, Russell. *The Domesticated Americans.* New York: Harper & Row, 1963.
83. MacFarlane, John James. *Manufacturing in Philadelphia, 1683–1912.* Philadelphia: The Philadelphia Commercial Museum, 1912.
84. Macrae, David. *The Americans at Home.* Edinburgh: Edmonton & Douglas, 1870.
85. *MacRae's Blue Book.* Chicago: MacRae's Blue Book Company, Selected Editions.
86. May, Earl Chapin. *Century of Silver.* New York: Robert M. McBride, 1947.
87. Mencken, August. *The Railroad Passenger Car;* an illustrated history of the first hundred years. Baltimore: Johns Hopkins Press, 1957.
88. Morton, Agnes M. *Etiquette; an answer to the riddle, When, Where, How?* Philadelphia: The Penn Publishing Co., 1892.
89. *Manufacturing and Mercantile Resources of Nashville, Tennessee.* n.p., 1883.
90. Okie, Howard Pitcher. *Old Silver and Old Sheffield Plate.* New York: Doubleday, Doran & Company, 1928.
91. Ormsbee, Thomas H. *Collecting Antiques in America.* Deerfield Books, Hearthside Press, 1940, 1962.
92. Phillips, John Marshall. *The Practical Book of American Silver.* Philadelphia: Lippincott, 1949.
93. Pleasants, J. H. and Sill, H. *Maryland Silversmiths.* Baltimore: Lord Baltimore Press, 1930.
94. Pollen, John Hungerford. *Gold and Silversmiths Work.* London: Kensington Museum. Published for the Committee of Council for Education by Chapman & Hall, 1879.
95. Prime, Mrs. A. C. *Three Centuries of Historic Silver.* Philadelphia: Society of Colonial Dames, 1938.
96. *Rhode Island Silversmiths.* Providence, R.I.: Rhode Island School of Design. Ackerman Standard Company, 1936.
97. Rogers, James Swift. *James Rogers of New London, Connecticut, and his Descendants.* Boston: Privately Published, 1902.
98. *Decorum, A Practical Treatise on Etiquette and Dress of the Best American Society.* Chicago: J. A. Ruth & Co., 1878.
99. Schlesinger, Arthur M. *Learning How to Behave.* New York: The Macmillan Company, 1945.
100. Schild, Joan Lynn. *Silversmiths of Rochester.* Rochester, N.Y.: Rochester Museum of Arts and Science, 1944.
101. Semon, Kurt M. *A Treasury of Old Silver.* New York: The McBride Co., 1947.
102. *Chicago Business Directory for 1864–65.* Chicago: W. R. Spencer, 1864.
103. *Etiquette for Americans by a Woman of*

Fashion. Chicago & New York: H. S. Stone & Co., 1898.

104. Taylor, Gerald. *Silver.* London: Penguin Books, Ltd., 1956.
105. *Thomas Register of American Manufacturers.* New York, N.Y.: Thomas Publishing Company, Editions of 1906 through 1920.
106. Thorn, C. Jordan. *Handbook of American Silver and Pewter Marks.* New York: Tudor Publishing Co., 1949.
107. Trollope, Anthony. *North America.* London: Chapman & Hall, 1866.
108. Trollope, Mrs. Frances. *Domestic Manners of the Americans.* London: Whittacher, Treacher & Co., 1832.
109. Van Voorhees Association. *Historical Handbook of the Van Voorhees Family in the Netherlands and America.* New Brunswick, N.J.: Thatcher-Anderson Co., 1935.
110. Veblen, Thorstein. *Theory of the Leisure Class.* New York: Macmillan, 1899.
111. *Mid-Georgian Domestic Silver.* London: Victoria & Albert Museum: Her Majesty's Stationery Office, 1952.
112. *Victorian and Edwardian Decorative Arts.* London: Victoria & Albert Museum: Her Majesty's Stationery Office, 1952.
113. Wardle, Patricia. *Victorian Silver and Silver Plate.* New York: Thomas Nelson & Sons, 1963.
114. Wenham, Edward. *Domestic Silver of Great Britain and Ireland.* New York and London: The Oxford University Press, 1931.
115. Wenham, Edward. *Old Silver for Modern Settings.* New York: Alfred A. Knopf, 1951.
116. Wenham, Edward. *The Practical Book of American Silver.* Philadelphia: Lippincott, 1949.
117. Williams, Carl Mark. *Silversmiths of New Jersey.* Philadelphia: G. S. McManus Co., 1949.
118. Wise, William. *Silversmith of Old New York: Myer Meyers.* New York: Farrar, Straus & Cudahy.
119. Wyler, Seymour B. *The Book of Old Silver, English, American and Foreign.* New York: Crown Publishers, 1937.
120. Wyler, Seymour B. *The Book of Sheffield Plate.* New York: Crown Publishers, 1949.
121. Yates, Raymond P. and Marguerite W. *A Guide to Victorian Antiques.* New York: Harper & Bros., 1949.

ARTICLES, BROCHURES, BULLETINS, PERIODICALS, ETC.

122. Alexander, Dr. A. E. "Tiffany's Sterling: History and Status." Pamphlet reprinted from *The National Jeweler.* 1963.
123. *Antiques Magazine.* Selected Issues, 1922 through 1964.
124. *From Colony to Nation.* Exhibition of American painting, silver and architecture from 1650 to the War of 1812. Chicago: Art Institute of Chicago, 1949.
125. Avery, Clara Louise. *A Study Based on the Clearwater Collection.* New York: Metropolitan Museum of Art.
126. *17th and 18th Century Silversmiths.* Exhibited at The Museum June to November 1906. Boston: Museum of Fine Arts, 1906.
127. Bridwell, M. M. "Kentucky Silversmiths before 1850." *Filson Club History Quarterly.* Vol. XVI, No. 2, April 1942.
128. Coburn, Claire M. "The Art of the Silversmith." *Good Housekeeping Magazine.* December 1906.
129. Conant, William C. "The Silver Age." Reprinted from "Scribner's Magazine" in *Description of the Works.* Providence, R.I.: Gorham Mfg. Co.: Livermore & Knight. (Second Edition) 1892.

130. *Connecticut Manufacturers.* No. 11. March 15, 1939.
131. *Connecticut Manufacturers.* No. 5; Additions. August 25, 1939.
132. Cutten, George Barton. *Silversmiths of Northampton, Massachusetts and Vicinity Down to 1850.* Pamphlet. n.p. n.d.
133. Cutten, George Barton. "Ten Silversmith Families of New York State." Booklet reprinted from *New York State History,* January 1946.
134. Cutten, George Barton and Ver Nooy, Amy Pearse. "Silversmiths of Poughkeepsie." *Year Book, Dutchess County Historical Society.* Vol. 30, 1945.
135. Defenbacher, D. "Knives, Forks and Spoons." Minneapolis, Minn.: *The Everyday Art Quarterly,* Walker Art Center. 1951.
136. *Bulletin of the Detroit Historical Society.* Vol. IX, No. 2, November, 1952.
137. *Good Housekeeping Magazine.* Selected Issues, 1890–1910.
138. *Gorham Salesman's Manual.* Providence, R.I.: The Gorham Co., 1930.
139. *History of the Gorham Manufacturing Co.* Providence, R.I.: The Gorham Company, 1945.
140. *Beautiful Tables.* (booklet) Providence, R.I.: The Gorham Co., 1960.
141. Parton, James. "Silver and Silver Plate." *Harper's New Monthly Magazine,* September 1868. Vol. XXXVII, No. CCXX.
142. Hill, Janet (compiled by). *Rumford Dainties and Household Helps.* Providence, R.I.: Rumford Chemical Works. n.d.
143. Holbrook, John S. *Silver for the Dining Room.* Cambridge, Mass.: Printed for The Gorham Company by The University Press. 1912.
144. *1847 Rogers Bros. Silver.* Meriden, Conn.: The International Silver Co., 1960.
145. *A Few Facts about The International Silver Co.* (booklet) Meriden, Conn.: The International Silver Co., 1937.
146. *The Story of Silverplate.* (booklet) Meriden, Conn.: The International Silver Co., n.d.
147. *The Jewelers' Circular.* Selected Issues, 1890–1910.
148. *The Jewelers Circular–Keystone.* Selected Issues.
149. *Jewelers' Review.* Selected Issues, 1887–1910.
150. *The Jewelers' Weekly.* Selected Issues, 1885–1900.
151. *Jeweler, Silversmith and Watchmaker.* Selected Issues, 1874–1880.
152. *The Keystone.* Selected Issues, 1892–1910.
153. *The Fine Art of Hand Chasing Kirk Repousse Sterling Silver.* Baltimore: Samuel Kirk & Son, Inc., n.d.
154. *Kirk in U. S. Museums.* (booklet) Baltimore: Samuel Kirk & Son, Inc., 1960, 1966.
155. *The Story of the House of Kirk.* Baltimore: Samuel Kirk & Son, Inc., 1914.
156. *Your Silver Notes.* Baltimore: Samuel Kirk & Son, Inc., n.d.
157. *Ladies Home Journal.* Selected Issues, 1894–1910.
158. *Life Magazine.* Selected Issues, 1884–1910.
159. *Early American Silver.* New York: Metropolitan Museum of Art, 1955.
160. *Hudson–Fulton Celebration.* Catalog of Exhibition. New York: Metropolitan Museum of Art, 1909.
161. Miller, V. Isabelle. *Silver of New York Makers, Late Seventeenth Century to 1900.* New York: Women's Committee of the Museum of the City of New York, 1938.
162. *Silver by New York Makers.* New York: Museum of the City of New York, 1937.
163. *National Jewelers' Speedbook No. 11.* Chicago: C. P. Engelhard & Co., n.d.

164. *Netter Collection Auction Catalog*. Cincinnati: n.p. 1881.
165. *Bella Landauer Collection.* New York: The New York Historical Society.
166. *New York Historical Society Silver Exhibit.* The Society, 1966.
167. *Designers Scrapbook.* Oneida, N.Y.: Oneida, Ltd., n.d.
168. *Exhibition of Old American and English Silver.* Philadelphia: Pennsylvania Museum and School of Industrial Art, 1917.
169. Stempel, Charlotte. "Proud Heritage at C. D. Peacock."*Guilds,* Vol. XVII. No. 8, September 1962. Los Angeles: American Gem Society.
170. Summers, Frances Rudolph (compiled by). *Mobile Craftsmen.* Mobile, Ala.: Historic Mobile Preservation Society, n.d.
171. *Silver Salesletter* (pamphlet). New York: Tiffany & Co., October, 1960.
172. *The oldest and proudest silversmithing tradition in America.* (brochure). Newburyport, Mass.: Towle Silversmiths, 1964.
173. *The Story of Sterling.* Newburyport, Mass.: The Towle Mfg. Co., 1964.
174. *Towle Silversmiths.* Newburyport, Mass.: The Towle Mfg. Co., 1964.
175. Correspondence and Interviews. N. D. Turner.
176. *Masterpieces of American Silver.* Richmond, Va.: Virginia Museum of Fine Arts, 1960.
177. Wallace, Floyd, Sr. "History of Wallace Silversmiths." *Wallace News,* June 1947. Wallingford, Conn.: R. Wallace & Sons Mfg. Co.
178. *Wallace Silverplate.* (pamphlet). Wallingford, Conn.: R. Wallace & Sons Mfg. Co., n.d.
179. *Watchmaker & Jeweler.* Selected Issues, 1869–1874.
180. *Early Connecticut Silver.* New Haven, Conn.: Yale University Gallery of Fine Arts. Yale University Press, 1935.

CATALOGS

181. *Annual Illustrated Price Lists and Catalogues.* Chicago: Benjamin Allen & Co., Editions of 1875, 1880, 1881, 1883–86, 1888–99, 1901–10.
182. *Morning Glory.* Sag Harbor, N.Y.: Alvin Mfg. Co., n.d.
183. *Silverware Catalog.* Bristol, Conn.: The American Silver Co., n.d.
184. *Catalog L.* Providence, R.I.: Baird-North Company, 1908.
185. *Catalogues.* Chicago: The Albert C. Becken Co., Editions of 1892 through 1904.
186. *The Verona Pattern.* North Attleboro, Mass.: R. Blackinton & Co., n.d.
187. *DuBarry.* New York: Black, Starr & Frost, 1905.
188. *Illustrated Catalogue and Price List of Electro-Plated Tableware, Nickel Silver and Britannia Spoons, etc.* East Haddam, Conn.: Luther Boardman & Son, 1880.
189. *Catalogues.* Chicago: Butler Bros., Editions of Jan.-Dec. 1895; Jan.-June 1900; Jan.-June 1905; July-Dec. 1910.
190. *Catalogue of Silverware, Jewelry, Watches, Diamonds.* Cambridge, Mass.: Carter, Sloan and Co., The Riverside Press, 1881.
191. *Catalogue.* Chicago: W. B. Clapp, Young & Co., 1888.
192. *Catalogue and Price List.* Birmingham, Conn.: Derby Silver Co., 1883.
193. *Catalogue of Flatware.* Birmingham, Conn.: Derby Silver Co., 1883.
194. *Illustrated Catalogue of the Jewelry Department.* Chicago: Marshall Field & Co., 1887.
195. *Illustrated Wholesale Price List and Catalogue.* Chicago: The Fort Dearborn Watch and Clock Co., 1910.

196. *New Illustrated Catalogue and Price List (No. 37)*. Chicago: R. Chester Frost & Co., 1891.
197. *Catalogue*. Chicago: Giles, Bro. & Co.
198. *Catalogue of Electro Plated Flatware*. Providence, R.I.: The Gorham Co., 1911.
199. *Catalogue of Sterling Silver Flatware by The Gorham Company*. Providence, R.I.: The Gorham Co., 1910.
200. *The Buttercup*. Providence, R.I.: The Gorham Company, 1900.
201. *The Marguerite*. Providence, R.I.: The Gorham Company, n.d.
202. *The Norfolk*. Providence, R.I.: The Gorham Company, n.d.
203. *The Virginiana*. Providence, R.I.: The Gorham Company, n.d.
204. *Catalogue and Price List*. Wallingford, Conn.: Hall, Elton & Co., 1867.
205. *Catalogue and Price List*. Wallingford, Conn.: Hall, Elton & Co., 1875.
206. *Catalogue*. Waterbury, Conn.: Holmes, Booth & Haydens, 1884.
207. *Catalogue*. Bridgeport, Conn.: Homes & Edwards Silver Co., 1885.
208. *Condensed Catalogue and Price List*. Bridgeport, Conn.: Holmes & Edwards Silver Co., 1895.
209. *Catalogue No. 26*. Bridgeport, Conn.: Holmes & Edwards Silver Co., 1903.
210. *Catalogue No. 24*. Chicago: Home Supply Association, 1880.
211. *Silver, Gold, and Precious Stones*. Chicago: M. Matson & Co., 1886.
212. *Catalogue*. Meriden, Conn.: Meriden Britannia Co., 1857.
213. *Catalogue*. Meriden, Conn.: Meriden Britannia Co., 1879.
214. *Catalogue*. Meriden, Conn.: Meriden Britannia Co., 1882.
215. *Catalogue*. Meriden, Conn.: Meriden Britannia Co., 1887.
216. *Catalogue*. Meriden, Conn.: Meriden Britannia Co., 1893.
217. *Catalogue*. Meriden, Conn.: Meriden Britannia Co., 1895.
218. *Catalogue*. Meriden, Conn.: Meriden Britannia Co., 1898.
219. *Illustrated Catalogue of Silver and Plated Ware*. Albany, N.Y.: Mulford, Wendell & Co., n.d.
220. *Catalogue*. Chicago: National Merchandise Supply Co., 1891.
221. *The New York Jeweler, Vol. III and trade price list No. 30*. New York: S. F. Meyers Co., 1889.
222. *The New York Jeweler*. New York: S. F. Meyers Co., 1900.
223. *The New York Jeweler*. New York: S. F. Meyers Co., 1905.
224. *Electro Silver Plated Tableware Catalogue*. Niagara Falls, N.Y.: Niagara Silver Co., n.d.
225. *Annual Price List for 1872*. Chicago: B. F. Norris Co., 1872.
226. *Community Silver Catalogue*. Oneida, N.Y.: Oneida Community, Ltd., 1910.
227. *Catalogue and Price List*. Cincinnati: Oskamp, Nolting & Co., 1895.
228. *Great American Jewelry Catalogue*. Cincinnati: Oskamp, Nolting & Co., 1906.
229. *Catalogue*. Chicago: Albert Pick & Co., 1910–11.
230. *Illustrated Catalogue and Price List*. Taunton, Mass.: Reed & Barton, 1877.
231. *Illustrated Catalogue*. Taunton, Mass.: Reed & Barton, 1885.
232. *Reed & Barton General Catalogue No. 47 in Four Parts*. Cambridge, Mass.: The University Press, n.d.
233. *Catalogue*. New York: Reed & Barton, n.d.
234. *23d Annual Catalogue & Price List*. Chicago: E. V. Roddin & Co.
235. *Abridged Pocket List No. 37, 1847 Rogers Bros.* Hartford, Conn. n.d.
236. *Catalogue No. 38*. Hartford, Conn.: 1847 Rogers Bros., 1891.

237. *Appendix No. 38*. Hartford, Conn.: 1847 Rogers Bros., n.d.
238. *Catalogue No. 43*. Meriden, Conn.: 1847 Rogers Bros., 1896.
239. *Catalogue of 1847 Rogers Bros. Silverware*. Meriden, Conn.: 1900.
240. *Rogers Bros. Price List; Spoons, Forks, Knives, etc.* Meriden, Conn.: 1904.
241. *Catalogue No. 70, 1847 Rogers Bros.* Meriden, Conn.: 1905.
242. *Catalogue*. Waterbury, Conn.: Rogers & Bro., n.d.
243. *Catalogue*. Waterbury, Conn.: Rogers & Hamilton, 1888.
244. *Catalogue*. Waterbury, Conn.: Rogers & Hamilton, 1889.
245. *Catalogue*. Meriden, Conn.: Rogers & Hamilton, 1909.
246. *Cutlery Catalogue*. Hartford & Wallingford, Conn.: Simeon L. & George H. Rogers Co., n.d.
247. *Catalogue*. Meriden, Conn.: Rogers, Smith & Co., 1885–86.
248. *Catalogue No. 47*. New York: Wm. A. Rogers, Ltd., n.d.
249. *Catalogue No. 50*. New York: Wm. A. Rogers, Ltd., n.d.
250. *Silver Plated Flatware, Catalogue No. 54*. New York: Wm. A. Rogers, Co., n.d.
251. *Catalogue No. 56*. New York: Wm. A. Rogers Co., n.d.
252. *Catalogue No. 57*. New York: Wm. A. Rogers Co., n.d.
253. *Catalogue No. 59; The Horeshoe Brand*. New York: Wm. A. Rogers, Ltd., n.d.
254. *Catalogue No. 61; Table Cutlery*. New York: Wm. A. Rogers, Ltd., n.d.
255. *1881 Rogers A-1; Catalogue No. 63*. New York: Wm. A. Rogers Co., n.d.
256. *Catalogue*. Hartford, Conn.: Wm. Rogers Mfg. Co., 1872.
257. *Catalogue*. Hartford, Conn.: Wm. Rogers Mfg. Co., 1892.
258. *Catalogue*. Hartford, Conn.: Wm. Rogers Mfg. Co., 1895.
259. *Catalogue*. Hartford, Conn.: Wm. Rogers Mfg. Co., 1897.
260. *Catalogues*. Chicago: Sears, Roebuck & Co. Editions of 1894, 1896, 1898 (No. 105), 1902 (No. 111), 1902 (No. 111R), 1903 (No. 112), 1903 (No. 113), 1905 (No. 114C), 1906 (No. 116), 1907 (No. 135), 1908 (No. 117), 1908 (No. 108), 1910 (Spring), 1910 (Fall).
261. *Christmas Catalogue*. Cincinnati: John Shillito Co., 1878.
262. *Catalogue*. Cincinnati: The John Shillito Co., 1884.
263. *Catalogue*. Troy, N.Y.: F. W. Sim & Co., 1897.
264. *Catalogue*. Wallingford, Conn.: Simpson, Hall, Miller & Co., 1878.
265. *Catalogue*. Wallingford, Conn.: Simpson, Hall, Miller & Co., 1901.
266. *What Shall I Give for a Present?* Boston: Steele & Sons—The Gorham Mfg. Co., 1877.
267. *Handwrought Sterling Silverware, The Stieff Company, Silversmiths. Baltimore, Md.* Cambridge, Mass.: The University Press, 1910.
268. Tilton, George P. (compiled by). *Newbury*. Newburyport, Mass.: The Towle Mfg. Co., 1904.
269. Tilton, George P. (compiled by). *Georgian (with catalog)*. Newburyport, Mass.: The Towle Mfg. Co., 1899.
270. *The Colonial Book* (*with catalog*). Newburyport, Mass.: The Towle Mfg. Co., 1910.
271. *Account of the Life of Marie Joseph Paul Yves Roche Gilbert Dumatier, Marquis de LaFayette* (*with catalog*). Newburyport, Mass.: The Towle Mfg. Co., 1910.
272. *Paul Revere* (*with catalog*). Newburyport, Mass.: The Towle Mfg. Co., n.d.
273. *Irian*. Wallingford, Conn.: R. Wallace & Sons Mfg. Co., n.d.

274. *Catalog*. Wallingford, Conn.: R. Wallace & Sons Mfg. Co., 1914.
275. *Catalog B 15*. Wallingford, Conn.: R. Wallace & Sons Mfg. Co., n.d.
276. *Catalogues*. Chicago, Ill.: Montgomery Ward & Co., Editions of 1872, 1876, 1877–78, 1881, 1895, 1904–05.
277. *Catalogue*. Brooklyn, N.Y.: E. G. Webster & Bro., 1879.
278. *Sterling Silver Wares of the Whiting Manufacturing Company*. Bridgeport, Conn.: Whiting Mfg. Co., n.d.
279. *Illustrated Catalogue*. Sheffield & London: Henry Wilkinson & Co., 1855.
280. *Williams Quality Silverplate*. Naugus, Conn.: Williams Bros. Mfg. Co., n.d.
281. *Illustrated Price List*. Chicago, Ill.: Otto Young & Co., 1895.

Index

Atlee, Charles, 238
Atmore, E. W., 238
Atmore, Marshall, 238
Attica pattern, 146, 387
Atwater, Edgar, 334
Atwell, G. E., 238
Audubon pattern, 75, 115, 173, 362
Aumont pattern, 387
Aurora patterns, 97, 136, 362, 387
Aurora Silver Plate Co., 35, 136, 334
Austen, David, 239
Autumn pattern, 125, 362
Auvergne pattern, 116, 362
Avalon patterns, 130, 142, 362, 387
Avon patterns, 94, 150, 362, 387
Ayers & Badger, 239
Ayers & Beard, 239, 241
Ayers & Dunning, 239, 257
Ayers, Socrates, 239
Ayres, Elias, 239
Ayres, T. R. J., 239
Azalea pattern, 362
Aztec pattern, 388

B (trademark), 317, 334
Babbitt & Crossman, 27, 342
Babbitt, Crossman & Co., 27, 342
Babbitt, Isaac, 25, 27
Babbitt Metal, 27
Babcock, James A., 239
Baby spoons, 174, 204, 218, 220, 222, 225–28, 406
Bacall, Thomas, 239
Bachman, A., 239
Backes, J. T. P., 239
Backstamps, 21, 67
Badger, A. M., 239
Badger & Lillie, 239
Baen, John, 239
Baggs, William, 239
Bagley, Abbott G., 239
Bailey, Banks & Biddle Co., 317
Bailey, Bradbury M., 239
Bailey & Bros., 239
Bailey, Charles, 239
Bailey & Co., 239
Bailey, Edward S., 239
Bailey, E. E., 239
Bailey, E. E., & Co., 239
Bailey, E. S., & Co., 239
Bailey, Hugh, 239
Bailey, James, 239
Bailey, J. T., 239
Bailey & Kitchen, 239, 278
Bailey, Major C. T. P., 13
Bailey & Owen, 239, 291
Bailey & Parker, 239
Bailey & Parmenter, 239
Bailey, Roswell H., 239
Bailey, Samuel, 239
Bailey, S. C., 239
Bailey, S. G., 239
Bailey, S. P., 239
Bailey, T. A., 239
Bailey, Thomas, 239
Bailey, W. E. J., 239
Bailey, William, 239
Baily, William, 239
Bain, Henry, 239
Baird, Pleasant H., 239
Baker, Anson, 239
Baker, E. G. A., 239
Baker, Eleazer, 239
Baker, Elias, 239
Baker, George A., 239
Baker, George M., 239
Baker, James M., 239
Baker-Manchester Co., 317, 324
Baker, S., 240
Baker & Shriver, 239, 301
Baldwin, Edgar, 240
Baldwin, Jedediah, 240
Baldwin, Stanley S., 240
Ball, Albert, 240
Ball, Black & Co., 240, 243, 332
Ball, Calvin S., Jr., 240
Ball, Charles, 240
Ball, David, 240
Ball, Henry, 240
Ball, S. S., 240
Ball, Tompkins & Black, 240, 243, 308
Ball, True M., 240
Ball Twist pattern, 116, 362
Baltimore mark, 31, 322, 333
Baltimore, Md., 19, 20, 31, 68
Baltimore Rose pattern, 102, 363
Baltimore Scroll pattern, 363
Baltimore silver, 67
Baltimore Silversmiths Mfg. Co., 317
Baltimore Sterling Silver Co., 317, 328
Balzac pattern, 98, 363
Bamboo patterns, 97, 108, 363
Banker, Benjamin B., 240
Bankers, silversmiths as, 17
Banquet Plate, 334, 337
Baptista, Edward, 240
Barber, James, 240
Barber, J. C., 240
Barber, Lemuel D., 240
Barber, William, 240
Barbere, Stephen, 240
Barbiere, G., 240
Barbiere, Stephen P., 240
Barbour Silver Company, 317, 334
Barclay, James, 240
Barclay, Orin, 240
Bard, Conrad, 240
Bard & Hoffman, 240, 272
Bard & Lamont, 240, 279
Barge, Thomas, 240
Barger, George, 240
Barlow, E. C., 240
Barnaby, S. S., 240
Barnard, Edward, & Sons, 349
Barnard, Samuel, 240
Barnes, James, 240
Barnes, James M., 240
Barnes, James P., 240
Barnes, Moses D., 240
Barney, James, 240
Barney & Valentine, 240, 309

Clark, Jonas C., 250
Clark, L. W. & J. C., 250, 251
Clark, Levi, 250
Clark, Lewis W., 251
Clark, Patrick F., 251
Clark & Pelletreau, 292
Clark, Philip, 251
Clark, Rackett & Co., 250, 295
Clark, Thomas W., 251
Classicists, 68
Classic Revival, 68
Clayton, Barns, 251
Clayton, Elias P., 251
Clayton, Richard, 251
Clematis pattern, 96, 110, 130, 364
Clement, James W., 251
Clements & Ashburn, 251
Clements, James, 251
Cleveland, Ohio, 80
Cleveland, Mrs. Grover, 37, 38, 39
Cleveland, President Grover, 37, 38, 39
Cleveland, William, 251
Clift, Josiah, 251
Clifton patterns, 117, 143, 364, 389
Climber pattern, 160, 389
Cline, B., 251
Cline, C. & P., 251
Cline, Charles, Jr., 251
Cline, J., 251
Cline, Philip, 251
Cline, Walter, 251
Cline, W. & J., 251
Clinton patterns, 103, 157, 365, 389
Cloeta pattern, 130, 365
Cloutman, Thomas B., 251
Clover Blossom pattern, 105, 365
Clover pattern, 117, 365
Clovis pattern, 138, 389
Cluny pattern, 95, 165, 365
Cluster, Isaac D., 251
Clyde patterns, 160, 389
CMR (trademark), 318
Coal, 234
Coan, A. L., 251
Coates, Isaac, 251
Coates, William, 251
Coats, A. W., 251
Coats & Boyd, 251
Cobb, Gould & Co., 318
Cobweb pattern, 365
Cochran, William D., 251
Cockrell, James, 251
Cocktail parties, 206, 208
Codding & Heilborn Co., 318
Codman, Willard, 251
Coe, H. H., 251
Coe & Upton, 251
Coeur de Lion pattern, 114, 365
Coffee sets, 206, 211, 215
Coffee spoons, 57, 181, 184, 191, 203, 204, 211, 406
Coffin shape handles, 15, 66
Coffman, William, 251
Cogswell, Henry, 251
Cohen, Albert, 251
Cohen, M. A., 251
Cohen, William, 251
Coin silver, 17, 18, 22, 30, 31, 32, 36, 44, 66, 67, 409
Coit, E., 251
Colbert pattern, 114, 365
Cold meat forks, 180, 183, 184, 194, 198, 203, 204, 207, 211, 406
Cold meat sets, 207, 211
Cole, Albert, 251, 252
Cole, John A., 251, 252
Cole, William Groat, 251
Coleman, Alvan, 251
Coleman, John, 251
Coleman, John F., 251
Coleman, Joseph, 251
Coleman, Nathaniel, 252
Coles, Albert, 251, 252
Coles, Albert, & Co., 91, 252, 318
Coles, John A., 252
Coles & Reynolds, 91, 318, 332
Colfax pattern, 94, 365
Coligni pattern, 97, 365
Coligny pattern, 389
Collectors, pointers for 230–35
Collette, Lambert, 252
Collings, Peleg, 252
Collings & Wallis, 354
Collingwood, Francis, 252
Collins, Blakely, 252
Collins, Patrick, 252
Collins, Selden, 252
Collins, W. A., 252
Collom, David W., 252
Colonade pattern, 147, 389
Colonial patterns, 91, 101, 115, 118, 127, 142, 143, 153, 365, 389
Colonial revival, 79, 82
Colon pattern, 235
Colser, Abraham, 252
Columbia, The (trademark), 340
Columbian Exposition, 47, 63, 78
Columbian pattern, 149, 389
Columbia patterns, 78, 150, 155, 235, 389
Columbine pattern, 123, 365
Colwell & Lawrence, 252, 279
Combination sets, 206, 211
Commel, William, 252
Commonwealth patterns, 122, 145, 365, 389
Commonwealth Silver Co., 318
Community Lake, 28
Community Plate, 47
Como pattern, 162, 235, 389
Compton, William, 252
Comstock Lode, 35
Comyns, Wm., & Sons, 350
Conant pattern, 157, 389
Concord pattern, 149, 158, 389
Conery, A., 252
Coney, John, 15
Connecticut patterns, 124, 365
Connolly, Patrick, 252
Conner, John H., 252
Conner & Stickles, 252, 306
Conning, James, 252
Connor, William J., 252
Conrad, George, 252

Drysdale, William, Jr., 257
DuBarry patterns, 93, 118, 366
Dubasee, Edward, 257
Dubois, Peter, 257
Dubois, Philo, 257
Dubois, Thomas, 257
Dubosq & Baton, 257
Dubosq, Baton & Co., 257
Dubosq, Carrow & Co., 248, 257
Dubosq & Carrow, 248, 257
Dubosq, Francis P., 257
Dubosq, George, 257
Dubosq, Henry, 257
Dubosq, H. & W., 257
Dubosq, Peter, 257
Dubosq, Philip L., 257
Dubosq & Scheer, 257, 299
Dubosq, Theodore, 257
Dubosq, William, 257
Duchess patterns, 79, 109, 128, 366
Duchesse pattern, 79, 112, 366
Duck knives, 184, 189, 207, 405
Duck sets, 207
Duck shears, 192, 207, 407
Ducommun, Henry, 257
Ducommun, Henry, Jr., & Co., 257
Duff, George, 257
Duff, George C., 257
Duffey, George Hurd, 257
Duffey, George Neilson, Major, 257
Duffield, George H., Reverend, 208
Duhme & Co., 257, 319
Duke of York pattern, 128, 366
Dumont pattern, 390
Dunbar & Bangs, 257
Dunbar pattern, 157, 390
Duncan, W. H., 257
Dundas, Pratt, 257
Dundee pattern, 148, 390
Dunham, Rufus, 27
Dunkerley, George, 257
Dunleavey, Robert, 257
Dunlevey, Robert, 257
Dunlevy, Robert, 257
Dunlevy & Dowell, 257
Dunlevy & Wise, 257, 314
Dunn & Cann, 248, 257
Dunn, David, 257
Dunning, ———, 257
Dunning & Crissey, 253, 258
Dunning, Edward, 257
Dunning, Julius, 258
Dunning & Knapp, 257, 278
Dunster pattern, 137, 390
Duplication, patterns in sterling and plate, 40, 76, 77, 82, 360
Dupuy, Bernard, 258
Durgin & Burtt, 258
Durgin, F. A., 258, 319
Durgin, William B., 258
Durgin, William B., Co., 79, 258, 319, 328
Duro Plate (trademark), 341
Duty, *ad valorum*, 24
Duvaine pattern, 366
Dynamo, plating, 49
Eagle Spoon Company, 319, 338
Eagle Sterling Company, 319
Eakins, Samuel, 258
Ealer, Joseph, 258
Earle pattern, 366
Earl Patent Fork, 222
Earnshaw, Alfred, 258
Easley, George, 258
Easter Lily patterns, 90, 112, 123, 135, 367, 390
Easterlings, 31
Easterling Standard, 31
Eastern Carolina Silver Co., 336
Eastlake, Charles L., 73, 74
Eastlake patterns, 73, 74, 139, 140, 155, 390, 391
East Lake patterns, 366
Eastman, Moses, 258
Easton, James II, 258
Easton & Sanford, 258, 299
Eaves, W., 258
Eaves, W., & A. Falize, 258, 260
Eaves, W. T., 258
Eckart, John, 258
Eckel, Alexander P., 258
Eckel, Andrew, 258
Eckert, Valentine, 258
Eckfeldt, Charles, 258
Eckhart, John, 258
Ecuyer, Lewis, 258
Edgewood pattern, 112, 367
Edler, Charles, 258
Edler, J. C., 258
Edmond, William, 258
Edmonds, Walter, 76, 77
Edwardian years, 9, 49, 57, 67, 216
Edward VII pattern, 114
Edwards, George, 28, 46
Edwards, Peter, 258
Egg, Edward, 258
Egg server, poached, 215
Egg spoons, 184, 191, 203, 205, 223, 406
Eglantine pattern, 101, 367
Egyptian patterns, 72, 108, 129, 138, 159, 367, 391
1847 Girl, 65
1847 Rogers Brothers, 44, 46, 63, 65, 108, 148, 149, 150, 170, 171, 231, 235, 327, 339
1865 William Rogers, 343, 344
1881 Rogers, 343, 344
1890 pattern, 149, 391
Eighty-eight pattern, 367
Eighty-three pattern, 100, 367
Ekstrom, John, 11
Elaine patterns, 116, 367, 391
Elberon patterns, 78, 154, 391
Elder, William, 258
Electricity, 40
Electroplate grades, 44, 45, 46, 47, 181, 182
Electroplate, flatware manufacturers, alphabetical list, 333–48
Electroplate, flatware pattern illustrations, 133–62
Electroplate manufacturers, Canadian, alphabetical list, 359
Electroplate manufacturers, English, alphabetical list, 354–58
Electroplating, 42–50, 51, 67–69, 410
Electroplating, home systems, 233, 234

F (trademark), 319, 336
Faber & Hoover, 259, 272
Faber, Otto G., 319
Faber, William, 259
Faber, William B., 336
Faber, William, & Sons, 336
Fabian, H., 259
Factories, 35, 36, 40
Faff, Augustus P., 259
Fagan, B., 259
Fahy Watch Case Co., 317, 345
Fairbanks, ———, 259
Fairbanks & Paul, 259, 292
Fairchild, Artemus O., 259
Fairchild, James L., 259
Fairchild, L. W., & Co., 320
Fairchild & Taylor, 259
Fairfax patterns, 94, 136, 367, 391
Fairfield pattern, 127, 367
Fairie pattern, 150, 170, 391
Fairoaks pattern, 145, 391
Falize, A., 260
Fancy pieces, 183, 232, 316, 360, 410
Fancy Tip pattern, 126, 368
Faneuil patterns, 115, 150, 368, 391
Farmelo, Andrew, 11
Farmington pattern, 141, 391
Farnham, Samuel E., 260
Farr & Co., 260
Farr & Gilbert, 260
Farr, John C., 260
Farr, John S., 260
Farr, Joseph, 260
Farrar, Mrs., 180
Farrington & Hunnewell, 260, 320
Farrington, John, 260
Fatman Brothers, 260
Fatton & Co., 260
Fay & Fisher, 260, 261
Fay, George H., 260
Fay, Henry C., 260
FCo. (trademark), 319
Feather Edge, 15, 410
Feather Edge pattern, 115
Feckhart, August, 260
Felger, Donna, 11
Fellows, Abraham Van B., 260
Fellows, Cargill & Co., 260
Fellows, Ignatius W., 260
Fellows, I. W. & J. K., 260
Fellows, J., & Co., 260
Fellows, James, 260
Fellows, James K., 260
Fellows, Jermiah Chichester, 260
Fellows, Jesse, 260
Fellows, John F., 260
Fellows, Louis S., & Schell, 260
Fellows, Louis Strite, 260
Fellows, Philip M., 260
Fellows & Storm, 260
Fellows, Storm & Cargill, 260
Fenno & Hale, 260
Ferguson, Elijah, 260
Ferrey, Lewis, 260
Ferris, Edward B., 260
Ferris, R., 260
Ferris, William, 260
Ferris, Ziba, 260
Fessenden, ———, 260
Fessenden & Co., 94, 235, 320
Fest, Alfred, 260
Fest & Bro., 260
Fiddle patterns, 66, 67, 85, 96, 368, 392
Fiddle Shell (Alden) pattern, 114, 368
Fiddle Tip, Tipped, Tip't patterns, 85, 109, 368
Fidler, James B., 260
Field, Alfred, & Co., 355
Field, Charles, 260
Field, David E., 260
Field, George, 260
Field, Marshall, & Co., 11, 331–32
Field, Peter, 260
Figured French pattern, 108, 368
Figured Shell pattern, 121, 368
Figured Tipped pattern, 121, 368
Filigree silver patterns, 78, 91, 368
Fillette, Francis, 261
Filley, Harvey, & Sons, 336
Filley, Mead & Caldwell, 43, 248, 261, 336, 339
Finch & Cagger, 248, 261
Finch, Hiram, 261
Finck, William C., Co., 320
Finefield, Samuel, 261
Fine silver, 410
Finn, Albert G., Silver Co., 336
Finney, Francis, 261
Fiorito pattern, 75, 110, 172, 368
First Empire patterns, 77, 102, 368
First Republic, 77
Fischer, A., 69, 71
Fischesser, Jean B., 261
Fish, Isaac, Jr., 261
Fish forks, 180–84, 190, 194, 200, 203, 205, 206, 211, 213, 233, 406
Fish, Willson, 261
Fish knives, 176, 180, 182–84, 189, 194, 200, 205, 206, 211, 213, 233
Fish sets, 176, 206, 208, 211, 213
Fish trowels, 176
Fisher & Champney, 249, 261
Fisher, George, 261
Fisher, George, & Co., 261
Fisher, Henry, 261
Fisher, William, 261
Fitch, Dennis, 261
Fitzer, James, 261
Fitzgerald, G. G. K., 261
Fitzgerald, James, 261
Five o'clock Tea spoon, 166, 167, 184, 191, 206, 223, 231, 406
Flach, George W., 261
Flagler developments, 78
Flanders patterns, 111, 149, 368, 392
Flask, 41
Flat dies, 73
Flat handles, 184, 205, 206, 223, 233
Flatware, 17, 409
Flatware manufacturers, alphabetical list, 316–48
Flatware pattern illustrations, 82–174
Flemington, Nora, 11
Flemish patterns, 124, 146, 159, 368, 392
Flersheim, L. H., 261

Haley, G. W., 268
Haley & Haley, 268
Haley, P., 268
Hall, Abraham B., 268
Hall, Almer, 28
Hall, Boardman & Co., 337
Hall & Bennet, 268
Hall & Brower, 246, 268, 321
Hall, Brower & Co., 246, 268, 321
Hall, Elton & Co., 28, 74, 138, 139, 168, 337
Hall, George, 268
Hall, George W., 268
Hall, Green, 268
Hall & Hewson, 268, 271
Hall, Hewson & Brower, 268, 271, 321
Hall, Hewson & Co., 268, 271
Hall, Hewson & Merrifield, 268, 271, 286
Hall, Ivory, 268
Hall, John, 68, 268
Hall, Ranson E., 268
Hall & Snow, 268, 304
Halleck, Alonzo Corwin, 268
Haller, ———, 268
Halliday, Hiram, 268
Halliday, James H., 268
Halliwell, George William, 268
Hallmarks, 31
Halsel, Charles, 268
Halstrick, Joseph, 268
Hamburg pattern, 101, 370
Hamilton & Adams, 237, 268
Hamilton, Daniel S., 268
Hamilton & Diesinger, 321
Hamilton, James, 268
Hamilton, M. F., & Son, 321
Hamilton Manufacturing Co., 337
Hamilton patterns, 89, 96, 119, 370
Hamilton, R. J., 268
Hamilton, Samuel, 268
Hamilton Watch Co., 330
Hamlet, 216
Hamlin, Cyrus, 268
Hamlin, William, 268
Hammet, Richard, 268
Hampshire pattern, 93, 370
Hampton & Palmer, 291
Hampton pattern, 120, 370
Hand, J., 268
Hand, Joseph S. K., 268
Hand-crafted patterns, 80, 82
Handicraft Shop, The, 80
Hand-Kraft pattern, 370
Handle, John, 268
Hands & Sons, 355
Hands, Thomas, 355
Hanis, Abraham, 268
Hannah, William W., 268
Hannum, John, 268
Hano & Co., 268
Hano, L., 268
Hanover patterns, 98, 153, 215, 370, 393
Hansbrough, Hamlet, 268
Hansell, James, 268
Hanson, Benjamin, 269
Happold, P. V., 11
Harbottle, George, 269
Harbottle & Smith, 269, 303
Hardeman, W., 269
Harding, C. H., 269
Harding, N., & Co., 269
Harding, Newell, 269
Hardman, Jacob N., 269
Hardman, William, 269
Hardy, Stephen, 269
Harker, William, 269
Harker, Willis, 269
Harkins, James, 269
Harlequin patterns, 152, 169, 370, 393
Harold pattern, 147, 393
Harper, Benjamin, 269
Harper, John M., 269
Harper, Thomas E., 269
Harper's Monthly Magazine, 176
Harpur, William W., 269
Harrington, Samuel, 269
Harrington, William, 269
Harris & Co., 269
Harris, C. S., & Sons, 350
Harris, Edward, 269
Harris, Edwin, 269
Harris, George, 269
Harris, Herman, 269
Harris & Kendrick, 277
Harris & Shafer, 39, 269, 300
Harris & Stanwood, 305
Harris & Wilcox, 269, 313
Harrison Brothers & Howson, 350, 355
Harry & Bear, 241, 269
Hart, Eliphaz, 269
Hart, Walter, 269
Hartford, Conn., 43, 44, 51
Hartford pattern, 155, 393
Hartley, Jeremiah, 269
Hartley, Samuel, 269
Hartwell, Samuel S., 269
Harvard College, 78, 180
Harvard patterns, 137, 149, 156, 161, 393
Harvey, Kathleen, 11
Hascy, Alexander R., 269
Hascy, Nelson, 269
Haselwood, George W., 269
Haselwood, William, 269
Hasey, Alexander R., 269
Hasey, Nelson, 269
Hassan, Charles, 269
Hassan, Moses, 269
Hassell, Charles, 269
Hastings, ———, 269
Hastings, B. B., 269
Hatch, B. B., 269
Hatch, Israel A., 269
Haterick, James R., 269
Hathaway, James L., 269
Hattrick, James R., 269
Hattrick & Shannon, 269, 300
Hattrick & Smith, 269
Haviland china, 57
Hawes & Co., 269
Hawkins, James, 269
Hawksworth, Eyre & Co., 350, 355

Hawley, Fuller & Co., 270
Hawley, H. H., & Co., 270
Hawley, H. & H. H., 270
Hawley, Horace H., 270
Hawley, John Dean, 270
Hawley & Leach, 279
Hawley, O. A., 270
Hawley, T. S., 270
Haws, John, 270
Hawthorne patterns, 101, 145, 370, 393
Hawthorn pattern, 121, 370
Hay, John, 270
Hay, William, 356
Hayden Brothers & Co., 270
Hayden, Gregg & Co., 266, 270
Hayden, H. Sidney, 270
Hayden & Whilden, 270, 312
Hayden, William H., 270
Haydock, Eden, 270
Haydock, James B., 270
Haydock, Thomas O., 270
Hayes & Adriance, 270
Hayes, C. B., & Co., 270
Hayes, Charles B., 270
Hayes, Edmund M., 270
Hayes, George, 270
Hayes & McFarland, 325
Hayes, McFarland & Co., 325
Hayes, Peter P., 270
Hayes, Peter P., & Son, 270
Haynes, David, 270
Haynes, D., & Son, 270
Haynes, J. R., 270
Haynes, LaFayette, 270
Hays, George, 270
Hazen & Collins, 270
Hazen, N. L., 270
HD (trademark), 321
HE (trademark), 321
Headman, William, 270
Heasley, Samuel, 270
Heat treating, 33, 40, 49
Hebberd, H., 270
Hebbard, H., 270
Heckman, Archimedes, 270
Hedge, George, 270
Hedger, George, 270
Hedges, David (Daniel), 270
Hedges, Daniel, Jr., 270
Heer, Schofield & Co., 102, 317, 321
Heffron, A. Judson, 270
Hegeman, James, 270
Heilig, John, 270
Heimberg, Gottlieb, 270
Heineman, Daniel, 270
Heineman, L. C., 270
Heineman, L. G., 270
Heiss, James P., 270
Helena patterns, 124, 154, 155, 370, 393
Helgefort, Henry, 270
Helgerfort, Henry, 270
Heller, 75
Heller, Jacob, 270
Helm, Thomas, 270
Hemburgh, George, 270
Hemming Manufacturing Co., 353
Hemphill, Thomas J., 270
Hempsted, D., & Co., 271
Hempsted, Daniel B., 271
Henderson, A. A., 271
Henderson, Adam, 271
Henderson & Lossing, 271, 281
Hendricks, John, 271
Hendrickson, William, 271
Henneman, John A., 271
Henry II pattern, 100, 370
Henry VIII, 31
Hepplewhite furniture, 80
Hepplewhite patterns, 80, 107, 370
Hequembourg, Charles, 271
Hequembourg, Charles Louis, 271
Hequembourg, Theodore, 271
Heraldic patterns, 127, 370
Herbel, A., 271
Hereford pattern, 370
Heringer, Charles, 271
Hermitage pattern, 370
Herrington, William, 271
Herschede Jewelers, 11
Hershey, Arlene, 11
Hewit, C. W., 271
Hews, A., Jr., 271
Hewson, John D., 271
Heyde, Charles, 271
Heydon, Charles W., 271
Hiawatha pattern, 393
Hickingbotham, H. J., 11
Hickman, John, 271
Higgins, F., & Son, 350
Higgins, George E., 271
Hilburn, Jonas Jacob, 271
Hildeburn & Bros., 271
Hildeburn, Samuel, 271
Hildeburn & Watson, 271, 311
Hill, E., 271
Hill, John, 271
Hill & Johnson, 271
Hill, William, 271
Hilliard, Christopher, 271
Hills, C. F., 271
Hillworth, Frederick, 271
Hillyartiner, Philip, 271
Hinckley, Richard, 271
Hinckley, Robert H., 271
Hindman, D. B., 271
Hindman, D. B., & Co., 271
Hindostanee pattern, 95, 370
Hindustanee pattern, 95, 370
Hines, Robert, 271
Hinkin, Benjamin, 271
Hinkle, Benjamin, 271
Hinsdale & Atkin, 238, 271
Hinsdale, Horace, 271
Hinton, William M., 272
Hirshbuhl & Dolfinger, 256, 272
Historic Mobile Preservation Society, 10, 22
Hizen pattern, 97, 370
HM (trademark), 321
Hobbs, Nathan, 272
Hocker, Willis, 272

Serving forks, 16, 37
Serving & place pieces, 16, 175–85
Serving & place pieces, illustrations, 187–205
Serving spoons, 174, 176, 191, 197, 200
Servoss, Joseph S., 300
Settle, Benjamin, 300
1776 patterns, 92, 102, 382
Seville patterns, 79, 157, 401
Sevrin, Lewis, 300
Seydell, Joseph, 300
Seymour, Edward, 300
Seymour & Hollister, 272, 300
Seymour, H. P., 300
Seymour, Joseph, 300, 326
Seymour, Joseph, & Co., 109, 300, 327
Seymour, Joseph, Mfg. Co., 327
Seymour, Joseph, Sons & Co., 109, 327
Seymour, Oliver D., 300
Shade, John V., 300
Shafer, Charles A., 300
Shakers, salt & pepper, 184, 185
Shakespeare, J., 300
Shakespeare, William, 216
Shannon, Robert, 300
Shaped dies, 32, 33, 35
Sharon pattern, 150, 213, 401
Sharp, George, 300
Sharp, George B., 300
Sharp, William, 300
Sharp, William & George, 300
Sharpe, William H., 300
Sharpley, R., 300
Sharrard & Ewing, 259, 300
Sharrard, James S., 300
Sharrard, Judson, 300
Sharrard, William M., 300
Shartle, Jacob A., 300
Shaver, Charles C., 300, 327
Shaver, Michael, 300
Shaw, Edward, 300
Shaw, George E., 327
Shaw, James, 300
Shaw, James W., 300
Shaw, John, 300
Shaw, John, & Co., 300
Sheed, William W., 301
Sheets-Rockford Co., 342
Sheets, R. W., 11
Sheffield, England, 25, 80
Sheffield patterns, 401
Sheffield Plate, 42, 49, 80, 233, 411
Sheldon, Alonzo D., 301
Shell patterns, 69, 85, 104, 105, 117, 125, 141, 152, 159, 160, 382, 383, 401
Shell Thread pattern, 140, 401
Shell & Thread pattern, 115, 383
Shell Tipped patterns, 108, 148, 383, 401
Shephard & Boyd, 245
Shephard, Thomas Jefferson, 301
Shepherd, Cumberland, 301
Shepherd, Ephraim, 301
Sheppard, George L., 301
Sheppard, George M., 301
Sheraton furniture, 80
Sheraton patterns, 94, 108, 142, 383, 401
Sherbet spoons, 184, 191
Sherman, Edward, 301
Sherwood, John, & Sons, 357
Sherwood patterns, 119, 153, 383, 401
Sherwood, Smith J., 301
Sherwood & Whatley, 301, 312
Sherwood, William, Jr., 301
Shethear & Gorham, 266
Shewell, Walter D., 301
Shiebler, George W., & Co., 79, 110, 111, 172, 318, 325, 326, 327
Shields, Jesse C., 301
Shimer, Anthony, 301
Shinn, ———, 301
Shinn & Baldwin, 301
Shipman, Nathaniel, 301
Shipp, ———, 301
Shipp & Collins, 301
Shipp & Woodbridge, 301, 315
Shirley patterns, 111, 162, 383, 401
Shirleysburgh, Pa., 217
Shoemaker, Abraham, 301
Shoemaker, Joseph, 301
Shoulder, spoon handle, 66
Shreve, Benjamin, 301
Shreve, Brown & Co., 301
Shreve & Co., 11, 76, 111, 327
Shreve, Crump & Low, 218, 301
Shreve, George C., 76, 301, 327
Shreve, Samuel S., 301
Shreve, Stanwood & Co., 301
Shriver, Thomas H., 301
Shuber, ———, 301
Shuler, John, 301
Shuman, John, 301
Shurley, John, 301
Sibley & Adams, 237, 301
Sibley, James, 301
Sibley, O. E., 301
Sibley, R. J., 301
Sidall, Joseph, 301
Siddons, John, 301
Siddons, Josiah C., 301
Siddons, Lawrence L., 301
Siebenlist, Michael, 301
Sigler, Amos, 301
Sigourney, Alanson P., 301
Sigourney & Hitchcock, 301
Sigourney & Turner, 301, 309
Sigourney, W. H. & A. P., 301
Sigourney, W. H., & Co., 301
Sigourney, William H., 301
Sikler, William, 302
Silberstein, A. L., 327
Silberstein, Hecht & Co., 327, 345
Sill, H., 302
Sill, H. & R. W., 302
Silver Applied, 345
Silver brazing, 34
Silver filled, 47, 48
Silver Fork school, 180
Silver-in-the-little, 32
Silver Metal (trademark), 341, 345
Silver mining, 35
Silver patterns, 137, 147, 157, 383, 401